The Making of Western Jewry,

The Making of Western Jewry, 1600–1819

Lionel Kochan

First published in hardback 2004

First published in paperback 2006 by
PALGRAVE MACMILLAN
Houndmills, Basingstoke, Hampshire RG21 6XS and
175 Fifth Avenue, New York, N.Y. 10010
Companies and representatives throughout the world

PALGRAVE MACMILLAN is the global academic imprint of the Palgrave Macmillan division of St. Martin's Press, LLC and of Palgrave Macmillan Ltd. Macmillan® is a registered trademark in the United States, United Kingdom and other countries. Palgrave is a registered trademark in the European Union and other countries.

ISBN-13: 978–0–333–62597–2 hardback
ISBN-10: 0–333–62597–8 hardback
ISBN-13: 978–0–230–50701–2 paperback
ISBN-10: 0–230–50701–8 paperback

This book is printed on paper suitable for recycling and made from fully managed and sustained forest sources.

A catalogue record for this book is available from the British Library.

Library of Congress Cataloging-in-Publication Data

Kochan, Lionel.
     The Making of Western Jewry, 1600–1819 / by Lionel Kochan
          p. cm.
     Includes bibliographical references (p.) and index.
     ISBN 0–333–62597–8 (cloth) 0–230–50701–8 (pbk)
          1. Jews – Europe, Western – History – 17th century. 2. Jews – Europe, Western – History – 18th century. I. Title

DS135.E82K63 2004
940'.04924—dc22   2004044689

10 9 8 7 6 5 4 3 2 1
15 14 13 12 11 10 09 08 07 06

Printed and bound in Great Britain by
Antony Rowe Ltd, Chippenham and Eastbourne

To my dear wife, as ever, for ever

Contents

Glossary

Bet(h) Din (pl. Batei Din)	court of law
Bet(h) Hamidrash	house of study
Cedaka	charity box or funds in Sephardi congregations
Halakhah (adj: Halakhic)	From Heb. halakh ('go', 'walk'), used of legal portions of Talmud and later rabbinic literature
Haskalah	Hebrew term for the Jewish enlightenment movement of the late eighteenth and early nineteenth centuries
Havdalah	ceremony to mark end of the Sabbath day and beginning of working week
heder	colloquial term for Jewish elementary school
herem	sentence of expulsion from a community for longer or shorter periods and of varying degrees of severity
herem ha-yishuv	prohibition against admittance of non-members to a community
Hevra(h) Kadischa	literally 'holy society'; term used to designate burial society which often had wider welfare activities
Judengasse	'street of the Jews'
Klaus	private 'house of study'
maskil (pl. maskilim)	adherent of the Haskalah (q.v.)
Midrash	elaborations of new meanings to scripture, often of legendary or ethical character
Mishnah	codification of Halakhah (q.v.) dating from the early third century
mohel	circumciser
Oral Law	authoritative interpretation of the Written Law (Pentateuch) and regarded as given to Moses at Sinai
schulklopper	communal official deputed to summon worshippers to prayer
Shulhan Arukh	sixteenth-century authoritative code of Jewish law
takkanah (pl. takkanot)	communal regulation or statute

Abbreviations

Biblical

Gen.	Genesis
Ex.	Exodus
Deut.	Deuteronomy
Ps.	Psalms
Jer.	Jeremiah

Other

AHRF	Annales Historique de la Révolution Française
AJSR	American Jewish Studies Review
AZJ	Allgemeine Zeitung des Judentums
b.	ben (Hebrew for son [of])
Ber.	Berakhot (Talmudic tractate)
BLBI	Bulletin of the Leo Baeck Institute
Git.	Gittin (Talmudic tractate)
HJ	Historia Judaica
HUCA	Hebrew Union College Annual
HZ	Historische Zeitschrift
JGGJCR	Jahrbuch der Gesellschaft für die Geschichte der Juden in der Çeskoslowakischen Republik
JJLG	Jahrbuch der Jüdisch-Litterarischen Gesellschaft
JJS	Journal of Jewish Studies
JPSA	Jewish Publication Society of America
JQR	Jewish Quarterly Review
JSS	Jewish Social Studies
Ket.	Ketubot (Talmudic tractate)
LBYB	Yearbook of the Leo Baeck Institute
MGWJ	Monatsschrift für die Geschichte und Wissenschaft des Judentums
Ned.	Nedarim (Talmudic tractate)
PAAJR	Proceedings of the American Academy for Jewish Research
PWCJS	Proceedings of the World Congress of Jewish Studies
R.	Rabbi
REJ	Revue des Etudes Juives
San.	Sanhedrin (Talmudic tractate)
SR	Studia Rosenthaliana
TB	Talmud Babli
(T)JHSE	(Transactions of the) Jewish Historical Society of England
VSW	Vierteljahrschrift für Sozial- und Wirtschaftsgeschichte
ZGJD	Zeitschrift für die Geschichte der Juden in Deutschland

Introduction

'The sceptre shall not depart from Judah'

To present an history of the Jews in central and western Europe from the sixteenth to the early nineteenth century is the aim of this book. More precisely, it is concerned with those Jews who lived in an area bounded to the east by an imaginary line that veers southwards from Danzig to the Adriatic, and is bounded to the west by Ireland. (This has not inhibited occasional sallies further westward, to Brazil and the Indies, and eastward to the Ukraine.)

It is the institution of the *kehillah* (Hebrew for a communal-corporate body; plural *kehillot*) that to each of these scattered settlements gives a degree of coherence and unity, over centuries of dispersion and migration. As an historical agent in its own right and as a sovereign power, the *kehillah* fulfils, relative to time and place, the Biblical promise that 'the sceptre shall not depart from Judah nor the ruler's staff from between his feet' (Gen. 49:10). In all its multiple guises it originated in Talmudic times as a vehicle of self-government during the dispersion to Babylon and elsewhere and in this capacity evolved into the basic unit of Jewish history. It groups together the Jews of a specific locality. Amidst expulsion, migration and resettlement in Europe and the Americas, the *kehillah* strove to uphold some semblance of self-government. The 'sceptre' sometimes buckles or is broken or blunted but is normally reconstituted, even if not always with its former power and authority. It necessarily evolves in accordance with time and place: what in sixteenth-century Prague is a compulsory and quasi-autonomous body is in eighteenth-century Berlin a government-controlled body of limited power; in eighteenth-century London membership is purely voluntary. Despite every variation the summons to self-government is ubiquitous and serves as a leitmotif that gives to the sixteenth, seventeenth and eighteenth centuries the semblance of a thread. No settlement of Jews, it is safe to say, is ever a chance agglomeration of individuals; rather they will display an inherent commitment to organization and self-assertion.

1

The *kehillah* is variously interpreted as a partnership of individuals, or as the semblance of a court of law that has coercive powers over the members of the *kehillah*.[1] The need for these powers arises in part from man's anti-social nature 'for, were it not for fear of the government, a man would swallow his neighbour alive' (Mishnah, Avot 3:2). Positively, the *kehillah* is committed to the realization of certain values, to be achieved through a further commitment to regulations ultimately derived from Biblical and Talmudic sources by a process of rabbinic ratiocination in accordance with the accepted hermeneutical principles. That is why every *kehillah* is normally designated 'holy'.

The *kehillah* ideally comprehends a governing body and an electoral system, enjoys tax-raising powers and juridical authority, exercises the right to impose sanctions and punishments on those members who transgress its rules, and encompasses a range of charitable, educational and communal fraternities. Above all, perhaps, the *kehillah* has the power to issue its own enactments – *takkanot*.[2] No *kehillah*, whether in a major urban centre – Amsterdam, Berlin, Prague, Trieste, London, Metz – or in the tiniest hamlet in outer Pomerania did not possess and exercise some of these powers.

Pari passu with the exercise of these powers, rabbis and other scholars debate virtually every topic in classical political theory. I do not wish to claim that the particular topic will necessarily take the form of a systematic treatise – rather, that it is through and amidst the clash of specific interests and viewpoints that the topic is debated. It is necessary to determine the distribution of power as between the majority and the minority, and between the rich and the poor; the system of elections and eligibility for office must be determined; machinery must be in place for the resolution of conflict, both inside the *kehillah* and also in the case of conflict between the *kehillah* and the gentile world. What state of emergency would justify the abrogation of certain safeguards? This contact with the concrete ensures that the *kehillah* (like the state) never acquires corporate status as a reified entity, having an existence distinct from that of its members or partners. The same situation also ensures that the notion of natural law and the abstract rhetoric of rights are rare in Jewish thinking – in fact, in classical Hebrew there is no term equivalent to 'right'.[3]

Who rules in and over the *kehillah*? This crucial question of leadership dogs every mode of organization to an extent that Leo Strauss has made it the 'most fundamental political controversy: the controversy as to what type of men should rule the community'.[4] Already in the exodus from Egypt the problematic arises: Jethro and Moses, his son-in-law, look among the Israelites for capable men, who are also God-fearing, lovers of truth, hostile to unjust gain, men of sagacity, percipient and well known (Ex. 18:21; Deut. 1:13). Leaders with no more than three of these seven qualifications were eventually found – men who were capable, wise and well known (Ex. 18:25; Deut. 1:15; see also Sifrei on Deut. 15). Between the ideal and what is available the discrepancy is unmistakable. If Jethro and Moses could not uncover properly qualified leaders, what chance have lesser men? In later generations the Talmud likens the rabbis to kings (TB Git. 62a; Ned. 20b). In a somewhat modified form R. Judah Loewe b. Bezalel (the Maharal of Prague), one of the dominating rabbinic figures of the late sixteenth century, repeats this comparison.[5] To no avail. However necessary in theory the rabbi's expertise in the laws and his role as communal judge or arbitrator, in practice his part in the government of the *kehillah* had normally to be exercised in conjunction with the elected leadership of the parnass (Hebrew, best translated as 'elder', though with a nuance of guardian, ruler, leader; pl. parnassim). The parnassim are sometimes referred to as 'the seven good men of the city'.

The distinction between the respective roles of rabbi and parnass is absolutely not between 'religious' and 'secular' but usually lies in the division of duties. Whereas, by the sixteenth century, the congregational rabbi is the norm and he will be engaged on a salaried basis to concern himself with legal adjudication, matters of personal status, education and synagogal affairs, the elected and (normally) unpaid parnass has administrative and financial responsibilities. But this distinction is very flexible indeed and their roles are interchangeable. Many an elected parnass will have rabbinical qualification and authorization, and many a rabbi will serve as a parnass. In a Jewish context it would be difficult, if not impossible, to assign any sort of discrete meaning to either term, 'religious' or 'secular'. It follows that a rabbi is as much of a lay leader as a parnass a religious leader, and though they may exercise their respective leadership in different spheres, they are both acting under the authority of the same Torah, and members of the same governing body to which the dichotomy holy–profane, religious–secular, is alien to the point of incomprehensibility. 'There can be no intrinsic duality in the law, and the phrase "secular law" is a contradiction-in-terms: if it is a law, it cannot be secular, and if it is secular, it cannot be a law.'[6]

In historical terms the distinction is socio-economic in that the *kehillah* is normally the employer of the rabbi; this implies that unless the latter has an independent source of income – which is by no means unlikely – he will be financially dependent on the parnassim, and this is a source of resentment and sometimes even of corruption. But this relationship has not always curbed the political sway of rabbis, dominant by virtue of their learning and character. At times conflict between rabbi and parnass will avert an undue concentration of power.

For all that, the answer to the question posed by Strauss is this: normally it is the wealthy who rule. Politically speaking, there are cogent and compelling reasons why it is essential that this should be so. The elected leader is by no means to be regarded primarily as the representative of 'his' *kehillah* but rather as its guardian, his wealth serving as a weapon, to be wielded for the benefit of all members. Much rabbinic testimony from at least the thirteenth century, formulated in various nuances, points to the importance of wealth as a political factor. Salo Baron has assembled some persuasive comments: 'Our taxes protect us', said R. Asher b. Yehiel (*c*.1250–1327) of Cologne and Toledo; R. Solomon ibn Adret of Barcelona (*c*.1235–1310) spoke of 'spending money in order to maintain the [governmental] privileges'; 'They only protect us for their benefit', declared R. Israel Isserlein of Vienna (1390–1460).[7] In the late sixteenth or early seventeenth century, R. Isaiah Horovitz of Cracow, Frankfurt and Prague (*c*.1565–1630) interpreted the dispute between Jacob and Esau (Gen. 32–3) in similar fashion:

> In the same way as he [Jacob] proceeded with gifts, prayer and war so do we in our generation deal with the sons of Esau and we have no strength but with our lips to pray to the Holy One at a time of distress. To wage war with the peoples is not appropriate for us but the purport of war against them is the power of intercession which the intercessors of Israel are obliged to wield against kings and princes and to intercede for Israel with all their strength and even if [kings and princes] meet them with wrath and thrust them away, they will come back and persist, and this is the support and pillar of Israel in the dispersion.[8]

In Venice, two or so decades later, R. Simone Luzzatto (*c*.1585–1663) would embellish this argument with all the apparatus of mercantilist theory and the politics of *raison d'état*. In his *Discorso circa il stato degli Ebrei et in particolar dimoranti nell'inclita Città di Venetia – (A Discourse on the State of the Jews, and in Particular Those Dwelling in the Illustrious City of Venice)*, addressed to the Venetian patriciate, Luzzatto sought to defend the community against a revival of antisemitism by lauding the role that Jewish mercantile enterprise had taken, and could increasingly take, in Venetian commerce. Luzzatto finds Venice in a state of decline, which he explained in terms of Macchiavelli's pessimistic conception of human nature, that is a challenge in the past had been successfully surmounted but satiety, slackness and complacency are the consequence, and in the case of Venice this had shown itself in the abandonment of the life of commerce in favour of an estate on the *Terra Ferma*:

> The despised Shylocks [Ravid writes] grudgingly allowed to settle in the city over a hundred years earlier, were no longer merely money-lenders, but were taking the place of the noble Venetian Antonios, who were withdrawing more and more from trade either because of the increasing difficulty of making profits, or because of the siren call of the mainland estates. The Jews, with their far-flung coreligionists, both of old-Jewish and also ex-Marrano stock, had resources that the once-mighty lion of San Marco could not match.[9]

This indissoluble bond between settlement and the economic imperative explains the need for plutocratic rule which in turn explains the electoral machinery. Though the parnassim do indeed require to be elected into office, communal statutes also make provision for cooption, and limit the franchise and organize electoral colleges in such a sophisticated way as to ensure that the representation of the poor is secondary to that of the wealthy. The quasi-universal result of every election is the emergence to power of the monied (though obviously the degree of wealth varies enormously).

The functioning of the *kehillah* was necessarily imperfect. 'Against unchastity there is no guardian' (TB Ket. 13b). Also to the abuse of power does this dictum apply. No set of institutions or power-sharing arrangement will permanently prevent the abuse of power, all the less so if it is concentrated in the hands of a few. This inherent source of tension is exacerbated for rabbis and parnassim and their fellow-Jews by the effects of congestion, multiple forms of discrimination, insecurity, vexation and harassment, and the incessant struggle to escape from poverty amidst a hostile milieu. Feuds and tensions proliferated (especially among those Jews confined to ghettos), even occasional physical violence, which rarely however went beyond scuffles and fisticuffs. There were 'tyrants' inside the ghetto, writes one of the most distinguished historians of an earlier century, David Kaufmann:

> Especially did capital attempt to assert within the community that authority which it did not dare to claim without and sought in the Judengasse honours denied it in the market-place ... there arose questions of authority and class interests as in a powerful state. Scholarship strove with wealth for supremacy; rabbinical prerogative endeavoured to maintain its ground against the arbitrariness of the Parnassim ... All the noisome brood of base passions – hypocrisy, treachery, corruption, bribery – rose to the surface.[10]

This was said of London Jewry in the early years of the eighteenth century where there was in fact no ghetto. If, of the London community these accusations could be made, what could then not be said of those cities where congested ghettos did indeed exist – of Frankfurt, Prague, Metz? Minor disputes easily swelled into major causes célèbres.

Virtually everywhere (London being a rare exception) a *Privilegium*, a *Stettigkeit*, a *Condotto*, a *Schutzbrief* will impinge – sometimes forcibly so – on the aspiration towards autonomy. But the challenge can to some extent be blunted through the application and implementation of the legal principle, 'The law of the kingdom is law' (*'Dina de-malkhutah Dina'*). This principle originated in the Babylonian exile, in the third century (TB Ned. 28a; Git. 10b), and later evolved into a means of adjustment and accommodation to the demands of the gentile state with the minimum of detriment to the legal sovereignty of the *kehillah*. The principle does not accept into Jewish law any decree of a gentile ruler but always remains selective. Three general

limitations operate: first, it is restricted to laws of property; second the duration of acceptance is limited; third, the law in question must be the work of a
properly constituted and acknowledged authority and be non-discriminatory.
It would otherwise be not 'the law of the kingdom' but 'the robbery of the
kingdom' and unacceptable except, of course, by way of force majeure.[11]

Similar in this respect to other political entities, the *kehillah* had secrets to
protect. In 1591, the council of the community in Padua unanimously
decreed:

> No son of Israel, whether a member of the [communal] council or of the
> community, shall make known any of the ordinances of the community to
> him who is not of our people. And he who contravenes will be proclaimed
> transgressor until he performs all that the parnassim impose on him.

In 1671 and 1684 the councils in Lithuania and Poland approved ordinances
couched in very similar terms – to preserve 'the secrets of Israel'. In Posen in
1652 and 1655 the communal *takkanot* threatened to impose the most severe
punishment on those informers who trafficked in the secrets of the *kehillah*.
In Bordeaux in 1735 the governing board – the Mahamad – of the Sephardi
community recorded: For our preservation it is not necessary that our affairs
become known *entre los Gentiles*.[12]

The *kehillah* stood out from its Christian milieu not only by virtue of its
particular objectives but also in its temporal reckoning. Its calendar is Jewish
and it lives in 'Jewish' time. Banking hours in Renaissance Verona, for example, took account of the times set aside for prayer; likewise at Lippiano in
Umbria. During the Passover festival, drovers suspend their delivery of
urgent supplies of horses to the French cavalry. Until the later eighteenth
century, private letters and communal documents commonly bear a date
according to the Hebrew calendar. Christian builders, engaged in the construction of a synagogue, must cease work for the duration of the Jewish
Sabbath. The cemetery at La Villette in Paris has tombstones engraved with
a dual date, for example, that of Rebecca Henrique, 'Deceased the 11th of
the moon of Adar of the year 5556 which corresponds to the 6th Germinal
of the Year Four of the French Republic' (that is, 30 March 1796).[13]

'Jewish time' is as much national as individual. This makes it misleading
to combine or conflate two different time scales such as would be, for example, contained in the use of the term 'modern Jewish history' to refer, say, to
the history of the last two centuries. What is 'modern' (or 'medieval' or 'early
modern' or 'late modern' or 'post-modern') does indeed have relevance to
general European history, but in referring to Jewish history these terms
impose an alien temporal division. Krochmalnik writes, precisely in reference to the period this book deals with, that in the Jewish calendar there is
no correspondence to such divisions as 'Renaissance', 'Humanism' and 'the
Modern'.[14]

Is there also 'Jewish' space? Only, it would seem, in reference to some structure such as a ghetto, synagogue, cemetery or ritual bath; otherwise, again until the later eighteenth century, it seems that the Jews conceived of space as territorially undifferentiated. For an Italian rabbi of the sixteenth century, R. Moses di Trani, anywhere outside Spain, Portugal and Italy is Ashkenaz.[15] For the Sephardim the wholly important distinction separated *terras de idolatria* from *terras de Judesmo*, that is, respectively those lands where Judaism could not openly be practised from those where it could; these distinctions change over time; France of the eighteenth century evolved from a land of idolatry to a land of Judaism. In the context of a Sephardi society for the dowering of poor girls, the operational area extended without distinction from Saint-Jean-de-Luz to Danzig.

The weakening of the sceptre that is not to depart from Judah is a recurring theme of this book. The corollary is assimilation. This dual process in central and western Europe moves amidst the destruction and recreation of old settlements and the establishment of new. This is a second theme to which I now turn.

Between expulsion and accommodation

'The earlier ones upheld the Torah amidst great hardship and the pressure of the peoples but now we sit in our dwellings, each one of us in peace and quiet.' R. Judah b. Bezalel, one of the outstanding rabbis of the late sixteenth century, wrote in these terms of the contemporary atmosphere in Prague and Bohemia. He was not alone: his friend and colleague R. David Gans published in 1592 an historical chronicle – *Tsemah David* – confessedly intended for those 'tired of the exile' and hopeful for a period of tranquillity.[16]

The comparative quiet in the Moravian and Bohemian countryside matched that in Prague; also in Poland where, wrote Meir Ashkenazi, many Jews 'live under the vine and under their fig-tree'.[17]

The two Prague rabbis were welcoming a moment when the widespread expulsions of the previous two centuries had seemingly come to an end. These had extended from Strasbourg in the west to Vienna in the east. The Jews of Prague barely escaped. In 1492 the expelled Sephardi Jews of Spain were at one with the Ashkenazim of central Europe and in 1497 the movement spread to Portugal, later to Sicily, Naples and southern Italy. Overall, the effect of these expulsions was to leave most Jews in the German lands dispersed in small rural groups, 'atomized', it is said; to reinforce the centres in eastern Europe and in northern Italy (Venice, Ancona, Ferrara); and to create a new centre in the Ottoman empire.

Towards the end of the century the expulsions slowly yielded to stability and in some cases to actual promise. The ghetto system, introduced as part of the Counter-Reformation in the 1550s, signified, with all its horrors, at least the antithesis to expulsion. In central and western Europe, either old centres took on new life or new centres came into existence. In Venice, whereas in the 1550s and 1560s the Talmud and other works of Hebrew literature had been ceremonially burnt in the Piazza San Marco, by the late 1580s the charters granted to the various Jewish 'nations' in the ghetto extended freedom of trade and religion and security of residence.[18] The example of Venice strongly influenced Livorno where the celebrated *La Livornina* of 1593, issued by Grand Duke Ferdinand of Tuscany, granted similar privileges, together with full internal autonomy in respect of religion, culture and legislation.[19] Frankfurt am Main stood out as a significant urban centre where the Jewish population increased in the sixteenth century, particularly towards the end of the century. The 900 Jews of 1569 became 1200 by 1580 and 2200 by 1600.[20] The number of houses in the Judengasse grew from 32 in 1530 to 147 by 1595. Overall, the proportional expansion in the number of Jews extended from *c*.1 per cent (1492) to *c*.15 per cent (1600). As a trading centre and home to the spring and autumn fairs, the city attracted displaced Jews from elsewhere in the Reich. In 1579 the Republic of the United Provinces came into existence and the Declaration of Utrecht proclaimed the individual's right not to be molested for his religious opinions. This provision of the Declaration applied to Christians and it could only be uncertain whether Jews with a Christian past would also be immune from interrogation on that score. Nevertheless it gave sufficient encouragement to a small group of self-styled 'Portuguese merchants' to take up residence in Amsterdam in the closing years of the sixteenth century. They could take the oath of citizenship and on payment of a modest fee qualify for its attendant rights.

By the end of the sixteenth century the Jewish presence was more or less at ease in three main and contrasting areas: the north Italian centre dominated by Venice; the Ashkenazi world of the rural areas of the German lands alongside the major towns of Worms, Frankfurt am Main and Prague; and the burgeoning Sephardi world of Amsterdam and Hamburg. The sceptre of Judah can resume some sort of sway. A major theme of this book is the fluctuating course of that revival, during and after the fourth century of the sixth millennium (by the traditional Jewish reckoning), that is, early modernity in terms of the Common Era.

1
Central Europe in Peace and War, 1600–48

Round about 1600 the Jews of the Holy Roman Empire consisted, at a rough estimate, of some 2000 families, say, 12000 persons. This was equivalent to one Jew per 1000 of the general population.[1] These Jews, 'tired of the exile', like David Gans of Prague, now had occasion to enjoy a somewhat more settled existence, certainly in relation to the earlier age of expulsions. There was some possibility that Jew and Christian could meet and engage in a shared scientific pursuit; and tension on religious grounds had somewhat abated. Some degree of confirmation came in the enhanced stability of Jewish residence. To communities large and small some degree of ease and security was returning. Perhaps the various *Judenordnungen* that territorial rulers in the central Rhine region issued in the sixteenth and seventeenth centuries also went to create a sense of stability – at least that was the intention, to transform a *ius incertum* into a *ius certum*.[2]

This point is not to be exaggerated. In extremity no laws protected the Jews. In 1601 Emperor Rudolf took advantage of the death of his banker, Markus Meyzel, to seize his entire estate, including that portion set aside for the poor. Meyzel had anticipated some such expropriation and taken the precaution of dispersing his assets, but to no avail.[3] In 1614–15 mob violence and agitation procured the spoliation and expulsion, albeit short-lived, of the Jews from the major urban centres of Worms and Frankfurt am Main.

All in all however, the process of acceptance prevailed. In 1603, these changing conditions united with internal Jewish disarray to persuade the leadership in the German states to undertake a major review of conditions 'at home' and the modalities of the relationship to the Christian world. One salient problem was the dispersion of jurisdiction over the small communities of the south and west. To the court at Frankfurt came litigants from East Frisia and the Mark in the north as well as from Speyer and Ansbach in the south; the court at Worms covered the Rhineland Palatinate; Hesse-Darmstadt, Upper and Lower Alsace; Friedberg covered Hesse-Cassel and Hesse-Marburg; Günzburg and Wallerstein covered Swabian Jewry; the rabbi to the Jews in the archiepiscopal see of Cologne was located in Bonn and the rabbi to those of Mainz in Bingen. In Fürth and Hildesheim there were local rabbinates.[4]

In part, in order to bring some order to this confusion, 26 communal leaders (of whom a quarter were rabbis) assembled at Frankfurt to debate matters relative to 'the needs of the people and the time'. The assembly explicitly accepted the principle that 'the law of the land is the law' and also promulgated ordinances on its own initiative: first, that legal disputes between Jew and Jew must be settled only before a Jewish tribunal and not a gentile court, a practice attributed to the wealthy. For this purpose the assembly proposed to establish five courts with supra-territorial jurisdiction – at Frankfurt, Worms, Friedberg, Fulda and Günzburg. This was not only an ancient right but would also avert discredit to the Jews. The assembly instituted a uniform and trustworthy system of taxation with designated assessors, collectors and depositaries; it repeated with increasing emphasis existing prohibitions against dealing in counterfeit or underweight currency or with thieves; fraudulent bankrupts would suffer expulsion from their community. In dietary matters the assembly called for strict supervision of animal slaughtering, prohibited gentile 'wine of libation' and cautioned against frequenting taverns. Rabbis must not be appointed to office except with the approval of three colleagues. The Jews must not dress like gentiles, in such a manner that they 'would not be recognized as Jews'. The assembly also imposed a form of self-censorship; in decreeing that no Jew must have a book printed in Basel or elsewhere in Germany, save with the permission of three rabbis from the five towns with established courts.[5]

In actual fact, none of the 'constitutional' ordinances was implemented. Wittingly or not, the Jewish leaders had involved the communities in the contentious and delicate issue of the relationship between the emperor and the territorial ruler at a time when power was passing fast from the former to the latter. The last imperial rabbi, R. Jacob b. Hayyim of Worms, died *c.*1574 and the absence of any successor suggests that the position was perceived to be redundant in view of the emperor's declining power. On the other hand, the fact that the five proposed courts were all to be located in imperial free cities (Frankfurt, Worms, Friedberg) or in cities close to the imperial power (Günzburg stood under direct Habsburg rule) suggests precisely the opposite – that is that the Jewish leadership sought to maintain the protective association with the emperor. In other words, it was a question of manoeuvring between two contending forces or perhaps creating a third force independent of either.[6]

In any event, this type of empire-wide body with a range of judicial and financial prerogatives creating a quasi-independent corporation could not be but provocative, both to the empire and the territorial rulers. There was nothing secret about the assembly's deliberations, though it may be that its conclusions were made public prematurely. That the decisions would be posted on every synagogue door in Germany was the hope, so that they might receive wide publicity and debate. This did happen, but hardly in the manner intended: the programme of the assembly provoked widespread anti-Jewish furore amidst accusations of treason, *lèse-majesté* and blasphemy. An embittered informer from Frankfurt, Leib Kraus, took the lead and succeeded in instigating an official enquiry, on behalf of the emperor, which lasted from about 1607 to 1612. The perennial hostility of the guilds to Jewish craftsmen provided popular support. The enquiry and the allegations of conspiracy created the utmost alarm in the Jewish camp. 1607 was a year of fear 'and a time of great distress'. There seemed no hope of relief, all the less so because 'the emperor refused all talk of mediation with emissaries from all Ashkenaz and hid his countenance'.[7]

Only for a time was the worst averted. The failure, it seems, of the emperor to protect his subjects encouraged the artisan guilds in Frankfurt and Worms to resume their campaign. Led by a certain Vincenz Fettmilch, in 1614 the mob forced the Jews out of the Judengasse in Frankfurt, and in 1615 from the Worms ghetto. The Jews found refuge in the Rhineland Palatinate, Darmstadt and Mainz, according to an eye-witness – Juspa Shammash ('Juspa the beadle', 1604–78) of Worms. As distinct from the mob, according to Juspa, the burghers and local rulers sought to protect the Jews. In the end salvation came from the *emperor*, following intercession by Leib Oppenheim, one of the Worms parnassim. Escorted by imperial troops, the Jews returned to Frankfurt on the very day that Fettmilch and the other ringleaders were executed. The three gates of the Gasse each bore a shield proclaiming that the ghetto stood under imperial protection.[8] A famous bilingual Hebrew-Yiddish historical song, 'Megillas Vints', records the expulsion and deliverance of the Jews and came to form part of the annual Purim festivities in Frankfurt.[9]

The new Stättigkeit of 118 articles issued by the emperor guaranteed the Jews of Frankfurt protection against any future expulsion but also limited the number of family households to 500; only 12 marriages were permitted annually and only 6 foreign Jews were admitted, who had in any case to marry into local families. The Stättigkeit also contained provision against any abusive treatment of the Jews by the town council or the guilds. After protracted negotiations the Jewish leaders renounced a compensation payment of almost 178 000 gulden promised by the imperial commission.[10]

The two rulers involved, Matthias and Ferdinand II, were tardy in renewing the Jews' charter of privileges. An internal revolt in the Frankfurt ghetto against the oligarchic rule of the Zehner ('Gang of Ten') did not help matters. Not until 1621/2 did Jakob Fröschel, the Jewish intermediary from Prague, receive confirmation of the renewal.[11]

Disastrous events of this nature did not typify the Jewish experience in the early seventeenth century. The precise contrary was characteristic, that is the extension to Jews by territorial rulers of authority to settle in their domains. This is much more marked later in the century (after the Thirty Years' War), but in the early decades it is not unusual and applies to locations as varied as Vienna, Trier, Hanau and Holstein-Schauenberg. Here and elsewhere a general *Judenordnung* and an individual *Geleit* or *Schutzbrief* ('letter of protection', 'licence') normally set out the conditions of settlement for community and particular individuals. In 1603 Duke Philippe Ludwig II of Hanau issued a charter (*Stättigkeit*) whereby all that distinguished Jews from Christians was the obligation to wear a yellow badge and the prohibition on the employment of Christian servants (apart from 'a Sabbath woman'). Otherwise, in respect of religious and economic freedom, tax, legal status, municipal obligations, nothing separated Jew from Christian; so much so that in 1609 a group of conversos from Venice made enquiry of the duke with a view to settlement. Only the refusal of Rudolf II to grant them free movement for their persons and goods aborted enquiries; they were Christians and should not be permitted to return to Judaism, it was held. In or around 1614, Jacob and Israel received *Geleitbriefe* from Ernest III, Duke of Holstein-Schauenberg. This entitled them, on annual payment of protection money, to settle and work in Altona, with the goodwill of the ducal authorities, so long as the said Jacob and Israel conducted themselves in accordance with the 'general privilege' granted to the Jews in Altona. In a somewhat more elaborate document from Vienna, 1615, Emperor Matthias extended imperial protection to Abraham Brodt, by virtue of his appointment as court-Jew; together with his wife and family, he was authorized to live and trade unmolested in Vienna, but he must not maintain an open shop, must attend on the court, buy and sell only in his dwelling, not conceal any foreign Jew, not purchase any stolen property. He pays the taxes, dues and fees of a Christian, is subject to the jurisdiction of the Office of the Hofmarschall. This freedom applies only during Brodt's lifetime and on his death the heirs must at once seek its confirmation. In 1618, Lothar, the archbishop and electoral prince of Trier issued a Judenordnung that forbade any Jew without an individual *Geleit* (see below, p. 95) to dwell in his territory; those Jews in possession of a *Geleit* must conduct themselves without arrogance, or quarrelsomeness; each Jewish household must consist of no more than husband, wife, children and the necessary servants; foreign Jews must pay a body tax, not remain longer than 4–5 days in the territory and not engage in trade without the permission of the local authorities; the Jews' ceremonies must not cause offence, and in consideration of the Christian religion, holidays and processions the Jews must conduct themselves discreetly. The *Ordnung* limited the economic activity of the Jews to trading in money, horses, silverware and jewellery and the cash purchase, in restricted quantities, of wine, fruit and other commodities; they must not maintain open shops. The moneylender must not lend to a husband without his wife's knowledge (and vice versa), and not to children, servants or students; properly signed and attested documents of indebtedness must be kept; arrears of interest must not be added to capital, nor weekly interest of more than one-half pfennig per gulden be levied; objects pledged as security for loans must be properly registered and redeemable against repayment; no loan contract must run for longer than three years; the Jews must not deal in any property suspected of having been stolen, especially chalice, monstrance or other object of Christian ritual.[12]

These documents, *Schutzbriefe, Ordnungen* and so on, had always to be paid for and this is the reality that determined the enormous role taken by the wealthy and their financial resources in Jewish communal and political life. Only the rich had the necessary funds to purchase the right to settlement. Without the wealthy there would be no community, said a late-seventeenth-century rabbi, R. Yair Bachrach of Worms: in the words of the Hebrew pun, no *binyan* (property), no *minyan* (community). Those many Jews who lacked the necessary funds led a dependent existence as servants in the household of a privileged Jew able to afford the cost of a *Schutzbrief*.[13] This relationship inevitably extended to the status of wealth inside Jewish society, to the detriment of the less favoured, but not without ambiguity. Social tension became much more marked as a result of the historical demands pressing on the *kehillah* in the seventeenth century. 'The people of Europe during the sixteenth and seventeenth centuries', writes one historian, 'became more money conscious than they had ever been before'.[14]

Among those people, it is safe to say, the Jews stood out. That 'breed of men … ready to devour the poor of the land' is already a theme in Proverbs (30:11–14). In the half-century after the Thirty Years' War it is likely that this 'breed' spread more widely as a consequence of the increased financial pressure from gentile rulers which they in turn transmitted to their Jewish subjects. For the moment, however, the problem posed by mass poverty seems to have been manageable and, paradoxical though it may be, the outbreak of the Thirty Years' War in 1618 did not, initially at least, interrupt the fitful process of consolidation. Historians, ancient and modern, generally agree that the destruction and depopulation in combat areas affected Jews less than Christians.[15] A geographical accident was of considerable help because the main areas of devastation – from the south-west to the north-east of the German lands – encompassed those territories where Jews were only thinly scattered. Some cessation of persecution provided a bonus. In this specific context, Jews enlisted as mercenaries, serving impartially in the armies of Mansfeld, Wallenstein and the Duke of Holstein and with the Swedes. They also appear from time to time in communal records. Juspa the beadle, of Worms, drew up writs of divorce in the early 1640s in two such cases. In the one, a mercenary who had abandoned his wife eight years earlier unexpectedly reappeared with his troop. Juspa indited the writ on behalf of the wife whose husband now wished to divorce her. The court disregarded its customary procedure, which would have involved consultations with the elders of Mainz and Speyer, and issued an immediate divorce so that the wife should not become 'an anchored woman' (*agunah*) and unable to remarry.

The widow of a Jew who died of plague while serving with Wallenstein's forces was given permission to remarry by the court.[16]

The Jewish communities enjoyed the protection of the Habsburgs and at times of other warring powers – Swedes, Dutch and French. This protection did not come cheap and had to be purchased by way of taxes, forced loans and the provision of military supplies to one or other of the warring parties. The protection and security enjoyed by Frankfurt Jewry, relative to the Christian population, was one reality. To this great Jewish centre with its population of some 370 households the first years of war brought some degree of prosperity. In the first six years the household tally rose in fact to 409. The number of marriages also increased. 'With our own eyes we have seen that amongst us there is a living God who performs wonders for us', exclaimed the Frankfurt rabbi, R. Juspa Hahn, 'and this is seen most clearly in relation to the soldiers who for some years now have passed over towns and villages ... it is impossible to inscribe both how much better our people were treated than the uncircumcised for (the latter) were sometimes made to suffer so much that in certain places they concealed their property in the houses of the Jews; and also the wonders performed for those people whom the enraged besiegers sought to take prisoner but in this they did not succeed ... and also some (Jewish) prisoners were easily rescued, most without paying ransom money and some for but small sums'.[17] Hahn was an eye-witness to the earlier stages of the fighting and completed his work in 1630. Had he been able to revise it, Hahn might well have qualified his initial appreciation, for from about the mid-1620s taxes and forced loans, demanded in turn by the imperial forces, the Protestants and the Swedes brought hardship to the community; so much so that in 1626 and again in 1632 loans had to be taken out with Christian lenders. The impoverishment was all the greater through the incapacity of borrowers to repay their loans to the moneylenders and pawnbrokers, with inevitable repercussions on the trade in second-hand articles. In these circumstances the Jews entered branches of trade in numbers that ignored the restriction imposed by the *Stättigkeit*, to the familiar complaints from shopkeepers, cloth-dealers, silk merchants and so on. To the tailors' protests, the Jews retorted that their undoubted decline followed from the disproportionate number of master-tailors, their inability to meet the demands of their customers for fashionable clothing, and their high prices – whereas the Jews were content to charge less, offered longer-term credit and willingly accepted payment not only in cash but also in foodstuffs, wine and fruit. Only in the horse trade could Jews engage without complaint, and demand from the warring armies ensured that this happily prospered. This of itself could not of course arrest the decline in the economy of the *Judengasse*. The population declined, partly through movement elsewhere but also through a fall in the marriage-rate; in 1631 and 1632 no marriages at all were celebrated and in 1636 and 1640 only one each year. Plague and disease killed off 222 people in 1635, including 160 children, according to the records of the Hevrah Kadischa. These varied factors account for remarkable demographic fluctuations. At the beginning of the war the city had 370 households; by 1639 this had shrunk to 285; by the end of the war in 1648 the total had increased to 329. The overall wartime loss amounted therefore to some 10 per cent.[18]

In Worms, the second most important urban centre in Germany, where some 1500 Jews had lived on the eve of war, the worst trials came in 1635/36, which lived on as 'the year of the great upheaval' (R. Yair Bachrach, 1638–1702, later rabbi in Worms).[19] A plague which killed 200 Jews was followed by demands from the magistracy for sums of 35000 and 40000 florins to billet and quarter the imperial troops. A number of the Jews' leaders were arrested as hostage. A protest to Vienna brought the release of the hostages, a warning to the city that the Jews enjoyed imperial protection and a negotiated settlement, confirmed by the emperor, to the demand for a war contribution. Much the same situation recurred in the early 1640s – as part of which, in 1641, imperial representatives mediated between Worms Jewry and the town magistracy so as to produce a revised *Judenordnung*. This still required the Jews to sport a yellow badge and to display on their houses an identifying shield, but in economic respects the Jews secured authority to buy any goods in the market (except fish on the fish market) and Jewish trade was liberalized in a very wide range of goods – foodstuffs, wines, fruits, spices, many varieties of textiles, cattle, gold, silver, jewellery and ironware. In return for a consideration they were permitted to graze their cows on common land. No doubt this *Ordnung* too had to be purchased by way of imperial loan; in 1643 Ferdinand III acknowledged a debt to the community of 9600 florins capital and 2919 florins interest. No imperial mediation or protection could, however, arrest the decline and impoverishment of the community; by the end of the war it consisted of no more than 400–500 people, somewhere between a quarter and a third of the pre-war total.[20]

From Prague, and the 'peculiar city of the Jews', the fortuitous loss of a bundle of 46 private letters manifests the preoccupations and concerns of at least some of the inhabitants. The letters were sent on 15 Kislev 5380 (= 22 November 1619) by certain of the more affluent inhabitants of the Jews' Town to friends and relatives in Vienna and Nikolsburg. Some are written in Yiddish, some in Hebrew. *En route* the bundle was seized from the courier and the letters never reached the people they were sent to. Löb Sarel Gutmans, a Prague merchant, was the organizer of this service but it was haphazard and ad hoc.

R. Yomtov Lippmann Heller writes to his sister-in-law Edel, widow of Salomon Malke in Vienna, who is arranging the betrothal of one of Heller's daughters (aged nine at the time); would a dowry of 800 florins rather than of 1000, be acceptable, Heller enquires? This would be without prejudice to the matchmaker's commission, he adds. (Heller was not a poor man, but since he had five daughters to marry off his concern is understandable.)

There is news of the betrothal of a son of the eminent Polish scholar and rabbi, R. Joel Sirkes ('the Bakh'); of a circumcision ceremony held in the Meyzel synagogue, with R. Isaiah Horovitz acting as *sandek* ('godfather').

There is an appeal from the Prague communal scribe in the name of the *kehillah* for help in efforts to ransom a Jew taken prisoner in Moravia; much anxiety is voiced at the news of destruction in Nikolsburg; a pawnbroker reproves his married son in Vienna for neglecting his scholarly duties through excessive involvement in the financial activities of his father-in-law; a Prague doctor writes that he is in such demand from Jewish and Christian patients that he has had to buy a horse to make his rounds; many of the women correspondents are preoccupied with their fur coats, veils, wimples and lacework, but two make mention of the capture of Nördlingen by Duke Maximilian of Bavaria (1573–1651), and the coronation of the Winter-King, 'the Heidelberger', and his queen, respectively on Monday 28 Heshvan and on Thursday 1 Kislev.[21]

Into the private–public world of these letters the Thirty Years' War violently intruded. But in Prague, Bohemia and Moravia it did not, on the whole, interrupt the consolidation of Jewish life and settlement that had, albeit fitfully, been in progress since the late sixteenth century. In certain respects it may well have accelerated the process. Normally, every *kehillah* had a bias in favour of the status quo. Here, in Prague, as nowhere else, sympathy for the empire abounded and this would have been reinforced by the pillaging of the Jews' Town that accompanied the early victory of the Bohemian rebels in 1619 and the 'loans' extorted by the new rulers. The community hailed with enthusiasm Emperor Ferdinand's victory at the battle of the White Mountain in 1620, and the reconquest of Prague, all the more so as the Jewish quarter of the city enjoyed effective imperial protection from the marauding soldiery. R. Lippmann Heller composed a number of penitential poems in thanksgiving and the community instituted a special festival of celebration, the Purim of Prague.[22]

Jacob Bassevi, the financier, had reasons of his own for welcoming the victory. In the early 1620s he entered into a syndicate with Karl v. Lichtenstein, governor of Bohemia; Wallenstein, the imperial general; and Hans de Witte, the Calvinist banker from the Netherlands, to lease the mint and provide currency for the Habsburg war effort. This in fact took the form of the debasement of the silver content of the florin. Bassevi's role was determined by his control over the operations of the Bohemian silver mines. In the heyday of the consortium, Bassevi's weekly income is estimated at 4000–6000 florins. But already in the early 1630s his position started to weaken. He enjoyed, however, the continuing protection of Wallenstein, on whose estate at Gitschin he took refuge in 1632. Bassevi died in 1634, shortly after Wallenstein's assassination.[23]

Like Meyzel before him, Bassevi was also the leading elder of Prague Jewry, and through his career, however chequered, was instrumental in enlarging the area of the Jews' Town. He not only was the recipient of adjacent houses by way of gift from Lichtenstein but on his own account also made purchases; he bought a house from the officers of the diocese of the Holy Cross at a cost of 5850 schilling. Two brothers, the rabbis Löbl and Markus Pecz, bought a house for 2750 schilling. The cheapest house cost Mauschl Löbl Konirz 200 schilling.[24]

During the years of war Prague Jewry did not benefit only through an extension of its living space but also economically. Jews were now permitted to travel and trade without hindrance throughout all Bohemia in all legitimate goods; and to attend, on the same footing as Christian traders, all public annual and weekly markets; were required to pay no higher tolls and taxes; and were free to acquire and to exercise any craft. An imperial privilege of 1623 also went some way towards rectifying the legal disabilities suffered by the members of Prague Jewry, inter alia, decreeing that only those persons who had incurred debts should be liable to arrest, that the Jews, their elders and judges should not collectively suffer should a Jewish malefactor escape punishment through flight, that to Jewish evidence in court be given the same weight as to Christian. The Jews fared better than the Protestants, who were expelled in their hundreds of thousands. In fact the community won permission to erect over its council chamber a tower crowned with a small belfry that summoned the elders to their sessions. This betokened some degree of stability and even acceptance.

In April 1623 the Jews of Prague mounted a spectacular display to welcome Ferdinand II on his visit to the reconquered city: three young girls, playing violin, lute and guitar, led a solemn parade of Jews garbed in their Sabbath finery. There followed the Jewish butchers, dressed in white, bearing two flagpoles each of which supported two small boys. The rabbi followed, carrying a Scroll of the Law. Behind him a group of Jews held aloft a canopy (*huppah*) sheltering a tablet of the Ten Commandments. Jewish schoolchildren sang psalms; one carried a silver plate, inscribed in letters of gold with an address of homage to the emperor. The procession halted from time to time, to enable one of the elders to read the address (in German).[25] The emperor confirmed the existing rights and privileges of the Jews and in 1625 and 1626 this was repeated.

The relaxation of political pressure had to be paid for, at a time moreover when traders were cut off from the fairs at Leipzig, Linz, Passau and Freistadt. In July 1623 the elders were first required to negotiate with the Bohemian Chamber over a demand for 50 000 Reichsthaler as a contribution to the war effort. After a prolonged and intense debate they managed to knock this down to 30 000. Shortly afterwards, in 1627, the Jewish quid pro quo for the concessions contained in the imperial privilege of 1623 and after was agreed at an annual contribution of 40 000 florins. It is generally agreed that in their taxation policy Ferdinands II and III were not overbearing or exacting or unfair. This does not take into account taxes levied by the local Bohemian authorities which at times more than doubled this total to 82 000 florins annually; also it does not take into account indirect taxes (on wine, grain, timber and so on), or head and house taxes. In the first Jews and Christians were treated equally but the head tax levied on Jews was four times that on Christians. Taxes sometimes took the form of deliveries in kind, for example meat, oats and corn or, as in 1645, equipping 500 soldiers with shirts and shoes.

In the early 1630s even the Chamber must agree that the community was suffering poverty and hardship, that its contributions were paid by certain wealthy members, that the community itself was burdened by debts of 120 000 florins.[26] This situation had political consequences to which the differential distribution of the tax burden significantly contributed, for an arbitrary limit turned differentiation into inequality. Fixed assets (*Vermögen*) and sums employed in trade and credit were both taxed at the rate of 1 dinar per 100 florins, but no further tax was levied on trade and credit once the sum due reached 4 dinars. Similarly, if the tax on fixed assets reached 6 dinars, then the taxpayer was also not liable to pay any further tax. Thus it was possible for a wealthy man to pay less than someone less well endowed, for example a person owning assets of 500 florins and liquid sums of 10 000 paid 5 dinars on the first and the fixed limit of 4 dinars on the second, 9 dinars in all. But a man with 600 florins in assets and also 10 000 florins employed in credit paid 6 dinars altogether, for these 6 dinars already brought him to the limit of his fiscal obligations. By the end of the war, poverty made it necessary to reduce the tax levels required to qualify for the franchise.[27]

During the years 1619–36 no less than four rabbis held the post of chief rabbinate in Prague – this is a sure guide to the degree of disturbance. An early victim was R. Moses b. Isaiah Menahem (in office 1621–3). His enemies apparently denounced him to the authorities on account of supposed irregularities in his residential permit and he left Prague to become chief rabbi in Posen. The most distressing fate overtook the very distinguished R. Yomtov Lippman Heller, the author of a classic commentary on the Mishnah. Born in Wallerstein (Bavaria) in 1578, Heller later studied at Friedberg in Hesse before entering on a long period of service as rabbinical assessor in Prague (1596–1624). Following short-term posts in Nikolsburg and Vienna, where his communal statutes and ordinances were of more than local importance, Heller returned to Prague in 1627 as chief rabbi and as head of the yeshivah. He also partook of the traditional Prague interest in astronomy and to a lesser degree the natural sciences.[28] In the absence of a central Jewish government, Heller actively tried to use the authority of the Prague *kehillah* as a substitute for such a government, specifically in order to mediate in conflicts elsewhere. In 1627 he wrote to the leaders in Glogau (Silesia) on behalf of a certain Yudel, aggrieved at his treatment by those leaders. Heller summoned them to attend a court either in Posen or Prague, on pain of *herem* if they refused. Prague he preferred, because the emperor had made Prague supreme over Silesia in tax matters and it was in any case the seat of the 'major rabbinic court'.[29] The next year Heller intervened in a protracted confrontation in Frankfurt between the so-called *Hevruta*, an oligarchy of self-perpetuating ruling families, and those who espoused a broader-based government. This dispute drew in not only the extremely influential Council of the Four Lands in Poland but also the emperor and the Frankfurt town council. Heller summoned the Frankfurt community to send two plenipotentiaries to Prague, again on threat of a general *herem*; also to no avail. His attempt to assert the supremacy of Prague was thwarted.[30]

Heller was at risk from local enemies. The rabbi who exalted imperial power fell victim to that very power, though machinations within the Jewish camp certainly set the wheels of imperial justice in motion.[31] Heller's central position in the *kehillah* but also his function as chairman of the commission required to apportion the tax due to the emperor of 40000 florins made him highly vulnerable and exposed, all the more because of his closeness to Bassevi, one of whose sons had married one of Heller's five daughters. In the spring of 1629 aggrieved persons had already complained to Emperor Ferdinand of inequality in the imposition of the tax burden, to which the emperor replied with a stern reproof for the elders, coupled with a warning against the use of the *herem* and threats of imprisonment to intimidate the complainants. A few weeks later Heller was arrested, his enemies denouncing him to the authorities for writings that allegedly blasphemed Christianity. Heller himself attributed the attack to the financial stress in repaying loans that the community had contracted at high rates of interest in order to pay its taxes. 'When the pitcher lacks barley, strife knocks at the door' – Heller quotes this Talmudic adage (Baba Metziah 59a) as a source of communal dissension. Heller was first taken to Vienna and imprisoned in the company of criminals on capital charges. Soon he was taken to another prison in the Jewish shopkeepers' quarter where local communal leaders could visit him. This was the prelude to hostile questioning: 'How could he praise the Talmud, when Popes had already ordered its burning?' one interrogator asked. Eventually rabbinical intercession secured Heller's release, on staggered payment of a ransom of 10000 gulden – 2000 at once, 1000 after six weeks and the rest in installments of 1500 gulden. Donors, guarantors and Heller himself jointly provided these sums and in 1629 after an imprisonment of 40 days Heller returned to Prague, on the eve of the Day of Atonement. He passed the remainder of his rabbinical career in Nemirov (Grodno), Wlodzimierz (Volhynia) and Cracow. In Volhynia, Heller made himself unpopular through his opposition to the sale of rabbinical posts.[32]

By coincidence or otherwise 'the Heller affair' preceded an intensified programme of conversion. Judaism remained a permitted religion, as distinct from all other non-Catholic religions after 1627.[33] But Jewish practice still had to confront attempts at its suppression, in the immediate sequel to

Heller's arrest and departure. At the initiative of Cardinal Khlesl of Vienna in 1630, the Jews of Vienna and Prague had to attend compulsory conversionist sermons, on penalty of a fine of one Reichsthaler if absent. Those in Prague were delivered in German, by arrangement with the Archbishop of Prague Cardinal Horrach, in the church of Our Lady. The Jesuit preacher gave his sermons, during which the Jews were forbidden to sleep or chat, on the (Jewish) Sabbath. This choice only reinforced the Jews' opposition. Rabbi Pinchas Horovitz, a former colleague of Heller, put himself at the head of the resistance and 'as the outstanding ringleader of the present-day disruption' was arrested and interrogated before a special commission. During this period also the Jewish printing presses were closed down (1630–3) and the Talmud once again became an object of suspicion.[34] Religious disputes were recurrent; for example, in 1646 the elders must petition the archbishop to silence the preacher of Sankt-Galli whose sermons were inciting the populace against the Jews. Genuine conflicts of interest existed; for example, not only did the guild of Jewish butchers compete with the Christian but its members also sold meat during Lent; there were Jewish musicians who not only played during Lent but were also sometimes engaged to play at Christian festivities (marriages, baptisms). On the other hand, in 1632 when Prague fell to the Saxon invaders the document of capitulation (article 6) provided for the security of the Jewish quarter.

By no means did the departure of Heller put an end to communal dissension. At one time three parties contended for power: first, the Bassevi party which, second, an opposing party accused of fraud and corruption, and third, a party of neutrals. But the emperor dissolved the 'neutralists'. The ruling, Bassevi party, used the weapon of *herem* against its opponents so much so that the Bohemian Chamber made this practice punishable by a fine of 1000 ducats. Bassevi's death in 1634 intensified distrust and enmity when his heirs accused the elders, especially Löbl Brandeis, of dishonest administration of the estate. In 1635 the emperor imposed on the community a new constitution and a new electoral procedure that called for elections only once every three years; electoral rights were made dependent on taxable capacity and three categories of electors created. These formed an electoral college of 200 persons from whom the council of some 20 members eventually emerged by way of a complex and indirect system of election. In the later 1640s voting was made compulsory and a secret ballot introduced using stamped and certified voting papers. The franchise was also enlarged to include those members whose taxable capacity had hitherto been too low to qualify them to vote; it was now argued that this might result in the tenure of certain offices by illiterate persons unable to read or write. In the community no one was unable to read or write, came the riposte.[35] In 1648, in the final stages of the war, 22 Jews were killed and 30 wounded in defending the city from the besieging Swedes, under Königsmarck. The Jews also dug trenches along the White Mountain, a participant recalls, and these were known as 'the Jews' rampart' (*Judenschanze*).[36]

Elsewhere in Bohemia and Moravia the Jews enjoyed 'a sort of respite for recuperation' (*Erholungspause*), partly because Protestants were seen as the more dangerous enemy, taking priority over the Jews.[37] In the 1620s, in return for annual contributions of 40000 gulden (Bohemia) and 12000 (Moravia), the emperor granted provincial Jewries exemption from all other taxes and tributes, and access to open markets (whether weekly or annual) in the royal and other towns; nor were the Jews required to pay tolls on duties in excess of what Christians paid; in their business affairs and conduct they were not to be 'hindered, disturbed or attacked' or their goods interfered with. Ferdinand III confirmed these privileges and instructed the authorities to extend their protection to Jewish traders in the royal towns.[38]

These privileges obviously did not safeguard the Jews from the general hardships and destruction of wartime, especially the sufferings inflicted by the Swedes after their victory over the imperial forces at Leipzig in 1642. Centres such as Brünn, Prossnitz, Holleschau, Leipnik and Kremsier were among the worst afflicted. At the war's end in 1648 the number of inhabited Jewish houses in Moravia was only somewhat more than double the number of those abandoned – 773 against 341.[39]

The fluctuating but generally favourable circumstances of war had parallels beyond Prague, Bohemia and Moravia. Conditions in the Upper Dukedom (Obergrafschaft) of Darmstadt indicate the improved economic situation in the early years of the war. The Jewish population increased from 26 families in 1619 to 30 in 1621. The intensified burden of taxes that the Jews were able to bear points in the same sense, as do certain data from Jewish socio-religious life. In 1623, according to Darmstadt municipal records, at the house of Hayyim guests at a wedding feast consumed almost 400 litres of wine; a circumcision at the son-in-law of Löw was celebrated with 80 litres.[40] In 1626 and the years immediately after, the new ruler, George II, who fostered an explicitly anti-Jewish policy, was unable to expel the Jews as he had resolved. He had to content himself with prohibiting Jewish trade in hides and skins and the engagement by Jewish employers of Christian workers. A new *Judenordnung* in 1629 inter alia reduced the permitted rates of interest, reintroduced the censorship of Hebrew literature and limited Jewish cattle-slaughterers to providing only for the needs of the Jewish community. In the middle 1630s the situation worsened in consequence of the billeting, burning, famine and plague that followed the defeat of the Swedish troops at Nördlingen. In 1635, 2200 people are said to have succumbed to bubonic plague in Darmstadt alone. Hence the dispersion of Jews to countryside and villages. This did not necessarily entail financial hardship, for the register of losses in cash and goods submitted by certain Jewish traders after the quartering of Franco-Swedish troops in 1645 exceeded those of the average merchant. Manasse, after the war, when the state stood in need of capital for reconstruction, claimed equality of rights in the market with other merchants, since he bore the same burdens.

Manasse enjoyed the sympathy of the authorities but failed to make good his demand.[41]

The years of war did not interrupt the process of resettlement, though this process was erratic and haphazard, in accordance with the incidence of epidemics and campaigns. In the province of Paderborn, in Westphalia, ruled by a prince bishop, some dozen localities supported 67 families. Warburg, in 1646 the largest community in Paderborn, sheltered 15 families and by the end of the war about 30. Here was the seat of the provincial rabbi, first mentioned in 1619. By 1628 these communities had organized themselves into some sort of federation which was fully functioning by mid-century. The four families admitted to Altona in 1611 grew to 30 by 1622 but dwindled to 10 in 1639. In Hohenems in 1617, 12 Jewish families from Rheineck were given permission to settle; in 1593 one Jewish family settled in Gunzenhausen, in Franconia, consisting of the family head, two married and two unmarried sons, a son-in-law, a teacher, together with children and servants; the *Judengasse* in Hanau in 1603 housed some 10 families who formed a total of 159 persons by 1607. These totals are not quite so limited as they appear, the family unit being better understood as a household. A tally of the 63 Jews made at Kitzingen, near Würzburg, in 1641 shows that one household consisted of husband, wife, three children, a brother, a manservant and a maidservant, eight persons in all. Only the schoolteacher and cantor lacked servants, their households in each case being limited to husband, wife and two children. During the war, Jews (horse-dealers in the main) returned to Durlach whence they had formerly been intermittently banned. At Emmerich, in the Duchy of Cleves, the number of Jews increased to the extent that in 1629 they acquired the ground for a cemetery; likewise in Wesel. Gumpert Salamon, founding father of a family of court Jews, had his base in Emmerich.[42] To the east, in the duchy of Pomerania Jewish peddlers and dealers took the place of their Scottish forerunners in bringing consumption goods to the isolated villages and estates of the area. The Scots either withdrew from the countryside during the war years or conducted their affairs from the suburbs of Danzig. The peddlers also bought village products; in the later seventeenth century this interchange evolved into the *Verlag* system whereby the *Verleger* supplied to the village weavers raw wool – the principal product of the duchy – for conversion into the finished garment, normally uniforms for the military. The predominance of Jews in this trade later brought restriction on their activity, instigated by the clothmakers' guild in Stargard and elsewhere. In Posen growing economic difficulties led to intervention by the community elders with the Polish king and the local duke to secure the reduction or remission of taxes due for the years of 'the tumult of war'.[43]

Further south, at Breslau, on at least two occasions, the emperor intervened on behalf of the Jewish traders at the fair. The first time followed a protest to Ferdinand II by Israel Benedikt, leader of Silesian Jewry and founder of the community at Glogau; he appealed to the emperor, in reliance on 'recorded old tradition', against a projected expulsion of the Jewish merchants who remained in Breslau for trading purposes beyond the prescribed duration of the fair. The immediate sequel is unclear but in 1627 an imperial privilege granted Bohemian and Silesian Jews equality of status with Christians, including the payment of customs duties. In 1635 when the imperial authorities again intervened on the Jews' behalf it was to require that the Jews be permitted to remain in Breslau for 14 days before and after each of the four annual fairs, and to this the council agreed.[44]

On the fringes of communal life, a young man born in Fulda *c.*1609 spent most of the years of war wandering with his wife and young son in the area of Wenings, Friedberg, Hanau and Bingen. He earned a precarious living as teacher. Wryly the young man comments: 'Teaching is certainly a holy occupation; yet God spares such occupation to him whom He will favour, especially if that man has a wife and children.' As Rabbi Judah Mehler Reutlingen the young man spent the last fifteen years of his life in Bingen as communal rabbi. He died in 1659.[45]

In Alsace and Metz the demographic revolution was perhaps most remarkable. The expulsions from Mulhouse, Obernai, Saverne and so on in the fifteenth and early sixteenth centuries were followed by the resettlement of small groups of 2–3 families in areas where they had no legal basis.[46] By midcentury these had reached a total of 100–115 in Upper and Lower Alsace. Renewed expulsions later in the century from Austrian Upper Alsace will certainly have reduced this total. Only with the onset of war was growth renewed, with, for example, new or enlarged settlements in Haguenau, Mulhouse, Westhoffen and Obernai. Whereas, at the beginning of the century, the number of Jews in Alsace was reasonably estimated at less than 1 000, this had increased to something between 1 500 and 2 000 by 1637.[47] The newcomers were no doubt peddlers and small moneylenders. On the other side of the Rhine, trading in the booty from sacked towns and the debris of the battlefield offered the chance of livelihood and profit. Grimmelshausen, in his satirico-picaresque novel of the war, *Simplicissimus*, refers to such Jews, and also to Jewish horse-dealers.[48] West of the Rhine these opportunities can be reasonably supposed to have been no less attractive.

A bilingual literary work in Hebrew and Yiddish originating in the lower Moselle district in the early years of the Thirty Years' War gives some idea of the social tension inside the *kehillot*. This is the Sefer Massah u-Merivah of Alexander b. Isaac Pappenhofen. This contains a debate between a rich Jew and a poor Jew. Underlying the debate, despite the opposition between the two (exaggerated for dramatic purposes), is wealth, and the question posed is not whether wealth or poverty is better, but whether wealth is good or bad. Wealth is not condemned and poverty is not praised. The rich Jew is self-assertive to the point of arrogance and accustomed to rule. The poor Jew is humble. The rich Jew has gained his wealth from moneylending and trade – 'his money earns good interest'. He deals in jewellery, precious stones, spices, unredeemed pledges. When he travels it may be on horseback and he is perhaps armed. The poor peddler goes on foot, staff in hand, pack on back. He lives on dry bread and a hardboiled egg. The rich man tells the poor man, 'Without money there's no living – you cannot give your sister or daughter in marriage.' Also, it is his very wealth that enables the rich Jew to fulfil many of the commandments. 'Without my money and my intercession', he tells the poor Jew, 'you would have nowhere to live. None of the taxes that I pay do you pay'. The rich Jew has the power of wealth to annul 'evil decrees' and to ransom prisoners. His philanthropy extends to the provision of dowries for the girls of poor families, facilities for study and relief for the poor of the Promised Land. The poor Jew is dependent on the wealthy Jew for his livelihood as servant or employee. The rich man sees himself as generous and open-handed. To the poor man he is a tightfisted money-grubber who will even shut his door in the poor man's face. The rich man complains that business is bad and money short; but to the poor Jew what is short is charity and kindness.[49]

In Metz in 1595 there were no more than 25 families (*c.*120 persons). By 1637 there were 85 families, comprising 349 individuals. In 1617 Metz was already considered important enough for its rabbi to join with colleagues from Hildesheim and Fulda in mediating between contending parties in Frankfurt am Main.[50]

Vienna would seem to have thrived most, from and during the years of war. In this period of 'the second ghetto' – 1625–70 – Vienna prospered in terms of scholarly repute and numbers. The Jews, not without stress and friction, established themselves amid a bitterly hostile population, a church fired with the anti-Jewish animus of the Counter-Reformation and the unreliable policy of the Habsburg rulers. Substantial payments, both regular and extraordinary, were a condition of this success. At the end of the sixteenth century the community apparently consisted of 31 families which in fact an expulsion of 1601 reduced to 12, when the community failed to make good a loan of 20 000–30 000 florins to meet the costs of war. The community had two 'synagogues' (what form they took is unknown) and a burial ground with some sort of permanent structure attached. The earliest grave dates from 1582. The members of this community enjoyed the status of *Hofbefreiter*, that is to say, they and their households were free from all local taxes and from duties on goods supplied to the emperor, also from the compulsion to wear the Jews' badge (a yellow circle on the left side); they could move freely wherever the emperor established his residence, and were subject only to the jurisdiction of the marshall of the court. The elders, led by Veit Munk in the early 1600s, without any rabbinical support, resolved internal disputes. This last was an extremely important provision, for it protected the *Hofbefreite* Jews from the jurisdiction of the Vienna magistrates or the governor of Lower Austria.

These Jews operated as retailers, selling from open shops. Their goods included fruit and wine. They also functioned as pawnbrokers with the right to sell unredeemed pledges after a year and a day (though this right had apparently to be negotiated separately). Other Jews made it their business to supply the mint with precious metals. The community also included servants in the households of the *Hofbefreite* Jews and an unknown and varying number of 'foreign' Jews – that is, those lacking residential rights.

None of this favoured status came cheap and the price took the form of extortionate taxation and forced loans. This did not diminish the attraction of Vienna, and by the early seventeenth century the number of household establishments had risen to about 40. The circumstances of war enhanced the importance of Viennese Jewry vis-à-vis the crown and its finances. This refers in particular to their role as sources of forced loans, suppliers to the army and operators of the mints, although it is not possible to be precise. There were forced loans of 10 000 florins in 1619 and of 17 000 florins in 1620.[51]

This relationship gave the Jewish leadership the leverage to secure important concessions from the new emperor, Ferdinand II. His accession in 1619 almost coincided with the outbreak of war in 1618, and its intense demand for finance. This weakness no doubt accounted for the alacrity with which the emperor reacted to Jewish complaints of maltreatment by soldiers. He instructed the Viennese magistracy to ensure that Jews were not 'molested' in the streets of Vienna. The Jews successfully requested the confirmation of their privileges (1622). Their petition for the same commercial status as that enjoyed by Christian court-purveyors also succeeded. This provided for protection from arbitrary arrest, freedom from collective liability for the misdeeds of individuals, exemption from billeting troops, and permission to establish a synagogue, as formerly granted to Veit Munk in 1603. In agreeing to this petition the emperor granted permission to the elders to appoint 'an impartial rabbi, cantor, *Vorsinger*, *Schulklopper* and butcher'.[52] (Why would the rabbi need to be 'impartial'? Because of the part he took in apportioning the tax burden.) Jewish protests induced the emperor also to silence the anti-Jewish sermons of a Catholic preacher in Hanau.[53] Jacob Bassevi in Prague was among the Dutch and Italian bankers who came to rescue the empire in 1623 from the declaration of partial bankruptcy accelerated by a weak currency and inflation. He took a mediatory part in securing for Viennese Jewry its new and enlarged privileges.

To wide sections of Viennese society – the populace, clergy and magistracy – the notion of a synagogue was abhorrent. The call was again raised for an expulsion of the Jews. This did not happen for the time being – on the contrary, in 1624 the designation of a special area in Vienna for Jewish residence actually strengthened their position. This development corresponded to, and reconciled, contradictory impulses among the Christian and Jewish populations of the city, respectively. To the first, if the expulsion of the Jews was for the moment unattainable, then at least let them be segregated, *faute de mieux*. To the Jews however, a segregated area offered enhanced security and in this very context Viennese Jewry sought its safeguard. At the end of 1624,

Ferdinand gave his approval and issued a patent specifying the area known as the 'Untere Werd' – later renamed Leopoldstadt – for Jewish residence. In his autobiographical memoir, *Megilat Eiva*, R. Yomtov Lippmann Heller, rabbi of the community and its senior judge from 1625 to 1626, exalted the emperor and enthusiastically welcomed the innovation: 'For then [the Jews] became united in one community...formerly they lived among strangers, each one for himself, they were not as one assembly until our master, the emperor – may his glory be raised on high – gave them a special place outside the city, and a fine synagogue was built and the place met all the needs of the community and of the Jews.' This ghetto was unusual, but not unique, in also including a prison among its buildings – for the punishment of transgressors.[54] Stabling was provided for the horses that were dealt in.

The patent establishing the ghetto was indeed generous for the Jews thereby secured freedom from taxes and dues to the Vienna magistracy, beyond those that Christian residents of the Untere Werd would have paid; the Jews in civil and criminal cases involving Christians remained subject to the authority of the *Hofmarschall*, but they must not shelter any *unbefreite* or 'foreign' Jews; they enjoyed the right to move unhindered in and out of Vienna, without the obligation to wear the Jew's badge; their religious freedom extended not only to the practice of all 'ceremonies' with attendant personnel but also to the right to maintain an abattoir and ritual bath and to elect their 'judges'; at all times and not only at time of war they were exempt from any obligation to billet (*Einlosen*) troops, mounted or on foot; lastly, the emperor commanded all ecclesiastical and secular authorities in no way to hinder the Jews in the exercise of their freedoms granted by the patent. Early in 1625 before actually taking up residence in the Untere Werd the Jews secured further concessions that included the right to trade at weekly and annual fairs, to maintain open shops and stalls in the inner city, and to work as tailors and furriers for the needs of the community. The ghetto was primarily a residential area, for the shops and storehouses of its dwellers continued to be in the city. The ghetto traders rented these from the Christian owners of the premises. The Jews had to return at night to the Untere Werd. Obviously, the concession embodied in the provision for a ghetto – especially when the emperor extended the area both for residence and trading – had to be paid for. Hardly, in February 1625, had these concessions been made than the bill came in June with a demand for 10 000 florins in 'voluntary aid'. In October 1626 came a further demand for 2000 florins outstanding and an additional sum of 5 000–6 000.[55]

The Jews had not only to meet these financial demands but also to withstand ecclesiastical pressure. In 1630, in partial satisfaction of Cardinal Khlesl's demand for their expulsion, the emperor ordered the Jews to attend conversionist sermons every Sabbath afternoon. Two hundred Jews had to attend, of whom one-third must be women and one-fifth children of both sexes. The Jews had recourse to passive resistance, that is, dozing off during the sermon.[56] In 1637, on the accession of the new emperor, Ferdinand III, the Viennese town council and burghers renewed their appeal for the expulsion of the Jews. A comprehensive petition accused the Jews of ruining the country, monopolizing trade, intercepting visiting merchants before Christians had a chance to deal, building a 'new Jerusalem' in Vienna, practising usury, debasing the currency, spreading infection through their unhygienic congestion and old-clothes dealing, evading taxes, and blaspheming the Saviour Jesus Christ and the Virgin Mary.[57]

For the time being these pleas went unheeded. Vienna during the years of war continued to attract Jewish traders; and the community prospered to the extent that its wealthier members (belonging to between two and eight families) supported a synagogue, Beth HaMidrash, hospital and a range of fraternities. By 1669 the ghetto comprised 120 houses and about 2000 persons.[58] Settlement in Vienna, Metz and Alsace paralleled that in Livorno, Hamburg and Amsterdam.

2
'A Little Jerusalem' and 'A Great Jerusalem'

In these terms the Sephardim of the seventeenth century referred respectively to Hamburg and Amsterdam.[1] In the resettlement of western Europe these port-cities were central to the incentives offered by the Atlantic economy. The conversos from Portugal, towards the end of the sixteenth century and beginning of the seventeenth, followed in the wake of the new to the blossoming or burgeoning commercial centres of Livorno, Amsterdam and Hamburg, and later of Bordeaux and London. In aggregate the number of these individuals was not large – it is unlikely that the total number of Portuguese individuals who adopted Judaism at these and other centres exceeded 4000.[2] Within these societies germinated and were debated some of the most contentious and radical ideas agitating recent Jewry. They are the Jews whose life, Schwarzfuchs writes, 'was dominated by this constant call of the sea'. To Sorkin they constitute the new social type of 'the port Jew'.[3] They created a new framework for Jewish practice; whether because of their troubled background or because of the economic emphasis on overseas trade and shipping is not clear. In any event, it has led to the description of Hamburg Jewry as 'perhaps the first really modern Jews, who sharply divided between their private (religious) and public (worldly) life'.[4] For the Sephardi world in general this distinction is indeed operative in the seventeenth and eighteenth century (and anticipates a similar distinction in parts of the Ashkenazi world by about a century). Thus a certain disregard for the Oral Law and its rabbinic exponents and practitioners marked the new settlement. This had already shown itself in Venice, and in Livorno would provoke a bitter clash.

The first contact between the Medici rulers and the Iberian conversos dates back to the 1540s. A half-century later, the celebrated *La Livornina* (1593), the charter of privileges issued by Grand Duke Ferdinand of Tuscany, invited merchants of 'any nation' to settle in Pisa and Livorno. But it was addressed in the main to Levantine Jewish merchants and to those New Christians who had reverted to Jewish practice. *La Livornina*, which the Venetian charter of 1589 strongly influenced, had a validity of 25 years, subject to renewal; it promised exemption from any enquiry into the Christian past of any new-comer; he enjoyed the same right as the Christian merchant of Florence and Pisa to engage in all forms of commerce and trade (except the trade in sec-ond-hand goods); he could own fixed property and need wear no distin-guishing garb, and La Livornina contained no provision for any ghetto. La Livornina granted the community full internal autonomy in matters of reli-gion, culture, administration and justice. In the Christian world this is said to be the first Jewish community to which no religious restrictions applied.[5] The community kept its records not in the customary Hebrew but in Portuguese and Spanish.

Fortified by its charter, the settlement in Livorno rapidly increased. It seems that the population of 114 in 1601 grew to 711 by 1622 and to 1175 by 1642 (out of a total population of 4403, 9745 and 12 484 respectively). It may well have reached c.3000 by about 1670. The overwhelmingly Sephardi community derived their wealth from the trade in coral and precious stones, often in conjunction with the East India Company based in London. Factories for the manufacture of soap and silk were another economic mainstay; the favoured profession was medicine.[6]

From 1607 the community had the status of a self-governing polity and also at this time began to organize itself independently of Pisan Jewry to whom it had been previously subordinate. Five massari whose names the grand duke drew by lot from among the members of the leading Iberian fam-ilies governed the community, through their exercise of legislative, judicial and executive authority. An electoral assembly of some 60 members con-firmed the massari in office. Italian, Levantine and other Jews had to con-tent themselves with positions of lesser authority – that is, if they sought at all to occupy public office. These 'lesser positions', however, were by no means unimportant in that in the main they comprised offices in the vari-ous fraternities of the community; and these fulfilled basic religious func-tions: charity to the native and foreign poor, the provision of special foodstuffs for the festivals (for example unleavened bread on the Passover), the welfare of the Promised Land, the ransoming of prisoners, the conduct of burials, the upkeep and extension of the synagogue (which had to keep pace with the growth of the community).[7] There also existed a fraternity, of which the warden is first mentioned in 1651, and the members of which assembled to recite penitential prayers, elegies and lamentations in the com-pany of the community's rabbis and scholars.

In education rabbinic influence predominated. The yeshivot, normally founded by the wealthy families, whose names they sometimes bore, were headed by distinguished rabbis – not only R. Jacob Sasportas but also R. David Nieto and R. Jacob Hagiz. Education was socially structured. Only the sons, nephews and grandchildren of the founders of the yeshivot might be educated in them. The instructors were forbidden to teach other boys below the age of fourteen. Private tutors and the Batei Hamidrash provided education at a lower level. The financial obligations of the community, as elsewhere, fell broadly into two categories: those due to the state and those required to meet the expenses of communal institutions and employees. Responsibility for the first was leased out by the duke to a Jewish tax-farmer. He raised the sums due from customs duties, stamp duties and residence tax. As to the second set of obligations, those destined for internal purposes, these were met by a form of self-taxation, supervised by specially elected collectors whose activities were subjected to punctilious scrutiny. Voluntary donations, synagogal offerings, legacies and bequests supplemented these funds.[8]

In Livorno, as generally in the contemporary Sephardi world, the rabbi had little independent authority. Like the synagogue officials, the cantor and the beadle, he was appointed and paid by the *massari* (that is, the parnassim to whose authority he was also subordinate). The Council, known as *Issur ve-Heter* ('Prohibition and Permission'), did indeed include at least one rabbi among its membership of three. But as a court of law its authority was limited to adjudication in matters of personal status and to the passing of judgements that had no more than advisory force. In commercial and mercantile law – obviously of major importance in a community such as Livorno – only the *massari* could enforce such verdicts as they thought fit to deliver. This was, in any case, part of their prerogative, as defined in *La Livornina*. But it was this very issue that provoked a major clash as between the Torah and *La Livornina*. A community *takkanah*, adopted in 1670, decreed that commercial disputes falling within the purview of the *masseri* were to be adjudicated 'in accord with the city's mercantile legislation which we take upon ourselves and confirm as if it were explicitly determined by the law of the Torah'. This decision not only replaced Jewish by alien, gentile law but also derogated from the authority of the rabbis in favour of communal leaders. In the Italian states this sort of relationship was by no means unfamiliar – Venice being a good example. In Livorno, hitherto, although a decision by the rabbinic Bet Din had no legal force unless and until it was approved by the *massari*, according to the *Livornina*, the *massari* had the authority to judge in accordance with Jewish law and could 'in certain cases' extend their power to judge in accordance with 'other juridical principles'. But it was by no means clear in which cases this extension would apply. There was also provision for the right of a litigant to claim adjudication in accordance with the Torah, but this had been progressively limited. Now, were the proposed decree to be accepted, the only civil cases to come before the Bet Din would be matters of marriage, kashrut, loans, mortgages and the like. In all other cases the *massari* would judge in accordance with local mercantile law. This decision, they explained, 'flowed from the desire to prevent obstacles in jurisdiction in commercial matters'. Sasportas, at one time a rabbi in Livorno, found this unacceptable, and reacted vehemently, not only in defence of the Torah but also of the Sages: 'Who has seen anything like this?', he exclaimed in a letter, 'The honour of God, and His Torah and the honour of its students profaned.' 'I will not rest', he added, 'until the Torah is restored to its former glory and the honour of its students and the community also.' He denounced the *masseri* as a coterie of self-selected oligarchs, eager 'to throw off the yoke of the Torah...Money reigns supreme.' Sasportas did however make an important distinction between those 'born in Jerusalem' for whom he reserved his most bitter attacks, as compared with the 'others', that is the ex-conversos. In the event, Sasportas gained a partial victory in that if one party to a dispute demanded a judgement in accord with the Torah then the other must agree.[9]

Like those of Livorno the port-Jews who followed the call of the sea to Hamburg had the source of their welcome in economic considerations. This was fluctuating. Even so during the first half of the seventeenth century a Portuguese community dominated by large-scale traders grew up. In the 1590s some seven households had established themselves as its nucleus. The early settlers included the famous court physician Dr Rodrigo (Ruy) de Castro who reached Hamburg by way of Antwerp and maintained a Catholic guise. His wife (d. 1603) was given a Christian burial. But that year the first official reference to the presence of the Portuguese already demanded an end to their toleration on the grounds of their Jewish belief. This was the first of a number of similar complaints made by the burghers and the clergy to the Hamburg senate. They did not hinder the growth of the colony. By 1610/12 'the roll of the Portuguese nation' listed 125 persons, included 26 married couples. About this time also, the community used three prayer-rooms in the houses of Rodrigo Pires Brandao, Alvaro Diniz and Ruy Fernandes Cardoso. This provoked the emperor Ferdinand II to complain to the senate that whereas the Catholics were denied 'the exercise of their religion', the Jews were allowed a synagogue 'for the sake of trade'.[10] But not until the early eighteenth century did the Portuguese win permission to establish a separate construction as synagogue. By 1652 the three groups of worshippers had formed themselves into one congregation.

In 1618 Hamburg allowed non-citizens of members of the Hanseatic League to become shipowners.[11] This permission further encouraged the overseas trading activities of the Portuguese; so much so that when the twelve-year truce between Spain and Holland expired in 1621 and trade came to an end and many merchants transferred their assets from Amsterdam to Hamburg, it seemed that the latter might eclipse the former.[12] This did not in fact happen but Hamburg continued to consolidate and prosper. A number of contracts between the community and senate signed at roughly five-yearly intervals – 1612, 1617, 1623 – and purchased for growing sums in cash – granted rights of settlement and residence. These contracts brought about some sort of balance between the Sephardim and senate in so far as they permitted the newcomers to engage in 'upright and honourable trade, similar to our burghers and other inhabitants'. But they made no concession in matters of religious practice and disallowed the acquisition of fixed property. The agreement of 1623 made particular provision for the protection of the Sephardim against 'insults, injuries and outrages'.[13] Plans for the erection of a synagogue had repeatedly to be postponed; it was forbidden to perform circumcision in the towns. By 1653 the 120 families equated to some 600 people, and under a Mahamad the united congregation of Beit Yisrael was formed and the community constituted itself as an organized, autonomous entity. The union of the three existing congregations, each of which was identified with a particular family, did not proceed without tension and feuding that survived the union. In 1662 this led to fisticuffs in the synagogue.[14]

The governing body, in an environment where the congregation was virtually coterminous with the community formed an oligarchy and enjoyed the plenitude of power, such that it could prohibit the establishment of any congregation other than the existing Beit Yisrael, and take any measures necessary for the well-being and effective functioning of the community. The Mahamad engaged R. Jacob Sasportas to fulfil the duties of rabbi, teacher and slaughterer; it introduced sumptuary regulations and measures designed to impose peaceable and, above all, unobtrusive behaviour on the community members. This rubric included measures of censorship designed to avert any written offence to the Calvinist clergy or theologians. In order to enforce these and its other regulations, the Mahamad had the power to impose fines and, in an extreme case, to exclude the offending member from the community. Between these powers and those exercised by the Mahamadim in the Sephardi communities of Amsterdam, London, Livorno and Bordeaux there was no substantial difference.

The Sephardim thrived, both in terms of numbers and prosperity. They helped to finance the Hamburg bank, founded in 1619, and by 1623, 46 members held 43 accounts. Antonio Falerio had the ninth-largest turnover.[15] The trade in tobacco and sugar from Brazil and with Spain and Portugal formed the basis of this prosperity. There were also trade links with the Baltic and Mediterranean. Among the members of Beit Yisrael this prosperity was unevenly distributed. The register and rolls of dues and taxes disclose extremes of wealth and, if not of poverty, at least of unremitting struggle to make ends meet. At one extreme the wealthy Abraham Senior Teixeira paid 600 marks; at the other Dr Yzaque Pereira paid 4 marks and others 1 mark. The stratum of household servants and communal employees may well have included persons unable to make any payment at all. One way to deal with the poor was to assist their emigration to South America and the Indies (Essequibo, Surinam, Barbados). Abraham Teixeira devoted some of his wealth to this purpose, making funds available, proportionate to the size of the migrating family, on condition that they did not return to Hamburg within three years.[16] In Amsterdam and London the Sephardim operated similar policies (see below). The motives in all these cases blend concern for the poor with concern for the good name of the community, which an immoderate number of indigent and demanding Jews would inevitably jeopardise. The declining years of Beit Yisrael in Hamburg overlapped with a growing Ashkenazi presence. Ashkenazim had begun to settle in Hamburg from the 1620s. They lacked a legal basis and depended on private personal arrangements and the connivance of the town council, as against the resistance of clerics and burghers. In 1649 this led to their expulsion and many Ashkenazim took refuge in Altona. Later, in the wake of the Danish–Swedish War, there was a return to Hamburg, again on the basis of private arrangements. Not until 1710 did an imperial commission lead to the legalization of their settlement rights.[17] The friction that the Ashkenazi presence generated made Hamburg less attractive to the Sephardim. This was by no means the sole reason for their withdrawal. The proposed imposition in 1697 of a special tax of 20 000 marks and an annual payment of 6000 for the right of residence persuaded certain of the wealthier and more respected merchant families to remove to Amsterdam, by way of Altona and Ottensen. The Hamburg bourse took several years to recover from the withdrawal of capital. Inside the community, disputes and feuds among leading families, which led to intervention by the senate (1703) and eventually demanded an imperial commission of enquiry for their resolution (1710), caused further disruption. Increasing financial weakness compounded the crisis of dissolution.[18]

Amsterdam, 'the great Jerusalem', offered to those in flight from persecution and an enforced uniformity of belief, a broad degree of religious freedom that made the United Provinces a haven indeed. Here was a uniquely favourable milieu, presented largely in negative terms: the absence of any subjection to discriminatory and extortionate taxation, of an enforced and congested residential area and of the compulsion to wear any distinguishing badge; on the positive side a wide degree of religious and economic freedom. Those occupational barriers that did exist were less burdensome than elsewhere, though they certainly impoverished the community. In no other city in western and central Europe did so beneficent a set of circumstances obtain (though they would slightly later in London). The promise of trade is again the key to settlement.[19] In 1579 the Union of Utrecht declared that on account of religion no one was to be persecuted. In 1585 the States General, by promising full freedom, sought to attract to Amsterdam the Sephardi merchants in Antwerp. By the turn of the century a few hundred Sephardim were already settled in Amsterdam. They constituted no more than one religious group among the myriad sects of Calvinists, Huguenots, Catholics of this merchant cosmopolis. In 1616 the magistracy took a major step towards regularizing the status of the Jews, demanding of their representatives not only that they live in accordance with the general legislation of the city, which included the prohibition on the construction of a synagogue, but also that they suppress any written or verbal attacks on the Christian religion;

refrain from any attempt to convert or circumcise Christians and refrain from sexual intercourse with married or unmarried Christian women, including prostitutes. Jewish marriages could be performed, but only those where the parties did not fall outside the officially permitted degrees of kinship (which negated of course large areas of Biblical law). The position of the Jews was economically limited in that they might not occupy any civil or military office, join a guild (except the brokers' guild) or engage in retail trade or peddling. This left in the main shipping and the wholesale trade. Citizenship was limited to the individual and was not therefore heritable.[20] By 1618 three congregations existed and in 1639 these united under the name Talmud Torah. The new congregation had provision for public worship, burial and the supply of kosher meat.

In the initial stages of the settlement there is no doubting the deep appreciation for these conditions. 'A tranquil and secure community dwells in Amsterdam today,' wrote one of the city's rabbis in 1616 to a colleague in Salonika:

> And the inhabitants of the city wish to increase the city's numbers, and have established laws and customs accordingly. Among other things they permit every man to believe in God as he pleases, and each lives according to his own faith, on condition that he not vaunt it about in the streets that he rejects the faith of the city's inhabitants.[21]

This was a private letter; the writer had no need to embellish his experience for any ulterior motive. The growth in population confirms the 'pull' of Amsterdam. In 1614 the number of families stood at about 160. The population doubled during the next decade, largely as a result of the favourable circumstances created by the 12-year truce with Spain (1609–21). About 50 new Sephardi families annually reached Amsterdam during this period, most remaining in the city. Of 124 marriages contracted in Amsterdam 1598–1630, 95 of the husbands were born in Portugal, 10 in Antwerp, 9 in Amsterdam, 3 each in Spain and France, 2 in Venice and one each in Jerusalem and Salonika.[22]

From the start, Venice, even in its seventeenth-century decline, exercised a sway over Amsterdam. The very name of the community – Talmud Torah – came from Venice and this is not nominal but indicative of the repute and prestige that Venice continued to command. This relationship derived from the status of Amsterdam as a virtual *tabula rasa* in terms of organized Jewish life and therefore receptive, and settlers who brought with them little or no recent experience of such life, neither from Spain and Portugal nor from the lands of their more recent diaspora. The status of Venice had multiple ramifications of a very wide stretch. There was migration and the dispersion of an extended family; commercial links encompassed the trade in jewellery, the Dutch financing of Venetian enterprise in North Africa and the Levant, and the role of the Venetian *zecca* as depository for Dutch funds. Two of the more influential Amsterdam rabbis – Joseph Pardo and Saul Levi Mortera – came from Venice. Venetian rabbis adjudicated and sought to resolve major theological debates in Amsterdam concerning matters of Biblical interpretation as well as the eternality (or otherwise) of punishment for the denial of central articles of belief. Electoral procedures and certain communal institutions came to Amsterdam by way of Venice.[23]

The founders of the new congregation couched its statutes in Portuguese, which was also the language of its records and, incidentally, also the language used by the congregation in everyday life. The membership embraced all Jews of the Spanish and Portuguese 'nation' living in Amsterdam in 1638. Those Jews of any other 'nation' were excluded and would require the Mahamad's permission to attend services. No other Sephardi congregation might be established in Holland. The governing body, the Mahamad, consisted of 7 members, elected in the first instance by the fifteen leaders of the three merged congregations and subsequently by the seven officers themselves, thus ensuring self-perpetuation. The Mahamad had the right to levy direct and indirect taxes, to regulate disputes among the members of the *Kahal* (who only as a last resort might turn to a non-Jewish court) and to impose a variety of punishment on transgressors and offenders. It operated a quasi-formal censorship in order to ensure that no controversial works appeared in print, especially any polemical works taking issue with Christian doctrine. Outside the synagogue, the Mahamad had ultimate responsibility for the conduct of the meat market, charitable distributions to the poor of the Amsterdam congregation and of societies for the relief of the poor in Palestine, for the ransom of prisoners and captives and for attending the sick and burying the dead. The community had three principal sources of income, their relative importance varying from time to time: the tax on kosher meat; the *finta*, a tax on wealth, subject to periodic adjustment by the Mahamad; and the *imposta*, a turnover tax on imports and exports. The *imposta* was first levied in 1622 at a rate of 1 per cent on the value of import and export transactions. There were certain provisions, variations and exceptions to cover the levy on brokers' transactions, funds on deposit, the profits of shipowners, dealings in certain commodities and in certain countries and so on. The proceeds of the levy were devoted to the general welfare of the community, including its representation before the civil authorities.[24] In this general context, the rabbi fulfilled his function in the conduct of synagogue services, and in preaching and teaching. Fortified with these powers, the members of the Mahamad looked on themselves as 'the peers of the city fathers', as absolute rulers over their subjects.[25]

In the seventeenth and eighteenth centuries the schools in Amsterdam excited the envy of Ashkenazi rabbis and scholars, mainly because of their graduated curriculum of study. R. Jacob Emden, like the Maharal of Prague a century earlier, made a most unfavourable comparison between Ashkenazi and Sephardi pedagogy. Whereas the latter began with Bible and Hebrew grammar, the former, he complained, 'turn the correct sequence upside down; they want the boy to learn the whole Torah while standing on one leg and be fitted to study Talmud before he knows the holy language competently'.[26] To Ashkenazi scholars, for example R. Shabtai Bass (Poland) and R. Sheftel Horovitz (Prague), the Sephardi schools served as exemplars. A curriculum that began with the study of the prayer-book moved on to the Pentateuch and its cantillation filled Bass with admiration. In the third class the boy learned to translate the Pentateuch into Spanish, and studied the weekly portion with Rashi's commentary. Next came the study of the Prophets and Hagiographa, also with their melodic cantillation: 'one boy reads the verse in Hebrew and then he explains it in Spanish and all the other lads listen to him'. The school devoted the fifth and sixth classes to the study of Mishnah and Gemarah with the traditional commentaries and standard codes, and to Hebrew grammar. Bass had special praise for the school's extensive reference library and for the fact that it was the community that appointed and paid the teachers. 'The teacher does not have to fawn on anyone and teaches all his pupils alike, whether rich or poor.' Those visitors made much of the fact that at each festival time the boys studied the relevant laws through the appropriate chapters in the *Shulhan Arukh*. 'This is kept up until all the boys are familiar with the holiday regulations', R. Bass wrote.[27]

Not only to Sephardim did Amsterdam offer shelter and settlement. During the Thirty Years' War more and more Ashkenazim found refuge in Amsterdam. The first immigrants hailed in the main from the Rhineland, the Palatinate, Swabia and Bohemia. By *c.*1640 there were perhaps no fewer than 500 German Jews in Amsterdam, most of whom were on the verge of destitution. To the existing Sephardi community these *Tudescos* were highly unwelcome, and ostracized as far as possible. In 1642 as much from self-interest as from benevolence, the Sephardim founded the Avodat Hessed society to teach the Ashkenazim a trade and rescue them from begging and poverty, and thereby also achieve a moral purpose. The Sephardim extended financial aid to, and subsidized the emigration of, the *Tudescos*. These measures denoted a blend of deterrence and assistance, born out of a concern with self-preservation and solidarity with fellow-Jews. In 1660 a fraternity, Talmud Torah, was founded, to provide education for the children of the poor. A movement away from direct election of the parnassim towards indirect election presaged an oligarchic style of self-government on the traditional model. In 1671 the Great Synagogue of the so-called 'High German' *kehillah* came into use. Many of the Ashkenazi Jews who reached Amsterdam did not take up permanent residence in the city but saw it as a halfway house on the route, say, to London or perhaps overseas, or perhaps to eastern Europe.

In the meantime, from the mid-1650s and for the next decade or so, Amsterdam became a reception centre also for many hundreds of refugees from Poland and Lithuania, mainly the latter. To the Sephardim they were known collectively as *Polacos*, as distinct from the earlier wave of *Tudescos*. The *Polacos* were in flight partly from the devastation wrought by Khmelnitski's Cossacks in Poland and the Ukraine but mainly from the depredations of the Muscovite forces in Lithuania. They came by way of the Baltic to Hamburg, Altona and Amsterdam. Here, it seems, most settled, and were in receipt of aid from the Sephardim. With their encouragement the *Polacos* founded their own community in 1660 and this followed the Lithuanian rite.[28]

The newcomers, whether from Poland, Lithuania or the German states, stood out from the sedulously cultivated image of the Sephardim which their poverty could not but threaten to bring into disrepute. They were Yiddish-speaking, culturally distinct and, above all, poor, verging on vagrancy and beggary. They are an early and particular instance of the growing number of beggar-Jews and vagrants in the seventeenth and eighteenth centuries (see below, chap. 11). To the Sephardim the *Tudescos* and the *Polacos* were almost equally unwelcome, which has led to the use of the term 'Jewish antisemitism' to characterize certain aspects of Sephardi policy in Amsterdam vis-à-vis the Ashkenazim.[29] This applied to the ethnic exclusivity which denied to '*Tudescos*, Italian Jews and mulattos' entry to the communal school; denied membership of the community and burial in the communal cemetery to the Ashkenazi consort of a Portuguese woman; and deprived a Portuguese Jewish male of membership rights in the case of his marriage to a Jewish woman who was not of the *nacao*.

The Sephardim included the *Tudescos* and *Polacos* in their policy of assisted emigration. Normally, as was made clear for example to R. Nathan Shapira on his visit to Amsterdam (1657), the Sephardim did not give money to Ashkenazim.[30] In view, however, of the threat posed by Ashkenazi indigence, this self-control was relaxed and in 1658–60 the Mahamad financed the emigration of some 200 *Polacos*, it is estimated. It is true that they received less monetary assistance than the Sephardi *despachos*. They also had different destinations. Whereas the *despachos* were sent to the Dutch colonies and possessions in the West Indies and South America, the *Polacos* were sent to Danzig, Frankfurt am Main, Mainz and Deutz. This was not necessarily the end of the emigrés' wanderings; Jewish residence both in Danzig and Frankfurt was uncertain because of either poverty or official restriction. After about 1670 the Mahamad discontinued this policy of assisted emigration.[31]

In the Sephardi world a small number of overseas traders dominated the 'great Jerusalem', economically and politically. For them this was the Amsterdam in the harbour of which 'the masts of 6000 vessels create the semblance of a forest'.[32] In Venice, Luzzatto had written in his *Discorso* (see above, p. 4), only a few Jews owned ships. But among those thousands of vessels in Amsterdam harbour, a number bore such names as *Het Huis Levi*, *Prophet Moses*, *Konig Solomon*, *Queen Esther*, *Mazal Tov*, *Schmuel Ha-Katan* (Little Samuel), and so on. In the 1620s and 1630s the register of the *imposta* tax already showed some 20–50 important merchants. Some had an annual turnover of 100 000 guilders or more.[33] Overseas trade sometimes went hand in hand with *haute finance*, diplomacy and army provisioning; for example, the Suasso family fathered a network of commercial, military and diplomatic interests. They seem to have originated in the small northern Portuguese town of Braganza. Antonio Lopes (later Isaac Israel) Suasso (1614–85) first engaged in the export of wool from Spain to Amsterdam, as part of a family network that had relations in Bordeaux, Rouen and Antwerp. In 1653 Suasso married into the de Pinto banking family of Rotterdam, and with his subsequent move to Amsterdam he developed interests in banking, the trade in precious stones and diamonds. His involvement in the overlapping world of finance and diplomacy followed by virtue of the common front that Spain and the United Provinces brought into being against the France of Louis XIV (the Hague Alliance, 1673). Suasso, it seems, handled the funds channelled northwards by Madrid bankers for the payment of German mercenaries and subsidies to those rulers sympathetic to the Spanish–Dutch effort. For his services Carlos II of Spain raised Antonio to the hereditary nobility as baron of Avernas-Le-Gras in the Spanish Netherlands. The second baron Suasso, Francisco (Abraham Israel, ?–1710) married into the banking family of Senior Teixeira of Hamburg and essentially continued in his father's wake in the intertwined world of *haute finance* and diplomacy. Francisco subsidized the election of an allied candidate to the bishopric of Münster, and on a number of occasions advanced payment to allied troops, particularly during the Nine Years' War, 1689–98. Perhaps his greatest coup was his involvement in the financial operation that preceded and accompanied the journey to England of William of Orange (William III) in 1688 (see below, pp. 83 ff.).

Most of the community worked in a variety of less colourful occupations related to the craft and service trades – as tobacconists (including tobacco-cutters), apothecaries, printers, sugar-refiners, diamond-polishers, silk-weavers, goldsmiths and brokers in various commodities. There were also some professional men such as doctors, and students of medicine at the university of Leyden.

Evidence indicates the presence of a distinctive Sephardi economic sector. New Christians and Jews constituted, for example, the great majority of the correspondents and agents of Jeronimo Nunes, and in the goods in which he specialized – tobacco and diamonds – relatively large numbers of Amsterdam Jewish artisans were employed.[34]

For the most part the prosperous merchant adventurers of the Dutch golden age were happy to enjoy the rewards of their enterprise. One striking exception was Abraham Israel Pereira, to whom wealth brought embarrassment and a yearning to shed the vanity of the world. Pereira's support for educational and philanthropic causes partially allayed his spiritual distress and turmoil.[35] Most of his contemporaries, it seems, when they welcomed home their cargo from the Indies, or when the broker and speculator returned from the turmoil of the Exchange, could anticipate modes of leisure pursuits much indebted to the Iberian model – for example the performance of allegories, poetry recitals, debates in the literary salons of Academia de los Sitibundos (Academy of the Thirsty, 1676) and Academia de los Floridos (Academy of the Flowery, 1685). These assemblies brought together the intellectuals of the community and its merchants.[36] Literary interests engaged with financial in the classic work of Joseph Penso de la Vega (1650–92), son of a wealthy banker, himself a man of letters. His *Confusion de Confusiones* (1688), in the fashion of a quasi-Platonic dialogue, but couched in Spanish, presents an erudite philosopher, a prudent merchant and a scholarly investor debating 'operations in stock, their origin, etymology, reality and all the devices of speculation'; and these business pursuits readily lent themselves to social intercourse: 'the big leaders consort in establishments called Coffee Houses, where a certain drink, known to the Dutch as *coffy* and to the Levantines as *café*, is obtainable. These houses are most convenient in winter because of their stoves and the variety of diversions they provide…In some we find books, in others draughts and chess, and in all of them entertaining gossip; the customers drink chocolate, coffee or tea, and most of them also take tobacco to mellow their conversation. News is exchanged and business discussed; thus warmth, refreshment and agreeable intercourse may be obtained at small cost'.[37] Reading matter, it may be assumed, will have included the *Gazeta da Amsterdam*, the Spanish-language journal that brought to the merchant community commercial and political news.

Both Venice and Amsterdam were hives of heterodoxy but, at its most simple, in Venice a person must live as Christian or Jew and belong to one or the other community; in Amsterdam it was possible to live as neither and belong to no community. The Jews thereby faced an unprecedented situation which, in view of the background of the conversos, their enforced estrangement from Judaism, Catholic upbringing and education and so on constituted a source of danger as well as of opportunity. As to the danger, it was precisely to their converso background that, for example, R. Sasportas had attributed the willingness of the Livorno *massari* to replace the Torah by local commercial law; as to the opportunity, I have tried earlier to demonstrate the creation *de novo* of a functioning *kahal* that provided all necessary facilities. If however, the public sphere is abandoned to an alien jurisdiction, what then remains of Judaism and Jewish practice? This lacuna was made good, in part at least, by an emphasis on synagogue attendance, decorum and worship to an extent that invested the building itself with an aura of holiness. This contradicted accepted teaching that denied to the synagogue as a building of brick, stone, wood and so on any degree or order of sanctity. In Amsterdam, however, precisely this quality was reserved to the synagogue of the Talmud Torah community, 'consecrated' in 1675.[38] Fortunately, at least according to Abraham Israel Pereira, one of the wealthiest traders among the parnassim, congregants were only too ready to break off and discuss the arrival of a cargo or a ship.[39] In any event, the synagogue became rapidly the object of a cult in which can be seen a certain Christianization of Jewish practice, even if the design of this *Esnoga* did derive from the supposed design of Solomon's Temple at Jerusalem.[40]

In the particular circumstances of the Portuguese Jews of Amsterdam, withdrawal from concern with the public sphere and the commercial world as an object of halakhic interest produced a religiosity determined by the synagogue service, the rite of circumcision, an immoderate exercise of the *herem* as a means of social control and a concentration on the private. The theological counterpart to this type of observance has been identified in the formula to which those girls and women seeking inclusion in the lottery for dowries had to subscribe: they must 'confess the unity of the Lord of the world and the truth of His Most Sacred Law'; and this formula, it is said, 'circumscribes the Marranos' [minimal] Judaism perfectly'.[41]

It is also true, however, that those Jews from Spain and Portugal who now, in the late sixteenth and seventeenth centuries, created in Venice, Livorno, Amsterdam, London, Hamburg and other cities and territories the Sephardi diaspora, did collectively bear in common the real memory of forced conversion, persecution at the hands of the Inquisition, pretence, subterfuge and a sense of exclusion. This complex of emotions, generated by a shared past, created a sense of identity that bound together 'the men of the Nation', no matter how scattered they might be or their theology attenuated. This bond was by no means commensurate with the task of establishing a *Kahal* of an unfamiliar type in which the led did not necessarily have to obey their leaders. They might in fact dissociate themselves entirely. It was perfectly possible in the heterodox environment of the United Provinces to live on the periphery of Jewish life and even in a sort of limbo. In 1643 Manuel Carvalho maintained that although he had settled in Amsterdam in 1603, not until 1616 had he 'openly practised the Jewish religion'.[42] Contemporary London had many a counterpart to Carvalho. The converso who discarded his Christian mask enjoyed autonomy and had no obligation to accept rabbinic authority and/or the discipline of the *Kahal*.[43]

The converso who transformed himself from a Manoel into a Manasseh had no need to identify himself as Jewish, join a community, practise Judaism or even accept its prevailing tenets. Such a person might even hold views that were irreconcilable with those tenets; or perhaps he was simply ignorant of them. In Spain and Portugal even works in translation would have alerted the Inquisition to the likely presence of Judaizers and this deterred enquiry and thwarted the quest for knowledge. The notions of

Judaism that did prevail among some conversos may well have been coloured by their sole access to the works of apostate Jews and Christian writers. This would be a further barrier to instruction. In Livorno the substitution of prevailing commercial law for that of the Torah removed from rabbinic scrutiny a salient sector of economic life. In Hamburg, given the overwhelming authority of the Mahamad, 'to determine and to decree, as it saw fit, what was most appropriate for the advancement of our holy community', there could be little, if any, scope for independent rabbinic jurisdiction. The Sephardi *Kahal* in Bordeaux would reproduce the same distribution of influence.

In Amsterdam, although distinguished rabbis and teachers such as Saul Mortera and Menasseh b. Israel engaged in what is known as 'the proselytization of the Marranos', they were unable to overcome the antinomianism, deism and scepticism of the seventeenth century. The *Voice of a Fool* was soon echoed in Amsterdam by Uriel da Costa, who was influenced by this work.

This treatise, which came to light in 1662 as the purported work of the unknown Amitai bar Yedaiah ibn Raz, but the true author of which has been unmasked by Talya Fishman as the distinguished Venetian rabbi R. Judah Leon Modena, proclaims a doctrine critical of the authority of the sages to determine the practice of Judaism. If the Torah 'is not in heaven' but entrusted to the fallibility of men, what those men make of the Torah, how they interpret the Torah and apply the Torah must *ab initio* be matter for controversy. Apart from all else, who will determine, and by what criteria, which men will be entrusted with this responsibility? The Talmud at times tries to overcome this whole *Problematik* by creating the category of 'law given to Moses at Sinai' and by attributing to Moses much subsequent legislation (cf. TB Ber. 5a). But the topic remained sensitive and questionable. Theologically speaking, the *Voice of a Fool* does affirm the existence of God, creation *ex nihilo*, providence and the doctrine of divine revelation – a corpus of teaching that is all intended for man as the purpose of creation. The doctrine of immortality follows the submission that it lacks Scriptural authority; that it could not be derived from reason; but only that 'analysis greatly inclines – if it does not compel us – to believe that the soul has existence after the death of the body'.[44]

In its plain and simple understanding, *Voice of a Fool* proclaims an attempt to remove from the Oral Law, as elaborated by the rabbis, distortions, misunderstandings, exaggerations and indeed the whole gamut of supposed divergence from the Written Law of the Bible. Whereas there is no question but that here is indeed the work of divine revelation, the Talmud and the codes of law and conduct are the work of fallible humans and therefore subject to error and an invitation to criticism. From this standpoint and within a modified understanding of the Pentateuch, *Voice of a Fool* calls for a reduction in the number of blessings, greater importance to be attached to prayerful intent, an end to the celebration of the second day of holidays, a pruning of the proliferation of precepts relating to the ritual slaughter of animals, circumcision and the dietary laws and so on. *Voice of a Fool* also scorns establishing the festival of Hanukkah by reference to the miracle of the long-lasting oil rather than by 'all the acts of heroism and the victories performed by the sons of the Hasmoneans in Israel'.[45] In Modena's view these projected reforms had a cosmic bearing in so far as the present corrupted legislation of the rabbis, in its deviation from the Bible, had hindered the diffusion of Torah and obscured its message and thereby positively prolonged the exile. This was for the long term. In the short term, *Voice of a Fool* reinforces that genre of literature sensitive to the tense relationship between Biblical and rabbinic law.

Uriel da Costa was born *c.*1583 in Oporto and after studying canon law at the university of Coimbra held modest positions in the church. In 1614 he fled Portugal with members of his family and lived variously in Amsterdam and Hamburg. Here he was circumcised and lived openly as a Jew. Da Costa's particular objection centred on the Talmudic and rabbinic tradition, collectively known as the Oral Law; more precisely, da Costa's critique bore on the status of the Oral Law in relation to Biblical Law and its interpretation of the latter. His first work on this theme was the so-called *Propostas contra a tradição*. These were submitted in manuscript form to the rabbinic authorities in Venice in 1615–16. This work led to his denunciation by R. Judah Leon Modena (in his traditionalist persona) as 'a heretic and complete epicurean who has spoken presumptuously against the words of our sages', alleging that that they are 'a chaos' and denigrating all who took seriously the words of the sages.[46] Da Costa was put in *herem* in Hamburg and Venice in 1618 and in Amsterdam in 1623 (though these sentences may later have been revoked). His work may well have been shaped through a reciprocal relationship with *Voice of a Fool*, if there was in fact transmission. In any event, the original critique became even more radical, so that the negative evaluation of post-Biblical teaching and legislation reduced Judaism to Biblical teaching alone. Essentially, da Costa took up a fundamentalist stance vis-à-vis the Biblical text and sought to nullify any attempt to innovate legislation or practice on the basis of rabbinic tradition and interpretation, whether formulated in the Talmud or anywhere else: 'There is no evidence or hint in the Written Law that there is another Law.' This, then, could only be a human creation and therefore qualitatively distinct from the divinely revealed law of Moses.[47] Moreover, da Costa accused the sages not only of falsifying the law but also of making this deliberate in order to exercise control over their communities. In later life he extended his attack on traditional teaching to deny Pharisaic views by siding with the Sadducees in denying the doctrine of reward and punishment, the existence of an afterlife and the immortality of the soul; for none could he find authority in the Torah. The law of Moses was not the law of God but a human invention.[48] Da Costa eventually compounded his heterodoxy by subordinating the Torah to natural law, rejecting revelation and denying the canonical status of certain scriptural works (for example the book of Daniel). He committed suicide in 1640, through the inability to accommodate or reconcile the conflicts and metamorphoses he had undergone as Catholic, professing Jew, Biblicist and quasi-deist. None of this argumentation went unanswered, and R. Menasseh b. Israel, for example, was assiduous in the 1630s in contesting the Sadducean views of da Costa and in putting the case for the immortality of the soul and resurrection. This did not repress heterodoxy or heresy. Da Costa was certainly not isolated in his views and only a generation later the Mahamad imposed its uniquely celebrated sentence of expulsion – that on Spinoza.

3
On French Soil

In 1394 the Jews were expelled from France and in 1615 this expulsion was reaffirmed. During all this period and until the Revolution, on papal territory in the south of France four 'holy communities' existed from the fourteenth century. Two centuries later two very different *kehillot* joined the papal Jews on French soil.

A papal decree of 1624 confined the four communities to *carrières* (Provençal for streets) in Avignon, Carpentras, Cavaillon and L'Isle sur Sorgue. Their numbers varied from 1500 to 3000. They corresponded, legend has it, to the four 'holy cities' of the Promised Land: Jerusalem, Hebron, Safed and Tiberias. This status did not preserve Avignon, at least, from the same sort of tension common elsewhere. In 1643 a proposed change in the communal constitution would have raised the financial qualification for the franchise. This reached a level (100 livres) that deprived the poor (or three-quarters of the Jewish population) of their electoral rights. An appeal to the papal vice-legate led to the successful withdrawal of the proposed *takkanah*.[1]

As in Rome, in papal Provence also, fines had to be imposed for the rowdy and riotous behaviour that the Jews indulged in during the conversion sermons. At Carpentras the Jews stuffed their ears with wax or ostentatiously chewed the plentiful chestnuts of the area.[2] The number of synagogues was limited, and Hebrew literature subject to censorship and seizure. This isolation and pressure went hand in hand with for the lax observance of the Sabbath, dietary laws and of the rules governing relations between the sexes. An emissary from Hebron, Abraham Guedaliya, denounced these infractions.[3]

Inside their *carrières* the Jews enjoyed considerable powers of self-government, including self-taxation, providing only that their communal statutes met with the approval of the religious and secular authorities. A council of *baylons* had executive power; it was elected, chosen by lot or simply coopted from the three economic groups or *mains* into which the inhabitants were divided, and this council represented the *carrière* to the authorities and also functioned as the representative body of the community. As elsewhere, communal power rested with the wealthy. In the eighteenth century a fourth class of poor developed which was denied entry to the council and to the holding of any communal position. The *baylons* had powers to levy taxes and in this way financed a wide range of charitable, benevolent and educational bodies. The *baylons de l'étude* collected school fees, on a graduated scale, from each of the three *mains*. The poor paid nothing. Boys attended school until the age of 15, under the instruction of the local rabbi. The statutes of 1558 exempted both teacher and pupil from the tax known as *capage*. The same statutes also exempted Hebrew books and medical treatises from taxation.[4]

The sums raised had normally to be supplemented by loans raised from Christian institutions. The financial burden that the service of these debts constituted led to the virtual bankruptcy of the community by the time of the Revolution. Earlier they gave the Christian lender a stake in the economic stability of the community and thus served the debtor's political purpose.

At the turn of the sixteenth–seventeenth century, two contrasting communities came to join those of Provence: Ashkenazi in Alsace and Lorraine and Sephardi in the south-west, in and around Bordeaux.

To the east, this particular instance of sixteenth-century resettlement had its origin in the protection that France exercised over the three Lorraine bishoprics of Metz, Toul and Verdun. The members of the new and tiny *kehillah* were welcomed for their help in sustaining and financing the garrison at Metz. They operated under royal auspices. The house of Bourbon shared little, if any, of the anti-Jewish animus that distinguished the house of Habsburg. In 1603, Henri IV, disregarding local hostility, took the Jews of Metz and their property *'sous sa protection et sauvegarde spéciale'*, having regard to the services they had rendered to the state. At this time the community consisted of *c*.24 families, perhaps 120 persons altogether. By 1632 when the community totalled *c*.370 persons (85 families), Louis XIII confirmed the Jews' privileges, again on the basis of their services and utility. To the Jews the attraction was the chance to traffic in wartime booty and the bric-à-brac and débris of the battlefields. The intendant Jacques-Etienne Turgot, writing at the end of the century, was explicit in his reference to the motive that inspired the policies of Henri IV, Louis XIII and Louis XIV in attracting Jews to Metz, 'by reason of their usefulness to the state'.[5] Letters patent of 1657 which required the chief rabbi of Metz to be approved by the king before his confirmation in office testify to the state's interest in the Jewish presence. On the Day of Atonement 5418 (7 September 1657) Louis XIV and his mother visited Metz. Some days later, on the first day of the Festival of Tabernacles, they visited the synagogue in Metz. During the visit, the Comte de Brienne, chancellor to the King, asked R. Moses Cohen of Narol who had escaped to France from the Khmelnitzky massacres in Poland (1648–9) and become rabbi in Metz, how could he, 'from another realm', officiate as rabbi without royal permission? Narol was too scared to answer, but was comforted by the count's assurance of the king's favourable disposition towards the Jews – even more so, no doubt, by the reconfirmation and extension of the Jews' privileges.[6]

The government's success in attracting Jews to Metz showed itself by 1679 in a population of 795. A decade later, when Jews from Worms and elsewhere took refuge in Metz from the devastation of the Palatinate, Louvois (1641–91), as minister of war under Louis XIV, not only authorized this inflow but also ordered that the Jews be prevented from sending their daughters abroad, lest their settlement decline. He would encourage the Jews to 'be fruitful and multiply' (in direct contrast to later French policy). By 1717 the Jews in Metz totalled *c*.2100, equivalent to some 8 per cent of the total population.[7] In 1718 the Conseil du Roi authorized the Jews already resident in the city to remain there but set their total at 480 families.[8] This severely qualified the policy of Louvois.

In Alsace resettlement took a broadly similar course, again with royal encouragement. Only by the peace of Westphalia of 1648 did France come into possession of most of Alsace (those areas formerly part of the Habsburg empire). By 1680, Louis XIV through his *chambres de réunion* had slowly annexed the remainder and in 1681 Strasbourg was occupied. Nevertheless, well before formal French control prevailed, by the later 1630s the Alsatian Jewish population already amounted to an estimated 300–400 families, amounting to a total population of *c*.1500–2000. After the Thirty Years' War growth quickened measurably. This resulted not only from natural increase but also from an influx of East European Jews, in flight from the Khmelnitzki massacres in Poland and the Ukraine, 1648–9. In 1689, 587 families were registered; in 1716, 1269; in 1740, 2125; and in 1784, 3942, equivalent to a total of some 20000 individuals. The overwhelming majority lived in a rural or semi-rural milieu – in villages, hamlets and small market towns. In the military centres of Thionville, Sarrelouis and Phalsbourg other small *kehillot* were established.[9] The Jewish communities had their administrative headquarters at Breisach in Upper Alsace, also the seat of the French tribunal which annulled the liberties and privileges of local lords and towns.

The haphazard settlement of Ashkenaz in eastern France gave rise to two distinctive types of *kehillot*: in Metz, a major urban *kehillah*, later to develop into 'a mother-city in Israel', and a multitude of small rural *kehillot* in the Metz countryside and in a scattering throughout Upper and Lower Alsace. The economic imperative of proximity to trading routes, and to the larger towns which refused to accept Jews, determined in part the precise location of many of these tiny communities.

This piecemeal process in the seventeenth century left largely intact the hereditary privileges of the feudal lords, bishops and knights who governed the admission of Jews into their territories and their juridical status. This eventuated in a multitude of quasi-independent *kehillot* in which the local ruler, secular or ecclesiastical, might sometimes have the power to nominate or appoint a rabbi or parnass in his particular territory. In Upper Alsace alone, in the mid-eighteenth century, no fewer than 50 communities fell into this category. With the singular exceptions of Metz and Nancy no Jews lived in the major cities such as Strasbourg, Colmar, Selestat. Not only did Strasbourg preserve its right to exclude Jews from overnight stays but those Jews who traded there on a daily basis (in cattle, old clothes, bric-à-brac and so on) had to pay a humiliating body tax – *péage corporel*. Rare exceptions in receipt of temporary residential permits included a chess-player, furnishers of cavalry mounts during the War of the Spanish Succession, a money-changer and bankers who were in any case associated with a local Christian financier.[10]

In the post-Westphalian period and into the first decade of the eighteenth century depressed agricultural prices, poor harvests and popular misery marked the area. This helps to account for the widespread popular hostility to the Jewish presence fostered both by the church and economic rivalry. Raphael Lévi from Boulay was burned alive in 1670 on a charge of ritual murder. The Conseil du Roi had forcefully to intervene to save Metz Jewry from the expulsion demanded by the Parlement of Metz. In 1698 three Jews, *vagabonds et étrangers*, were tortured and burned alive for having robbed the chapel of Saint-Hippolyte in Obernai of certain objects and precious fabrics. The Jews had to appeal to the commandant of Alsace for protection against molestation and attacks on the synagogue.[11]

In the late seventeenth and early eighteenth centuries the Jews lived largely in Lower Alsace, dispersed over more than 100 localities. Westhoffen (37 families), Marmoutier (20 families) and Haguenau (19 families) were among the more important communities. Ribeauvillé (18 families) was in Upper Alsace the most important community. These latter communities and their fellows had the simplest of structures – normally, it seems no more than a *préposé* (or parnass) who might be elected (*préposé particulier*) or appointed by the local suzerain (*préposé seigneurial*) on payment of a certain sum. There is mention of a formal meeting of five *préposés* in 1702.[12] In 1784 the 473 Jews who lived in the village of Bischheim, and who constituted more than 50 per cent of the population, were attracted by its proximity to Strasbourg (where the Jews could trade only on a daily basis).

In the bishopric of Strasbourg the three *préposés* met twice a year. These assemblies would be a rough equivalent to the corporate assemblies (*Landjudenschaften*) on the other side of the Rhine. The duties of a *préposé* hardly went beyond tax-collecting (that is why they were sometimes known as *Einnehmer*) and maintaining order in the *kehillah*. The *préposé*, whether *particulier* or *seigneurial*, had only limited powers of constraint and on recalcitrants he could impose no higher a fine than 3 livres. When it was proposed to raise this to ten, the letters patent of 1784 rejected any such increase (see below, Art. 23). The locally elected *préposés* assembled from time to time and in their capacity as representatives of their individual communities elected the rabbis of Upper and Lower Alsace, based respectively in Ribeauvillé and Haguenau. These appointments always required royal approval. At an election in 1753, 50 local *préposés* were present. This procedure did not always avert bitterly contested rivalries. In 1753, for example, the death of

R. Samuel Baruch Weyl (of Upper Alsace) occasioned an acrimonious struggle for his succession between his son-in-law Jacob Gugenheim and the Frankfurt-born rabbi, Süssel Henes, from Creutznach in the Palatinate. The latter had the support of one of the *préposés généraux*, the wealthy Lippmann Moïse of Ribeauvillé. Gugenheim lost the election, which was no model of probity. Weyl's widow (née Esther Philippe) took the case to the provincial authorities in defence of Gugenheim, her son-in-law. Esther's complaint reached the *conseil royal*, by way of the intendant and Cardinal Mazarin but she was apparently unable to prevent the confirmation in office of Henes.[13] The duties of a rabbi included not only judging disputes between Jew and Jew but also drafting contracts and wills, resolving disputes among heirs, appointing guardians to orphans and determining 'the permitted and the forbidden' in other religious matters. In these rural and semi-rural *kehillot* of Alsace and Lorraine, the rabbinate coalesced with the seigneurial parnassim, either through the purchase of office or through the hereditary principle. 'The rabbinate of the Lower Rhine was dominated by the Aron family for nearly two centuries, and in Mutzig the communal rabbinic post passed from father-in-law to son-in-law over a period of nearly one hundred and fifty years (1716–1864)'.[14] To this coalescence however, in pre-revolutionary times, the divergent sources of authority acted as some sort of check and balance in that it was the king who authorized the rabbi to officiate whereas the parnass was often a local seigneurial appointment.

In the dozens of *kehillot* in villages and hamlets that were home to the pedlars, moneylenders and petty traders, poverty was the norm. A fortunate man had a horse and cart (making him a *colporteur renforcé* or *marchand forain*); the others peddled on foot, carrying their goods on their backs (*porte balle*). The Jews had to be versatile and turn their hand to whatever came their way: 'Some are reduced to money-lending', observed the Prince de Birkenfels in 1716, 'others trade in animals and others deal in all sorts of goods, in retail, and in running commissions. All of them, nonetheless, are not so attached to particular trades, that, as time and occasion demand, they do not follow one or the other indiscriminately, all the more so as they are very often obliged to take in payment all sorts of merchandise...no matter what kind, which they make it their job to re-sell'. Samuel of Bollwiller functioned as deputy cantor in the synagogue, tended the sick, was a storyteller, barber, marriage broker and 'commissionnaire'. This was no path to affluence; nor was peddling, but it became something of a hereditary calling. Ben Lévy, a former peddler, almost one hundred years old in 1841, published his memoirs of life in the mid-eighteenth century. He was born in a Lorraine village, the son of a *colporteur*. 'I was taught to read Hebrew, to translate the Bible and the Talmudic works.' At thirteen, the age of his religious majority, Lévy joined his father on his rounds. At eighteen he married the daughter of the local rabbi – 'in the presence of the community, assembled to the sound of the violin'. The villagers collected a dowry of 200 livres; and Lévy's

father handed over his own wedding outfit, 'which he had carefully preserved'. At 20, Lévy was the father of two and peddling on his own. 'The
Jewish peddler', he recalls, 'was at the time (that is *c.*1760) the sole bond
linking one village to the next; he brought news, he supplied the necessary
and the superfluous, he ran messages and arranged deals (*commissionaire,
courtier*), he was an expert in coins and medals, he bought and sold cattle
and harvests, he procured cash and he gave advice in major events – in a
word, he was the pivot on which turned all important transactions. And yet
despite, or perhaps because of, these numerous services, the Jewish *colporteur*
was the butt of incessant harassment and perpetual persecution not without
a clutch at my heart do I remember that I did not enter the smallest village
without the urchins running after me; throwing stones and shouting "Look,
the Jew, the Jew!"' Lévy's great consolation was the Sabbath day he passed
with wife and children. He arrived home Friday afternoon, amidst family
jubilation. 'I put down my heavy bundle and I dressed for the evening service. In the synagogue, friends and neighbours came to shake my hand. We
sang with delight the song 'Lecho Dodi' [Sabbath Bride] which promised
24 hours of rest and domestic bliss... Saturday was spent in the synagogue,
at the sermon, in visits and in promenading and night arrived always
too soon; as soon as the wine of *Havdalah* was drunk, I put on my clothes
for the road, took up my bundle and set off, for I often had to cover 8 or 10
leagues at night in order to reach a market next morning where I earned
something to satisfy my family needs for a week'. Between the struggle for a
livelihood and Sabbath rest among the family the lack of congruity is a feature that marks the accounts of peddlers' lives.[15]

   This was no way to live, and again and again the Jewish leadership in
Alsace agitated for permission to diversify away from the trade in old clothes,
second-hand goods, cattle and moneylending to which their Christian competitors in Strasbourg and elsewhere had largely confined the mass of Jews.
In 1717 a group of Jewish merchants submitted a petition to the State
Council (*Conseil d'État*) in which they argued strongly in favour of free
trade, economic equality, permission to enter the retail trade, whereby they
would enhance the prosperity of a devastated area and increase the tax
yields. The Jews also petitioned for leave to bring in girls from outside as
marriage partners for their sons; and for the exclusion of Jews from
elsewhere, unless the king or the seigneurs gave express permission. Where
they were at least six families, they sought to maintain a butchers' shop, selling the hindquarters at six *deniers* per pound cheaper than the Christian
butchers; to open synagogues without obstruction; to have access to
common pasture lands for their cattle. None of these demands was an innovation, the petition stressed. In the name of divine charity, the law of nature
and the rights of peoples, the Jews petitioned for redress from injustice and
prejudice.[16] The Council of State rejected this petition, like its fellows,
and until the Revolution no substantial change was made to economic

confinement. Evasion and subterfuge alleviated the confinement, and in this the state tacitly connived. Officially, 'Jewish' trade was virtually limited to the trade in money and every sort of second-hand goods. But it was an open secret that certain Jews, both rich and poor, flouted the law – simply because the poor could live no other way;[17] the Jews of Metz, Lorraine and also of Alsace engaged in the contraband trade of smuggling specie from one territory to another, in these areas of varied jurisdiction and currency systems. Swiss, Italians and Alsatians also took part in this *billonage*. The Jewish community in Metz more than once (in 1712, for example) attempted to suppress, on pain of *herem* 'the entry of specie from Lorraine into the country, since the king forbids it', but the trade undoubtedly flourished.[18] It was an obvious and convenient adjunct to peddling in the vicinity of the towns and further afield.

In eastern France the Jews created not only a variety of rural or semi-rural *kehillot* but also a major urban centre in the ghetto of Metz. This developed into a true 'mother-city in Israel'. From 1614 onwards the earlier requirement to live away from the public gaze gave way to the compulsion to live in the district of Saint-Ferroy. This lay to the extreme north-east of Metz and was the only area where Jews were permitted to buy houses. It had the shape of a rough quadrilateral about 280 metres long and of variable width of about 100 metres. During the eighteenth century the population fluctuated around the 2000 mark. Saint-Ferroy was in effect a ghetto, though the degree of physical separation from the Christian world was less than in the classic ghettos, of say, Frankfurt, Venice or Rome. Inside the ghetto enormous disparities of income and life-style prevailed.

Jacques-Etienne Turgot, the intendant at Metz 1696–1700, well describes the ambivalent milieu in which the ghetto found itself – under royal protection but intensely unwelcome. Turgot writes of the *'grandes jalousies'* of the Metz (Christian) traders whose only desire was to expel the Jews, 'although it is, so to speak, in the interest of the state that there should be some in Metz, but in a certain limited number'.[19] The Christian merchants fought to expel the Jews because, on the basis of the royal letters patent, they were engaging in branches of trade in competition with the established guilds and corporations (whose eventual restrictions will have contributed to the hardship and poverty from which most of the ghetto-dwellers suffered). The Jews had no permission to keep open shops (*boutiques-ouvertes*) and had to sell their goods from home; their right to sell new goods made in Metz or the *pays messin* was challenged. In virtually every decade from the 1630s to the 1670s, the Jews had to rebut the accusations and complaints of this or that guild, allegedly the victim of Jewish infringement. Mercers, butchers, tanners, shopkeepers, goldsmiths – these were among the more vociferous accusers. Jewish traders on the streets were not immune from harassment and might well be searched to ensure their goods were not new but second-hand. Following a protest at one such incident in 1704, the Parlement banned this practice (by virtue of its status as a court enjoying civil and criminal jurisdiction over the three bishoprics, Metz, Toul and Verdun). To rebut these charges added to communal expense for each case had to be fought and this required the engagement of a local advocate. Pierre Brandebourg, a Metz attorney, was paid over 600 livres in 1729 for his role in 15 trials. The Jews of Metz suffered disproportionate taxation; in 1695 they represented about one-twentieth of the population but contributed one-fifth of the capitation tax paid by the city.[20] What, though, of Turgot's other point, that 'the interest of the state' required in Metz the presence of Jews, albeit in limited numbers? This is a reference to the support that merchants and entrepreneurs in this frontier zone gave to the French military effort, to the garrison and to the provisioning of Metz. This commerce is what made the Jews welcome and ensured their security of tenure, and to a few brought considerable wealth. This is a French version of the association simultaneously developing in the German states between the court-Jews and the military policies of their respective rulers. Metz was a garrison town in a period of recurrent warfare, as well as of crop failure and food shortages. There was war with Holland in 1672, with the League of Augsburg in 1688 and the War of the Spanish Succession in 1702. Turgot justly sighed, 'the kingdom is almost always at war.'[21] In this context, in the late seventeenth and early eighteenth centuries, Metz Jewry found its *métier* in the supply of grain and horses to the French cavalry. This was the work of the so-called *étapiers* – military suppliers.[22] In 1698 at a time of near-famine in Metz Jewish suppliers (Cerf Lévy and Abraham Schwabe) achieved perhaps their greatest coup, albeit unwillingly. Under pressure from Turgot, they reluctantly agreed to supply 17 000 sacks of grain from Franconia and Germany to meet the needs of the town and of the troops stationed in the department. On the grounds of expense Louis XIV cancelled the agreement, to the relief of the Jews. At this point the Jews offered to bring in the grain, without commitment, on two conditions: first, that Louis intervene with the German princelings to secure free passage up the Rhine; second, that they retain the freedom to sell the grain throughout the province at whatever price it would fetch. With Turgot's support French diplomacy brought its resources into play, though without giving formal support to the Jews or accrediting them with royal authority. The grain was shipped from Mainz along waterways that traversed the territories of four feuding rulers – the Elector of Mainz, the Elector Palatine, the Elector of Trier and the Landgrave of Hesse. The intervention of Aaron Beer, Resident of the Elector Palatine and an important financier at Frankfurt on Main, and the French ambassador to Mainz formed part of the operation. It may well not have been profitable, in money terms; it at least relieved the famine and had a political bearing that, as Turgot remarked, enhanced the status of the Jews, 'to have themselves tolerated and strengthen their position' (*établissement*).

In supplying horses for the cavalry and cartage duties, the dealers of Metz were outstanding. 'They are the only people', declared Taillard, the Metz military governor in 1694, 'by means of whom we can bring horses from Germany.' In one respect this general activity created a privilege in that, although normally letters patent forbade Jews to own or rent any premises outside the ghetto, when '*le service du roi*' was at stake this restriction fell away; and this concession is generally taken to refer to granaries and stables. The demand for horses was unremitting and intensive, amounting some-times to 3000 to 4000, especially of course in time of war. At such a time, typically 1702–05, the intendant met with those whom he termed 'the heads of the synagogue' that is the elders and commercial élite, '*les grands juifs*'. The latter then assembled their horse-dealers, '*les petits juifs*', who were enjoined 'to do all that is possible for the service of the king and our satis-faction'. This was very much a Jewish monopoly, at all levels. Olry Cohen, a communal leader, saw the community in 1715 composed of 'a small num-ber of families in a position to undertake business ventures' and 'day-workers who are used by being sent into neighbouring states at the peril of their lives to collect what is needed for the support and supply of the horses for the king's armies'.[23]

Inside the 'synagogue', a banker and a supplier jointly organized the sup-ply chain. The banker provided the funds and negotiated with the purchaser, who was sometimes a minister in Paris; the *étapier* provided the animals. In one such operation the accounts of the banker Marc Terquem show that he put up 3000 livres in a syndicated venture with Lyon Cerf, the actual sup-plier. This sum was deposited in a chest, with an account book, in the banker's home. Lyon Cerf held the key to the chest and used his contacts with the mass of peddlers and small-time dealers to purchase the actual steeds in the *plat pays messin* and in Alsace – perhaps even from across the Rhine, although this entailed all the hazards inseparable from circumvent-ing export bans. Lyon Cerf was also required to arrange for the feeding of the horses. In 1701, 310 horses are supplied; 1702, more than 400 (at 260 livres apiece) for the cavalry in the army in Italy; in 1704, 1600 horses; in 1705, 1000 horses for the army of the Moselle.[24] If any of these deliveries conflicted with Jewish requirements, they were suspended. Turgot wrote in 1699: 'They are very religious in their holidays and whatever need one has of them, even for the service (that is, of the state), they never engage in any dealings the day of their Sabbath'. Saint-Contest, intendant at Metz (1701–15) wrote to Chamillard, the *contrôleur-général*, reporting the depar-ture of 107 horses out of 400 destined for the French armies in Piedmont: at Lyons the drovers will have to be replaced – otherwise 'they would be obliged to travel on their feast day, which they would not do for all the gold in the world'.[25]

Here and there mention is also made of espionage, 'pour le compte du Roi', undertaken by a Jew from Boulay, David Marchand (1702); other Jews supply tents and advance the troops' pay. There are Jews who supply meat for the troops (1709); two brothers, Moyse and Abraham Alphen, supply clothing for a regiment (1712); two Italian Jews, from Cazal (in Genoa), Raphael and Moses Sacerdotte (Italian for *Cohen*), maintain and equip hospitals for the French troops during the campaigns in northern Italy (1705–06).[26]

The supply services that the Jews of Metz and Alsace rendered to the French armies and civilians strengthened their *établissement* and merited countless tributes from the various intendants; and any order or even intimation of a local expulsion aroused their concern and at times also that of Louis XIV. The community was also an important taxpayer and from 1715 liable for the arbitrary tax due to the Brancas family which survived all protests till the Revolution.[27] Even the bishop of Metz, who complained that the permitted total of 400 Jewish families was too high, yet made an exception for the bankers, horse-dealers and 'certain others' (unspecified). But not for 'vagabonds'.[28] The end of the War of the Spanish Succession (1701–14) reduced the importance of the suppliers based in Metz; later in the century, it seems that suppliers from Alsace, who dealt directly with d'Argenson, the secretary of state for war, superseded those from Metz.[29]

It was no part of French thinking to nurture on French soil a studious Ashkenazi community. When the nascent French state came to encourage the repopulation of a devastated but coveted area, it did not envisage the creation of 'a mother-city in Israel'. Yet the willing help of kings and intendants, whose motives were quite other than the glory of Ashkenaz, had much to do with this consummation. Obviously, this is another of those instances where the two parties in the implementation of a common policy cherish very different hopes. Likewise, it was no part of that community's thinking to further the cause of the French monarchy; initially, that is – later the economic élite turned staunchly monarchist.

There is some evidence to suggest that in the same way as the state extended its control over the newly acquired portions of Alsace, so too did Metz Jewry find its liberty restricted. Although initially the Jews of Metz enjoyed freedom of movement outside their quarter in the Saint-Ferroy district, decrees from the late seventeenth century obliged them to remain inside the quarter on Sundays and feast-days.[30] Numbers were limited to 480 families in Metz. This limitation was applied selectively. The French authorities made a very clear distinction between those Jews of substance who could be useful to the state and the impoverished. This is *raison d'état* at its most refined. Bernard Creutznach, a German Jew and horse-dealer, wanted to settle in Metz in order to marry the daughter of Jacob Halphen, the banker. His application (1727) for permission to settle in Metz makes explicit the differential treatment of rich and poor. The minister of war approved Creutznach's application on the grounds that a distinction must be made between those Jews, who were 'so ragged that they barely have enough to live on', useless to the country, and those, like Creutznach, who were useful to the king.[31] To impose the wearing of a yellow hat also showed increased control. It had however, a chequered history. None of the early letters patent mentions costume. Apparently, not until the first half of the seventeenth century was it introduced. Even then there were exceptions and the Jews disregarded the order until it fell into disuse after 1715.[32]

What remained unaffected by growing control was the chief rabbi's need for royal approval before his confirmation in office. From the early years of Metz communal existence the rabbi could normally count on governmental backing. In 1624 and again in 1627–8 those members of the *kehillah* opposed to the rulings or election of R. Joseph Lévi and R. Moses Cohen were reminded of their duty to submit, by the Duc de la Vallette, governor of Metz, Toul and Verdun.[33]

R. Moses Cohen had previously served in Prague as a rabbinical assessor and thus inaugurated an impressive relationship. Metz looked not to Alsace but eastwards, and with the *Judenstadt* in Prague developed a special rapport, mediated through the rabbinate. Metz was the westernmost outpost of the Ashkenazi world, and in this capacity its rabbi, by virtue both of his enjoyment of royal approval and of his role as head of the yeshivah took a central part. The *kehillah* was able to attract some of the most distinguished scholar-rabbis of the late seventeenth and eighteenth centuries. These included R. Jonas Frankel (?–1669), R. Gershon Ashkenazi Oulif (1670–93), R. Gabriel Eskeles (1694–1703), R. Abraham Broda (1703–09), R. Jacob Reischer (1716–33), R. Jacob Joshua Falk (1733–40), R. Jonathan Eibeschütz (1742–50) and R. Aryeh Loew (Asser Lion) (1766–1785). Eskeles was related by marriage to the famous court-Jew at Vienna, Samson Wertheimer. These rabbis all came from elsewhere in Ashkenaz. Oulif was a pupil of R. Menahem Mendel Krochmal of Moravia, whose daughter he married after the death of his first wife. One of his most famous pupils was the future chief rabbi of Bohemia and Moravia, R. David Oppenheim. Metz adhered strongly to the principle that its rabbi must be free from family or other attachments in the area of his jurisdiction, that is he must come from 'abroad'. Of the some dozen chief rabbis of Metz from the seventeenth century until the Revolution, six had associations with Prague and/or Bohemia. Others came from Vienna, Cracow, Mannheim and Frankfurt am Main. A specially convened tribunal that might have up to 50 members, composed of elders and representatives of all classes of the community, drawn by lot, elected the chief rabbi into office. An equal number of persons was selected from each of the three classes of the *kehillah* – apart from those dependent on public relief. The same electoral procedure operated in the choice of the governing council and in both cases of course ensured that the wealthy would be represented disproportionately to those possessing middling and minimal assets. The successful candidate still of course required royal confirmation, which was in fact never withheld. The electoral procedure was designed to remove any chance that candidates might try to bring to bear on the electors undue pressure, for who could know in advance whose name would be drawn from the electoral urn? This precaution was not always successful. In the interval in 1703 between the departure of Eskeles and the appointment of Broda, much intrigue was deployed. 'A book could be written of all that each party did to obtain its own end,' wrote Glückel, the diarist and wife to one of the Metz elders. This gave her an insider's view.[34] It is quite clear that an unseemly dispute also preceded the appointment of Falk in succession to Reischer in 1733 (Falk had previously served in Lemberg and Berlin). The contract that these rabbis concluded with the community varied in detail, but invariably it defined the three obligations of the chief rabbinate: to teach, to deliver sermons, and to preside, flanked by two deputy-judges or assessors, over the rabbinical court that adjudicated disputes. He received a salary, accommodation, the opportunity to earn supplementary fees (for example for officiating at marriages, certifying the transfer of property, administering of oaths, delivering writs of divorce and so on). The contract normally had a validity of three or six years and was renewable. Chief rabbi Broda's basic salary was 750 livres per year. Later the chief rabbi's salary was raised to 1000 livres p.a., making him the highest paid communal employee.[35]

The support given to education exemplifies the piety of the *kehillah*. In the face of perceived degeneration in biblical studies, the inability of members, for financial reasons, to have their children educated, and increasing ignorance, the twelve administrators, in agreement with the chief rabbi, issued in 1689 a communal regulation that required all children up till the age of fourteen to attend heder daily. Boys aged 14 to 18 need attend only one hour per day. Exams were held twice a week, on Thursdays by the chief rabbi and on Friday by the teachers. Only those boys engaged to be married were exempt from the weekly exams. Responsibility for attendance devolved on the father, who could be fined or in an extreme case expelled from the community should he fail to fulfil this obligation. This schooling, free to those unable to pay, was financed from special communal taxation and private benefactions.[36] At the highest level of education, Abraham Schwab Grumbach and his wife Jachet (daughter of the court-Jew of Cleves, Elia Gomperts) founded a yeshivah in 1704. The endowment supported five rabbis, preferably poor, and their individual students. In his will Grumbach bequeathed sums for the continued maintenance of this institution which lasted into the nineteenth century. In 1751 another school was founded and in 1761 the wealthy *étapier* from Alsace Moïse Belin donated to the community a capital sum of 25000 livres, the interest on which (1250 livres at 5 per cent p.a.) was to be devoted to providing higher education for 24 poor children from Metz and three from Alsace. These and similar foundations, established by wealthy benefactors, also served to provide status and income for learned relatives who were employed as teachers. By the end of the eighteenth century, Metz is estimated to have supported some 40–50 full-time students in accommodation and premises provided by patrons and benefactors.[37] This compared favourably with the provision for advanced education in other centres such as Mainz and Frankfurt am Main. This was in part a function of the degree of wealth at the disposal of communal leaders. Belin, for example, left a fortune of 60 000 livres. The education dispensed in Metz was concerned exclusively with 'religious' matters. This applied also to the printing shop founded by Moses May in 1765. Since none of the Jews could work openly as an *imprimeur breveté*, the Hebrew fonts were imported from Frankfurt, composition took place in May's residence in the ghetto and the sheets were pulled in the shop of a local printer. The local and national authorities connived at this enterprise. But May went bankrupt, and took flight from his creditors. His son-in-law, Goudchaux Spire, revived the operation.

The chief rabbi, for all his eminence, shared power with the syndics or parnassim. Here too, Metz followed the pattern common to Ashkenaz, despite its isolation and recent foundation. From the outset the wealthy were politically dominant. Observers, Jewish and Christian, saw an entity characterized by the familiar coexistence of a small group of families of bankers, army purveyors and traders with a mass of pedlars, horse-dealers, petty traders and petty moneylenders. Marshall Belle-Isle saw 'a fair quantity of families of bankers, traders and merchants with a number of poor who work for the rich as domestic servants and run their errands' (*c.*1728).[38] The absence of qualified artisans and craftsmen and the limited number of professional men (teachers, doctors, rabbis) allowed of no more than a tiny 'middle class'. There is no mystery here – only men of property could wield, through their property, the power to preserve the *kehillah* as a taxpaying entity and at the same time maintain its multifarious institutions. This is the simple truth formulated in the lapidary phrase of the contemporary scholar, R. Yair Hayyim Bachrach (1638–1702): 'Without the wealthy there would be no *kehillah*,' or, 'No *binyan*, no *minyan*' (see below, p. 106).

The earliest Metz constitution extant, dating from 1699, provided for an electoral college of 40 members nominated by the taxpaying members of the community. The 40 chose 11 others who nominated the governing body of the community, which consisted of 12 persons – 5 administrators and 7 tax assessors, all of whom normally served for 3 years. After 1702 the numbers were reduced to 4 administrators and 5 assessors. Only the college of 40 members had the authority to alter the regulations of the community which its elected officers were bound by oath to uphold.[39] In the mid-eighteenth century, no doubt to take account of the increase in the size of the community, the number of members in the electoral college grew to 99, of whom one-third were elected by each of the three economic strata – wealthy, middling and poor. 21 electors out of 99, 7 from each order, drawn by lot, now elected the communal administrators, the parnassim. Not only did this system give to the order of the wealthy disproportionate power, but only those who met certain financial criteria were eligible to serve as syndics (parnassim) – primarily, they had to own assets to a minimum value of 5000 florins, to enjoy residential rights in the city, and to have served previously as one of the commissioners of charity. These various conditions ensured the perpetuation of oligarchy – all the more so as the duties of a parnass were unpaid and obligatory. What householder of poor or middling means could absent himself from gainful activity? At the turn of the century in the early constitutional document there is already among the parnassim a pre-eminence of the wealthy; and in the last two and a half decades of communal existence (1753–89) these positions were monopolized by perhaps a dozen families. These parnassim sometimes enjoyed office for two, three, or four decades, for example the horse-dealer Hirtz Halphen (Cerf Goudchaux) who was elected to office 11 times and was first a syndic in 1756–9 and again without a break from 1762 to the Revolution. By then he was aged 82 and the average age of the council was 61, giving it the air of a gerontocracy. Many of these leaders were also men of education; of the 68 mentioned in the *Memorbuch* of Metz, 41 had rabbinical qualifications.[40] The advanced age of the syndics is no doubt the consequence of the demographic stagnation in Metz in the later eighteenth century.

The parnassim in Metz and elsewhere had wide powers and responsibilities. Vis-à-vis the state and the intendant, its local representative, their task was to maintain order and discipline inside the community. In the 1690s for example the Metz council enacted sumptuary legislation that limited display in dress, coiffure, jewellery, the number of musicians and guests at festivities, the wearing of perruques by unmarried men or ostrich plumes in the headgear of young boys and girls.[41] This is not necessarily to be construed solely as a product of a need to repress lavish competitive and debilitating expenditure but is also to be understood as a product of anxiety lest the display of wealth arouse the envy of Christians.

Above and beyond all else, the council must ensure that the community meet its fiscal obligations, which were indeed one of the *raisons d'être* of the community. In the case of Metz in particular and *le pays messin* these obligations included the especially burdensome Brancas tax of 20 000 livres annually. This formed the subject of particular resentment and the *kehillah* repeatedly protested (1735, 1739 and 1746), but always in vain. The sheer volume of taxes and other outgoings forced the *kehillah* to take out loans with the wealthy Metz bourgeoisie, both Christian and Jewish. They were repaid by way of annuities. This created a growing indebtedness, especially from the 1740s, that survived the Revolution, dragged on and on, and was not finally liquidated until 1854.[42] As a fiscal authority the body of parnassim had to apportion and collect taxes in such a way as to provoke among the taxpayers the least possible dispute. Because the principle of collective liability for taxes operated, the dominance of the wealthy was reinforced. In a very real sense it was they who funded the continuing existence of the *kehillah*.

The budget of the community also had to cover the salaries of its employees (not all of whom were full-time): these included three or four doctors, scribes, cantors, a beadle and of course the chief rabbi and his *dayanim* (assessors). The activities of these persons overlapped with those of the *Hevrot* (fraternities) each of which had its own elected officers, by-laws and sources of revenue. Some *hevrot* had a limited life; others endured longer and these belonged to three broad categories: those concerned with the care of the dead (coffin-makers, gravediggers); those devoted to study; and those dedicated to alleviating the distress of the sick, the bereaved, the poor and prisoners. From at least the mid-seventeenth century the community maintained a hospital and employed a doctor. By the mid-eighteenth century there were two hospitals and four to five doctors under contract to the community, about 1 to every 500 of the population. The doctors, unable to train at French universities to which only Catholics were admitted, were products of Padua and certain German universities (for example Mannheim, Giessen and Halle-Magdeburg). Ad hoc bodies met special needs, for example providing dowries for poor brides, sending relief aid to Ashkenazi communities in distress (Cracow, Buda, Prague in 1744). Some of this activity would necessarily impinge on that of the *shtadlanim* (intercessors), who combined their commercial activities with the representation of the community's interests at Paris or Versailles, sundry German courts, and the imperial chamber at Speyer. In the early eighteenth century this activity, apparently, lacked coordination and was subject to the arbitrary initiative of individuals. Thus in 1712 the official communal envoy to Paris and Versailles, Israel Lambert (Willstadt), a wealthy banker and communal leader, had to contend with the individual activities of Itzik Speier. The former's letters bear the Hebrew date (for example 10 Kislev (5)473 = 2 December 1712), are written in Judeo-Lorraine and are said to reveal 'a community torn apart by rivalries, conflicts of interest and tensions'.[43] Later, perhaps, control from the centre was exercised more effectively; in any event, continuously, from 1760 to 1780 Metz also maintained an *'agent à la Cour royale'*, for the modest fee of 60 livres. This was Meir Hadmir (also Mayer Hadamar), a merchant in draperies and jewellery. He had in the main, it seems, to hold a watching brief on behalf of the syndics and keep them informed of any 'worrisome measures' (*mesures fâcheuses*) that might be in preparation.[44] Rarely is the precise intent of any individual intercession made explicit. Sometimes it amounted to no more than simple public relations mediated by a plump Alsatian goose. In 1786 the agent in Paris, Moïse Weill, remitted 1000 livres (and also three geese) to Marshal de Broglie. In 1789 Weill reported to Metz the arrival in Paris of nine geese for presentation to the minister of war and other ministers. He was still awaiting the arrival of two further geese for Necker, the minister of finance. The pâté de foie gras prepared by the Jewish butchers enjoyed wide renown.[45]

Among the wealthy the *étapiers* were a small minority. The evidence suggests that the most profitable enterprises were in banking and the trade in foodstuffs. Opportunities for investment hardly existed, which helps to explain the importance of moneylending as a vehicle for the employment of surplus cash. Debts frequently figure among the assets bequeathed in the will of a deceased householder. In 1714 one Metz Jew bequeathed 49 debts to his heirs; the estate of Lehman Hirtzel of Bouxwiller included debts outstanding from 53 debtors. Seligmann Wittersheim left a large estate of almost half a million livres; most was in loans but it also included assets derived from dealing in wood and candles, and from Wittersheim's share in a river barge business. A scrutiny of *c.*1500 rabbinic decisions dealing with Metz inheritances shows that outstanding loans formed the substance of the estate.[46]

The will of the banker Marc Terquem (d. 1777) shows that he lent money both to rural workers in the villages of the *plat pays messin* (millers, vine-growers, farriers), and in Metz itself to glovemakers, locksmiths, innkeepers, booksellers and glaziers. Most of these loans in the later period of Terquem's life (1770–7) were for sums between 100 and 600 livres. Larger loans of more than 1000 livres constituted about one-quarter of the loans outstanding. Sometimes the loans were secured on future wine harvests.[47]

Both the royal and the Jewish authorities sought to control and regulate the money trade in regard to interest rate, clientele, registration of loans, the interval that must elapse before unredeemed pledges could be sold or loans called in and so on. One very sensitive aspect of the trade in money was loans to minors, particularly to cadets of the large military garrison in this strategically important town. This the community tried to suppress, and had on several occasions to prohibit the practice, for fear lest it add to the prevalent antisemitism. In 1786 the Jewish leaders obtained from the head of the garrison a list of the debts incurred by the men under his command and undertook to force their Jewish creditors to accept repayment of the loans without interest.[48]

Supplying the needs of the military and the garrison for horses, fodder, and so on was inseparable from 'normal' trade. The enterprise of Alexandre Hesse is perhaps an example; active between 1754 and 1772, he specialized in importing into Metz draperies and cotton goods from Rouen, Troyes, Reims, Zurich, and elsewhere. These were sold on, either to individuals or to other traders. Hesse extended credit and also himself took loans from Paris bankers. On occasion he combined the import of textiles with that of supplier of foodstuffs to the military. One grievance all these merchants shared – the need to obtain a travel permit every time their business took them to Paris – for example, to negotiate a loan or letter of credit or lobby a minister or claim payment for services rendered. More than one intendant complained that this restriction hampered trade. Probably the only permanent Jewish resident at Versailles was Samuel Hirsch, the ratcatcher.[49]

In a number of the sermons that chief rabbi Jonathan Eibeschütz delivered in Metz he took issue with certain symptoms of assimilation: in dress, in diet (for example drinking tea and coffee), in language (for example learning French and German to the neglect of Hebrew), in shaving the beard, in mingling with the nations (ref to Ps. 106:35). Perhaps however, the most telling symptom is apparent in his condemnation of the litigant who resents an unfavourable decision in the Jewish court and at once resorts to a civil court to complain at the Jewish judge. This is not, Eibeschütz emphasizes because the litigant rejects the Torah – he is acting out of purely personal rancour.[50] Even at this personal level and even if the degree of assimilation that Eibeschütz deplored in Metz is perhaps exaggerated for rhetorical purposes, his reference to the resort to gentile courts is undoubted and significant. This is indeed a pointer to the morale of the wealthier members of the *kehillah*, for only the wealthy could afford the costly process of initiating litigation outside the *kehillah*. At the centre of the friction stood the willingness of wealthy and well-connected Jews to take their disputes with each other to the secular courts, should they feel aggrieved at the decision of the syndics and the Beth Din of the chief rabbi and his assessors (*dayanim*).

The authority of the rabbinical court was certainly not absolute and was occasionally sidelined. Vis-à-vis the community the rabbinical letter of appointment made the exercise of its strongest sanction, the penalty of *herem*, dependent on the assent of the syndics. This was not at all unreasonable in so far as the syndics were coresponsible with the rabbinate for the good order of the community. However, this degree of legal autonomy was at risk from 'the determination of wealthy individuals to assert their independence from community control, especially in areas concerning their financial security and business activity'.[51] Such individuals would appeal to the Metz Parlement which used the occasion to diminish the powers of the community and thereby, *pari passu*, enhance its own. Berlin offers a parallel (see below p. 212).

From its earliest days in the sixteenth century the community had insisted on its authority in reserving to itself the power to judge civil disputes between Jew and Jew.[52] But disaffection from within encouraged outside intervention from at least the end of the seventeenth century. In 1694 Alexander Lévy was informed, despite his wishes to the contrary, that he must bring his case against fellow-members of the *kehillah* before the rabbinical court. This followed intensive lobbying in Paris by the community. Such situations still recurred during the eighteenth century, within a framework that called into question the right and power of the community to sentence any of its members to the penalty of *herem*.

Already during the rabbinate of Gabriel Eskeles (1694–1703) certain dissidents attempted to remove from the rabbi and the council their power in civil matters between Jew and Jew. When R. Abraham Broda took office (1703–9) the royal letters patent confirming his nomination also confirmed his authority in civil and religious matters and the Parlement acknowledged that in cases of 'Jew against Jew judged by the rabbis of the synagogue' it had no standing. Nevertheless, in 1709 Jacob Schwab, at odds with his brothers and brothers-in-law over the estate of their mother and mother-in-law, the widow of Abraham Schwab (founder of the yeshivah at Metz), initiated action in the secular courts which eventually involved the *procureur du roi* and intervention in Paris. In the upshot the Metz Parlement recognized the legal powers of the community, but in terms that made its jurisdiction dependent on the agreement of the parties concerned.

Five years later, in 1714, Salomon Cahem, a wealthy banker, appealed to the Parlement against an allegedly unjust fine and threat of *herem* in its extreme form imposed on him by the community. In 1715 and again in 1718 royal letters patent reaffirmed the juridical autonomy of the community but not in such unambiguous terms as entirely to preclude infringement by the Parlement, especially of course if a Jewish litigant aggrieved at his (or her) treatment by the communal authorities actively solicited the intervention of the Parlement.[53]

Three cases involving the financial affairs of women belonging to prominent families disturbed this uneasy relationship and considerably weakened such juridical autonomy as the community retained. The will of Merlé, the deceased wife of Joseph Worms, disinherited her husband in breach of Jewish law but was upheld by the civil court in Metz (1739); Madeleine Bernard Cohen, in the care of guardians and now about to be married, demanded her dowry of 3600 livres and a quantity of silver, as provided for in her late father's will (1742/43); Rozette (Reisele), widow of Bernard Spire Lévy, was named sole heir in his will, again in defiance of Jewish law (1759). All these situations generated contentious references to the Metz Parlement, as a result of which the community had to meet the demand of the Parlement for '*un recueil en langue française des Loix, coutumes et usages*' that the *nation* observed. Obviously, if the Parlement was to judge cases between Jew and Jew it must be familiar with Jewish law. In its 33 sections, this *recueil*, a most comprehensive document, dealt with virtually every aspect of property law.[54] It was three years in the making – 1740–3 – given the delaying tactics employed by the community. In its later stages the newly appointed R. Eibeschütz participated. The *recueil* fulfilled the same purpose as the corresponding document in Prussia of 1776 (see below, p. 213).

This by no means put an end to the friction between Parlement and community. In 1745 the Jews appealed to the king for the restoration of their jurisdiction first, on the grounds of common law which conferred the right of disciplinary jurisdiction on every community; second, the royal letters patent authorized the practice of Judaism. But in 1759 an arrêt by the Parlement banned the community's use of the punishment of *herem*. This provoked a counter-offensive in which the syndics called for a restoration of the provisions of the letters patent of 1715 and 1718. Their arguments, and no doubt the syndics' intervention in Paris, succeeded in alerting the king to the contradiction between the arrêt of 1759 and the letters patent of 1718. Thus in 1767 the Parlement was instructed to inform the newly appointed R. Aryeh Loew that his powers under the letters patent remained in force.[55]

These debates between the spokesmen of the Parlement and the community are doubly significant; first, they indicate the presence of persistent centrifugal forces in the *kehillah*. It is losing control of some of its more influential members; second, and by association, the very existence of the *kehillah* as even a quasi-autonomous body is being called into question. These debates precisely rehearse the rhetoric of the early revolutionary period and its hostility to Jewish autonomy. Was there a distinction between the religious and political laws of the Bible? Was a denial of the latter not also a denial of the religious freedom of the Jews and thereby a breach of the terms of settlement? Did the Jews not form a state within a state? How could a rabbi have more power than a bishop? Were the community to be deprived of the major sanction of the *herem*, how could it maintain order among its restive members?

In south-west France, the decrees of expulsion of 1394 and 1615 had a force that was of far greater consequence than in the newly acquired territories of the east. Here, therefore, settlement had from the outset a somewhat clandestine air. This was also evident in Paris.

The freedom granted to Eliyahu Montalto (Felipe Rodrigues) stands out from this twilight phase: in 1611, as personal physician to Queen Marie de Médicis, he secured permission to live openly as a Jew in Paris with his wife and two children. Montalto had studied medicine at Salamanca and later practised at Florence and Venice. He dedicated his *Archipathologia* (1614) to the queen. At the court Montalto will have found a small contingent of conversos – among others Manuel Mendès, born in Braganza, the royal perfumer, and his nephew, Francisco Alvarez, doctor-in-ordinary to the queen. Close to Richelieu stood the soi-disant Morisco, Alphonse Lopez, known to Richelieu as 'seigneur Hebreo' and Richelieu's agent in a variety of confidential ventures. It was Lopez who persuaded Richelieu not to expel the crypto-Jewish community of Rouen (detected in 1633 in the performance of Jewish practices) but rather to extract a monetary payment. Something of a 'Richelieu cult' was in the making: Manuel Fernandez Villareal (later burned at the stake at Lisbon) dedicated a number of panegyrics to Richelieu; the poet Joao Pinto Delgado, head of the Judaisers in Rouen, dedicated to

Richelieu his French versions of the books of Ruth, Esther and the Lamentations of Jeremiah. In 1633 the Sorbonne pronounced in favour of Jewish settlement at Charleville and, by extension, France.[56]

During the late sixteenth and early seventeenth centuries, as distinct from individuals more or less settled, Portuguese communities took shape in south-western France. A ritual bath (mikveh) at Labastide-Clairence dates from 1600. At the turn of the century and in consequence of a renewal of persecution, more and more conversos and New Christians crossed the Pyrenees to Saint-Jean-de-Luz or Biarritz, or, by way of sea journey along the north-west frontier of Spain, reached Bayonne and Bordeaux. By the early 1630s there are 80 families at Labastide; more than 60 at Bayonne; more than 40 at Peyrehorade; about 10 at Dax. To the north, some 20 Judaizing families are estimated to have settled in Rouen, 10 in Paris and 6–7 in Nantes; there was no more than a stable total of *c*.5 at Bordeaux between 1609 and 1650. In the 1630s of 52 family heads 6 were French-born, and of the approximately 260 individuals, 93 were indigent. In all south-west France the total number of these families cannot have exceeded 300, say 1600 to 2000 individuals.[57] How many of the New Christians remained Christian, as against those who reverted to Judaism, is uncertain and much disputed. Those in France who did revert, like their fellow-Sephardim of London, Amsterdam, Venice and Hamburg, had heeded 'the constant call of the sea'. In Bordeaux and Bayonne their communities came to rank alongside other centres of the Sephardi diaspora.[58]

These communities enjoyed the benefit of letters patent issued in the first instance as early as 1550 by Henri II. These were subsequently renewed by Louis XIII and Louis XIV. They referred to 'the merchants and other Portuguese called New Christians', for Jewish practice was never authorized and in the France of the *ancien régime* no more than tolerated; and at this stage of the *ancien régime* that toleration would be covert and by no means overt. In 1619, in Saint-Jean-de-Luz, an elderly Portuguese lady, Catherine de Fernandes, suspected of insulting a host, was burned alive. In 1685 in Toulouse the Parlement decreed the public burning of a number of 'Jews styling themselves Portuguese merchants'. This sentence was passed *in absentia* (and may not in fact have been carried out), but it does convey something of the atmosphere.[59]

Those Jews from Portugal who settled in south-west France exposed themselves to the reproaches of their fellows. These communities, while lacking at least some of the traditional institutions, had necessarily a clandestine air and outwardly conformed to Catholic rites. This was the occasion for certain rabbis from Venice and Amsterdam bitterly to reproach these crypto-Jews for not choosing to leave a *terra de idolatria* where Judaism was proscribed and to which travel was forbidden.[60] Not until the early eighteenth century did France lose its odium as a *terra de idolatria* and become a *terra de judesmo* where Jewish observance could be freely engaged in, even if it was merely tolerated by the state.

Already however in 1655 the bishop of Aire complained that at Saint-Esprit de Bayonne and Peyrehorade 'three hundred Portuguese families openly practise the Jewish religion'. This is certainly an exaggeration. In 1679 the celebrated *femme de lettres* Mme d'Aulnoy was shown 'the Jews' synagogue in the [Bayonne] suburb of Saint-Esprit', in which, however, she saw 'nothing of note'. She did, however, appreciate the dried fruit (*confitures seiches*) she was served, and then adds, 'The Jews who pass for Portuguese and live at Bayonne have them sent from Genoa; they supply the whole country with them.'[61]

Sundry official documents in 1684 acknowledge the presence of Jews in all the main areas of settlement in the south-west of France – Bordeaux, Bayonne, Dax, Bidache. On the other hand, and until the last few decades of the seventeenth century, children continued to be baptized, and weddings and funerals conducted in accordance with Catholic rites.

The last marriage of a Jewish couple performed in accordance with Catholic rites took place in 1705. The eventual emergence of the Portuguese as acknowledged Jews was precipitated in 1722 by a decree that called for a census of the Jews in the generalities of Bordeaux and Auch and the registration of their properties with a view to their seizure. This decree, to all appearances, presaged the expulsion and dispossession of the Jews. French opinion, nationally and locally, by no means unanimously supported the decree which was in fact withdrawn in 1723; a payment of 110 000 livres secured the issue of new letters patent of protection which confirmed earlier letters patent from the sixteenth century onwards and at last explicitly equated Jews with Portuguese and New Christians: for the recipients of the letters patent were 'the Jews of the said generalities (Bordeaux and Auch) known and established in our kingdom under title of Portuguese, otherwise New Christians...'[62]

None of this was achieved without friction and tension, especially perhaps at Bayonne. Thus the Bayonne municipality prohibited Jews from living in the town centre or even spending the night there; they were forced to live in the suburb of Saint-Esprit.[63] In 1705 the synagogue in Bayonne was forced to close because it was so located that its proceedings were audible from the local church; to the inhabitants and canons of Saint-Esprit it was 'a scandal' that they could simultaneously hear the sounds of Jewish and Christian worship. In 1710 the Jews then sought permission to worship 'in the last house of the suburb, remote from the church'. The Marquis du Rozel, lieutenant-general of Bayonne, supported this request: a positive response would reconcile 'the friendship of the Jewish people' and encourage them to make advances, that is, loans. In 1729 Jacob Silva, an apothecary in Saint-Esprit, was refused leave to send drugs and medicaments for loading on ships at Bayonne bound for the French islands in America:

This would be to deal a blow at the different regulations which have been made in order to set limits to the trade of the Jewish nation, by enabling this individual to enjoy indirectly the privileges of the bourgeois of the town of Bayonne.[64]

In 1733 Jewish funeral services had sometimes need of special escort for fear of popular insult.[65]

What was it that enabled the New Christians to overcome these and other obstacles and to establish themselves? The answer, it seems, is to be found in the mercantile role of the Portuguese Jews. Their struggle to survive in a hostile environment was appropriate to French economic objectives. (Not only in the south-west, by the way: in 1665 Colbert, minister of finance and commerce, inaugurated at Marseilles a small settlement of Sephardim from Livorno, in the hope of stimulating French Mediterranean trade.) The expulsion of the Jews in 1682 put an end to this experiment. The needs of the state were necessarily more apparent to the central power than to the Jews' local trading rivals. Hence for protection they must look primarily to the king and his officials. This was all the more so after the revocation of the Edict of Nantes in 1685 and the expulsion of the Huguenots. In the next few years de Bezons, the intendant at Bordeaux, showed himself sensitive to the further harm that the state might suffer in the aftermath of the Huguenot expulsion should the Jewish economy also be jeopardized. The fairs at Bordeaux cannot dispense with the trade generated by the Jews, he wrote in 1688.[66]

In the same year de Bezons warned the *contrôleur général*:

Trade has already diminished so much because of the daily departure of new converts that the government should not consider expelling the Portuguese from the realm at this time. They supply most of the money for bills of exchange here. I have long believed that nothing should be done about the Jews until new converts get over their desire to flee.

In 1718 the sous-intendant of Bordeaux wrote of the Jews' 'great utility to the city; they were the only people who understood something about commerce, especially banking. Without them the commerce of Bordeaux and the provinces would infallibly perish'. He singled out the role of certain Jews in financing the winegrowers of the region and made a special point of the interest-free loans granted to the town for the purchase of grain at a time of shortage – in 1709, 1710 and in 1712 when the loan amounted to 100 000 livres.[67]

Jews worked as shoemakers, wigmakers, porters, domestic servants. But the big money was in trade and this was the forte of the Portuguese. As Colbert recognized, they could contribute to the fulfilment of the state's mercantile aims. In the early years – the 1620s and 1630s and even more so after the peace settlement of 1648 – the Sephardi families in exile doubled as trading links in the contraband trade between Amsterdam and Portugal and Spain. The Bayonne Sephardim in association with those at Peyrehorade, Labastide-Clairence and Dax formed part of an involved overland route from south-west France along which exports from Amsterdam of valuable products such as linens, tobacco and spices were conveyed over the Pyrenees for eventual disposal through Sephardi trading partners in the markets of Madrid, Barcelona and Saragossa. Wool was exported from Spain by way of Bordeaux, Rouen, Antwerp until it finally reached Amsterdam. The trade was later broadened to include also such commodities as salt, pepper and sundry foodstuffs (nuts and cocoa). For some individuals this trade proved immensely profitable – especially for those engaged in shipping (including privateering), banking, marine insurance, and freight services. As early as 1720 the merchant banker Joseph Nunès Péreire acquired a title of nobility and was metamorphosed into Seigneur Vicomte de la Ménaude et Baron d'Ambès.[68]

The government and its intendants regarded the Sephardi presence in relation to their preoccupation with the needs of the state. The experience of south-west France reproduced the 'trade off', already familiar from Venice and Amsterdam, between acceptance and economic utility, the implication being that those unable to be of use had no place in France. This had special reference to the Bordeaux of the seventeenth century and the economic crisis it was suffering from. Given the reluctance of the local French traders to engage in risky overseas ventures, despite all Colbert's encouragement, foreign seafarers and entrepreneurs were welcome – not only Dutch, Italian and Hanseatic but also the Portuguese New Christians.[69]

The range of entrepreneurial activities had a twofold importance. First, they generated the sums that legitimized, by way of taxation, the presence of the Portuguese *tout court*. In respect to royal taxation, the *nation* paid capitation tax as a corporate body, the total being suballocated among the general body of taxpayers. In Bordeaux this tax increased from 2000 livres to more than 10 000 over the period 1720 to 1780; and at Bayonne from 3000 livres in 1704 to 13 329 in 1783. The *vingtième* tax on land, commerce and salaries had also to be discharged. Second, in terms of their existence as 'holy communities', the Sephardim of the south-west had to maintain a range of facilities.

They looked initially to Amsterdam as their mentor. Venice, the erstwhile 'mother-city in Israel', was in decline. Amsterdam took its place. Family links abounded. Rabbinic works printed in Amsterdam were submitted to R. Raphael Meldola in Bayonne for his approbation (*hascamah*), including the important collection of responsa of R. Jacob Sasportas (*Ohel Ya'akov*, 1717); certain of the French rabbis were trained at Amsterdam; at least three rabbis of the Bayonne community Nefutsot Yehudah (The Dispersion of Judah) came from Amsterdam: Abraham Vaez, until 1691; Ishac de Acosta, at first cantor and teacher in Peyrehorade, then rabbi in Bayonne, until 1702; Isaac Ibravanel de Souza until 1752. This takes no account of lesser communal personnel; through Amsterdam funds collected in Bordeaux were channelled to institutions in the Promised Land; from Amsterdam Hebrew works were supplied to France (where the printing of works in opposition to Catholic teaching was prohibited); cemeteries in Peyrehorade and Paris were purchased in part with the aid of Dutch subsidies; communal disputes in the French settlements were referred to Amsterdam for advice. Outside this framework but indicative of the relationship falls the case of Joseph Henriques, taken prisoner in 1734 by the Spaniards when they captured the vessel in which he was sailing from Amsterdam to Curaçao. Amsterdam called on Bayonne to intervene through the influence of those members of the Bayonne community with interests in the Curaçao company. After about a year Henriques was released and returned from San Sebastian to Amsterdam (but it is uncertain what influence Bayonne brought to bear, if any). There was traffic also in foodstuffs between the two centres: kosher wine from Bordeaux and kosher cheese from Amsterdam. In 1706 Rachel Mendès Colaço sent 80 barrels of kosher wine from Peyrehorade to her sons Abraham and Solomon in Amsterdam.[70]

On the Amsterdam model, the structure of the communities must necessarily favour the wealthy because only they could provide the means to meet communal expenses and commitments. An electoral body composed of all taxpayers formed the major instrument of the communal structure, that is, to the exclusion of the poor and the recipients of charity. A syndic or *gabbay* and two deputies stood at the head. Their duties encompassed 'all matters which may concern our community'. This body, the Mahamad, held office for one year. In 1716 the electoral assembly of taxpayers gave way to a narrower body:

> In order to avoid unpleasantness, when the time comes to elect a *gabbay* and his deputies, no one may participate at the election meeting, or in deciding any question that concerns our poor, except those who have already held the office of *gabbay*.[71]

This decision did make provision for that situation when a father and son or two or more brothers might cast the same vote but the change unquestionably denoted a further concentration of power at the disposal of the wealthy. This was all the more the case because the elders also functioned as tax-assessors and determined an individual member's liability (although this was subject to challenge). For fiscal purposes *La Nation Juive Portugaise* of Bordeaux divided itself into four categories: the poor who were communally aided, the non-aided poor who were exempt from tax, taxpayers, and elders who had already held office. The commitments included one or more cemeteries in the larger centres and a school, and the salaries of a rabbi, teachers and perhaps, as in Bordeaux, a doctor and, later, of the community's agent in Paris. The Mahamad imposed its authority and maintained discipline by the use of the *herem* and also took recalcitrants before the royal intendant or the local magistrate.

This concern for the preservation and transmission of identity was satisfied, as in Amsterdam, by the operation of the dowry society, known as *dotar*. In preserving a sense of ancestral individuality 'amidst the alien corn' of France, *dotar* brought Amsterdam together with other centres of the western Sephardi world. The society's operational area stretched 'from Saint-Jean-de-Luz to Danzig'. Beyond its location in Amsterdam, *dotar* had members and agents virtually all over south-west France and seems to have aided young girls in France soon after its foundation in 1615. In 1617, the list of approved applicants already contained the names of 37 girls from Saint Jean-de-Luz.[72] The marriages were celebrated sometimes in Amsterdam, sometimes in France; if the latter, the local communal authorities would supply to the society a dossier with authenticating details of the marriage. In 1688, for example, a dowry of 300 florins that Ester, the orphaned daughter of Simao Nunes Neto of Bayonne, had won in the draw, was paid over in Amsterdam to Isaac Nunes Belmonte (Manuel Belmonte), who evidently had some power of attorney to receive the money. The dossier presented by Belmonte comprised 'a certificate of the Haham, *hazan*, and parnassim' to the effect that Ester Nunes Neto had married Joseph Netto de Fonseca 'professing our Holy Law'. The dossier sometimes contained a short *curriculum vitae* of the girl; in 1732 it was certified that Ribla de Sáa Da Costa, aged 22, orphaned daughter of the late Abraham de Sáa, had come from Portugal with her family, was now living with relations and had 'no other resources than the work of her hands and the aid that is given to her as to other poor Portuguese'. She was 'truly Jewish and observant of His Holy Law'. Three parnassim of Bayonne and the celebrated rabbi, R. Raphael Meldola, signed this document.

This system of arranged marriages had its counterpart among the wealthy. Here, not only was endogamy at stake but also economic interests. Marriage strategy accordingly was designed not only to prevent young people, usually daughters, from contracting some sort of *mésalliance* but also to preserve and enhance a family's socio-economic standing. The *ascamot* of Bayonne as early as 1700 and 1703 annulled secret marriages and ordained a sentence of *herem* on the parties concerned and the complicitous witnesses. As in London, aggrieved parents had sometimes to take their children to a public court. In 1743 Moïse Robles, citing the communal ordinances, took his son Abraham to a court in Bordeaux for having married, against the father's will, Sara, daughter of Moyse Rodriguès. The Bayonne community passed a sentence of *herem* on the guilty couple and their accomplice witnesses, but the Bordeaux court upheld the validity of the marriage. The concern for family honour through the determination of marriage partners extended to the disinheritance of those children who converted, as happened in the wealthy Gradis family of Bordeaux. In another family, in 1739, Abraham de Souza-Henriques in his will ordered his children 'to honour and respect their mother as they are obliged to do, and to marry only members of their Nation with the explicit consent of their mother'.[73]

Poor girls who lacked a dowry were, however deserving, no more than a limited aspect of a major and continuing problem. The poor were a paramount responsibility, not only for social but also for political reasons. Their immoderate increase or prominence had the power to jeopardize the very survival of a community whose acceptance and wellbeing depended on economic utility. This problem existed from the outset, for in the main only those exiles who could not afford to travel any further settled in the small towns over the Franco-Spanish border. The poor had always had (and would continue to have) a significant social presence so that inevitably the *cedaka* (Hebrew for charity, and, by extension, poor chest) took a central part as nucleus of the future organised community. The precise dimension of the problem is unavailable but of the significant social presence of the poor there is no doubt. 'Less than 40 years ago', wrote a local inhabitant of Bayonne in, probably, the third quarter of the seventeenth century, 'there were not 6 families of this religion in [Bourg] Saint-Esprit. And now there are more than 400 but of this number there are not 10 who are of reasonable means, all the rest living only from each other's charity and the funds sent to them by their brethren in Holland and England.'[74] In 1718, the subintendant at Bordeaux reported that of the approximately 100 Jewish families in the city 30 depended on the charity of the remaining 70. In 1744 there were Portuguese in the towns whom the syndic and his deputies had to prohibit from buying and selling old clothes. This is no sign of prosperity. There were also *'vagabons et gens sans aveu'* among them.[75]

To support the poor cost the Bordeaux Mahamad 3000 livres per annum in 1726, and rose to 9000 in 1782. This did not include the cost of free *matzot* at Passover and of kosher meat. The poor could also call on support from fraternities that supplied clothing, medical aid and sundry other services to those in need.[76]

In 1684 the Bayonne community sought and obtained permission from the Conseil Royal to expel 93 families of the poor from Bordeaux, Bayonne, Dax, Bidache and Peyrehorade. The royal decree of 1685 justifies the expulsion of the 93 families on the grounds that *'elles ne sont d'aucune utilité au commerce, mais à charge ... à cause de leur pauvreté'*. The same decree also withdrew from expulsion two inhabitants of Dax (Jacques Léon and his father Anthoine Lopes Léon) who had been mistakenly included among the 93 families, on the grounds of their *'commerce très considérable dans ladite ville de Dax, duquel le public reçoit une grande utilité ...'* In c.1735 the Bordeaux Mahamad limited to a maximum of 80 the number of families it would support. It also subsidized the despatch of the poor to Amsterdam and elsewhere – which was not without detriment to relations between the two centres. The expulsion of 1685 set a precedent for a similar expulsion in 1749.[77]

From early in the new century the Jewish nation of Bordeaux identified itself with the destiny of France. In 1706 the community prayed publicly and in Hebrew for the success in battle of Louis XIV. Permission was given for the publication of a printed translation. In 1744 and 1748 the community prayed for the recovery of Louis XV and the queen respectively. The royal acceptance of the text signified of course their toleration. In the seven synagogues of Bordeaux the Jews, according to an aide to the intendant (1733), practised their religion 'with the same display, the same ostentation, the same security and liberty as can apostolic Roman Catholics'. They celebrated circumcisions and marriages with the same openness, including the 'remarriage' of new arrivals from Spain:

> From Friday evening until the same time the next day, householders, their wives, children, employees and servants go regularly to pray in their synagogues, like Christians...That day their shops are closed as on Sunday and they do not engage in any business. All the said householders, their wives, children, and so on publicly carry in their hand when they go to synagogue, their prayer-books, their white veils [that is, prayer-shawls] and other types of adornment that the exercise of their religion requires. Sometimes they go there barefoot, their feet in slippers and ungartered, sometimes with the brim of their hats turned down [that is, on the Day of Atonement]. All that takes place in the sight of Christians, without any sort of concealment [*mistère*]. They have beadles and sacristans as in our churches. They never begin prayers in their synagogues unless the rabbi has arrived.[78]

By the first few decades of the eighteenth century the former conversos of south-west France had long discarded their Catholic guise and asserted the power openly to practise their Judaism, and established the necessary institutional apparatus, reached a *modus vivendi* with their Christian neighbours and proved their economic utility to the state. This did not mean either that a sense of security prevailed or that the Portuguese were popular – at least if de Boucher, the intendant at Bordeaux is to be believed. They lived in a state of apprehension at decrees the king might issue; they were also unpopular, 'and if the nation maintains itself with so much success, it is only by reason of the utility drawn from it by several persons of authority'.[79]

Hardly had the Portuguese reached a position of at least semi-acceptance than fellow-Jews from Avignon and the Comtat Venaissin came to threaten their hard-earned wellbeing. From the early years of the century a few Jews from Avignon had been living in Bordeaux, for example, Lange-Mosse, Joseph Dalpuget and Joseph Petit. For them to venture beyond the Comtat was certainly not without hazard. In 1687 the bishop of Orange secured the expulsion of all Jews from the town and principality of Orange; in 1709/10 a group of merchants from Avignon were detected trading in Provence on the basis of forged documents, and expelled forthwith; in 1716 the king overruled the Parlement of Toulouse and revoked permission it had given to certain traders from Avignon to trade and move freely in the province of Languedoc.[80] Between the seventeenth and eighteenth centuries the economic status of Provençal Jewry improved to the extent that they were no longer dependent on short-term, small-scale moneylending and petty trading but had moved into banking, and trading in the products of the nascent industries of the region, for example, paper, wool, and silk. After the 1650s the ban on trading in new goods (as distinct from second-hand) fell into disuse and this opened up further opportunities. The increase in the size of dowries is one index to their increased prosperity.[81]

The expansion of Avignon commerce in the 1730s and 1740s brought the Jewish traders into running battles with rivals at Montpellier, Nîmes, Tours, Nevers, Gien and further afield in the provinces of Poitou, Normandy and even Lorraine. The opposition that they provoked is a measure of their success and geographical spread. The Jews from the *carrières* were dealing in horses, donkeys and mules – a branch of commerce which in Languedoc they virtually monopolized; in draperies, cloth and textiles; and in watches and jewellery. The retail sale of draperies 'is almost all in the hands of Jewish merchants', reported the *inspecteur des manufactures* in Burgundy in 1726. The Jews split up into small groups, he declared, and moved from town to town. Their goods were inferior, he added, for the Jews never bought them at the factories but dealt in rejects, bankrupt stocks, or stolen property. They sold these inferior goods at cut-throat prices, undercutting other traders. Not every official was unsympathetic. At least by the 1740s a group of intendants (except in Tours) accused the exclusion-minded merchants of 'having no more than their own interests in mind'; that to exclude Jews, ambulant traders and so on 'would be contrary to the public interest'; and that 'the Jews should be left with the freedom they have always had to attend fairs, in accordance with the customs of each generality'.[82]

Bernage, the intendant of Languedoc, stood out as perhaps the most forthright advocate of Jewish commerce. The high price of animals caused harm to agriculture, he argued, and he defied every counter-pressure to invite a group of Avignonnais into the province to sell mules and horses at competitive prices at the fairs and markets. The initial invitation covered six months but became well-nigh permanent and was extended to include the sale of draperies, silks, and old rags.[83]

To the Portuguese Jews of Bordeaux the Jews of Avignon were no less unwelcome than to the traders of Tours, say – all the less so, as they sometimes passed themselves off as Portuguese. The reasons differed in each case: whereas in Tours commercial rivalry was at issue, in Bordeaux it was feared lest the Avignonnais besmirch the reputation for probity and respectability that the Sephardim cherished. Eventually, as the Avignonnais prospered, the Sephardim would have to make their peace with them. But not yet. For the time being, that is, in the 1720s, in this intra-Jewish conflict the French authorities generally sided with the Sephardim. The Avignonnais, one official wrote in 1722, had no authorization to live in Bordeaux, generally traded in old clothes and braid (*galons*), had no connection with the Portuguese and were 'merely tolerated'. At this time there were 22 Avignon families in the town and it does not seem that any decree of expulsion was in fact carried out; in 1724 a meeting of the Bordeaux Jewish leaders rejected any contact with an emissary from Avignon who had come to Bordeaux in pursuit of communal debtors from Avignon living in the city. 'It is our duty and our interest to take no part in the dispute of the said Avignonnais still less in their alleged arrangements', the leaders proclaimed, 'which we regard as a foreign matter and into which we must not enter in any way at all'.[84]

Despite the hostility of the Portuguese, some at least of the Avignon Jews must have prospered, for in 1730 they donated to the treasury 4000 livres. Thereby they hoped to secure for themselves the same rights as the Sephardim enjoyed under the letters patents of 1723. Three Avignon traders that same year – Lange Mozé, David Petit and Jacob Dalpuget – acquired from the Parlement of Dijon the right to trade outside Bordeaux for one month in each season but the merchants of Dijon got this right annulled.[85] Evidence from the 1730s suggests that some of the Portuguese had so reconciled themselves to the presence of the Avignonnais that they were covertly financing their trade.[86] If confirmed, there could be no greater testimony to the ultimate acceptablity of the *comtadins*.

In 1734/35 another expulsion from Bordeaux was decreed. Again it could not be fully effective because the affected families moved no further than to neighbouring areas. Moreover, the Petit group of families had leased the estates of the Duc de Gramont, military governor of the province. It is also by no means clear that the intendant, de Boucher, fully acquiesed in the policy of expulsion. Certain of the Avignon families, for example, the Dalpuget family who dealt in silk goods and draperies, enjoyed not only the highly placed protection of the Princess de Conti and the Princess de Rohan but also that of the Parlement of Bordeaux.[87]

4
Resettlement in London

The re-creation of a *kahal* (or *kehillah*) in the London of the mid-seventeenth century forms part of the turbulence that assailed the economy of the Dutch Sephardim. From the Americas to the Mediterranean, a complex interplay of disparate factors created a serious threat to its wellbeing. In Brazil the successful revolt of the Portuguese planters against Dutch rule, in 1645–54, put an end to the prosperity of the Sephardi colonies in Recife and Mauricia. During this decade c.200 families from Brazil, many impoverished, had to find refuge in the Dutch Republic. In 1645 the outbreak of prolonged war-fare (until 1669), between Venice and the Ottoman Empire, undermined Venetian Sephardi commerce with the Levant, both by sea and overland to Constantinople and Salonika. In a different sense the intensified persecution of the New Christians in Spain and the financial collapse in Madrid – both events of the 1640s – led to further mass emigration from the Iberian penin-sula. This not only increased the population pressure on existing Sephardi settlements in the west (Amsterdam, Livorno, Hamburg), but also strength-ened these settlements, for the newcomers included men of financial stature and outstanding intellect.

This context accounts in part for the 'more enlargement' that the Mahamad in Amsterdam sought; in particular for the establishment of a bridgehead in London through the foundation of an entirely new *kahal*. This is the 'push' factor. But why London, and whence the 'pull'? This derives from the partic-ular position of privilege that England took in relation to trade with Portugal and the Caribbean, especially the plantation colony of Barbados, pre-eminent for the production and export of sugar to Europe. But if the Dutch were to participate in this trade they would have to circumvent the obstacle erected by the Navigation Act of 1651. This Act aimed to ensure that trade between Britain and the colonies be conducted in British ships or in vessels belonging to the country where the goods originated, that is, to secure for English traders a monopoly of colonial trade and squeeze out the Dutch, including of course the Dutch Sephardim. Only the establishment of a Dutch bridge-head in London could overcome this obstacle.[1]

In what sort of world, 'Jewishly' speaking, were the Dutch Sephardim proposing to venture? Tiny groups of Jews in London and elsewhere survived the general expulsion in 1290. Newcomers were few in the following centuries and appeared in various guises, virtually never as professing Jews; for example a troupe of visiting musicians from Italy at the court of Henry VIII; converted Jews engaged in various branches of Hebrew studies at the universities of Oxford and Cambridge.[2] Two crypto-Jews took minor public roles: Dr Hector Nunes worked with Sir Francis Walsingham, secretary of state 1573–90, as intermediary in peace negotiations with Spain and provided intelligence from Portugal; Dr Rodrigo Lopez, a graduate of the University of Coimbra, came to England *c.*1559, worked at St Bartholemew's Hospital and in 1586 was appointed physician to Queen Elizabeth's household. His enemies at court exploited Lopez's Iberian connection, his quasi-political activities and his expertise in poisons to secure his execution on a charge of conspiring with Philip II of Spain to poison the Queen (1594). In 1605 some seven people celebrated the Passover festival in London, at the home of the (?) unrelated Jeronimo Lopes.[3] A small group of overseas traders lived a clandestine life in the guise of Catholics (see below, p. 77).

Curiously at odds with the crypto-Jews and the conversos are the fictional creations – Marlowe's Barabas and Shakespeare's Shylock – who flaunt their Jewishness. The former does so as a caricature, revelling in his villainy; the second is a far more ambiguous figure who lends himself to a wide variety of interpretations. Both share a readiness to reject the taunts of their Christian enemies. To the knight's charge that the 'first curse' of Barabas 'falls heavy' on his head and is born of his 'inherent sin', Barabas retorts:

> What, bring you Scripture to confirm your wrongs?
> Preach me not out of my possessions.
> Some Jews are wicked as all Christians are;
> But say the tribe that I descended of
> Were all in general cast away for sin,
> Shall I be tried for their transgression?[4]

That this image of the unregenerate Jew should overlap with a certain philosemitism that had accumulated in England since about the turn of the century is also curious. It is plausibly conjectured that this turn towards philosemitism is exemplified in Bacon's choice of a Jew for the original of Joabin, the merchant who is a spokesman for Solomon's House in the *New Atlantis* (1627) and an exponent of the general good; this original was Joachim Gaunse, from Prague, possibly related to R. David Gans (see above, p. 7). As a mining engineer and industrial chemist Gaunse had come to England in 1581 to advise on the smelting of copper.[5] This 'economic' argument accorded with renewed Christian appreciation, in the seventeenth century, for the purported commercial acumen of the Jews. By the time of

Cromwell and the Protectorate, Harrington looked forward to a Jewish settlement *en masse* in Ireland. In his *Commonwealth of Oceana* (1656) he envisaged such a settlement as a mutually beneficial bargain, 'as is not to be found otherwise by either'.[6]

Irrespective of those factors that favoured the extension to England of the Jewish presence, and in spite of its urgency from the Dutch Sephardic viewpoint, grave impediments called for careful diplomacy. Paramount among them were probably the recurrent hostilities between Britain and Holland. The first Anglo-Sephardi contacts were made in Amsterdam in 1651–3, principally with R. Menasseh b. Israel, a rabbi, millenarian thinker, printer and pamphleteer, with many correspondents in the world of Christian scholarship. He took a central part in the life of the 'Great Jerusalem'. A letter describes his congested schedule:

> Two hours are spent in the Temple (Synagogue) every day, six in the School, one and a half in the public Academy (Bet HaMidrash) and the private one (Yeshivah) of the Senhores Peréyra, in which I have the office of President, two in the corrections of my printing press, which all passes through my hands. From eleven to twelve I give audiences to all who require me for their affairs and visits. All this is precise, judge then how much time remains for domestic cares and to reply to the four or six letters which come every week, of which I keep no copy, for the time fails me.[7]

Menasseh had somewhat earlier presented an indirect appeal for the readmission of the Jews to England in messianic terms (as in his pamphlet *Esperança de Israel* [*The Hope of Israel*], 1650). Moses Wall, a friend of Milton, translated Menasse's Latin version of this work (*Spes Israelis*) into English in 1652. The explicit connection with England is indeed slight but the urgency of Menasse's messianically oriented analysis of contemporary events might well be calculated to appeal to English enthusiasts similarly inclined.[8] The Mahamad held itself aloof for it could not openly align the community with a venture that might jeopardize the acceptance of the community in Amsterdam. Cromwell's Council of State did issue Menasseh with safe-conducts for England in 1652 and 1653 but these proved abortive and it was an associate, Manuel Martinez (David Abrabanel) Dormido, who came to London in 1654, together with Menasseh's son, and petitioned Cromwell for the readmission of the Jews to England. Dormido, born in Andalusia of Portuguese conversos, was a financier and trader who had left Spain after prosecution and imprisonment by the Inquisition. He settled in Bordeaux and then Amsterdam where he rose to prominence in the community. The fall of Brazil to the Portuguese brought severe loss to Dormido and in one petition he sought Cromwell's intervention with the Portuguese king, John IV, now allied to England, to secure compensation for his confiscated property. Cromwell did accede to this request. In petitioning for admission to the Commonwealth and its dominions Dormido emphasized the economic benefits that the newcomers would bring to the state. This petition of 1654 failed to move the Council of State.

In September 1655, after the conclusion of the First Anglo-Dutch War (1652–4), Menasseh himself ventured to travel to England and to join Dormido, with, it seems, the covert approval of the merchants of the Mahamad in Amsterdam. When Menasseh arrived in London, his *Humble Addresses* to Cromwell (1655) made explicit a messianic appeal – 'therefore this remains only in my judgement, before the Messiah comes and restores our nation, that first we must have our seat here likewise' (that is in England). Menasseh therefore sought permission for the Jews to establish public synagogues, exercise their religion freely subject to their own laws (with the right of appeal to English civil law) and acquire a cemetery. By no means was the messianic appeal the only string to Menasseh's bow: in the *Humble Addresses* and a subsequent petition to the Council of State, he made much of the economic benefits that the trading activity of the Jews would infallibly bring to the Commonwealth. Merchandizing was their 'proper profession', and this Menasseh attributed

> in the first place, to the particular Providence and mercy of God towards his people: for having banished them from their own Country, yet not from his Protection, he hath given them, as it were, a naturall instinct, by which they might not onely gain what was necessary for their need, but that they should also thrive in Riches and possessions; whereby that they should not onely become gracious to their Princes and Lords, but that they should be invited by others to come and dwell in their Lands.

Many of Menasseh's arguments he owed to Luzzatto's *Discorso* on the Jews of Venice: that the receipts from tolls and customs would swell; that goods from remote countries would become available; that 'mechaniqs' would be provided with the raw materials of their craft; that the export of manufacturers would be facilitated; and that peace would be fostered 'between neighbour nations'. In a very wide-ranging survey of the diaspora, intended to demonstrate those mercantile virtues of the Jews that made them profitable and therefore welcome to others, Menasseh took care to strike an occasional note of apologetics:

> As for usury [he wrote, for example], such dealing is not the essential property of the Jews for though in Germany there be some indeed that practise usury; yet the most part of them that live in Turkey, Italy, Holland and Hamburg, being come out of Spain, they hold it infamous to use it.[9]

Menasseh's messianic appeal certainly found resonance in England in millenarian circles of similar enthusiasts (though for different reasons), for example, Henry Jessey, John Dury and the Fifth Monarchy men. They lacked political weight, however. To welcome Gaunse for his expertise in mining or to propose mass Jewish settlement in Ireland in the framework of a utopian novel was one thing; quite another to accede to the arguments of Dormido and Menasseh and admit into London an unspecified number of Jewish merchants. Whatever Cromwell's sympathies may have been, his response had to take the form of the Whitehall Conference, an ad hoc body constituted of clergymen, lawyers, diplomats, merchants and Hebrew scholars. After much debate the Conference concluded there was no legal impediment to Jewish resettlement. Opposition to the reality of readmission, largely it seems from the clergy and merchants, dissuaded Cromwell from issuing any sort of invitation or charter such as the Sephardi leaders hoped for. William Prynne's 'Short Demurrer' (1655–6) made much of the argument that the Jews' 'Synagogues of Satan' contravened the Gospel and the 'Redemption of our Lord Jesus Christ'. Even worse perhaps, given that Prynne and others thought religion to be in decline in England,

It was now [he wrote] a very ill time to bring in the Jews, when the people were so dangerously and generally bent to apostasy and all sorts of Novelties and Errors in Religion; and would sooner turn Jews, than the Jews Christians.

As for the supposed economic benefits expected from the Jews, even if they were valid, which Prynne denied, this would still be nothing more than 'a renewed betrayal of Christ', on the model of Judas Iscariot. In an antisemitic poem addressed to Menasseh, Edmund Gayton accused the Jews of planning to buy St Paul's Cathedral and turn it into a synagogue.[10]

In the meantime, the disclosure that in London a small number of Jewish merchants were living already, *sub rosa*, masquerading as Catholics, took the initiative away from Dormido and Menasseh. Antonio Fernando Carvajal and Antonio Rodrigues Robles headed this secret group. The outbreak of war with Spain in the autumn of 1655 brought their presence to light. Denounced as Spaniards in March 1656, these Jews found their goods and property were liable to confiscation. They chose to reveal their Jewish identity, disclaiming any Spanish affiliation. The group's subsequent petition asked for no more than permission to live unmolested in London, to practise their religion freely and to acquire a cemetery. Menasseh himself, still awaiting a positive response from Cromwell, headed the list of signatories which also included Carvajal and Dormido. Robles, who submitted a separate petition, had his property and ships restored, even though the fact that he was not circumcised and, before hostilities, had regularly attended Mass in the chapel of the Spanish ambassador, led the commission of enquiry to suppose that he was 'either no Jew or one that walks under loose principles'.[11]

In October 1656 Menasseh returned to Holland, saddened at his failure to secure a charter that would define the conditions of the cherished readmission. He had secured no more than Cromwell's verbal assurance of the Jews' right to worship freely in a private house and to bury their dead in a separate cemetery. Menasseh was not alone. 'Those few Jews that were here, dispairing of our expected success, departed hence,' Menasseh had earlier written. 'And others who desired to come hither, have quitted their hopes, and betaken themselves to Italy, some to Geneva.'[12]

This pessimistic assessment was in fact unwarranted. John Evelyn, the diarist, had a surer grasp of the situation when he wrote 'now were the Jews admitted', for it had been established that no legal hindrance debarred them from entering Britain.[13] Menasseh in fact shared the misconception of several other Jews, that also in London their position would need to be regulated by a charter or some such document. But they were projecting on to London their experience of Amsterdam or Prague.[14]

By the end of 1656 the tiny community already had premises for worship in Creechurch Lane, London, in which to read from the Scrolls of the Law (newly arrived from Amsterdam at the earlier instance of Menasseh); and its first rabbi, Haham Moses Athias, had arrived from Hamburg. At this time the number of families stood at *c.*20, by 1660 at *c.*35. Two years later John Greenhalgh visited the synagogue premises: he found more than one hundred men 'most of them rich in apparel' and the ladies in an adjoining room 'with muffs in one hand and books in the other'.[15] This was the first congregation of the Sephardi settlers in England and first fruit of the discussion with Cromwell in the 1650s. The newcomers hailed from the many quarters of the Sephardi diaspora – Holland, the English and Dutch colonies in the Caribbean, the Canaries, France and Iberia. Not only to Greenhalgh was the community an object of curiosity, it may be assumed; an early supplement to the communal statutes (September 1663) decreed that during religious ceremonies the presence of English ladies and gentlemen was to be ignored, in order to 'avoid scandal and hindrance'.[16] This did not deter Pepys, who happened to visit the synagogue during a festival service for 'The Rejoicing of the Law'. He was appalled by 'the disorder, laughing, sporting and no attention'.[17]

These unwelcome visits were certainly among the least of the community's concerns. There was however no ghetto or residential restriction. That London Jewry lived in about six City parishes was a matter of choice. They could not participate in political and public life, but this exclusion (shared with Catholics and Protestant Nonconformists) was no more than an incidental function of the inability to take the Sacrament in accordance with Anglican rites, and, in any case, accorded happily with Sephardi preference. As aliens they could not inherit real estate or hold absolute title to land (though legal opinion was divided on this point). As traders, only by taking out letters patent of endenization could they engage in the colonial trade. Between 1655 and 1680, 91 Jews did take this course, despite its cost.[18] In terms of legal status, whereas Menasseh b. Israel's initiative had at the very least confirmed the absence of any impediment to the readmission of the

Jews to England, his failure to secure any sort of charter of privileges created a situation of limbo, qualified, however, by the Christian character of the state. 'The Jewish religion', declared Lord Hardwicke, the Lord Chancellor, in 1744 'is not taken notice of by any law, but is barely connived at by the Legislature' (whereas, for example, the Toleration Act of 1688 had rendered legal the religion of the Dissenters). Access to the courts was unrestricted; a Jew could serve as witness and had the right to sue; there also is an instance (1677) when a court sitting scheduled for a Saturday was rearranged for the convenience of Jewish witnesses. The Jewish community enjoyed a status whereby it constituted a separate and distinct corporation, with the power to regulate its affairs in accordance with its own statutes and laws. This applied primarily to matters of private law. Hardwicke's Act of 1753 (26 Geo. II, cap. 33) which sought to suppress clandestine marriages, explicitly excluded from its purview any marriage between two persons both of whom professed the Jewish religion.[19] 'The Jews, though *British* subjects', ruled Sir William Scott in 1798 in a case brought before the ecclesiastical consistory court of London, 'have the enjoyment of their own laws in religious ceremonies'. Scott, therefore, as duly advised by rabbinic experts, proceeded to apply Jewish law in the case at dispute.[20] The limited parallel here is with those courts in Metz, Berlin and Halle which had the benefit of manuals of Jewish law in adjudicating disputes involving Jewish litigants. In England not until the Marriage Act of 1836 did the state take any interest in the registration of Jewish marriages.[21]

This makes a violent contrast with the position in Austria and France, for example, where every effort was made to enforce state marriage law on the Jewish communities (see below, pp. 244, 280). Even in England, however, this unconcern had its limits and this stemmed from the Christian character of the State. Thus, in the case of *Da Costa* v. *De Paz* (1744), Hardwicke held that a bequest in favour of the maintenance of a yeshivah was 'not a good legacy':

> This is a bequest for the propagation of the Jewish religion [he added] and though it is said that this is a part of our religion, yet the intent of the bequest must be taken to be in contradiction of the Christian religion, which is a part of the law of the land.

In the case of *Isaac* v. *Gompertz* (1783–6) the court sanctioned annuities in favour of Jewish education and charitable welfare but not those for the support and maintenance of a synagogue.[22]

The Sephardim took advantage of these uncertain boundaries to establish in London a *kahal* that imposed a high degree of discipline. This corresponded to their sense of insecurity. Wrote one Sephardi historian:

> The heads of the Jews were constrained to remember that they were strangers in a foreign country, surrounded by a population which, if not openly hostile, at all events eyed them with distrust and jealousy, and

where the slightest offence against the laws of the land might entail misery and expulsion to all their race.[23]

The same sense led the *kahal* to obscure the community's Commonwealth origins; in 1705 the Mahamad in London strongly deprecated in a letter to the Amsterdam bookseller and publisher Ishac Abraham Cohen de Lara his proposed republication of the works of Menasseh b. Israel, 'until circumstances improve'. It fostered the legend that it was founded under the monarchy of Charles II and not the Commonwealth of Cromwell and dedicated a special annual service to the commemoration of this legend.[24]

In 1663 the Sephardim constituted themselves as an independent congregation under the name Saar Asamaim – Portal of the Heavens. The preamble to the constitution locates the community within what has been termed 'a universal political context': 'experience has shown that it is a necessary thing in all republics and nations to have statutes wherewith to be governed'. The preamble now asserts: 'all copy the example of our nation's government', thus it is now claimed that whereas contemporary states might indeed refer to Biblical precedents for their institutions, only did Jewish society enjoy immediate and unbroken access to those precedents. Second, the preamble locates the *Ascamot* (statutes) of Saar Asamaim in the context of those observed in Amsterdam, 'wherein they have included the usage of that of Venice'.[25]

The statutes themselves of the new congregation 'serve for the Jews of the Spanish and Portuguese Nation who are at present in this city (London) and later may come to it'. The first prohibits the establishment in 'London, its district and environs' of any other congregation. This was of enormous importance for it not only maintained the unity of the congregation but also had the indirect effect of imposing on the Mahamad responsibility for the good and loyal conduct of members, and this the revised version of the aim of the *Ascama* made explicit in 1677 – 'to avoid causing scandal to the natives of this City as we are recommended by His Majesty (Charles II) whom God preserve'.[26]

The other *Ascamot* provided for the self-financing of the congregation by means of a regular subscription and a form of turnover tax on trading activities (*imposta*). Charitable institutions for the ransom of prisoners and the poor of the Terra Santa were organized. The statutes also provide for the creation, by election, of the governing body, the Mahamad. Distinctive is the power wielded by this body: it enjoyed 'authority and supremacy over every thing and no person shall rise in the synagogue to reprobate the decisions which they may take', under pain of *herem*. The Mahamad regulated the conduct of synagogue services; maintained the right to arbitrate business and brokerage disputes; forbade the consumption of all meat save that from animals examined and slaughtered by the community's designated officials; disallowed the printing of any books by any member without the Mahamad's express permission; prohibited 'dispute or argument on matters of religion with *Guim*' (gentiles) who must also not be urged 'to follow our holy Law'. The statutes also prohibit any *yahid* (member; pl.: *yehidim*) to speak 'in these realms in the name of the Nation or general affairs thereof' – this was a prerogative the Mahamad reserved to itself.[27] These statutes were adopted in 1664 and at the same time the Mahamad invited R. Jacob Sasportas of Amsterdam to take office as its Haham, at a salary of £50 p.a. (later raised to £70). His duties were to preach on all Sabbaths and holy days, to teach the Talmud, and read the prayers 'as the Mahamad may ordain'. Out of his salary, Sasportas was required to employ his son Samuel as teacher (two hours morning and afternoon), and also as inspector and slaughterer of cattle (*Bodek* and *Schochet*). By 1690 the c.35 families of 1660 had risen to 70–80.[28]

The discipline the *yehidim* imposed on themselves served to facilitate political activity in the interest of their acceptance and to disarm their enemies. This was imperative on the part of the Mahamad for the first two or three decades of the existence of Saar Asamaim: but it did not involve personal and overt identification with a political cause. This precisely paralleled the policy of the Ashkenazi court-Jews among whom it was altogether exceptional to assume any ministerial role. The Sephardim went further and from overt political action they explicitly demanded abstention. From 1688 and at least until 1819 those of the congregation who took part in such matters or voted in any political contest rendered themselves liable to *herem*.[29]

The Sephardim had to confront the hostility of the economist, Sir William Petty. The frugality of the Jews enabled them to undersell other traders, he alleged; and because they dealt so much in bills of exchange, jewels and money, and practised fraud they evaded customs and other duties.[30] The London merchants already under the Protectorate had helped to thwart Cromwell's hopes for the resettlement. This hostility did not abate and demanded from the Sephardim constant vigilance and recurrent battle against threats of expulsion, and/or of extortionate taxation, and threats to religious practice (which of course at this time had economic repercussions). In 1660 the Lord Mayor and City Corporation of London used the restoration of the monarchy to petition the king to expel the Jews. At a meeting in the house of Antonio Carvajal's widow, the Sephardim organized a counter-petition. Both were submitted to Parliament in December 1660 and the *status quo* was maintained. No doubt this benefited from the defence fund that the elders of the *kahal* raised at Carvajal's house. Its size is unknown but the community's records show that Antonio Robles (known to the *kahal* as Isaac Barzilay) claimed back £80 from the *Cedaka*, 'which I paid in advance on the *Impuesta* for the action which the traders brought against us in order to drive us from the kingdom, and there fell to my share the said £80 of the sum expended in its defence'. That Charles during his exile in Holland had incurred some sort of obligation *vis-à-vis* the Dutch Jews such as would later incline him to extend to Anglo-Jewry his protection is very likely. It is clear, in any event, that Duarte da Silva, the administrator of the queen's dowry, was associated with other Sephardim in discounting, in advance of the due date, the king's drafts and warrants exercisable on the dowry.[31] In 1664 the Conventicle Act, as an anti-Puritan measure, prohibited religious gatherings the conduct of which did not conform to the Book of Common Prayer. 'We thought that the evil decree would fall on us also...', wrote the newly arrived R. Sasportas, 'but against our people they said nothing.' 'Another miracle was added in these days and at this time', he continued. Sasportas was referring to moves by Peter Rycaut, whose brother Paul was an associate of the Levant Company (from which Jews were excluded), and by the Earl of Berkshire. Both men represented to the London Jews that in the name of the king they had been given power over their persons and property. The Jews played for time and informed Charles. The king assured the community, relates Sasportas, that 'no evil decree had ever gone forth against us, nor would it, that they should not look for any other protector apart from him, and so long as he lived let them not fear... he would be their advocate and help them with all his power'.[32]

The diplomacy of the Sephardim extended to the cultivation of Pepys, to the annual presentation of wine or a silver dish to the Lord Mayor, and to unitemized expenditure in political circles: in 1671 the community charity accounts record an outlay of £22 8s. 10d. 'for various expenses on solicitors and goings and comings to the Parliament and bottles of wine that were presented'. In 1673/4 Charles II was persuaded by a group of leading Sephardi merchants to quash all proceedings alleging that Jews engaged in worship technically constituted a 'riot'. The next year the sum of £10 17s. 6d. is recorded, 'by outlay in the house of Ishack Alvarez with the Duchess of Bokingham [sic]'. The Duke of Buckingham was a member of the 'Cabal'; Alvarez the court jeweller and also a senior member of the Mahamad. In 1678 the Mahamad entertained the daughter of Lord Arlington, another member of the 'Cabal' to a banquet costing £9 5s. In 1680 the Bishop of Lincoln and Sir Peter Pett proposed for the Jews a special legal regime headed by a 'justiciary' with special responsibility for the taxes due from the Jews and for their relations with the crown. This scheme went no further than the Privy Council. In 1681 it was the turn of Princess Anne (the future Queen Anne), who visited the synagogue during the Passover festival and was subsequently entertained at home by the treasurer of the congregation, Abraham (Francisco) de Liz. Sephardi leaders not only presented the new king, James II, with a loyal address but were also repeated visitors to the palace. At the end of 1685, writs were issued against 48 Jewish merchants of whom 37 were arrested at the Royal Exchange. They were charged with recusancy, under an Act of 1581. In return for the Mahamad's outlay of 200 guineas the second Earl of Peterborough presented a petition at court which eventually secured the cessation of all proceedings, 'His Majesty's intention being that they (that is, the Jews) should not be troubled ... but quietly enjoy the free exercise of their Religion while they behave themselves dutifully and obediently to his Government'. The Declarations of Indulgence issued by James in 1687 and 1688, 'for the increase of trade and encouragement of strangers', were sufficiently vague to encompass the Jewish presence. In 1696, both the London Jews and the French Protestants had to petition the House of Commons to thwart efforts by the City merchants to exclude even endenized or naturalized aliens from the colonial trade.[33]

Obviously, the *yehidim* must be monarchists to a man, be the monarch Protestant or Catholic. But in support for the House of Orange political and financial interests coincided. The Amsterdam firm of army contractors, Machado and Pereira, provisioned the Irish campaign of William of Orange (1689–90); this required the mobilization of some 28 bakers, 700 to 800 horses and 300 to 400 wagons. Solomon de Medina (*c.*1650–1730), who settled in London in 1672 after a childhood and early adulthood in Bordeaux and Amsterdam, acted as a sort of agent and subcontractor to Machado and Pereira. William III knighted Medina in June 1700. The community enthusiastically espoused William's cause, to the extent of prohibiting Jewish brokers from taking out insurance policies that covered the holder against the government's fall, or reverses in war. Members succeeded in frustrating William's efforts both to levy on them a special tax of £100 000 and also to impose a forced loan of £20 000. To achieve the former cost almost £200.[34]

Whence came the funds that financed these *douceurs*, and communal expenditure in general? From the trading activities of a small number of wealthy merchants. The founders of Sa'ar Asamaim and their successors prospered from the trade in West Indian sugar, Brazil-wood, wine from the Canaries, fish from Newfoundland and cloth from northern Europe. Diamonds were the most important item in their import and export trade. The raw, uncut stones were imported from India, sent to Amsterdam for cutting and polishing, and reimported into London for sale. The trade in diamonds and other precious stones had such importance that as early as 1663 and 1665 the *imposta* on rough or cut diamonds was singled out for special mention (together with gold, silver and minted coin) in the *Ascamot*. The retail jeweller was a by-product of this trade. Another occupation was commodity broking on the Royal Exchange. There is also mention of an occasional 'doctor of physick', for example David de Paz. In 1701 of the 107 proprietors of the Bank of England who held £4000 or more of stock, which was the qualification for governorship, one-ninth were of Spanish and Portuguese origin. Between 1694 and 1725 some 350 proprietors of Bank of England stock were of Jewish origin (though these figures also include a growing number of Dutch Sephardim from Amsterdam). Jewish investors also held stock in the Royal African Company, the South Sea Company and the East India Company.[35] 'The thriftier they live the better example to our people,' wrote Josiah Child, president of the East India Company, 'there being nothing in the world more conducing to enrich a Kingdom than thriftiness.' He called for more Jews to settle in England, for their naturalization, with the security they enjoyed in Holland and Tuscany.[36]

Later, it seems, instability and insecurity came to characterize the trading world, as shown in the large number of Jewish bankruptcies.[37] Always, however, the gentlemen of apparent affluence whom Greenhalgh admired, and the ladies 'richly attired', were a minority in the community. The *kahal* suffered from the unremitting presence and influx of the indigent who thwarted every effort that the Mahamad made to limit their numbers. As early as 1669 the Mahamad complained to the Lord Mayor at the presence of impoverished foreigners and mendicants, and ordained: 'All foreigners who were in this city and those who should come for the future in expectation that the *Ceddacka* would support them, should within five days depart from the country...and for their passage the *Ceddacka* will aid them with what may be possible'; a week later, it was agreed that since 'it appeared to all to tend greatly to the preservation of the Nation in this city', no person would be admitted to the synagogue or congregation, 'unless he should bring an order, arrangement or business for a lawful livelihood'. In 1674 the Mahamad imposed a fine on any member who 'interceded for any foreigner'.[38]

In the 1670s only 54 per cent of households paid any *imposta*. About one-quarter of households received relief from communal funds. The Mahamad devoted approximately one-third of the synagogue's total income to the relief of the poor.[39] The Mahamad dare not abandon the immigrant poor to their own devices, for this would endanger the community's cherished repute. Not for nothing did it proudly claim that none of the Spanish and Portuguese poor was a charge on the public funds.

The physical problem of poverty and its attendant repercussions on the repute of the community can be seen as an 'external' threat; as an 'internal' threat there emerges the issue of deviant conduct among the *yehidim*. The *kahal* was not a happy one. Subject to their vigilance, *yehidim* enjoyed security of property and religious liberty. In these respects London did indeed compare favourably with the centres of those other Sephardi port-Jews in Bordeaux, Amsterdam, Livorno and Hamburg who also had 'heeded the constant call of the sea'. The port-Jews of London, like their confrères, created a communal structure and form of religious expression that met their needs. But that was precisely the point. R. Jacob Sasportas held positions not only in London but also in Livorno, Amsterdam and Hamburg and in every case his zeal for the Torah in an inhospitable environment brought him into conflict with the particular *kahal*. In London Sasportas spent little more than a year. He returned to Amsterdam in 1665, in flight from the plague. Sasportas's letters to relations and rabbinic colleagues show a decidedly mixed community. Their *kahal* was indeed traditional in its practice but members had a variety of backgrounds and were unfamiliar with tradition and in many cases with Hebrew, so that normative observance was by no means general. Sasportas found not only linguistic deficiencies but also members of such weak attachment to the Torah that although they worshipped in the synagogue, once outside they posed as Christians. Sasportas accused others of denying divine providence, challenging the Oral Law, harbouring false beliefs and neglecting the commandments. Above all, there were those who refused to fulfil the commandment of circumcision, 'the most important and weighty of all in relation to the transition from forced conversion to Judaism', writes the editor of these letters. To the emphasis of Sasportas on this commandment may well be attributed a by-law of one of the community's principal charitable societies: this disallowed the burial of any uncircumcised man (or any one of his family or person dependent on him) until the society's elders and the Mahamad had considered the matter. In one of his letters Sasportas relates that he dismissed from his presence one of these uncircumcised men and others, 'and they left the house of prayer, for an uncircumcised and impure person shall not enter the house of the Lord'. In short, the London Jewish community of former and present conversos as it existed in the 1660s had a decidedly mixed composition of believers and unbelievers, circumcised and uncircumcised, observant and unobservant, Judaizers as well as Christianisers. Between 1657 and 1684 no more than 54 per cent of the deceased of the community were buried in the community cemetery.[40]

These pointers to the considerable presence of the attached/unattached generated counter-measures. The Mahamad constantly strove to extend its authority over any Jew, 'whether he be among those who attend the synagogue or those who do not', and in the case of those who failed to observe the Sabbath rest the Mahamad imposed the penalty of *herem* for a greater or lesser period. The force of the sentence was necessarily limited, first, if the Jew concerned did not belong to the congregation, and second, if communal discipline remained, as it did, subordinate to the need for economic cooperation among the members of this trading fraternity. The Mahamad overestimated its power. But it is also true, at least according to Joshua da Silva (haham of Saar Asamaim, 1670–9), that malefactors sometimes had powerful protectors, so that although the Mahamad had the authority, it lacked the will to impose a sentence of *herem* on those who desecrated the Sabbath by attending the theatre and handling the money to pay for their seats. Some of those who flouted the Sabbath regulations were accompanying the young Pepys to the theatre.[41]

In a letter to Sasportas, his successor Haham Solomon Aailion (1690–1700), from Amsterdam, discloses a body of Jews who traded on the Sabbath and festivals and flouted rabbinic teachings – even though 'they live now in a place where they can observe all the commandments of the Torah publicly and with no fear'. But at least they had their sons circumcised. Some of the concern with the lack of observant practice had defensive and apologetic overtones. Into the mouth of a sympathetic Christian critic Haham Aailion puts this reproach: 'What are these wretched Jews doing on their day of rest, their holidays and Sabbath? Where is the observance of their religion? Where then are the scholars of their Torah that they do not protest against it?'[42]

5
At Peace in the Post-War World

A sixteenth-century chronicler, Joseph Ha-Cohen (1496–1578), a physician from Avignon and Genoa, saw in Luther 'a man of understanding and wisdom ... [who] ... spoke openly and aloud against the Pope and against his dreams and the morals of the Popes – only to that man [Jesus] did he cleave – and many rallied to him ... and they did not follow the religion of the Popes and to this day their doctrine has become two doctrines'.

R. David Gans (1541–1613), in his chronicle *Tsemah David* (first published Prague, 1592) wrote with unmistakable sympathy of the Peasants' Revolt of 1525 and its anti-clerical impetus. In Luther he saw

> a great scholar [who] ... walked in the path of John Huss ... He broke the laws of the Pope, destroyed the unity of the Christians and prepared to destroy and burn the statues. He believed one should not pray to Mary, the mother of their Messiah, nor to the twelve apostles.[1]

These writers, and their contemporary sympathisers, would have found their views vindicated in the seventeenth century, though not precisely in the way they had hoped. Following the Treaties of Westphalia of 1648, in major areas of the heartland – in Brandenburg-Prussia, Saxony, Hanover – as a result of religious division, Jews no longer constituted the sole minority and therefore did not stand out as sole dissenters from the majority. Important also in ameliorating their situation was the spread of the politics of *raison d'état*, which called for support, irrespective of source, and which is effectively equivalent to a secularization of politics and the neutralization of the religious factor. The spread of mercantilist ideas and the extension of the cash nexus between Jew and Christian gave further impetus to both these aspects. The work of Bodin and the 'politiques' in the sixteenth century and of Hobbes, say, in the seventeenth, pointed to the dangers associated with a religiously dominated polity.

These factors were to be less influential in those areas (for example the Habsburg empire) where the Counter-Reformation prevailed, the consequences of which can be seen in the expulsion – albeit short-lived – of Jews from Vienna (1670–1) and from Prague (1744–5). Negative also was the liberty that territorial rulers enjoyed to determine the religion of their subjects (*cuius regio ejus religio*). Conversionist policies did re-emerge at the end of the seventeenth and beginning of the eighteenth centuries.[2] In Rome, Carpentras and Vienna this task was well under way. In the German states many a ruler not only cared for the spiritual welfare of his subjects but found in the Christian ordering of the state and the enforcement of the Christian calendar a means to foster politico-social harmony which the Jewish presence would *eo ipso* disturb. Hence the numerous attempts to segregate Jews and Christians at times of religious fervour and celebration, and the censorship of Hebrew literature. Thus religious preoccupations on the ruler's part determined to a large extent the content of the *Ordnung* or terms of settlement. In the duchy of Hesse-Darmstadt for example, a toleration patent of 1692 disallowed worship except in private dwellings, remote from church or school. The services must not be audible from the street and the ram's horn must not be sounded in public. Elsewhere movement was generally restricted, especially on the Christian Sabbath and holidays. The letters of protection in the duchy were distributed individually dependent on the possession of assets to at least the value of 600 gulden and the ability to write and read German (1728, 1737). Numerous decrees prohibited Jews from trading on the Christian Sabbath or required them to remain indoors during Christian festival processions. In Pforzheim in 1672 a Jew who drove cattle through the town on a Sunday during the midday sermon had to pay a fine of 6 kreuzer. The Jews of Worms could not leave their ghetto on Christian holidays except for funerals. The counts of Erbach in the Odenwald not only prohibited Jewish trade on Christian Sabbaths and holidays but also banned Christians from entering Jewish dwellings at those times.[3]

In conformity with this approach the destruction of the post-war community of Vienna in 1670–1 exemplifies the negative effects of the Treaties of Westphalia. The Jews shared in the fate of the Protestants, for the Treaties of Westphalia gave Emperor Ferdinand III *carte blanche* to impose Catholic uniformity in Bohemia, Moravia and the Austrian duchies. This constituted a partial victory for the forces of the Counter-Reformation and implied the acceptance of Protestant dominance to the north as a *quid pro quo*. The emperor was free to expel the remaining Protestants from Bohemia, to force the Lutheran peasantry of Lower Austria to choose between conversion and exile and to suppress the Protestants in Hungary. In 1666 Leopold engineered the expulsion from Vienna of the Danish minister for his part in authorizing the secret celebration of a Lutheran service.[4] It was hardly realistic to suppose that Austrian Jewry would escape untouched, all the less so as the policy of the state converged with popular antisemitism. Not that the court itself was also not rife with superstition – that the Jews had poisoned the well used by the court, that they had engineered the empress's miscarriage, that they were conspiring with the Turks, the Swedes and the French and Prussian armies.[5]

In 1668 there were already anti-Jewish riots in Vienna and the question was raised whether the number of Jews could not be reduced. In February 1670 the emperor decreed that by the following Corpus Christi Day the Jews in Vienna and Lower Austria must have departed. By now some 477 families were settled in the countryside of Lower Austria and about 3000 persons in Vienna.[6] The ghetto of the Untere Werd had grown immeasurably over the past three or four decades or so. By the late 1660s it contained three synagogues and 300 houses which their inhabitants owned and had therefore no need to rent dwellings in the city. The well-endowed yeshivah, headed by R. Meir Isserles, supported 24 students of the Talmud. For the most part the rabbinate stood firm and did succeed in containing most overt expression of sympathy for the pseudo-messiah Sabbatai Zvi.[7] Two celebrated office-holders were R. Sabbatai Sheftel Horovitz (1658–60), who had earlier served in Prague, Fürth, Frankfurt am Main and Posen, and R. Gershom (Ulif) Ashkenazi (1664–70), who came from Nikolsburg and was married to a daughter of R. Menachem Mendel Krochmal, the regional rabbi of Moravia. Perhaps a pointer to the respect which the Viennese court enjoyed was Krochmal's readiness to defer to its judgement in a case in which a woman sought leave to remarry; Krochmal readily submitted his permissive opinion to Vienna for a final decision.[8]

Trade, local and international, provided the material base for the existence of the Viennese community. Moneylending had lost its earlier importance. Commerce in wool linked the Jews of the Untere Werd with Venice, Padua, Reggio, Poland and Turkey (until the outbreak of war with Turkey in 1664). Marcus Lazarus traded with Belgrade in tin and clothing. Moses Frankl dealt in jewellery and precious stones, often for the court. The trade in horses took a special place; in 1648 Abraham Levi Epstein, also known as Leubusch Hecht, was authorized to bring in 70 horses from Hungary; in 1656 Hecht took 15 horses to Frankfurt and brought back 30 others for the imperial stables. Wine was imported from Hungary. The trade in cattle and grain is said also to have been important. Only eight families enjoyed any financial ease and these were coresponsible for the vast majority who were unable to make any worthwhile contribution to the fiscal demands that the state made on the community.[9]

From the 1650s onwards the community fell into arrears with its payments and was absolutely in no position to compete with the German and Italian bankers of Vienna. This weakened financial position of the Jews made them all the more vulnerable. The full exposure was not obvious at all in the early years of peace. In 1659, two years after his accession, the new emperor Leopold I confirmed the privileges of the Jews and protected them from the accusations and attacks of the Vienna magistracy. In 1663, over the latter's opposition, he permitted Jewish families, during a threatened Turkish advance, to take refuge in the inner city and rent the necessary accommodation. In 1665, when a woman's corpse was found in the proximity of the ghetto and the populace accused the Jews of her murder, their leaders appealed to the emperor. Leopold responded with an order to all authorities, including the rector of the university of Vienna, not to harass the Jews in any way, in print, lampoon, pamphlet and outcry. The responsibility for the poverty and hardship of the bulk of the community cannot be imputed solely to the fiscal demands of the state, onerous though these were. A commission of inquiry into the community's accounts for the years 1659–66 found that even after discharging its regular payments to the state and city, and paying interest on its loans and meeting communal outgoings, the community should have enjoyed a financial surplus. The fact that it did not resulted from mismanagement, financial abuse and the self-serving policies of the elders. These had so weakened the community that most members had virtually been forced into vicious competition with each other and into doubtful business practices.[10] Since the results of this inquiry were utilized in a document that sought to justify the expulsion of the Jews, its conclusions are necessarily suspect but not altogether disputed. Beyond doubt is the presence in the communal leadership of corruption and abuse. Much of this – although the details are obscure – centred on the dispute between the Viennese rabbi R. Gershom (Ulif) Ashkenazi and Hirschel Mayer, a wealthy notable. The former was a Sabbatian sympathizer, the latter a decided opponent. This was not the only and certainly not the most important issue between them. Mayer was foisted on the community as tax collector on behalf of the Emperor and for his own safety removed from the jurisdiction of the Jewish courts. He made himself odious to the community as a traitor and informer (*moser*) – their 'scourge', says one historian. He was arrested in 1667 for embezzlement but saved himself through informing on fellow-Jews.[11] The full extent of Mayer's denunciations and informing is by no means clear but they certainly contributed to the weakening of whatever influence the community possessed. In 1668 the ghetto endured mob rioting. Could the number of Jews not be reduced, it was once again asked? This weakness of the Jews at home coincided with their weakness 'abroad', that is, the vastly diminished reliance of the state on the Jews. There is a fair degree of positive correlation between the privileges enjoyed by Habsburg Jewry and the needs of the Habsburg empire – the more of the one, the more of the other; the less of the one, the less of the other. In the late 1660s the international situation of the empire was such that Leopold and his state and war machine no longer had need of the services rendered by the Jews of Vienna and lower Austria or of their contribution to the state budget. To the east, a conciliatory policy towards the Turks brought a relative degree of peace; to the west, France and the empire had reached an accommodation in regard to the disputed Spanish succession. At court, the prejudices of highly placed individuals such as Chancellor Hocher and Bishop Kollonich combined with the prejudices of the empress, the Infanta Marguerite-Theresa and her confessor, a Spanish Franciscan.[12] This is not perhaps the whole story. The report of the Jews' Investigation Commission (*Judeninquisitionskommission*) divided the *kehillah* into three categories: first, those foreign Jews who had illegally 'slunk' into Vienna; second, those Jews who had a legal right but were 'quite poor' and contributed nothing or very little to the general tax assessment, their several hundred families forming the majority; the third category consisted of eight wealthy families. The whole community contributed no more than 10 000 florins annually to the state budget.[13] Thus, although the commission found compelling reasons to recommend to the emperor the expulsion of the Jews, there is perhaps an intimation to the effect that had the Jews been financially stronger the commission might have taken a different view. The eventual decision to expel the Jews was by no means unanimous and met opposition from Prince Wenzel Lobkowitz (1609–77, president of the War Council), and from Count Jörger (1624–1705, vice-president of the *Hofkammer* and regent of lower Austria). Jörger pointed to the loss of confidence in the government that the arbitrary withdrawal of 'dearly bought rights' would cause.[14] They did not press their objections against the empress's encouragement for the expulsion. In July 1669 the emperor introduced one decree of expulsion and in August a second. By 6 June 1670 all the Jews must quit Vienna, and the rest of lower Austria by 11 April 1671.

First to go were the poor and needy – estimated to total 1346 according to Andreas Neumann, the Prussian resident in Vienna.[15] In September the remaining Jews desperately petitioned the emperor for permission to stay; and in March 1670 they turned for help to Isaac Senior Teixeira of Hamburg, the Sephardi banker, merchant and diplomatist with European-wide connections. Contact between Vienna and Hamburg was made through R. Jacob Sasportas of Hamburg, it seems. Two important letters were found among his legal rulings. The first, sent in the name of R. Gershom Ashkenazi and some other Viennese notables, implored Teixeira to prevail on the 'duke of Saxony', the confessor to the queen of Spain, 'and similar personages...to write letters of intercession on our behalf to the emperor, the empress and the latter's confessor'. Teixeira reported back to the Viennese, 'I have written to great men in Spain, some of whom have promised me to devise appropriate means through a prince...important to the empress's confessor'; perhaps respite could be added to respite, during which time, Teixeira hoped, 'the Lord of Hosts would show His grace'. But he wrote also to the Duc de Condé, the Austrian field-marshall Count Montecuccoli, to Cardinal Azolino in Rome, to Queen Christina of Sweden in Rome, to the apostolic nuncio and to the consort of the Duke of Saxony whom he had entertained. Teixeira's letter is dated 12th of Iyyar, (5) 430 = 2 May 1670.[16]

None of this had any effect. The Jews secured no more than an insignificant delay, until 26 July 1670. Two days earlier the Swedish minister-resident in Vienna had written to Queen Christina:

> [T]his alone is worthy of the highest wonder that among the 3000 to 4000 souls who have emigrated this half-year and will mostly set out for Bohemia, Moravia and Silesia, no one was found who even considered in this their extreme hardship that they might change their faith.[17]

This expulsion brought to an end the period of 'the second ghetto' in the history of the Jews in Vienna. Most enthusiastic at this conclusion were the smaller shopkeepers and tradespeople who had most to suffer from Jewish competition. The exiles found a Moravian refuge in communities such as Austerlitz, Kremsier and Prossnitz; in Bohemia, Prague was a natural destination where many had family connections. Others had to travel further, to Fürth in Bavaria, to Berlin in Brandenberg; some few went east to Poland. R. Gershom Ashkenazi accepted an invitation from Metz where his appointment as chief rabbi was approved by Louis XIV and the Metz Parlement (1670/71). The wealthy exiles found it far easier than the poor to secure refuge. This was made explicit in the case of the newcomers to Brandenberg. This northward exodus showed itself to be the most significant of all.

Very soon, the emperor had to overcome opposition to the expulsion: voices of dissent came from the estates in Lower Austria (1672) and in Moravia (1673). In his response to the latter's request that Jews be allowed to attend markets and fairs the emperor relaxed the terms of the expulsion and permitted Jews from Moravia, Bohemia and Silesia to trade at certain Austrian fairs and markets beyond the Danube. At this time also, at Wischau in Moravia, Austrian negotiators apparently discussed with Jewish representatives led by Hirschel Mayer and associates the conditions for the return of a limited number of wealthy Jews. A total of 250 families is mentioned against an advance of 300000 florins.[18] The theology faculty of the University of Vienna found in favour of the proposed readmission but at this time no readmission took place. In any case an outbreak of plague in Vienna in 1679 must have proved a deterrent.

Apart from this notorious exception the post-Westphalian world encouraged rapprochement at a variety of levels. Christian clergy and laymen alike came to interest themselves in Hebrew and Jewish literature. Students of Hebrew included the rulers of Saxony, Darmstadt and Hesse. Christian Hebraists familiarized themselves with Jewish writings and the missionary activities of the Pietist movement were well informed and far removed from the programme of subjecting the Jews to compulsory sermonizing.[19] In 1704 in Hanover a disputation between Jew and Christian took place, unprecedented, in that, first, secular authority was the sponsor, and, second, the

Jewish spokesman, R. Joseph Samson Stadthagen, enjoyed the same freedom of discourse as his Christian opponent (a converted Jew).

Rapprochement extended into social intercourse, at varying levels. Jewish and Christian thieves had their meeting place at a tavern in Hamburg. At Cleves in c.1674, Prince Frederick of Prussia (the future king of Prussia, 1701), and Prince Maurice of Nassau and his entourage attended the wedding of Zipporah, the eldest child of the diarist Glückel, to the grandson of the wealthy R. Elia Cleve. At Mannheim in the 1670s the local rabbi R. Isaac Brillin and Duke Karl Ludwig, the elector Palatine, were on friendly terms and frequently met to converse on what are termed 'intellectual matters'. What these were is not reported but an anecdote conveys the tenor of the relationship of the two men. The duke complained that his Jewish subjects not only broke the laws but also corrupted the judges with bribes. This was conduct that Brillin condemned from the standpoint of the good order of the state as well as from a Jewish standpoint. The matter did not end there. Brillin put bribery in the context of actuality: it could not be assumed, he said, that the person who gave the bribe did so in order to secure a verdict favourable to himself, no matter whether this was justified or not:

> but he who gives the bribe is giving it in order to secure a truthful ver-dict ... it is well known that there is no hatred like religious hatred ... so that if a Jew and a Christian come to court, without doubt, the heart of the judge will be inclined to exculpate the Christian and incriminate the Jew and suspect him of lying and deceit. The Jew therefore thinks that he will correct the scales of justice ... the bribe that he gives is not to pervert justice but, on the contrary, to uphold justice.

This was an argument that Karl Ludwig accepted but he then asked: 'What do you say when it is two Jews who are fighting each other in court and each offers a bribe? Your last answer falls down here.' Each party, Brillin replied, gives a bribe only because he suspects the other is doing so 'and it is only to uphold justice and each one, if he knew that the other would hold back and not give a bribe, he too would refrain'. And the duke laughed and said 'Your words are gracious, with my knowing that the gates of the answers are closed neither to truth nor to falsehood.'[20]

For their part Jewish thinkers came to view Christianity and the Christian world in general with less antagonism. (This does not apply to the Sephardim, for whom the church remained a fount of idolatry.) In the Ashkenazi world, noteworthy are the anecdotes of generous Christian help to Jews in trouble, that Juspa (Joseph) Hahn of Frankfurt published towards the end of the seventeenth century.[21] Juspa gives his contemporary version of the classic Talmudic question, 'What is the answer to Epicurus?' Whereas Epicurus and his followers were indeed heathens who denied the divine government of the world and worshipped the stars, sun and moon, 'of the peoples among whom we live today it can be said that even the zealous among them are not epicureans because although they associate one other matter with Him', they acknowledge the living God, King of the universe and Creator of heaven and earth. In dispute with Christians, Hahn pre-scribed three guidelines: first, make it clear to the Christian disputant that he was using a translation; second, show the meaning of a disputed verse in its full context (and that, Hahn explains, is why he never travelled without all the 24 books of the Bible); third, be familiar with the Gospels so as to be alive to their contradictions.[22] Contemporary gentiles 'are not idol-aters', for this referred only to those 'who denied the Creator', declared R. Yair Hayyim Bachrach of Koblenz and Worms (1638–1702), an authority of the period.[23]

In this post-war world of the later seventeenth century the Jews of the German states at least made good their wartime losses in terms of popula-tion and settlement. By about 1700 the Jews numbered some 25 000.[24] The overwhelming majority of those approximately 25 000 Jews lived as hitherto in rural areas, villages and hamlets. In Baden, Hesse, the Palatinate, Bavaria, Swabia, Franconia and Westphalia the Jews, almost without exception, lived in small villages. In the seventeenth and eighteenth centuries, more than 90 per cent of the Jews in the German lands lived in the countryside, it is estimated.[25] Many would, it appears, willingly have exchanged countryside for town.[26] They were in effect displaced townspeople, eager to resume urban life not least because, with all its restrictions, it offered an enhanced liveli-hood. The average assets of a resident in the city of Darmstadt were demon-strably higher than those of a village-dweller – so much so that the latter have been likened to 'something resembling a Jewish proletariat'. Outside Hesse, in Moravia and Prussia, the same pattern of demographic distribution held good.[27]

The rural population was atomised and the *kehillot* were constituted of groups of families. sometimes amounting to no more than a handful. In Heidelberg the number of families was 5 (1660); in Buchen there were 5 pro-tected Jews and 1 widow (1668); in Fellheim (Swabia), in 1670, 5 families received letters of protection to settle in the village, almost burned to the ground by the Swedes. Eighteen Jewish families lived in Bruchal by 1685, and were entitled to buy houses and vineyards. In Stühlingen there were 32 families by 1710. In Oettingen Wallerstein (1687) there were 35 families, of whom 17 lived by dealing in horses and cattle. In the villages in Württemberg where the Jews lived this dispersed and fragmented existence it was customary for them to reside in a separate Judengasse.[28] Over the decades little change took place. In Hesse-Cassel (1744), 842 families lived in 177 localities and in 148 of those localities the number of families did not exceed 5.[29]

With the best will in the world it was barely possible for the minuscule atomized communities of dwellers in villages and hamlets to maintain all the facilities that religious life ideally required – schooling, law-court, cemetery, ritual bath, slaughterhouse and so on.[30] That explains why one theme of the contemporary Yiddish song is the mockery directed by urban Jews at the ignorance of *Dorfjuden*, village Jews. Already in the late sixteenth century this formed the basis for an unfavourable comparison made by R. Hayyim b. Bezalel between the Polish communities and the scattered settlements of the German lands. A century later a rabbi who came from Meseritz in Moravia to Bamberg, R. Samuel Halevy, lamented the absence of concern with study: 'Torah unopened lies in a corner and in the whole country nobody cares to instruct his son in the Torah that he should spend as long as possible in the Yeshivah to uphold and strengthen knowledge of the Torah.' At a more popular level, the satirical poet Elhanan Kirchhan uses a 'Polak' (Polish Jew) to make an incisive critique of observance in the German village:

When they come together on the Sabbath for services,
They begin to laugh,
Their mouth does not stand still.
One speaks of his filly, one of his horse –
Do I have to say more?
Often they even come to blows in the synagogue.[31]

Such degrees of acceptance and security as these sections of Ashkenazi Jewry did secure in the seventeenth century never came cheap and had to be paid for both by way of agreeing to certain restrictions on self-expression and also by way of cash payment. Even to an established *kehillah* did this apply. In 1663 Worms Jewry paid Emperor Leopold I 1000 florins in crown tax and poll tax in return for his confirmation of the privilege that Ferdinand III had granted in 1641.[32] At its crudest the local rulers might regard the Jews purely as a means to enrichment. In an anonymous 'Discurs' of 1670 an imperial knight discusses the means whereby 'one can make use of the Jews', that is how best to squeeze them, through demanding protection money, New Year money, synagogue fees, meat supplies, funeral taxes and so on.[33] With more sophistication, a *Judenordnung* would need to be purchased defining the conditions of settlement, in terms of religious observance, dues and taxes, occupation, numbers, and access to common pastureland.

In addition to purchasing his privilege under a general *Judenordnung*, each individual head of household would need to purchase his *Geleit* or *Schutzbrief* ('licence', 'letter of protection'). There are variations on this broad distinction. Sometimes, for example, the distinction between a general privilege and an individual 'letter of protection', *Schutzbrief* or *Geleit*, is not clear. In the mid-seventeenth century in the Westphalian territories the *Generalgeleit* replaced the individual *Geleit*, and thus the community acquired the status of a judicially recognized public body, under the protection of the territorial ruler. In Warburg in the late seventeenth century an unusual blend of general and individual *Geleit*, normally with a validity of 10 years or the lifetime of the ruler, listed the names and dwellings of all Jews in the territory. On the ruler's death a renewal had to be purchased from his successor by the general body of Jews. A Jew could also not without permission change his residence, or transfer, or sell or bequeath his *Geleit*; it was strictly personal, even though included in a general list.[34] An application for a *Schutzbrief* from the widow of a protected Jew offers an interesting variation on the normal procedure: in about 1750, Arendt Lambert died in Würhden, in the duchy of Oldenburg, and his widow sought from the Danish king, the overlord, Frederick V, a *Schutzbrief* on behalf of Herz Israel Schwabe of Bremen, her intended second husband, evidently a butcher who engaged also in money-lending. Frederick granted his protection, on condition that the couple lived in either Würhden or Butjadingen, that Schwabe paid an annual protection fee of 10 Reichsthaler and all dues and tolls, conducted his trading and slaughtering operations honestly, and did not levy an excessive rate of interest. The king promised Schwabe protection against hindrance or interference from any 'foreign Jew'. This document had a validity limited to the lifetime of the king.[35]

This system of *Judenordnung*en, 'licences' and 'letters of protection' expressed the power of the territorial ruler to appropriate a revenue that had formerly been the prerogative of the emperor. This was one factor in the reinvigoration of a Jewish representative organ, the *Landjudenschaft*, or corporation, a regional assembly of the Jews of a given territory. It obviously facilitated the implementation of a state's Jewish policy if it dealt with one authority – the corporation – rather than with a multitude of minor authorities. This corresponded also to the increasing centralization of the state's apparatus. To the small *kehillot* the same corporation gave an opportunity to confront the local territorial ruler as a more or less united body. Certainly, this system did not encompass every territory and not every Jew. The imperial and free cities (Frankfurt am Main, Worms, Friedberg) did not belong to any of the *Landjudenschaften*; and only those Jews who had a *Geleit*, 'a licence' (i.e. were *vergleitet*), or had a 'letter of protection', a *Schutzbrief*, were included. This of course, severely qualifies the claim to comprehensive representative status, in excluding the poor and those unable to afford the required 'protection fee'. Even so, apart from Bohemia and Moravia, the major territories of the empire, from Pomerania to Strasbourg, contained some 30 *Landjudenschaften* during the two centuries 1616–1821. The many others in minor territories were sometimes not easily to be distinguished from purely communal organizations.[36]

The assembly of *vergleitete* individuals comprising the *Landjudenschaft* met at a *Landyom* or *Landtag* every 3, 4 or sometimes 5 years, for example as decided at Aschaffenburg in 1721.[37] In an ideal situation, in the larger territories such as Hesse-Cassel (1690), the assembly operated through a council composed of 12 men, selected by a complex process which began by drawing 13 names from an electoral urn and ended with election by a majority. Only those persons were included in the initial draw who fulfilled four conditions: held the modest title of *Chaver* for their learning; were aged at least 50; were assessed for 200 Reichsthaler tax; and had no debt outstanding to the *Judenschaft*. This comprehensive body drew up the statutes of a quasi-autonomous entity – which governed the appointment of a rabbi and the specification of his duties; tax assessment; the election of officers and matters of internal discipline; the means to settle disputes; regulations for the admission of newcomers; educational policy and standards; the control of economic activity; the fixing of a marriage broker's fee; the support of yeshivah students.[38] The elected council normally required to be confirmed in office by the ruler; it held office for three years during which period it conducted the affairs of the *Judenschaft*. Sometimes the protocols were kept in Hebrew. They were certainly dated in accordance with the Hebrew calendar.

From the ruler's point of view the *Landjudenschaft* provided a central body through which taxes, the annual protection money and so on could be collected, at a time when the responsibility for meeting these obligations was passing from the individual Jew to the collective body of which he was a member. For this reason the ruler normally took a keen interest in the workings of 'his' *Landjudenschaft*, especially so in the choice of its leaders, rabbinic and other. As an institution the *Landjudenschaft* is another example of a body that fulfils for the Christian ruler one function and for the Jew an overlapping but different function. The heads of the *Landjudenschaft* had the unenviable task of reconciling these two standpoints. Moreover, given the function that the *Landjudenschaft* took in the government of the state, the ruler had an interest in its subordination and this sometimes conduced to his actual nomination of its leaders. It was sometimes 'made known' to the relevant Jewish body that at the forthcoming *Landtag* the existing president must be confirmed in office with undiminished rights, and without the need for an election. In 1651 the prince-bishop Christophi Bernhard v. Galen appointed Nini (or Nino) Levi of Warendorf to be 'commander and leader' (*Befehlshaber und Vorgänger*) of the assembly and specified his powers in relation to the Jews of the bishopric of Münster. The prince-bishop gave Levi powers to settle disputes among the Jews of his 'constituency' and to collect the annual 'protection money' (*Schutzgeld*). He could call on the power of the state to secure obedience. Levi himself and his family and household enjoyed freedom from payment of 'the annual tribute' and had all the rights of a protected Jew. Priebatsch quotes the case of the rulers of Öttingen who always required their court-Jew to preside over the *Judenschaft*, and even prohibited a minor innovation in the synagogue service that a new rabbi from outside wished to introduce. There were two rulers in Öttingen, one Catholic and one Lutheran, so that people spoke of 'their' respective Jewries as Catholic or Lutheran.[39]

By way of extension to his interest, it was not uncommon for the gentile ruler to intervene on behalf of his nominees, favourites or supporters. In

1678 the bishop of Bamberg-Würzberg issued a patent protecting the rabbi of Heidingsfeld against competition from 'foreign' rabbis. In 1731 the *Oberlandesrabbiner* (senior regional rabbi) of Mainz, R. Issachar Bär b. Gabriel Wiener from Prague, confirmed to the authorities of the electorate that the Jews of certain districts were not only not taking their disputes to him but were taking them to the state's officials, and also circumventing his authority in religious matters. Thereupon the officials were instructed to adhere to the regulations and direct all disputes to the rabbi for resolution; in 1732 Moses Feist, senior elder of the Jews in Gernsheim and Starkenburg, complained that the officials were not giving him due support in his struggle against Jewish dissidents (*widerspenstige Juden*) and were infringing on his jurisdiction; Feist was rewarded with a rescript that instructed the officials, first, to give him all due assistance against these dissidents and, second, not to hamper the jurisdiction of the rabbi and the elders.[40]

The poor had no direct representation at the *Landtag* or *Landyom*; the elders and the rabbi must be confirmed in office, if, indeed, they were not actually installed in office. It is quite true of course that the rules governing the election of the Jewish elders invariably took account of the limitations imposed by consanguinity, but these could not of themselves resist the influence created by the combined forces of self-interest and dependence. The system was not immune to abuse and this as usual took form in the main in the inequitable distribution of financial burdens among the members of the *Landjudenschaft*. The leaders, during their period in office, were subject only to intermittent scrutiny. Financial and taxation matters unleashed most disputes. At Darmstadt in 1701 a *Landtag* summoned to apportion taxes 'exploded'. A second meeting was preceded by the decree that all Jews must appear without exception and towards the elders conduct themselves 'modestly and decently' (*gebührlich*). In 1704 at a similar *Landtag* at Gross-Gerau some of those present were so 'disobedient and unseemly' (*ungebührlich*) vis-à-vis Benedikt David, the old-established court-Jew and elder, that a fine of 15 gulden was imposed. At a *Landtag* in Spangenberg in 1726 three of the prince's officials found 'considerable confusion and inequality' in fiscal matters; this resulted from the activity of earlier Jewish elders, since removed from office: 'They were mostly the wealthy and had assessed lightly the Jews of means but the poorer Jews very heavily.'[41] In Paderborn the court-Jew Behrend Levi exercised, it is said, 'a tyrannical and dishonest control over the treasury of the corporation'. In 1650 the community at last succeeded in securing his dismissal on grounds of embezzlement. This did not prevent the later introduction of a system of tax assessment that favoured the wealthy at the expense of the poor and those of middling wealth, for example by raising from one-fifth to one-half that proportion of an individual's property exempt from taxation.[42]

The atomization process and the growth of the territorial unit as the unit of government in the German states necessarily altered the composition and disposition of the rabbinate, most conspicuously in the further development of the so-called *Landrabbinat* or regional rabbinate. The tasks of a regional rabbi – *Landrabbiner* – differed little from those of a communal rabbi, and the terms of his contract (*Rabbonusbrief*) corresponded likewise to the various functions of self-government, that is he exercised his authority primarily in a judicial, educational and synagogal capacity. At Ansbach in his capacity as a member of the Lesser Council, he will also approve and sign the ordinances of the parnassim. In many cases he will also supervise the conduct of elections, as a sort of scrutineer, and administer an oath of integrity and fair dealing to those elected to office in the *Judenschaft*.[43]

During the seventeenth century, *Landrabbinate* were created in the bishopric of Paderborn (1619); in Münster (1649); in the duchy of Cleves (1650); for Halberstadt, Minden and Ravensberg (1650). Aron Bär Oppenheim from Frankfurt, court-Jew of the prince of East Frisia in Aurich, was entrusted with the dual office of state-rabbi and senior Jewish elder (1687); at much the same time Duke Ernst August created in Hanover a *Landrabbinat* for Brunswick-Lüneburg. In 1706 the Jews of Jülich-Berg broke the traditional link with Cologne and appointed their own rabbi.[44]

Because, in the context of territorialism, the number of rabbinates multiplied, their respective jurisdictional areas diminished. Round about the mid-seventeenth century the jurisdiction of the Worms rabbi extended from members of his own community to the surrounding villages, Darmstadt, Speyer and its neighbourhood, Upper and Lower Alsace (Haut-Rhin and Bas-Rhin), Switzerland, the region of the Neckar river. In these areas no marriage could be contracted without rabbinical authority, or divorce writ issued, or release from levirate marriage secured, or marriage settlements sworn. The rabbi also had a role in resolving religious and civil disputes among the local Jewries.[45] In 1650 R. Samson Bachrach of Worms is reported to have settled a taxation dispute at a communal assembly in Rüsselsheim.[46] This *modus operandi* entailed periodic visits to outlying areas. During the seventeenth and eighteenth centuries this system came largely to an end, and the 'parish' of the Worms rabbinate shrank considerably, losing the Palatinate, Hesse-Darmstadt and Speyer. If the function and composition of the parnassim must conform to the dictates of territorialism, so too must rabbinical jurisdiction be geographically circumscribed.[47]

Obviously, no *Landjudenschaft* in 1750, say, will be the same as in 1650. A loss of power over this period will be the most notable difference. There is a transition from that stage when the gentile ruler signified his approval of those elected to office to that later stage when the ruler himself appointed communal leader or rabbi. This was the case, for example, in the Franconian communities of Scheinfeld and Marktbreit in 1764 where the local ruler reserved to himself the right to install rabbis and parnassim.[48] This converted the corporation into a quasi-organ of government. To some extent this had always been the case – now it was blatant. It remained nonetheless a *Landjudenschaft*, albeit shorn of much of its autonomy. This evolution paralleled that of the urban *kehillot*, which similarly declined in the eighteenth century into governmental agencies while also functioning as instruments of Jewish preservation. Berlin offers an excellent example (see below, p. 138). With all their faults and weaknesses the *Landjudenschaften* survived for over two centuries, until the later eighteenth; and during this period they served as some sort of buffer to protect the atomized and isolated rural communities from the arbitrary sway of the gentile ruler, even if the arbitrariness came sometimes from within the *Landjudenschaft* itself. This body made it possible, in unfavourable and straitened circumstances, to create the necessary organizational framework for the exercise of a Jewish life.

That 90 per cent of German Jews who lived in rural areas, no less than the 10 per cent of towndwellers – these totals are of course only approximations – benefited from the conjoined phenomenon of a secularized polity and a less hostile Christian world. What of the urban population? In the process of resettlement that is an outstanding feature of these centuries entirely new communities came into existence; older ones were enlarged or expulsions rescinded. Before the eighteenth century there were no Jewish settlements in East Prussia, Mecklenburg or Saxony. Centres to be revived or created or enlarged included (apart from Vienna) Mannheim, Karlsruhe, Dresden, Leipzig, Cassel, Stuttgart, Hanover, Bayreuth, Magdeburg, Berlin, Halle and Königsberg. Across the Rhine, in west-central Ashkenaz, the same process of expansion through dispersion operated in Alsace and Lorraine.

Characteristic of the post-war period is not the expulsion of Jews rather their attraction. Overwhelmingly, settlement or resettlement came about by way of invitation. This reversal was grounded in the socio-economic condition of the German states in the seventeenth century. There was reconstruction needed to make good the ravages of war; natural resources called for exploitation; trade and development would revive the broken economy; there was a princely way of life to be supported, all the more costly at a time when the splendour of Versailles set the standard; lastly, there were wars to be waged, again at a time when not only did wars last longer than in previous centuries but their prosecution demanded ever more costly investments in manpower, armaments, fortifications, uniforms and equipment.[49]

By no means to any and every Jew did the German rulers extend their invitation – only to those whose abilities and resources and contacts enabled them to provide the means to satisfy the manifold wants of the hundreds of ruling establishments. This excluded the poor Jew, anathema to all. The German princes had nothing to learn from the French intendants in this respect. The very criteria of settlement ensured that admission was the prerogative of the wealthy. To settle in Berlin the Jew needed to be 'prosperous' and possess assets that he can invest in the economy; in Mannheim he needed the resources to build a two-storey house in the shattered city; in Fürth 5000 Reichsthaler; and in Warburg 1000 Reichsthaler. Urban settlers in the electorate of Cologne needed at least 1000 Reichsthaler, in the villages at least 600. However genuinely philosemitic some of these rulers were (for example Frederick William, the Great Elector, or Duke Karl Ludwig of the Palatinate), to poor and vagrant 'semites' their philosemitism did not extend. It was highly selective. No ruler is interested in the *schnorrer* or beggar-Jew, and neither were many of their fellow Jews. The fortunate few who, again in Mannheim, had the resources to build a house of two storeys, enjoyed much the same trading rights as other dwellers; no religious restrictions were imposed – a synagogue and ritual bath were erected in 1664, and in 1674 a *Hevra Kadischa* founded; there were no residential restrictions; no yellow 'Jews' ring' need be worn. A town map of 1663 shows 15 houses inhabited by Jews, including two Portuguese. In 1680, 78 Jews were taxed for war contributions of whom the wealthiest were the two Portuguese, Astrouque and Carcassone. As distinct from the Ashkenazi settlers, the Sephardim enjoyed freedom from the travel tax (*Taschengeleit*) and the requirement to build a house. Hostility to this growth on the part of the town council, and of certain guilds (for example the butchers') did not prevent a lift in the number of officially permitted families to 200 (1717). Newcomers now had to swear to the possession of assets totalling 1000 thaler. The number of families did not in fact reach this total but at 160–180 formed about one-eighth of the total population.[50]

In many cases settlement or resettlement, as the case may be, took place under the auspices of a court-Jew. His entourage stood at the heart of the community and he himself stood at its head. He merited the title and rank of 'court-Jew' (and its concomitant privileges) through fulfilling the expectations and meeting the demands of his ruler. The title denotes that Jew who rendered, in a personal or family capacity, any of a variety of services to his employer-patron-protector as ruler or as individual. These services normally belonged to the domains of private banking, trade, diplomacy, personal provisions and military supplies. In principle, there seems to have been no limit to the variety of demands that had to be met. Moses Kauffmann, an important supplier to the electorate of Cologne from the 1720s onwards, provided the court with forage in time of peace and war, also timber, writing materials, tallow, liveries, beer, oil, flowers, furniture, costly fabrics as well as ordinary draperies, and shoes and stockings for the archbishop. In 1746/47 Hirsch Baruch, Alexander Löw and Samuel Süsskind were engaged by the court at Ansbach as court chess-players. The bishopric of Paderborn engaged a court dentist, Samuel Levi, who claimed to be able to replace missing front teeth, whiten stained teeth and fill hollow teeth with cold lead or gold.[51]

Towards the end of the seventeenth century the needs of the warring armies took on a speciality of their own. This created fresh opportunities for the court-Jews and in general for the Jewish economy. Obviously, exclusion from many activities led to concentration in others, and the case of war offered particular advantages for not only is conflict a more and more significant feature of European society in the late seventeenth and eighteenth centuries, not only is armed conflict more and more demanding in its requirements – it has also the advantage that the very nature of these requirements (for example horses for the cavalry and baggage trains) is such as to make control difficult and therefore hamper any efforts at control by such hostile bodies as the guilds. Where this was possible, however, the guilds did raise their voice, for example in decrying the boots that the Jewish saddlers in Berlin made for the Prussian cavalry (see below, p. 204).

During the Thirty Years' War, Protestants had been the principal military entrepreneurs.[52] In a very small way they did have Jewish counterparts; for example in 1622 a certain Joseph from Zwingenberg delivered lead to the arsenal in Giessen for the casting of guns.[53] At much the same time the Gomperts family entered on its long reign in the duchy of Julich-Cleves, supplying foodstuffs and tobacco to Dutch troops – a step towards the family's appointment as court-Jews to the Hohenzollern dynasty in Brandenburg. Five generations of this family served six Hohenzollerns – from the Great Elector to Frederick William III. In 1732 Frederick William I of Prussia appointed Jakob Gomperts to provide 'handsome young recruits', to be delivered to Wesel. Payment started at 300 Reichsthaler for a recruit of six feet tall, and rose in proportion to the recruit's height.[54] These recruits required uniforms and this was instrumental in creating or at least stimulating a specifically 'Jewish' branch of the economy. In the seventeenth and eighteenth centuries uniforms became *de rigueur* for the modern soldier, as means to distinguish between friend and foe in hand-to-hand fighting. Badges and emblems were no longer enough. This opened the way to the mass procurement and provision of uniforms. In a small way the new settlers in Pomerania already presaged the future. The duchy fell to Brandenburg after 1650 and restrictions on Jewish residence were removed. The new settlers engaged in the wool and skin trades in the 1660s and 1670s. Early entrepreneurs were Abraham Arndt and Levin Joseph from Stargard. These merchants took a large part in developing the *verlag* system: the *verleger* financed the purchase of the raw wool by the primary producer and bought it back from him in the form of the woollen uniforms that the new standing armies required and which the *verleger* disposed of through his foreign connections. By about 1705 there were 45 Jewish families in the duchy, forming a *Landjudenschaft* which was headed by a rabbi and three elders. Most were propertyless peddlers, subject to expulsion.[55] In the 1680s and after, the operations of Leffmann Behrens (1634–1714), known to his fellows as Lippmann Cohen, court-Jew to the elector of Hanover, far outclassed artisan production through the cloth factories that he established in Lüneburg (for a time in association with the Huguenot Antoine de Pau). Other associates included Hayyim Gundersheim from Mainz and Hertz Cassel, specialists in military equipment. Their factories supplied the Hanoverian (and other) troops with greatcoats and uniforms.[56] Leffmann Behrens also prospered through his credit operations (including the transmission of subsidies from France to Hanover), his manufactories (textile, tobacco) and the trade in gold, jewellery and precious fabrics. About half the protected Jews in Hanover-Neustadt belonged to Behrens's entourage. He had family connections with the Oppenheimer and Wertheimer families in Vienna, Liebmann in Berlin, Gomperts in Cleves-Mark and agents of various categories in Amsterdam, Hamburg (for example the Sephardi bankers Teixeira and Musaffia), Paris, London, Frankfurt am Main and Brussels. These links enabled Behrens to satisfy not only the demands of a court that was prodigiously extravagant but also the demands of an electorate that maintained a standing army of more than 15 000 men. Only the empire, Bavaria, Brandenburg and Saxony, could muster larger forces.

Unquestionably the most impressive example of a resettlement initiated and maintained by a court-Jew is that of Samuel Oppenheimer (1630–1703) at Vienna. Through Oppenheimer's instrumentality and under his auspices, barely a dozen years after the expulsion, in Vienna a *kehillah* was re-established, albeit tiny in comparison with its predecessor. Known as 'The Jews' Emperor' (*Judenkaiser*), Oppenheimer developed a financial and supply network that made him the most redoubtable, influential and far-flung court-Jew in all Ashkenaz. The new *kehillah* in Vienna developed amidst the Habsburg wars with France and the Ottoman empire of the later 1670s and early 1680s. (The emperor did not abrogate the earlier degree of expulsion.) This *kehillah* differed fundamentally from its predecessor; whereas the latter had acquired mass proportions, its successor was strictly controlled and according to the census of 1752 no more than 452 persons were included in the privileges granted to 12 heads of families.[57] Samuel Oppenheimer dominated its early decades. His first contact with the finances of the empire went back to 1674. As early as 1677 military commanders found his services indispensable.[58]

Oppenheimer came from the Rhineland, of a rabbinic family that had been expelled from Frankfurt and then settled in Worms. His wife, with whom Oppenheimer had nine children, came from the Sephardi Carcassone family of Mannheim. A sister was married to R. Brillin of Mannheim, the friend of Elector Karl Ludwig (see above, p. 93). In 1660 Oppenheimer entered the elector's service. In 1676 during the French siege of Philippsburg he began to make his first deliveries of food and ammunition to the imperial armies, coming under the patronage of Margrave Armand of Baden and from this point grew into the all-powerful 'monopolist', familiar to his enemies. During the struggle of the Habsburgs against the French in the west and the Turks in the east, Oppenheimer's supply system provided the imperial armies with clothing, munitions, foodstuffs, cavalry, draught animals for the artillery, bridging materials and shipbuilding equipment. He also organized the transmission of subsidies. Oppenheimer had suppliers and agents in Holland, Poland and Russia (gunpowder), Bohemia, Moravia, Hungary and Silesia (saltpetre), Styria and Carinthia (arms), Kremsier (boots for the dragoons), Salzburg and Bavaria (horses and floats), Holland (cloth), Austria, Bamberg, Mainz, Trier (wheat and corn), Hamburg (spices), Rhineland, Neckar and Mosel (wine) and Siebenbürgen (oxen). Most, but certainly not all, of these suppliers were themselves court-Jews, factors, purveyors and the like, and included a number of Oppenheimer's immediate family in Donauwörth, Breslau, Frankfurt and Heidelberg. Oppenheimer also ensured that the emperor and his court were supplied with jewels, silverware, livery and cash loans. State loans during the period 1695–1740 were provided in alliance with the approximately fifteen members of the Oppenheimer circle in Vienna. They included Emanuel Drach, Oppenheimer's son-in-law, Lazarus Hirshel, Moses Isak, David Lebl, Simon Michael, Moses Lemle, Lebl Pollak. Oppenheimer also acted as 'front man' for credits advanced by the rulers of Mainz, Trier and Saxony.[59]

Oppenheimer and his family and associates were not popular. His residence in Vienna was attacked and plundered in 1700. He himself was arrested from time to time and on these occasions the warning bell sounded as far away as Hamburg; brokers on the Bourse refused to deal in Oppenheimer's bills, as Glückel found to her cost.[60] An observant and pious Jew, Oppenheimer was refused permission to pray publicly and must content himself with somewhat less than a prayer-room in his house – and that only grudgingly conceded. Cardinal Kollonitsch stood out for his enmity to the Jewish presence in Vienna, all the more vehement because of his failure to organize a syndicate of Christian bankers to counter Oppenheimer's influence.

The prosperity of the *kehillah* survived Oppenheimer's death in 1703 and the bankruptcy of his firm. In 1719, R. Samson Wertheimer, nephew to Oppenheimer and in some respects his heir, was visited by a 17-year-old relation, Abraham Levy (from Horn in Lippe-Detmold). 'The Jews in this city of Vienna are the richest in all Europe', the boy reported:

> First, the great, respected and renowned R. Samson Wertheimer has 10 soldiers of the emperor standing guard at his gate all the time, and he has been favoured by the emperor with many other freedoms. This Wertheimer owns many palaces and gardens in Vienna ... He has also had many synagogues built and distributed much money among the poor Jews in all Europe, as far away as Poland and Jerusalem in the holy land ... And he is the rabbi of Hungary ... He is now an old man in the seventies. He dresses like a Pole and has a long white beard. He is often with the emperor ... Foreign Jews may not stay overnight in Vienna without the permission and written attestation of Herr Wertheimer.[61]

The status of this small group did not match its wealth. Given the hostility of the populace, and of influential churchmen, not even personal safety was always available. In 1715 a pamphlet alleging ritual murder required an official warning to the Viennese magistracy against 'any violence or uproar' directed at the Jews. They suffered a range of vexatious restrictions, for example the prohibitions against appearing on the street before 10 a.m. on Sundays and Christian holidays. During religious processions in the streets no Jew must show himself at the window of a house. They were subject to forced loans, held collectively responsible for those community members detected dealing in stolen property, and required to curtail music and dancing in public places when celebrating weddings and festivals – this was all the more reprehensible as Christians might be attracted, which was 'in itself punishable and forbidden'.[62] The regime made every effort to maintain the separation between Christian and Jew; and certainly no synagogue might be erected. To Oppenheimer's biographer, 'the political situation of Viennese Jewry was incomparably more unfavourable than a century earlier in the ghetto of the Untere Werd'.[63]

This decline in status was not characteristic of the institution in general. Leffmann Behrens of Hanover, for example, had no ambition to accommodate himself or his way of life to the gentile world. He remained an observant and studious Jew, who refused to conduct business on the Sabbath, and fostered Jewish life in multitudinous ways: in 1687 he secured permission from Ernst August to establish a state rabbinate empowered, inter alia, to adjudicate conflicts between Jew and Jew and impose fines and even the sentence of *herem* (but not of course to infringe on the state's jurisdiction); in 1703/04, the existing but cramped synagogue was replaced by a more commodious building financed by the Behrens family; in his own premises, Leffmann Behrens had a Bet HaMidrash ('house of learning') installed where he himself studied in the company of like-minded scholars. These men he supported with board and lodging. He also financed the publication of Talmudic commentaries and arranged for the transfer of the library of R. David Oppenheimer (his son-in-law) from Prague to Hanover. Here it would be less exposed to censorship and harm. He actively intervened in the effort to suppress Eisenmenger's antisemitic *Entdecktes Judentum* ('Judaism Unmasked') and in the movement to thwart the threatened expulsion of the Jews from Kremsier in 1699, following an appeal from Oppenheimer.[64]

This was the sort of diplomatic intervention that in the view of certain rabbis entitled the court-Jew to special consideration in regard to the laws, on the principle that in the interests of the Torah, the Torah can itself be disregarded. Rabbi Joseph Stadthagen (d. 1715) in his commentary on the Talmud (Gittin 14b), counselled a lenient and permissive attitude to those who concerned themselves with the public welfare. This applied at all levels – to those who were 'close to the kingdom' no less than to those who, at a lower level, 'worked among judges and officials for the good of the many and the few'. 'There is no greater act of righteousness than this', wrote R. Lippmann Heller in his commentary on the Mishnaic Treatise 'Chapters of the Fathers' (2:3), 'that they exert themselves for the community for the sake of heaven'.[65]

The very existence of the Jews, as individuals and as collective, depended on their financial utility and standing. This is what secured their wellbeing, as a necessary if not always as a sufficient condition. 'Without money there's no living,' the rich Jew reminded the poor Jew in a poetic dialogue of the early seventeenth century (quoted above, p. 24). In later decades this tension assuredly did not slacken. A Jew who lacked the resources to purchase a *Geleit* or *Schutzbrief* lived in a sort of limbo, outside the protection of any law:

> To the Jews of the eighteenth century [*of the seventeenth also, I would add*], their 100 thalers meant not only nourishment but also momentary security from falling into nothingness, and therefore signified an expression of their precarious independence and to some extent offered a substitute for that security and freedom which the guild-burgher sought and found in his group and in his estate.[66]

Every *kehillah* certainly had its charitable fraternities to help those of its members who fell into need. But these resources were plainly inadequate, especially given the growth of the Jewish population and the westward flight from Poland (as Chapter 11 will show).

What applied to the individual applied also to the *kehillah*. In a dispute over the payment of 'exit' fees due from those leaving a certain *kehillah*, R. Yair Hayyim Bachrach of Coblenz and Worms (1638–1702), one of the most distinguished authorities of his generation, explicitly declared:

> The existence of every *kehillah* is more dependent on property (*binyan*) than on the number of its members (*minyan*) and that is why R. Asher b. Yehiel ruled that in respect of taxes which are raised in proportion to wealth [that is, progressively: LK] the minority of the wealthy are considered the majority.

Rabbinic jurists disagree as to whether this situation thereby signifies the wealthy 'majority' is also entitled to advance its position at the expense of the poor 'minority' in a political sense, that is dominate political power in the *kehillah*. Bachrach for his part is doing no more than make a statement of fact; that is, without cash, no *kehillah*.[67]

This responsum lends itself to an understanding in terms of a continuation of the trend that, in existence ever since the medieval rabbis and the seventeenth century of Isaiah Horovitz and Luzzatto, has identified the coincidence of Jewish security and material benefit. The activity of the court-Jews is to effect a reinforcement of this trend in that – and here I quote a great historian of this period, Felix Priebatsch – in the view of the Jewish trader his dealings with his Christian counterpart take place within 'the neutral domain' of commercial intercourse. That is the reason, Priebatsch continues, why the Jewish merchants were emboldened no longer to accept slights, constraints and indignities, especially in the imperial cities; in Worms (1702) they complained that the police deployed at the time of Jewish festivals were ragged and tattered; in Frankfurt (1715) they rebelled against having to wait longer than the Christian merchants for their mail, and thereby secured in the *Judengasse* their own delivery system; also in Frankfurt the Emperor Charles VI, in order to facilitate the dealings of the Viennese court-Jew Emmanuel Oppenheimer with his correspondents in Frankfurt (Löw Menasseh and Isaac Moses Goldschmidt) ordered that when Oppenheimer's bills fell due they should be settled on the premises of the creditor; in Leipzig, led by a court-Jew of Lauenburg, the Jewish traders threatened to boycott the fair unless there was an end to insults (1687); in Fürth the *kehillah*, against the opposition of a hostile burgomaster, secured representation on the town council.[68] Examples with a similar purport abound; thus in 1695 an edict of toleration that was extended to a small group of money-lenders and military purveyors in Hesse-Darmstadt legitimized the undisturbed practice of Judaism in houses of prayer: it 'recognized the connection between taxpaying capacity and intellectual religious freedom'; in the margravate of Bayreuth, under the protection of the margrave and the court-Jew Samson of Baiersdorf, a 'Jews' corporation' was organized in 1709 which subsequently bought additional privileges in regard to rabbinical jurisdiction, the power to exclude 'foreign' Jews and to establish two cemeteries; in Halle, Assur Marx, an associate of the Prussian court-Jew Bernd Lehmann, was instrumental in securing the construction of a synagogue (1700), and in 1704 the Prussian king granted Halle Jewry a 'general privilege' that gave it recognition as a legal personality with the right to exclude newcomers.[69]

In all these cases resources are being deployed in a way that reinforces 'the neutral domain' by transmuting a political into a commercial relationship. If the Jew can acquire by purchase from its ruler the right to settle in a particular territory, say, then it is clear that the relationship to the Christian world was mediated through cash, though not through cash alone because, as I hope to show, common patriotism also operated as a factor. Also, negatively speaking, 'the neutral domain' is by no means as 'neutral' as it may appear to have been, for to a greater or lesser extent antisemitism persists as a complicating factor and what is known as the 'royal alliance' may have to face local hostility. Even so, cash, I would say, was king and this argument will later encompass discussion of the improvement in the Jews' general political status.

The genesis of a neutral domain had its precondition in the instrumental relationship of the Jew to the prince. Political life, as mentioned earlier, became secularized in the seventeenth century. All that is known of the outlook of the court-Jews indicates their acceptance of this secularization, their services being seen in pragmatic terms as the fulfilment of a variety of demands. Those Jews who served princes and rulers did so in an instrumental spirit, initially at least, and developed a personal and dynastic loyalty. Only in the second half of the eighteenth century did patriotism develop. With equal fervour court-Jews served Catholic and Protestant rulers, secular and religious authorities. 'Habsburg Jews' came to grips with 'Bourbon Jews'. The principle of utility, neutrality and instrumentality finds apt expression in a ruling of the sixteenth century code:

> Where Israel is dwelling among idolaters and has concluded a covenant with them it is permitted to sell weapons to the king's servants and to his armies because they will be used to make war against the enemies of the state and preserve it – they will protect the Jews living in the state.[70]

This instrumental stance required complete abstention from overt political involvement. The execution of Joseph Süss Oppenheimer (*c.*1692–1738), court-factor in Württemberg but also finance minister, served as a dreadful deterrent. When his patron, Duke Karl Alexander, died, the minister lost his protection, succumbed to popular hostility and was publicly hanged.

Into Jewish society, a value-free economic life penetrated first into the Sephardic world of Amsterdam and Livorno. The law of the market-place replaced the Torah. Ashkenazic society proved more successful in its resistance to secularization. Even so, the increasing entry of the cash nexus into the economy of the *kehillah* is perhaps evident in the development of the *mamran*, or at least its spread from eastern to central Ashkenaz. The Hebrew term *mamran* is derived from the Latin *membrana* (parchment) and denoted a document that functioned very much as a bill of exchange or letter of credit, payable to bearer. One side bore the signature of the debtor, the other the amount of his indebtedness and the due date of payment. No witnesses were needed and it was transferable without endorsement. According to the Moravian rabbi R. Menachem Mendel Krochmal (who had formerly held office in Cracow), it was widely used at the fairs in Lublin and Yaroslav. The *mamran* was a negotiable instrument and could be used to settle a creditor's debt to a third party or sold. Difficult legal problems might arise from its use; if, for example, a man who issued several *mamranim* then went bankrupt, which of his creditors would have prior claim on any remaining assets? In any event, from eastern Europe the use of the instrument spread to the German lands.[71] The *mamran* belonged to the transitional stage of a Jewish economy that was formerly based on moneylending and credit operations but now, in the later seventeenth century, turned increasingly to trade and industry.

The extension of the *ma'arufiyah* is perhaps also another pointer to the operation of the cash nexus in Jewish society. This ordinance, first promulgated by Rabbenu Gershom of Mainz (*c.*960–1028) established that a Jewish trader, moneylender or supplier to a non-Jewish client enjoyed a monopoly right to the non-Jew's custom.[72] The *ma'arufiyah* seems to have undergone a revival and extension in the seventeenth century and after. In Hesse in 1663 a decree of the *Landjudenschaft* prohibited the formation of a partnership between a native Jew and a foreign Jew with a view to introducing the latter into the territory of the *Landjudenschaft*. In 1690 a *Landtag* in Spangenberg decreed:

> If a Jew lives in a small place, then no one from an outside locality is to offer his goods for sale there, or bring in meat for sale, except once in 30 days; other trade however, for example with cattle and horses or the purchase of yarn, is not disallowed.

On 25 Iyyar, 5530 (= 20 May 1770) a *Landtag* at Aschaffenburg in Mainz imposed fines on any trader who 'talked down' the cattle or other goods that a rival trader might have on offer; or if one Jew were in the house of a prospective customer negotiating a deal, no other Jew must enter until the first had left.[73]

The success of this measure in reducing competition among Jewish traders is unascertainable. But there are unmistakable signs of a social malaise. The envy generated by the favoured position of the court-Jew is one such sign. The agreed evasion of the *ma'arufiyah* as described by R. Bachrach exemplifies a symptomatic breakdown in commercial restraint, the flouting of a communal ordinance and the emergence of a neutral and unrestrained value-free economy; Bachrach writes of a group of dealers in cloths and draperies who set aside a few hours every day to study with a learned man. They were in agreement among themselves that disputes arising from the infringement of their respective trading rights be brought before their teacher and rabbi for settlement. But the disputes multiplied and the costs of litigation became increasingly burdensome until their convenor, a pious and God-fearing man, asked:

> Why do you waste money on legal fees and also lose much time? ... Apart from the fact that there are infringements concealed from each other when one [of us] breaches the monopoly rights [*ma'arufiyah*] of another, decries his goods and has made himself culpable in the eyes of heaven. But because it is impossible to make good this breach which has already become entrenched in sinful fashion let us agree to allow us all to infringe each other's trading rights no matter how it happens and we will forgive each other the loss of income caused in this way; the law of man will be unconcerned and the law of heaven stay silent.[74]

Again unknown is the extent of this sort of commercial conduct but it is not difficult to suppose that it will have conduced to a sharpening of rivalry among traders; all the more so because this was precisely the time when the number of poor and vagrant Jews was increasing. They were necessarily pressing on the livelihood of the more established.

To this process of disintegration the emergence of a caste of court-Jews also contributed. It is indeed ironical that the *kehillah* which in many cases owes its very existence to the activities of a court-Jew also experiences dislocation through that court-Jew. By way of sequel to the process of caste formation an increased polarization of rich and poor came to mark Jewish society and to determine its polities. In any of his varied roles as banker, entrepreneur, military supplier, mintmaster, diplomat or 'fixer', the court-Jew enjoyed an opulent life-style, akin (*mutatis mutandis*) in many respects to that of the court he served. Samuel Oppenheimer made a notable exception to the vogue for conspicuous consumption, but his nephew R. Samson Wertheimer in Vienna was a boon hunting companion to Prince Eugene of Savoy, the military leader. The dowry and trousseau of a bride in Bayreuth was truly princely. It comprised a range of jewellery, *objets d'art*, clothing and finery.[75] That rulership and the leadership of Jewish socio-political organizations in town and countryside should belong to the wealthy was no novelty; so that its pervasiveness in the seventeenth and eighteenth centuries denotes no upheaval. On the other hand, the exceptionally favoured status that communal leaders enjoyed, the comparative absence of representation of the poor, and the ability of the court-Jews to absorb the rabbinate do seem to have added to the earlier pattern of plutocratic rule a fresh dimension. This was all the more so were the communal leader a court-Jew, as well as head of a *Judenschaft*, and benefit from such privileges as equality of status at fairs with Christian merchants, direct access to the ruler and his court of law, freedom from the compulsion to wear the yellow badge and so on. This contrast with the poverty and insecurity of the many made the court-Jew the frequent focus of much of the tension inside the communities:

> If the community records of that century [17th–18th] are filled with endless charges, suspicions, intrigues and quarrels between the classes, if the lower class rebelled against the patricians, the underprivileged (*unvergleitete*) against the privileged (*vergleitete*), and if the entire community opposed the successful court-Jew, we do not have to look far for the cause. At a time when money was the only weapon a Jew possessed in his struggle for existence, when it was the only means to win the goodwill of the authorities and to settle in a city, it was small wonder that the lower and middle classes should look with envy and bitterness at the patricians who were exempt from most of the crippling regulations, who alone were in a position to engage in foreign trade, to found factories and to gain for their children the right of domicile.[76]

With perhaps one or two exceptions no court-Jew established a dynasty, and – again with very rare exceptions – none occupied an overt political position. This picture would not do justice to their political importance. An early attempt (1911) at an estimate led only to Sombart's antisemitic and racially tainted argument that through their part in providing the state with military supplies and finance the court-Jews were indispensable to the creation of the modern state: in a grandiose image Sombart has the prince and the Jew 'striding arm in arm into the centuries that we call modern'. He likens the pair to Faust and Mephistopheles (that is, the Faust who sold his soul to the devil).[77]

In a vein less colourful and more limited, in the activities of the court-Jews can be discerned at least the prelude to Jewish emancipation, through their contribution to the mercantilistic secularization of politics. Towards the end of the eighteenth century Mendelssohn in Berlin (in his treatise *Jerusalem*, 1782) will articulate and develop what was initially the merely pragmatic concept of 'a neutral domain' into the 'Jewish' version and programme of a secular state. Essentially, Mendelssohn transfers into the Jewish context the theory of the separation of church and state. This was a presupposition of the eventual emancipation of the Jews. Long before that stage was reached however, the activities of the court-Jews in extending the range of Jewish economic activity and enterprise and opening up hitherto forbidden areas of settlement had significantly contributed to that presupposition. But no more than that. To this there is a negative side: the benefits of this activity accrued overwhelmingly to the court-Jews themselves. A vast increase in the number of poor and vagrant Jews, and Jews on the margin of criminality, accompanies their rise. If the court-Jew has one arm linked in that of the prince, the other points to the beggar-Jew.

6
Prague and Bohemia: From Recovery to Reduction

The Thirty Years' War brought to the Jews of Prague, Bohemia and Moravia hardship and death as well as enhanced economic opportunities. The war came to deprive Prague of the predominance it had earlier enjoyed as 'a mother-city in Israel'. Of the Jews' losses in physical terms no estimate can be made. The communities of Ungarisch-Brod, Prossnitz, Holleschau, Leipnik, Nikolsburg and Kremsier were among the worst affected. In 1648 the number of inhabited Jewish houses in Moravia was only somewhat more than double the number of those abandoned – 773 against 341. In 1653 a census of the Bohemian population (evidently outside Prague) gave a total of 3589 Jews (out of a total population of about 130000). Those over 20 years of age accounted for 2619 and those of over 10 years of age for 970.[1]

Amidst this world of death and destruction the Jews of Bohemia and Moravia prolonged their 'respite for recovery', as the war years have been called. In the fight against an expulsion that was as yet no more than projected this effort was crucial. Close to the centre of this struggle stood R. Menahem Mendel Krochmal, born in Cracow *c.*1600, rabbi in Kremsier 1636–46 and chief rabbi of Moravia with his seat in Nikolsburg from 1648 until his death in 1661. Krochmal's responsa give some notion of the disruption in the immediate aftermath of war (and of the social conflict inside the Moravian *kehillot*). As a pupil of R. Joel Sirkes (the 'Bach'), Krochmal was widely respected in the rabbinic world of his day and corresponded with Rabbis Lippman Heller (Prague and Vienna), Ephraim Kohen (Vilna) and Gershom Ashkenazi (Prague and Metz). He took an active part in the synods of the Moravian elders.[2]

In 1646 Krochmal's court had to deal with the case of two Jewish traders and a younger man who disappeared on their return journey from Vienna to Nikolsburg – murdered, according to the testimony of a Christian. This was accepted by the court and the widows given the freedom to remarry. An ambulant trader from Austerlitz failed to return from a business trip – he too was found murdered. In 1650 we read of a wife who is captured, imprisoned in Constantinople, but ransomed and eventually reunited with her husband in Lublin. (It was first thought that in order to save her life she had apostasized – later this was found not to be the case.) A widow recounts the death of her husband in an attack by robbers in Polna in south-east Bohemia. In another case, a husband leaves his wife after their wedding, 'for a distant land to supply the military with food and provisions'. He is absent five years until his wife confronts him to demand 'either that he should remain with her and no more follow the soldiers or he is to divorce her absolutely'. She fears becoming an 'anchored wife', that is, that on his hazardous journeys her husband might disappear in such circumstances that no absolute proof of his death will be obtainable and she will therefore become an *agunah* and not be free to remarry. But the husband, Krochmal writes, has no wish to divorce his wife: 'she is the love of his youth', he adds, but the husband also does not wish to stay behind with her, for he is set on enriching himself in the war, after which he will return to the land of his birth and live with his wife. But to reduce the risk of her becoming 'anchored', the husband promised to return within two years. The court decided that the husband unconditionally divorce his wife but, before doing so, it also stipulated that the couple agree on oath that should the husband return within two years (from the date of the divorce) they would remarry. In fact, the husband followed the armies, did not return and about four years later the divorced wife remarried on the strength of the writ of divorce issued by the former husband.[3]

In this uncertain world the Bohemian and Moravian *kehillot* had to preserve in the post-war years the improved status they had secured in the war years. They did so in a position of isolation. Now that Anabaptism and Protestantism no longer threatened Habsburg and Catholic supremacy in the Czech lands and Moravia, the Jews were, religiously speaking, isolated. The success of the Counter-Reformation and the extirpation of the Protestants in these areas of central Europe left the Jews vulnerable and exposed. In 1669–70, this weakness had facilitated their expulsion from Lower Austria and Vienna. In Prague it encouraged the censorship and burning of Hebrew literature, intensified conversionism and encouraged plans to limit, or at least reduce, the size of the Jewish population. On the other hand, in the landed nobility the Jews had a staunch ally, to whom their taxable capacity, at a local and imperial level, could not be indifferent, especially amidst a devastated economy.

In the earliest post-war years these conflicting trends already showed themselves. In 1648 Emperor Ferdinand III confirmed the existing privileges of the Jews in Bohemia, though with certain minor qualifications. He limited to the royal towns their right to unhindered residence and protection from expulsion. Interest on money loans against pledges was restricted to the customary 6 per cent; no lending on fixed property was permitted. Ferdinand sanctioned Jewish trade in a comprehensive range of goods and foodstuffs, the opening of shops and stalls 'in squares and markets so far as is customary', and attendance at fairs on the same terms as Christian

merchants. He also, in the ever-thorny matter of Jewish artisans and craftsmen, confirmed their right to operate inside the Jewish community but not
to employ Christian journeymen or apprentices, or sell their wares outside
the Jews' Town in the flea market. Those crafts associated with the war, for
example, the manufacture of rifles or armoury work, were forbidden to
Jews.[4] In 1657, in the last year of his reign, the emperor confirmed the privileges of Moravian Jewry again, demonstrating his aim to assure to Jewish
traders free access to markets, fairs and so on, and also protection from the
hostility of his Christian subjects, especially towndwellers and burghers.

The emperor allied the policy of confirmation and protection to its precise
antithesis in relation to those Jews of Bohemia and Moravia who lived on,
or were economically associated with, the estates of the nobility. Here no
protection operated, in so far as in 1650 Ferdinand III demanded of the
Landtage of Bohemia and Moravia that they expel the Jews from all those
locations where they had not been living on 1 January 1618.[5] Jews must also
not be further admitted as lessees of customs posts and tolls; the Bohemian
Jews were prohibited from employing Christians (as domestic servants,
drovers, journeymen and so on). The Moravian Estates succeeded in delaying the implementation of this decree – so much so that in 1681, Leopold I,
successor to Ferdinand III, had to advance the base-date from 1618 to 1657.
Here was a significant withdrawal, for by 1657 the areas of Jewish residence
had increased; all the more so, as refugees from the atrocities perpetrated by
the Ukrainian Cossack hordes in 1648–9 and some of those expelled from
Vienna and Lower Austria in 1669–71 found refuge in Bohemia and Moravia.
Even so, Ferdinand's demand in itself had elements of foreboding that later
attempts at reducing the size of the Jewish population made real. For the
moment the differential view taken of urban and rural Jewry corresponded
to the respective interests of the emperor and the land-owning nobility.
Ferdinand's proposed expulsion of 1650 expressed the fear that the nobles'
economy would benefit from the Jewish presence, whereas the opposition
to Jews in the royal towns deprived them of this beneficial presence. This
was a conflict of interest that Jewish diplomacy could not fail to profit from.[6]

The letters that Jewish merchants, middlemen and artisans exchanged
with members of the Czernin family and their agents go to explain their
mutually advantageous relationship. Aron Hradistsky is offered a consign-
ment of goose fat, to which he replies that although there was no demand
for fat at this time, he is not disinclined to buy it. But what is the price,
Hradistsky asks, so that he can plan accordingly and not make a wasted journey (1637)? Salomon Buchtrucker has been arrested for a debt owed to
Hermann, Count Czernin. From prison he appeals to be released for four
weeks so that he can attend to his business and collect those monies owing
to him; otherwise, the longer he is imprisoned, the less likely it is that the
debt to the count will be paid. Czernin agreed to recommend to the imperial judge that Buchtrucker be released for two weeks, during which period he

must settle the debt or return to prison (1640). A lady buys an estate, part of the purchase price being her obligation to pay off a mortgage debt of 5000 florins secured on it. The intending purchaser lacks the ready cash and seeks someone who will take over the mortgage. Salomon Elikum offers the business to Count Czernin, who is ready to take over the debt but not for cash – rather, against the delivery of a quantity of iron and the rest in fine wheat and butter (1642). Three elders of the Prague community confirm collectively a debt to the count for wool bought on six months' credit, the debt to be discharged at regular monthly intervals; failing which not only would 6 per cent interest be levied on the outstanding sum but the three also become liable to arrest (1643). Four Jewish butchers of Prague Old Town owe the count 300 Reichsthaler and accumulated interest of 45 Reichsthaler. In a letter signed by the count and countersigned by the four butchers (in Hebrew script), the parties agree to defer the payment of the capital sum to the following year, the interest to be paid off by the daily delivery to the count's household in Prague of good quality beef and tripe (1647). Moyses Brandeis, a saddler, contracts with the count to deliver within six weeks a luxury six-seater coach to be furnished on the same model as the coach earlier delivered to Count Coloredo (1648). Jakob Levita Tuschkauer, Götzl Mändl Lichtenstadt, Adam Götzl Lichtenstadt and Baruch Weisel are among Prague Jews who negotiate on the count's behalf his purchase of landed property (1650–2). Items supplied to the Czernin household include buttons for the uniforms of the liveried servants (1670). A tanner, Löbl Schebkes, on the ground that in Prague he cannot satisfactorily support his wife and family, asks Humprecht Johann Count Czernin for permission to settle on one of the count's estates and exercise his craft, in return for appropriate protection money, and for permission also to slaughter cattle in the manner prescribed by Jewish ritual. Schebkes rejected the count's first offer and proposed another location where the water supply, necessary for his craft, was more readily available (n.d.). A mattress-maker, Israel Baroch, complains to the count that his steward has beaten and abused him when asked for payment in return for mattresses, bedcovers and bolsters. The count is therefore graciously requested to order his steward to pay (n.d.). Godl Israel Zappert informs the count of an estate in Austria near Vienna ready for purchase and offers to make available a sum of 50 000 or 100 000 florins at 6 per cent interest, to be repaid by instalments. In a second letter the count is reminded that, though he would certainly be able to obtain a loan in Austria, because the Czernin estates and properties were all located in Bohemia and not in Austria the conditions could not be the same (1686). Other letters relate to the count's dealings with horse-dealers, leather merchants, and military outfitters supplying uniforms for recruits. Moyses Gitschin, evidently a large-scale importer and exporter, both wholesale and retail, of cloths, silks, and raw wool, drew the count's attention to the loss that both the count and the imperial treasury would incur, should the rumour that Jews were to be excluded from the annual market at Linz actually be confirmed; for, Gitschin explained, he paid excise duty and sundry other tolls and taxes at the borders, in Prague, en route, and in Linz itself. At the very least he should have been notified in advance and his voice listened to; the prohibition would absolutely not benefit the generality (1709).[7]

Prague, post-war, remained 'a mother-city in Israel' and the Jews' Town the largest such urban centre in all Ashkenaz. But for the majority this was a metropolis of poverty, disease, congestion and insecurity. The effects of the Thirty Years' War showed themselves less in loss of population than in impoverishment. In 1647, the financial qualification for the exercise of the franchise had on this account to be reduced. In the declared inability of Prague and the provinces to meet an extraordinary tax demand of 8000 and 4000 florins respectively, the extent of mass poverty again showed itself. These sums were demanded by the Bohemian Kammer in 1650–1 and when they were not forthcoming, the elders and chief rabbi R. Aron Simon Spira-Wedeles were arrested as hostages and imprisoned in the Hradčany castle. (Wedeles was arrested by virtue of his responsibility for the thankless task of apportioning the burden.) From prison the elders addressed numerous petitions to the emperor, arguing, inter alia, that the extraordinary sums demanded by the Kammer would make it impossible to pay the sums due to the emperor, who was in any case their liege lord. They complained also that the authorities had barricaded the synagogues and stationed musketeers to supervise them. This attempt to play off the emperor against the Bohemian Kammer succeeded to the extent that the elders were released and the synagogue blockade lifted through an offer of 500 florins weekly.[8]

'When the pitcher lacks barley, strife knocks at the door.' The Talmudic adage quoted in the 1620s by R. Lippmann Heller (p. 19 above) had lost none of its thrust two or three decades later. Four courts operated in Prague to deal with 'strife' and maintain harmony inside the Jews' Town. At the system's summit stood the appellate court; next in importance came the Beth Din Rabo for the more important court cases; then the Beth Din Zuta for lesser civil claims. A special court dealt with property disputes. The division of houses, their multiple occupation and ownership, engendered manifold disputes over hereditary rights and repairs.[9] This arrangement could only mitigate but not overcome social tension. Thus inordinate tax demands at a time of economic distress necessarily impinged on the political and social structure of the *kehillah*. Already in 1647, amidst denunciation and dissension, rabbis and parnassim issued a joint declaration imposing the penalty of *herem* on those guilty of factionalism or electoral fraud.[10]

Fiscal pressure, economic weakness and the political disarray in the Jews' Town of Prague conduced to a major constitutional change: for a number of years provincial leaders had complained that they had no voice in determining the level of the burden of taxation that the Prague elders imposed on them. The latter in effect suffered taxation without representation.[11]

The repeated complaints of these rural elders eventually persuaded the authorities (1654) to appoint some of them as tax-collectors. This provoked counter-protests by the Prague elders, who were barely calmed by an official assurance in 1656 that the role of the provincial leaders was limited to fiscal matters. Only three years later, however, the Prague leadership had to reconcile itself to the reality of a group of provincial elders assembled in the capital, engaged in devising statutes for an organization claiming sovereignty over non-metropolitan Bohemian Jewry. The Prague leadership successfully insisted that should the provincial body be required to mediate in Prague on behalf of its members, it must record the proceedings in a document to be confirmed and attested not only by its own leaders but also by those of Prague. The latter, in other words, would still retain some degree of control over access to the Christian authorities.

Even so, this new body was an authentic organ of Jewish self-government. It had a constitution modelled in part on the ordinances governing Moravian Jewry, and approved by the Bohemian Kammer. This necessarily varied over time but in its essentials provided for five elected deputies (at their heads a 'primas' or 'primator') and five associates (*'Beisitzer'*) who would each serve in office for two (later three) years, and also for a salaried representative in Prague. The electoral system was indirect and operated partly by ballot and partly by lot. Though weighted in favour of the wealthy, it came to enlarge the composition of the electorate so as to permit wider numbers to participate in the elections. The primator and deputies had the power to instruct the rabbi to issue writs of excommunication, to settle civil disputes among Jews, and, above all, to organize the apportionment and collection of taxes from provincial Bohemian Jewry. The global sum to be raised from the Jews was determined at one-forty-fifth of the total tax burden born by the province and the specific sum determined by the Bohemian *Landtag*. The Prague Jewish elders and those of the provinces divided this between them, though on an unknown basis. The two parties met every three years in the Prague suburb of Smichov, to negotiate their respective contributions, this interval corresponding to the provincial elders' period in office. The total was then further subdivided at a joint gathering of the members of the provincial electoral college and representatives from each provincial region, making forty-five persons in all. At the level of the individual community in each region this procedure was repeated, and the apportioned sum finally demanded from the individual taxpayer. There were all sorts of provisions and safeguards for appeals, supervision, record-keeping and checking of accounts, and remission in case of duly confirmed hardship or disaster (for example, fire, robbery). Provision also had to be made for the taxpayer who migrated from one locality to another, so that neither did he pay twice nor altogether evade his obligations. Despite every safeguard, it does seem likely that there were those among the wealthy who did abuse their position to secure disproportionate relaxation from the tax burden. The records of Kolin, the most important provincial city outside Prague, in the 1760s, which had 200 taxpayers, reveal this practice on the part of the primator of the period.[12]

These non-metropolitan Bohemian communities acquired their own chief rabbinate soon after 1689 when the elders decided to fill the vacancy. The primator, Abraham Aron of Lichtenstadt, secured the election of R. Abraham Broda of Prague as incumbent of the post. Broda had previously held office and conducted yeshivot in Jungbunzlau and Lichtenstadt. The former was at the time the largest Bohemian community outside Prague and an important trading centre. A celebrated pupil was R. Jonathan Eibeschütz, who claimed that Broda had taught most of the contemporary luminaries of the rabbinic world.[13]

But Broda, although he enjoyed the patronage of Primator Abraham Aron, had to share office with R. Wolf Wedeles when the latter's youngest daughter, Schifra, married Solomon Lichtenstadt, son of Abraham Aron. In June 1691, the two contestants for office temporarily shared power in that Wolf Wedeles was given authority over eight Bohemian regions (*Kreise*) and Broda over seven. This was inherently an unstable arrangement, to which the appointment of R. David Oppenheimer, formerly chief rabbi of Moravia with his seat in Nikolsburg, as chief rabbi in Prague and Bohemia, put an end (1718). More than 100 of the Prague electoral body signed Oppenheimer's letter of appointment. The party leaders had only very recently been in Vienna and it is credibly suggested that David's uncle, Samuel Oppenheimer, the immensely important banker and court-Jew in Vienna, was not without influence on his nephew's appointment.[14]

Be that as it may, David Oppenheimer had the learning and personal authority required to officiate in Prague and needed no extraneous endorsement. In 1718 Oppenheimer added to his position in Prague that of chief rabbi to provincial Bohemia. There were reservations at the loss of independence from Prague, but the provinces had to be content with twelve regional rabbis (*Kreisrabbiner*) whose written agreement with Oppenheimer authorized them to supervise the slaughter of animals, to sanction betrothals and 'fulfil matters relating to the religion and laws of our sacred Torah'. These *Kreisrabbiner* had of course to be acceptable to Oppenheimer as well as to their respective regional leaders.

Political dissension was unremitting and Prague justified its repute as a centre of factionalism. In the Jews' Town two parties developed, known respectively as Catena ('Chain') and Liga ('League'). The first represented the wealthy, and the second those families of middling substance. Their initial differences centred on taxation policy, Catena arguing in favour of uniform contributions whereas Liga espoused a system of progressive taxation, proportionate to income and assets. But by the end of the seventeenth century the socio-economic distinction had yielded to a struggle for power among family clans and clients. Bunzl and Bondy stood out in Catena; Lichtenstadt and Märle in Liga. These allegiances fluctuated in accord with marriage policy and at times a third party emerged, especially at election time. In 1657 an imperial order brought some sort of stability to the intermittent feuding (that accompanied disputed elections) by ensuring the elders of three years in office, after which period they would cease to be eligible again to stand for office. This was barely a provisional solution, for in 1678 Leopold I had again to intervene in communal affairs, again with a view to the enforcement of communal unity.

Until at least the early eighteenth century conflict was endemic. After 1679, when chief rabbi Aaron Simon Wedeles died, factional disputes seized on the succession and brought electoral deadlock. Neither Catena nor Liga proved able to secure the election of their favoured candidate. After a hiatus of more than a decade only a decision in 1692 to elect two chief rabbis for Prague broke the deadlock: this followed Leopold I's dissolution of the Prague governing body and a decree ordering new elections.

This disunity and internecine feuding left the Jews' Town the more vulnerable at a time when emperor and church and commercial rivalry threatened its continued existence. Forces were even at work to make Prague a city without Jews. From the end of the Thirty Years' War, Evans writes, 'Central Europe's Counter-Reformation could be resumed with greater intensity, on a firmer base, and it continued to enjoy the wholehearted support of the emperors.'[15] The demand of 1650 to limit the location of Jewish settlement to the area of 1618, and the census of 1653 already presaged the future. In the later 1650s and 1660s the community had to combat a proposed ban on the sale of kosher meat on Sundays and Christian festivals and halt the circulation of antisemitic pamphlets. The campaign featured the censorship of Hebrew and Jewish literature. By order of the archiepiscopal consistory, two printing houses in Prague were closed 1669–72 – no doubt because they were producing forbidden literature, including perhaps even the Talmud. Two decades later the Prague elders had to contend with a confiscation of Hebrew and Jewish literature instigated by the Jesuit, Father Wolfgang Preissler, professor of theology and Hebrew at the University of Prague. Preissler, on the qui vive for blasphemous attacks on Christianity, also took to attending the sermons of Jewish preachers. The two hundred books seized fell into three main categories: Talmudic and Kabalistic treatises; biblical commentaries; legal codes. At one point it was suggested that the Jews engage with Preissler in a public disputation over the supposedly blasphemous passages. Citing Preissler's incompetence the Jews refused, proposing in his place professors from Leyden, Basle, Leipzig and Wittenberg. It was also argued that only recently had the very works seized and condemned by Preissler been republished in Venice, Ferrara, Metz, Cracow, Frankfurt and even in Prague itself, and with the permission of ecclesiastical authorities at least as competent as Preissler. Further: if they, the Jews, were to be deprived of their literature they would no longer be able to practise their religion – which would contradict the terms of their privileges. The court-Jews in Vienna, newly readmitted in 1683, also made their influence felt. The censorship operated with particular rigour in the early eighteenth century; in 1714 many copies of the first Frankfurt printing of the Talmud were confiscated and burned. The chief rabbi of Prague and Bohemia, R. David Oppenheimer, a celebrated bibliophile and collector of Hebrew and Yiddish manuscripts – whose library is now one of the treasures of the Bodleian Library, Oxford – had to keep a large part of his library in the house of his father-in-law in Hanover. A particularly zealous customs officer confiscated from R. Jacob Emden, en route from Prague to the village of Blau, copies of his father's responsa.[16]

The Jesuits stood out in a reinforced campaign of conversion. The enforced attendance at sermons, as instituted in 1630 by Ferdinand II, was long discontinued. Incomplete figures for the later decades of the century show that in the years 1661–78, 174 Jews were converted by the Jesuits: 132 in Bohemia, 25 in Moravia and 17 in Silesia. Other figures show a total of 116 Jews baptized between 1691 and 1710 (75 men and 41 women). Most neophytes on a list drawn up in 1720 belonged to the lower and lower-middle classes (barbers, soldiers, baker's assistant, mattress-maker and the like).[17] In the later seventeenth and early eighteenth centuries the university of Prague supervised not only Jewish writings but also Jewish doctors. At this time, they studied mainly at Padua – later at the Protestant universities of Halle, Heidelberg and Frankfurt on the Oder.[18] Whatever their qualifications, these doctors required the authorization of the Prague medical faculty in order to practise, and this was in any case limited to Jewish patients. In 1684, 1686, 1692 and 1706 this limitation was made explicit in a number of individual cases. In order to avert confusion or deception by Jewish doctors the university required them to wear a special ruff (*Halskrause*). In Moravia, in 1709 a decree prohibited Jews from selling to Christians medicaments, saffron and olive oil. Not until 1784, following an audience that Emperor Joseph II granted to Dr Jonas Jeitteles, were Jewish doctors allowed to practise outside the confines of the Jews' Town.[19]

In 1679 the Jews' Town had a total population of some 11 000; the plague of 1679–80 reduced this figure by about 3500. Commerce came to a complete halt. The protocols of the court that arbitrated between contending parties in minor cases give an idea of the economic paralysis. This court sat every day (except Friday, Saturday and from 26 Elul to 2 Heshvan on account of the High Holydays and from 8 Nissan to 23 Nissan on account of the Passover festival). The sub-lessee of a stall in the flea market denied owing anything for the plague years (5439–5441) because the market had been deserted. In another case, a newly married couple died from the plague within a year of their marriage, and left no children. Kopel Schocket, the father of the bride, therefore demanded the return of the dowry of 200 gulden in accordance with the terms of the marriage contract (dated 13th day of Kislev, 5440) which did indeed provide for such an eventuality. But Chaya, widow of the butcher Selig Kalman Katzev and mother of the deceased bridegroom, argued that the dowry had taken the form of settling the debts of her son. The court decided that she need make no repayment; should, however, Kopel be able to prove that he had indeed paid the debts of his deceased son-in-law, then he could take over his stall in the flea market.[20]

The authorities hoped to exploit this catastrophe further to reduce the size of Prague Jewry and/or altogether to secure their removal from the city. At the initiative of the Jewish Reduction Commission and in cooperation with the elders, a list of 1337 names of family heads was drawn up, composed of those who had sought refuge in Prague from the plague outside, and of the poor. They were to quit Prague by April 1680, it was planned. Nothing came of this project, given the further ravaging of the plague. An overlapping plan to construct a new 'Jews' Town' at the nearby village of Lieben also failed. In this case Jewish cooperation was lacking: the Jews took to delaying tactics and passive resistance to the Lieben commission. The elders were absent when its members, together with architects and one carpenter, met at Lieben to plan the new 'Jews' Town'. The commissioners had to content themselves with its 'delineation' and a provisional plan for 100 houses.[21]

In 1689, a fire usually attributed to arson burned down most of the houses in the Jews' Town. Amidst much recrimination most, about 200, were rebuilt by 1700. Despite reiterated protests and bribes it was only in defiance of an imperial ruling that the Jews rebuilt eight synagogues as against the six officially permitted. Not until 1700 could the undamaged Alt-Neu Schul be reopened and gates installed to enclose and protect the Jews' Town from marauders. Not until 1714 did rebuilding restore the town to its original composition. Before the fire 34.6 persons occupied one building on the average, in 1703 about 54.

Outside Prague, the town of Kolin was the only other significant centre. The remainder of Bohemian Jewry lived in small, scattered settlements numbering about 200. In Moravia the dispersion was far less, no more than some 50 settlements accounting for the bulk of the population. The major centres were Nikolsburg and Prossnitz. On the landed estates, the devastation and depopulation of the war years made all the more welcome the economic activity of the Jews. Here, as elsewhere, there is a suggestion that Jews might take the place of the expelled Protestants. The participation of Moravian Jewry in the rural economy was no novelty and preceded 1648. After the war, to an increasing extent it was Jews who helped to provide the manpower and expertise that enabled estate-owners and landed magnates not only to revive the rural economy after the devastation of war and repopulate the countryside but also to overcome the critical problem of surplus production on the landed estates. In the transition to a money economy, the estate-owners derived their main income not from agriculture but from the operation of monopolies in such products as beer, meat, wool and skins; these were sold to the inhabitants of the seigniorial towns.[22] But on the enlarged estates of the Counter-Reformation period the problem of surplus production in the manorial economy became all the more acute.

The guilds were unable or unwilling to undertake the role of rural entre-preneur or middleman or concessionaire, even had the division into estates not made inconceivable the unmediated cooperation of noble and artisan. The guildsmen lacked either the capital or the entrepreneurial spirit and for this very reason in a mercantilistic economy incurred gathering criticism. In these circumstances Jewish traders, merchants, leaseholders increasingly took on the role of rural entrepreneur or middleman or concessionaire. Jewish traders and estate-owners contracted a *mariage de convenance*, grounded in their mutual benefit.

A contract normally governed the relationship between the estate-owner and the Jewish factor or whatever. This provided for the payment of 'pro-tection money', determined by reference to the size of the enterprise. The contract was in effect a licence to trade. Prince Schwarzenberg's bailiff in Wodnain, where the Jewish presence was an innovation, was thus informed, in precise terms, that 'protection money is fixed according to the capital employed in their business ... since it is customary to increase or reduce the account of protection money according to the increase or reduction in business.'[23] This was of much lesser importance to the landowner than the function that his Jewish 'partner' performed.

In 1694 Prince Schwarzenberg, the greatest territorial magnate in southern Bohemia, wrote to his steward that he intended 'to settle some Jewish fam-ilies (on his village of Vresna) to populate it and for the better retailing of the vendibles'. 'The Jews were accepted in Frauenberg', wrote, in respect to 1678, the steward of another village belonging to Prince Schwarzenberg, 'in order to turn vendibles into cash.'[24]

These 'protection letters' (*Schutzbriefe*) would contain a clause whereby the Jewish trader committed himself to purchase (sometimes on credit) at a high fixed price and at fixed intervals such products as cheese, linen, wool, cattle, hides, leather, butter and fish. This system of compulsory purchase constituted the primary condition of Jewish residence and accommodation and ensured magnates of a regular income (though this would to some extent necessarily depend on the fluctuations of the market). Part also of the Jewish trader's com-mitment might be to supply goods not available on the estate but which he was required to provide 'without excessive profit', as one contract puts it. Such goods were wines, spices, groceries, silk, paper and tobacco. The trader was, however, by far rather a purchaser than a seller in his relation to the estate.[25]

The question arises: if the trader must pay a high price for certain goods and sell others at a low price, how does he survive and earn enough profit to meet the demands of taxation, not to mention a livelihood for self and family? This question is best answered in terms of the creation of an economic sector in which a privileged and protected purchaser functioned as a sort of wholesaler and even exporter, selling his goods not only to local villages and market men but also at some distance from their point of origin, through intermediaries if necessary.

What the Jews also brought to the rural economy was the capacity to operate various of the quasi-manufacturing facilities to be found on many feudal estates – especially distilleries, tanneries and potash refineries. These too were brought into the service of the market as a means to enhance the landowner's income and provide cash for the estate. This task was not susceptible to fulfilment by the guild member, first because the necessary capital would be lacking and second because again the contemporary order of the relationship of the estates would have been infringed. In these circumstances, the prospective lessee could effectively be none other than that Jewish entrepreneur with access to adequate capital. A non-economic factor, relevant to the sociology of religion, is also held to account for the reason why a Jew should be best fitted to operate a distillery – his sobriety.[26] The terms of the lease normally included provision for unpaid or low-priced deliveries of the product to the feudal household. Even so, there was clearly opportunity for profit, especially in the operation of a distillery, given the demand for its products. In the distillery at Meseritch, according to a young autobiographer of the 1680s, the author's father was provided by the estate-owner 'with 7 great kettles, and he gave him servants to do the work and grain to prepare brandy. For this my father paid him at the end of the year a specified amount, in addition to paying a certain percentage of the income in taxes, as was customary'. In 1724, of 410 Jewish lessees on landed estates in Bohemia, 328 leased distilleries, 56 potash refineries and 26 tanneries.[27]

On the 'sales' side the protected Jew might be a peddler and have a contract that guaranteed him monopoly rights to peddle in a certain district. Prince Schwarzenberg's contract of 1699 with Izak Abraham assured him that 'foreign Jews whom Izak Abraham does not wish to allow to peddle and who have received from the prince's office no written permission therefor, are forbidden to sell door to door in Bzi and Zimutice and their goods will be confiscated after they have been cautioned.' In 1749 Count Czernin divided his estates into 'peddling regions' so that the three groups of Jews settled in different areas should not encroach on each other's preserve.[28]

The Jewish retail sector comprised not only peddling and hawking but also large-scale merchanting, for which markets and fairs served traditionally as outlets. A pointer to their importance: in 1682 Nikolsburg changed the date of its St Michael's Market from 2 September, because this would coincide with the Jewish New Year (5443) and the consequent absence of the Jewish traders. Even in places where Jews were not allowed to live – for example, the southern Bohemian mining town of Ratibor – the elders petitioned for their unhindered access to the local fair, lest the town's revenues otherwise suffer. Frequently, at fairs and markets the trader disposed of finished products which he had himself commissioned. The situation obtained in Jung-Bunzlau, where Jewish traders supplied twenty Christian artisans with the raw material for their craft, in the form of the putting-out system (*Verleger*). In 1714 Emanuel Bachracher commissioned tailoring guilds in different Moravian towns to manufacture uniforms for the army. Even more striking was the situation in Pirnitz, part of the estate of Count Vinsiguerra Thomas von Collalto. The community in 1746 consisted of 56 families (262 individuals), with its own synagogue, community room, cemetery and hospital, and employed a schoolteacher and other communal servants. Twenty of the 56 householders were mainly dealers or sub-dealers, with a couple of shopkeepers and taverners. Economically dominant in Pirnitz was David Löb Austerlitz, not only as moneylender to his fellow-Jews and lessee of a tannery and distillery, but also as a major proponent of the putting-out system of cloth production. Austerlitz bought the raw wool, delivered it to guilds of clothmakers in Pirnitz, Triesch, Pilgram, Iglau and elsewhere, bought back the finished product which was either delivered in fulfilment of his orders (sometimes regimental uniforms) or marketed at fairs or the like. Austerlitz's commercial activity was certainly not popular; the guilds bitterly resented their dependence on a single supplier and purchaser, all the more so when that supplier was a Jew; the Jews also resented Austerlitz's activities, for by dealing *directly* with cloth-makers and so on outside his own 'domain', that is, Triesch, he was acting in clear breach of the Moravian statutes, jeopardizing the livelihoods of the Jews of Triesch.[29]

Because the privilege granted in 1648 by Ferdinand III was ambiguous in specifying whether or not Jewish craftsmen could sell their wares to Christian customers and thereby infringe the guilds' monopoly, the position of these craftsmen is complex and obscure. It is at least clear, however, that their range was extensive and embraced tailors, shoemakers, tanners, furriers, glaziers, seamstresses, mattress-makers, cap-makers, butchers, bakers, goldsmiths and stockingers. Tailors and butchers were the most numerous, followed by tanners and shoemakers. It appears that urban craftsmen worked primarily for the Jewish market, those in villages mainly for the Christian peasantry.

Within the setting of the principle – 'The law of the land is the law' – halakhic considerations governed all economic activity. Sometimes, where all parties to a dispute are Jewish, the two systems are blended. Disputes were referred to R. Krochmal for a decision: Reuben, who belongs to the *kehillah* of Dresnitz, purchases skins from Shimon who belongs to the community of Gidung, and transfer of the goods takes place in accordance with Jewish law, that is, by the purchaser 'lifting' the goods. As part of the contract, Shimon the vendor commits himself to deliver the goods to Dresnitz at his own expense and responsibility. The toll-collector in Gidung, who is also Jewish, now demands payment of the toll on the skins. Who is liable? Shimon claims that since he is contracted to deliver the goods to Dresnitz at his own expense and responsibility, they have in fact not yet left his 'domain' and by the law of the land he is not liable to pay a toll on his own goods in the very town he lives in. But Krochmal ruled that in spite of these factors, it is indeed Shimon who is liable for the duty, on the grounds that 'the substance' of the property has passed to Reuben, the purchaser, who is not a local inhabitant. In another case – the trade in exports over the Moravian-Hungarian border – Krochmal refused to allow traders from Nikolsburg to use their horses to transport their goods on the Sabbath, even though this would be supervised by the Christian carters whom the traders employed. The latter, in their approach to the rabbi, argued that the practice was customary elsewhere. Krochmal remained adamant: 'I searched out the matter from each and every side and I toiled and I found no way to permit this sort of thing.'[30]

Krochmal, until his death in 1661, necessarily took part in the continuing elaboration of the '311'. These had three dominant aims: first, to impose exclusive access to sources of livelihood; second, to avert rivalry between one Jew and another for monopoly rights to a facility and thus diminish any opportunity for the estate-owner to exploit intra-Jewish divisions; thus Ordinance 259 sought to prevent one Jew approaching the landowner so long as the right of another Jew to operate a certain facility on his estate, for example a customs post or a distillery, had not yet expired; and third, these ordinances aimed to constitute so far as possible an economic entity closed to outsiders, Jew or other. At the Lundenburg synod in 1697 delegates introduced a statute that proclaimed stringent measures to prevent traders from other regions, 'such as Bohemia, trading and circulating in the villages near the community, buying up goods, for example, flax and feathers... and destroying the livelihood of the community members.'[31]

For reasons of good neighbourliness as much as the ideal, intense concern with the honesty of the lessees of customs posts and toll booths also characterizes the '311'; lessees are warned to expect the most serious penalties if they should wrongly accuse [Christian] carters and traders of smuggling; 'and if at times some incident should arise then they must agree among themselves that it not come to court, for their overlords will support them [that is, the Christians] and cause a great outcry'. The lessee of a toll booth or customs post must display his tariff, translate it into Yiddish, have the translation authenticated by the signatures of two communal leaders and not levy more than the tariff specified. Obviously the odium attaching to these unpopular functions fell on the Jewish lessees and not the landowner or his agent. Here, perhaps, is a further reason why the Jewish authorities in Moravia took the utmost care to ensure that the exercise of this function attracted to their 'subjects' no more odium than was inevitable.[32]

Into the rural areas no less than into Prague itself the penetration of the cash nexus and the exploitation of the landed estates on a commercial basis entailed an increasingly significant economic differentation between rich and poor. There are those who see this development in terms of the class struggle. This is not limited, for example, to the joint work of the two Marxist historians who write of 'the social contradictions' discernible in Krochmal's responsa. The same framework of ideas gives shape also to the rabbi and historian of the community of Kremsier who talks of 'the class struggle in the ghetto'.[33] But the undoubted growth in the division between rich and poor can by no means be interpreted as conducing to a struggle – all the less so as the poor shared precisely the same aspirations as the rich (but in which they were frustrated). This does not mean though that social tension and conflict were not present, and to their presence Krochmal's responsa are indeed an indispensable guide.[34] In general terms, he used his influence in Moravia to redress the balance as between rich and poor, to secure unanimity in the event of a contested communal decision and to ensure that all members of the *kehillah* enjoyed a share in the distribution of power; basically, that *binyan* (property) would not dominate *minyan* (numbers). Thus, when Krochmal first came to Kremsier, a community of 50 taxpaying households (in 1636), he faced a situation in which the five wealthy families who paid three-fifths of the taxes wanted to introduce a change in the communal statutes that would give them a deciding voice in deciding on the appointment of rabbi, cantor, beadle, and so on as against the majority of the community who paid the remaining two-fifths of the taxes. Krochmal reconciled the two factions by demonstrating that in fact the numerical majority paid the bulk of the projected salary of the communal employees and therefore *minyan* and *binyan* were of one opinion and neither need coerce the other. In another responsum Krochmal had to confront a situation in a certain *kehillah* where those who paid the higher taxes and the learned sought to exclude the lesser taxpayers and the unlearned from a share in the government of the *kehillah*. They based their argument on the fact that since most of the *kehillah*'s business concerned its outgoings, the precedent applied, to the effect that 'in all matters supported by taxes raised according to wealth, wealth is decisive and the wealthy who are a minority are considered the majority.' Also, maintained the wealthy, this was the custom 'in all large and important communities'. Krochmal rejected both arguments: first, that 'to exclude the poor who are the absolute majority...is certainly not right, for the little that the poor give is equivalent in each case to the large amount given by the rich'. He also could not accept the argument from comparison elsewhere: 'If so there would be no end to the matter...and disputes, heaven forfend, will multiply in Israel.' Above all, he feared the consequences should the poor be excluded from the decisions of the community – 'They will certainly become hostile and build a platform for themselves and separate themselves from the community and thereby multiply dissension in Israel.' Krochmal carried this policy into a dispute in Prossnitz; he ruled that when the community decided to pay to the commander of troops requiring billets a sum of money rather than physically accommodate the troops, contributions to this total should be determined according to wealth and not per head of community members (this decision being subject to repeal should the minority of the wealthy be successful in having this ruling reversed on appeal); in a communal dispute over payment for installation of an improved water supply Krochmal ruled that since the rich would benefit more than the poor the expense should be apportioned as to three-quarters on the basis of the town-dweller's property and assets and one-quarter in equal shares from the individual householder.[35]

Despite the efforts of the *kehillot* in Bohemia and Moravia and of their leaders, such as Krochmal and his successors, to preserve a degree of autonomy in their internal arrangements, in the early eighteenth century they succumbed to the state. Partly, as in the case of Prague, this was in consequence of a disastrous fire in the Jews' Town of 1689 and of internal dissension. In 1703 Emperor Leopold intervened dramatically, suspended the constitution of 1635 with its provision for the rotation of leaders and replaced what remained of the Jews' Town's autonomous regime by a regime modelled on the permanent magistracy of the Christian town. In the 1720s the growing power of the state brought self-government in Moravia also to an end, when the elected leadership under the provision of the '311' lost the power to issue new ordinances.[36]

Not censorship, conversion, taxation or fire threatened the Jews of Prague and Bohemia so much as expulsion. The demands of 1650 and 1681 made respectively by Ferdinand III and Leopold I for the expulsion of Jews of recent settlement from Bohemia and Moravia anticipated the future, it is now clear. The expulsion from Vienna and Lower Austria in 1669–71 formed a precedent. In Prague only the utmost exertion of certain court-Jews and of the Bohemian nobility averted an even greater catastrophe.

7
Early Decades in Brandenburg-Prussia: The Last Resettlement

The menace of expulsion that loomed over the Jews of Bohemia and Moravia from the mid-seventeenth century coincided with the beginnings of Prussian Jewry. This was the last major episode in that great movement of resettlement to the north and west. In 1571 Joachim II, elector of Brandenburg, had expelled the Jews from his territory 'for all time'. Less than a century later the depopulation and destruction of the Thirty Years' War called for the reversal of the decision. By the 1650s small communities already existed in the dispersed Prussian territories in Minden, Cleves and Ravensberg, as well as in Berlin itself. The Great Elector, Frederick William (1640–88), was something of a philosemite in the hope that this would facilitate the Jews' conversion. In 1650 he issued letters of protection to 10 families entitling them to reside and trade in the bishopric of Halberstadt. This formed part of the territories acquired by Brandenburg under the peace of Westphalia (1648). By 1669 the number of such families had reached 55, comprising 284 persons lodged in 25 houses. In 1678 Frederick William was giving financial support to two Jewish medical students from Poland at the university of Frankfurt an der Oder, Gabriel Felix b. Moses and Tobias Kohen.[1]

In Berlin itself the family of Israel Aron was well established. From a modest beginning as suppliers to the Hohenzollern troops during the Polish–Swedish War (1655), the family used its contacts with importers at Hamburg and Amsterdam to become a purveyor of silver to the mint at Königsberg and thence to providing the court with horses, wines, carriages, and so on. Aron earned the right in 1663 to take up residence in Berlin and in 1665 the Great Elector granted him 'special protection'. At about this time he married Esther Schulhof from Prague, *en secondes noces*. Their united household in Berlin embraced several generations of an extended family. Aron died in 1673, and bequeathed to his widow a tangled and debt-ridden estate.[2] Esther did not extricate herself from these complications until 1684. She inherited some part of her late husband's prerogatives and the elector granted her the title of court-Jewess. Glückel's memoirs of this period show that for women to trade in concert with their husbands was by no means unusual, but the number of court-Jewesses is very limited and apart from Esther the total is more or less confined to Cecilia Hinrichsen (Mecklenburg), Klara Gompers (Prussia) and Madame Kaulla (Bavaria). In 1676 Esther married Jost Liebmann (known also as Judah Berlin), for whom she used her good offices with the elector to secure his entrée to Berlin. As traders in precious metals and jewellery, Esther and her second husband prospered. They annually visited the Leipzig fair with an entourage of servants, accountants, book-keepers and so on. They were instrumental in effecting the exile from Berlin of a prospective competitor, Moses Benjamin Wulff. In 1684 the family's power was further enhanced when the elector authorized Liebmann (together with the mint master Bendix Levi) 'to attend Jewish courts and all assemblies to observe their proceedings and punishments' and to inform the appropriate authorities including the *Hausvogt* (police chief) 'of all happenings'. They had in particular the task of dividing the community into rich, middling and poor Jews for the purpose of collecting the protection money due to the state, to report thefts, to maintain a register of objects pawned and to prevent the open display of goods.[3] The family was popularly regarded as the wealthiest in Prussia.

In 1688 the Great Elector died, but this did not diminish the power of the Liebmann family or of Esther. She enjoyed unrestricted access to the newly titled Frederick I as king of Brandenburg-Prussia and used her wealth, influence at court and masterful personality to secure exemption from all the restrictions applying to Jewish merchants and also from the jurisdiction of the Jews' Commission of 1708.[4] Members of the family came to occupy key rabbinic positions. Her stepson, R. Abraham Liebmann, even had rights of inspection over the 'house of study' established in Halberstadt by Berend Lehmann, one of the most important court factors in north Germany and royal Polish resident in Brandenburg. Also, all the students were obliged to attend Abraham's Talmud classes in May and June, October and November. Not until 1713, by when Esther Liebmann had died, did Lehmann succeed in removing Abraham from any position of control.[5]

Among those families whom Leopold I had expelled from Vienna and Lower Austria in 1669–70, some of the wealthier and most respected found refuge in Berlin. Vienna's loss was Berlin's gain. Others of the exiles found refuge in Kremsier (Moravia) to which they brought economic benefit. These 'Viennese' also claimed the right to have their own regional rabbi.[6] To those 50 families who came to Brandenburg-Prussia belonged the most momentous future. Who made the first approach that would lead to an invitation is uncertain. But it seems that the notion of a settlement first occurred to Andreas Neumann, the Brandenburg resident in Vienna, who was well aware of the need to repopulate the Mark and revive its economy. This was in the early spring of 1670, but certain family heads may well have been in touch with Neumann earlier. In any case in April 1670 a rescript from Berlin informed Neumann that Frederick William was 'not disinclined' to admit 40 to 50 families into his territory, 'in so far as they were wealthy prosperous people, who would wish to bring their assets into this country and employ them here'. There is a suggestion also that this economic initiative might weaken the conservatism of the estates and the guilds. The Prussian–Jewish relationship, like many of its contemporaries, had its *fons et origo* in mutual advantage and reciprocal benefit. These Habsburg Jews, hand-picked for their affluence, inspired the willingness of Frederick William and his successors to facilitate the entry of 'the Austrians', as they came to be known.

Not until a year later did Abraham Ries, Hirschel Lazarus and Benedict (Baroch) Veit – the representatives of the Viennese Jews – appear in Berlin in order to negotiate the terms of a general privilege and of individual letters of protection. Their wives and children remained on the Moravian–Austrian border. These terms were not finalized until May 1671. Opposition to the proposed resettlement on the part of the existing Berlin court-factor, Israel Aron, and his wife Esther, accounts for at least part of the delay. The Aron family feared the economic rivalry of 'the Austrians'. Thus the three negotiators had to undertake to refrain from any activity that might harm the interests of the Aron family and their associates. The 50 families did not all settle in Berlin; about seven did so. Three families settled in Landsberg an der Warthe, others at Königsberg and Frankfurt an der Oder.[7]

The terms that had determined settlement in Halberstadt (1650) served in part as a model for those applying to Brandenburg as a whole. They governed the material conditions of resettlement. The Austrian negotiators secured terms that permitted them to settle in any convenient area. They might also rent, buy or build residences; the edict required

> all the elector's subjects and servants … to allow the said Jews to pass in freedom and security everywhere in the whole of our electorate and other lands, to attend the public fairs, depots and places of trade, to offer all their wares for sale publicly, and to give them facilities without let or hindrance for honourable trade and such traffic as is not forbidden, and not to molest them.

The edict exempted the Jews from the body tax and imposed on them the same duties and excise taxes as all other subjects, but also required 8 Reichsthaler per annum per family in protection money and one Gulden 'whenever one of them [that is, the Jews] marries'. In civil cases the Jews were subject to the jurisdiction of the local burgomaster; criminal cases must be brought to the elector personally. The edict disallowed a synagogue and only in private dwellings permitted worship; it did, however, authorize the employment of a (ritual) slaughterer and schoolteacher. Against payment of an 'equitable fee' the edict enjoined local magistrates to assign land for a cemetery. The edict had a validity of 20 years.[8]

These terms were certainly generous – to one historian 'a Magna Carta'; to another, 'extremely lenient and favourable for the times'. They were not as generous as those that would be extended to the Huguenots, even before the revocation of the Edict of Nantes in 1685, or to other Protestant settlers from Bohemia, the Palatinate and Switzerland.[9] Also, the status and terms assigned to the community deteriorated markedly in the eighteenth century. For all that, to the emergence of Berlin in particular and Brandenburg in general as major centres of Ashkenazi life, they gave a powerful impetus.

Not everyone in Brandenburg welcomed the entry of the Jews. Whatever sympathy there may have been in ruling circles, settlement in Berlin and elsewhere was protracted, painful and highly unpopular. In 1669, in Halberstadt, even before the settlement of 'the Austrians', eight carpenters, accompanied by 50 armed musketeers, solemnly demolished a school building used as a synagogue. Elsewhere, barely a year after the first families had taken up residence in 1672, the estates protested to Frederick William that the Jews were allegedly dealing indiscriminately in all sorts of goods, irrespective of guild regulations, for example wool, cloth, silk, canvas, shoes, clothes; selling unsupervised meat, hawking their goods in village and town, enticing purchasers with low prices, trading on Sunday, engaging in secret usury and exploiting their exemption from many of the burdens borne by the rest of the population; lastly, the estates asserted, were an enemy to attack the country, they, the Jews, would 'infallibly' turn out to be traitors. In 1673 all the guilds in Berlin and Kölln made similar allegations; likewise the merchants in the new city of Brandenburg. The Great Elector was unconvinced and defended Jewish trading activities as 'not harmful but beneficial'.[10] Again, however, in 1714 the Berlin community must challenge and refute allegations of 'unfair' competition, 'underhand' dealing, and trading in forbidden items such as new gold, silver, silk and woollen goods. Both the native Prussian and the newly admitted Huguenot merchants made these charges.[11]

These interchanges took place in the context of enduring internal feuding. The community became an arena for intra-Jewish conflict which lasted well into the eighteenth century.[12] Elections did little to solve the problem of dominance. In 1698 Jewish leaders sought and received from the elector permission to elect 'elders and leaders'. A few months later, however, aggrieved members complained to the authorities not only that were the elections to the communal council rigged but also that those elected were corrupt and incompetent. The elector thereupon annulled these elections and the Berlin *Hausvogt* (police chief) and the rabbi were called upon to supervise fresh elections. For a time at the turn of the century two synagogues confronted each other in the Heidereutergasse – one for the Liebmann family and its adherents, the other for their bitter enemies, headed by Koppel Reiss.[13] In these circumstances it was of the utmost difficulty to reconcile the parties and in 1712 after several years of debate, Bartholdi, an official with special responsibility for Jewish matters, had reluctantly to conclude that if 'unity, peace and calm' were ever to be achieved, then each party must have its own *Schule* and its own body of elders, even if this should entail the duplication of all those bodies in the bureaucracy dealing with Jewish matters.[14] In actual fact the synagogue issue *per se* resolved itself. What was known as 'Esther Liebmann's empire' – *der Liebmannin Reich* – had reached its zenith and in May 1712, in the twelfth year of the reign of King Frederick I, on the 3rd day of the month of Iyar in the year 5472 the foundation stone was laid of the new synagogue, amidst a ceremonial address from the cantor, Hirschel Benjamin Fränkel.[15] On payment of 3000 thaler the new king, Frederick William I, authorized its construction and at the New Year festival 5474 (= 1714), the building was formally inaugurated. The congregation enhanced the occasion with a celebration to honour the betrothal of a daughter of Aaron Isaak, the court embroiderer. In 1718 King Frederick William I with his consort and the future Frederick I, and political and military leaders, attended a service during the intermediate days of the Passover festival.[16]

The erection of the synagogue was doubly significant: it testified to the standing and prosperity of the *kehillah* and also facilitated its supervision and control. The somewhat free-and-easy days of the Great Elector had passed. The erection of the synagogue with the permission and even encouragement of the state may seem in contradiction in that the original charter of 1671 had expressly prohibited public worship. But in fact the reverse applies, because the new synagogue, grouping all the Jews, would eliminate the so-called *Winkelschulen* – corner-synagogues – that is those maintained by private individuals in their own dwellings, necessarily removed from scrutiny.

The state had a vested interest in the maintenance of order in the community and in the community's role as tax-collector, and, generally, as executor of the state's policies in matters Jewish. It had an interest in reinforcing the authority of the communal elders and in defending them against 'incitement'. This dual factor converted the *kehillah*, in the eyes of the state, into a blend of fiscal and religious body, the taxable capacity of which made it of growing importance to the state, no less than did its contribution to the state's mercantilistic aims. Already in 1697 a state commission of enquiry defended the traders Moses and Jacob de Jonge in Memel against the accusations of the local guild of merchants.[17]

The decade of the 1690s was crucial. Prussian Jewry had to contend with decrees that, inter alia, regulated the interest rate permitted to money-lenders; required them to accept the marriage laws of the state; prohibited the entry of any Jews without a *Geleit*; and sought to centralize religious life by limiting the number of synagogues to no more than two. There was a degree of flexibility in the implementation of these measures; for example in 1702 David Elias secured from the king 'a dispensation' that allowed him to marry, in accordance with 'the Mosaic laws', his deceased wife's sister, even though this conflicted with the civil law, and R. Simon Berend, son of Jost Liebmann, was authorized to officiate at the betrothal.[18] As a further measure of control the Jews' Commission was formed in 1708. The head of the Commission, a senior bureaucrat Freiherr v. Bartholdi, was required to ensure that the number of licensed families in Berlin never exceeded 100; that any foreign Jew wishing to settle must possess a capital of 4000 to 6000 Reichsthaler. The Commission had power to settle all disputes either *Jud contra Jud* or between Jews and Christians involving sums of 100 thaler or less. Disputes involving larger sums must be submitted to the civil courts.[19] In 1723 Frederick William I brought a further decree of centralization to his governance through the combination of the military and fiscal agencies into the Directory General. This brought with it an extension in public law and a corresponding reduction in the ambit of private or traditional law. Prussian Jewry could not hope to escape these innovations.

This was a prosperous *kehillah* in Berlin and precisely this prosperity excited the interest of the state. By 1705 the Berlin Jews were already paying 117 437 thaler in excise taxes (internal duties and tolls) as compared with the 43 865 thaler paid by Christian traders. A differential remains, even when account is taken of the fact that the Jews paid twice as much excise duty as did Christians. In actual fact this went beyond the payment of double excise duty but encompassed a multitude of indirect exactions: the funds needed to raise and supply a foot regiment of 1200 men; birth, marriage and divorce taxes; in 1713, 1500 thaler to secure exemption from the obligation to wear red hats; taxes on election to office; and taxes to compensate for exemption from military service. In 1728 the government introduced a global system of taxation of the Jews, partitioned among the various provinces and communities, to be paid quarterly into the general treasury and no longer into the royal purse.[20]

The income of community members also had to cover the outgoings arising from their obligations to support the sick, the poor, the bereaved and all the apparatus of an observant *kehillah*: school, slaughterhouse, synagogue, ritual bath and so on By the 1730s the Berlin *kehillah*, numbering not more than 100 families, had a generous authorized establishment of 3 cantors, 8 unmarried schoolteachers, 2 slaughterers, 2 gravediggers, 1 scribe, 2 *schulkloppers*, 2 medical attendants, 2 midwives and 2 nurses for the sick and women in labour. The community owned not only a synagogue but also a cemetery and a *hekdesh*, a sort of combined hospital, hospice and shelter, just outside the city walls. The fraternities included a burial society and societies for the care of the poor, for attendance on the ceremony of circumcision, for the visitation of the sick and for the provision of dowries for poor brides.[21] In 1737, it is reckoned, only 10 members of the 120 individually licensed and tolerated Berlin Jews possessed assets worth less than 1000 Reichsthaler, so that the majority enjoyed above-average wealth. All the others owned assets to a value of between 2000 and 20 000 thaler.[22] This *kehillah* diverged greatly from the structural norm.

Trade was overwhelmingly its mainstay. This was obviously an extremely narrow economic base but virtually inevitable, given the exclusion from public employment, guild membership and difficulty of access to the professions (though medicine was a partial exception). There were shopkeepers, selling silks, 'white goods', woollen goods and clothing; dealers in gold, silver, jewellery and fancy goods (*Galanteriewaren*); pawnbrokers; mint suppliers; money-changers; one book printer; and one horse-dealer. Not until 1730 does a significant manufacturer appear – in the person of David Hirsch from Prague, the owner of a famous velvet and silk factory in Potsdam.[23] In 1734 'foreign' Jews from outside Berlin, on business visits to the capital, included Hersch Abraham, a goldsmith from Dresden en route for the Frankfurt fair; Bernd Michel from Frankfurt to sell leather; a seller of Hebrew books, 'a learned Jew from Hamburg'; Moses Kohn from Frankfurt who had business with Jablonsky, the court preacher, in connection with the Hebrew printing shop; a bookbinder; Hirsch, a protected Jew from Halberstadt, in connection with the local kosher slaughterers; and a widowed lady, Hundeln from Mittenwalde, selling 'lambs cheese' (*Lammkäse*).[24]

The *kehillah* owed its prosperity in these early decades in part not only to the industry and forcefulness of the members but also to the initial discriminatory policy of the state in allowing only 'people of substance' to enter and settle; and the Jewish leaders had collaborated from the first in this policy, pledging themselves to prevent 'incapable people from slinking in'. Those who tried were turned back at the frontier.[25]

The interest of the state must also extend to the choice of rabbi. In the early decades of the *kehillah* provision was made for a legal presence not only in Berlin but also in Frankfurt an der Oder to adjudicate any disputes arising out of transactions at the fair.[26] When the influence of the Liebmann family waned after 1714 the procedure became regularized and rabbinic appointments required royal approval. This *modus operandi* was halakhically acceptable, ruled the sixteenth century Polish authority, R. Moses Isserles, provided that the person in question was qualified and acceptable to the community.[27] The elders of the community elected their rabbis and determined their terms, remuneration and fees, prior to royal approval. In 1714 for example, the elders, led by Marcus Magnus, requested the king's permission to appoint R. Michael Levi Hassid as rabbi in Kurmark Brandenburg and Pomerania. He was a renowned author of mystical works (and for a time also a covert follower of Sabbatai Zvi). The king took 10 days to signify approval in a letter that also authorized the rabbi to impose on disobedient Jews a sentence of *herem* and promised him the support of the state in maintaining discipline.[28] In 1715 R. Mordecai Toklas was elected to office on a three-year contract and an annual salary of 150 Reichsthaler, in 1731 R. Jacob Joshua Falk of Cracow was similarly elected on a four-year contract and a basic salary of 4 Reichsthaler per week, with the use of a residence. Falk's contract required him to teach and to judge all civil disputes arising inside the *kehillah* with the aid of two assessors whom the elders appointed. Both Toklas and Falk were distinguished for their Talmudic scholarship and erudition. This did not protect Falk from summary dismissal. In 1734 he was forced to leave Berlin for Metz after he had run foul of an influential and combative elder (Veitel Ephraim; see below, p. 203) in a dispute between the latter and one of his business competitors, according to one source.[29] In 1729, on one celebrated occasion, Frederick William I unilaterally appointed R. Moses Aaron from Leipnik (Moravia) to office in Berlin. Some elders agreed and the communal record (*pinkas*) officially noted the appointment but the entry was later erased: the hostile reaction, including fisticuffs and jostling in the synagogue, forced Aaron to withdraw in less than a year. The elders appointed in his stead R. Esaias Hirsch from Poland, but at a cost of 1500 thaler.[30]

The 'dispensation' granted to David Elias to marry his deceased wife's sister did not in any way signify a general accommodation to Jewish law and practice, still less any relaxation in the official supervision of the community. Certainly, in a state such as Prussia friction on religious grounds was rarely a feature in the Jewish–Christian dialogue. Virtually the sole exception, it appears, was the *Aleynu* prayer in the daily liturgy. This prayer contained the phrase, 'they bow down to vanity and nothingness and pray to God who cannot save them', and at least since the sixteenth century had been erroneously regarded as a blasphemous reference to Christianity.[31] At Landsberg the prayer was banned, an official supervising the service to ensure the congregation's compliance. The *reglement* of 1730 (see below, p. 138) repeated earlier prohibitions of 1703 and 1716 (para. 19).[32] What did create dispute was the extent of rabbinic jurisdiction. At no time, it is safe to say, did a clear distinction come about between the legal competence of the state and that of the communal rabbinate. This was partly because different organs of the state held different views on the subject, and partly because the state wished to maintain a special legal regime for its Jewish subjects at the same time as it also made them subject to the general law. Again, not all Jews were united in their choice of jurisdiction: some indeed brought their own disputes with each other before the rabbinical court but others of the *kehillah*, even in a case involving a fellow-Jew, preferred to bypass the rabbi and take the matter before the civil court. As early as 1719 a widowed lady, Rachel Frenkel, in her capacity as guardian of her daughter Rosine, and in regard to a dispute with her son-in-law over the dowry, sought to take her case to the Jews' Commission. In 1720 Aaron Riess applied to the king for release from the jurisdiction of R. Michael Hassid, again in favour of the Jews' Commission. The Jewish elders refused Riess's request while undertaking to investigate his grievance against the rabbi.[33]

Neither alleged blasphemy, nor even the extent of rabbinic jurisdiction, but the increase in the number of Jews caused the Prussian authorities most concern. All the greater would be the concern lest it should be the Jewish poor who constituted the increase. This fear had already inspired the original charter of 1671 which limited the newcomers to 50 families who must not only be of substance but must also commit themselves to keeping out the poor. These precautions proved insufficient in that they did not take into account natural increase; nor the attraction of Berlin in particular and Prussia in general: in 1699 the three overseers of the poor in Berlin reported that every week 70–80 poor Jews passed through the city some of whom undoubtedly remained.[34] The growth was indeed remarkable, from the end of the seventeenth century and beginning of the eighteenth. By 1688 in Berlin, when the Great Elector died, the number of Jewish families is estimated at about 40. By 1700 the total had reached 117, of whom 70 held letters of protection, the remainder being unlicensed. In 1704 the government limited the total to 96. In Landsberg an der Warthe the 3 'Austrian' families admitted in 1671 had grown to 21 by 1690 and in 1717 the *kehillah* comprised a total of 417 persons: 96 men, 93 women, 210 children and 18 *Gesinde* (that is domestic servants). Outside Berlin the urban *kehillot* almost rivalled Berlin in size. The rate of growth was rapid indeed. In Halberstadt the 10 families of 1650 grew to 97 by 1699; in Frankfurt an der Oder from 43 families in 1688 to 74 by 1700; in Halle, which had 2 Jews in 1692, there were 20 families by 1713; in the Duchy of Cleves the 49 families of 1661 almost doubled by 1711. In Königsberg, where a community only came into existence at the beginning of the century, there were 26 families by 1710, and 38 by 1716. They included artisans, old-clothes dealers and merchants. In the rural areas of Pomerania in *c*.1700 there were 36 families with 175 persons and in 1706 45 families. These tiny communities overcame their isolation by establishing a *Landjudenschaft* which held its first session in Stargard in 1706.[35]

By no means to Prussia alone was fear of Jewish increase in general and of the Jewish poor in particular confined. In the Habsburg empire alarm had shown itself in the immediate aftermath of 1648. Here, and also in certain of the other German states (for example Bavaria), and in France, this fear inspired legislation that in one way or another prohibited marriage to certain classes of Jews (especially the poor) or imposed limits on the size of the Jewish population or demanded from those setting up separate households onerous financial guarantees with a view to limiting the number of such households. Legislation of this type is generally known as 'Pharaonic' (after Exodus 1:8 ff.). It lasted in Bavaria until 1861, and, given that the proportion of the Jewish population in any country was everywhere tiny, this legislation is best regarded as antisemitic in intent. Pomerania yields an early example: in 1694 legislation prohibited the marriage of servants in a Jewish household.[36] This legislation was taken extremely seriously. In 1710, for example, Bartholdi, head of the Jews' Commission, demanded advance notification of every Jewish marriage, not only in order to collect the requisite tax but also to ensure, principally, that the number of Jews did not increase beyond all measure (*über die Massen*) through a secret arrangement (*Zusammengebung*). The privilege of 1714 allows as many teachers as the *kehillah* required, but they must remain celibate.[37] In 1726 Hanna Salomon of Landsberg, whose failing health made it impossible for her to continue in her occupation as an exporter of cloth to Poland and Silesia, was refused permission to bring her son-in-law, Meyer Benjamin, into her household, on the grounds that all Jewish domestics must be unmarried.[38]

Pharaonic legislation formed part of a continuing tendency to subordinate the *kehillah* to the state, if not actually to turn the *kehillah* into a department of state.

Continuing dissension within the Berlin *kehillah* facilitated the government's encroachments and the deterioration in its legal standing. Feuding and financial disorder outlived *der Liebmannin Reich*. An official enquiry of 1722 into the accounts of the community disclosed abuse, '*viele Malversationes*', diversion of public monies to private purposes, and 'great animosity' between the two senior elders, Marcus Magnus and Gumperts. This was the background to a *reglement* (1722) which declared that, following a period of 'disorder, conflict and hostility', the elders were unambiguously and emphatically required to act 'in furtherance of the royal interest and ensure good order' in the community. Other clauses of the *reglement* defined in the most meticulous and painstaking detail the responsibility of the elders *vis-à-vis* the community's accounts. These must be submitted to the Jews' Commission and kept in German as well as Hebrew. The elders must also report to the Commission the presence of foreign Jews and ensure that they did not outstay their permitted visit.[39] Two subsequent decrees reinforced his message; the first prohibited the entry of beggar-Jews while the second instructed the Jews' Commission to refuse a *Geleit* (letter of protection, or *Schutzbrief*) to any Jew who lacked assets to the value of 10 000 thaler. The continuing preoccupation of the state with its Jewish subjects ensured that the *reglement* of 1722 would soon be superseded. Towards the end of the decade a revised *General Reglement* was in fact in the making and the *kehillah* used this interval to challenge certain clauses of early drafts. In debates and interchanges with the king and his ministers the elders were not inactive. Obviously in a mercantilistic polity, their memoranda appealed to commercial concerns and stressed their share in the promotion and extension of trade; they had not tolerated any unlicensed Jews; and reductions in their privileges would harm their credit at home and abroad and thus the country's trade; Christian borrowers and traders would suffer were there any interference with the supply of credit or goods; the royal interest in the revenue from tolls and excises would also suffer through any diminution in Jewish trade and the number of Jewish families; as for demography, in Hamburg, Frankfurt am Main, Prague and Amsterdam did there not live thousands of Jewish families who were 'rewarding and beneficial' to these cities?, the elders asked rhetorically; they protested at any imposition of a general privilege covering all the Prussian provinces, since conditions varied from one to the other; and they strongly advocated the retention of the existing procedure for the ritual slaughter of cattle; they advised the authorities that to require communal employees to be unmarried (for example, cantors, ritual slaughterers and gravediggers) would make it impossible for them to perform their religious duties and thus breach the community's conditions of settlement:

> For we are concerned that unmarried persons easily sin through weaknesses of the flesh and might therefore become unsuitable for our worship so that we would have no communal servants at all, if these must remain unmarried and consequently be unable to observe our rites.

The elders offered to limit the number of marriages in the Berlin *kehillah* to 10–12 per annum as a means to meet the state's demographic concerns.[40]

In the event the *General-Reglement* of 1730 dealt with matters of trade, pledges, purchase of property and interest rates; limited the number of families in Berlin to 100; excluded the Jews from all artisanal crafts except engraving; prohibited the entry of further Jews unless they could show assets of 10 000 thaler; defined rabbinical power and the Jews' legal status; authorized a family to maintain one male and two female domestic servants (or two male and one female), all of whom must be unmarried. Finally, it stipulated that if a father wished to include one or two sons in his *Schutzbrief* and allow them to marry then the first son must be able to show assets to the value of 1000 thaler and the second to the value of at least 2000. When the sons married they must not set up separate households which would exceed the specified limit. The marriage of a son must be scrutinized 'with all diligence' to ensure that it did not breach the fixed quota of *Schutzjuden* in a given location.[41] The implication of this clause (no. 12) was correctly seized on by the community; they protested that a son would not be able to marry until an existing quota member died, by which time he might very well have reached the age of 50.[42] This measure alone, to say nothing of the multiple restrictions on trade and property, dramatizes the deterioration in the status of the *kehillah*.[43] The objections of the Jewish leaders may perhaps have succeeded in averting the danger that the imposition of celibacy on communal employees would entail – at least it is not mentioned in the final version of the *reglement*; otherwise the *kehillah*'s counter-proposals did no more than secure an extension from 100 to 120 in the number of families allowed to live in Berlin. The General Directory selected the 120 from among 'the best and wealthiest'. By 1737 the Jewish population of Berlin totalled 1198, leaving 593 to be expelled.[44]

In 1734 the elders in Pomerania, Borchard Philip and Loyser Marcus, showed how the prohibition on the continued residence of married sons in the households of protected Jews positively harmed the royal interest. The 65 families in their area, who were required to discharge an annual tax of 1000 thaler, included those of the married sons. Without the latter the total number of families would shrink to barely 30, among whom some were impoverished and quite unable to contribute towards the tax. Further, it was Jews who supplied most of the serge and woollen factories, argued the elders, and these would collapse if the Jews were forced to leave.[45] This petition had little success, it seems. It was premature. Three or even four decades must pass before Prussian Jewry could translate its economic prowess into political advancement.

8
Amsterdam: From Turmoil to Decline

The economic crisis that overwhelmed the Sephardim in Amsterdam in the mid-seventeenth century, and encouraged a bridgehead settlement in London, began soon to subside. The Sephardi economy in general survived and overcame the upheavals of the mid-century, and to such good effect that in the 1670s, in both Amsterdam and Livorno, the communities rose to unprecedented levels of wellbeing and activity.[1] Both cities had the notably large Jewish population of about 3000 each at this time. Amidst much *éclat*, in 1675, after a delay caused by the French invasion of 1672, the Amsterdam Sephardim ceremonially opened their magnificent new synagogue. But this did no more than once again draw attention to the synagogue-centred nature of Sephardi practice. In terms of Judaism, the building was as much a token of taste and 'monumentality' as of the particular character and degree of synagogue–centred Judaism of the type practised in Amsterdam. The building was a 'monument to the detriment of the concept that it illustrates, indeed the residence in the place of the Presence'.[2] It was this situation that gave some degree of rationale to the turmoil that culminated in the Amsterdam community's most celebrated *herem* of all – that of Spinoza (1656). In that 'Great Jerusalem', what was known as 'the proselytization of the Marranos' was limited to no more than the defence of the doctrine of immortality, the reconciliation of apparent contradictions in the biblical text, the proclamation of the Oral Law and what are called 'discreet theological polemics', that is, the critique of certain Christian teachings, such as trinitarianism and the mutability of the Sinaitic covenant in Menasseh b. Israel's *Conciliador* (1632).[3] This could not silence the doubts and challenges of sceptics, dissenters and the heterodox. (Though in the absence of orthodoxy, what is heterodox is necessarily questionable.) There is some reason to suppose that already in Spain and Portugal those forcibly converted had claimed in justification that religion was a personal matter and its mode of expression unimportant.[4]

The heterodoxy of the ex-conversos centred on the status of the Oral Law and on this front the communities of the port-Jews, given their particular arrangements, were indeed vulnerable. Some were located, after all, in centres of free thought. The most recent assault had come from Venice in R. Leon Modena's *Voice of a Fool*. Here the limited sway of the rabbinic courts and of the scope of the Oral Law, and therefore of rabbinic authority *eo ipso*, favoured antinomian thinking. In Livorno the struggle of R. Jacob Sasportas against the *massari*, especially those of Sephardi origin, is a further sign. In Amsterdam also the authority of the rabbinic court 'appears to have been limited to strictly religious matters'. It certainly did not concern itself with economic activity. The communal agreement of 1639 in regard to the settlement of disputes between members of the *nacao* 'conform', it is said, 'to those already customary in mercantile circles in general'.[5] Spinoza's teaching both encouraged and benefited from this tradition, for he would argue that in the contemporary absence of a Jewish state, Jewish law was redundant.

Both in Venice and Amsterdam, though to differing degrees, critics profited from this limited application of the Oral Law to espouse various theories of deism, scepticism and antinomianism. The work of da Costa was one instance. Spinoza himself could have reached some sort of *modus vivendi* with the authorities but he refused and in July 1656 the Mahamad put him in *herem*. In February 1658 the Mahamad similarly expelled Dr Juan (Daniel) de Prado, a former converso and associate of Spinoza in Amsterdam, where he had found refuge only in 1655.

The Mahamad couched its decree against Spinoza in the gravest of terms. 'In order to take account of the horrible heresies which he practised and taught, and of the monstrous actions which he performed...we order that nobody should communicate with him orally or in writing, or show him any favour, or stay with him under the same roof, or come within four ells of him, or read anything composed or written by him'. This decree did not, unusually, bear the signatures of the parnassim. This is not the only lacuna, for neither does the decree specify 'the horrible heresies' which were practised and taught nor 'the monstrous actions' which were performed.[6]

An ensemble of factors would constitute, as some sort of unit, the grounds for Spinoza's expulsion. They combine philosophical and socio-political issues, the denial of immortality and of a personal God. It appears that both de Prado and Spinoza participated in a gathering, at which they were heard to say:

> They were circumcised and had observed the law of the Jews and they had changed their opinion because the said law was not true and souls died with their bodies and only philosophically speaking was there a God... and thus they had no need of faith.[7]

The position of the Mahamad had a strong political dimension because a precondition of Jewish settlement in Amsterdam demanded a considerable degree of conformity to the religious criteria determined by the Christian authorities. The views of Prado and Spinoza precisely threatened this conformity and they might thus jeopardize the status quo enjoyed by the Portuguese. Juan de Prado's teaching had negative relevance to Christianity as much as to Judaism, for example the dismissal of the Biblical text as an assemblage of isolated documents or the denial of personal survival.

As an extension of the same anxiety, lest scandal erupt in the Christian community, with unforeseeable political consequences, the Mahamad must also be concerned at any breach of those of the 1639 ordinances which proscribed religious discussions with Christians, as would also be the case in London. On this score Spinoza was vulnerable. If, as was perhaps the case, in the year preceding his expulsion he was already in contact with English Quakers in Holland, his activities could not but render him even more suspect to communal leaders as a socio-religious liability. Certainly, Spinoza has been identified as 'a Jew at Amsterdam that by the Jews is cast out' whom the English Quaker, William Ames, less than a year after the expulsion, met in Amsterdam. If, in addition, the conjecture is valid that already before the *herem* of 1656 Spinoza had occupied himself with the condemned philosophy of Descartes, then this would reinforce the demand for his expulsion.[8] However, at the very heart of the reason for the punishment imposed on Spinoza surely lies his denial of a personal providential God, the immortality of the soul and the truth of the Torah.[9] For the first of these, with its corollary of a Jewish survival attributable to natural causes, there is authority in earlier Jewish sources.[10] But the doctrine of the immortality of the soul, despite its uncertain status, had in Amsterdam a psychological relevance that made it a central and controversial theme, above all in respect of reward in the hereafter. At issue stood not only the veracity of a theological doctrine but also the intensely personal and human concern that the fortitude of those who had resisted conversion and suffered torture and death at the hands of the Inquisition should be acknowledged in the hereafter, in contrast to the ultimate fate of those who had accepted conversion. Why be a martyr if both martyr and converso were promised salvation? Was it worthwhile to shed one's Christian belief if in Judaism the doctrine of eternal damnation was again met with? What of the kabbalistic view that the souls of all Jews would merit ultimate salvation?[11]

Spinoza's eventual critique of Biblical and rabbinic teaching took him far beyond that of any of his predecessors and into an entirely novel area of political rejection, for his presentation of Biblical Law as essentially political ('merely the law of the individual Hebrew state') and of Moses as a political leader entailed the consequence that 'it was binding on none but Hebrews and not even on Hebrews after the downfall of their nation'.[12] In the contemporary world therefore Jewish autonomy was some sort of aberration, anomalous and without *raison d'être*. To maintain this position gives Spinoza his historical importance as a pioneering theorist of the *kehillah*'s demise. The argument to the effect that the political existence of the Jews had long before come to an end and therefore that the laws had lost their validity was taken up by Mendelssohn a century later, though in a form that was severely qualified. Mendelssohn did not at all disavow Biblical legislation, which remained binding but left uncertain which laws remained applicable – and to a Jewish political existence since the destruction of the Temple he certainly denied any reality. Even so, Mendelssohn's position was fundamentally less radical than that of Spinoza.

Spinoza's naturalistic understanding of Jewish history did not prevent him from contemplating the possibility – 'so changeable are human affairs' – that the Jews might restore their state and God again choose the Jews.[13] This was a reference to the Sabbatian pseudo-messianic movement of 1665–6 which threw on Sephardi religiosity a revealing light. At least from Talmudic times onward rabbis had feared and sought to neutralize the messianic appeal. The Talmud at one point assembles a collection of diverse and contradictory traditions concerning the messianic advent, as a means to demonstrate an agnostic stance, and calls for a curse on those 'who calculate the end' (TB San. 97a ff.). This, though, had little effect. An important differentiation did later emerge, whereby the Ashkenazi world showed itself less susceptible to the messianic appeal than the Sephardi. Messianic literature and speculation proliferated in Sepharad to a far greater extent than in Ashkenaz. From the twelfth century onwards enthusiasts formulated a series of scenarios which envisaged contemporary history in terms of an apocalyptic and self-destructive clash between Islam and Christianity whence Israel alone would emerge as *tertium gaudens*.[14] In the seventeenth century Menasseh b. Israel's 'Hope of Israel' (1650) projected the return to their Land of the supposedly lost tribes of Israel together with the tribes of Judah and Benjamin. Menasseh used contemporary events and Biblical texts to predict that all would be 'governed by one Prince who is Messiah the Son of David; and without doubt that time is near'.[15] A decade or so later a feature of the excitement generated by the messianic career of Sabbatai Zvi was the comparative indifference of the Ashkenazi centres:

> The Sabbatai Zvi movement at its crest had very little impact indeed on what was the largest Jewish community at the time and the home of the overwhelming majority of Ashkenazi Jewry, namely the Jewish community of Poland...there is no convincing evidence that the movement caused any interruption whatsoever in the day to day affairs of that Jewry.

During the crucial years 1665–7, it was 'business as usual'.[16] In favour of the Sephardi excitement, it was admittedly not difficult to read selected events of the mid-seventeenth century in the light of a proto- but predetermined messianic spectacle. The Westphalian treaties of 1648–9 presaged liberty of conscience, an end to Spanish dominance and therefore of Catholicism, and of the Inquisition as defining influences in the life of the conversos; second, in Poland and the Ukraine the massacres perpetrated by the cossacks of Khmelnitzki could be interpreted as part of the disasters that traditionally would herald the messianic advent; third, the execution of Charles I was surely symptomatic of a 'world turned upside down'. Not only Sephardim could read the signs of the times. For entirely different reasons Christian millenarian enthusiasts in Holland and England shared in the hopes of the Jews, inevitably reinforcing the expectations in the Sephardi centres.[17] When therefore in 1665 a supposed redeemer, Sabbatai Zvi, did appear, existing messianic hopes joined hands with the ex-converso emphasis on the centrality of faith as a religious value to ensure for the pretender a rapturous welcome.

In Amsterdam, Hamburg and Venice and other centres of the Sephardi world, between the converso experience and vulnerability to the messianic appeal there was an existential bond. The effects of antinomianism, the emphasis on faith and the Christian past of the conversos contributed to this vulnerability. Further, the pretender's cause offered to the conversos welcome occasion to repent and compensate for their sin in apostatizing to Christianity by flocking to the pretender's support.[18] In Smyrna 'messianic perceptions' were already a feature of the Sabbatai Zvi circle 'and thus it appears that the conversos contributed to, or even caused, the emergence of the movement'.[19]

The Amsterdam Jews 'abandoned themselves to great rejoicing, beating drums and dancing in all the streets', according to R. Jacob Sasportas, a hostile but attentive observer from nearby Hamburg. 'The Scrolls of the Torah were taken from the Ark with their beautiful ornaments without fearing the danger of arousing a feeling of jealousy and hatred among the gentiles. On the contrary they announced (the news) in public and informed the gentiles of it.' Not all rejoiced, for a decree of May 1666 issued by the Mahamad in Amsterdam confirms not only the enthusiasm of the leadership but also the presence of sceptics: the decree rendered liable to a sentence of *herem*

> any person or persons who composed or helped to compose a certain document which was printed about those lacking in faith and was today on sale in the Bourse amidst much scandal, against the honour of the Holy One blessed be He, and against the hopeful expectations in the advent of our messiah.[20]

In Hamburg in December 1665 the *Pinkas* of the Sephardi community records

> its thanksgiving to the Lord of the world for the news from the Levant, confirmed from Italy and other regions, that He in His divine grace and mercy has given us a prophet in the Land of Israel in the sage R. Nathan

Ashkenazi and an anointed king in the sage R. Sabbatai Zvi ... chosen to redeem His people from exile ... May the God of Israel cause the truth of these tidings to be confirmed and grant us the inheritance of our Land.[21]

There were those in Hamburg who put their money where their mouth already was, so much so that in March 1666 the communal leaders required R. Moses Israel, their rabbi, to proclaim from his pulpit an immediate prohibition on 'all wagers on the coming of our salvation'; the penalty for infringement was a fine of 5 Reichsthaler (if the wager was laid with a fellow-Jew, 10 if with a Christian).[22] Among the Sephardim in London the same fervour led believers to offer odds of 1–10 (according to Pepys) on the wager that 'if a certain person now at Smirna be within these two years owned by all the princes of the East ... as the king of the world ... that this man is the true Messiah'.[23]

Only were belief and faith to be exalted at the expense of the Oral Law, and rabbinic doctrine of the criteria that the messiah must satisfy be disregarded, could the claims of Sabbatai Zvi become acceptable. At the heart of the anti-Sabbatian attack that Sasportas and his allies waged stood this argument. Sasportas, a veteran of the fight against antinomianism in Livorno and London, justifiably maintained that not only had the alleged messiah failed to punish sceptics and unbelievers, as his office and mission required, but that he had also failed to give any affirmative demonstration of his proclaimed messianic status, as Maimonides, for one, had demanded. Sasportas quotes the relevant passage, and comments: 'It seems that his deeds prove and establish the presumption that he is the king messiah'; in default of deeds, 'all was dependent on faith in the prophesy'. Faith, in such circumstances, aroused the fear of Sasportas that here was inherent the possibility of a 'new Torah', as proclaimed by Jesus. R. Joseph Halevi of Livorno, a fellow-campaigner of Sasportas, contrasted 'the principle of Torah and good deeds', which gave to its exponents the promise of life in the world to come, with those who 'believe that a man can save souls'.[24]

After the débâcle of Sabbatai Zvi's apostasy to Islam in 1666 the Amsterdam Portuguese *kahal* did its utmost to remove from its records all trace of its earlier enthusiasm. But merely to expunge the record of error was insufficient to repress all trace of Sabbatianism, adherents of which later emerged in the important Ashkenazi centres of Prague and Metz.

Sabbatianism was not the only symptom of disintegration to show itself in the seventeenth century. Another strain of antinomianism appeared in 1712 when the Mahamad had to impose a sentence of *herem* on three members of the community – David Mendes Henriques, known as David Almanza, and the brothers Aaron and Isaac Dias da Fonseca. Their 'Karaite' views led them 'entirely to deny the Oral Law which is the foundation and underpinning of our Holy Law'. The three men refused an invitation to repent, so that, lest their 'poison' infect others, the sentence was passed.

About 18 months later, Almanza did recant; publicly, from the synagogue pulpit, he sought pardon for his actions, and the sentence was duly annulled. But the two da Fonseca brothers became converts to Calvinism. This was the most extreme of all steps. Even in the absence of evidence relating to *herem*, still less conversion, it seems that views such as these were by no means confined to the fringes of the Amsterdam Sephardim.[25]

Their adherents aligned themselves with the growing deistic and Spinozistic currents of the eighteenth century, inside and outside the synagogue. This was certainly the case in the London *kahal* (see below, p. 150). The problem of a successor to the Haham Abendana de Britto in 1760 and the eventual need to leave the choice to Constantinople illustrates congregational weakness in Amsterdam.[26]

Outside the 'synagogue' also, so to speak, disintegration became apparent, for example in the unwillingness of the ruling group to rule. This decline in morale had its parallel in other major urban communities (for example Berlin and Bordeaux). Perhaps in Amsterdam this symptom showed itself earlier than elsewhere, for as early as 1694 and over several decades (in 1706, 1722, 1739) the same regulation had repeatedly to be introduced: the imposition of fines on those who refused to take up the offices in the *kahal* to which they had been elected. This inherent weakness was compounded by the limits on the power to decree a sentence of *herem* that the municipal authorities imposed on the *kahal* in the 1680s and by the latter's recurrent need to turn to those authorities for help in executing its own decisions.[27]

About this time also precipitate messianic enthusiasm gave way to contentment with the customs of the status quo. 'I found many who lacked knowledge and belief who were so intent on profit as to doubt the words of our sages', wrote R. Moses b. Jacob Hagiz, an emissary from the Promised Land to Amsterdam and the diaspora in the early eighteenth century:

> They are 'epicureans' – and because they live in lands where they have freedom, as well as the wealth that is preserved for their peril, they remove from their necks the yoke of the rabbis.
>   I have heard them say that every town and country where they live is today like the holy land, like the cities of Israel and Judah…they see themselves living in peace and security, each man under his vine and fig tree.
>   They quote scripture, God's words to Jeremiah (29:4 ff.): to guide those exiled from Jerusalem to Babylon – 'build houses and live in them … take wives and beget sons and daughters … multiply there and do not decrease. And seek the welfare of the city to which I have exiled you'.

Hagiz continues: whereas the exiles in Babylon could not sing the song of the Lord in a strange land, their successors call the city where they dwell in peace 'my Jerusalem'. 'They eat and drink and parade in carriages, in gardens and orchards...they are at home with the children of foreigners. At the approach of a bearded emissary from Jerusalem, they say "here comes another one...we must flee from them as from a snake."'[28]

The call of the sea grew fainter and fainter and more and more the erstwhile merchant-adventurers renounced the active pursuit of trade and converted themselves into simulacra of the wealthy Amsterdam burgher, content to rely on the income from his investments. Already in the 1650s the de Pinto family began to invest its wealth in interest-bearing securities, such as Dutch bonds and the stock of the East and West India companies, and in Venetian and other banks. About a century later, according to R. David de Raphael Mendoza,

> here in the city of Amsterdam most of the wealthy and the gentlemen have all of their monies abroad for from early times they placed all or most of their wealth in another kingdom to bear interest or to trade with overseas and these funds never saw this country.[29]

The general wellbeing of the Jewish community was obviously inseparable from that of the Dutch economy in general. The wars against England and the more protracted wars with France (1672–8, 1689–97, 1702–13) prepared an age of decline in the early eighteenth century. They created financial burdens and were a source of increasing economic impoverishment. Military provisioning did indeed benefit certain specialized branches of the Sephardi economy; for example the house of Machado and Pereira, which had taken a leading part in equipping the Dutch armies of William III and the States General. In the years after 1713 even this activity suffered, when the Treaty of Utrecht put an end to the period of warfare, and also limited such associated activities as banking and diplomacy. In the general field of commerce English and French traders provided growing competition. The Dutch lost their virtual monopoly of the Baltic trade and the wool-producing centre of Leyden declined. In the Levant trade, Marseilles thrived at the expense of Amsterdam. In terms of specific commodities, the industrial processing of sugar and tobacco, a staple of the Dutch Sephardi economy, suffered when it was transferred to the north-eastern European area. The number of tobacco-processing workshops in Amsterdam collapsed from about 30 in 1720 to no more than 8 in 1750. Not all were Sephardi-owned, but the overall decline is certainly significant. The harmful economic effect was all the greater since the artisans in these workshops were themselves largely Sephardi. Trade and prosperity must also suffer from the renewed persecution of the Inquisition in the 1720s, which finally destroyed those surviving nuclei of New Christian merchants in Lisbon, Seville, Madrid and elsewhere with whom their relatives and associates in Amsterdam and Livorno had been cooperating. The *relative* prosperity of the Sephardim did not suffer from these changes. An assessment of 1742, when there were about 3000

Sephardim in Amsterdam (from a total population of 240 000), reveals that 283 had an annual income of 800 florins or more and that on average the Sephardi population was more prosperous than the rest of the population, and much more so than the Ashkenazi community.

In absolute terms however, the Amsterdam Sephardim were clearly in a state of crisis in the mid-eighteenth century. A number of new charitable societies had to be founded to provide winter coats, bread, fuel and matzot for the poor and needy.[30] This support was increasingly burdensome and in their extremity the Mahamad took to petitioning the government for freedom from taxation on fuel and bread and for permission to sue those members who failed to pay their share of the tax for poor relief.[31] They also resorted to an earlier remedy for poverty: sponsored emigration. In his pamphlet *Reflexoens Politicas* of 1748 Isaac de Pinto (1717–87), the political economist and director of the East and West India Companies, and advocate of national debt on the English model, expounded the benefits of emigration in the context of pauperization. In the past 25 years the number of contributing members to the Portuguese Jewish congregation had fallen from 629 to 610, de Pinto calculated; and this at a time when the number of families living from communal funds increased from 115 to 415, a burden that increased taxes to the state and the community rendered all the heavier. Not in Holland alone but throughout the diaspora poverty became the norm. De Pinto correctly saw no prospect of escape from impoverishment and depression so long as the Jews continued to be excluded from the craft guilds, retail trade, agriculture and public service. In this extremity he advocated the assisted emigration of the poor, especially to Surinam, the most prosperous Dutch colony. This would, de Pinto expected, bring benefits to all concerned: relieve the burden on the community's charity funds; relieve also the members of the community; help the emigrants to start a new life; and release resources that could then provide greater help to those of the poor who remained. This policy was adopted. As in earlier years the prospective emigrants received financial assistance, part of which was disbursed on their departure, with the bulk en route or on reaching their destination. For his part the emigrant undertook not to return to Amsterdam for a specified number of years, usually 15, and these details were recorded in the Registro dos Despachos. Between 1759 and 1814 more than 400 Sephardim, often with wives and children, left Amsterdam for the Sephardi Mediterranean communities in North Africa, Italy and the Near East, or London, Hamburg or Bordeaux. The Dutch colonies, especially Surinam, accounted for almost half the *despachos*. More precisely, almost two-thirds of those dispatched to Surinam between 1759 and 1802 were young, single and male (22.7 per cent married and 15.2 per cent widowed). The parnassim brought those who refused to leave before the city authorities with imprisonment as the sequel or forcible deportation.[32] With regard to *their* poor (if they could not be prevented from coming altogether), the London

Sephardim took much the same steps so that in the middle and later eighteenth century a class of transient and impoverished Sephardim emerged, shuttled from Europe across the oceans of the world.

The policy was in any case not at all successful. By removing the young and unmarried it effectively ensured demographic decline. It also did nothing to stem economic hardship: 'Our nation becomes poorer from year to year', wrote an anonymous Portuguese Jew in 1770. His sober assessment pointed to bankruptcies and 'ever increasing luxury and extravagance. The middle classes have to be very cautious in their expenditure'. Business was becoming 'more and more insecure, especially the share transactions in which our most important men are solely concerned. Taken all in all, the Portuguese Jewish nation has had her summer and approaches her winter.' This observer ended with an envious (but erroneous) glance at the Ashkenazi Jews who had come to Holland in poverty, were despised but are 'in truth more industrious and economical than we are... We fall and they rise.'[33]

By this time – say the mid-eighteenth century – it is estimated that there were *c.*10 000 Ashkenazim in Amsterdam. They were poorer as a group than the general population but had undoubtedly benefited, according to tax figures, by comparison with their state in 1674. In 1737 and again in 1747 the municipal authorities required the parnassim to issue sumptuary regulations. These governed, inter alia, the number of guests permitted at the celebration of a circumcision or wedding and the type of refreshments served. However, this evidence of affluence is reconcilable with the presence of a large proportion of poor Ashkenazim dependent on the charity of their fellows. The Ashkenazim, like the Sephardim, suffered of course from the same economic disabilities, that is exclusion from agricultural life, virtually all guild-controlled activities and the retail trade. These were not always strictly enforced, but they did tend to limit the range of occupations to such activities as diamond-cutting, tobacco-drying, engraving, moneylending, unskilled labour (sailors and porters) and the selling at retail of cloths, spectacles, second-hand goods, jewellery, fish, old clothes and so on. There were also itinerant musicians.[34] The same factors that account for the poverty of the Sephardim, as expounded by Isaac de Pinto, account also for the poverty of the Ashkenazim. This explains why the parnassim repeatedly sought remission from the tax on fuel and breadstuffs, for the benefit of the poor. In 1748 the parnassim found 1335 poor families in their *kehillah*, equating to some 5300 persons.[35] These absolute and relative totals increased towards the end of the century.

9

From London to the Provinces

The conflicts that bedevilled Amsterdam were in London less acute but no less real, and at one time almost powerful enough to divide the Sephardi community. The synagogue, newly opened in 1701 in Bevis Marks in the City of London, became an arena of conflict. The Sephardim numbered *c.*700 at the turn of the century. They reproduced in London the continuing ferment in Amsterdam. Initially it centred on the writings and speeches of the Haham David Nieto, whose appointment followed shortly on the inauguration of the synagogue in Bevis Marks. Born in Venice in 1654, Nieto was among the most distinguished scholars to occupy a London pulpit. He was educated at the University of Padua, where he graduated in medicine, and later moved to Livorno where he held office as community judge, preacher and physician.

Hardly had Nieto taken up office in London than he came under attack in a controversy that the alleged pantheism of Spinoza and contemporary deists had provoked, in the last resort. It may also be the case that covert supporters of the pseudo-messiah Sabbatai Zvi exploited the furore aroused by the sermon to discredit the rationalism of Nieto. On the Sabbath reading of Parshat Vayeshev, 5464 (20 November 1703), barely two years after his arrival in London, Nieto delivered a sermon in which he seemed to some of his audience to have equated God with nature, much as Spinoza had apparently argued (as well as pantheists among the contemporary deists). In actual fact, deistic thinking was precisely Nieto's target, for the 'nature' familiar in that context, that is as an entity distinct from God, Nieto equated with divine providence. It was not made sufficiently clear that the 'nature' Nieto had in mind was absolutely not *natura naturata* but *natura naturans*. Nieto referred to Psalm 147 with its invocation to God 'who covers the heavens with clouds, provides rain for the earth' and so on as a formulaic concept of the identity of God and *natura naturans*:

> From these passages it is clear that everything attributed by modern thinkers to nature is due to the action of God; so that in fact there is no

such thing as Nature, what they call Nature being nothing other than the providence of God. And so, as I said, God and Nature and Nature and God are one and the same.

On the basis of a putative misunderstanding the sermon became a *cause célèbre* in the Sephardic world, and led to accusations of heresy against Nieto to the extent that an independent rabbinical adjudication was called for. The Amsterdam Bet Din refused to become involved and Haham Zvi Ashkenazi of Altona, the father of R. Jacob Emden, was entrusted with the task of adjudication. In a judgement signed by two other *dayanim*, the Haham's report completely vindicated Nieto against any charge of heresy and welcomed his 'disclosure of the errors of the philosophers'. For the significance that Nieto's sermon had attributed to natural forces, Zvi Ashkenazi found ample precedent in the *Kuzari* (*c.*1135) of Judah Halevi and the *Two Tablets of the Covenant* (*Shnei Luhot ha-Brit*, 1648) of R. Isaiah Halevi Horovitz.[1]

Nieto could now freely continue unhampered in office and take up the outstanding theme in contemporary Sephardi theological discourse – the defence of the Oral Law against its detractors. In his *Matteh Dan* (1714), written in Hebrew and Spanish, Nieto outlined his task and foresaw

> disaster following disaster, for there has arisen a rabble of men wise in their own eyes who have never seen the light of Torah, who say our words are our own, who is Lord over us? What do we care about the arguments of the *tannaim* and *amoraim*, about the arguments of Rav and Shmuel? For this is the Torah which Moses set before the Children of Israel, as pure as the sun, enlightening the eyes; none shall be weary or stumble in it; for the book of God's Torah is clear and can be grasped by reason.[2]

In his last years Nieto polemicized against apologists for the Inquisition.

This stands, for all its succinctness and *parti pris*, as a classic statement of the distinction made by the Sephardi 'neo-Karaites' between the Judaism of the Bible and that of the Oral Law. Not only is it contended that the plain sense of the biblical text, 'the Torah of Moses', is accessible to the uninstructed reader but also that the apparatus of Talmudic and later rabbinic commentary and legislation, derived from the Bible in accordance with the accepted rules of hermeneutics, has somehow become irrelevant to the contemporary world.

'Neo-Karaism', whether articulated or present only in the form of unreflecting disregard for rabbinic teaching and interpretation, threatened the coherence and wellbeing of Sa'ar Asamaim. It does not seem that Nieto's writing and efforts had much success in arresting the spread of deistic ideas, still less of indifference. This may be regarded as an internal source of weakness and even disintegration. The symptoms barely differed from those denounced by R. Sasportas some four decades earlier. This came to such a point that in or about 1705 some of the *yehidim* found the conduct of certain fellow-members so reprehensible in its flouting of Jewish norms that their dissatisfaction led them to contemplate seceding from Sa'ar Asamaim and joining the newly founded Ashkenazi congregation in London. The gravamen of the complaint can be reconstructed from the ensuing correspondence. There were Jews, it was said, who

> perform acts that should not take place among the Israelites [and] attend prayer services there and go up to read from the Torah and [participate in] all the other rituals that are customary in the synagogue – this being a thing that they [the complainants] and other God-fearing persons cannot accept. And they demand that an agreement be made that anyone who commits one of these major sins in public shall not be present in God's congregation until he repents – and no one heeds their words.

This controversy later showed itself to be of momentous importance in the emergence of 'orthodoxy'. For the moment there was little resonance; only in 1730 did a group of members secede from the Sephardi congregation and join the Ashkenazi.[3]

The congregation developed in two contrasting directions. On the one hand, the struggle in the late seventeenth century to maintain a distinction between those Sephardim who identified fully with the *kahal* and those marginal or ambivalent Sephardim began to weaken in the eighteenth. The process that Todd Endelman has stigmatized as 'radical assimilation' finds at this time its exemplar. Mirabeau drily noted: *'C'est un fait singulier, mais constant, que les juifs en Angleterre ne parviennent jamais à un certain degré d' opulence sans désirer de passer pour chrétiens dans la société.'*[4] Less indulgent and more scathing is the auto-critique articulated in the writings of Dr Meyer Schomberg (1690–1761), a German-born physician who became a celebrated practitioner in London. He made the most scathing attacks on London Jewry – essentially the London Sephardim, it seems. 'They are entirely devoted to multiplying riches and property,' he wrote in his Hebrew pamphlet, *Emunat Omen* (1746). On the Sabbath day they frequent Exchange Alley 'to enquire and find out on that day from merchants and brokers if there has been a rise or fall in the price of the Indian securities...' They fail to help the poor and needy. 'They love whoredom and adultery. Not only do they lie with women, daughters of the gentiles ... but they also ... reject the kosher daughters of Israel who are our own flesh and blood.' Tale-bearing, envy, false pride are other charges brought by Schomberg against London Jewry. This is the view of an informed moralist, sharpened by personal animosity and conflict who may well also be attempting to justify his own withdrawal from the community and the defection of his own children from Jewish practice.[5]

On the other hand, as an accompaniment to assimilation, the construction of a *kahal* was an urgent and continuing need, especially as a means to care for the poor. The policy of deterrence failed. In 1692 and again in 1710 the Mahamad warned, cautioned and threatened intending immigrants to London. To no avail: even when reinforced by the civil authorities, dissuasion was ineffective. The synagogue in Bevis Marks came to serve as a welfare centre that provided the Sephardi poor with free medical and burial facilities. From the end of the seventeenth and into the eighteenth century, communal charities offered specialized services to the sick, the bereaved, mothers in childbirth, and the aged. From 1703 the Sephardim also maintained an orphanage, one function of which was to apprentice boys to useful trades. Sometimes the masters were Jewish, sometimes not. The masters' occupations covered virtually every London trade – carpenter, cooper, 'lapidary' (jeweller), watchmaker, barber and barber/surgeon, bricklayer, cordwainer, engraver, perukier and so on. The number of trades practised by Jewish masters amounted to *c*.100. The number of masters in each trade shows a preponderance of jewellers and watch and clock makers – both *c*.21 per cent. The girl apprentices, very much in a minority, were articled to milliners, mantlers, glove-makers and drapers in the main.[6]

In the 1720s a revival of the Portuguese Inquisition and a mass exodus stretched charitable and philanthropic facilities to the utmost. Between 1720 and 1735 some 3000 persons are estimated to have fled to England. In 1726 communal expenditure on behalf of the poor reached its peak: £1639 6*s*. 0*d*. on the home poor and £744 4*s*. 4*d*. on the foreign poor. Relief also took a form that encouraged the emigration of the poor, especially in the 1730s, provided that they agreed to be circumcised within 15 days, in the absence of any compelling counter-reason. Travel subsidies and participation in the Crown's charter for the colonization of Georgia in 1732 enabled the Mahamad to dispatch the families of poor Sephardim to Barbados, Jamaica, Georgia and Carolina. This takes no account of the sums disbursed in favour of communities and individuals (mainly Sephardi) throughout the Jewish world.[7]

These efforts and policy barely diminished the extent of poverty. In 1731 the number of families of the sick and poor attached to Bevis Marks still amounted to 254, probably more than half the total Sephardi population. This was the context to the establishment of a hospital in 1748, funded by synagogue members. First situated in Leman Street, the hospital had a medical staff that included a dispenser, a matron, an apothecary, a nurse and two midwives: 'the first hospital in England designed from the outset to include care for maternity cases', it has been claimed. The average total of infant burials showed a rapid decline: in 1734–43, it was 32.9 per annum; in 1744–53, 20.5; and in 1754–63, 17.3.[8]

Trade supplied the vast bulk of the community's income. This ranged from peddling in the streets of London to government loan contracting at the highest level. The entry into crafts and the apprentice system may perhaps have corrected the normal occupational pattern whereby a very small number of the wealthy ruled a community of the poor and indigent. Overseas trade in diamonds, coral, bullion and the foreign exchange markets and stockbroking and stockjobbing were the principal branches of trade.[9]

'On the whole the Dutch Portuguese Jews who came to England did not find a permanent place in British finance', writes one economic historian.[10] But for all their ephemeral importance in *this* respect, two of the financiers are of lasting significance in the Jewish context. Gideon Samson (1699–1762) exemplifies the complexities in the process of 'radical assimilation'. Gideon's father, probably born near Hamburg (of the Abudiente family of Portugal) was active in the West Indian trade, and settled in London from Barbados towards the end of the seventeenth century. Samson acquired fame and fortune as a skilled dealer and speculator in government securities and the stocks of the Bank, the East India Company and the South Sea Company. In 1742 and after, with the outbreak of the War of the Austrian Succession (1742–8) and the Seven Years' War (1756–63), Gideon's activity came to embrace government loan contracting, through an association with chancellor Henry Pelham. While still remaining a member of the Sephardi congregation, he married a Protestant lady, acquired various country seats and had his children baptized shortly after their birth. Special Acts of Parliament were passed to enable Gideon, while still remaining a member of the Sephardi community, to purchase landed property. In 1757 he married off his daughter Elizabeth to Viscount Gage with a dowry of £40 000. In 1759 he secured a baronetcy for his son, a schoolboy at Eton. He resigned from the community when the Mahamad made unauthorized use of his name in its advocacy of the 'Jew Bill' of 1753 (see below, p. 156). Gideon's will contained a legacy of £1000 to the community with the request that he be buried in the Jewish cemetery in Mile End, London. At his death it was also disclosed that since his resignation Gideon had anonymously donated to the community an annual sum equal to the value of his membership fees.[11] Gideon's career overlapped with that of his successor, Joseph Salvador (1716–86), who enjoyed ephemeral success, not only in government loan contracting but also in the trade in coral, diamonds and in silver. But Salvador's lasting importance is embedded in his efforts, though abortive, to exploit economic success for political advancement.

An alien or a Jew enjoyed in England a wide degree of economic freedom, but it was still hedged in. In the late 1720s and 1730s the Sephardi communal élite had to confront a reality that was not consonant with their economic role but which was embedded in statutory and/or corporate legislation. In 1727 Anthony Moses da Costa, a wealthy, English-born member of the Mahamad (unlike his converted father Alvaro da Costa) and a freeman of the East India Company, applied for membership of the Russia Company. The company rejected da Costa on the grounds of his religion. In 1737 a senior member of the Bevis Marks congregation applied to become a freeman of the City of London. This would have permitted his entry into retail trade in the City. Again on grounds of religion the application was rejected.[12]

The status of alienhood produced perhaps the worst disability of all, for an alien was excluded from the colonial trade, and had to pay special fees and customs duties. Endenization, secured by means of a royal letter, removed some of these burdens, but not alien duties. In 1714 a petition for endenization submitted by Elias Paz and Solomon de Paz explained that the lack of 'Denization ... maketh them incapable of being Owners of Shipping, and several other Inconveniencys they lye under in their Trades and Businesses upon the Import and Export of Goods and Merchandise ...'[13] In the middle decades of the eighteenth century, when about one-half of the Sephardi mercantile aristocracy was foreign-born, therefore alien, and therefore subject to some degree of commercial disability, even if endenizened, the need for British nationality was self-evident. But to a Jew naturalization was not available because it required the applicant to have received the Sacrament within the previous month. British *raison d'état* dropped this requirement in 1740 when an Act freed from the sacramental test those Jews who had served in the Royal Navy or those who had lived in the American colonies for seven years. Over the period 1740–53 185 Jews of whom 130 lived in Jamaica were naturalized with the benefit of these provisions.[14] In 1743/4 the Mahamad in London made use of contacts in the Dublin Parliament, perhaps to inspire but at least to encourage a number of bills that would have facilitated the naturalization of the Jews in Ireland. These bills the Irish House of Commons accepted, but in the Irish House of Lords the Irish peers and Primate ensured their defeat. The margin of defeat was, however, so small that in 1746 the Mahamad in London felt encouraged to invite the elders 'to devise measures to gain more liberty for their nation whenever occasion should offer'. This produced a group of *senhores deputados* and a Committee of Diligence, composed of five leading City merchants and Sephardi notables. Benjamin Mendes da Costa took the presidency.[15]

The question of a Jew's right to own land came to be involved, comprehended in the 'more liberty' mentioned in the programme of 1746. The question first arose, it seems, in relation to the Sephardi acquisition of a new burial ground in 1724. Philip Carteret Webb, attorney, antiquary, Whig politician, and legal adviser to the Sephardim, took legal opinion of eight counsel who all confirmed that an English Jew had the same right to purchase land as any other Englishman. But in 1738 the historian D'Blossiers Tovey brought to light a decree of 1271 which prohibited the acquisition of land by Jews and inevitably rendered the earlier positive opinion problematic. Of course Jews did own land and if Chief Justice Lord Ellenborough bought Abraham Goldsmid's estate at Roehampton it may be assumed that the title was good. But it is also true that Benjamin Goldsmid (1755–1808), Abraham's brother, registered *his* property in the name of an employee. In

1830 Moses Montefiore was unable to purchase an estate at Ramsgate and had instead to rent the property for three years.[16]

In the eighteenth century the uncertainty must be all the greater. The intent of the agitation to ease the conditions for naturalization can be understood as a benefit not only to alien Jews but also to native-born English Jews whose power to acquire a good title to the land they wished to purchase would be reinforced, in so far as the removal of the requirement to take the Holy Sacrament in the one context, would 'establish by inference the legality of property ownership for Jews born in England'. In other words, the Sephardim sought to remove the distinction between, one, being English and, two, being English *and* in a position to take the Sacrament. Henceforth, were the Sephardim to succeed, in order to enjoy all the rights and powers of an Englishman, it would only be necessary to be an Englishman *tout court*. The preferential position hitherto enjoyed by an Englishman who was also able to take the Sacrament would have been eliminated.[17]

The primary agent in this campaign, Joseph Salvador, had during the panic-ridden crises of the Jacobite rebellion of 1745, together with other Sephardi financiers, backed the government: only a few years later it would not be unreasonable to expect a quid pro quo. In January 1753 Salvador wrote to the Duke of Newcastle, one of the triumvirate dominating the government (the others being Henry Pelham, Newcastle's brother, who was close to Samson Gideon and the Lord Chancellor, Lord Hardwicke):

> It is desired that it be enacted that any person professing the Jewish religion whom it may in future be thought proper to Naturalise, shall in lieu of taking the Holy Sacrament, take the Oaths of Supremacy and Allegiance, or such other oaths as may be thought proper, on or before the Second Reading of the Bill for Naturalising him in either of the Houses of Parliament.

Salvador used the pseudonym Philo Patriae to pamphleteer on behalf of the Bill and in this capacity introduced the 'land question': some of the native-born Jews, he writes, 'had turned their thoughts to buying landed estates and might be willing every obstacle should be removed before they purchased'.[18] Salvador himself had an estate in Tooting in the southern vicinity of London. Not all Jews supported the Bill; according to Mirabeau there were 'zealots' who feared a weakening of doctrinal teaching.[19]

The accounts of the Mahamad show that Philip Webb, during the years 1742–53 disbursed several hundred pounds 'in relation to the application to Parliament concerning Naturalization'. These sums could not nullify the effect of a grave misjudgement on the part of the Sephardi leadership. The Bill was indeed approved by the House of Lords in April 1753 and by the House of Commons the following month. But powerful opposition, instigated by the City mercantile element fearful for its share in the Portugal trade, won such support – all the more so as the Bill became an issue in party-political debate – that the government was forced to repeal the measure in December 1753. The most irrational outbursts, many of which centred on the fear of circumcision, and on the Jew as vengeful, cruel and lustful, entered into political discourse and completely overwhelmed the cautious and discreet diplomacy of Salvador and his associates.[20]

They had overlooked the arrival of mass political participation and the ideology of Olde England. This lesson in political reality ensured that not until 1829 did Anglo-Jewry again take up the land question: in the form of a proposed petition to the House of Lords that should include a request for 'the full protection in holding and conveying of landed property and etc.', advised Nathan Mayer Rothschild.[21]

Was the 'land question' even more than a matter of ownership? I believe that in fact it embodied a desire to belong, in the sense that to possess a stake in the country (irrespective of those other financial and social benefits a landed property might yield) would convey with it the right to participate in the government of the country. In other words, it had a strong political relevance. The economic and the political cannot, in this context, be dissociated. This bond became more and more explicit in the nineteenth century when the exercise of the franchise was dependent on the possession of property. Even if a less far-reaching interpretation is acceptable, then so long as even the native-born and therefore British Jew lacked this special power available to a Christian compatriot, his 'Britishness' must be suspect. To own an estate by unquestionable right may well be considered a part of naturalization – otherwise naturalization would be incomplete in a most important respect and frustrate one of Salvador's arguments to the Duke of Newcastle in favour of the Naturalization Bill that thereby the Jews would 'be more closely connected' with the government, for 'they have no connection or tie with any other Government or state whatsoever'.[22] This is indistinguishable from the patriotic emotion evoked a few years later during the Seven Years' War. A Jew without at least the right to own land could not be a whole-hearted patriot, and this was deeply felt. Conversely, to withhold this power was equivalent to impugning the injured party's patriotism.

The débâcle over the 'Jew Bill' in 1753, and its disclosure of a widespread antisemitism that lent itself to rapid mobilization for political purposes, exacerbated the already troubled state of the Sephardim. The process of 'radical assimilation' was unremitting.[23] The demographics of decline are apparent in the slight population increase between 1700 and 1764, when the individual membership of the congregation Sa'ar Asamaim increased from an estimated total of 200 to no more than 238. The annual number of burials in the congregation's cemeteries fell by 30 per cent and that of children under 10 by 47.4 per cent between 1710 and 1760. Over the whole period 1740–1800 the annual number of marriages at Bevis Marks dropped by 42.7 per cent. The approximate total of 2000 Sephardim in 1750 remained more or less unchanged over the next 80 years, it is estimated, even though Sephardim continued to immigrate into Britain. Intermarriage, assimilation, migration overseas and the marriage of Sephardi men to Ashkenazi women account for the stagnation (even though in 1766 the *kahal* prohibited marriage between a Sephardi and an Ashkenazi woman); no wife or widow would be eligible to claim relief from the charity chest (Cedaka).[24]

The fall in numbers had its counterpart in a fall in educational standards. Although the college (*Medrash*) of the synagogue had at this time 18 students of the Talmud, in 1775 of the 64 pupils in the school attached to the synagogue at Bevis Marks, scarcely one-eighth could read Hebrew and nearly all were unfamiliar with the daily prayers.[25] From 1784 until 1806, when Raphael Meldola from Livorno took office as Haham, the community lacked ecclesiastical leadership. 'In this *Kahal*', the Mahamad remarked in 1803, 'the study of the Law will be entirely lost and the *Kahal* will become an object of contempt and ridicule.'[26]

The decline of the Sephardim in London was accompanied by the rise of the Ashkenazim. From *c.*1710 the former must share with a growing influx of poor, Yiddish-speaking Ashkenazim the same half-dozen City parishes. This transformed London into a replica of contemporary Amsterdam, especially in the tension and friction that marked the interface of the two communities. Already in the late 1670s the Mahamad resolved to exclude any Tedesco – perjorative term for Ashkenazi – from synagogal office, and no Tedesco should be the recipient of a synagogue honour or permitted to pay the *imposta* or contribute to charity, without the approval of ten elders. Only exceptional wealth could release a Tedesco from these constraints. If even from Ashkenazim of moderate means the Sephardi leadership held aloof, how much more must they shun Ashkenazim who were indigent. Those dependent on charity were given five shillings and sent off to Rotterdam, Amsterdam or Hamburg.[27] This aloofness could not survive the decline of the Sephardim. In 1745 the two communities held a joint conference on problems in the provision of kosher meat. In 1751 they exchanged letters agreeing to repress any attempt at the making of proselytes and to punish any offending member with the withdrawal of burial rights and 'all other privileges appertaining to the Jewish religion'. In 1760–1 this collaboration moved towards a quasi-statutory character: 'Whenever any publick affair should offer', the Sephardim resolved, 'that may interest the Two Nations We will on our part communicate to the Committee of the Dutch Jews synagogues what we think proper should be done And that we desire the said Gentlemen may do the same.' The combined body of 1761 included two *senhores deputados*, who had been active in earlier interventions – Benjamin Mendes da Costa and Jacob de Moses Franco.[28]

In the meantime nothing could halt the inflow from Ashkenazi centres elsewhere – from Holland, the German states (particularly from the southern and western), Bohemia and Poland. No more for Ashkenazim than for

Sephardim were the streets of London paved with gold, as we shall see. They possessed, however, an irresistible 'pull' factor compounded of their freedom from at least the grosser forms of antisemitism and their capacity to offer a wider range of economic opportunities. The 'push' factor was a function of the deteriorating conditions for the poor in central Ashkenaz and anti-Jewish outbreaks in Poland, in the late seventeenth and even more in the eighteenth century. For the young bachelor, 'push' came also from the imposition of population control and limits on the marriage of younger sons in Prussia, Bohemia and Moravia and some of the German states. Of those immigrants who settled in Plymouth in 1745 and after, 30 were aged between 20 and 26, and almost all the rest 16–19 or 27–30. This breakdown shows the effect of population control and restriction on the formation of separate households in forcing young men to emigrate in quest of marriage and livelihood.[29] In 1695, it is fairly reliably estimated, the London Askenazim numbered 255. This total grew at a tremendous pace – to some 6000 by 1730–50.[30]

The uninterrupted Ashkenazi influx made London the most populous city in the whole Jewish world (apart from Prague). The Ashkenazi leaders made certain modest efforts to halt the inflow. In 1766 two parnassim of the Great Synagogue, Naphtaly Franks and Naphtaly Hart Myers, both American-born, petitioned the government to remove the facilities for free immigration offered by Post Office packet boats. The lord mayor at the same time offered free passes to any poor Jew desirous of returning to his native land. In 1771 free passages on the mail boats ceased altogether. These measures had little effect.

In the best of circumstances this influx of culturally distinct, impoverished Jews would have created severe social problems. In the particular context of late seventeenth- and early eighteenth-century London, the absence of communal welfare bodies or synagogal infrastructure exacerbated the distress. The first establishment of premises for worship in the London 'ghetto', in or about 1690, was apparently located in the large upper room of a house.

The influence of Hamburg largely determined the character of the nascent Ashkenazi community. If the Sephardi community was an offshoot of Amsterdam, the Ashkenazi was an offshoot of Hamburg. The early benefactor of the community was born in Hamburg, Benjamin Levy. He was a prosperous merchant, and wealthy enough to be allowed to join the Sephardi congregation. He was later admitted as one of the 12 Jews licensed to operate as a broker on the Royal Exchange. Levy was a subscriber to the Bank of England, held shares in the East India Company and was also a member of the Royal African Company. About 1695, the Ashkenazim founded a Burial Society (Hevra Kadischa) and Levy was instrumental in acquiring the ground required for a cemetery. This was contiguous with the Sephardi cemetery. The first rabbi came from Hamburg, R. Judah Leib b. Ephraim Anschel Cohen, and the congregation followed the Polish and north German rite as observed in Hamburg.[31]

R. Abraham (known as Reb Aberle), also a leader of the new congregation, was a son of one of the Hamburg parnassim. He was a wealthy overseas trader and dealer in precious stones, renowned also for his learning. The scholars and teachers of the community came from Ashkenazi centres in Moravia, Pinczow (Poland) and Posen, and one from Amsterdam. Moses Hart from Breslau, Benjamin Levy's kinsman and eventual successor as virtual Ashkenazi leader, initiated and financed the construction of what became known as the Great Synagogue, in Duke's Place, in the City of London. The official opening took place in 1722. Here too, the Polish and North German rite, as observed in Hamburg, prevailed.[32]

'The Great' was not the only Ashkenazi synagogue established in London. Despite every effort to maintain its unique status, it could not prevent the establishment of another congregation. The Ashkenazim were prone to division and variety in way that markedly contrasted with the control that the Sephardi authorities exercised. David Kaufmann talks of 'a faction-split communal life'.[33] Of course, this is in part due to the sheer number of Ashkenazi newcomers as compared with the fairly static corpus of Sephardim. Reb Aberle, described by Kaufmann as 'the tyrant of the community', certainly tried to enforce, on pain of *herem*, any secession from 'his' congregation, and he did prevail on the rabbinical court to forbid the establishment of any separate *minyan*. This proved impossible to uphold. An opponent of Reb Aberle, a certain Mardochai Hamburger, took the lead in the secessionist movement and used a disputed decree of divorce issued by Reb Aberle's chosen rabbi as his weapon. This decree was conditional and had been issued in secret to a heavily indebted member and incorrigible gambler who hoped to escape his creditors by fleeing to the West Indies. A sentence of absolute *herem* (the so-called '*herem* of Rabbenu Tam') was imposed on Hamburger and the tangled conflict that now ensued involved the Mahamad, the Court of Aldermen of the City of London and the rabbinical courts of Amsterdam, Rotterdam and Altona. Hamburger emerged vindicated and in 1707 in defiance of the London leadership and its prohibition of the establishment of other congregations, he opened a synagogue in his own house. He engaged as rabbi his former teacher, R. Johanan Holleschau, who had studied at Nikolsburg in Moravia and was one of the original scholar-teachers of the community. This new foundation came to be known as the Hambro' synagogue and from 1725 occupied permanent premises in Fenchurch Street in the City of London. Holleschau, who witnessed much of the whole episode at first hand, combined his appreciation for the incorruptibility of the English judiciary and the generous treatment of the Jews in England with condemnation of certain lax practices current in Anglo-Jewry, especially its prevailing anarchy: 'they do not have a mentor, guardian and ruler ... and afflict each other in a way such as is not to be found in all the cities of Israel'.[34]

The membership of the Great Synagogue consisted largely of printers, pen- and pencil-makers, diamond-polishers, tailors, watchmakers, painters, hatters, butchers and poulterers. Wolf Liebmann, grandson of the Berlin court-Jew Jost Liebmann, founded the Westminster synagogue in 1760. Here were represented what its historian calls 'luxury trades such as high-class tailoring, jewellery, gold-embroidering for military and court uniforms; callings such as portrait-painting, engraving, antique-dealing and the like – all those are found among the early Jewish settlement'. These men were merchants, artisans and shopkeepers. When the synagogue moved to new premises in 1797, a jeweller, button-dealer, auctioneer, mercer, sealing-wax maker, salesman and embroiderer figured among the signatories to the lease.[35]

Less formal bodies for worship constituted themselves in attachment to the Great and Hambro synagogues. Sometimes, as quasi-adjuncts to these synagogues, individuals formed study circles. 'About eight years ago' (that is in the 1760s), Levi Nathan, an old-clothes man from Hamburg, wrote in his autobiography, 'one Mr. Mordicai Mordicai and myself formed a society, for the benefit of our own people, in which we used to read the word of God to them, every evening.'[36]

Among the Ashkenazim the structure of religious life closely resembled that of the Sephardim. A 'communal aristocracy' (Roth) of wealthy jewellers, wholesale merchants, stockbrokers and stockjobbers set the tone. This was not conducive to scholarship, at least if the testimony of the two leading Ashkenazi rabbis – R. Hart Lyon (1756–62) and R. Tevele Hacohen Schiff (1765–92) is to carry weight. Both felt themselves isolated amidst alien corn. The recollections and records and activities of the rabbinate confirm that beyond their synagogal role and participation in marriage ceremonies and decisions in matters of personal status, little was asked for. The pattern of conduct required in the synagogue and its very purpose reinforces this argument. Thus, 'divine worship in the synagogue should be so conducted', according to one of the *takkanot* of 1722 governing the Ashkenazi Great Synagogue, 'as to ensure the decorum and devotional feeling so essential to the elevation of the mind and the purification of the heart'.[37]

'In London I had money but no Jews,' Hart Lyon recalled in retrospect. 'In Mannheim Jews but no money. In Berlin no money and no Jews.' He bitterly challenged the priorities of his London congregation: 'instead of gathering in the houses of learning, people go to operas, plays, concerts and clubs'. They had no respect for learning or the learned. He himself, Hart Lyon, had no pupils, 'not even a colleague with whom I could pursue my studies. Even the learned men in the community fail to train their children in the study of the Torah'. 'There is no Talmud Torah for children, and what will be the future of Judaism if this state of affairs continues?' The women were immodest, Hart Lyon continued: the older ones sported wigs and the younger ones décolleté dresses, front and back. Their whole aim was not to appear like daughters of Israel. His pessimism reached its apogee in adding to the denunciation of assimilation, the denunciation of its correlate, a deistic universalism:

> On the one side we claim with pride that we are as good as any of our neighbours ... and we want to be like them and want to make everybody forget that we are Jews. But on the other hand we are too modest and say: we are not better before God than the gentiles, we all come from the same stock, are all descendants of Noah's three sons, and need not keep more than the seven precepts which the sons of Noah are obliged to observe. Know you not that ideas like these are the ruin of Judaism? We must be conscious that we are the chosen people of God, the kingdom of priests, and behave as it behoves Israel, the princes of the Almighty.

R. David Tevele Schiff, who came from Frankfurt am Main, lamented his intellectual loneliness no less than Hart Lyon. 'I have no intercourse with scholars and pupils ... You imagine there is a *kehillah* in London. No! Far from it!' (1780). The next year Schiff seems to suggest in another letter to his brother in Frankfurt that the only laws of concern to the London Ashkenazim related to matters of family life, marital conduct and personal problems. Schiff's correspondence includes reference to couples who went through a form of betrothal before witnesses but without the appropriate blessings. Later they wished to live 'in accordance with the law of Moses and Israel', but could their precedent relationship be overlooked when the time came for a proper betrothal, and could the couple be considered in every respect a 'bridal couple'? Mention is also made of Jewish men who had children by gentile women, had the boys circumcised and brought them up in every particular in accord with Jewish faith and customs, but now the boys wished to enter into a Jewish marriage.[38] In 1781 and 1782 Schiff unsuccessfully sought appointments in Rotterdam and Würzburg. He remained in office in London until his death in 1791. Not until 1802 was a successor appointed. This meant that for more than a decade the major Ashkenazi and Sephardi synagogal offices in London both went unoccupied. Obviously, the disturbed conditions of the contemporary wars with France were largely responsible for this hiatus. Beyond that, all is conjecture. Both in Bevis Marks and Duke's Place members must submit their disputes to the communal leaders for arbitration and not resort to the courts. The rabbi's authority was similarly defined in both places: without the authority of these leaders he could not impose a sentence of *herem*, officiate at a marriage or divorce, or intervene in a private dispute.[39]

This resemblance in structure between the two congregations extended also to the Ashkenazi organs of philanthropy. Bevis Marks had its orphanage and the Great Synagogue its Orphan Charity School under the name Hevra Kadisha Talmud Torah (1732). The early records have not survived; the first detailed information dates from 1788, when its governors were pre-eminently wealthy merchants and bankers. The programme proclaimed that

[T]he committee shall admit into this school as many (German) Jew boys, as they shall judge the funds will allow; the boys shall be instructed in the accustomed manner (under the control and direction of the committee), Hebrew-Reading and writing; also Gemara to such whose capacity will admit; and English-Reading, Writing and Ciphering.

The object was to preserve 'the morals of the boys, that they may become useful members of society'. The boys remained at the school only until the age of religious majority – 13 – when they were normally apprenticed to such craftsmen as tailors, glaziers, watchmakers, pencil-makers and sometimes helped to emigrate to the colonies. The school had a strong vocational emphasis. Towards the end of the century other charities provided for the distribution of bread, meat and coal to the poor; for the support and clothing of orphan boys and girls; and for the education of destitute children between the ages of 4 and 7 or 8. The regulations of the Orphan Charity School stress selectivity in favour of children of 'approved character' who are also required to be 'lawfully begotten'.[40] These institutions served the respectable poor whose offspring would become industrious apprentices, the school defraying the cost of their indentures.

To the overwhelming majority of the newcomers this opportunity was not available, and in any case the school hardly had more than 20 pupils at any one time. Most of the newcomers arrived unskilled and they remained unskilled. Peddling therefore became the principal occupation. So ubiquitous was the Jewish peddler in eighteenth century London and the home counties that the newly founded pottery firm of Minton made him its first figurative porcelain object. The peddler sold an enormous variety of objects – sealing-wax, brushes, writing materials, needles, thread, combs, trinkets, handkerchiefs and foodstuffs such as lemons and spices. The same man peddled hardware at one time and anchovies at another. There is some suggestion that the peddlers 'traded up', as it were – the pencils, combs and sealing-wax at the beginning of the eighteenth century later gave way to bits of jewellery and silverware. There is also a suggestion that Sephardi peddlers specialized in slippers and medical drugs (rhubarb), the Ashkenazi peddlers in old clothes and hats.[41]

Outside London, it was peddlers who were probably instrumental in extending the range of Jewish settlement to the ports of the south and east coast. The more venturesome and successful peddlers settled in the more rewarding areas they worked in. As early as the late seventeenth century it was worth while to produce almanacs or pocket calendars giving dates of the festivals, coach timetables, dates of fairs and market days, addresses of synagogues and their officers, bath-houses and so on. They were first produced in Hebrew and Spanish for the Sephardi peddlers and then in Yiddish for the Ashkenazi. From the beginning of the nineteenth century, the almanacs appeared entirely in English.[42] Perhaps shopkeepers and craftsmen responded to competitive economic pressure in London by transferring their activities elsewhere. Whatever the cause, though London remained overwhelmingly central to Anglo-Jewry, in the 1730s and 1740s tiny provincial communities came into being. By mid-century there were synagogues or at least facilities for worship in Birmingham, Bristol, Dover, Falmouth, Hull, Ipswich, King's Lynn, Norwich, Penzance, Plymouth, Portsmouth and Yarmouth. In port towns the Jewish newcomers formed a commercial link with naval personnel, especially seamen. These traders supplied the seamen with old clothes, slops, trinkets, cheap watches and jewellery. They also functioned as agents who discounted the sailors' wage tickets for cash and goods.[43]

This was another variety of those port-Jews who heeded 'the constant call of the sea'. In this case they were mainly Ashkenazim and this was of political importance in synagogal terms. The expansion of the peddling network helped to make the Ashkenazi 'Great' authoritative in Anglo-Jewry. Events in Portsmouth, the most important Ashkenazi community outside London, are conclusive: the communal ordinances (1766) demanded of members that 'they live in strict accordance with Jewish law'; should a dispute arise among them

> they must not dare to go to the non-Jewish tribunal, but it is to be settled by our congregation. If it should be a hard matter however, then they should bring it before R. Tevele (Schiff) HaCohen, chief rabbi of the Great Synagogue in London.

Only after a protracted quarrel among members, led by the community's German-born mohel, Reb Leib Aleph (Judah Leib), was this decision reached. This divided the community to the extent that a secessionist synagogue was founded; but it only lasted for some twenty-odd years. Other seaport communities such as Plymouth and Chatham also acknowledged Schiff's authority.[44]

In 1753 the controversy over the 'Jew Bill' disclosed an antisemitic dynamic that overwhelmed the government and its Sephardi supporters. Even so, it was in these years that the two branches of Anglo-Jewry developed a closer relationship to the state that verged on patriotism. This would be encouraged by the ideology of the nation-state. The classic formulation of Jeremiah (29:7) continued to prevail, obviously: 'And seek the welfare of the city to which I have exiled you and pray to the Lord in its behalf, for in its prosperity you shall prosper.' But did Anglo-Jewry feel itself to be in exile in the prophet's sense? Did London differ in this respect from north Germany, Bordeaux and Amsterdam where observers such as R. Jacob Emden and R. Moses Hagiz deplored the loss of the sense of exile? Was it not part of Salvador's argument to the Duke of Newcastle in favour of the bill (1753) that thereby the Jews 'will be more closely connected' with the government,

having no connection or tie with other government or state?[45] The awareness of exile is yielding to identification with the state.

This certainly did not signify that either Ashkenazim or Sephardim
refrained from intercession for threatened Jewries elsewhere. In 1744, representatives of both communities jointly petitioned George II to use his influence with Empress Maria Theresa on behalf of the Jews of Prague whom
she planned to expel. In 1766 deputies from the two communities petitioned the Duke of Richmond (one of the secretaries of state) to secure for
the Jews of Port Mahon (Minorca) permission to re-establish a place of worship such as they had enjoyed before the island's capture by France and its
recapture by Britain. Incipient identification with the state emphatically did
not preclude the pursuit of special Jewish interests. But it is also true that
this had to take account of the obligation to patriotism.

In 1757 or 1758 R. Hart Lyon preached a sermon on a novel occasion –
a national service of intercession ordered by George II in the early and fateful days of the Seven Years' War (1756–63). The rabbi warmly commended
the king's decision to call for a service of this particular type for it showed
that he 'acknowledged the First Cause and His providence'. Horses alone
were no guarantee of victory. Jews, above all, were obliged to pray for the
welfare of the king and state: 'for how else can we serve the king under
whose protection we live?' And was not their own welfare bound up with
that of the land where they lived, even though war brought high prices and
economic distress? Hart Lyon drew an analogy between war abroad and
war at home – that is, the inner man. The macrocosm had lessons for the
microcosm:

> Aristotle wrote in his *Ethics* [a mistaken reference to the *Politics*] that war
> is utterly hateful because of its essential nature, killing many people. But
> if it is waged for the sake of a peace for which all citizens hope, then it
> may be praiseworthy.

Similarly, war for the sake of peace must be waged against the impulse to
shave the beard, to engage in forbidden sexual relations, to profane the
Sabbath. Hart Lyon invoked God to protect the king and his ministers, 'give
them respite from their enemies and…may He lead the navy upon still
waters'. The peroration called for the rebuilding of Zion and the reign of universal peace. Services on such occasions now become customary. In 1776
Moses Cohen d'Azevedo, Haham of the Sephardi congregation of Bevis
Marks, called for 'Divine Assistance' to support the armies of George III in
their suppression of the American provinces 'that have withdrawn their
Allegiance and raised a Rebellion against their lawful Prince…' These were
'deluded fellow-subjects', whereas the Jews of England must not weaken in
their allegiance to George III, 'not only as loyal subjects and true Israelites
(whose character has always been in every place of their dispersion, that of

true and faithful subjects to their sovereigns) but likewise as being confor-
mant to what our Holy Law enjoins us'. When George III fell ill in 1788,
R. Schiff celebrated his recovery with a sermon based on a text from Ps. 21:1 –
'O Lord, the king rejoices in Your strength.' There were sermons in thanksgiving for naval successes in 1797 and 1798. Most momentous of all, the
Sephardim and Ashkenazim of England used an identical order of service on
the 14th day of Kislev 5566 (= 5 December 1805) in national thanksgiving
for victory at Trafalgar.[46]

To conjoin 'loyal subject' and 'true Israelite', in the manner of Haham
Cohen d'Azevedo, and to stress their reciprocal confirmation belongs to the
traditional formula of the exilic consciousness. But from its particular context it acquires the ring of genuine patriotism and transcends a time- and
place-bound allegiance and prolongs a sentiment first apparent during the
Seven Years' War. To what extent this applied generally, as distinct from
the moneyed élite, I shall try to determine later (Chapter 11). Within this
limitation, it is clear that the Ashkenazim and Sephardim of England
rejoined fellow-Jews throughout the Continent in creating a synagogue-
based community, largely indifferent to the tradition of exile and the
Oral Law.

10
Expulsion from Prague (1745–8)

In 1744 George II of England received a petition soliciting his intervention with Maria Theresa on behalf of the expelled Jews of Prague. The Ashkenazi leaders of London, Aaron Franks and Moses Hart, were acting jointly with Joseph Salvador of the Sephardim. Their petition was one act in a vast movement of intercession.

A series of measures that aimed to segregate Jew from Christian, to reduce the number of Jews and/or to procure their removal at least from Prague culminated in their actual expulsion. The formation of a Jewish Reduction Commission in the late seventeenth century foreshadowed this policy, all the more so when it was accompanied by a proposal to transfer the Jews' Town from Prague to the village of Lieben, to expel 1337 families of poor and foreign Jews, and to 'freeze' the Jewish population in existing limits. In 1700 there was already talk of introducing a costly marriage licence. An intensification of censorship after a comparative lull further confirmed these portents. Censorship now required priests to attend sermons in the synagogues and included the seizure of literature such as the Talmud. In 1714 the authorities confiscated and burned a large number of copies of the first Frankfurt am Main printing of the Talmud.[1]

In January 1714 a rescript of Emperor Charles VI called into existence a Jewish Commission. The commission had a broad brief to reduce the number of Jews in Prague, limit their economic influence and separate them from the Christian Old Town. A return of the plague later in 1714 effected part of the commission's task in that it reduced the Jewish population to some 7800. The next year the commission went further and reported in favour of a reduction in the number of Jewish families to 620 (equivalent to some 3000 persons). To the Jewish elders would be deputed the task of selecting the wealthy few permitted to remain. The poor, because of their lesser taxable capacity, were to be expelled. In order to forestall any future natural growth and family formation, the commission further advised that the number of Jewish marriages be limited and the formation of a new family be permitted only when an existing family became extinct. The commission justified its recommendations not only in terms of the economic benefits that would accrue to the Christian burghers and craftsmen of Prague through the limitation of their Jewish rivals but also in terms of the supposed hatred of Christianity that Jewish teaching inculcated; this 'reasoning' also led the commission to recommend that Jewish doctors be forbidden to treat the Christian sick, many of whom these doctors were said to have poisoned. Baron Brandlinski of the Bohemian Kammer withdrew from the commission, on fiscal grounds. Serfs also did not have the right to marry, other commissioners pointed out.

The Jewish elders emphasized the harmful fiscal implications of the report. They rejected all the accusations of shoddy goods and shady practices made against the Jewish tradesmen and artisans; refused to accept any diminution in the overall area of the Jews' Town; maintained that the size of its population at 7633 (not including children under 10) was lower than at the end of the Thirty Years' War; and emphasized the value of their contribution to the overall tax burden and the profit that Christians made when they leased their premises to Jewish tradesmen. This report was not implemented, partly because of opposition from the Bohemian Kammer, partly because of bureaucratic cross-currents and partly because of an additional complicating factor introduced at a late stage: a projected extension of the reduction programme from Prague to the Jews in the countryside. In any case, Emperor Charles II confirmed the Jews' privileges in 1719 and this effectively nullified the commission's report, together with any reduction plans.[2]

As it turned out, whatever the emperor's confirmation may have implied, it actually provided no more than a short respite, for in 1726–7 the emperor introduced the *Familiantengesetze* (Family laws). These imposed a fixed quota on the number of permitted families in Bohemia (8541), Moravia (5106) and in Austrian Silesia (119). Limits on the number of Jewish families permitted to settle in any particular location existed already before the *Familiantengesetze* and were specified in local privileges.[3] The new legislation gave systematic extension and imperial support to these precedents and the associated marriage legislation would ensure the preservation of the demographic status quo. This determined that in each family only the eldest son could marry and then only after the death of the father. A younger son could inherit the 'family number' only on the death of an older brother. If a family had only daughters then the family and its 'number' became extinct. The term for marriages contracted in defiance of this law was 'Bodenhochzeit' (ground/earth wedding). These marriages, proclaimed R. Noah Mannheimer in the Austrian Reichstag, 'are sacred before God, if also not before man'. On the pattern of legislation proposed from 1650 onwards, the regime enforced also geographic immobility on the Jews and disallowed settlement in any location where Jews were not living in 1726; it also prohibited Jews from acquiring new residences. A number of censuses ascertained the exact size, location and occupation of the Jewish population, for example in 1724,

1729, 1783, 1793, 1799 and 1811. A quota of families for each location was determined – that for Kremsier being 106, for example.[4]

Pharaonic legislation of this type existed already in Prussia (see above, pp. 136–7). Bavaria and France followed later in the eighteenth century. In 1733 in Mantua (then under Habsburg rule) it was seriously proposed to prohibit marriage to Jews below the age of 30; in Darmstadt in 1757 a demographic *numerus clausus* was introduced. From Bayreuth and Mantua in the south to Halberstadt in the north, community leaders and their members had to engage with these attempts to limit their very survival. When, at the end of the eighteenth century and beginning of the nineteenth a new relationship between the *kehillah* and the state was negotiated, the salience of the freedom of marriage was unmistakable. Only in the broadest outline can the gravity of this policy be suggested. In essence however, by striking at the inviolability of marriage, the state was also striking at an institution indispensable to the preservation of Jewish continuity. The clear inseparability of continuity and marriage is shown in the capacity of marriage as an institution to 'include', as it were, an extra-marital relationship. A married man whose wife proves infertile, or is otherwise incapacitated, is permitted under certain conditions to take a concubine (Hebrew: *pilegesh*) whose children will enjoy precisely the same rights of inheritance and status as his other children, if any. The disenfranchisement or exclusion from communal positions of the unmarried adult male in many *kehillot* (for example Verona, Padua, Jerusalem, Carpentras) confirms the importance of marriage. In the best of cases, bachelors were regarded with suspicion.[5]

In Bohemia and Moravia the legislation had demoralizing consequences for family life, and delayed the age of marriage particularly for the poor. (This was also the case in Alsace.) Where it was disregarded, it increased the number of vagrant families, unattached to any community and with no secure legal existence, poised between beggary and crime. It encouraged the fragmentation of family life, through the emigration of the young, particularly to western Hungary, at an estimated total of 30000 between 1700 and 1800 (and to other more hospitable countries such as Britain). Overall, the legislation, though it will have hampered the growth of the Jewish population, altogether failed to halt its expansion. When the Family laws lapsed in 1848 a census the following year found a total of 75000–76000 Jews in Bohemia as compared with *c.*42000 in the 1720s; for Moravia the corresponding totals are 38000–39000 and *c.*25000.[6] The *Familiantengesetze* compromised between the catholicizing and centralizing policies of Vienna and the opposition of the Bohemian and Moravian estates, concerned for the economy and their income; that is to say, they would go some way towards satisfying Vienna without at the same time depriving landowners of their factors, lessees, intermediaries and agents. This compromise proved unsatisfactory to Empress Maria Theresa who took the policy of reduction and stabilization a stage further and in 1744 initiated the complete expulsion of

Jews from Prague, Bohemia and Moravia. On 18 December 1744 the empress issued an order requiring all Jews to quit Prague by the end of January 1745 and the rest of Bohemia by the end of June; if they failed, the military would be brought into use. Leopold I's expulsion of the Jews from Vienna in 1669–70 served as a precedent.[7]

To expel Jews *en masse* from major urban centres (and even rural areas) was rare but not unknown in the eighteenth century, especially if the affected Jews were poor. To the authorities, whether in Prussia or Alsace, the poor were no more than a burden on the state and therefore had no claims on its tolerance. This argument is best exemplified in Berlin in 1737 and again in Prussia in 1773, after the first partition of Poland. Maria Theresa ordered an expulsion of a different magnitude altogether – of approximately 13 000 Jews from Prague, 40 000 from Bohemia and 20 000 from Moravia.[8] This shocked Jewish diplomacy into action on the widest scale, far exceeding the Viennese precedent. The reason is simple: if not even Prague was safe, 'a mother-city in Israel', with a population of thousands and a history of centuries – then where was? Could any Jew under Habsburg rule feel safe?[9]

To the empress's revulsion at the presence or appearance of a Jew is generally attributed this radical step. 'Her aversion to the sight of a Jew was too great to be concealed,' observed Sir Thomas Robinson, the British ambassador to Vienna,

> when at Pressburg she could not pass from the town to her palace, but through the very street that was thronged by that people, and the first order she gave upon her arrival at Prague the year before last [i.e. 1743], was that no Jew should presume to enter into the precinct of the palace during her residence there.[10]

The atmosphere generated by the War of the Austrian Succession (1740–8) gave cover for the expulsion. Maria Theresa, allied to Britain and the United Provinces, had to defend the indivisibility of the Habsburg territories against Prussia, France and Bavaria. This was not without the Austrian loss to Prussia of upper and lower Silesia. During the campaigns, first the French and Bavarians occupied Prague (1741–2) and then the Prussians (1744). The supposed collaboration of Prague Jewry, and their trafficking with the foreign invaders, provided a pretext to saddle the Jews with the odium of treachery and espionage. The departure from Prague, under French auspices, of R. Jonathan Eibeschütz in 1743, to assume the position of chief rabbi in Metz, gave colour to these allegations.[11] The homage that some of the Bohemian nobility paid to the elector of Bavaria, King Charles VIII, during the Bavarian occupation added to the odium, in view of the *mariage de convenance* that united the noble and his factor, and gave it a political dimension. To some extent the Jews fell victim to the tension between Habsburg centralization and Bohemian particularism.

The Prussian occupation, particularly, exacerbated the animosity of the Christian population and gave rise to further accusations of Jewish treachery and to the Jews' enjoyment of favourable treatment at the hands of the Prussian invader. It was indeed a fact that the Prussian troops protected the Jews from would-be plunderers. Towards the end of 1744 rumours of an impending expulsion, as soon as the Habsburg forces reoccupied the city, were circulating in the press. When the Prussians did evacuate the city in November, the first threat of disaster became real in the form of an anti-Jewish outburst. The mob killed some 20 Jews in Prague and injured many more. From his residence in Munich, Wolf Wertheimer, son of the Viennese court-Jew R. Samson Wertheimer, was already in touch with relations and colleagues in Vienna, rebutting allegations of Jewish treachery and seeking an audience with the queen and her ministers. The Prague leaders sent their own envoy, Samuel Koref, to Vienna, for the same purpose. He was still en route when news reached him of the edict of expulsion in the form of a rescript to the royal governors in Prague. The rescript gave no reason for the expulsion, merely declaring that 'the most compelling causes' had persuaded the queen that 'henceforth no Jew shall any longer be tolerated in our hereditary kingdom of Bohemia'. By 31 January 1745 all Jews must quit Prague; those unable to settle their affairs by then could remain in the environs until 30 June 1745, with permission to enter Prague by day for business reasons (but not stay overnight); by 30 June 1745 all the Jews of Prague must quit Bohemia; by the same date must all Bohemian Jewry likewise leave. Maria Theresa charged the vice-president of the royal Bohemian Kammer, Count Philipp von Kolowrat, with the execution of the decree and assured him of any necessary military assistance. In the event, the end of January became the end of February and then the end of March; otherwise the decree took effect as intended.

On no account did this policy enjoy the support of many of the queen's advisers. Before the rescript was made public, Chancellor v. Kinsky of Bohemia wrote in opposition, on grounds of humanity and economics: not only was the expulsion precipitate, not only did it deny Christian values, but it was over-comprehensive, since although there was a case for the expulsion of the poor who made no contribution to the state and, he added, lived by deceit, the economic activity of the Jews earned foreign currency for the state and furthered internal trade. Some Jews should in limited numbers be favoured with special privileges, as in Vienna.[12]

The Bohemian nobility had long challenged the centralizing policy of the empire. During the first Silesian war of 1741, Bohemian nobles had rendered homage to the Bavarian Elector Charles Albert (Emperor Charles VII) at the time of his short-lived occupation of Prague; and from the first intimation of the expulsion Bohemian institutions had shown their hostility (the *Statthalterei*, Bohemian *Hofkanzlei* and the Estates). The protest of the *Statthalterei* of 31 December 1744 included in fact verbatim extracts from the protest of the Jewish leaders. The queen's policy of expulsion came to appear to the nobility as further Habsburg encroachment on Bohemian noble wellbeing. It threatened not only the profitable operation of their holdings but also the state's revenue. The protest of the *Statthalterei* did not fail to remind the empress that the Jews bore one forty-fifth of the total tax burden in Bohemia, not to mention their annual supplement of 12 000 florins; that some of their tax payments were outstanding and these the conditions of exile would make it impossible to collect; that the community and private persons were indebted to private (Christian) creditors for substantial sums. The *Statthalterei* did not take up the cause of the poor majority with whose expulsion it undertook to cooperate to the extent of offering armed assistance, but only that of the wealthy and men of affairs. In July and August 1745 further memoranda pointed to the loss occasioned by the rupture of commercial and credit relations between, on the one hand, the lessees of the breweries, distilleries and so on. and the dealers in wool, feathers and cattle, and, on the other, the foreign and home purchasers of these agricultural products. To such vulnerable partners who would extend credit or have dealings with?[13]

'The whole ministry is most certainly against the manner of the present proceedings, yet nobody seems to be against the necessity of coming to some sort of regulation or other', reported Sir Thomas Robinson, British ambassador to Vienna. Where her revenue was concerned, Maria Theresa might well 'affect an absolute indifference'. But, Robinson added, 'there is hardly a man of estate in Bohemia and Moravia, who will not suffer greatly in his private economy'. These 'men of estate' were not isolated; early in January 1745 the Saxon-Polish government intervened on behalf of the Leipzig merchant body; the Nuremberg town council swiftly followed.[14]

Desperate pleas for intervention to avert expulsion came from Prague; from the community president and rabbi of the Klaus synagogue, for example, R. Samuel Lasch. On the 18th day of Tebeth (5)505 (= 23 December 1744) he wrote of this 'unbelievable' misfortune to his relation R. Eisik, rabbi of the *kehillah* of Schwabach (Bavaria):

> Now, you, brethren and children of the exile, whom God has spared in Ashkenaz, on you falls the duty of deliverance and help, of aiding us in the time of affliction, and of trying to obtain appeals from mighty princes to the court of the Queen, from princes in the Netherlands where many are indebted to us, from the Prince Elector [i.e. archbishop] of Mainz, and the Prince of Würzburg for intervention in our behalf to delay the date of expulsion for some months.[15]

Wolf Wertheimer, resident in Augsburg, son of the late Viennese banker and court-Jew Samson Wertheimer, and himself chief court factor to the emperor, took a forceful part in the campaign. Wolf Wertheimer was all the better equipped to do so; not only had he further developed the house's banking contacts from 1709 onwards but he also had a son resident in Vienna, Samuel, who kept his father *au courant* with Habsburg policy. Hardly was the edict of expulsion issued than on 28 December Wolf Wertheimer wrote to his brother-in-law in Bamberg, R. Moses Loeb Kann, head of the yeshivah in Frankfurt-am-Main and court factor to the Archbishop of Mainz. He advised Kann to intervene with the Archbishop, with Tobias Boas, the Sephardi banker of The Hague (to whom Wertheimer was also related), with George II of England:

> And yet a third thing [Wertheimer added in his letter to Kann], would it not be advisable to make all efforts to obtain a letter of intercession from the lord Pope [Benedict XIV, 1740–58], which could be done in the best and shortest way if the famous community of Frankfurt were to send an emissary to him?

R. Jonathan Eibeschütz of Metz was in contact with the Roman community, to the same end.[16] Kann replied to Wertheimer that letters had been despatched to Rome, to Turin and to the Sephardi and Ashkenazi communities in London, Amsterdam and the Hague. Vienna was silent, Kann complained, with the singular exception of Baron Diego D'Aguilar, the converso.[17]

The Estates-General in Holland and the British government, allies of Maria Theresa in the continuing War of the Austrian Succession, conducted a strictly diplomatic offensive through their respective ambassadors in Vienna, Baron Barthold Burmania and Sir Thomas Robinson. In Robinson's case the initiative came ultimately from Aaron Franks and his father-in-law Moses Hart, both wardens of the Ashkenazi Great Synagogue in London. Their connections, as fashionable jewellers and government financiers, merited an audience with George II. (Appeals reached Hart from Innsbruck, Hanover and Frankfurt am Main.) Joseph Salvador, also a government financier and later the chief protagonist of the 'Jew Bill' of 1753 (and relative of D'Aguilar), represented the London Sephardim (who collected £843 in relief funds). The sole exception of major importance was Berlin. This was deliberate: Maria Theresa could hardly be expected to listen to any intervention that emanated from the capital of her sworn Prussian enemy. Jewish leaders also attempted to use the South German press, through the insertion of sympathetic reports.

In the first few weeks of January 1745 appeals reached Vienna from most centres, Ashkenazi and Sephardi, in the form of a diplomatic *démarche*, or a personal, private missive. The Archbishop of Mainz, the Hamburg Senate, the Venetian Senate, Maria Theresa's mother and grandfather, the court at Dresden and the Danish king – all interceded in favour of Prague Jewry. Pope Benedict's letter reached Vienna at the end of March:'and although it is not for us to care for the affairs of the Jews, We nevertheless, out of neighbourly love, commend this also to your Majesty that they be not expelled in so hasty a mood.'[18] In April 1745 the Sultan's emissary also arrived in Vienna.

By 23 February 1745 some 6000 Jews had left Prague; by the end of the month more than 14000. The children and the sick were not spared the expulsion, amidst an exceptionally severe winter – 'a fearful sight', observed the rector of Prague university. In the morning of 31 March 1745 the communal leaders locked the synagogues, schools, town hall and assembly hall and in the afternoon they handed the keys over to von Kolowrat. Apart from a small number of pregnant women and the infirm and those deputed to care for them, and the exceptionally favoured family of the army supplier Markus Löwi, those Jews still remaining in Prague now left. About 1000 were dispersed among friends and relatives in existing Jewish communities in the countryside. The remainder, numbering at least 10000, did not move far from Prague but found some sort of shelter in neighbouring villages and towns, living in stables, barns and attics. Some small towns were suddenly flooded with Jews, for example Brandeis where *c.*2000 assembled, including many of the former communal leaders, and neighbouring Celakowitz, where some hundreds formed a Jewish quarter.

On 8 April 1745, Maria Theresa ordered the Jews of Moravia to prepare for their exodus at the end of June 1745. At this very time the cost of the state of exile began to show itself, for in mid-April, only two weeks or so after the final exodus from Prague, two families and their respective entourage were permitted to return to the Jews' Town: the families of Markus Löwi and of the widow of Herz Pisek, both of whom worked as army suppliers and whose services were now required. This was the prelude to a sensational volte-face: on 15 May 1745 a rescript radically modified the expulsion order of December 1744, proclaiming that 'for a further period' the Jews could be tolerated; 'in manifold ways' they were involved in credit operations with the inhabitants that could not be settled by 30 June 1745 – 'consequently the required removal would cause the most suffering to the Christian inhabitants of the country'.[19] From the Jews of Bohemia and Moravia this took away the immediate threat, but it did not mean that those expelled from Prague could return.

What brought about this significant relief? So deep-rooted was the queen's aversion to her Jewish subjects that sympathetic ministers to whom Jewish leaders in Vienna (for example the converso Baron d'Aguilar) had access could not approach her with their memoranda, still less could any Jewish envoy;[20] and it was certainly not Jewish diplomacy of the type embodied in the appeals and petitions to sympathetic personages and members of the queen's family. As early as February 1745 Samuel Wertheimer in Vienna complained to his father in Augsburg:

> There is no co-ordination of the efforts…the delegates from Prague are
> themselves confused in their interventions…You will hear a thousand

opinions at every meeting... Everybody keeps his activity a secret, as if it were a business and is afraid that the other may frustrate his steps.[21]

Later research has indeed reinforced the impression of unrewarded effort that was not only uncoordinated but also ineffective. Writes one historian: 'The scope of the foreign interventions and their influence on the fate of those expelled is as yet but little clarified... so far as the Viennese and Prague archives make clear these interventions had hardly any influence on the decisions of Maria Theresa.'[22]

More plausible, and in the present state of knowledge more persuasive, is the argument that a fortuitous twist to the international situation gave Wolf Wertheimer a favourable opportunity to influence the queen. From February 1745 onwards, in the context of efforts to avert the expulsion from Moravia and Bohemia, negotiations to achieve an accommodation between Austria and a previously hostile Bavaria were under way. The two powers conducted their negotiations, in which the major European states also participated, in Augsburg and nearby Füssen, and Augsburg was of course the residence of Wolf Wertheimer. This assembly followed the death of the Holy Roman Emperor, the elector of Bavaria, and this presented Maria Theresa with an opportunity to recover the imperial crown for her consort. These negotiations ended on 2 May with the signature of a treaty of peace. Barely a fortnight later, the queen postponed indefinitely the expulsion from Bohemia and Moravia. Is there any connection between these two events? Given Wertheimer's earlier actions on behalf of Bohemian Jewry it is inconceivable that he would have failed to exploit the opportunity and not continued to press their case on the assembled diplomats, with many of whom he had had financial and diplomatic dealings. The virtual absence from Wertheimer's papers of any documentary evidence that would confirm any such activity is neither here nor there – this was the sort of *démarche* that might well not lend itself to written record.[23]

The exiled Jews of Prague enjoyed no relief from that granted to the Jews of Bohemia and Moravia. The Christian population was indeed under instructions not to harass or molest the Jews and to make cheap shelter available, but some landowners refused the Jews entry to their properties, and in other cases (for example in the royal mining town of Görkau) Jews were forbidden to observe the Day of Atonement or the festival of Tabernacles in the house of a local coreligionist: the town enjoyed the privilege of not tolerating a synagogue, the magistracy argued. In Karlsbad where, in the autumn of 1745, 66 exiles – later reduced to six families – found refuge, the Bohemian *Statthalterei* forcefully insisted that if it were to tolerate the exiles a similar privilege would not be infringed, especially as the onset of winter made the departure of women and children not 'fitting' (*nicht füglich*). Not all were so fortunate – in December 1746 there were still many 'without shelter, hundreds of poor people are wandering from town to town, from village to village ... many die in the carriages, many die on the roads', before they could reach hospital.[24]

Those Jews who found refuge in the vicinity of Prague were able to maintain some sort of trading relationship with the city by daily visits, and sometimes they illegally spent the night in the city; otherwise, with the exception of the Sabbath, it was a question of leaving the countryside each morning early, on foot or with a loaded wagon, and returning late, with articles for consumption on the land. The authorities protected this trade – not so the Prague traders. Their harassment of the Jews drove the latter to protest again and again. In any case a new rescript of 20 June 1746 sharpened the conditions of expulsion and severely hampered this trade, by requiring all Jews to quit towns within a two-hour radius of Prague by the end of July 1746. A new exodus now took place, not so terrifying as the first, for it was summer not winter, and the Bohemian *Statthalter* succeeded in reducing the number of prohibited towns to 25.[25] To the worsening conditions of the exiles in the countryside this brought no lasting benefit. The hospitals in Brandeis and Wolschan could not cope with the sick, and serious disputes flared up among the Jewish leadership. In the Jews' Town buildings were deteriorating through neglect; looters and pillagers were rife.[26]

Against this background, Maria Theresa performed another volte face – this time a volte face that could seriously herald an end to the expulsion from Prague. She now decreed, in August 1746, so complex were the commercial dealings of Jews and Christians that only a phased annual expulsion of the Prague Jews from Bohemia would be possible. She projected a six-year period at the expiry of which 'no Jew would it be possible to find in the kingdom of Bohemia'. The new programme of a phased expulsion sharply divided the Jewish leadership: would it mean the mere prolongation of their suffering, or would this very prolongation not offer the chance for time and events to make yet further extension possible? Salomon Koref took the latter view, which proved correct but not until the summer of 1748. In the interim he had more immediate demands to meet and in May 1747 won permission to impose on the exiles a head tax to provide medical attention and facilities for the sick and poor. Koref also acquired the right to use remaining communal funds for this purpose. The leadership had entrusted Koref with the task of representing the exiles to the authorities and the administration of the Jewish hospital. In this capacity he enjoyed the confidence of v. Kolowrat, president of the expulsion commission, who supported Koref in his attempt to raise funds. Not all acquiesced – among others the wealthy Fränkel brothers, David and Israel, refused – maintaining that Jewish law prohibited an individual from handling communal funds.[27]

What was it that persuaded the queen to substitute a phased expulsion for an immediate expulsion? There is little doubt that the economic factor was decisive. The guilds were prominent in specifying the losses caused by the absence of the Jews as suppliers or consumers. By the autumn of 1747 the guilds of Prague's Old Town, New Town and *Kleine Seite* almost as one man came to regret the expulsion. They had earlier given it welcome. Now, in the third year of the expulsion, in a questionnaire completed by the masters of 61 guilds, the overwhelming majority expressed dismay at the loss of business following the expulsion. Only the merchants argued against the return of the Jews and some were indifferent (for example waggoners, pewterers).[28]

More compelling as an economic factor was the influence of the landed nobility. From the outset the *Statthalterei* had opposed the expulsion and in some degree sought to mitigate its sufferings. This was very much the reaction that Sir Thomas Robinson, the British ambassador to Vienna, had foreseen from those whom he called 'men of estate' (see above, p. 172). To the Jewish leadership also this factor was no less familiar. 'The greatest income of the higher classes comes from the Jews ... the subsistence of the public, especially commerce, depends upon them', Wolf Wertheimer wrote to Moses Hart (London) in December 1747. The estate-owners in Moravia, through Count Leopold v. Dietrichstein, according to Wolf Wertheimer, were the first who 'put a halt to the expulsion and reminded everyone that their main revenues came from the Jews.'[29]

This factor determined the issue. Diplomatic intervention, no matter how high the level, could not rival the cumulative effect of the impetus that the hundreds and thousands of lessees, stewards, peddlers, moneylenders, brewers, distillers and factors gave to the manorial economy and persuaded the landed nobility of the necessity of the Jewish presence.

In the spring of 1748 at a conference in Prague the Estates made their agreement to raise their contribution to the military budget for the following decade dependent on the return to Prague of the exiles, 'also [that] those Jews in the countryside were to continue to be tolerated'. The complete expulsion of either would be most damaging to the country. The Estates would otherwise not meet the financial demands made of them. If needs be, the Estates would be content with the return of at least 500–600 of the wealthier and more industrious families, each of whom would be made responsible, at their own expense, for securing the departure of three or four of the poorer families. In later negotiations between Vienna and Prague, Salomon Koref had some sort of contact with the Bohemian delegates who pressed the case for the return of some 600 wealthy families, made subject to an appropriate tax assessment. In order, however, to arrest an immoderate increase in the size of the Jewish population, the delegates made two proposals: first, let only one son in each tolerated family be allowed to marry in the country; second, let the existing expulsion commission be entrusted with the gradual removal of the non-tolerated Jews.[30]

This was the message that Count Haugwitz, the queen's plenipotentiary to the Estates, had to return to Vienna with. It was simply out of the question to drive the Jews over the frontier by force, he informed her; this could lead only to complications with neighbouring states, who would, in any case, refuse the Jews entry. With a reference to the teaching of Sts Augustine, Thomas Aquinas and Bernard of Clairvaux, the Bohemian delegates sweetened the pill and sought to dissipate the queen's religious scruples. Had not all three saints argued that the toleration of the Jews was required, so that 'they might remain among us Christians as witnesses to the Old Testament and its prophecies and divine wonders'. Had not the pious emperor Ferdinand II, despite his oath to exterminate all heretics, 'not only retained the Jews but also extended to them sundry privileges?' the delegates asked. Maria Theresa yielded and in July 1748 granted the Jews a 10-year stay of expulsion. This permitted the Jews in Bohemia, Moravia and Silesia to remain *in situ* and those from Prague to return to the Jews' Town. This concession was accompanied by a change in the assessment of the tax burden – from one forty-fifth of all taxes to an annual global total of 300 000 florins.

Jewish leaders in Vienna intently followed these negotiations. On 7 July 1748 at two hours after midnight a messenger brought news of their successful conclusion to R. Simon Wedeles in Brandeis. Two days later they elected plenipotentiaries to represent Bohemian Jewry and negotiate with the delegates from Moravia and Silesia over the apportionment of the tax burden. The Bohemians included Salomon Koref, Israel Fränkel, Abraham Pressburg (former president of the Prague community) and the primator of provincial Jewry, Wolf Bresnitz. Dissensions inside the Bohemian delegation, the precise reason for which is obscure, led to the initial exclusion of Pressburg and Duschenes, 'because they had held themselves aloof during the period of expulsion and thereby disqualified themselves from standing at the head of exiles'.[31]

The formula that determined the tax payable by each of the three communities of Bohemia, Moravia and Silesia on the import of palm branches (Heb., *lulavim*) and citrus (Heb., *etrog*) for the festival of Tabernacles was applicable also to the apportionment of the new tax. Thus, Bohemian Jewry would have borne seven-twelfths of the new tax, Moravian Jewry four-twelfths and Silesian Jewry one-twelfth. The Bohemian delegates vigorously challenged this formula on the grounds that their most important component – Prague Jewry – had suffered far more than any other. It required Maria Theresa's intervention to resolve the conflict; she now insisted on the most rapid return possible, the better to enable the Jews to discharge their tax obligations, 'before the onset of the forthcoming military-year'. The empress also permitted, at the request of the Bohemian Jewish representatives, some 40–50 Jews (but without their families) to re-enter the Jews' Town and serve as guards to prevent further damage. In case of need these guards were promised military assistance.

In order to avert recourse to Christian courts, 36 of the Jewish leaders assembled on 9 August to establish a court of arbitration. This would handle the multitude of claims involving property and inheritances that had accumulated during the expulsion, but not cases involving money-changing operations or bills of exchange. The first group of 101 families re-entered the dilapidated Jews' Town at the end of August and the remainder in groups of 30–50 daily. By mid-September 1748 several hundred families had returned and by the end of the month restoration was virtually complete. The exiles could now resume some sort of normal life among their derelict and sometimes looted homes and synagogues.[32]

Politically speaking, the Jews had their most pressing and urgent task in establishing between themselves and the empress a degree of confidence, for it was the former's alleged lack of patriotism that in the early 1740s had reinforced an existing antisemitism. Some sort of reconciliation did indeed take place – at least to the extent that during the Seven Years' War (1756–63) the Jews were left unscathed, 'handled with velvet gloves', it is said, even though their enemies again accused them of spying and treachery.[33] As a 'bridge-builder' the newly appointed chief rabbi of Prague and Bohemia, R. Ezekiel Landau (1713–93), took a prominent part: hardly had the Seven Years' War broken out than he composed special prayers for an Austrian victory and imposed the *herem* on any Jew who might aid the Prussian enemy and cause harm to 'our most gracious Queen'; the text of both proclamations was issued in German. Landau also introduced sumptuary laws to limit entertainment and attire; in 1767 when Maria Theresa fell ill he called for a public fast and offered thanksgiving prayers for her recovery; on her death in 1780 the Meyzel synagogue in Prague encompassed a ceremonial gathering of distinguished governmental and military figures assembled to hear Landau eulogize the late empress. This sermon too was distributed in a printed German text.[34]

These efforts, in one important respect, had no success. The empress died an unregenerate antisemite who reintroduced the yellow badge that Jews must wear:

> I know no worse plague for a state than this nation, she wrote in 1777, because of deceit, usury and money-lending, bringing people to beggary, all performing evil actions which another honourable person would despise; therefore, as far as possible, they are to be kept away from here [i.e. Vienna] and their numbers reduced.[35]

As I have shown, it was not possible to keep the Jews 'away' from Prague. To Vienna the same applied. Even here, in the capital, the very capital of the Counter-Reformation, a small, select but irreducible settlement of Jews had to be lived with, but at least they were infinitely less prominent than in Prague. An enormous number of imperial decrees, directed at would-be immigrants from Galicia and Hungary, limited the community to no more than 500–600 throughout the eighteenth century.[36]

The Habsburg authorities had to tolerate not only an Ashkenazi grouping but also a Sephardi community. Paradoxical is it that the defeat of the Turks in 1685, to which Oppenheimer's supply system had decisively contributed, brought to Vienna a colony of Jews from Turkey. By virtue of the Austro-Turkish treaty of Passarowitz (1718) and the treaty of Belgrade (1739) these traders, as Turkish subjects, were exempt from the restrictions imposed on the Ashkenazim and enjoyed freedom of settlement, movement and trade. The origin of this Sephardi community belongs to the late 1730s, when the members acquired premises for a house of prayer. Among the earliest members were Naphtali Kamondo from Constantinople, Aaron Nissim, Naphtali Eskenazi, and Aaron Samuel Nissimi. The founder of their congregation as such was a Portuguese converso Diego D'Aguilar (known also as Moses Lopez Pereira), the holder of a Portuguese barony. He left Lisbon in 1722 for London and then moved to Vienna where he joined the Oppenheimer-Wertheimer circle and enjoyed the favour of Charles VI and Maria Theresa. In 1732 he participated with Löw Sinzheim and Samuel Simon Michael (also known as Samuel Pressburger) in raising the loans that saved the Wiener Stadtbank. He advanced 300 000 florins to the empress to construct the palace of Schönbrunn. He was involved in the negotiations in 1743 over the £300 000 in subsidies that Austria had to remit to England where D'Aguilar was represented by his brother, Baron Ephraim, who was married to Sarah Mendes da Costa, a niece of the Sephardi grandee and financial adviser Joseph Salvador. D'Aguilar rendered his main service to the Habsburgs in reorganizing the tobacco monopoly in the 1740s so as to enhance its tax yield to the treasury. In Portugal, with his father, D'Aguilar had earlier functioned in a similar capacity. In Vienna the tax revenue suffered from the large quantities of tobacco imported and sold by the Spanish, French and Turkish ambassadors as well as the Papal Nuncio. This competition was one reason why D'Aguilar returned to London in 1749. He found the toleration tax too high, it is also said, and that the Spanish government demanded his extradition. D'Aguilar died in London in 1759.[37]

The Sephardi Jews and their successors among the Christian population of Vienna were as unwelcome as the Ashkenazim. In the 1760s, at a time when Maria Theresa eagerly projected a new ghetto, the government made no distinction between Sephardim and Ashkenazim; from both must the Christian be protected.[38] However the Sephardi, or 'Turkish Jews', as they now began to style themselves, enjoyed the Sultan's protection. Perhaps the regime also turned a blind eye to their presence; to discriminate in favour of Turkish Muslims and against Turkish Jews would have been virtually impossible. Until 1778 there is, apparently, no documentary evidence to prove the existence of an officially recognized and organized *kehillah* in Vienna. But by then a synagogue already existed and in June 1778 the Habsburg authorities issued regulations determining the government of the *Türkisch–Israelitische Gemeinde*. This document covered the financial responsibility of the congregation, the mode of election to office, and the hours of prayers. The president was required to be able to read and write in German. The general assembly of the Turkish Jews approved these regulations without dissent. The community also established a school where the Bible was taught in German and had its own welfare fraternities.[39]

By no means did the existence of a Sephardi *kehillah* encourage the formation of an Ashkenazi equivalent. Perhaps the very contrary applied. In any event, throughout the eighteenth century the 'Jewish' legislation of Joseph I, Charles VI and Maria Theresa aimed to reinforce or at least maintain the barriers to entry to Vienna. Those Jews who were not deterred – and they came mainly from the outlying eastward areas of the empire – had to resort to any number of devices and subterfuges in order to gain entry; for example they posed as Catholics (complete with rosary) or provided themselves with a Turkish passport or obtained employment with the Venetian embassy. A Jew who did have a temporary permit but which was on the point of expiry could 'kosher himself' – as the phrase had it – by going to the border controls, greasing the official's palm, securing a renewal, at once re-entering the city by another route. This procedure was accepted and recognized and the amount of the bribe a fixed sum.[40]

Some of those who entered Vienna in these devious ways later achieved the status of notables by virtue of their economic enterprise. This applied to the Schlesinger brothers (Markus and Marx), to Adam Oppenheimer, great-grandson of Samuel Oppenheimer, and to a certain Benedict Heybach who had allegedly 'slunk' into Vienna under the protection of the envoy of the Elector-Palatine. An anonymous informer reported these instances to Maria Theresa. Despite all the ingenuity exercised by the Jewish aspirants to entry, the authorities certainly succeeded in limiting the number of Jewish residents: in 1753 they totalled no more than 452 out of an overall population of 175 403.[41]

This was a settlement of some score of wealthy householders with an entourage of servants, employees and clerks surrounded by a floating, marginal and insecure body of Jews who were scarcely tolerated. The indebtedness of the *Staatsschuldenkasse* in 1746 to certain individuals indicates the extent of their wealth: Diego d'Aguilar was a creditor for 157 077 florins; the Israel Arnsteiner estate for 320 092; Leidesdorff for 105 924; and the Löw Sinzheim estate for 110 454.[42] In 1753 a *Judenordnung* limited the economic activities of the Jews to moneylending, banking operations and the jewellery trade. They were instrumental in the great money-changing operation of 1754 when Maria Theresa declared invalid all Saxon coins minted since 1749 and ordered their replacement by imperial specie.[43] At this time, of 57 prominent Jews in Vienna, jewellers and coin-dealers numbered 7, moneylenders and money-changers 33. Of the remaining 17, 2 were visiting rabbis, 1 a tutor in the Wertheimer ménage, 1 a hospital attendant. The rest followed unknown occupations. For the generality of Jews, according to a report (1762) from the *Hofkanzlei* to the empress, poverty was the norm.[44]

Through the instrumentality of the church, this body of Jews was refused a synagogue, had no corporate existence and no legal standing in the state's perspective and lacked perforce the normal communal institutions. This anomaly lasted until 1763 when a group of 76 young Jews from leading families (Wertheimer, Oppenheimer, Schlesinger, Arnstein, Drach, Wetzlar, Eskeles, among others) formed a *Hevrah Kadischah* – a burial society. This was a vehicle – as was customary elsewhere – not only for performing the rites attendant on the burial of the deceased, but also for textual study and general philanthropy. In the particular circumstances of Vienna the *Hevrah* came to resemble a student corporation and such religious obligations as would normally be incumbent on its members (for example the visitation of the sick or the recital of psalms in the house of the bereaved) were discharged by a deputy, or commuted for payment.[45] It is likely that to these young people a member of the Council of State was referring when he noted with dismay 'young Jewish men contrary to all previous custom, now go about in public dressed indistinguishably from Christians, some even with swords at their side'.[46] They were to be found in public places in the company and consort of young Christians:

> Likewise one sees Jewish women and girls dressed little differently from a lady, walking publicly in the company of Christian men and women … Jewish people, indistinguishable from others by their garb, now frequent inns, ballrooms and theatres, and mix with Christians who are there.[47]

The formation of the *Hevrah Kadischah* did not stand entirely isolated as a symptom of change: only the next year a new *Judenordnung* provided for an expansion of the Jewish colony in Vienna. It reiterated many of the existing restriction concerning rights of residence, the number of permitted servants (one coachman and two clerks), the obligation to maintain a household register, the prohibition of any rabbinical jurisdiction or the erection of a synagogue, the ban on leaving house before midday on Sundays or Christian holidays or witnessing a procession of the host, either at street level or from an upper window or whatever. A married Jew or widower must wear a beard as a mark of identity. House-to-house selling was absolutely disallowed. These measures of discrimination and stigmatization were accompanied, however, by provisions that favoured and encouraged the settlement in Vienna of Jews able to pay acceptable tolerance tax, who possessed demonstrable assets in cash and paper, and who also could 'undertake to be of value to the common weal especially by way of establishing factories (in which however the work force is always to be Christian)'. This *Judenordnung* did not confer any heritable right to settlement. The son or daughter of any tolerated Jew in the event of marriage, and the establishment of a separate household, must secure an individual privilege or quit Vienna. Also in 1764, and after some two years' debate, the government allowed Jews to deal in domestic goods, thereby enabling them to dilute their existing specialization in the money trade.[48]

Two of the Viennese magnates – Adam Isaak Arnstein and Leib Isaac Leidesdorf – tried to turn this economic opening to political advantage. They raised the issue of corporate representation, protesting that they lacked the right to form a community such as the Jews of Bohemia and Moravia enjoyed.[49] They did not succeed in these precise terms but the protesters did at least have some part in thwarting the project for the establishment of a 'third ghetto'. This was a project dear to the heart of the empress; and to certain government organs 'a greater degree of decency' required that the privileged and tolerated Jewish families 'had no cause to dwell among Christians from whom they should, so far as possible, be segregated'.[50]

Departments and officials exchanged protracted *mémoires* and memoranda over some five years but no third ghetto came into existence. Practical reasons made it impossible to recreate in the Leopoldstadt or elsewhere a ghetto for the 594 Jews then estimated to be living in Vienna. This inability had another dimension in the position held not only by the Viennese magnates but also by their Bohemian counterparts, for example the families of Hönig, Dobruschka and Popper, who were all participants in one or other of the state monopolies (tobacco, salt). In Vienna the Arnstein family and Karl Abraham Wetzlar took the lead.[51] They were prominent not only in the operation of the tobacco lease but also in banking and military provisioning. In 1768 the Arnsteins threatened to quit Vienna for Holland if they were forced into unwelcome accommodation and also if they were not released from collective liability for the rent payable by Jewish tenants to their Christian landlords. In the end the empress had to give way.[52]

In 1776 the Jewish population of the province of Lower Austria, including Vienna, totalled 337. When Maria Theresa died in 1780 the 50 or so families in the capital accounted for 'perhaps 570 family members and servants'.[53]

In Prague reduction and expulsion gave way to readmission. When their next trial came, Habsburg Jewry had to face not exclusion or expulsion but almost its contrary, their very integration into state and society. The empress's successor and former co-regent, Joseph II (r. 1780–90), initiated a policy of social engineering designed to germanize his Jewish subjects. To the Habsburg–Jewish relationship this brought renewed tension. In pitting himself against the emperor, Chief Rabbi Ezekiel Landau had to fight to make the new policy acceptable.

11
The Old and the New *Kehillah*

The abortive expulsion of the Jews from Prague, Bohemia and Moravia has a significance beyond the local: its demonstration, not of the diplomatic backing that the Jews could command, but of the empress's isolation throughout Europe and no less of the appreciation they enjoyed in landowning circles points to a turn in their status. This is not to be exaggerated – expulsions from Prussia took place after the partition of Poland in 1773. Even so the events of 1744–8 suggest that in the stability of the Jewish settlement in central and western Europe (first noted about 1600) a further stage has been reached – so much so that the mid-eighteenth century can be regarded as a vantage point to suggest those features that mark the transition from the old *kehillah* to the new.

From Prague to London, from Danzig to Trieste, traversing multitudinous hamlets, villages, townships, or the seafaring centres of Sepharad; in and out of the ghettos and *carrières* and *Judengassen*, an old world is dying and a new one coming to light. This new world is long in the making in its evolution towards a modified *kehillah*.[1] This institution, its leadership, its powers, its claim to loyalty, its prestige are increasingly called into question and in many instances found wanting. Given the variety of circumstances in which the Jewries of central and western Europe find themselves, no uniformity of process is to be expected. But it is possible to discern, without overmuch simplification, symptoms of disintegration and change at the level of rich and poor.

Poverty on a mass scale comes increasingly to mark Jewish society in the eighteenth century. This is the major factor that subjects the *kehillah* to unbearable strain and makes it incapable of sustaining its inherited role. The eighteenth century was in any case marked by widespread poverty in France, the Habsburg empire and the German states. The Jewish case was no different, though the causes would differ. In Holland, when the political economist, Isaac de Pinto, asked himself why the Jews were so poor, he had no doubt that the answer was to be found in their exclusion from public life, agriculture and the skilled labour of the guilds. This situation, no less than restrictions on trade, prevailed throughout the eighteenth century. Not without a certain sardonic humour do the archives of Worms, among the oldest *kehillot* in Ashkenaz, retail the community's unremitting fight with merchants and guilds. The Jews were dealing in leather, complained the tanners in 1705. (But this their imperial privileges permitted, came the riposte.) In 1717 the shoemakers complained that the Jews were selling new shoes in public; the tailors would only agree to Jews selling new clothes made by Worms craftsmen. The bakers complained that a Jew was dealing in grain, infringing their ancient right. The Jews must not deal in buttons made of gold, silver, tin or horn, demanded the button-makers. The coopers would not tolerate Jews trading in barrels because they were bringing in wine from the countryside to the detriment of the local vintage. In 1757 the shopkeepers protested that Jews were selling tea, sugar and coffee from which they must be debarred; and in any case they must be permitted to sell only in their *Gasse* and except on fair days forbidden to display their goods publicly.[2]

Elsewhere in Ashkenaz, in France, barely did the situation improve when the French authorities took steps to break the monopolistic powers of the guilds. In 1767 a royal decree went some way in this sense and created new vacancies that would also be accessible to foreigners; the Jews of Metz, Thionville, Sarrelouis, Sarreguemines and elsewhere who now hoped, despite fierce opposition, to enter hitherto forbidden occupations engaged an advocate to plead their cause. The same year five Jews from Avignon, born in Bordeaux and who had been living and trading in Paris for 30 years, sought to enter the corporation of merchant mercers through the purchase of *brevets de marchands*, as authorized by the king. The five – Israel Salom, Joseph Petit, Moyse Perpignan, Salomon Petit and Moyse Dalpuget – had been naturalized in 1759, which accorded them the same status as other subjects of the crown. They had always conducted their business affairs '*avec l'exactitude et la probité nécessaire à des commerçants*', according to the authorities. This failed to overcome the intense resistance of the guilds and corporations of Paris and by 1774 the five lost their case against the guilds. The next year, Turgot the newly appointed director of finance, as part of his campaign against the powers of the guilds, reversed this decision. But the intense opposition to his policy forced Turgot out of office in 1776. The Jews could claim a partial victory in that, although refused admission to the mercers' corporation, they retained the right to unhindered trade in Paris.[3]

Familiar also to de Pinto, though perhaps he would not have perceived its full dimensions, was the immigration of poverty-stricken Ashkenazim from the disintegrating kingdom of Poland and the growth of the Jewish population of the West through natural causes. The sponsored migration of the poor could have only a limited effect. At any one time in the eighteenth century a rough calculation has a total of 10000–15000 vagrant Jews from Poland in the German lands, apart from an unspecified number of 'local' Jews.[4] There seems no way of computing the extent of immigration; the increased presence of the Ashkenazi poor in such centres as Amsterdam and London is unmistakable. But demographic decline or stagnation in Bordeaux, Berlin and Metz towards the end of the eighteenth century cannot obscure unusual overall growth. The phenomenon is Europe-wide. The Jewish population in all Europe in the eighteenth century grew from *c.*719 000 in 1700 to *c.*2 million in 1800, it is estimated. In eastern Europe at the beginning of the seventeenth century the Jews of Poland-Lithuania numbered less than a quarter of a million; by 1764–5, *c.*750 000; and by the end of the eighteenth century *c.*1 000 000.[5]

In the German territories the total rose from *c.*25 000 in 1700 to 60 000–70 000 by the 1750s.[6] In Bohemia between 1754 and 1785 the Jewish population doubled – from 21 000 to 42 000; in Moravia and Silesia over the same period it grew from 20 000 to 26 000 (almost 30 per cent).[7]

The sources of livelihood did not expand in proportion to the growth in population; obviously, therefore, from the same limited and static range of occupations ever larger numbers of Jews had to support themselves, so that the effect was to exacerbate all the more the existing level of poverty. Adventitious factors were also at work to depress economic activity, for example the destruction of the Seven Years' War, poor harvests (Hesse, 1760–70); cattle plague (Saar-Moselle area, 1770s). 'Have not the poor multiplied into thousands and hundreds and circulate in all corners', wrote R. Judah Hurwitz (d. 1797) in the 1760s. He was born in Vilna, studied medicine in Italy, and in Berlin attracted the warm sympathy of Mendelssohn.[8] In Mantua, the proportion of communal expenses devoted to the poor grew from 21 per cent in 1686 to 25 per cent in 1757. The number of paupers did not change markedly, but their percentage among the total Jewish population did increase and expenditure on medicines for the poor swelled sevenfold, from 1000 lire per annum in the mid-seventeenth century to 7000 lire per annum half a century later.[9] In Frankfurt am Main, in the mid-century almost one-quarter of the community could not make ends meet or lived on charity. Most of the community, well into the second half of the eighteenth century, lacked means of their own and had a hard struggle to gain their daily bread. In eighteenth-century Paris, despite all the efforts of Péreire to ensure that only communally recommended individuals entered the city, it is clear that a high proportion were poor, if not positively indigent or dependent on charity. Of the 171 Jews in Paris whose decease was officially recorded (1717–89), 77 were children under 3.[10] In Darmstadt, in the early eighteenth century, the Jews were forbidden to shelter vagrants. The latter were assembled in one of the city's squares, given some payment and sent on their way. In Amsterdam, towards the end of the eighteenth century, a stratum of 3000–4000 prosperous Jews had to support 17 000–18 000 paupers; half the Sephardim depended on public assistance. This explains a curious link between Amsterdam and London: to the Dutch Ashkenazi poor, London offered posts as domestic servants for their daughters; Yehudah b.

Isaac Katz of Amsterdam, who is related by marriage to R. Aaron the Scribe of London, asks the latter to keep an eye on his daughter Blimche. She once worked for Joseph Levy, a wealthy Hamburg jeweller settled in London; where she is at present working, the father does not know. Let her be careful with her earnings and not waste them on fancy goods, and 'have something worthwhile in mind, she will not be in service all her life'. Katz also asks: does the rabbi know of a job in London for a second daughter, Breinche, unemployed in Amsterdam, but 'a brave and handy girl and she knows how to work?' A relative, Leiser of Naarden, would also welcome news of a job in London.[11]

It is unlikely that Yehudah Katz's hopes for Blimche and Breinche were realized, still less those for Leiser – simply because London, like Amsterdam, was already home to thousands of impoverished immigrants, despite the efforts made by the Ashkenazi leadership to halt the inflow of newcomers. This was the Anglo-Jewish version of the *Herem Ha-Yishuv*. As I mentioned earlier (p. 159), in 1766 the parnassim of the Great Synagogue, Naphtaly Franks and Naphtaly Hart Myers, both American-born, had petitioned the government to remove the facilities for free immigration offered by Post Office packet boats. The lord mayor at the same time offered free passes to any poor Jew desirous of returning to his native land. In 1771 free passages on the mail boats ceased altogether. These steps had no perceptible effect in mastering what became a major migratory movement. In mid-century the Ashkenazim numbered *c.*6000, by the beginning of the nineteenth *c.*20 000. This indicates, taking account of natural increase, an immigration of not much less than 10 000, doubling the population in no more than half a century. In 1800 there may have been 1000–1500 old-clothes dealers in London. 'A great crowd of dirty ragged people, to the number of some hundreds' confronted an American visitor to London in 1805. 'They appeared to be very busy in displaying and examining the old clothes which they were pulling out from bags.' This was Rag Fair – 'held every evening for the sale of old clothes which are collected all over London, principally by Jews who go about with bags on their shoulders crying with a peculiarly harsh guttural sound "Clothes, clothes, old clothes"'. Joshua van Oven, honorary physician to the Ashkenazi Great Synagogue, conceived the creation of a 'house of industry' that would break the cycle of deprivation and poverty by teaching handicrafts and trades. He proposed that part of the general rates in certain London areas be appropriated to finance the project or a form of Jewish self-taxation introduced. The Sephardim rejected the proposal and in Parliament it languished.[12]

Indigence and hardship in rural areas matched that in major urban centres. In the later eighteenth century Clavé, the bailiff of Altkirch (Alsace), divided the Jewish population in his area into five groups: 35 families were moneylenders and almost all also traded in heavy animals – they were the best able to bear the charges due to the king and the communities;

36 families were engaged in the same trade, made enough to live on and to contribute to tax demands, but much less so than the first; 58 families traded in cloth, Indian (fabrics), silverware, groceries, beds, ink, iron and old clothes; the baker and the six schoolteachers also had enough to live on; there were six butchers and six 'foreign' dealers; in the fifth group of 29 poor families the women knitted, sewed and carded wool and the men ran errands on commission – they were also supported by alms from the communal charity chest. 'The Jewish nation, generally speaking, lives very badly,' Clavé concluded, 'and many of them content themselves the whole day travelling the villages for their trade with a lump of bread, or apples, pears or other fruit in season.' Among the poorest traders were those who dealt in rabbit skins, old bones to make glue, and beehive shelves to make wax with.[13]

The peddlers, ambulant traders and travellers had a special hazard to face – random attack – to which their isolation made them especially vulnerable. Glückel writes of the casual killing of a Jewish traveller by a poacher on the road from Hanover to Hildesheim. The murderer went undetected despite all the efforts of the local community to have the crime investigated; Jews travelling from Vienna to Nikolsburg to celebrate the New Year were robbed and murdered by Polish soldiers (1683); soldiers from Würzburg attacked and robbed a Jewish courier (1723); R. Ezekiel Landau of Prague reports the killing of a peddler on the open road; a Jew was robbed at an inn in Hounslow, near London (1751); two emissaries travelling from Nikolsburg to Brünn were captured and mishandled (1742); a French official in Alsace writes: '*Les Juifs ne peuvent voyager sans courir risque de leur vie, un Juif ayant été depuis peu assassiné sur le grand chemin par des paysans*' (1747).[14]

These circumstances, taken as a totality, intensified the prevailing tendency towards the polarization of Jewish society into a few wealthy and many poor. This showed itself in *kehillot* large and small. In eighteenth-century Metz of the three groups into which the community was divided, the middle group was fading away, whereas the distance between the highest and lowest deepened. At the beginning of the century, three-quarters of the Jews lived from day to day, or on the charity of the better off; at the end of the century the position had barely changed, according to Isaie Berr-Bing. So great was the distress that in 1782 rabbis took the extreme decision to divert to the relief of the local poor funds originally raised for the Jews of Palestine. In the hamlet of Niedenstein in Hesse economic differentiation developed to the extent that by 1809 (when the community consisted of 20 families and 87 persons altogether) 5 of these families controlled seven-eighths of the estimated wealth of all families combined.[15]

The *kehillot* were less and less able to support their own needy members, let alone the 'foreign' poor, who were deterred and kept at bay. Whereas, as a matter of course, they readily supported their own poor, even perhaps, albeit for a limited period, the transient and unaffiliated poor, they could not extend their scanty resources to such persons on any sort of enduring basis. The *herem ha-yishuv* of the medieval period still operated. The Hamburg *takkanot* of 1726 even prohibited 'public collections on behalf of the poor', not even to ransom captives or dower a poor bride (with certain exceptions). In 1746 in Eisenstadt, about 40 miles to the south of Vienna, the communal statutes prohibited any member from giving even a *peruta* to those vagrants who came knocking at their doors, 'shouting abuse and insults'.[16] In 1741 the parnassim of Bordeaux, in receipt of a decree from the Conseil d'État, resolved to expel 68 vagrant Jews at 24 hours' notice, '*sans qu'il leur soît permis d'y rentrer sous quelque prétexte que ce soît, et faute par eux de le faire, il a été convenu que nostre Sindicq et ces adjoints prendront les voyes les plus sévères pour les y contraindre*'.[17]

To Berlin in particular, and to Prussia in general, the authorities, aided by the parnassim, did their best to deny entry to poor Jews. This duty, remember, was a commitment under the original charter of settlement (1671). It could not, in fact, be carried out , either then or later. In the 1770s in Berlin, it is estimated, some 100 residents were in receipt of poor relief; case-studies of the sick and indigent show that 'a whole milieu' of Jews in Berlin were unable to support themselves.[18] At the Rosenthaler Gate to Berlin the community maintained a *hekdesh* for vagrants and the sick. The society for the care of the sick – *Hevrat Bikur Holim* – supervised its operation: the *hekdesh* had been reconstructed in 1753 with a loan from the *kehillah*. Here hopeful entrants to the city could be intercepted and diverted elsewhere if found undesirable. In the 1770s when Solomon Maimon, the philosopher prodigy from Lithuania and exponent of the new philosophy of Kant, arrived at the *hekdesh* he found it full, 'partly with sick people, partly with a lewd rabble'. A Berlin elder cross-examined Maimon, gave him a pittance and sent him on his way. On another occasion, the Jewish police all but chased him out of Berlin. The communities in Berlin and elsewhere, maintained the *hekdesh* more or less exclusively for vagrants; no wealthy or middle-class Jew would seek shelter or medical treatment here.[19]

A most significant measure of the pressure on the resources of the *kehillah* was the limit on the number of marriages it would permit. That the gentile state (French, Austrian, Prussian) imposed a quota on its Jewish population and therefore also a limit on the permitted number of marriages was a familiar eighteenth-century phenomenon, as I have shown, and related to the state's interest in protection from the presence of the poor. If the *kehillah*, the Jewish 'state', imposed such a policy – as some did – the difference was twofold: first, because the limitation was an ad hoc response to an emergency and had no status as policy; second, because it was motivated by a concern for its own financial viability and not by any notion of demographic limitation as an aim of policy. Early examples date from the seventeenth century; in Rome, for example, in 1618 the community would support no more than 12 brides annually; in Brest-Litovsk, Grodno and

Pinsk the Lithuanian council would support 12, 10 and 8 brides respectively per annum.[20]

Much later in the century, indebtedness forced the *kehillah* in Posen to make its approval for a marriage dependent on the level of the dowry (1670); in Lomnitz a bridal couple was required to show a capital of 300 florins, which was considered the minimum amount needed to cover their taxes and to live on; in Halberstadt, in a petition to the Prussian king of 1711, the community claimed that 'bitter poverty' forced it to allow only those couples to marry who had assembled 'a specific dowry' so that the new household would be able to cover its share of the taxes (and not be a burden on an already impoverished *kehillah*). In Berlin a *hevrah* founded in 1721 for the support of poor brides provided dowries, as did private philanthropists such as the banker and communal leader Daniel Itzig, who is reputed to have financially facilitated the marriage of 50 orphans and who also bequeathed sums for this purpose. In Metz in 1750 a couple needed a dowry of 2400 livres before permission to marry was granted. In Hamburg, insistence on the discharge prior to marriage of all taxes and dues served the purpose of population control. As a result, in 1802 Jewish couples accounted for one-seventeenth of all births to unwed mothers, although the Jews formed only one-twenty-eighth of the city's population. This also applied to Berlin and Frankfurt am Main. Another result of the restrictions was a differentiated marriage pattern in Berlin of rich and poor: grooms from the wealthy 'generally privileged' families were on average 9 years younger than those from the less favoured 'extraordinary' families; brides were 5 years younger. There is a later instance where political considerations were invoked to strengthen the case for limiting the number of the poor: in 1808 Elkan Henle, a Prussian notable, who aimed to make Jews 'citizens of the Jewish faith' advised that in order to prevent 'the progressive increase' in the number of the poor, marriage be made dependent on the resources of the intending couple.[21]

In eastern Europe social tension and the decline of authority generated actual outbursts of violence in such centres as Vilna, Opatov, Vitebsk, Cracow and Minsk.[22] To the west violence was apparently rare, but there was certainly no shortage of ugly scenes. Miserable and desperate as was the state of the attached poor, they could at least turn to their respective *kehillot* for some degree of support. But in the late seventeenth and eighteenth centuries unaffiliated Jews and gangs of beggar-Jews and of criminal Jews emerged. In Franconia and Swabia they are said to have been especially numerous.[23] As I have already mentioned, certain *kehillot* (for example Hamburg and Eisenstadt) forbade almsgiving or the unauthorized collection of funds for the vagrants. This was no deterrent. From all parts of the diaspora and throughout the eighteenth century examples of vagrancy abound, from the North Sea to Provence. At Ansbach in 1707 rarely did the communal shelter accommodate fewer than 30–40 beggar-Jews per day; Hamburg in 1721 was visited by 700–800 beggar-Jews in a period of four months, moving in groups of 10, 15 or 20, according to a contemporary observer. In 1763, 1773 and 1775, reports from Avignon, l'Isle-sur-Sorgue and Carpentras speak of groups of destitute Jews roaming the streets, begging for alms, turning belligerent when refused. At Carpentras (1775) the *baylons* of the *carrière* appealed to the local Christian authorities for their aid in 'protecting the persons and goods' of the Jews of the town. Carpentras already had enough poor of its own: of the population of about 1000 in 1789, 240 were paupers dependent on communal support.[24] In 1769 the inhabitants of Gross- and Kleinenglis petitioned their leaders to dispatch to neighbouring Fritzlav those beggar-Jews sent to them on carts; here there was no support for them, they argued, whereas Fritzlav had three nearby localities to help. The Metz community in 1772 requested additional guards at the ghetto entrance to prevent an influx of the rural poor.[25] About one-third of the Jews living *c.*1780 in the territories of the electorate of Cologne had no *Geleit* to validate their residence. Quite a number came from Moravia and Bohemia, in flight from the Pharaonic family laws.[26]

Not only did the Jewish authorities exclude the beggar-Jews from their domain – the same goes for gentile rulers. Nobody wanted the beggar-Jews. They are shunted from one *kehillah* to the next, their life a veritable 'dance of death'.[27] The consequence was sometimes a descent into criminality. It is not without a degree of reason that precisely at this time the antisemitic stereotype of the Jew as criminal flourishes. Wrote one contemporary Christian observer in 1783 (probably Christian Wilhelm Dohm):

> As soon as a Jew through some mischance loses his capital then he has only the choice – either to become a wandering beggar or to become a robber … Generally he follows the first way of life – but the transition from this to the second is so easy, especially when the Jewish beggar is again and again turned back from one border to another that all our support is insufficient to restrain the poor from begging and the beggar from stealing.

Fences among the Jewish peddlers were 'not infrequent', Mendelssohn admitted, 'but genuine thieves are very few in number and these are mostly people without "protection" who have nowhere to settle … to the poor Jew all "protection" and residence is refused.'[28] This repeats what the rich Jew said to the poor Jew a century earlier: 'Without money there's no living.'

In the late seventeenth and eighteenth centuries gangs composed mainly of Jews were at work in Holland, northern France and Belgium, central Germany and Pomerania. They specialized, in Holland at least, in pocket picking at markets and fairs, stealing gold and silver from artisans' workshops, and robbing churches, directing their violence against priests. In two respects the Jewish gangs had an advantage over their gentile colleagues. First, they had more benefit from the information conveyed by peddlers and house-to-house hawkers whose activities lent themselves to the spying-out of likely spoil; second, the role of fellow-Jews in the trade in second-hand goods made it easier for the thieves to dispose of stolen property. Fencing had the characteristic of a Jewish speciality (see Fagin). The number of London Jews sentenced to death or transportation almost doubled from the 1760s to the 1770s – from 35 to 65.[29]

With the blurring of the distinction between the beggar-Jews and an underworld of crime and violent behaviour a certain assimilation of this stratum of Jewish society to the actuality of low life took place. Assimilation and emancipation from the *kehillah* were by no means limited to the young men and women of Vienna, dressed indistinguishably from elegant Christians, wearing swords and frequenting inns, theatres and ballrooms in the company of Christians. At a lower level assimilation took shape not only in a common way of life but also in mixed concubinage,and mixed Jewish–Christian criminal gangs; already in the early eighteenth century such gangs existed in Metz and Hamburg, jointly frequenting drinking and gaming taverns. But it is also true that certain gangs observed the dietary laws. In the German demi-monde so close was the association of Jews and Christians that Yiddish expressions made their way into German criminal jargon, for example *gonif*: thief; *chevrusa*: gang; *kochem*: wise guy.[30]

From the late sixteenth century Jewish social structure was characterized by a very small number of the wealthy and a very large number of the poor. A middle stratum certainly existed but it was everywhere and always relatively weak. 'Today, whoever is not rich is poor – this has long been a curse that rests upon us,' wrote R. Isaac Noah Mannheimer of Vienna in 1835.[31] A rough analysis of eighteenth-century Germany – which is all that is possible – divides the population into at most 2 per cent of court-Jews, a thin middle tier of merchants with their own trading capital, 75 per cent of the remainder a mass of petty traders, peddlers, people living on charity and approximately 10 per cent of beggar Jews.[32] During the eighteenth century all the evidence points to increasing differentiation along these lines and to the consequent alienation of the poor from Jewish society.

If 'money meets all needs', according to R. Jacob Emden, what will be the fate of the men without money? The fear of R. Menahem Krochmal in the seventeenth century was realized in the eighteenth: the alienation of the poor. 'The rich Jews prefer to go around in magnificent clothes rather than help the poor,' a group of vagrants told a Christian missionary whom they chanced to meet on the road. Conversion was indeed, it seems, one symptom of response to alienation, for at this time it involved mainly the poor (by contrast with the later eighteenth and early nineteenth centuries). Thus, among Christians, the saying was current: 'What good can come of the Jews? Aren't the converted ones all tramps?' A student of missionary journals found most converts to be 'nomadic and impoverished, showing the symptoms of severe disorientation and isolation'.[33]

The note of social protest is one more expression of alienation. The rejection that Solomon Maimon met with at the Rosenthaler Gate in Berlin had parallels elsewhere, for example Frankfurt am Main: 'Listen, dear people, to what is happening nowadays,' runs a Yiddish song, first published Hanau, 1708:

> When we, poor folk, travellers, come marching to Frankfurt, they do not let us pass through [their] doors. We are met by Jacob Fulvaser ... He asks: 'how long have you been here, and what is your name?' ... They are in great fear – forbid it – that through their charity, the wealth of the community will soon vanish ... They make us poor strangers stand in the same spot in the sun, so that we almost melt and are scorched.[34]

At the other socio-economic extreme disengagement from the *kehillah* and alienation from its values showed itself in a reluctance to take public office. This factor cannot be separated from the deterrent effect of exposure to unpopular duties (for example tax-collecting) attendant on public office. In Rome the reluctance to take office in the communal board, the *Congrega*, in the eighteenth century was perhaps associated with the leadership's role as tax-collector. In the 1730s Pope Clement XII and his officials had at times to intervene in communal matters and direct the attention of members to designated individuals.[35] This factor is certainly inseparable from a simple refusal to undertake at all the burden of public office. It is likely that this first showed itself in the Sephardi world. In 5461 (= 1701) Solomon de Medina in London refused the office of parnass in the Sephardi congregation. On occasion counter-sanctions must be enforced. In 1717 in Bordeaux two members of the ruling group, Pedro Gomes Silva and Joseph Lameyre, refused to accept office and were fined 100 livres. Earlier the fine would have been no more than 20 livres. In Amsterdam, in the years after 1713 members of élite families refused office in the Mahamad – 'in endemic proportions', it is said. Solomon Halphen in Berlin was not alone. In London similar defections also took place in the eighteenth century. In Livorno the situation was no better. In a variation on this theme, Israel Samson Popert of Altona, a wealthy manufacturer of serge, employing 150 Christian workers, bought his freedom from the jurisdiction of the Ashkenazi *kehillah* in favour of the less demanding Sephardi (1768). In 1769 the utmost pressure had to be exercised on Gumbrich Meyer to take up office as communal leader in the domain of Runkel. He maintained that he lacked the necessary ability in writing and reading (which the rabbi would confirm).[36]

If to the *kehillah* and its institutions commitment was waning, where, if at all, was the political replacement? If the hazardous attempt were ever made to construct the *mentalité* of a wealthy Jew, or even a Jew of middling means, of central or western Europe in the mid-eighteenth century, to acknowledge his patriotism would be unavoidable. Allegiance to a national state that is not yet in being stands out. The cosmopolitanism of the *Aufklärung* passed the Jews by. The new patriotic ideal has an amplitude that transcends both the traditional injunction to pray 'for the welfare of the city to which I have exiled you' (Jer. 29:7; see also Ezra 6:10) and even the personal loyalty to a particular ruler. Manifestations of loyalty and thanksgiving are becoming *de rigueur* on royal occasions, for example those Hebrew elegies composed by Joseph Abendanon on the death of Queen Mary II (1694) and of William III (1702);[37] or the poetic laments on the death of Louis XV in 1774 and other poems dedicated to the welfare of the French royal family (which were among the first publications in French of translations from the Hebrew); or even Mendelssohn's bridal song to celebrate the betrothal of Princess Wilhelm of Prussia in 1767, which was recited to musical accompaniment in the Berlin synagogue. Can demonstrations in this key be altogether separated from demonstrations of patriotism *tout court*? In regimes where the sovereign is all but identified with the state, for example in Prussia and France, homage to the one becomes homage to the other. Thus:

[I]n the process of praying for those who embodied the state, Jews construed sovereign power and their relationships to it. They participated in the sacred 'center' of royal charisma and simultaneously sanctified, that is to say legitimized, the governments of which they were subjects or citizens. They constructed narratives through which to understand their historical situation, and used these stories to explain themselves to gentiles, whose religious or 'enlightened' assessments of the Jews were marked by ancient and modern misperceptions.[38]

The phenomenon of those Bourbon monarchs ruling by divine right lent itself readily to a parallel reminiscent of the biblical monarchs. (Disraeli well understood the 'conservative' tendencies of the Jews when he wrote of 'their bias to religion, property and natural aristocracy'.) In Avignon, Metz and Bordeaux rabbis customarily apostrophized the Bourbon monarchs, on significant occasions in the life of the dynasty, as God's anointed. In Carpentras, on the festival of Simchat Torah (the Rejoicing of the Law), the Jews prayed for the welfare of their ruler, the pope.[39] The Seven Years' War (1756–63) gave much impetus to this phenomenon. In London at the Ashkenazi Great Synagogue, R. Hart Lyon (= R. Herschel Levin) delivered a number of war-time sermons, in the first of which he argued that the sovereign must be trusted and supported even if his decisions are inscrutable. In a second Hart Lyon made the point that though to God all nations are objects of concern, certain of those nations might turn aggressor; over them victory might legitimately be celebrated. From his pulpit in the Alt-Neu synagogue in Prague, R. Eliezer Landau mobilized support for 'our most gracious Queen', Maria Theresa, and offered thanksgiving to God for those very successes that in London R. Hart Lyon lamented. In London,

Berlin and Prague, the sermons 'point to the striking psychological transformation within major Jewish communities of western and central Europe preceding the emancipation that might be called an incipient patriotism'.[40]

The degree of emotional identification with the welfare of the state of itself introduces the further notion that the Jewish fate and self-perception will be less distinctive than in the pre-patriotic world. The one is the counterpart of the other. Only the Jewish Enlightenment, the Haskalah, towards the end of the eighteenth century, will articulate this notion within an ideology, but its beginnings already appear in a participant identification with the perceived welfare of the existing state order. To that extent the integrity of the awareness of exile and the messianic redemption is compromised. Of course, there is no agreed messianic 'scenario' but it is certainly inseparable from a distinctively Jewish future. Precisely that concept is now jeopardized. Mendelssohn, in Berlin, showed a degree of ambivalence, it is true, but at a time of transition this would have been inevitable and, in any case, he finally relegates the redemption to a prayer. At one time he denied that he had a fatherland; at another, he hoped for a change in the political circumstances of the Jews that would enable him to share in the pride of his fellow-countrymen; at yet another, he reproached Frederick the Great for writing his poetry in French, not German; but was the messianic idea at all relevant to political reality? 'The hoped-for return to Palestine ... has not the slightest influence on our behaviour in society,' Mendelssohn assured the anti-Jewish theologian, Johann David Michaelis (1717–91):

> Experience has always taught that wherever Jews have enjoyed toleration and this is in accord with the nature of man who, if he is not an enthusiast, loves the soil where he is at ease, and if his religious views are in opposition saves these for the church and prayer and thinks no more of it.

Mendelssohn then refers to the Talmudic warning against any violent attempt at redemption and re-establishment of the nation in the Promised Land, and he quotes the traditional passage from the Song of Songs: 'Do not wake or rouse love until it please' (2:7; 3:5).[41]

This warning is by no means irreconcilable with cherishing the idea of the messianic redemption – but it is irrelevant to its abandonment. A number of rabbis had however to confront precisely this latter position and also Mendelssohn's ambivalence, in Ashkenaz elsewhere than Prussia and in the Sephardi world. Two rabbis have special importance – R. Moses Hagiz (1671–1751) and R. Jacob Emden (1696–1776). Both were outsiders, the latter rarely having any fixed rabbinical appointment, being reduced to adventitious occupations as moneylender, printer or wool merchant. Hagiz was an emissary from the Promised Land, charged with raising funds for its institutions from the communities in western and central Europe. Both had experience of Ashkenazi and Sephardi communities in London, Holland and north Germany. Early in the eighteenth century Hagiz wrote of London and Hamburg in the warmest of terms: no more than two or three other communities in the diaspora 'were so securely and confidently established and enjoyed such wealth and honour'. But the wealthy flaunted their possessions to engage in 'sinful doings – consorting with women, riding splendid carriages, indulging in choice dishes, building homes and courtyards'. Hagiz developed his critique of Jewish society into a scornful portrayal of the ideology that comfort, wealth and ease had engendered. The emissaries from the Promised Land were despised and their appeals derided. The wealthy justified their rebuff by refusing to allow any superior status to the Promised Land in the present exile, for did not the Shekhinah ('the indwelling presence of God') accompany the Jews wherever their wanderings might take them? Hagiz makes a telling and bitter contrast: the exiles in Babylon wept when they remembered Zion and they asked: 'How can we sing a song of the Lord on alien soil?' (ref. to Ps. 137). But now, Hagiz continues, 'Each one in his city says, I am at peace, for this is my Jerusalem.' In the last resort, this rebellion culminates in the conscious dismissal of the messianic hope. 'I myself have heard some of them say, in the boorishness and complacency bred by wealth: "If the messiah should come, and make rich and poor equal, what need have we of him?"'[42]

The share of R. Jacob Emden in this critique belongs in part to his polemic against the study of philosophy, 'Greek wisdom', and in part also to his associated campaign against accommodation to gentile society. To both phenomena he attributed disaster and exile. In Emden's view, Spanish Jewry succumbed to ease and forsook the centrality of the Promised Land and conducted themselves as though they 'had already found another Land of Israel and Jerusalem'. With the same weapon Emden attacked the Jewry of his own mid-eighteenth century. The present reproduced the past: his contemporaries, he wrote, 'are no longer mindful of the fact that they are in *galut* – exile; they mingle with non-Jews, adopting their customs and are a great disgrace. The holy seed mixes with the peoples of the earth.'[43] Emden generalized his critique of Jewish society through the vision of Ecclesiastes (10:19): 'They make a banquet for revelry; wine makes life merry and money answers every need.' Emden's experience was limited in the main to the communities along the North Sea and Baltic, but he was widely travelled elsewhere and his remarks tally with those of other observers. Emden found that violent and powerful individuals interfered in legal proceedings; that rabbinic judges were bribed; that the parnassim of Ashkenaz were arrogant and 'little gods'; that rabbis obtained their posts through the manipulation and intrigue of the wealthy; that it was 'a robber's profession' the bankers, brokers and money-changers of Altona and Hamburg were engaged in.[44] In these sallies there is unquestionably an outsider's personal resentment. But by no means can they be discounted entirely, given the evidence from other

sources. Emden's strictures are largely reproduced in the ethical writings of
R. Judah Hourwitz.[45] Of particular concern to Isaac Wetzlar (1680/90–1751),
a pupil of R Abraham Broda's yeshivah in Prague and later a successful busi-
nessman, was the lack of educational facilities for the children of village Jews
in Ashkenaz. The picture presented by Wetzlar in his ethico-autobiographical
memoir *Liebes Brief* (1749) is indeed qualified and far from monochrome. Yet
Liebes Brief gives a dominant impression of a society struggling to ensure its
future amidst ignorance, insensitive and corrupt leadership, poverty, and a
body of rabbis less interested in teaching than in the fees to be earned from
officiating at weddings or supervising the ritual slaughtering of cattle and
sheep. Wetzlar's main target is the parnassim, so much so, writes one student of the work, that in the whole of the *Liebes Brief* 'there is not one positive comment about parnassim'.[46]

The disengagement from the *kehillah* showed itself also in the resort to
gentile courts and the quest for freedom from rabbinic jurisdiction. Not only
in Berlin but also in Metz and Halle, local (Christian) judges required manuals of Jewish law to enable them to judge cases of *Jud contra Jud*. In
eighteenth-century London in such cases, rather than presiding in their own
Batei Din, both Ashkenazi and Sephardi rabbis were reduced to advising
Christian judges in their courts and serving as expert witnesses. In Hamburg
in 1716 an addition was made to the *takkanot* of the combined communities of Altona, Hamburg and Wandsbek that prohibited one Jew citing
another before the non-Jewish court, 'and also not in claims on a bill of
exchange'. This practice would not have been banned had it not been current. The prohibition was in any event ineffective: only a few decades later
Chief Rabbi Jonathan Eibeschütz of Metz had to admit its prevalence,

> and it is likewise [he added] in the other communities of Germany
> that the ordinances have permitted litigants in disputes over bills of
> exchange to take their disputes to non-Jewish courts. Who permitted this
> to them? ... This practice appears very evil to me but I lack the power to
> abolish it because it is ingrained through this ordinance.[47]

In contemporary London, the status of the rabbinate was such that the
Ashkenazi communal leaders could at their own discretion revise synagogue
takkanot during the interregnum of 1791–1802, separating the death of
R. David Tevele Schiff (1791) and the election of R. Solomon Hirschell (1802).
In the Judeo-German text of these *takkanot* the rabbi becomes the *Dienst* or
Meshubed – the servant of the congregation: 'The tone of these *taqqanoth* is
on the whole one of patronage, demanding subservience from those who
were meant to obey.' The same terminology marks the revised regulations of
1788 for the Orphan Charity Society (originally founded in 1732).[48]

By the mid-eighteenth century the *kehillah* is losing its power to attract
and retain its natural leaders; increasingly the point of political reference is

becoming patriotism and the institutions of the gentile state in which ease is found – like the sixteenth-century contemporaries of R. David Gans, this too is 'a generation tired of the exile'; judicial authority yields to the civil courts; the growing numbers of the poor overwhelm the resources of the *kehillah*. In aggregate, these features signal a crisis of survival.[49] There is much variation in the extent to which any of these circumstances affected any individual *kehillah*; otherwise, the picture in general holds good. The effect is compounded by the rise of the Jewish Enlightenment – the Haskalah – and its resort to the support of the enlightened despots Frederick the Great and Joseph II for rescue from rabbinic tradition.

12
'Jerusalem' in Berlin

The Jews of Prussia from the time of their readmission in 1671 willingly engaged themselves in the economic development of the state. This participation was for some a means to prosperity, no less than a means to the creation of a cultural centre, of such magnitude that to the reign of Frederick the Great, 1740–86, has been ascribed the beginnings of modern Jewish history.[1] Less doubtful is the reciprocal benefit that accrued to each party, the price being paid by the *kehillah* as an institution.

During Frederick's reign the particular role of the Jews was accommodated to Prussian mercantilist theory in the sense that to favoured Jewish entrepreneurs, manufacturers and traders was entrusted the task of furthering the objectives of a closed protectionist economy, that is, to exploit the resources of the state, earn foreign currency and reduce imports to the minimum. As part of the same mercantilist policy the Prussian state made the organized *kehillah* into its own instrument. The community in general, no less than all other subjects of the crown, must be put to the service of the state. Thus the *kehillah* served as a tool of the state, for which it collected taxes, performed a policing role and kept at bay the poor, and therefore unwelcome, Jews. The Jews' Commission long kept a watching brief on the number of Jewish marriages. In 1737, the state extended its control through the appointment of an official from the Department of War and Domains to supervise the assessment, apportionment and collection of taxes. Either through its own officials, or designated Jewish leaders, the state introduced similar modes of control into other major Prussian communities, Halle, Frankfurt an der Oder, Königsberg and Landsberg an der Warthe.

So burdensome and multifarious were the taxes, excise duties and tolls imposed on the community that this measure alone took the state into its very heart. This degree of intrusion must necessarily compromise the factor of self-government, the authority of the court and the extent of rabbinic jurisdiction. However, despite the share of the state in its domination of the *kehillah* and its commanding relationship to the economic élite, in neither respect did it rule supreme: in Berlin the familiar, Janus-like existence of the *kehillah* was as apparent as elsewhere; and the entrepreneurs displayed a capacity to react and transmute economic success into political advancement. Between them and the state the relationship was dynamic. Also, economic success was a factor in cultural efflorescence.

Given the instrumental role of the *kehillah*, what 'space' remained within which to wield 'the sceptre that shall not depart from Judah'? And how was the 'sceptre' organized? Essentially a system of indirect elections, inevitably evolving over the lifetime of the community, called into being a governing board. Every three years, to coincide with the triennial tax assessment, and during the intermediate days of the Passover festival, in the presence of 15 men, the rabbi, deputy rabbi and their learned assessors, an electoral body of 7 persons was chosen by lot: 3 (or 4) from the wealthy; 2 from those of middling income; and 2 (or 1) from the poor. These 7 (or 8), after being 'sworn in', then elected the members of the board, taking account of the obligatory requirement not to elect any person ineligible by virtue of family connection – though the electors did not always observe this restriction, and property qualifications varied to take account of the community's increasing wealth. In 1780 senior officers of the *kehillah* needed taxable assets of 4000 Reichsthaler to be eligible for election and lesser officers 2500. In Frederick the Great's time the state also confirmed in office a senior elder who enjoyed jurisdiction not only over Berlin Jewry but over all other Prussian communities. Invariably the wealthiest stratum of bankers and entrepreneurs provided these senior elders, for example, Nathan Veitel Heine Ephraim (1750–75), Jacob Moses (1775–92) and Daniel Itzig (1775–99) (see below).[2]

Nowhere more than in the oligarchic nature of the *kehillah* regime did the traditional structure show itself as a plutocracy of related families. This resulted from, and was reinforced by, a marriage policy concerned with capital formation and retention, distribution of risk and enlargement of the economic network. This brought Berlin families into alliance with similar families strategically located elsewhere in Ashkenaz, for example Hamburg, Amsterdam, Vienna and Königsberg. 'Much brother-in-lawed', it was remarked of London Jewry in the eighteenth century. No less 'brother-in-lawed' were the Prussian and Berlin families of Gomperts, Friedländer, Ephraim, Itzig, Ries, Levy, Wulff, among others.[3] These relationships did not always obviate commercial rivalries, or perhaps simple struggles for power, of the type common to both Ashkenazim and Sephardim, in Prague, Bordeaux or London. In 1750 a dissident faction headed by Philip Lazarus Mendel and Mayer Ries complained to the king, 'We are groaning in slavery ... under the despotic rule' of interrelated elders. This faction took special objection to the impropriety and breach of (Jewish) law inherent in the relationship between the current senior elder, Veitel Heine Ephraim, and the second rabbi, R. David Fränkel, whose sister was married to Ephraim, which disqualified them from serving together; the board as a whole was trying to postpone new elections, it was further alleged.[4]

On the one hand, the board functioned as 'the elongated arm of the state authorities' (Meisl, *Pinkas*, p. xxii). But in its capacity as one of Judah's 'sceptres', the board must concern itself also with issues beyond the purview of the state and other than those determined by the state, regardless of how deeply the latter penetrated into its workings. The board had three fields of activity: the general administration of the *kehillah*, including its finances; religious, synagogal and educational matters; and care for the poor. From the 1720s and until the early nineteenth century, the communal *Pinkas*, in a mixture of Hebrew and Yiddish, records the activities of a functioning *kehillah* that comprises a synagogue, house of study, cemetery, school, slaughterhouse and a *hekdesh* – a kind of combined hospice, hospital and welfare centre. The elders organized elections, both to their own ranks and to subordinate bodies, fixed the wages of those employed therein, imposed a form of social control through the prohibiting of private gatherings for worship and the offering of individual gifts to the authorities, introduced sumptuary legislation covering apparel and entertainment, and distributed special meal for the Passover festival; the Fraternity for the Succouring of the Poor (*Hafsakat Evyonim*) was given the monopoly of producing sugar for the festival; special tax regulations applied to widows, orphans and the unmarried. Other fiscal measures included the levying of a special tax on the occasion of the Russian occupation of Berlin in 1760, raising loans from the Berlin nobility to cover the Jews' share of the occupation costs, and the release of 'Moses Dessau' (Moses Mendelssohn) from all taxes; through an emissary the elders agreed to make two annual payments to the poor of the 'Holy City of Hebron'; they took shares in the East India and Levant Company and a bolting-cloth factory; they arranged payment so that merchants from Berlin attending the twice-yearly fairs at Frankfurt an der Oder would enjoy the facilities of the local synagogue, and they approved a contract between two doctors, Markus Herz and Benjamin Bloch, to care for the poor.[5]

This was an observant community. It insisted on the provision of meat that was *glatt* kosher, that is, meat derived exclusively from cattle the lungs of which had been examined for any growth. Only from communities which maintained the same standards of inspection as Berlin could meat be bought. In case of transgression the official responsible was fined and the vessels used to convey the offending meat were not to be used again. And if, as was indeed the case, the *Pinkas* used the Jewish calendar and made allowance for the messianic advent, so that loan contracts and the like had to provide for the contingency of enforced redemption before the due date, then it can be concluded that the subjects of the *Pinkas* lived in 'Jewish time'.[6]

The rabbis exercised their role solely within the community. To themselves alone the elders and parnassim reserved the conduct of all dealings with the state's authorities. Religious life in the narrow sense defined the rabbinical field. The rabbis' principal functions were bounded by the court and the Beth Hamidrash (House of Study). The court normally sat on the afternoons of Monday to Thursday and reached its decisions by a majority vote of the presiding rabbi and his assessors of whom there were four. The presence of the chief rabbi might be limited to one sitting a week, his position on the bench being taken at other times by the second rabbi. The Berlin Beth Hamidrash, founded 1743–4, met the need for study of the Talmud and other texts. This institution maintained a staff of three rabbis who were engaged in instructing young men and interested members of the public, on a formal and informal basis. Privately financed institutions existed side by side with the Beth Hamidrash, for example the later *Lehranstalt*, conducted on the lines of a yeshivah and financed from the income of a trust fund established by Veitel Ephraim in 1774. The trustees of the Beth Hamidrash also kept their minutes in a Germanized form of Yiddish, and dated their proceedings by reference to the Jewish calendar.[7]

Outside his role as judge (or arbitrator) and teacher, the rabbi participated in the discussions on the allocation of seats in the synagogue, organization of religious festivities, exclusion of a member from certain positions of honour, taxation of widows and the unmarried, measures against counterfeiting and against libel or slander (*pasquille*), and electoral regulations; the rabbinical court decided in its own right the raising of the tax on kosher meat and the scale of betrothal and burial fees for the childless and unmarried. Two instances are recorded in the *Pinkas* where the court intervened in financial matters: in the first, in 1742, R. Toklas and his assessor, R. Naftali Herz Wolf, determined the taxes to be paid by the heirs to the estate of Zalman Baruk; in the second, in 1748, R. David Fränkel, sitting with Rabbis Wolf and Joel Sachs, determined the mode of repayment of a loan of 300 Reichsthaler made by the *kehillah* to a deceased member, Meir Rintel, and now due for repayment from his estate.[8]

By the early years of the reign of Frederick the Great (1740–86), the Berlin community had shown, despite every effort at repression, numerical growth, and this continued during his reign. In 1737 the total stood at 1198 persons; in 1744 at 1836; in 1754 at 2510; in 1764 at 3626; in 1800 at 3322; and in 1812 at 3493. At about this time the three largest communities were still Hamburg (*c.*7000), Breslau (4400) and Frankfurt am Main (4300). In Berlin the proportion of the Jewish to the non-Jewish population varied between a minimum of 1.93 per cent (1750) and a maximum of 2.88 per cent (1770).[9] The fluctuations, despite the marriage laws, show some success in repressing population growth over limited periods only.

In 1749 community members owned 41 houses, one in excess of the permitted total of 40. Bankers and dealers in silk goods predominated among the house-owners, followed by moneylenders, and traders in jewellery, and livestock; other house-owners included an embroiderer in gold and silver, a ribbon manufacturer, a jeweller, a velvet manufacturer and a *rentier*.

Some of the bankers combined their principal occupation with a sideline, for example dealing in silk fabrics, or women's clothing. These were the wealthy stratum who constituted 9 per cent of those household heads gainfully occupied. Roughly another quarter enjoyed a more or less secure existence as traders and craftsmen; and slightly under two-thirds led a marginal, insecure existence as peddlers, hawkers, tolerated domestic servants and employees. In all cases this structure had been reached amidst the opposition of Christian traders and craftsmen (both native-born and members of the Huguenot colony). Necessarily negative also was the effect of 'special' and regular taxes and limitations on those goods Jews might trade in.[10] The very few factory owners included Veitel Heine Ephraim and Herz Gomperts. They showed their ability as industrialists in the operation of a lace factory which they took over in 1749. This enterprise employed 200 orphans from the state orphanage in Potsdam. Gomperts came from the family of court-Jews in Cleves whose fortunes were originally founded on trading in battlefield booty of the Thirty Years' War. David Hirsch's velvet factory in Potsdam enjoyed wide renown, and also employed orphans. Isaac Joel had a factory in which orphan girls were taught to embroider white and coloured muslin. The manufacturers also included Moses Riess and Isaak Bernhard. Jewish silk manufacturers had to contend with the opposition of Spitzgerber and Gotzkowsky, Christian entrepreneurs who aimed to monopolize the production of silk.[11]

Frederick's esteem for the acumen and abilities of these industrialists and their contribution to the Prussian economy had to overcome his antisemitism. In his political testaments of 1752 and 1768 he made his detestation explicit and stressed the vital need to limit the growth in numbers of families and individuals. He denounced the Jews as 'usurers, smugglers and swindlers' whose activities endangered burghers and Christian merchants, but Frederick also appreciated the merchandising role of the Jews in small-scale trade with Poland. In the later testament there is, perhaps, a slight mellowing of the hostile tone in that here Frederick prides himself on never having persecuted the Jews, in favourable contrast to Maria Theresa; also the reference to demographic control is less harsh and the earlier mention of the need to keep the Jews away from 'large-scale trade' (*Grosshandel*) is absent.[12] His alarm at any increase in Jewish numbers was shown on several occasions. In 1747 he allowed a protected Jew, Isaac Abraham of Fürstenwalde, to include only his eldest son, Samuel Isaac, in his *Schutzbrief* (and therefore confer on him settlement rights); to include two children would defeat the aim of 'reducing the number of Jew-families' who would multiply and in 20–30 years exceed 'the fixed total'.[13]

In 1778 two of Frederick's most highly favoured associates, Veitel Ephraim and Daniel Itzig, petitioned for the admission of more Jews to Breslau. Frederick retorted: 'Where their trade is concerned let things stay as they are, but that they bring entire tribes (*Fölkerschaften*) of Jews into Breslau to make a whole Jerusalem out of it – that cannot be.'[14] The same fear of any 'out-of-hand increase' in Jewish numbers inspired in large part the crucial *reglement* of 1750. This legislation combined favours to the wealthy, the increased subordination of the *kehillah* to the state and the repression of the poor, including their demographic limitation. It also aimed to avert harm to the Prussian Jews themselves, 'through unlicensed foreign Jews of no fixed residence slinking in'; the *reglement* was designed to maintain a balance between Jewish and Christian merchants.[15]

In earlier Prussian legislation all these themes and objectives had precedents. But if the *reglement* contained nothing new, it codified and elaborated earlier decrees to the extent that it constituted a major statement of policy, which remained substantially in force until 1812. It was in the making from the late 1740s, and this period gave interested parties a chance to influence the government. The Christian leather-dealers in Berlin complained that their Jewish rivals had supplied badly cured leather to the cavalry for bridles and saddlery, which would 'not last in the field and withstand hard wear'. The Berlin merchants' guilds complained that Jewish traders were selling forbidden goods and engaging in smuggling and usury. This was *vieux jeu* of course – save for the absence of one significant theme, the religious. When, for example, the Prague or Viennese artisans and guild merchants attacked the business practices of their Jewish rivals they could not but help associating these practices with accusations of blasphemy, irreligion and deicide.[16] Not so in Prussia – here the rivalry was undisguisedly economic.

The submissions of the Jewish elders had a twofold thrust: the need for relief from the economic constraints under which they suffered and the value they attached to legal autonomy. To be more specific, the Jews' submissions concentrated on obstacles to their commercial activities, the request for a joint consultative commission, permission for a second child to enjoy the same advantageous legal position as the first, the rejection of collective liability for trafficking in stolen goods and for fraudulent bankruptcies, and freedom from the body tax – *Leibzoll* – throughout all the Prussian territories. This was the Prussian equivalent to the French *péage corporel*. The sum involved was small, payable when the Jew crossed from one Prussian province to another, but *Leibzoll* had a humiliating effect in forcing the Jew to levy a duty on himself as though he were an animal or an item of goods. The elders also objected to a proposed paragraph which imposed on all the members of a Jewish family collective liability should any one of its members (for example, a pawnbroker or moneylender on pledges) be found in possession of goods that were stolen or illegally acquired, and be unable to compensate the true owner to the full extent of the loss; if the family could not make this compensation, 'then the entire Jewry of the town is officially held to be liable for cash payment in compensation'. A memorandum in December 1748, in the name of all the Jews in Berlin and the Prussian provinces, argued that such a provision would not only make the innocent suffer with the guilty but also damage their credit standing – and thus, although this was not explicitly stated, also the interest of the Prussian economy.[17] Collective liability continued also to apply to the payment of taxes.

As for legal autonomy, communities throughout Prussia sought to sway the king in its favour. In Cleves, Halberstadt and Rhineland-Westphalia they urged the government to preserve their religion and its associated laws, 'on which their whole weal and woe depended'. The elders of the Berlin community and of all provincial communities submitted a similar plea to Cocceji, Frederick's chancellor: let disputes between Jews be decided in accordance with 'the Mosaic laws', in order to thwart those Jewish litigants who were bypassing the Jewish courts and turning at once to the civil courts. The memorandum denounced 'certain ruthless and obdurate persons among us who merely in order to avoid a judgement according to the Mosaic laws and to withdraw themselves from a decision of the rabbi and his assessors immediately bring their claims of Jews v. Jews to a civil or secular forum'. These were 'untimely leaps into a secular jurisdiction'.[18]

Frederick gave nothing away. The Jews secured no more than a six-year delay in the promulgation of the reglement. This 'concession' indirectly acknowledged its possible repercussions on their creditworthiness, for the reglement, more than ever before, made the elders into servants of the state. Now, from the middle of the eighteenth century, they must maintain a register of all Jews in Berlin, supervise and regulate the activities of visiting and transient Jews, keep lists of births, circumcisions, marriages and deaths, control the economic activities of the community's members, apprehend their illegal activities, record the sale and purchase of property, organize and supervise elections to the numerous communal bodies and – perhaps most burdensome of all – draw up tax lists and assess, apportion and collect the taxes and multifarious payments due both to the state and to communal bodies.

Essentially, the revised reglement of 1750 defined six categories of Jews in terms of their utility to the state, and in terms of the economic activities in which each group might engage. It maintained the distinction between ordinary and extraordinary protected Jews in that the former could install one child with a letter of protection (Schutzbrief) whereas the latter were entitled to protection only for their lifetime and could acquire a letter of protection for a child only if they could endow it with assets to the value of 1000 Reichsthaler.

To population control and the limitation of marriage the reglement devoted special attention. Basically, in order that the existing Jewish population be not exceeded, every proposed marriage must be first investigated. Domestic servants, male and female, were not allowed to marry – if they did they lost their tolerated status. On the other hand, the two teachers for the girls' schools must both be married, but not the other teachers. Paragraph vii of the *reglement* disallowed marriage of an employee to the daughter of a protected Jew until he had spent three years outside the town where he had been employed. This provision met the demands of merchants concerned lest a former employee bring knowledge of confidential business matters to a possible competitor.[19]

The *reglement* made no concession to the plea for legal autonomy – it may in fact have reduced the already exiguous authority of the rabbi to no more than the power of arbitration. The *reglement* (by paragraph xxxi) empowered the rabbinical court to resolve only those conflicts arising out of 'Jewish ceremonies and religious customs'. It was not empowered to impose a sentence of *herem* on transgressors or impose a fine of more than 5 Reichsthaler without the foreknowledge of the magistrate. The rabbi and elders had no 'real jurisdiction' in civil cases: these were to be referred to the competent civil authorities. The regulations did permit the rabbi and his assessors to take 'some sort of judicial cognizance' in matters between Jew and Jew such as marriage contracts, wills, inheritances, inventories and appointment of guardians, 'which must be settled by them solely in accord with the Mosaic laws' – but this was only by way of arbitration. This did not satisfy Cocceji, Frederick's chancellor and a proponent of legal uniformity. He used an argument that Spinoza had expounded in his *Theological-Political Treatise* (Chapter xix) and which Mendelssohn in Berlin and Zalkind Hourwitz in Metz echoed a century later, that is, how could civil and political laws exist in the absence of a polis? Cocceji maintained not only that the 'Republic of the Jews' and consequently its civil law had ceased to exist more than 1600 years earlier, but also that Mosaic law made no reference to such matters of contemporary dispute as inventories, guardianships or inheritances. Frederick comforted his chancellor: '[N]o one will be harmed by it [paragraph xxxi] for it is really only arbitration against which anyone can lodge an appeal with the judicial authorities.'[20]

Overall, it is by no means clear precisely to what extent rabbinical jurisdiction did survive the encroachment of the state. That is why, when R. David Fränkel in 1752 was appointed senior rabbi in Prussia, he had to enquire of Frederick how to conduct himself as judge in cases of conflict that the legislation did not provide for. The king, replying through Cocceji, drew Fränkel's attention to paragraph xxxi of the 1750 *reglement*.[21]

The debate over a rabbinic presence at the fair at Frankfurt an der Oder in 1775–6 shows the continuing concern with which the state regarded any exercise of independent rabbinical jurisdiction and the recurrence of friction at the interface. The Jewish merchants from Poland, who took a prominent part in Poland's foreign trade, requested the services of the Berlin chief rabbi, Hirsch Levin, to judge their disputes, aided by the Frankfurt rabbi and Polish rabbis as assessors. Levin refused. The matter did not end there, for the Prussian Directory General welcomed the merchants' request, arguing, pragmatically, that 'the flourishing of the Frankfurt fair depends largely on the

Polish Jews', whose wishes should therefore be heeded. But the Prussian Fiscal-General opposed the request, as did the Kammergericht and the Frankfurt magistracy:

> To exempt some part of the merchant body, whatever confession they belong to, from the ordinary jurisdiction of the state and to grant them a legal adjudication independent of the highest authority of the state, is so peculiar an idea, precisely contradicting all maxims of state administration, that in our opinion it could only have been invented by Jewish heads.

In the end the proposal came to nothing – the state rejected 'such a fateful innovation'. On the other hand, according to the historian of the Berlin rabbinate, until the death of R. Hirsch Levin in 1800, a rabbi from Berlin did attend the fair three times a year, and judged cases in civil law as well as cases of divorce and levirate marriage.[22]

The limits, constraints and financial exactions which Frederick imposed on his (wealthier) Jewish subjects had to be accommodated to the particular demands that he made on the entrepreneurs among them. They, for their part, could turn this situation to their advantage. Already in 1731 David Hirsch, the famous velvet manufacturer, had secured exemption from the body tax for himself, his children and his servants, on the ground that it hampered his business travel.[23] A generation later Prussian participation in the Seven Years' War (1756–63) offered opportunity on a scale without precedent. In Prussia, as also in England and France, the war accelerated and reinforced the attachment to the burgeoning nation-state. In the Prussian version this dynamic rapport derived from the share that the 'mint-Jews' (*Münzjuden*) took in financing the war. Outstanding among them were Veitel Heine Ephraim, Daniel Itzig and Itzig's brother-in-law Moses Isaak. The former two had backgrounds respectively in the retail trade in Berlin (Ephraim was the court jeweller) and the Leipzig fair; Itzig was born in Berlin but the family came from Poland where it had specialized in supplying the Polish nobility and the Prussian cavalry with their mounts. The three families, who had first to overcome competition from a rival consortium led by the families of Gomperts and Fränkel, were already prominent in pre-war Prussia, for example as lessees of the mints in Cleves and Aurich. In the early 1750s this was enhanced when the king quadrupled the number of mints from 2 to 8 and made concessions available to entrepreneurs who would supply and operate the mints. The famous mint-Jews were born. They needed access to the supply of silver necessary for the increased volume of coins. The bulk of the silver came by way of imports arriving at Hamburg and Amsterdam where Ephraim and Itzig had close family contacts. Ephraim had family connections through his son, Benjamin Veitel Ephraim, with the metal-smelting family of Levin Moses Philipp. To some extent the mint-Jews procured their raw material also from the multitude of Jewish peddlers and itinerant traders who thronged the fairs at Frankfurt on the Oder and Leipzig. (This repeated the pattern of supply in the horse trade in Alsace and Metz.)

Within a year of the first mint concessions the outbreak of the Seven Years' War not only vastly increased the demand for specie to finance the war but also created the occasion which, *derrière les coulisses*, Frederick instigated and encouraged – to debase the currency, by decreasing the amount of silver in the coinage. By 1760 all the Prussian mints were making 30 thalers out of one fine mark of silver against a pre-war proportion of 18 : 1. The use of captured dies engraved with the head of Elector Augustus of Saxony and king of Poland imbued the debased specie with pre-war authenticity. Inflation resulted from this policy and in the crash of 1763 even so powerful an entrepreneur as Gotzkowsky lost his fortune. These operations proved invaluable however, to the Prussian finances and the income derived from the activities of the mint-Jews is estimated to have covered slightly more than 20 per cent of the total cost of the Seven Years' War.[24] Moses Isaak also negotiated on Frederick's behalf with the British government and bankers over subsidies for the Prussian war effort.

Currency depreciation was inherently a risky pursuit, but the rewards matched the risk, and Ephraim and his associates, particularly Itzig, emerged from the war in a vastly enhanced position and were able to acquire palatial residences beyond the customary area of Jewish residence in Berlin. The share of the tax burden borne by the wealthiest members of the community underlines their financial paramountcy: in 1754 (that is pre-war), 21 per cent of the communal taxes were contributed by the wealthiest 5 per cent of the Berlin community; in 1764 that 5 per cent paid 43 per cent, that is more than twice as much. The three families – Ephraim, Itzig and Izaak – paid 26 per cent of all communal taxes in 1764. The weekly taxes paid by Daniel Itzig over the decade 1754–64 rose almost twentyfold.[25]

Not only did the Seven Years' War lead to a significant growth in socio-economic differentiation – it also contributed to the growth of Prusso-Jewish patriotism. The two may well be connected; in any event, the mood in Prussia re-echoed to the same refrain as in England and France. For a service of thanksgiving for the unexpected Prussian victory over superior Austrian forces at Leuthen (1757), Moses Mendelssohn composed a sermon for R. David Fränkel to deliver. It combined universalistic and patriotic sentiments: not to rejoice at the defeat of the enemy but to express thanksgiving, by helping the widows and orphans of those killed or wounded in battle; to appreciate the role of divine providence in victory, without neglecting the need for bravery and sound tactics; to remember that 'we are all children of the one living God. They who declare themselves our enemies are equally the work of His hands, and love and fear Him'; and we should love them were they not seduced by perverse passions to disturb the tranquillity of 'our dear sovereign'. This was published in Berlin in German and in London in an English translation, for the benefit of Prussia's ally in the war.[26] It may also be a symptom of patriotism in Mendelssohn and his circle that in 1760 he sent to his bride a pair of earrings and a medal, designed by himself, commemorating the recent Prussian victory at Liegnitz. Two years later Mendelssohn designed another medal, to celebrate the peace treaty between Prussia and Sweden (1762). This was engraved by the famous Jacob Abraham at the order of Veitel Ephraim.

How far did this mood extend? Was it limited at most to an economically successful élite, partners in executing Frederick's economic projects; or is it meaningful to talk, certainly not of Prussian patriotism, but at least of a general 'Fritzische Gesinnung', as does one historian? I am inclined to doubt its widespread prevalence and to argue that, in that vast majority of Jews who were anathema to Frederick because of their poverty and 'parasitic' nature, it would be difficult to detect any trace of Fritzische Gesinnung.[27] And if volunteers in the War of Liberation against Napoleon (1813) were primarily the moneyed, then here is further support for the class-bound distribution of Fritzische Gesinnung.

The beneficiaries of the Seven Years' War were not fully at liberty to engage in conspicuous consumption. The burden of taxes in the second half of the eighteenth century grew heavier. Also, Frederick 'encouraged' the beneficiaries to invest at least some of their gains in industry and a range of new factories came into existence as well as other enterprises, for example Daniel Itzig's iron works and lead factory at Sorge in the Harz, Moses Isaak's silk factory in Potsdam, the muslin factory of Ephraim and Jacob Borchgard, the poplin factory of Israel Marcus. After the Seven Years' War Jews owned 70 houses in Berlin as compared with the prewar 40.[28]

To the same degree as did their Christian colleagues, these industrialists benefited from state subsidies, advances and the allocation of factory sites and manpower and thus, in a crucial, if limited sense, enjoyed equality of status, so to speak. They took full advantage of the ideology of the Frederician regime. This can be interpreted, in a trivial sense, as a reward for economic prowess and promise. But this, I believe, would fail to do justice to the political implication in that here, first, is a move towards a state where status is determined solely by the extent of the individual's usefulness to the state; second, where the useful individual is a Jew he will, as a consequence of his success, secure and enjoy a degree of emancipation from the disabilities and constraints imposed on the generality of his fellow-Jews. At work is a process of auto-emancipation. This interpretation will qualify and even overturn the widespread view that it was the absolutist rulers and their officialdom who initiated the process of emancipation and even brought it to a conclusion.[29]

Between the policies of these rulers and their exploitation by the Jewish beneficiaries the bond is undeniable. The ideal of a pure utilitarian society was central to a petition submitted to the General-Directory by Israel Marcus (1783). He already had a privilege of general protection (*Generalschutzprivileg*) but this did not include full freedom of trade. Marcus was to all appearances a pugnacious, enterprising and successful manufacturer of semi-silk goods. His factory had 20 looms in 1777; by 1783 it had between 120 and 150 and employed some 300–500 workmen. He had export markets throughout Europe, and also in the West Indies. Together with a partner, he took over Moses Ries's silk factory in Potsdam and that of Isaac Benjamin Wulff in Bernau, both of which were on the verge of bankruptcy:

> I am asking for general freedom of trade not as Jew but as manufacturer [Marcus wrote to the king]. It is quite clear that, if I receive permission to trade with foreigners in their products I can create a considerable market for my factory goods and also enlarge the factory itself...If I were to be treated as a Jew and therefore prevented from entering on this path of commerce, then I would have to renounce a large part of the trade in exports and the future outlook for the preservation of the degree of perfection to which I have brought my factories would look unpromising.

Marcus reminded the king that, unlike others, his factory enjoyed no subsidy yet employed more than 500 Christian workers,

> and was it not all one whether the founder of the factory was a Jew or a Christian, especially when there was no Christian who made the effort and bore the costs of developing an establishment of this sort to the degree that I have done. And yet, because I am a Jew, should I be held back from being of further... benefit to the state in the future... I seek the benefit of unrestricted trade and the direct distribution of my manufactured goods abroad not as a Jew but as a manufacturer, and manufacturers in my modest judgement must enjoy the same privilege without consideration of person or belief if they, as is the case with me, bring to the state a vital benefit.

In the event, the General Directory turned down Marcus's request and he was refused the freedom to engage in direct trade with foreigners in Königsberg, Memel and Elbing. It is not clear whether this followed from the fact also that Christian manufacturers normally did not enjoy this facility or whether the Christian traders in Königsberg complained that too many Jews were in receipt of privileges.[30]

Already in 1750 Frederick made privileges for individual Jews dependent on their establishment of new factories.[31] Between economic usefulness to the state as mint-master, industrialist or exporter and the extent of personal and economic freedom there was a trade-off, in a dynamic and reciprocal relationship. This is what Abraham Marcuse ('court agent' in Strelitz) took advantage of, when he informed the king of the 'quite considerable fortune' he could bring into the country (1761). Frederick thereupon ordered the judicial authorities to extend to Marcuse and his heirs the same status, inside and outside the courts, as that of a Christian banker, together with permission to purchase a house and also to settle his children. This was, *mutatis mutandis*, comparable to a patent that granted Itzig and Ephraim a 'general privilege of Christian merchants and bankers'. This was their share of the politico-economic quid pro quo. The patent freed the two men and all their descendants from the restrictions imposed on Jews in trade, commerce and the legal system and granted them the same freedom to acquire property, to settle and to trade as that enjoyed by Christians. Some 23 other families also received a 'general privilege' from Frederick. Most came from Berlin, others from Rathenau (Pinthus Levi, a purveyor of grain and horses during the war), from Halberstadt (Michael Abraham), from Breslau (the mint-master Moses Heumann). Also from Breslau came R. Joseph Jonas Fraenckel, honoured with a general privilege and the rights of a Christian banker. He merited this distinction through his part in the export of silk goods to Russia, Poland, Lithuania, Moldavia and Wallachia, and in his financing of Silesian wool manufactures. Fraenckel's general privilege cost him 4000 Reichsthaler in 'old' coin. Jacob Moses, a merchant and banker, who followed Veitel Ephraim as senior elder in 1775, was awarded the legal status of a Christian banker, with the right to settle and trade anywhere in the kingdom.[32] In 1791 Daniel Itzig won a grant of naturalization which applied also to his 16 children (but not to the second generation).

These titles and privileges concerned not only individuals but – and this is indeed meaningful – the oligarchs were able to secure certain concessions that applied to second children as a collective. In return for their yielding to governmental pressure to assume full responsibility for the operation of a factory in Templin making caps and stockings, the second children of *Schutzjuden* were granted, inter alia, certain tax and excise reliefs, monopoly rights on the sale of the factory's products, permission to purchase wool at the regular fairs and the right to settle in the area of their parents. The oligarchs – Veitel Ephraim, Daniel Itzig, Abraham Marcus, Hirsch David and Jacob Moses – negotiated with the authorities not in their own name but in that of all Jewry in all the territories of the Prussian crown, except for Silesia.[33]

This degree of 'emancipation' was not of course general. Frederick limited Jewish occupations to trade and commerce and certain manufactures. Thus he ordered that Christians replace those Jews who operated distilleries and taverns on the estates of the Polish nobility in Upper Silesia. In Prussia the state preserved the distinction between the wealthy and useful Jews who were to be welcomed, and the poor and useless Jews for whom Prussia had no place, for example 'the useless Jewish rabble' in Breslau were to be expelled; and in 1775, (that is after the first partition of Poland) in defiance of his own mercantilist *raison d'état* Frederick disregarded a memorandum from the senior elder, Jacob Moses, cautioning the king that his policy of expelling the Jews from the Netze district of West Prussia jeopardized the

Jews' taxpaying capacity and endangered Prussian trade with Poland. Frederick distinguished between 'the well-to-do commercial Jews', who must be retained and cherished, and 'the beggar Jews in the countryside as well as the towns who must be removed, one by one, and without violence'. By 1786 'only' about 7000 of the *c.*25 000 Jews had been expelled.[34]

In the Jewish sources the voice of the poor is rarely heard. To Christian missionaries, vagrant and expelled Jews, condemned to wander with wife and children from one *kehillah* to the next, did vent bitterness and resentment. The wealthy in their 'magnificent garments' dismissed the poor with a pittance, the latter complained, and even demanded payment for entry to their *kehillot*. The *hekdesh* by the Rosenthaler gate in Berlin served as a sort of interrogation centre for intending entrants who could thereby be 'persuaded' to move elsewhere.[35] Measures such as these enabled Berlin Jewry in the 1780s to maintain an unusual degree of affluence. An uncharacteristic proportion of Jews enjoyed middling wealth – 239 families, probably over one-third of all Jews in Berlin, it is estimated. The family head would be a petty merchant, pawnbroker or old-clothes dealer. In good years he made a living; in bad years he might fall into bankruptcy.[36]

Unmistakable symptoms of decadence accompanied this unusually favourable socio-economic distribution. Towards the end of the century the earlier dynamism began to flag. In Berlin alone the evidence from the late 1770s suggests a decline in population. The second and still more the third generation of the 'founding fathers' typically lacked the dynamism of their fathers; for example, Benjamin Veitel Ephraim, the youngest son of Veitel Heine Ephraim, composed dramas and political pamphlets and established a collection of Jewish art. In the early years of the French Revolution he also served as some sort of diplomatic agent on behalf of Prussia. Isaac Daniel Itzig, the eldest son of Daniel Itzig, had cultural interests which led him to take part in the foundation of the Jews' Free School in 1778. Even members of the Ephraim and Bernhard families went bankrupt and fell into dependence on communal aid. There are the first signs of conversion: already in the 1770s a doctor in Königsberg took this step, and in 1786 Rebecca and Blümchen, two daughters of the wealthy mint-Jew Moses Isaac, did likewise (and married Prussian noblemen).[37] This presaged the same phenomenon among the 'Salondamen' of *fin-de-siècle* Berlin. Disaffection from Judaism and the *kehillah* showed itself in a variety of ways; for example, in the refusal of elected *kehillah* officials to assume office and to accept, as did Solomon Halphen in 1765, the alternative of a fine. In 1783 Aaron Wessely appealed, unsuccessfully, to the authorities to free him from the office of communal tax assessor.[38] Part of the same disengagement from the *kehillah* was the resort to gentile courts; so much so that in 1770 Frederick ordered the Berlin leaders to supply the civil court with a statement of Jewish ritual law to enable such courts to adjudicate between Jewish litigants. In their embarrassment the elders turned to R. Jonathan Eibeschütz of Metz, who had had to supply in French to the Parlement a statement of Jewish law (*Hoshen Mishpat*) in the same circumstances that now obtained in Berlin. There is no record of any reply from Metz. The Berlin version eventually appeared in 1776, the joint work of R. Hirschel Levin and Moses Mendelssohn. It is best described as a compilation of guidelines in relation to inheritance, guardianships, bequests, wills and the property rights acquired by each party to a marriage contract. But the preamble also made it clear that these guidelines could hardly guide a judge who, in his endeavour to apply Jewish law to a particular case, did not know Hebrew, had not studied the Talmud and law codes and could not therefore, where necessary, draw on the sources of the laws. The authority of Jewish law was limited to matters of personal status and family concerns. This is borne out by the testimony of R. Hirschel Levin. In 1798 when the aged chief rabbi sought from King Frederick William III some alleviation of his duties, the only cases he directly mentioned concerned 'inheritances and divorces'. It is clear that in these respects Jews were subject to their own jurisdiction – but not without significant protest, another sign of disarray: in 1802, Elias Jacob Moses, a banker from Friedberg in the Neumark, and in 1803 the banker Ruben Samuel Gumpertz, one of the presidents of the Berlin stock exchange, sought permission from Goldbeck, the Prussian chancellor, to make wills in accordance with the laws of the land, even if, to quote Gumpertz, this 'should run counter to the Jewish ritual laws'. Moses did indeed have the right to make his will in a Christian court, in accordance with the general law, Goldbeck informed him. But testamentary dispositions in relation to his heirs must be so formulated as to conform to the prescriptions of the Jewish ritual laws.[39]

In 1775 in an obscure but telling submission to the Prussian authorities the rabbis and elders in all the Prussian provinces jointly requested protection from the 'lack of respect' shown to them. In 1778 Daniel Itzig and Jacob Moses, the senior elders in Berlin, reported that whereas certain individuals paid the taxes due to the state, these Jews also took the view that they did not have to make annual contributions to the charity-chest, hospital, fund for foreign Jews, upkeep of the rabbi and cantor, 'and other communal needs'. Heirs of protected Jews, the report added, were also refusing to take on their proportional obligations of charitable dues which the deceased had discharged during his lifetime and which his successors had, as it were, inherited. The Directory-General at once responded with an emphatic rejection of all such efforts to evade communal obligations.[40]

The *kehillah*, as the seat of learning, worship and rabbinic jurisdiction, could not escape the general decadence. The translator of the Hebrew prayers into German (first edition, Königsberg, 1786) wrote:

> How deplorable is it, dear friend, that if we are to hold fast to the pre-
> scribed and traditional prayers, which are uttered in a language of which

we understand not a word, almost all the women, and most of the men of our nation will be unable to savour this delight.

Mendelssohn's translation of the Pentateuch into German (though printed in Hebrew characters) was in part intended to remedy the loss of Hebrew for which reason it was welcomed by R. Hirschel Levin.[41] The yeshivah in Berlin no longer functioned. The historian of the Berlin rabbinate commended chief rabbi Hirschel Levin who came to Berlin in 1772 for his achievement 'in teaching many students in his great yeshivah'. But about a decade later, this institution was no more and David Friedländer, of the Jewish Enlightenment, the Haskalah, could claim that in Berlin 'true Talmudism' had disappeared, and the rabbis had lost their power.[42] In accord with this view, the Jews' Free School, of which Friedländer was part-founder with Isaac Daniel Itzig, had a curriculum which reduced the study of Judaism to 'religion'. This was a leitmotiv of the Haskalah, and in the next generation encouraged the composition of children's catechisms which distinguished between the moral teachings of religion – 'its non-juridical categories' – and 'those that were increasingly seen as truly juridical ones'. This pioneering process of 'delegalization' also served an apologetic purpose in that it disarmed those critics who denounced Judaism as a religion of legality.[43] This was not the only symptom of a sentiment of inferiority *vis-à-vis* the contemporary non-Jewish world.

Towards the end of Frederick's reign in 1783, Mendelssohn published his *Jerusalem, or on Religious Power and Judaism*. This work has the character of a *pièce d'occasion* which yet became a major contribution to the contemporary debate on the *kehillah* in the context of the ongoing struggle for release from discrimination. *Jerusalem* takes into account the diminished role of the *kehillah*, the increased proximity to the state, such acceptance as had been achieved, and, lastly, the demand of the Enlightenment for a rational Judaism. And this whole programme Mendelssohn combined with an adherence to the revelation. Of course Mendelssohn's espousal of the Enlightenment, as Rosenzweig pointed out, left German Jewry 'defenceless'.[44]

Jerusalem belongs to its time as a manifesto. It takes the form of a rejoinder to a tract by August Cranz, *The Searching for Light and Right in a Letter to Herr Moses Mendelssohn Occasioned by His Remarkable Preface to Menasseh b. Israel* (1782). The work in question was a German translation of Menasseh's treatise *Vindiciae Judaeorum* of 1656. Mendelssohn's preface had been read in a hostile spirit as an acknowledgement on Mendelssohn's part that the Judaism he practised was incompatible with the admission of the Jews to civil society, by reason of the fact that the laws relating to the Sabbath, marriage and diet, for example, separated the Jews from their fellow-subjects to such an extent as would prevent them from participating in the life of the state as equals. Thus the issue at stake between Cranz and Mendelssohn was eminently political, and the latter's rejoinder to a particular polemicist assumed a general importance, not only from the standpoint of those gentile authorities who saw the Jews as constituting 'a state within a state' but also from the standpoint of those *maskilic* Jews to whom the laws formed a barrier to their political admission, on an equal basis into gentile society. There is yet a third perspective in which to regard *Jerusalem* – as a positive response to the challenge presented by the decline of the contemporary *kehillah*. Mendelssohn sought to salvage the essential and in this he anticipates the stirrings of the Napoleonic period and the *modus vivendi* of the nineteenth century.

In his introduction to *Vindiciae Judaeorum*, Mendelssohn had already broached the one basic theme that was to dominate the first part of *Jerusalem*: the denial of authority in worldly matters to any church and the similar denial to the state of any right to associate the enjoyment of earthly goods with the profession of congenial opinions; a right that the state itself did not possess, it obviously could not grant to any body of its subjects and sanction the exclusion of those who held dissident or offensive opinions that were not congenial.[45] Thus, in the first part of *Jerusalem*, Mendelssohn takes up the arguments earlier expounded by Locke and the English deists in favour of the separation of church and state, so that neither would enjoy a position of power outside their respective realms. *Jerusalem* here postulates an ideal division of authority where

neither church nor state has a right to subject men's principles and convictions to any coercion whatsoever. Neither church nor state is authorised to connect privileges and rights, claims on persons and title to things, with principles and convictions, and to weaken through outside interference the influence of the power of truth upon the cognitive faculty. Not even the social contract could grant such a right to either state or church. For a contract concerning things which, by their very nature, are inalienable, is intrinsically invalid and cancels itself.[46]

This argument is presented in terms that transcend Judaism or Christianity (neither of which is at all mentioned) or indeed any specific religion, state or society (save for a passing reference to the Anglican church and the Thirty-Nine Articles). It is wholly abstract and ideal. Only in the second part of *Jerusalem* does Mendelssohn engage with the particular problem of presenting Judaism in such terms as to make it amenable to the ideal scheme of the first part, that is, that it lacks any temporal claims or political demands. This required a rewriting of Jewish history, on the lines that Spinoza had pioneered. Mendelssohn followed Spinoza in his reading of Jewish history in so far as he also made a very sharp distinction between the period before and after statehood.[47] Only with the destruction of the Temple and the loss of a political entity could modern, enlightened Judaism emerge: 'The Mosaic constitution did not persist in its erstwhile purity.' What was initially a theocracy, which brought together civil, political and religious power in one governmental entity, became through force of circumstances an entity that was purely religious: 'The civil bonds of the nation were dissolved; religious offences were no longer crimes against the state; and the religion, as religion, knows of no punishment, no other penalty than the one the remorseful sinner *voluntarily* imposes on himself.' This signified the end of the authority to impose any sentence of *herem*. The Mosaic constitution no longer existed. Moreover, Mendelssohn added, since Judaism possessed no dogmas or articles of belief it had no need of any coercive machinery or enforcement. It was already in a position to enter that ideal situation where the practice of religion would be confined to the private sphere.

Thus far Mendelssohn could agree with Spinoza without overmuch difficulty. But whereas the latter, rejecting altogether the notions of election, and of a personal God, and seeing the whole *raison d'être* of the Sinaitic revelation primarily in its political import, could attribute no further validity to a continuing Jewish existence, for Mendelssohn the 'personal commandments', also proclaimed at Sinai, as distinct from the 'political commandments', continued to retain all their authority.[48] Here there is a decisive break from Spinoza of overwhelming importance. It required Mendelssohn despite his purpose in emancipating his people from discrimination, to impose conditions that the Christian world was called on to accept, on the admission of Jews to the enjoyment of legal rights. He mentions no more than those laws relating to Kashrut and marriage (more or less, the prevailing situation), but the message is clear: in the near-peroration to *Jerusalem*, Mendelssohn addresses the Christian world:

> Should you believe that you cannot have us in return as brothers and unite with us as citizens as long as we are outwardly distinguished from you by the ceremonial law, do not eat with you, do not marry you … which we cannot suppose of Christian-minded men – if civil union cannot be obtained under any other condition than our departing from the laws which we still consider binding on us, then we are sincerely sorry to find it necessary to declare that we must rather do without civil union.[49]

There is an inconsistency here which Solomon Maimon, although a great admirer of Mendelssohn, quickly pointed out: how could Mendelssohn, who denied to religion any authority in civil matters, legitimately protest at the action of R. Raphael Cohen, chief rabbi of Hamburg, in imposing the sentence of *herem* on Samuel Marcus for his public transgression of the law? On the one hand, Maimon argued, Mendelssohn proclaimed the permanency of 'the Jewish-ecclesiastical state'; on the other, he denied to this state power in civil matters. 'What is a state without rights?', Maimon demanded.[50]

So long as the Sinaitic revelation was still in force, as Mendelssohn maintained, then did its recipients not remain committed to it, not free to choose and subject to sanction in case of infringement, Maimon asked? The notion of a voluntary adherence was untenable.

But why should this be a barrier to a *bürgerliche Vereinigung* – civil union – that did not require a *Glaubensvereinigung* – union of belief, Mendelssohn could respond. All the more so, he might add, in the light of the many legal devices that reconciled the demands of the state with those of Jewish law. In these pragmatic-political terms, events vindicated the model that Mendelssohn projected. In a few years' time, in the early years of the French Revolution, Mendelssohn would first find true disciples in the Jewish leaders of Metz and Alsace. (He had none in Germany.) This would be confirmed in the Napoleonic settlement of 1806–7. Judaism must indeed sacrifice its own political claims but would in return receive a *locus standi* that left intact much of its other legislation. This solution to the problem posed by emancipation from the *kehillah* and incorporation as a citizen was endorsed in France and throughout the nineteenth century came to prevail elsewhere, haltingly and painfully. The first test, however, came in the Habsburg empire, more particularly through its role in the renaming of the Jews.

13

On the Eve, in France

In the decades preceding the revolution the three communities on French soil pursued their separate existence, but to a diminishing extent. The major change was the disappearance of the earlier status quo as between the Sephardim of the south-west and the Jews of the Comtat, the Avignonnais, in favour of parity of esteem. As late as 1752, according to the intendant de Tourny, 'The enmity between the Portuguese and the Avignonnais is greater than between the Catholics and the Portuguese.'[1] However, by the mid-1760s a small group of six families from Avignon had secured the right to establish their own community in Bordeaux. They were authorized to exercise self-government to the extent that an *arrêt* permitted them to elect their own syndic and deputies and to impose their own taxes. In 1775 three more Avignon families were admitted to the privileges enjoyed by the original six. At least by 1777, the Avignon Jews had their own synagogue in Bordeaux.[2] This success followed the increasing economic enterprise of the Provençal Jewish traders. Christian complaints make it easy to follow their tracks throughout Provence and Languedoc – they come from Montpellier, Toulouse, Nîmes, Narbonne, Aix and Marseilles; from many lesser centres as well as further afield; from Brittany, Normandy, Poitou, Burgundy and the Dauphiné. In Paris, Israël Bernard de Vallabrègue became 'secrétaire interprète du roi pour les langues orientales'.

The traders from the Comtat had to overcome or circumvent the rivalry of the Christians. In Languedoc in 1738 this rivalry took the form of not only a ban on the sale of their animals but sometimes also the actual seizure of the mules the Jews were trading in. In 1775–6 and 1784 the Parlement at Aix issued expulsion orders against the Jews and tried to ban their trade (except at fairs) at Grasse, Draguignan, Lorgues and Fréjus.[3]

These Jews were trading in draperies, silks, cattle, horses, hides, jewellery, olive oil and grapes. On the 33rd day of the 'Omer' 5512 (= 2 May 1752) David de Milhaud the younger wrote to a certain Asher of Prague, then living in Turin:

> Last year at the fair in Beaucaire I met some Jews from Turin. If your Honour could make it your business to find out if they are returning this year to the fair they could bring some goods that I have asked for... If I had contacts at Turin we could perhaps join together in the future for the sale of woollen goods which I am engaged in. Every year in fact I sell them in large quantities at Aix, Nice, Lyons and elsewhere. These goods include thick winter blankets, heavy clothing for prisoners of war and soldiers, and thick, coarse canvas to wrap up packages loaded on to mules and carts, as well as woollen decorations hung on the necks of pack horses.[4]

There was also a certain amount of moneylending, sometimes in large sums, for example in 1772–3 the young Mirabeau was indebted to Daniel de Beaucaire of l'Isle-sur-Sorgue in the sum of 40 000 livres.[5]

In the concessions forced on the Sephardim in Bordeaux two factors stand out: the demographic and the religious. A certain degree of demographic stagnation began to show itself from about mid-century, and also assimilation. Between 1752 and 1787 at Saint-Esprit there were more deaths than births – 1032 against 992; in Bordeaux between 1758 and 1802 the comparable figures were 1870 as against 1878. The population was ageing and the number of marriages declining – at Saint-Esprit, for example, from 100 (1751–65) to 75 (1771–85). The size of families also dropped; in Bordeaux, couples with five children or more which accounted in 1751 for 22.5 per cent of all couples were 19.59 per cent in 1808. In Bordeaux also there was a distinct decline in the number of individuals born between 1768 and 1783. This is probably to be attributed to voluntary birth restriction and/or to a slowdown in immigration. From the mid-eighteenth century the birth-rate at Bordeaux was no more than 16.66 per 100.[6]

As for the religious factor, much contemporary evidence points to a synagogue-centred *kahal*, on the Amsterdam model, that certainly extended to the observance of the Sabbath. Not only did major communities purchase exemption from certain security commitments on the Sabbath (for example guard duty), but well-attested sources confirm the refusal of individuals (for example David Gradis) to sign contracts on the Sabbath.[7] For all that, it would not seem unfair to say of the Sephardim – of their leaders particularly – that they wore their Judaism lightly: rationalism and the values of the Enlightenment had seemingly coloured the views of such communal leaders as Abraham Gradis, Salomon Lopez, Abraham Furtado, Lopez-Dubec and Jacob Robles. Never had he 'believed in any other religion than that which nature has engraved in their conscience', Jacob Robles declared in his will. This antinomianism and internalized source of value was by no means unusual. Salomon Lopez was another leading Sephardi who did not believe in the Oral Law of the rabbis and, according to R. Hayyim David Azulay, 'considered himself a philosopher'. Azulay described Abraham Gradis as 'one of those great heretics who do not believe in the Oral Law and eat forbidden dishes in public'.[8]

To this form of observance the Oral Law had little, if anything, to contribute. On the contrary, 'The rabbi will take no part in the affairs of the *Nation*, and he will limit himself [*se contentera*] to everything that touches on his ministry,' decreed the Bayonne communal statutes of 1753 (article xxxiii); the same statute forbade him to attempt to augment his salary, 'on any pretext whatsoever'. At Bordeaux the rabbi authorized marriages, supervised the preparation of kosher wine and *matzot*, administered oaths, and taught at the Talmud Torah school, which he may also have directed. The *Nation* decided of its own accord whether to call a sitting of the rabbinical court. When Haham Falcon, the first rabbi at Bordeaux, was replaced in 1738 by Jacob Atias, the communal record specified that 'he can at no time and under no pretext whatsoever impose any penalty or publish anything whatsoever against any member of the *Nation* without the express and written permission of the parnassim, the *gabbay* and of the two elders of the *Nation*.' One member of the Bordeaux rabbinate had to approach the intendant to intervene with the community and secure for him a greater degree of respect. At Bayonne when R. Raphael Meldola left in 1741, no successor was appointed.[9]

This outlook also largely governed the curriculum of the Talmud Torah school. It was maintained partly by communal taxes and individual contributions and partly by a surcharge on the sale price of kosher meat. This school existed in 1731 and in the 1760s and 1770s but its uninterrupted existence is not established. No boy was admitted below the age of five. There were two classes: in the first the boys studied Hebrew up to a level where, after an examination, they could enter the second: here pupils learned to translate into Spanish the Pentateuch, Prophets and Psalms. The statutes ruled out corporal punishment. A beadle saw to it that truants were detected. The regulations of 1774 made an important addition to the curriculum by including instruction in arithmetic and written and spoken French, to be taught at a time 'the least harmful to the study of Hebrew'. Provision also existed for a third class devoted to Biblical studies which were, however, restricted to

> the insight (*l'intelligence*) of our best commentators, that is to say, those who, being themselves the best grammarians, have most attached themselves to the literal meaning of the text, the sole means to discover the true duties prescribed to us by God.

This constraint and the dismissal of rabbinic teaching disturbed and even alarmed contemporary scholars. They study only the Bible [exclaimed Azulai in 1788]. 'They do not want to teach Rashi's commentary because it contains

Midrashim and the explanations of the rabbis. Not even Maimonides do they want. Woe to the eyes which see such things'.[10]

To judge from the schools at Saint-Esprit (Bayonne) and Peyrehorade and perhaps Bidache, the scholastic situation was there no different. Education in Judaism, here, as elsewhere in the Sephardi diaspora, was bibliocentric, confined to the inculcation of certain moral values and linguistic competence to the exclusion of the Oral Law. For the graduated curriculum of the Sephardim there was certainly admiration among Ashkenazi scholars but also certainly not for its limitation. Classes met from 7 to 11 and 2 to 6 in summer and from 9 to 11 and 1 to 4 in winter.

To some extent the school in Bordeaux served not only as a medium of instruction but also as a means of social control and even public hygiene. Thus, those families on the communal poor roll would be struck off should their children fail to attend school. Those families in appropriate circumstances would be required to provide their children with the Bibles and other books necessary for their studies. Only the children of the poor, unable to purchase books, would have their needs met. The teachers were to take care to instruct first those children of the poor who sold thread and braid and other goods in town: this would enable them to leave without delay (*pour qu'ils puissent sortir soudain*), though not in advance of other pupils. The new regulations of 1774 showed concern for the hygiene and medical condition of the pupils: the doctors employed by the *Nation* must examine each pupil on the first Sunday of each (Hebrew) month for signs of infectious disease. As an additional precaution against contagion, mothers were made responsible for seeing that pupils changed their chemises at least twice a week. Chemises and shoes would be provided for the most needy. Abraham Gradis took a central role in fostering the school's vocational purpose by encouraging the study of French and '*les chiffres*'.[11]

The children of the wealthy tended to be educated at home. But the same sort of educational constraints applied: 'I was born on 28 April 1743,' writes Salomon Lopès-Dubec of Bordeaux, in an autobiographical memoir which also describes his financial successes as shipper, overseas trader and Sephardi political leader. In 1815 he was appointed deputy mayor of Bordeaux:

> I was taught to read French and Hebrew; to write, arithmetic and exchange operations. This was at that time the only instruction given to Israelite children, who, finding themselves excluded by the laws of the kingdom from all the professions, even the arts and crafts, for the exercise of which it was necessary to be Catholic, were exclusively destined for commerce.[12]

With those Jews in the *carrières* of Provence and the ghetto of Metz, the Sephardim shared a common patriotism and a devotion to the monarchy.

When Louis XV fell ill in 1744, when he was the target of a would-be assassin in 1757, when he died in 1774 – concern was general. Synagogues organized special services, as the occasion demanded, to call for divine intervention; there was fasting and the public recital of psalms and abstention from all normal activity. In 1782 'patriotism and loyalty to the king' led the *Nation*, following an invitation from the Bordeaux chamber of commerce, to subscribe more than 60000 livres for a new ship of the line.[13]

Patriotism on these lines was one of the few features common to the Sephardim of the south-west and the Ashkenazim of Metz and Alsace. But the latter combined their patriotism with a much greater emphasis on an autonomy that served religio-political purposes. As a result, in Alsace and eastern France in the mid-eighteenth century two worlds confronted each other. In the same way as certain Jewish leaders sought to make an amalgam of the scattered Ashkenazi *kehillot*, so too did the French state seek to extend and centralize its control in the east. In the long run, the two aims were in obvious conflict. The state, whether monarchic, republican or Napoleonic, refused to tolerate or acknowledge an independent jurisdiction and source of authority. When the military purveyor Cerf Berr (1726–93) became *préposé général*, a degree of centralization that was undertaken gave political meaning to the concept of the 'Nation juive d'Alsace', creating from dispersed Alsatian Jewry a united force.

This was by no means the only vision of the future *kehillah*. A model that had affinities with those of both Spinoza and Mendelssohn was presented by Zalkind Hourwitz (b. near Lublin 1751 – d. Paris 1812). He was a self-styled *juif polonais*, a journalist and interpreter in oriental manuscripts to the Bibliothèque Royale. Hourwitz wrote in response to a competition organized in Metz in 1785. La Société Royale des Arts et des Sciences offered a prize for an essay on the theme 'Are there means of making the Jews more happy and more useful in France?' As a deist, Judaism to Hourwitz meant no more than 'praying to the supreme being in Hebrew'. Hourwitz espoused the notion of a natural religion. In his relationship to Judaism as a political construct, Hourwitz, much like Spinoza and Mendelssohn, vigorously denied that the Jews, since the dispersion, had any 'political laws'. This created a certain ambivalence in respect of collective Jewish existence: on the one hand, Hourwitz recommended the destruction of 'Jewish quarters' (*les Juiveries*) but not that of the communities: '[L]et them, therefore, continue to exist with their synagogues, their hospitals and their cemeteries; those who wish to benefit from them will contribute to all their expenses, as in the past.' Jews must also be permitted to acquire property ('which will attach them to the country'), to practise all liberal, mechanical and agricultural arts, and to enjoy full freedom of trade and manufacture. But they must be forbidden the use of Hebrew and Yiddish in their book-keeping and contracts; the public schools must be made accessible to their children for the learning of French; and in order the better to intercourse further with Christians, the rabbis and communal elders must be 'strictly forbidden from arrogating to themselves the slightest authority over their fellow-Jews outside the synagogue...'[14] This was the voice of an outsider to whom only the Revolution would bring any sort of influence.

In Alsace itself, in the last years of the *ancien régime*, only the activity of Cerf Berr had any importance. In political terms, he stood out among a group of powerful *préposés* such as Moïse Belin, Aron Meyer and Lippmann Netter who used their status and wealth to try to enhance the occupational and social standing of the Ashkenazim in France. Cerf Berr was born in the hamlet of Medelsheim (hence he sometimes signed with 'Hirtz Medelsheim') to a merchant family in comfortable circumstances and received an advanced education. All his life he remained punctilious in his observance of the laws, and a staunch monarchist. A contemporary portrait in oils shows him clothed in a costume of dark-green velvet, edged with pink taffeta, set off by a delicate lace jabot. He is wearing a white powdered wig.[15] Of Cerf Berr's early years little is known beyond the fact that he entered the service of German rulers allied to France with possessions in Alsace and Lorraine – the Duc de Deux-Ponts, the Landgrave of Hesse-Darmstadt and the Prince de Nassau-Sarrewerden. At the age of 30 he was a protégé of the Duc de Choiseul as military supplier at the beginning of the Seven Years' War (1756). As a military contractor in Alsace and Lorraine Louis XVI granted him letters of naturalization in gratitude for his services as *'entrepreneur des subsistances aux Armées de Sa Majesté'* (1775). In 1785 Cerf Berr relinquished control of his extensive banking and commercial interests to his sons and sons-in-law (by his first wife, Julie Abraham, he had four sons and four daughters) so that he could concentrate on supplying the military. He used some of his wealth to establish a school for the study of the Talmud, an endowment for poor young girls and also a pious foundation, and he subsidized the publication of religious works. He was also the main financial support of the impoverished Jewish communities of eastern France in the years before the Revolution, especially Metz. Cerf Berr exemplified his concern for scholarship through his interest in the welfare of the yeshivot at Bouxwiller and Ettendorf conducted by R. Wolf Reichshoffer. A provision in the marriage contract (1790) of his orphaned niece Demoiselle Bella Berr endowed the young couple with an annual income of 1000 French livres for 10 years, on condition that the husband refrain entirely from commerce and devote himself exclusively to study.[16]

Cerf Berr's political campaign had a mixed character. In one respect he fought to assert a right to residence in the forbidden city of Strasbourg. The authority to collect the *péage corporel* was farmed out, to the banker Moïse Belin (1736–54) and to Cerf Berr (1763–75). During the latter period Cerf Berr used his influence as a military contractor, with Choiseul and Louis XVI, to break the resistance of the Strasbourg local authorities and convert his residence in the city from temporary into permanent. During 1767–8 he prolonged a permitted stay, first leasing a house and then purchasing adjoining property through the employment of a Christian 'front', the French ambassador to Prussia. This enabled him to accommodate the households of his sons and sons-in-law – 68 or 70 persons in all, including domestic servants. By letters patent of 1771 the king authorised Cerf Berr to reside and acquire property anywhere in the kingdom. The suit brought against Cerf Berr by the Strasbourg magistrates dragged on, amidst the thrust and counter-thrust of *mémoires*, until 1791 when political events put it out of court.[17] A breach had been made in the city's defences against the Jews, and Strasbourg alienated from the court.

This formed no more than part of Cerf Berr's activity and perhaps not the most important. Rather, if he were to establish the Nation Juive d'Alsace then the reform of its communal structure must precede and buttress its political aspirations. In 1770, Cerf Berr in his capacity as *préposé général* of the *Nation*, advanced the work of centralization with a requirement that candidates for the office of local *préposé* be subject to the approval of the departmental rabbi and of the *préposés généraux*, who would have the right to exclude those individuals whom they did not find capable; further, that any other Jew claiming to be *préposé* by virtue of seigneurial choice be subject to those *préposés* who had been 'elected, recognized and installed in accordance with the above ordinances'. This policy advanced with the summoning of a number of general assemblies of the *Nation Juive d'Alsace*. They had an obvious affinity with the *Landjudenschaften* in the German states to the east. In 1777, delegates representing 42 communities met at Niedernai where they codified earlier communal regulations and added others. The 'protocol of the *Nation* of the assembly of Iyar 21 (5)537' (= May 28, 1777) has two main themes: religious and political. The first is concerned to provide funds, raised by indirect taxation, *inter alia*, for two schools of Talmudic study at Ettendorf and Sierentz and for the establishment of a *Klaus* offering a three-year study cycle, the necessary funds to be raised from fines imposed on those who failed to make true declaration of their assets, from a tithe raised on dowries and from sundry appeals throughout Alsace. In politico-organizational terms the Niedernai assembly resolved that in external matters the Jews remained subordinate to the seigneurs; that the *préposés généraux* and rabbis were responsible for matters of internal Jewish discipline, the former also being recognized as 'heads of the *Nation*'; that the election of local *préposés* was without prejudice to the right of the seigneurs to nominate their own *préposés* empowered to impose their taxes. They had the power 'to punish whomsoever disregards their authority with a fine of 50 crowns, to be paid into the treasury of the *Nation*'. Against whomsoever committed an irreligious act, they could, in the presence of a tribunal of three rabbis, and subject to the approval of the intendant pronounce a sentence of *herem* and *niddui*. In 1778, given the continuing inability of the *Nation Juive d'Alsace* to meet absolutely unavoidable expenses, Cerf Berr was requested to raise a loan in Paris of

40 000–50 000 livres at the cheapest possible rate. This was approved by the intendant. The loan would be secured on the property of the *Nation*. The general assembly summoned for 1780 in Bischheim also concerned itself with financial matters – more specifically, with raising, for communal purposes, 28 800 livres from 51 communities in Upper Alsace and 12 000 livres from 47 communities in Lower Alsace. The ordinances issued by these and other assemblies had the highest sanction in that they were equated with 'the law of our holy Torah, which has been transmitted to the august rabbis, parnassim and to the *shtadlanim* of the *Medinah*' (= 'the nation's intercessors').[18] Two years later, in a letter dated 12 Av 5542 (= 23 July 1782), Cerf Berr (signing himself Hirtz Medelsheim) called on R. Reichshoffer to summon an assembly of all parnassim, again to debate the budget of the *Medinah*.

The *Nation* did not neglect local issues. In the name of the *Nation*, Cerf Berr led a triumvirate of *préposés généraux*, in their protest at the profanation of the cemetery in Ettendorf. They demanded that the curé and all others 'be enjoined not to put rabbits, to hunt or to cut the grass' in their cemeteries (1773). At another time (1780) the *préposés* requested that a Jew, imprisoned in Saverne for not paying the body tax be released on the grounds of his feeble-mindedness.[19]

In Metz the incidence of poverty was no less than in Alsace. This followed from the burden of communal outgoings, legal expenses, gifts in aid, and the increasing indebtedness of the community. The Brancas tax alone cost the community one and a half million livres over the 70 years of its existence (1718–90). The average tax burden per household increased from 150 livres 1700–14 to 215 livres by the outbreak of the Revolution. Even so, the sums raised were far from matching the total of communal expenses. The loss of their 'primacy' by the Metz élite of military purveyors aggravated the situation. They lost ground to Cerf Berr or other suppliers such as Mayer Marx of Landau or Berr Isaac Berr of Nancy. Two brothers from Sarrelouis, Hayem Olry Worms and Cerf Olry Worms, stood out in the Seven Years' War as purveyors of meat, fodder and horses to the French forces.[20] Further, between 1740 and 1789 a Christian merchant house (the Dosquet family) took the place of the Jews as suppliers of grain. By way of exception, in 1770–1, Cerf Berr and the Worms brothers imported grain 'at great expense and risk' to avert shortages in Strasbourg and Sarrelouis.

From about the mid-century outgoings gravely exceeded communal receipts. To cover the deficit the leaders took out loans with Christian financiers in return for the issuance of annuities. Between 1748 and 1789 the community took out 990 of these loans, to a total of 526 000 livres, and the annuities payable grew from *c.*17 000 livres (in 1750) to 47 000 livres in 1789. (A political motive also operated, for the Christian creditors and annuitants now had an interest in the continuing stability of the *kehillah*.)

All sorts of expedients were resorted to, as a means to reach financial equilibrium. The Metz syndics introduced indirect taxes on meat, wines and liqueurs, on horse sales and inheritances. In 1750, in order to avert the growth of the poor, those couples where the bride's dowry did not total at least 2400 livres were forbidden to marry. (This parallels similar measures in Posen and Hamburg – see p. 190 above.) They tried to increase the proportion of the taxes paid by those smaller communities in the *généralité de Metz*, but in 1772 of their 334 taxpayers 185 lacked a secure income. In 1769 and 1779 sumptuary regulations would enforce economies. To this extremity a further guide is a decision of the communal council, sanctioned by the rabbinical court, of 1782 ('on the 25th day of the month of Adar, 5542') on the basis that 'the poor of one's own city come first', donations, originally destined for the poor of Palestine, were diverted to the local poor. To fiscal pressure and financial hardship the sequel was the polarization of the community – probably to a greater extent than elsewhere – between a tiny minority of extremely wealthy families and a mass of impoverished and pauperized peddlers and moneylenders. The 'middle class' tended to disappear. The tax rolls for 1790 show that 15 family heads paid more than 500 livres whereas 582 (83 per cent of all taxpayers) paid less than 100 livres and of these 416 paid less than 50. This had a political consequence in making it difficult to recruit sufficient members for the second college of 'middling' electors.[21]

Poverty was accompanied by demographic stagnation. From the 1770s a decline set in. In the 1760s the population had totalled 2500–2700 but by 1789 was barely more than 2200 (593 families). This total was virtually unchanged from 1739. The demographic weakness in the 1770s and after was a consequence of the poverty that afflicted young men in particular. Not only did they suffer from lack of employment – accommodation became more and more scarce in the ghetto of Metz. No new houses were built in the decades 1739–89 and limits were set to the construction of additional storeys. The daughters of the poor, on the other hand, had the benefit of the fraternities that provided poor girls with dowries and of bequests for this purpose. This was an Ashkenazi version of the *dotar* society among the Sephardim. In Metz the male–female differentiation shows in the relative number of celibacies: in the period 1760–89 of those persons who died celibate aged 50 or over, 56 were men (12.6 per cent of males) and 31 were women (7.6 per cent of all females). The governing council of the community resembled 'a gerontocracy to a certain extent', the average age being 61.[22]

The affair of 'the forged receipts' made the poverty and distress in Alsace, among the Christian peasantry no less than among the Jews, a political theme. In 1778 a sworn and avowed antisemite, Jean-François Hell, a bailiff from Landser, orchestrated a campaign among the impoverished and indebted peasants of the Sundgau whereby they were provided with forged documents, in Hebrew, purporting to be receipts for the debts outstanding to their Jewish creditors. Hell also published antisemitic pamphlets. The creditors took their case to the court at Colmar and the perpetrators of the forgeries were hanged, or sentenced to the galleys for varying periods or to imprisonment and exile. This did not quell the fermenting antisemitism. At its peak the scandal of poverty and distress among the peasantry engaged the attention of the Conseil d'Etat and the Sovereign Council of Colmar. Baron de Spon, first president of the Conseil Souverain d' Alsace, proposed that Christians and Jews be prohibited from 'contracting fresh obligations or redemptions otherwise than in the presence of public persons' and that the 'multiplication' of Alsatian Jewry be arrested.[23] Hell was elected to the Estates General in 1789, and guillotined in 1794, as an unregenerate monarchist.

In 1780, amidst continuing antisemitic agitation, Cerf Berr turned to Moses Mendelssohn in Berlin for aid in making known the plight of Alsatian Jewry. Cerf Berr submitted a memoir on this topic together with proposals for the removal of the Jews' worst grievances. The memoir was passed on by Mendelssohn to Christian Wilhelm Dohm, a young ministerial counsellor, known to Mendelssohn through their common work in the circles of the Berlin Enlightenment. This resulted in Dohm's publication the following year of his *Über die bürgerliche Verbesserung der Juden*, in which Cerf Berr's memoir is reprinted.[24]

The memoir argued that exemption from the annual habitation tax should be granted to the infirm and elderly, and to rabbis, cantors and schoolteachers, as 'officers of the *Nation*' without fixed residence; next, that the right of residence should be transmissible from father to son: no longer should the latter, on marriage and the foundation of a new family, be required to purchase anew this 'right of the citizen'; the *péage corporel* (body tax) of 3 livres per day, especially in relation to Strasbourg, 'as onerous as it is humiliating', should be abolished. The memoir protested at length at the obstacles to the resolution of the affair of the 'forged receipts'; the Jews of Alsace should enjoy a 'freedom of commerce' comparable to that of their brethren in Metz, Nancy, Bordeaux and Bayonne; the right to purchase landed property without constraint or hindrance should be granted; likewise the right to take up residence anywhere in Alsace. The memoir demanded that rabbinical judgements in civil and ritual matters not be subject to appeal before other courts, that the *préposés* have the power to impose fines on transgressors against 'good order' and that a court of two *préposés* and two rabbis enjoy the power also to pronounce sentences of *herem*. The memoir concluded with a request that children baptized against their parents' wishes be given the freedom to abjure their new religion up to the age of 12 (following letters patent of 1728, a decree of the Rouen Parlement of 1769 and of the Conseil Souverain of Alsace, 1752).

By 1783 the memoir had solely achieved the irrevocable abolition in perpetuity of the *péage corporel* as a tax which ranked Jews with animals – 'it is repugnant to the feelings we have for all our subjects to allow a tax on any of them to remain which seems to degrade mankind', ran the royal decree. Cerf Berr made available to Strasbourg the sum of 48 000 livres which at

5 per cent interest per annum produced an income of 2400 livres and thereby indemnified the city for the loss of its revenue from the tax. Hertzberg points out that, in all the legislation of the *ancien régime* this is the only decree to refer to the Jews of eastern France as 'subjects' of the French crown and not as resident aliens, liable to arbitrary expulsion, at least in theory.[25]

In the declining years of the *ancien régime* the Jews of eastern France confronted two hostile thrusts: one was directed at their autonomy; the second at what Baron de Spon, first president of the Conseil Souverain of Alsace, had called their 'multiplication' (see above, p. 227). La Galaiziere, the intendant of Alsace, already in 1783 proposed that the title and function of the *préposé général de la Nation Juive* be suppressed and that the other *préposés* be denied the right to speak in the name of the Jews. Another critic, tentatively identified as the marquis de Ségur (secretary of state for war), denounced the '*régime* [commun] *subsistant sous le nom de Préposés Généraux de la nation juive*' as a communal edifice that had

> no legal base … The league, which naturally exists between the *préposés généraux* and the rabbis, unites in the hands of the former the springs both of civil power and ecclesiastical power and in a nation where all laws are mingled [*confondues*] in the same code, this power is superior to all other powers and is necessarily independent.

'By what title and right do the Jews in Alsace', this critic asks, 'have any sort of permanent representation in a province where no order of citizens enjoys this prerogative?' Here is a 'clandestine regime which unites all Jews among themselves'.[26]

As for the second thrust, the Jews of Alsace had indeed 'multiplied', from *c.*580 families at the end of the seventeenth century to *c.*3600 a century later. But with a total in 1784 of *c.*20000 persons altogether they still accounted for no more than some 3 per cent of the population of the province (684000). The major cities – Strasbourg, Colmar, Mulhouse – had no Jewish residents, though peddlers and merchants might ply their wares during daylight hours. Bischeim, in the lower Rhine, on the outskirts of Strasbourg, was the largest community, with 473 members. Most communities had anything between 100 and 300 members. Because however, many Jews lived in small villages, their small absolute total might still represent some 15–25 per cent of village-dwellers. The average size of a Jewish family in 11 localities of Lower Alsace was 2.96 children as compared with 2.60 in a Christian family. In accordance with the norms of a poor society the men married late: of 14 fathers at Herswiller one was 24 when his first child was born; 2 were 27; 11 were aged 30 or more.[27]

The Habsburg Jews had already faced the fact of population control in the form of limitation on the right to marry, and marriage had also been prohibited to certain classes of Prussian Jewry. Now came the turn of the

French Ashkenazim, especially if they were poor – the overwhelming majority. The first proposals to this end limited the number of marriages to 72 per annum and to none at all in those localities where Jews formed more than 10 per cent of the population. In any case all marriages would be subject to and require royal approval. Cerf Berr, when aware of these projects, at once protested on the grounds of equity, humanity and 'the wish of nature'. In the event the subsequent letters patent of July 1784 prohibited marriage to Alsatian Jewry without royal permission – on pain of immediate expulsion – and forbade rabbis to officiate at such marriages (articles 6–7). A census of Alsatian Jewry carried out in connection with the letters patent gave a total of 3910 families in Alsace, comprising 19 624 individuals dispersed over 182 towns and villages. It is generally assumed that to this total must be added *c.*2500 Jews living illegally in the Province. These latter had no fixed abode in Alsace, paid no taxes and were to be expelled as vagabonds. By other articles of the letters patent the leaders retained the power to apportion and levy taxes. Only where a general Jewish interest was at stake might they undertake collective action, that is, not where a particular grievance called for remedy. French was made the language of commerce. Henceforth the intendant would supervise the proceedings of the general assemblies as well as the apportionment of taxes. Also, of course, the leaders could levy only small fines (3 livres) by way of punishment. The extension of economic opportunity – for example the right to lease farmland or vineyards, exploit a mine, own real property – had no relevance to the impoverished mass of Alsatian Jewry, only to a happy few. In general terms, the letters patent brought communal organization under tighter control as well as private and commercial life, and residential rights. The Jews engaged an advocate, M. de Mirbeck, to challenge the letters patent before the Conseil du Roi, especially on the issue of marriage limitation. Mirbeck had no success. No more could be achieved than to bring about repeated delays in the expulsions from Alsace of vagrant Jews, that is those who had not purchased their right to 'réception'.[28]

The edict of 1787 'concerning those who do not profess the Catholic religion' restored to the Calvinists, who had been deprived of a legal existence since the revocation of the Edict of Nantes and the expulsion of the Huguenots (1685), their civil status and the right to maintain separate official registers for births, deaths and marriages. This reopened and renewed the debate on the civil status of the Jews and gave new hope. Not that the edict applied to them, in fact the Parlement of Metz refused to extend to Jews the benefits of the edict, but any extension of civil status to one group of non-Catholics could not but react favourably on another.[29] This is what showed itself in the formation of the 'Malesherbes Commission' of 1788, an enquiry, on behalf of the Council of State, into the status of the Jews. Malesherbes, minister of the royal household and a former treasurer of the *Encyclopédie*, was largely responsible for the 'Protestant' edict. By extension, he was perhaps also contemplating some sort of arrangement that would entitle the Jews to register their personal status separately from the communal register and thus weaken their ties to the community. He likened the Jews not to an *imperium in imperio* but – *'les Juifs sont dans l'Univers entier Imperium in Imperiis'*. Malesherbes looked forward to a physiocratic future that would convert the Jews into peasants and agriculturalists.[30]

Both Sephardim and Ashkenazim took part in the discussions in Paris initiated by Malesherbes. Salomon Lopes-Dubec (1743–1837) and Abraham Furtado (1754–1817) were the principal representatives of the former, aided at times by the historian Louis Francia de Beaufleury. Cerf Berr represented the Ashkenazim of the north-east; Berr Isaac Berr, Lorraine Jewry; an unidentified deputy from Alsace was also present. Although the policies of the Ashkenazim are hardly documented, it seems that a *mémoire* of Cerf Berr called for the maintenance of communal autonomy and for some sort of federal arrangement grouping together Alsace, Lorraine and the *généralité* of Metz. For entirely different reasons the Sephardim also insisted on the need for a separate existence, especially for an existence separate from that of the Ashkenazim. Clearly, any proposed intention that applied to the totality of Jews in France, such as Malesherbes was thought to cherish, must at the least necessarily jeopardise the favourable status that the Sephardim enjoyed relative to the less favourable status of the Ashkenazim. Therefore, to avert this danger, Moses Gradis, of the Bordeaux shipping family, reminded Saint Maur, a former intendant in Bordeaux and associate of Malesherbes, of the 'very ancient line of demarcation' which separated Jews of Iberian origin from those others 'with whom they have never mingled, even by ties of marriage'; and this reminder was subsequently enlarged so as to emphasize the distinction between the customs, usages, and rites of the Sephardim and those of other Jews who are 'to some degree so enslaved to all kinds of superstition and bigotry which has further lowered them in our eyes to the point that we are never permitted alliance with them by way of the ties of marriage'. In this light the Sephardi policy aimed to reinforce the separatist status quo in conjunction with the right to own and work landed property, to enter colleges and universities, and to hold municipal office.[31]

Within a few months the 'Malesherbes Commission' was no more. Sephardim and Ashkenazim would soon have to confront each other and to engage with the revolutionary pressure to assimilate on the floor of the Assemblée Nationale.

14
The Rabbi and the Emperor: Ezekiel Landau and Joseph II

In the debate on the Jews and their autonomy that engaged French Sephardim and Ashkenazim and the government alike in the 1780s, all parties had in mind Joseph II's policy of toleration. It gave support to the *Apologie des Juifs* (1786) of Zalkind Hourwitz. Ashkenazim and Sephardim in France referred appreciatively to this or that component of the policy. It served Cerf Berr in his campaign against *péage corporel* and it featured in a *mémoire* that the Sephardim submitted to the Malesherbes Commission in 1788.[1] These repercussions are explicable in terms of the magnitude of Joseph's project.

Joseph II involved his empire in a highly ambitious attempt to engineer a socio-economic and even cultural transformation of Habsburg Jewry: 'to regenerate this people', said the emperor, 'that has hitherto concerned itself only with usury and led a wandering life'. His contacts with Turgot in Paris had persuaded Joseph that the revocation of the Edict of Nantes and the expulsion of the Huguenots had contributed to the political and economic decline of France. Per contra, the tolerance extended to minorities in England, Holland and Prussia helped to account for their prosperity and economic advancement. Nearer home, the success of toleration in Trieste strengthened the argument. The case for the 'civil betterment' of the Jews that Dohm advanced in Berlin gained ground in Vienna. Joseph was in any case an admirer of Frederick II, and would attempt to follow the Prussian model in enabling the Jews to serve the state. But the humanitarian component, combined with the ideology of toleration, distinguished Joseph's policies from those of his predecessors or contemporaries. 'Inside the *kehillah*', so to speak, it is generally agreed, Joseph's programme, with all its limitations, created a fresh and less tense atmosphere for debate. Despite every reservation, Joseph established a fresh agenda or at least gave impetus to an older agenda.[2]

A series of patents, edicts and decrees dealt with the Jews' circumstances in all the varied Habsburg territories – from Vienna to the Jews' Town of Prague, the villages of Moravia, the port of Trieste, and newly acquired

Galicia. Each was the subject of specific legislation. Overall, the principle of toleration proclaimed that without distinction of 'nation and religion all our subjects, so soon as they are accepted and tolerated in our states, take a common share in the public welfare which we desire to increase through our concern'. In the case of Vienna the edict emphasized a policy of education and the need to enlighten youth 'through their direction [*Verwendung*] towards the sciences, arts and artisanry'. This included permission to take up an apprenticeship with Christian masters. Others were encouraged to open factories and engage in wholesale trade (as *Grosshändler*), and to employ unlimited numbers of Jewish and Christian servants (the former to be unmarried). There is particular mention of reading, writing and arithmetic, to be taught either in the existing German-language primary and secondary schools or in schools established by the communities. Hebrew was banned from all public transactions in favour of the vernacular. The compulsory wearing of beards as well as forms of special clothing and badges and the ban on attendance at public entertainments were all removed. This extended to the need for special permits and passes, the body tax and double judicial fees. Wholesale merchants and their sons could carry swords. Jews were permitted to leave their homes before midday on Sundays and holidays.[3] This edict applied primarily to the Jews of Vienna and Lower Austria but it had relevance throughout the empire, especially in educational matters. Separate patents issued by Joseph during the 1780s corresponded to the circumstances of the particular communities. The patents for Prague and Bohemia emphasized the need for German-Jewish schools. These would be under the supervision of state-approved teachers and follow a state-approved curriculum that included 'secular' subjects. Where the community lacked the resources to establish its own school, the children would be directed to Christian primary and secondary schools. The poor would devote themselves to agriculture. They could also enter the haulage trade and work in the textile factories. In Austrian Silesia, a less generous patent required Jewish children to attend Christian schools (although the wealthy might engage private tutors) and merchants could trade only with the agreement of the guilds. The patent for Moravia made it easier for Jews to lease land and engage in agriculture. Here they could become master craftsmen, whereas in Bohemia this required the agreement of the guilds. It made school attendance obligatory. In Galicia, to which the Bukowina was incorporated in 1785, the number of Jewish agriculturists was higher than in any other province and the relevant patent aimed to strengthen this trend. The Galician patent of 1789 was the most comprehensive and liberal of all and freed Jews to become members of municipal councils. The patent abolished all limits on the growth and size of the Jewish population and declared that 'all occupations, vocations and all branches of livelihood are open to them as to all other inhabitants of the province; and all restrictions hitherto in effect and applicable to Jews only are hereby revoked'. This applied to handicrafts, trade in all commodities, peddling, membership of artisanal guilds and to the lease or purchase of estates (except those of the peasants). To enhance the attractions of Galicia would encourage its inhabitants to stay put and not migrate to Vienna, it was hoped.

For the Jews of Trieste the authorities in Vienna issued no special edict. In its stead, the governor, Zinzendorf, was sent draft proposals in May 1781 which he translated into Italian and then submitted to the Jewish leaders and the Triestine police and judiciary. The translation incorporated certain significant divergences from the German original for, in view of the favourable conditions already enjoyed by Triestine Jewry, the emperor's proposals would have had a retrograde effect or were simply irrelevant, for example there was no need to dismiss the wearing of badges and so on because this requirement had long fallen into disuse; similarly, it was pointless to foster agriculture in Trieste or to relate the ownership of land to conversion to Christianity because the rights of land ownership already extended beyond this. In replying to Zinzendorf, therefore, the Jews of Trieste made much of the three primordial benefits they already enjoyed: the free and public exercise of their religion, unencumbered ownership of fixed property and participation in wholesale and retail trade.[4]

Edicts and patents without territorial limitation imposed the use of German for commercial and official purposes, the use of Hebrew being restricted to liturgical and religious purposes (1782); the Jews were made liable to military service (1788); by a patent of 1787 they were required to discard their inherited Jewish names and take on German given and family names. The registers of births and circumcisions must also be kept in German. These new names must be reported to the authorities. In Nikolsburg the regional rabbi and communal elders performed this task. On the 22nd day of the month of Av, 5544 (= August 1784), in the dating of a contemporary Prague chronicle the Jews lost their power to judge cases in civil law, which included the division of estates, the appointment of guardians to orphans and minors; magistrates descended on the Jewish town hall in Prague and removed its court records.[5] The marriage patent of 1783 and the civil code of 1786, though general in their application, had highly important implications for Jewish life, not all of which were favourable. The universities were already open to Jews since their withdrawal from Jesuit control in 1773 and secularization in 1782. Joseph enhanced his educational policy in 1786 by making it a condition of permission to marry that the bridegrooms demonstrate attendance at a *Normalschule*. In 1790 this condition was extended to their brides.

This body of legislation, for all its extent, left intact the Family laws. It also retained the limit on movement – there was no freedom of movement into Vienna and the Edict of Toleration expressly proclaimed that 'in the places where Jews never resided they will not in the future be granted the right of residence'. Joseph had to reassure the Council of State: 'It is by no means my intention to spread the Jewish nation more widely in the hereditary lands or to introduce it afresh there where it is not tolerated but only to make it useful to the state there where it already lives and in the measure to which it is tolerated'. The only exception applied to those Jews who established a factory in an undeveloped area.[6]

Every variety of response greeted the emperor's legislation. In Bohemia Peter Beer, the *maskil* (1758–1838) saw in Joseph II a second Cyrus. The edict of toleration made the emperor into 'a friend crowned with humanity'. When the emperor died in 1790, *Ha-Me'assef* lamented his passing with an emphasis on his benevolence and educational aims, in preparing 'the children of the sons of Israel ... to achieve goodness and greatness in the land'.[7] At the other extreme stands the judgement of Rabbi Wolf Boskowitz of Hungary (1740–1818), a leading Talmudic scholar and student of the natural sciences:

> If the nations desired us to assimilate with them only externally, then we would have some excuse for shedding the heavy yoke of exile and becoming like them. But this is not the case ... their true desire is not for us to change our garments and the like, but they desire our souls and our religion, for they wish us to be like them in our inner selves and not only outwardly.[8]

It is indeed as a vast exercise in social engineering that the Josephine legislation is best interpreted, but with the qualification that for the mass of Jews the various patents did little more than reinforce existing relationships. The legislation favoured the wealthy, it is generally agreed. The enhanced economic freedom that the patents provided for must necessarily intensify socio-economic differences among the Habsburg communities. The historians are unanimous.[9] If the patents did not make the poor poorer, they certainly made the rich richer. Freedom of movement favoured the rich; so did freedom from military service – it was more rewarding to make a uniform than to wear it. Official encouragement helped to create a class of *Grosshändler* in Vienna and industrialists in Bohemia. This was no novel concept and there was already precedent; in 1763, even Maria Theresa encouraged Jewish entrepreneurs to open factories, stipulating that the workforce must be exclusively Christian. Vienna exemplified the effects of Joseph's policy in fostering the wealthy and economic diversification; here, by 1789, only about one-third of the 74 household heads still dealt in money and jewellery. To counterbalance this decline, the numbers of *Grosshändler*, and of merchants in sundry miscellaneous goods (wool, leather, silks, horses), had much increased. The roster of occupations also included three doctors. By 1804 of the 119 tolerated Jews in Vienna only 6 were money-dealers; and the number of *Grosshändler* had doubled from the 8 of 1789 to 16. There was a correlated diversification in the range of goods that the merchants dealt in. The Emperor Francis ennobled three banking leaders in 1797 – Nathan Arnstein, Bernard Eskeles and Salomon Hertz. Of course not all this enterprise is attributable to the toleration patents of Joseph II. Certainly the important *Grosshändler* component derived from Joseph's policy. An industrial exhibition in Prague in 1791, attended by the new emperor, Leopold II, showed further results. The products of Jewish manufacturers merited special mention: those from Isaak Liebstein's woollen goods factory in eastern Bohemia; from the silk factory of Joachim Lederer and Schwabach, and from the Joachim Popper-Frankel whalebone factory (both in Prague). By 1807 of the 58 Bohemian factories making linen, cotton and calico, 15 were Jewish-owned.[10] As a new industry in contrast to the old-established wool industry, cotton enjoyed freedom from guild regulations and also governmental encouragement. It flourished during Napoleon's continental blockade of 1806 and the larger establishments survived even the Austrian state bankruptcy of 1811. The Jewish entrepreneurs benefited in some cases from the fact they took a variety of economic roles: they combined manufacture with *Grosshandel*, banking and export, and perhaps participated in the tobacco-leasing operation. The wars of these years also created a demand that military suppliers of all types could profitably satisfy. To a varying extent this applies to Popper, Laemel, Hönigsberg and Feith Ehrenstamm. The latter founded the first woollen goods factory in Moravia, at Prossnitz in 1801. The workforce of 3000 men, women and children used the most modern Dutch and English machinery. Ehrenstamm and his family lived in the factory complex, that is outside the Prossnitz ghetto in defiance of the law. As the most important military supplier to the imperial Austrian forces, from the Turkish wars of the eighteenth century to the Napoleonic wars of the nineteenth, Ehrenstamm, at times in partnership with the Prague *Grosshändler* Simon Edel v. Laemel, provided leather goods and foodstuffs and the clothing for entire regiments. Feith Ehrenstamm's children succumbed to luxury and inherited wealth. The *Grosshändler* also went into partnership with the feudal nobility.[11]

The poor benefited little from Joseph's various edicts and patents, despite the emperor's hopes. In Bohemia and Moravia the restrictions on movement remained, as did the restrictions on household numbers. The encouragement to enter the crafts and agriculture could also not be of much effect if, first, Christian master craftsmen were under no compulsion or obligation to take Jewish apprentices, and if, second, the condition and status of the peasantry was depressed.[12] The mass of Habsburg Jewry at the beginning of the nineteenth century endured worse living conditions than had their ancestors a century earlier – not only because of economic hardship but also because of the Family laws, the position of younger sons and the liability to military service. In Prague there was a marked deterioration in living conditions to the extent that one building which in 1729 had accommodated 40–50 persons, in 1790 sheltered 140. A committee of visitation, following an epidemic in the ghetto, found the living and sanitary conditions to be unbearable and described the houses for the Jewish poor as 'death-traps' (*Mordgruben*).[13] The Bohemian tax arrears that had accumulated by 1797 and the 70 per cent shortfall for that year amply confirm the extent of poverty. At Nikolsburg by 1811 two-thirds of the community had fallen out of the taxpayers' roster.[14]

The reinforcement of the status quo makes a strong contrast with the cultural revolution that was its accompaniment.

Mendelssohn, writing before the full scope of Joseph's programme of regeneration was made public, took up a position of cautious welcome. His initial assessment was measured, and in 1781 in a letter to R. Avigdor Levi of Glogau he warned against undue excitement and quoted 'Do not wake or rouse love until it please' (Song of Songs 3:5). But in a Hebrew letter dated 23 Iyar 5542 (= 7 May 1782) to Joseph Galico, secretary of the Jewish community in Trieste, he enquired sympathetically what progress had been made in setting up a *Normalschule* for the children; were the necessary schoolbooks ready? he asked. Mendelssohn described his dismay at the hostility to the emperor's plans ('who was gracious to his subjects') and expressed fear at

the absurdities and errors of our brethren among the children of Israel ... who are trying with all might and main to destroy the plans of the wise ruler and to turn his good will into anger, for he will say – this is an uncomprehending people of unwanted fools who do not know what is good for them.

But in a Hebrew letter (of 28 Marcheshvan 5546 = 1 November 1785) Mendelssohn took care to warn Moses Wiener (1748–1814), a teacher at the principal Jewish school in Prague, against immoderate praise for the emperor. This warning was accompanied by praise for a pamphlet by Wiener extolling the need for public schools that Jewish and Christian pupils would attend alike and learn tolerance.[15] The amplitude of the programme gradually showed itself. If children are to be exposed to a Germanophone and secular educational curriculum, if the system of communal jurisdiction is demolished, if the distinctiveness of apparel is removed, if the adoption of German forenames and surnames is imposed, if military service is required, if extensive occupational restructuring is enjoined – then *en bloc* the only consequence can be to 'make over' the Jews. Their very identity comes under threat.

The requirement in the patent of 1787 that the Jews take on German forenames and fixed family names is symptomatic of this threat to the extent that it merits a diversion – all the more so because Joseph was the first ruler to impose this demand and thereby set the precedent for rulers in Prussia, and France and Holland under Napoleon. Between 1787 and the mid-nineteenth century at least 28 pieces of legislation concerned themselves with 'Jewish' names as well as names for the Jews. The politics of onomastics is perhaps the most visible sign of that evolution in policy which from the 1780s onwards alarmed the Jews of central Europe and the French empire.[16]

To the best of my knowledge Joseph II was the first ruler to introduce this type of measure and to complement his educational programme for the Jews with a policy for their renaming. This legislation required the Jews to take on German forenames and definite family names and for all registers of births, circumcisions and marriages to be kept only in German. A supplement to the patent included a list of approved male and female names, to be borne 'according to the German or Christian pronunciation', that is, the Jewish, Hebrew or Yiddish version, even of a permitted name, was prohibited. The list was sufficiently eclectic to include Nebuchadnezar, Iphigenia and Semiramis, side by side with names from the Hebrew Bible and the New Testament.[17]

The state confronted the problem that the Ashkenazi Jews of eighteenth- and early nineteenth-century France, Holland, the German states, Bohemia and Moravia limited the cognomen to forename and patronymic (for example 'Isaac son of Abraham' or simply 'Isaac Abraham'). The Jew had no family name and it was therefore not at all unlikely that more than one person would have the same name. Second, the same Jew might well be known under at least two different names, depending on context. There might well be two Jews with one name and one Jew with two (or more) names. There is the philosopher known to the learned world as Moses Mendelssohn and the member of the Berlin *kehillah* known as Moses Dessau, sometimes Moses from Dessau and then again as R. Moses Dessauer.[18] There is Rabbi Hart Lyon in London who is variously known in Mannheim and Berlin as Hirschel Loebl and Hirschel Levin and as Zvi ben Arye Löb Berlin. Would Frederick the Great recognize in Veitel Berlin his associate Veitel Heine Ephraim? In April 1789 when Cerf Berr wrote to Necker, the minister of finance, his signature 'Cerf Berr' was accompanied by 'Hirtz Medelsheim' in Judeo-German characters. To his fellow-Jews he was known as Medelsheim de Bischheim.[19] In seventeenth-century Frankfurt am Main a boy might well receive a Hebrew name at his circumcision and a Yiddish name when his mother next visited the synagogue.[20] The flexibility of nomenclature flouted the state's need to identify its subjects/citizens. In an extreme case, a Jew at Teplitz was carried in the municipal records under six different names.[21] At a time when the state was conscripting the Jews, marshalling their young into state schools, and registering their marriages, the problem of identification necessarily became more acute than ever.

But it is not solely a matter of administrative convenience. Also at stake is a claim to appropriate an identity, to which sensitivity was extreme. Those conversos from Spain and Portugal who, on their escape, discarded their Christian names, were signifying a renewal of continuity. Manuel Dias Soeiro became Menasseh b. Israel; Tomas Rodrigues Pereira became Abraham Israel Pereira; Captain Miguel de Barrios became Daniel Levi de Barrios. In 1646 when the de Pinto family arrived in Rotterdam on leaving Portugal, the boys were circumcised and André, Rodrigo and Inigo respectively became Jacob, Moseh and Aaron. When the uncle Rodrigues Alvares was circumcised he became David Emanuel.[22]

The bond between name change and assimilation is not a concern limited to recent centuries. Büchler quotes the Talmudic sage, Bar-Kappara (3rd century CE): 'Four merits made Israel in Egypt worthy of redemption: they had not changed their names or their language, they were not informers or lewd.' Funkenstein refers to the following midrash (Shoher Tov, 114): 'They [the Israelites in Egypt] did not change their names, they did not change their language, they did not divulge their secrets, they did not abolish circumcision.' Funkenstein comments:

> The list rather sounds to me as hidden polemics against hellenized Jews who changed their names into Greek ones, spoke Greek better than Hebrew in the best of cases, translated the Bible (usually referred to as the Jewish mysterion in various midrashim) and sometimes even hid their circumcision.[23]

A warning against change of name, language and dress is traditionally found in the verse, 'Jacob arrived safe/whole/in peace (*Shalem*) at Schechem' (Gen. 33:18).[24]

In the event, the politics of onomastics as espoused by Joseph contained enough 'Jewish' and 'German' names to be acceptable and the Prague leadership (Gabriel Franckel and Joachim Popper) did not press any very strong objection (though there were certainly protests at the loss of an inherited forename and fears on economic grounds lest the confidence of traders abroad be disturbed at the apparent change in the identity of their trading partner). The chief rabbi in Moravia, R. Gerson Abraham, also made objection.[25] This was all to little effect. The intent of the policy remains unmistakable – especially since it was joined to limitation on the use of Hebrew and Yiddish and the compulsion to attend germanophone schools. The Jews were being robbed of their names, their language and their self-government.

The ensuing debate, as Joseph's programme unfolded year by year, encompassed virtually every theme of public discourse from the previous two centuries. The gamut ran from educational policy (especially topics outside the inherited curriculum) to economic restructuring, and took in the role of the *kehillah* in a gentile world, the choice of language, rabbinical prerogatives, the Talmud and Oral Law as barriers to social advancement, and the messianic idea. Given the scope of the Josephine programme and the challenge to identity and survival that regeneration presented, it could not be otherwise. In the classroom the opening battles took place; first, because the various patents not only modified the accepted curriculum but also removed educational control from the rabbinate; second, because of the widespread fear and awareness of the absolutist aim in the eighteenth century to make the schools 'an instrument for exacting obedience', a means of social control.[26] The other battle took place around the *huppah*, the marriage canopy. Later, the conflict moved to the issue of military service. In all cases Chief Rabbi Ezekiel Landau of Prague and Bohemia had to engage with Joseph's legislation, no less than with enemies in his own ranks.

In a general way Maria Theresa in 1776 had already anticipated Joseph's educational policy, by proposing to introduce *Normal*-type schools for Bohemian Jewry. The latter successfully objected that the religious study and prayer required of Jewish children left them no time for other studies. This skirmish was no preparation at all for the furore some five years later. Hardly had Joseph in 1781 issued the first edict of toleration and the edict calling for compulsory elementary education for all his subjects than the *maskil* Hartwig Wessely published a Hebrew pamphlet, *Words of Peace and Truth*. Like Mendelssohn, his mentor, Wessely stressed the need for a command of German, which might be acquired through the study of Mendelssohn's translation of the Pentateuch. Wessely went beyond this, in at least seeming to make what he called 'the law of man' (by which he meant profane studies) the indispensable preliminary to a life of piety and to the study of 'the law of God'. Wessely also called for simple textbooks and manuals to introduce pupils to ethical concepts.[27] The pamphlet was written in haste, as a *pièce d'occasion* and to some extent repeated earlier criticism of the prevailing educational system, and David Friedländer was quick to translate it into German, making much use of paraphrase. Wessely later became disillusioned both with the fact that his programme for a modernized teaching of the Torah was not realized and also with the acceptance of the ideas of the contemporary European Enlightenment by his own supporters. He became alienated from traditionalists and *maskilim* alike.[28]

Some of Wessely's terminology lent itself to misunderstanding, and his praise of 'the great emperor' might well be considered fulsome. The pamphlet created a scandal. In Lissa, Posen and Frankfurt am Main, leading rabbis denounced its pernicious effect in undermining the traditional system of education and associated values. In Lissa and Posen, communal leaders made attempts to silence Wessely through intervention with Chief Rabbi Hirsch Levin of Berlin, where Wessely was then living. Levin was unresponsive; he himself was something of a *maskil*, and welcomed Mendelssohn's translation of the Bible. If Mendelssohn presented him with a Hebrew translation of Aristotle it can be assumed that he was no enemy of 'Greek wisdom'. Reference to Aristotle had also featured in one of Levin's sermons at the Ashkenazi Great synagogue in London.[29]

In Prague, Ezekiel Landau launched the most significant attack. 'I have seen the world turned upside down,' he exclaimed to his congregation in a sermon on the Great Sabbath preceding the festival of Passover 5542 (= 23 March 1782). 'How can one be zealous in the study of Torah, when an evil man has arisen from our own people and brazenly dared to assert that the Torah is not at all important … ?[30] Essentially, Landau's denunciation bore on the attribution to secular subjects of study a religious value; he did not in principle condemn Mendelssohn's translation, though he certainly feared its putative side-effects in serving as an incentive to learn German, thereby not only diverting the student's attention from the supremely more important text but also giving access to material capable of disturbing belief.

News of the uproar also reached London, where R. Tevele Schiff of the Ashkenazi Great Synagogue praised Landau's sermon for being in a 'very pure language, full of pious and wise words, careful not to offend the majesty of the Emperor'. Schiff also showed himself *au courant* with the widespread rabbinic hostility to Joseph's policy in Posen, Lissa and Vilna.[31] The task was indeed for Landau not to offend Joseph but also only to accept his policy in a form that removed its danger.

The furore over Wessely's pamphlet overlapped with the controversy over the new type of school that Joseph had proposed. In Vienna the Jews refused to cooperate with the regime's demand for a Jewish *Normalschule*. The children of the poor already attended the German *Normalschule*, it was argued; private tutors educated those from the better-endowed families. Besides, how could a non-existent community establish a communal school? And no communal fund existed with which to establish a school, which in any case the 'community' would not be able to support.[32] In Pressburg objections came on grounds of tradition but financial considerations also took a part.[33] Trieste stood out for its support of imperial educational policy. The local leaders, in concert with Chief Rabbi Isacco Formiggini, also had no hesitation in proclaiming their sympathy with Wessely's programme of educational reform. This was in part because the curriculum already included subjects such as Italian and mathematics, side by side with Hebrew and religious studies. The curriculum also moved by stages of difficulty, beginning with the Bible and advancing to the Talmud, to which, in any case, not every student attained or even aspired. Wessely hoped to use Trieste as a sort of springboard for the dissemination of his ideas throughout other Italian communities and in this he did have some success, for rabbis from Venice, Ancona and Reggio did, though with varying degrees of enthusiasm, applaud his ideas. Those who most warmly welcomed *Words of Peace and Truth* were not uncritical or undiscriminating, especially over the relative priority attached to the 'Torah of Man' as against the 'Torah of God'. Rabbi Formiggini in Trieste maintained that from the ages of 5 to 10 studies other than the Torah would 'confuse the children's minds'.[34] The new school in Trieste, the *Scuola Pia Normale Sive Talmud Torah*, opened in May 1782 under these auspices. It had approximately 35 pupils. This was one example of the hundred or so schools established at the state's behest by 1790 throughout the empire. All taught the same basic curriculum: reading and writing in German, and mathematics. Only later did the curriculum of these state schools verge on religious matters. Until then they functioned harmoniously alongside the traditional *hadarim*. After its initial rejection Mendelssohn's biblical commentary came to be accepted as an auxiliary to instruction in the Bible.

In Prague Landau could not of course simply reject Joseph's policy. Rather, he engaged in a process of damage limitation, cooperating to the utmost with the imperial dictate while preserving the integrity of the Torah and its study, as he understood it. The smoothness of this operation owed much to the tact of Joseph's commissioner for education, Ferdinand Kindermann v. Schulstein (1750–1801). He had made Landau a party to the government's plans from the outset and settled with him details of the curriculum. Landau developed sympathy for the study of the vernacular (German) and its grammar (finding support in Nehemiah 13:24 and from law 10 in chapter II of Maimonides's codification of the laws related to the utterance of the prayer 'Hear, O Israel'). Not only did Jewish self-respect count; there were also pragmatic grounds, since 'most of our labour is in the area of trade and commerce, which requires the ability to write and to speak the language of the country'. This accomplishment, however, Landau warned, gave access to a body of literature and scholarship, 'that are not aids in learning the language but philosophical inquiries pertaining to matters of Torah and faith, which may lead you to harbour doubts about the faith, God forbid!'. This could be the work of Jews, no less than others 'who deny individual providence over the affairs of men, who deny the revelation of the Torah and supernatural miracles, who say that religion was not given by the Creator'. Landau could at least find comfort in the limitations imposed on the new schools – in that they existed 'solely for the purpose of teaching children language, writing, mathematics, ethical behaviour and etiquette, and not to speak calumnies against our religion'.[35]

Only a few months later the new school (financed in part by Lazar Grünhut) opened in Prague, amidst much pomp and ceremony. Fireworks spelt out *Vivat Josephus secundus*. Jewish and Christian dignitaries, ecclesiastical and civil, honoured the occasion. Landau could be satisfied with the outcome, for not only would pupils not enter the 'German' schools until the age of 10 but, once there, the hours of instruction would be limited to 4 per day in summer (10–12, 5–7) and 2 per day in winter (5–7), except of course for Friday and Saturday. Meanwhile, the *hadarim* attached to the synagogues, purveying education in traditional religious matters, continued to function. Statistics that are not entirely clear suggest that in 1784 Jewish pupils at the Prague *Normalschule* totalled 347, with 584 at the Bohemian *Trivialschulen*; in 1787, 559 pupils were attending 25 rural Jewish schools; in 56 other localities 278 Jewish children were attending Christian schools. At the Prague schools in 1790 there were said to be 215 boys and 63 girls.[36] The regime was concerned to ensure that these measures proved palatable to the Jews. Thus Jewish pupils at Christian schools were dispensed from attending school on festival days and could keep their heads covered, and their teachers were required to ensure tolerant conduct on the part of their Christian fellow-pupils.

Compulsory military service stretched to the utmost Landau's policy of cooperation with the government – in other words, his effort to minimize the harm it entailed for the community. This was an innovation; in medieval times, as part of the legislation that aimed to demean the Jew, the bearing of weapons (for example a sword or a dagger) was prohibited. Conversely, when the Edict of Toleration of 1782 included permission for the Viennese *Grosshändler* and their sons to wear daggers the effect was to enhance social esteem and status. Jews had indeed fought as mercenaries (as in the Thirty Years' War) or served in the Royal Navy with a view to becoming British. In 1813 in the War of Liberation young Prussian Jews would volunteer *en masse* to fight against Napoleon. Normally, however, Jews confined their participation in combat to the supply of horses, forage, recruits and uniforms or perhaps to advancing the troops' pay, or espionage. This limited role was insufficient, at a time when the newly emerging corporate state in principle required military service from all its subjects, whether in Joseph's Habsburg empire or revolutionary France. The matter did not become controversial until C. W. Dohm took it up in his work on the 'Civil Improvement of the Jews' (1781) with which he associated military service. Dohm not only referred to the participation of Jews in the defence of Prague against the Swedes (1648), of Ofen against the Austrians (1686) and to the more recent role of Portuguese Jewish seamen in a naval engagement with the British (1781), but also quoted (with Mendelssohn's assistance) the Sabbath laws of Maimonides (Ch. 2: 23–5) to the effect that the Sabbath need not inhibit military operations. 'I do not see why in our armies the Jews should not conduct themselves as well as they once did in the Greek and Roman,' Dohm concluded. Controversy at once followed, especially when the professor of oriental studies at Göttingen, J. D. Michaelis, claimed that the obligation to observe the Sabbath, even in wartime, must a priori exclude any notion of military service by Jews. But this lacked any halakhic backing and did no more than provide a vent for Michaelis's antisemitism.[37]

In the contemporary Habsburg empire the nobility enjoyed exemption from military service – likewise clergy, state employees, physicians, free peasants and their first-born sons. Under Maria Theresa the Jews had been able to commute military service for money sums – in 1764, 65 florins per head, reducing to 50 in 1771. This indulgence was not possible under Joseph II or his successors, whose wars against revolutionary France and Napoleon demanded more and more manpower. They required the actual men under arms – and all the more so as the Habsburg recruiting base from among the enserfed peasants shrank through evasion and flight. Perhaps also it may have been thought that military service would further the cause of assimilation and also remove the resentment of the peasantry at the right of the Jews to purchase exemption from what was in effect a long-term sentence. It was only gradually reduced to 25 then 14, and finally 12 years. Communities varied enormously in their reaction to conscription. At one extreme, in Galicia, the decree of 1788 was seen as a calamity. Some of those affected sought refuge in Poland and Hungary. At Brody, on one occasion, Jews armed themselves with clubs to resist a press gang. Recruits sometimes took to flight: at Teplitz in northern Bohemia 13 out of 14 conscripts fit for service were reported absent. A mission to Vienna from Buda and Lemberg, led by Zvi Hirsch and Zvi Margoliouth, hoped in vain to persuade Joseph to withdraw his decree. It was not the undoubted halakhic problems that agitated such communities but rather the consequent alienation from Jewish practices and society that might well follow the conscription of young men. The Italian communities (for example Trieste and Mantua) rejected all cooperation with the mission, and here rabbis and communal leaders welcomed the emperor's initiative. They construed the decree as a demonstration of the emperor's trust in his Jewish subjects and evidence of his goodwill. Greater confidence could not be shown in the Jews than if to them was entrusted the defence and safety of the realm.[38]

Almost to a man the *maskilim* supported the call to arms. Significant exceptions included Saul Ascher, Elia Morpurgo and Mendel Lefin. They proclaimed the injustice of imposing conscription on those denied equality in the very state they were called on to defend. The *maskilim* themselves, by virtue of their socio-economic and financial status could, and did, successfully claim exemption. This differentiation between the poor and the others precisely anticipated the situation that would obtain in Russia in 1826 and later, when Tsar Nicholas I also made Jews subject to conscription.[39] In neither empire did the possibility of exemption exist for the poor, marginal and 'undesirable' persons who thereby came to make up the bulk of the Jewish conscripts. (If, by some mishap, the son of a rich father was called up, a commission could often be bought. 'Day one, a private; day two, a sergeant; day three, an officer', Asher Lehmann [1769–1858] wrote in his unpublished memoir.)[40] Unlike in Russia, however, boys below the age of 18 were not conscripted and in fact the government made efforts to resolve the problems created by military service and, for example, provided uniforms free from a mixture of animal and vegetable fibres (*Shaatnes*, see Lev. 19:19); organized *Kameradschaften* where the Jewish conscripts could jointly prepare kosher meals; and undertook to require the Jews to perform no more than necessary tasks on the Sabbath. The court chancellery also requested the War Council to ensure that if gravely wounded Jewish soldiers in a military hospital asked to see a rabbi, 'for their last comfort', their request must at once be granted. A soldier on his death-bed would do well to recall the reassurance of a leading *maskil*, 'There is no nobler way to depart this world than through a hero's death in the combat for fellow-citizens and freedom under the law' (thus Herz Homberg, senior supervisor of the German-Jewish schools in Galicia (1787–1800) and later censor of Jewish books in Vienna[41]).

R. Ezekiel Landau, even in the face of conscription, did not luxuriate in patriotic effusions. Of his consternation there is no doubt, even if he did, initially at least, accept, however unwillingly, the need for accommodation to government policy. In 1789 he gave a farewell address in Yiddish in a Prague barracks to the first 25 conscripts. Landau reluctantly accepted that the exigencies of military life might make impossible the observance of the Sabbath or the dietary laws. He nonetheless exhorted the soldiers 'always to remain loyal to God in their heart' and to serve the emperor 'with goodwill and unremitting effort'. Landau found perhaps some modest comfort in that through the readiness of the Jewish conscripts to serve and, if necessary to offer up their lives, 'the semi-fetters…which still in part oppress us' might be removed. The priestly blessing ended the address and at this point Landau broke down and wept. This was clearly no endorsement of conscription but it was also no protest or rejection. It may be however, that within a year Landau came to align himself with the enemies of conscription, though he would not wish openly to manifest his hostility.[42]

Only in one significant respect did Landau openly take issue with imperial policy – marriage law. Obviously, only a matter of the utmost gravity could precipitate a conflict of this magnitude, especially since Landau's general instinct normally persuaded him to seek a means to accommodate the legislation of the state. But the marriage patent of 1783 and the civil code of 1786, though applicable generally, encroached on an institution central to Jewish society. This would be in addition to the existing encroachment embodied in the 'family laws'. Even in Trieste, where relations between the state and the community were certainly more harmonious than elsewhere, the conflict between the halakhah and the patent led one historian to expound the community's defence against the state in terms of control over its present and future identity: 'Determining who the legitimate members of society will be, who will form legally and socially recognised units for the purpose of procreation and transfer of property, marriage is a legal and symbolic act that defines the next generation of a society.' To lose control over marriage law was to lose control over the vitals of collective identity.[43] The threat to Triestine Jewry was of course no different from that to other communities in the empire. Against the encroachment of the state Landau was therefore defending the general future. Given the assimilationist thrust of the state's policy, Landau's stand was all the more challenging.

The marriage patent of 1785/86 amounted to something of a hybrid: it regulated the civil contract of the union but did not introduce civil marriage, which remained, as hitherto, subject to a religious ceremony. On the face of it, therefore, the state could legitimately demand of the Jews that

> because the marriage patent applies only to the validity of the civil con-
> tract, which for all religions, including Jews, must be equal in its effect, the
> Jews in their marriage procedures are to be treated and dealt with in every
> respect in accordance with the marriage patent. What concerns however,
> their further bond (*vinculum*) of religion, in that the government is to
> intervene as little as in the sacramental union of the Catholics.[44]

But the problem arose out of the fact not only that Jewish marriage law could not be distinguished in this way but also that its provisions partook of the nature only of a civil contract (and not of a sacrament), which under the new legislation fell within the purview of the state.

The gravamen of Landau's critique inevitably bore on the 'civil' aspect of a marriage. He submitted to the emperor a lengthy memorandum in German that expounded in summary form 'the laws of marriage according to Moses and the Talmud'. Part I of the memorandum outlined those laws; part II compared them point by point with the provisions of the patent, indicating agreement or disagreement. This confrontation of the two systems showed a decisive irreconcilability in certain varied and salient respects, for example the age of majority (13 as against 24) and the validity of a marriage for which the contracting parties had not secured the court's permission, as the patent required – in the Jewish case a marriage in these circumstances would be valid and only a writ of divorce could annul the marriage, and without such a writ 'the married woman is in no way permitted to marry another man'. Landau directed perhaps his most cogent remarks at those provisions of the patent which extended the forbidden degrees beyond those in the Torah and thereby gave to the law of the land an authority rightfully belonging to divine law:

> It is a great and revered principle among us that everything that is not
> prohibited to us is permitted ... for example, marriages with the daughter
> of a brother or of a sister were never forbidden and all the more so with
> the daughter of the brother of a father or a mother.

Landau supported his argument from Biblical precedent (see Num. 36: 10, 11; Josh. 15, 16, 17). Not even the Sanhedrin of 70 elders could forbid something that the Torah explicitly or implicitly sanctioned. Landau also pointed to the social consequences if the projected terms of the marriage patent were actualized and the prohibition on marriage with relations extended (as the patent required): in that eventuality, who would be willing to marry the offspring born of marriages hitherto within the permitted degrees of consanguinity but which were now no longer permitted? They would be 'separated from the congregation of Israel', Landau concluded. The thrust of the argument was clear – 'The Kaiser's Jewish subjects would try to comply with the law of the state but Jewish law remained paramount.'[45]

In this complex debate Landau, it seems, did secure certain concessions. In relation to the 'civil contract' of a Jewish marriage, when a Jewish couple, within the otherwise forbidden degrees of consanguinity, wished to marry they could put their case to the civil authority and secure permission for their marriage; second, 'the president of a synagogue' was given a status corresponding to that of a clergyman or priest in relation to marriage (that is, in accordance with the Jewish law, there was no need for a rabbi); third, a marriage could be dissolved only with the consent of both parties.[46]

These were significant conclusions which helped to reconcile the marriage patent with Jewish requirements. They also exemplify success for Landau's general inclination to preserve the essential through accommodation to the inevitable or the *fait accompli*. He was able to preserve the *heder* alongside the enforced introduction into the curriculum of 'secular' subject-matter and attendance at Christian schools. Conscription he could not avert, but at least provision was made for certain Jewish necessities. In the celebrated and vehement conflicts that centred on the dispute between rabbis Eibeschütz and Emden (1751 and after), and in the furore over the Cleves divorce case (1766–7), Landau took a conciliatory and mediating role.[47] He carried this accommodationist and even lenient outlook into everyday decision-making. His halachic methodology, which made it a cardinal principle to acknowledge no other authority in the corpus of the Oral Law than the Talmud and its expositors, facilitated Landau's policy in seeking to meet the demands of his time and his questioners. In the case of an allegedly defective writ of divorce received by the wife of a Jew who had converted, Landau made his decision to disregard the alleged defect by reference to the fact that the matter was

> of great urgency for she [the wife] would remain an 'anchored wife' [and therefore unable to remarry – LK] and therefore it is necessary to argue … that perhaps in all the prohibitions on defective instruments imposed by the rabbis one should exercise leniency in cases of *ex post facto* urgency, and all the more so here for I have already written that in the opinion of all the decisors this is not a prohibition imposed by the Torah, a prohibition imposed only by the rabbis, and according to Rashi not even a rabbinical prohibition.[48]

Landau also allowed a pawnbroker whose premises were located on the outskirts of Vienna (with the benefit of an imperial privilege) to operate on the Sabbath provided that he leased the premises to a gentile who would also be entitled to a percentage of the takings on Sabbaths and festivals, including the intermediate days of the festivals. If the premises were closed then the privilege would be forfeit and the licence holder suffer 'great loss' – which Landau intended to avert. The economic aspect stood out also in the permission granted by Landau to a factory-owner to operate his factory on the Sabbath. The factory, making 'cartons', was located away from the Jewish quarter of the town and the work force was composed wholly of gentiles. They were paid not a regular sum but on a piecework basis. The factory required to operate non-stop: therefore 'cessation of work would create considerable loss, for the workers would not wish to be without work and the Jew would have to pay them their wages for nothing'. Of course the owner must refrain from entering the premises on the Sabbath. This leniency had its limits. Israel Hönigsberg, the wealthy communal leader and industrialist, asked of Landau whether he could find a way to permit him to instruct a non-Jew to use a seal to stamp his signature on documents that came before 'the important ministers' with whom Hönigsberg deliberated on the Sabbath on communal matters. Landau refused, for in this procedure most commentators saw an action forbidden by the Torah on the Sabbath; 'it could not be permitted, even if great loss was involved'.[49]

In addition to the problems created by economic developments, and the Jew's changing relationship to the state, Landau must also contend with the continuing presence of believers in the messianic claims of Sabbatai Zvi. He apparently intervened with Maria Theresa to prevent the return to Prague of R. Jonathan Eibeschütz, an alleged secret adherent of the pretender. Landau certainly prevailed on Joseph II to prohibit the import into Austria of works of Kabbalah.[50]

Towards the end of Landau's career, the movement known as Hassidism began to spread from the east. Its search for hidden meanings in familiar prayers and commandments, the physical movement in prayer to express enthusiasm, the elevation of the tsaddik ('righteous man') to a position as mediator between man and God, the weakness for feasting – all were repugnant to Landau. Their individualism was excessive – the Hassidim had cut themselves off from the two Talmuds

to hew for themselves cracked cisterns and raise themselves up in the arrogance of their heart; each says I am the one who sees and to me were opened the gates of heaven and on my account the world exists. These are the destroyers of the generation. But to this orphaned generation I say the ways of the Lord are upright and the righteous will walk in them and the Hassidim will stumble.[51]

Ongoing concerns related to the misuse of economic power on the part of the rich to shuffle off their fair share of the tax burden or to exploit the weakness of the poor by burdensome and unredeemable loans, secured on property which was subsequently distrained. Shopkeepers and wine merchants used false weights and measures, traders took advantage of letters of credit to create fictitious partnerships in order to evade the prohibition on taking interest from a fellow-Jew. Landau and his rabbinical colleagues had also to challenge the misuse of leisure epitomized in the frequenting of coffee-shops, taverns, the-atres and opera-houses, and in card-playing. One responsum in this respect has acquired classic status – Landau's rebuke to a wealthy Bohemian Jew who had acquired an estate and wished to go hunting. Landau condemned this pursuit, not because he espoused any abstract notion of animal rights ('since all living things are given to man for his needs') but because it was wanton destruction and cruelty on the part of he who has no need to make a livelihood from hunt-ing, and whose hunting 'has nothing to do with his livelihood'. It also involved gratuitous exposure to danger. Landau's sermons dealt also with infractions of the sexual norms (unwed mothers, pregnant brides, the unauthorized con-sorting of men and women, whether married or single, and prostitution).[52]

Landau died in 1793 after almost 40 years in office. Towards the end of his long career he will have had some cause for satisfaction in that his campaign in support of Jewish marriage law and against that of the state achieved some success. In 1790 three communal leaders – Samuel Landau, Marcus Karpelis and Seligmann Kalmus, all from Prague – personally handed to the new emperor, Leopold II, a petition in which protest at the incursion of the state into the Jewish law of marriage and inheritance accompanied other sources of grievance:

> Marriage in the case of the Jews, is so bound up with religion and so defined by Jewish laws [they argued] that not only when marriages are concluded or dissolved, but also in the case of disputes between marriage partners, procedure follows only these laws and the prescription of learned and experienced rabbis and jurists.

At some interval, the emperor agreed to relax the limit on the marriage of consanguineous partners apart from that on marriage between brother and sister; second, a validly concluded marriage could only be terminated through the husband handing to the wife a writ of divorce in the presence of the authorities.

The new legal code of 1800, it was pointed out, 'passed over in silence' the approved exemptions from the general marriage laws in regard to the for-bidden degrees and divorce procedure. In 1811 these were incorporated in the civil code, but with other regulations which ran counter to Jewish mar-riage law, for example the need to announce the marriage in the synagogue over three successive Sabbaths, and the need for a rabbinical presence at the betrothal, apart from the two witnesses.[53] In Trieste R. Abram Eliezer Levi and the communal leaders, the *Capi*, issued a *takkanah* in 1805 which did in effect accept the provisions of the marriage patent while clothing them in halakhic garb.[54]

At one time Landau considered returning to his birthplace in Poland, and it does not seem that he died in contentment for in an address on the Sabbath of Repentance (preceding the Day of Atonement) Landau lamented: 'the words of rebuke I reproach you with year after year are not heeded. And for all that I add by way of chastisement, the transgressions multiply.'[55] In 1782 Landau had found 'the world turned upside down'. His writings in general give no indication that he ever reconciled himself to those powerful and inimical forces that were seeking to germanize Habsburg Jewry and undermine their traditions. Landau remained sensitive to these features of the contemporary world that curbed the use of Hebrew and Yiddish in favour of German and thereby facilitated access to literature that might disturb belief, and introduced secular subjects into the accepted school curriculum; and imposed conscription; and encroached on the marriage laws.

Landau's efforts to retain some elements of identity against the contrary efforts of the state and to establish a *modus vivendi* with Joseph II were increasingly compromised by the Haskalah and religious reform, with the ascent to influence of Herz Homberg (1749–1841), already known for his work in reconciling Jewish conscripts to their fate (see above, p. 244). After a traditional Talmudic education in Prague, Pressburg and Gross Glogau, Homberg, partly under the influence of Rousseau, resolved to devote himself to pedagogy. He worked for a time as teacher in Mendelssohn's household in Berlin before entering state service as senior inspector of all Jewish schools in Galicia with his seat of office in Lemberg. In this capacity, and by virtue of his relationship with the authorities, Homberg was able to reinforce their hope to the extent that the contribution of the individual Jew in the localities to the upkeep of the rabbi would become a voluntary matter and thus further weaken the communal structure. He saw in the Talmud 'a bottomless sea of casuistical and useless conceits which utterly deaden the feeling for beauty, order, regularity and simplicity'. Homberg argued for the censorship of this type of literature; and for its practitioners and exponents – the rabbinate – had nothing but contempt. He saw a solution to the Jewish economic plight in a return to the soil on Rousseauistic lines, and in the crafts. Instruction on these lines would over a period of six years qualify a Jew to become an equal member of society. Homberg's 'Children of Zion' (Bnei Zion, 1812), which became a compulsory catechistic manual in the Jewish schools of the Germanophone territories, more or less reduced Jewish teachings to the obligation to see in complete and utter obedience to the secular ruler a Jew's whole duty, and affirmed that this would ensure his bliss not only in this world but also in the next. A Jewish bride and bridegroom seeking permission to marry had first to pass an examination in 'Children of Zion'.[56]

The outbreak of revolution in France confronted the Jews of Alsace and Bordeaux with a new relationship to the state even more challenging than that offered by Joseph II to Habsburg Jewry.

15
Revolution and War, 1789–1805

The turmoil of the *ancien régime* in Europe, the Revolution in France and the Napoleonic wars left no *kehillah* untouched. The Anglo-Jewish community combined its patriotism with aloofness from overt political activity in its own specific interest. Anglo-Jewry would fight not for the rights of man but for the less politically loaded rights of Englishmen. A very rare if not unique example of political initiative was Abraham Tang's pamphlet of 1770 in defence of John Wilkes and democracy, *A Discourse Addressed to the Minority*. The lasting memory of the débâcle over the 'Jew Bill' of 1753 (see above, p. 156) and the anti-alien agitation of the 1790s combined to still any overt pressure on the part of the leaders.[1] This quiescence certainly did not inhibit intervention on behalf of Jews abroad (for example at the Congress of Vienna). But not until 1829 did communal leaders prepare a petition calling for some relief from the Jews' civil and political disabilities. It was then suggested (by Nathan Mayer Rothschild) that their petition should also call for 'full protection in holding and conveying of Landed Property'.[2] This may well be interpreted as a step towards political emancipation, for if a man who possesses a stake in the country cannot share in its government, then who can? This was the rationale that justified attaching financial conditions to the franchise. In Prussia any notion of political activity in response to the French model would have to overcome the suspicious taint of revolution.[3]

Communities in France, Ashkenazi and Sephardi, were the first to confront the swift succession of events. The deepening financial crisis of the state led to the royal convocation of the Estates-General for February 1789; in June, the Third Estate in the Tennis-Court Oath refused to disperse until its demands for greater constitutional power were acceded to; in July, Necker, the Genevan banker and financial mainstay of the government, was dismissed; the troops summoned to Versailles to disperse the Third Estate refused to quell the mass revolt in Paris; on 4 August the Estates-General voted to abolish all the privileges of the different orders; the Estates-General converted themselves into a Constituent Assembly and on 26–27 August adopted the Declaration of the Rights of Man and the Citizen. 'No person shall be molested for his opinions, even such as are religious', proclaimed article x, 'provided that the manifestation of these opinions does not disturb the public order established by the law'.[4]

No Jews participated in any of these events. But it is reasonable to suppose that they intently followed their course, all the more so in eastern France because here the local peasantry exploited the decay in authority to run riot in a series of anti-Jewish disturbances. Two Metz publications went some way towards keeping the Jewish population of Alsace *au courant* of developments in Paris. The first was a *Beschreibung* which provided a digest of events from the meeting of the Estates-General until 5 November 1789; it was followed by a weekly journal, called simply *Zeitung*. This appeared until April 1790. The language was a blend of Yiddish and German, printed in Hebrew characters. The author-editor-publisher of *Zeitung* was Abraham Goudchaux Spire, grandson of Moses May, the founder of a Hebrew printing works at Metz in 1764. May had intended to relieve the community's dependence on Germany and Poland for works of scholarship. But he was overcome by debt and fled to Hamburg in *c*.1770. Spire, the grandson, restarted the enterprise some three years later under letters patent granted by Louis XVI.[5] *Zeitung* had about 100 subscribers; with an estimated 15–20 readers per copy it is reckoned to have reached all the potential readers in Metz. (Still, to what extent this can serve as a measure of political awareness in rural areas, where of course most Jews were living, is unclear.)

In their *cahiers de doléance* the Christian inhabitants of eastern France, with rare and qualified exceptions, reviled the Jews as aliens, usurers and the bearers of a corrupting religion whose presence should be reduced if not removed. The nobility were less inclined to be hostile than the clergy and the Third Estate. The *cahier* of the nobility of Metz, for example, expressed the wish that 'all *régnicoles* would enjoy the right of residence (*droit de cité*) in the kingdom, irrespective of their belief'; the *cahiers* from Metz made almost no mention of Jews; from the bailiwick of Toul the nobility, 'desiring and demanding that the Jews be permitted to practise the liberal and mechanical arts', deplored the enforced predominance of moneylending among the Jews. As for the purchase of land, this required further thought.[6] The *cahiers* elsewhere made little, if any mention, of Jews. Of the *c*.40000 *cahiers de doléance* only about 300 mentioned Jews. The 'problem' was localized, but for that very reason all the more intense. Events of the summer showed how intense. At intervals in July, August and September, during *la grande peur*, peasants attacked Jewish homes and property in Alsace and Lorraine. They caused 'considerable damage' and forced the inhabitants to seek refuge in Bâle and Mulhouse.[7]

The Revolution exacerbated existing differences among the communities of Alsace, the south-west and Paris. In Bordeaux there was little question but that the Sephardi and Avignonese communities possessed the right to elect their deputies to the Estates-General. The *Jurat* did indeed have reservations, but these did not hinder the Sephardim in their election early in March of four representatives: Azevedo the elder, Solomon Lopes-Dubec, David Gradis and Abraham Furtado. A week or so later the Third Estate of Bordeaux included Gradis and Furtado among its 90 electors. By only a few votes did Gradis fail to secure election as one of the four Bordeaux deputies to the Estates-General. At Saint-Esprit lès Bayonne the Christian inhabitants refused to permit the Jews to hold their own primary assembly. The *Nation* protested and in the eventual compromise of April 1789 elected two representatives (as against the original four): Jacob Silveyra and Mordecai Lopes-Fonseca. The Sephardim thereby asserted and confirmed their right to possess the status of *régnicoles* and to participate as equals in the formation of a new regime. The Avignon Jews in Bordeaux elected two representatives, Daniel Astruc and Salom. There was a general resolve not to submit any *cahiers de doléance* lest they gratuitously jeopardize their favoured status by drawing attention to themselves. For the Sephardim the issue must be to preserve rather than to acquire, especially if the process of acquisition should entail any sort of cooperation with the Ashkenazim. This was precisely the reason why David Gradis wrote to Dupré de Saint-Maur, in April 1789, and pointed to the satisfactory state enjoyed by the Sephardim so that they should not be included in any new legislation that Malesherbes was thought at the time to be preparing for the Jews of Alsace and Lorraine. In August the Sephardim wrote to Abbé Grégoire (spokesman for the Ashkenazim) in the same sense. They must at all costs avoid being tarred with the Ashkenazi brush, though without harming the Ashkenazi. This letter was printed and published as a token of its importance.[8]

In 1789, when the king took the initiative and summoned the Estates-General, the Ashkenazi Jews of north-eastern France, at the behest of the minister of war, were not able to take part in the local assemblies or to draw up *cahiers*. But they were *régnicoles*, and not foreigners, subject to the civil laws of the kingdom, as well as taxpayers, the Jews of Metz, Alsace and Lorraine protested; and were not also 'non-Catholics' (that is, Protestants) to be represented in the Estates? In the name of the three generalities, Cerf Berr wrote to Necker, director-general of finance, on 15 April 1789 and proposed a form of indirect participation whereby one or more deputies to the estates would be charged with representing Jewish interests. The king accepted this proposal and the Jews in the three generalities elected their deputies: for Alsace, R. David Sinzheim and Samuel Seligmann; for Metz, Goudchaux Mayer Cohen and Louis Wolff; for Lorraine, Mayer Marx and Berr Isaac-Berr. Sinzheim took the Alsatian *cahier* to Paris where it was amalgamated with the two others and presented to Abbé Grégoire, the nominated spokesman of the Ashkenazim. Grégoire, one of the prizewinners in the Metz contest of 1785, enthusiastically espoused the 'regeneration' of the Jews through their reeducation and emancipation from their religion. In the longer term he looked forward to their conversion but in the shorter term his advocacy of the Jews' cause at the Estates-General and the National Assembly and elsewhere was of inestimable value.[9]

These *cahiers* are couched in the spirit and values of Cerf Berr. They formulate a policy in keeping with his earlier support for a strengthened communal body in Alsace and for the retention of communal institutions as earlier propounded by C. W. Dohm (*Über die bürgerliche Verbesserung der Juden*, 1782). Cerf Berr, it is said, was even ready to sacrifice emancipation to the maintenance of communal autonomy.[10] But for the moment at least, between full citizenship and communal autonomy no incompatibility was envisaged. The three generalities jointly demand an end to enforced protection payments, and uniformity of taxation with other citizens; the Jews should be able to practise all arts and crafts, acquire fixed property, cultivate the land and enjoy freedom of movement without being required to live in segregated districts; they should be free to practise their religion, retain their rabbis, syndics and communities, 'and their jurisdiction ... without any change in their present constitution in everything which might refer to their religion and the Jewish law'. The Jews of Alsace asked for permission to employ Christian servants for help with agriculture and for freedom to marry (that is, without the need for royal permission) subject to the self-imposed condition of owning 1200 livres in town and 400 in the countryside. The Jews of Metz argued for an end to the Brancas tax and for the right to participate in communal facilities. The *cahier* from Lorraine spoke of the demand for synagogues with no external sign to mark them out as places of worship; for rabbis empowered to pronounce divorces, administer estates and serve as judges of first instance in cases of Jew versus Jew; for the right to enter colleges and universities; and required that every Jew seeking to establish residence in Nancy show assets of 100 000 livres (3000 elsewhere in Lorraine and 1200 in the villages) – this would keep at bay paupers and vagabonds. The Jews of Nancy enjoyed an unusual degree of affluence; about half the 97 families were prosperous.[11]

When the six deputies from eastern France came to Paris they learned 'with much joy, of the rights of man', wrote Berr Isaac Berr (from Lorraine):

> All men are born equal and free. We found then that not only was our mission pointless but we judged that this decree ... granted us rights far beyond those that our *cahiers* entrusted us with requesting ... We decided by general demand to obtain the rights and title of citizen.

In an *Adresse* published on 30–31 August, the eastern Jews therefore modified their policy and, in addition to protesting at unfair taxes, also introduced a thoroughly new concept in requesting from the Assembly an explicit pronouncement conferring on the Jews 'the title and rights of citizens'. This was also the position of the Jews of Paris with, however, a significant difference from the Alsatian Jews. In Paris a small group of Ashkenazim and Sephardim moved fast to spell out the implications of the Declaration of the Rights of Man:

> We are henceforth certain to lead an existence different from that to which we have hitherto been dedicated [*dévoués*]. In this empire, which is our homeland, the title of man guarantees us that of citizens; and the title of citizens will give us all the rights of the city and the civil faculties which we see are enjoyed, alongside with us, by the members of a society of which we form part.

These Paris Jews, in return for the rights of a citizen, renounced their own jurisprudence, police, laws and tribunals and their own leaders in favour of 'a uniform plan of police and jurisprudence'.[12]

Whereas the Paris Jews willingly renounced all forms of communal organization, the deputies of Alsace, Lorraine and Metz insisted on the retention of 'our synagogues, our rabbis and our syndics in the same way as all exist today', and 'to be maintained in the free exercise of our laws, rites and usages'. They drew the deduction that since the Declaration of the Rights of Man prohibited discrimination on religious grounds, then, provided the exercise of religion did not disturb public order, the Declaration gave positive protection to religious practices and so on. Soon Zalkind Hourwitz and Jacob Lazard, a fellow-spirit from Metz, would accuse the Alsatian leaders of 'tyrannizing the conscience of their fellow-Jews with a rabbinical inquisition'.[13]

The agenda proclaimed at the end of August 1789 included not only the new status of citizenship but also freedom of residence; abolition of arbitrary taxation; and freedom of religion with particular reference to the retention of the synagogue in Metz. Two objections had been raised. First, at a time when feudal privileges were abolished, was it not provocative to seek to retain the judicial administrative privileges of the communities? Second, the Metz community, concerned about the problem of its debts, sought to prevent its members from leaving. How could this be reconciled with the freedom of residence that was also sought?

On 14 October 1789 Berr Isaac-Berr of Nancy in an invited address at the bar of the Assembly called for a total reform in the Jewish condition, which would of course include admission to citizenship. The Jews did not fail to remind the president of the Assembly that they had been waiting for two months, and that the prolongation of this period of uncertainty had contributed to the unsettled conditions in Alsace. At this time also Grégoire republished significant extracts of his original essay in favour of the 'regeneration of the Jews' through their integration in society. A month later the deputy from Aix, Charles Bouche (1737–95), demanded for the Jews of Avignon an end to all discriminatory taxation, and to the compulsion to wear a distinctive badge, the authority to buy property and the recognition of their rights as citizens. But this would all be dependent on the decision of the Assembly.

In the continuing debate in the Assembly on the constitutional question of the franchise and the prerogatives of an active citizen (as distinct from those of a passive citizen), it was apparent that, though the qualifications for active citizenship might include economic criteria, the Rights of Man would completely exclude discrimination on religious grounds. This validated the circumspect Sephardi strategy of avoiding explicit mention of the Jews with all the odium that this might provoke. In September 1789 Lopez Dubec wrote to Zalkind Hourwitz and explained that 'In the Rights of Man and the Citizen (the Jews) will find their security and their happiness'; thus, if Cerf Berr and the Paris Jews understood this truth then they would withdraw the memoranda they were supplying Abbé Grégoire with. No law specifically applying to Jews was needed.[14]

This strategy of relying on the Declaration of the Rights of Man was perfectly reasonable but it failed to allow for the antisemites in the Assembly. The Ashkenazi strategy also proved abortive, in this eventuality. The decisive confrontation came in a debate in December 1789 on the eligibility of Protestants for active citizenship. When it was accepted that religion could not be regarded as reason for exclusion, the antisemites in the Assembly – primarily Reubell, a Jacobin from Colmar, Abbé Maury, the bishop of Nancy, La Fare, and Prince de Broglie – distinguished between the Jews and the Protestants and derived their opposition to the acceptance of the Jews as active citizens not from their religion but from the alleged foreignness of the Jews in their constituting a separate nation by virtue of their communal autonomy. They are people 'who demand to be Frenchmen', wrote Reubell a few days after the Assembly debate, 'but still wish to preserve Jewish administration, Jewish judges, Jewish notaries…their particular laws on heritage, marriage, tutelage, majority, and so on.'[15] In the debate itself the objection arising from Jewish autonomy became joined to the inherent status of Jew *qua* Jew. If the Jews were to become citizens, then they must cease to be Jews: 'To call the Jews citizens,' declared Abbé Maury, 'would be as if one would say that without letters of naturalization and without ceasing to be English or Danish, the English and Danes could become French.'

Clermont-Tonnerre's answer has deservedly attained classic status; it did not reject Maury's argument and in fact it accepted the premiss that only a Frenchman could be a citizen. But for Clermont-Tonnerre the criterion of 'Frenchness' was adherence, or rather the lack of adherence, to some sort of organized independent body within the state whereas religion was purely an individual and private matter. This position was markedly less deterministic than the presupposition of Abbé Maury, for whom the Jewish religion was also a nationality. Clermont-Tonnerre rejected antisemitic allegations of Jewish misanthropy and usuriousness and then offered both a promise and a threat: 'everything must be refused to the Jews as a nation and everything granted to them as individuals. Their judges must be refused recognition; they must have none but ours; legal protection must be refused to the supposed laws of their Judaic corporation. In the state they must form neither a political body nor an order. They must as individuals be citizens'. If they do not wish to be citizens, let them say so, 'and then let them be banished. It is repugnant that there should be in the state a society of non-citizens and a nation within the nation ... Certainly the Jewish nation, as nation, cannot be received and admitted to citizens' rights (*Droits de Cité*) and preserve its laws, customs and political principles.' So much for the threat; now for the promise: 'but every man, Jew or not, who personally fulfils the conditions fixed by our laws ... must no longer be excluded from public positions and the elections by reason of his religious opinion'.[16] In the upshot the Assembly agreed to accept the eligibility of non-Catholics as electors but to reserve judgement on the status of the Jews. The debate, however, had at least served to uncover the position of the Jews' extreme opponents, that is, in order to be eligible for citizenship it was not enough for the Jew to forswear any corporate existence whatsoever but he must also take the further step of ceasing altogether to be a Jew, this condition being regarded as a nationality in itself. The Revolution happily rejected this position and contented itself with the delimitation of Jewish corporate existence.

The adjournment vote at the Assembly led to intense distrust between the respective Ashkenazi and Sephardi leaderships. The latter was particularly sensitive to the fact that the debate had made no distinction among Jews. It had also shown the political activity of the Sephardim in Bordeaux to be *ultra vires*. The Sephardim therefore abandoned the policy of laissez-faire, withdrew from their quasi-common front with the Alsatians and organized a separate campaign that would legitimize explicitly their status as citizens. As early as 30 December, the leadership formed a rapid reaction force of 8 members – 1 from Avignon and 7 from Bordeaux; these deputies were soon to be fortified by the authority to act also in the name of the Bayonne community. In a petition of 31 December 1789, the Sephardim reproached the Ashkenazim with aspiring 'to live in France under a special regime, to have their own laws, and to constitute a class of citizens distinct from all others'; were this in fact to come about, then it could be attributed only to 'the effervescence of a poorly intentioned religious zeal', from which they themselves were free. This separatism the Sephardim juxtaposed to their own status as naturalized Frenchmen, acknowledged as *régnicoles* by letters patent going back to 1550. They owned and disposed of property as a matter of right; they had no laws or courts special to themselves; they paid the same taxes as other Frenchmen; David Gradis had been admitted as one of the 90 electors of Bordeaux; they had joined the 'Regiment Patriotique', in whose ranks several had reached the rank of captain and lieutenant. What more could be demanded of us 'so that our quality of active citizens be recognized'? the Sephardim asked. 'Should the barely considered demands of some Jews of Alsace and Lorraine ... have the power to have us deprived of our rights?'[17] In the first few days of 1790 the Sephardim took to lobbying and canvassing and made contact with perhaps one hundred deputies, mainly from the Third Estate, including Mirabeau, Sieyès, Roederer, Robespierre, Barnave and the Protestant pastor, Rabaut-Saint-Etienne. This entailed domiciliary visits because of deputies' preoccupations with the sessions of the Assembly. Contact was also made with the antisemites from Alsace and Lorraine, Abbé Maury and the Jacobin, Reubell. The Sephardim centred this campaign on the bishop of Autun, Talleyrand, by virtue of his status as *rapporteur* of the committee on the constitution.

The final breach between the Sephardim and the Ashkenazim took place when, under pressure, the latter admitted that 'if they were granted the rights of a citizen with the power to acquire fixed property, to sell and dispose of it at will, with the faculty also of practising any branch of commerce, arts and crafts', then they would not aspire to those citizens' rights 'which would render them capable of becoming electors and eligible to take up places in the administration and civil or military posts'. Nevertheless, in the address that the Ashkenazim were planning to put to the Assembly, 'they would demand the rights of a citizen with all the extension that this quality entails'. This did not satisfy the Sephardi interlocutors, 'because it was more than presumable that in their verbal solicitations [the Ashkenazim] would not demand that extension of rights, and that several members of the Assembly had understood it thus, they told us'.[18]

In what seems to have been a last-minute attempt to delay the Sephardi momentum, a letter and petition to the Assembly prepared by Jacques Godard, at the instance of the Ashkenazim, maintained that no distinction be made among Jews and that all obtain the rights of citizenship without discrimination. Should that be withheld, further debate must be postponed, with regard to both Ashkenazim and Sephardim. It could not be the intention of the Assembly 'that men whose religion and principles are the same should lead a different existence in France, because they do not inhabit the same province'. The signatories shared in principle the same demands, with the difference that what 'they are seeking to preserve, we are seeking to acquire'. This document pleaded for a recognition of the distinction between 'citizen' and 'Jew' and the absence of any conflict between them. The same person would, in the former capacity, fulfil all the requirements of his citizenship and in the latter all his duties as a Jew.[19]

This document, made public in 28 January 1790, had no practical effect, for the previous day Talleyrand had already told the gratified Sephardim that 'it was not his intention' to seek an adjournment until such time as the question of both Ashkenazim and Sephardim could be resolved in unison.

Precisely on 28 January 1790, Talleyrand put the Sephardi motion to the Assembly: All the Jews known in France under the name of Portuguese, Spanish and Avignonese Jews

> will continue to enjoy the rights which they have enjoyed hitherto and which are sanctioned in their favour by the letters patent and in consequence they will enjoy the rights of active citizens when they meet the conditions required by the decrees of the Assembly.

There was immediate tumult, '*réclamations vives*', says the official report. Would Sephardi success not prove the thin end of the Ashkenazi wedge? 'The exception for the Jews of Bordeaux would soon entail the same exception for the other Jews of the kingdom', complained Reubell, one of the antisemitic deputies from Alsace. Another such deputy, Schwende, sought to add an amendment which would explicitly declare that 'in no way had the Assembly intended to prejudge anything in regard to the Jews of Alsace'. The Assembly eventually accepted the motion by a majority of 374 to 224 (about one-third were absent).[20]

To the Sephardim the retention of their existing corporate status yielded to the status of citizenship and thus the dissolution of the *Nation* followed the vote within a matter of weeks; on 18 February 1790 the *Nation* ceased to exist, at least in its previous form, and became an 'association of charitable benevolence'. The *Nation* at Bayonne took the same action.

The Sephardi success was felt by Abraham Spire in Metz as 'an affront to the Jews of the other provinces'. He saw no hope but in 'divine providence', he wrote in his journal.[21]

This pessimism was unjustified. Berr Isaac-Berr had by no means abandoned his hope of a *modus vivendi* between some degree of political rights and some degree of autonomy. In April 1790 he suggested to Bishop de la Fare of Nancy that if the Jews of Alsace and Lorraine were voluntarily to relinquish their rights to occupy offices in the municipality and magistracy, by virtue of the Declaration of the Rights of Man and the Citizen, then, as compensation, the National Assembly should permit these Jews to constitute a '*communauté particulière*'. This body would have its own rabbis and leaders, as much for the civil as for the religious order, and enjoy also the power to adjudicate disputes between Jew and Jew, subject to appeal to a higher court, furnished with a certified translation of Jewish civil law and customs. Jacob Berr, nephew of Berr Isaac-Berr, denounced his uncle's offer of a separate regime as 'a dangerous proposition', and an 'abuse of power'. He rejected in principle the rabbinical union of civil and religious authority, apart from which the syndics would in any case enjoy an excess of power. Jacob Berr thought in terms of a balance of power.[22]

The new conception of the nation created by the revolution erected the obstacle that the Ashkenazim in general faced, and Berr Isaac-Berr in particular. In essence it united emancipation and nationality. It went beyond any difference of religion and made 'citizen' and 'Frenchman' one.[23] The Sephardim overcame this obstacle relatively early but the Ashkenazim must wait till September 1791 before they too were admitted to the rank of citizen; and then the problem was overcome only by recourse to abstract constitutional principles.

In 1791, work on the constitution, the flight of the king and the death of Mirabeau necessarily overshadowed the 'Jewish question'. Only some minor but significant successes could be achieved: the Assembly explicitly extended to Alsatian Jewry the protection of French law; and abolished the Brancas tax. Not until 27 September 1791, on the eve of the very dissolution of the Assembly, did Adrien Duport (of the Jacobin Club) call for the removal of all discrimination in terms of the freedom of religion which could not countenance any distinction among citizens on account of their faith. To remove discrimination on this account would alone complete the Revolution, and conform to the constitution, adopted just a few days earlier. This argument, drawn from the very principles of the Revolution, the deputies accepted with virtual unanimity:

> The National Assembly, considering that the conditions requisite to be a French citizen and to become an active citizen, are fixed by the constitution ... annuls all adjournments, restrictions and exceptions contained in the preceding decrees affecting individual Jews who will take the civil oath.

The next day, Reubell and de Broglie, the unreconciled antisemites of Alsace, persuaded the Assembly to add to the decree the phrase, 'which shall be considered as a renunciation of privileges and exceptions introduced previously in their favour'. This contract takes the form of a quid pro quo. Reubell also persuaded the Assembly that the Alsatian Jews be required to submit to local officials lists of their credits.[24] This demand was never complied with.

Not with a bang the struggle ended, but with a whimper. Until the end the Ashkenazim fought to enforce a conception of citizenship that would be reconcilable with some degree of communal autonomy. They had to yield, while leaving details in a sort of limbo. Only during the reaction under Napoleon and his successors did the Jews recover a form of acknowledged self-rule. For the moment, in the wake of defeat, Berr Isaac-Berr executed a partial volte-face, that involved the deity and the monarch. On the very morrow of the decree of 28 September 1791, he invoked the former who, he maintained, 'has chosen the generous nation and King Louis XVI to reintegrate us into our rights ... the title of active citizen that we have just obtained is without contradiction the most precious quality that a man can possess'. This enthusiasm Berr Isaac-Berr tempered with the acknowledgement that the Jews must change their manners and customs and acquire a perfect command of the French language, if they were to obtain the esteem of their fellow-countrymen. In respect of religion they must 'abandon that *esprit de corps* and of community for all those civil and political aspects, which are not inherent in our spiritual laws; there we must absolutely be no more than individuals'. He called for a translation into French of the Bible, on the Mendelssohn model, so that young people would learn Hebrew and French: 'We are French Jews.' 'Our attachment to our Sovereign, to our king ... has never been equivocal.' But Berr Isaac-Berr also pointed out that these very laws which restored the Jews' rights and placed them on the same footing as all other Frenchmen also granted the Jews 'full liberty to profess [their] religion and to follow [their] mode of worship'. He balanced this accomplishment with a warning to his fellow-Jews not to exercise to the full their newly acquired political rights until they had acquired more familiarity with French circumstances, facility in the language, and an education on the lines recommended by Wessely in his *Words of Peace and Truth* (1782).[25]

In actual fact the process of emancipation was not completed until 1831, when the French government agreed to pay the salaries of rabbis, thereby aligning them with the Catholic and Protestant clergy. Earlier, the debts of the Jewish communities were treated differently and less favourably than those of other corporations. This emerged in 1797. In 1791 and 1793 decrees had nationalized the debts of those corporations earlier dissolved in 1790. The Jewish leaders hoped that nationalization would apply also to the debts of the Jewish communities which were likewise corporations, they argued, and which in September 1791 had been dissolved. In 1797 the Council of Five Hundred destroyed this hope, maintaining that the communities had never been recognized as corporations.[26]

For all that, the admission of the Jews to citizenship in 1791 had vastly more than token importance. This process lends itself to two different interpretations – roughly speaking, a 'French' and a 'Jewish'. The first sees the outlines of a bargain: one party, despite every effort, has had to sacrifice its claim to autonomy, reduced Judaism to a 'religion', assumed all sorts of obligations (for example military service, 'regeneration') and for this has been rewarded with admission to the body of citizens (though it is as a Jew that this admission takes place). The second interpretation locates the projected new relationship of the Jews of France to the French state, that is their putative status as citizens, in the evolution of the *kehillah*, and then the notion of contract or bargain yields to the notion of a fresh phase in that evolution, mediated by the conceptual principle that 'the law of the land is the law'. Of course, the decree of the National Assembly that annuls all the legislation affecting those Jews who take the civic oath refers only to 'individuals of the Jewish persuasion' and makes no specific allusion to any collective association for example the *kehillah*. Even so, it is surely understood that this institution will forfeit its remaining legislative power.

The Jews, some at least, are able to understand the implications of citizenship (as promised by the Declaration) in terms of the enforced evolution of their *kehillah* from a quasi-autonomous body with varying powers of coercion into a non-coercive voluntary body, as proclaimed by Mendelssohn less than a decade earlier. To be more precise: if, in consequence of the implementation of the Rights of Man the Jews are to be made subject to an alien law and thereby to forfeit their own, then their executive-communal body, the *kehillah*, is undergoing a painful and enforced mutation to the extent that it is losing its most distinctive prerogative. In this light, the loss of that remaining degree of sovereignty that had survived the earlier incursions of eighteenth-century absolutism denotes no more than further evolution and an accommodation to the reality that 'the law of the land is the law'. This does not have to be a 'bargain', 'contract' or 'quid pro quo', rather the continuing application of an accepted principle, however painful and drastic and debilitating. Only Napoleon will make clear precisely how painful and drastic. The transition from one source of sovereignty to another and the consequent diminution of the existing *kehillah* was by no means clear-cut. In many cases, certain sections of Jewry, in France and elsewhere, especially the Sephardim and the Jews of Paris, positively sought and welcomed the right to be subjected to the general law of the state. To others the conditions attached to inclusion in the Rights of Man betoken a sacrifice and not an advance. Therefore, when the time came in 1806–07 for Napoleon and Cerf Berr's brother-in-law, R. David Sinzheim, to negotiate the degree to which the actual terms of the eventual transfer of sovereignty would impinge on the *kehillah* the result was not without ambiguity and ambivalence, given the need to satisfy different Jewish constituencies.

Not the least bewildering aspect of the formal dissolution of the *kehillot* is in fact the need for their continued existence, so that taxes could be collected, in order to pay off the communal debts. Already in August 1789 the Metz deputies, Louis Wolff and Goudchaux-Mayer-Cohen, had sought legislative power to prevent any Jew 'from leaving the district where he lives without having discharged his share of the common debt'. Pressure from Christian creditors reinforced the demand for the preservation of communal integrity. In February 1792 the *directoire* of the Metz district authorized the maintenance of the special taxes that the former leaders levied on the community for the repayment of its debts,

> ordering that the same former syndics will be required to oppose, with all their power, on pain of personal responsibility, the abandonment by any Jew of his domicile in this city ... until he has satisfied the commitments imposed on him by the former community i.e. until he has remitted to the *caisse* the one-eighth of his fortune for the discharge of his contingent share in the common debt.[27]

Special factors operated in Metz in that some of the communal debt was due to Cerf Berr, who in pre-revolutionary days had given financial support to the Alsatian communities. Whether this factor influenced his policy in support of the existing *kehillah* structure is of course an open question. His conduct and belief as an observant and pious Jew would in any case predispose him in favour of the status quo. In 1792 and again in 1793 Cerf Berr claimed from the Strasbourg authorities a sum of at least 30 000 livres which was admitted and apportioned among the taxpayers of the Alsatian communities, which no longer had any official existence. Metz, which already before the Revolution was a depressed area, suffered even more after its outbreak and in 1792 had to issue to communities throughout Europe an anguished appeal for assistance.[28]

The measures taken to ensure that the community discharged its debts can have only added to its hardships. The clash of claim and counter-claim endured well into the nineteenth century. For the moment, despite the failure of an antisemitic centre such as Strasbourg to reconcile itself to the new status of the Jews, the enthusiasm of many was unabated. They swore an oath of fidelity to 'the nation, the law and the king and to uphold with all their power the constitution of the kingdom, decreed by the Constituent National Assembly of 1789, 1790 and 1791'. At Nancy and Lunéville the Jews took the civic oath 'amidst great pomp', from as early as January 1792. Their enthusiasm flowed into a *fête civique* held in the Metz synagogue in October 1792 to celebrate the victory at Thionville. Rabbi Oury Cahen spoke patriotically to the assembled soldiers of their bravery. France, he emphasized, 'had the right to count on the efforts of all her children, no matter what their faith'. Cahen then presented the mayor with a civic crown; and an orchestra swung into the notes of the *Marseillaise* – but a *Marseillaise* the text of which Rouget de Lisle would hardly have recognized. The *maskil* of Metz and Berlin, Moses Ensheim, had rendered the original into a Hebrew version that used biblical discourse and imagery to convey to an audience unfamiliar with the language and concepts of the original French something of the new era they were living through. Isaiah Berr Bing rendered Ensheim's Hebrew text into the French revolutionary idiom of patriotism and republicanism.[29] This can serve as a token of the sort of national identification to which the Jews of France had committed themselves. Not all, of course; the Jews, like everyone else, were subject to the constitution of 1791, which limited the condition of active citizen to taxpayers above a certain level. There were Ashkenazim of inadequate means who saw no advantage in exchanging their inherited status for an uncertain novelty that was in any case restricted. In Nancy, the list of Jewish citizens who took the oath shows that these were the better-off.[30]

In the transition from the *ancien régime* to the consolidation of the Revolution continuity was not absent. After '2000 years of oppression', was it realistic to expect rapid change in a mode of life, Abraham Lambert of Uffholtz (a newly arrived immigrant from Mannheim) asked of Euloge Schneider in 1793? Was there more reason to encourage wealthy Jews, whether merchants or manufacturers, to take to agriculture, if Christians of the same occupations were not to be touched?[31] The data point both towards continuity in occupation and towards novelty. Circumstances were predisposing factors. If an army marches on its stomach, as Napoleon famously proclaimed, then certain Jewish entrepreneurs, once suppliers to the armies of the *ancien régime*, retained that role, but now the stomachs they nourished belonged to the armies of the Revolution. Based in Tomblaine-Nancy at the outbreak of the Revolution, Cerf Berr supplied the armies with forage and foodstuffs, which he combined with his political activities. Theodore, the youngest son, was appointed *régisseur* of the Army of the Rhine in 1792, with particular responsibility for the Rhine-Moselle region; Baruch, the same year, was appointed *régisseur* of purchases for the army of the Rhine; Lippmann become *régisseur* to the army of Dumouriez; Marx Cerf Berr, the eldest son, and the first Jew to be admitted to the Jacobin Club of Strasbourg, became director of purchases for the Marine with special responsibility for the provisioning of the coastal warehouses of the Channel, Mediterranean and Atlantic. In 1795 the company contracted with the Comité du Salut Public to supply the armies of the republic with the enormous total of 40 000 horses within 6 months – 13 000 of them in the first 3 months alone following the signature of the contract. Baruch Cerf Berr needed a network of about 500 subcontractors to fulfil a contract for the supply of wheat and barley. On the eve of the Revolution (1773–90) the account books of the Cerf Berr family show business links with 67 Jewish suppliers. This was *par excellence* a military family. Cerf Berr himself had 22 grandsons, serving on the staff, in the imperial guard and in the artillery; 9 were decorated with the Legion of Honour for their feats of arms.[32]

Other provisioners included Ulry Hayyim Worms (later de Romilly, 1759–1843) from Sarrelouis. In 1792 he contracted with the ministry of war to supply, inter alia, mutton, beef, rice, cheese, wine, oil and dried vegetables to certain strongpoints along the Rhine (Neuf Brisach, Fort Louis and Huningue). This was about a month after the outbreak of war with Austria. Berr-Léon Fould from Boulay (1767–1855) was another important provisioner. The profits from this activity went into property – inevitably so at a time of inflation – and later financed entry into banking. As early as 1797 Fould became the principal partner in the Caisse des Comptes and in 1800 one of the principal shareholders in the Banque de France, side by side with Worms de Romilly.[33]

There was continuity also in money and the credit trades. The need for funds to purchase or deal in property nationalized by the Revolution fed the demand for credit. The depreciation of the currency increased the hazards inherently attached to moneylending, but this did not deter the Jewish lenders.[34] They also had to compete with Christian landowners and affluent peasants who, through the acquisition of large parcels of land, sought to enlarge their own holdings of nationalized properties whereas the Jewish moneylenders dealt largely with the poorer peasants whose purchases, because they were small, threatened the integrity of the larger parcels of land. *In toto* the financing of these smaller holdings amounted to a very considerable proportion of the credit operations in Alsace. According to the data assembled by Roland Marx, for year X (1801–02), it appears that in the Strasbourg registration area 33.48 per cent of debts, representing 42.6 per cent of the sums borrowed by rural proprietors, were owed to Jews; at Sélestat the respective proportions were 55.67 per cent and 48.45 per cent. These figures were some 2 or 3 times larger than in 1791 and illustrate the dimensions of this aspect of Jewish economic activity. This is confirmed in the steep rise in the advances made by Samuel Levy of Balbronn, 1792–93. As for speculation in the nationalized properties of the registration district of the Lower Rhine, most of this was conducted in the secondary market. The total superficial area of the land knocked down to Jews in this district between 1791 and 1811 amounted to less than 1300 hectares, hardly more than 2 per cent of the total sale of *biens nationaux*. Only 12 Jews (as against 344 Christians) acquired more than 30 hectares. These public purchases were complemented and vastly exceeded by purchases in the secondary market which doubled and perhaps trebled the number of properties handled by Jews. Of the 148 large-scale buyers of properties of more than 20 arpents, 42 were Jews (28.38 per cent), their purchases representing 11.91 per cent of the properties. Of these 42 Jewish purchasers a breakdown shows that the more numerous held less land: thus they accounted for only 22.81 per cent of the purchasers of 100 arpents and more, and 28.89 per cent of purchasers of 50–100 arpents and 34.78 per cent of those buying 20–50 arpents. Of these 42 Jews, 15 came from rural areas, 16 from Strasbourg (including Seligmann Alexandre, a son-in-law of Cerf Berr), 6 from Ribeauvillé (including the brothers Abraham and Isaac Wormser) and 4 of the remaining 5 from Hagenau. Almost all the properties bought were for resale. In some cases land speculation turned out to be immensely profitable, yielding gains of 40–80 per cent over two months. But there were some lenders and land speculators who were ruined through the repayments of loans in the form of worthless *assignats*.[35]

Where change did take place it was not necessarily in the direction of 'regeneration'. This became clear during the few years following the emancipation. Far from turning to agriculture some Jews took advantage of the freedom of movement to settle in the urban centres of Strasbourg, Paris and Marseilles and to disperse more widely. Between 1784 and 1808–10 the Jewish population of Alsace increased by 24 per cent. There was an increase both in their dispersion and in their urban concentration. In Strasbourg the Jewish population grew from *c*.68 in 1784 to 1476 in 1807; Jews were also living in 15 per cent more communes than in 1784. In 1809, the census showed a total of 2908 Jews in Paris, whereas at the outbreak of the Revolution there were barely an estimated 500.[36]

The Jewish leaders in Alsace and Lorraine always cherished the hope that emancipation and 'regeneration' would reinforce each other. This was inherent in the educational programme propounded by Berr Isaac-Berr under the inspiration of Wessely's *Words of Peace and Truth* (which he had himself translated from Hebrew into French). The Thus, in order to quit that 'mercantile and trading inspiration', Berr Isaac-Berr called for the establishment of 'charity workshops in which we will have poor children, and those who are not born for a higher destiny, instructed in all the crafts and mechanical arts which society needs, let us train from among us carpenters, locksmiths, tailors, etc'. An artisanal qualification would become a condition for marriage.[37]

The themes of the Berlin enlightenment, conceived amidst Prussian and Habsburg absolutism, reechoed strongly in revolutionary France. To some extent this call was indeed answered; for example by 1806 there were some 190–200 gainfully employed family heads in Strasbourg; of these some 60, it is calculated, were neither peddlers nor second-hand dealers but licensed artisans including butchers, bookbinders, watchmakers and innkeepers as well as shopkeepers. Antisemitism had much to do with the slow entry of the Jews into a wider spread of occupations, at least according to one French official, sub-prefect of the Département de la Meurthe (1806). In his *arrondissement* there were about 400 Jews, he reported to the prefect. Most of the economically active were traders in draperies, cloths, horses and cattle. There were also some butchers:

> If [added the sub-prefect] they do not devote themselves to the liberal or mechanical professions, it is not because of lack of goodwill; the strong religious prejudices which the multitude entertain in their regard, would always reject them and in these professions they would die of starvation.[38]

It takes two to 'regenerate'. But the slow rate of change was also a function of the backward agricultural provinces of eastern France where the bulk of French Jewry continued to live well into the nineteenth century.[39]

During the Terror and the Reign of Reason the Jews of France shared in the fate of their fellow-citizens. They had to witness the despoiling of the synagogue at Metz. In November 1793 the Strasbourg District Commission prohibited the practice of circumcision, the wearing of a beard and the use of Hebrew, and ordered the destruction of all books in Hebrew, particularly the Talmud. 'They had declared that they would destroy all the books written in Hebrew,' wrote R. David Sinzheim, brother-in-law of Cerf Berr and later a leader in the negotiations with Napoleon.[40] He himself took refuge in Winzenheim (near Colmar) before moving to Switzerland. 'I live between hills and valleys, in the midst of peasants, with few pleasures and many expenses,' he wrote to a friend. In 1794 there were 177 Jews from Alsace among 5540 refugees in Karlsruhe, Baden and Bühl.[41] Sinzheim was not arrested but a number of rabbinical colleagues were less fortunate (for example Simon Horchheim and Benjamin Hemmerdinger). The students of the yeshivah of Metz had to take refuge in Germany to complete their training, so that until 1840 men trained in Germany held virtually all the rabbinic positions in France. Berr Isaac-Berr remained a monarchist to the end and in 1792 joined in a petition of the aristocrats of Nancy to save from demolition the statue of Louis XV in the Place Royale. The emigré movement included also Jews.

The guillotine did not discriminate among Jews, converted or otherwise. Its victims included the Frey brothers from the Dobrushka family of Moravia. Converts to Christianity, they were the followers of the messianic pretender Jakob Frank. They had taken part in the attack on the Tuileries in August 1792 but were arrested on allegations of espionage in November 1793 and executed the following April, together with Chabot (their brother-in-law), Danton and Camille Desmoulins. The heretical messianism propagated by the Frey brothers had led them to associate with the messianic hopes of the Revolution. Other victims included two members of the wealthy Calmer family and the picaresque adventurer Jacques Peyrera, a one-time associate of Beaumarchais. Political participation took the Sephardim of the south-west into support for Girondins, Jacobins and some few Montagnards. Abraham Furtado, one of the Sephardi leaders and a future protagonist in the negotiations with Napoleon, had to leave Bordeaux and take to flight because of his Girondist sympathies; likewise Lopes-Dubec. By way of contrast, Jean Mendès was condemned to death for his criticism of the constitution, which he found irreconcilable with his religious principles (20 July 1794). At Bayonne opinion may have been less moderate, although Fonseca Neveu did become president of the Montagnard Society. Here the general body of Jews supported the Jacobins. Rabbi Abraham Andrade proposed that the suburb of Saint-Esprit be renamed 'Jean-Jacques Rousseau'.

16
Beyond the Rhine and Over the Alps

The aura of freedom that accompanied the Revolution did not necessarily ensure it a welcome in the communities of Holland, the German and Italian states, the Habsburg empire and among 'the Papal Jews' of Provence. Even for the Alsatian Ashkenazim it was a second best. Every variety of response was met with elsewhere – hostility in Amsterdam and euphoria in Venice. If, in some cities, Jews danced round liberty trees, in others they held aloof; and of course, no community is monolithic in its attitude. In a general sense, communities must be alive to the odium that any association with revolution might bring to their political aspirations as Jews. In the reason why Markus Herz, the Kantian doctor of Berlin, was refused membership of the Berlin Academy of Sciences in 1793, there is more than a hint of the link attributed to Jews and revolution: Herz's membership, it was said, 'would be too much in favour of the new ideas, which are overturning the order hitherto established and which bring too close that which this order has kept at a distance'.[1]

In the *carrières* of Avignon, Carpentras and the Comtat Venaissin welcome and doubt first showed themselves. Their former inhabitants, released together with the Sephardim of the south-west, made manifest their revolutionary enthusiasm by taking office in local administrations, and by joining such groupings as La Société des Amis de la Liberté de l'Egalité et de la République. The promised freedom of movement, the opportunity to discard the yellow hat and the removal of economic restrictions spoke an unmistakable language. There were Jews who did not passively observe events but actively participated in political developments even though their presence was not always welcome, and Sabbath and other religious observances provoked suspicion at the very least. Jews holding official positions in their commune refused to breach the Sabbath by signing reports of debates in which they had themselves taken part. Also enthusiasm declined, particularly in Avignon, when the more radical turn of the Revolution threatened the economic interests of certain merchants.

The enhanced freedom of movement favoured the wealthy so that the depopulation of the *carrières* and their consequent impoverishment followed political freedom and advancement. Even before the Revolution, wealthy merchants were leaving Carpentras, Montpellier, Nîmes and Aix-en-Provence. The effects of this emigration of the wealthy showed in a report to the Carpentras municipality of March 1791: 'Most of the wealthy families of their *carrières* have had their houses emptied of all their effects, linen and jewels, and transported to France, and they left this city about a month ago.' This had two consequences: first, these families thereby relieved themselves of their share in the repayment of the communal debts owing to Christian lenders, both corporate and individual; second, the withdrawal of the mobile wealthy deprived the static poor of the support that the community had hitherto provided. In 1795 an anonymous writer proposed that the community be reconstituted as a purely charitable body: how could the 240 poor Jews of the locality be abandoned – they included 38 infirm old men, 78 children below 14 years of age, and 44 women? The same story in Avignon: in January 1793 the poor appealed to the municipality for aid, citing their loss of 'the resources which they found among their former corporations and their wealthy brethren whom the Revolution had largely removed from this city'.[2] In Metz special measures were enforced to prevent precisely this sort of situation (see p. 254 above).

The French incursions to the east and into the north-Italian states exacerbated intra-Jewish tension as between Jacobins and traditionalists. This was compounded by fluctuating regimes as between French revolutionary conquest and Habsburg reconquest. Communal leaders must bear in mind the possibility of popular violence, amid any pro-French enthusiasm they might display. In Savigliano, in 1796, only the intervention of French troops saved the Jews from attack; in Verona Austrian troops protected the Jews. In the Cisalpine Republic of 1797 anti-Jewish posters denounced the constitutional equality of religion. At Modena the populace tried to prevent the enrolment of Jews in the National Guard. In the reaction of 1799 the mob sacked the ghetti of Pitigliano, Lugo and Arezzo, and in Arezzo and Sinigaglia 13 Jews were murdered or burned at the stake. In Trieste alone perhaps did simplicity and order prevail. The French occupation in the 1790s and again in 1809–13 produced little change beyond the admission of Jews to the public service and their right (shared with others) to be elected to the municipal council, the French judging 'Jewish status in Trieste to be sufficiently close to the Emancipation they were legislating elsewhere'.[3]

In Livorno, another favoured trading centre, with a Jewish population of *c*.5000, sympathy for the French was unnecessary, given the generally protective policy of the Tuscan grand dukes. This was also the case in Florence, where Jews already participated in the municipal government and the conservative-minded Sephardi mercantile leadership had little sympathy for ideas of equality and democracy. The Jacobin Aron Fernandes was exceptional. To the *massari* in Livorno the status quo was preferable to revolutionary change and they were assiduous in repressing or removing the few instances of revolutionary sympathy. On the other hand, the promise of emancipation on the model of 1791 must appeal, so that one French official found 'very large numbers' of the wealthy Livornese Jews seemingly 'well enough disposed towards the French'. This cautious and guarded attitude prevailed during the actual French occupation of 1796–7 when only 8 young Jews enlisted in the French forces and no more than 6 joined the masonic lodge Amis de l'Union Française, founded in 1796. In 1799, during the second French occupation, republican sympathy proved more pronounced in the Jewish 'street', now that the French presence promised to be longer lasting; moreover, the Jews had won a representative in the new municipality. Jews enlisted in the Garde Nationale in proportionately larger numbers than the Catholic population; two communal notables, Salomon Bonfil, a *massaro*, and Daniel Vita de Medina, became captains in the Garde. In the synagogue Rabbi Mosé Vita Milul offered a prayer for the French armies. A calculation gives the figure of 17–26 per cent as the proportion among the Jacobins of adult Jewish males. Again, however, Jewish Francophilia must be qualified – all the more so because French economic exactions and general economic hardship intensified the recurrent anti-Jewish animus of the general population. Certain Jewish leaders warned the editor of the republican *Amico della Patria* against any undue emphasis on Jewish patriotism, lest it add to this animus. Not for nothing did some of the wealthy, hardly had the French arrived in March 1799, take flight from Livorno. The careful stance of the communal leadership had to take into account the repercussion of the French presence on the internal Jewish struggle. Those who danced in celebration around the tree of liberty in the ghetto were mainly the poor, that is the Italian and Levantine Jews. Daniel Vita de Medina used the same occasion to call publicly for harmony between Jews and Christians and an end to prejudice. The poorer Jewish stratum hoped to exploit the French presence to weaken the rule of the Sephardi plutocracy. Their spokesman, the intellectual Salomon Michel, published an article in the journal *L'Amico della Patria* denouncing the *massari* and their confirmation in office by French citizen-general Miollis: 'Is that liberty? Is that justice?' he asked. In fact, it had to be; yet collaboration with the French had also to be weighed against the odium that would follow the possible return of Tuscan rule, not to mention the coincidence of French occupation with economic crisis and commercial stoppages.[4]

In Mantua the community already benefited from the Habsburg reforms of Emperor Leopold II, which aimed to equalize the economic status of Jew and Christian. The virtual abolition of the guilds made it possible for Jews to enter a variety of trades (for example as saddlers, tailors, glaziers, carpenters, barbers, printers and bakers). The community also included surgeons, physicians and manufacturers. They could not live outside the ghetto, although they might own land beyond its walls. In 1797 when Mantua fell to the French, the community, fearful of reprisals, pleaded for the provisional retention of the ghetto gates, as a measure of protection. (The Jews of Modena and Reggio made the same request.) The Mantua community also asked the French not to accelerate their emancipation and not to appoint Jews to serve on public bodies. These pleas failed, in so far as the gates were torn down in 1798 and Jews were called on to serve on the new municipal council and enlist in the militia. The Habsburgs and their Russian allies retook Mantua in 1799, and sentenced to 10 years' exile three revolutionaries from the former ghetto. The eventual Austrian return to Mantua in 1814 left virtually unaffected the reforms that the French had imposed over the previous decade.[5]

On the 19th of Messidor Year IV (7 July 1797) the gates of the Venice ghetto were demolished to great rejoicing – 'the immortal Bonaparte ... has broken the bonds of Italian servitude'. The leaders of the former Universita of the Jews became deputies of the Jewish citizens and three Jews sat in the municipal government. The total of such citizens had dwindled to no more than 1620 (820 men, 800 women) of whom *c*.30 families (say, 200 people) were affluent. About one-third were comfortably off and the remainder more or less indigent. Their enthusiasm for the French may well have been encouraged by the revised charter of 1777, which had strengthened a range of economic restrictions. After the first French invasion and subsequent return of Austrian rule it was only in the Napoleonic kingdom of Italy (1804–14) and after that the ghetto regime came finally to an end.

The Jews of Rome, and the papal states, greeted the entry of the French with an enthusiasm no doubt unmatched elsewhere. The regime imposed by Pope Pius VI (1775–99) must encourage this reaction. He banned the study of the Talmud; forbade the Jews to open shops outside the ghetto area, to stay overnight outside the ghetto, to sell meat, bread and milk to Christians and to employ Christian domestics. Jews must wear the yellow badge and attend conversion sermons. An anonymous chronicle of the period (*c*.1792–7) from Ancona (part of the papal territories) describes the initial tension at the French invasion when for example on the 24th day of the month of Adar (= 8 March 1793) an attack on the Jewish quarter was narrowly averted. The mob accused the Jews of aiding the French 'with weapons of war, food and sustenance, against the wishes of the pope'. The eventual victory of the French inspired the community to send three of its leaders to Milan to thank Napoleon in person, 'for all the good deeds he had wrought for us, that he will strengthen and confirm our freedom'.[6] With the foundation under French auspices of the Roman republic in 1798 and the planting of a tree of liberty the cockade of the revolution replaced the yellow badge. Jews entered the National Guard. These improved circumstances survived the return, in 1814, of the new pope, Pius VII, and brought an end to the exodus of the wealthy to neighbouring Tuscany, which had begun in 1805. It was now possible to open shops outside the ghetto, perhaps even to live outside, and invest liquid capital in landed property. With the accession of Leo XII in 1823 this liberality was lost and emigration resumed.[7]

The impetus that the Revolution gave to Jewish political activity fostered internal differences. In France the Revolution sharpened the conflict between the Jews of Paris, who (like Zalkind Hourwitz) eagerly looked for an end to communal structure, and the conservative-minded leaders of Metz, Lorraine and Alsace, who sought to maintain the existing structure allied to an extension of the Jews' existing economic and personal freedoms. In Livorno the opposition to the *massari* led by Solomon Michel showed a similar pattern. It was in Holland, however, and especially in Amsterdam in the late eighteenth century, that the two themes of internal Jewish dissent from the ruling oligarchy became involved with the impact of revolutionary politics. The Jews in the Dutch Republic in the late eighteenth century numbered *c.*30 000, of whom *c.*20 000 lived in Amsterdam (18 500 Ashkenazim, 2800 Sephardim). This equated to 10 per cent of the city's population. The Republic's wars with England and resultant economic crises, combined with restricted entry to many occupations and the retail trade, caused increasing hardship to the overwhelming majority of Dutch Jewry. This community reproduced the familiar pattern whereby a small number of wealthy Jews confronted a mass of hawkers, peddlers and petty tradesmen whose numbers also included a criminal element. No significant difference separated Ashkenazim from Sephardim in these various respects.

In the 1780s the manifest difficulties in the Republic gave rise to the Patriot movement and its effort to remove the ruling House of Orange and the Stadholder, William V, in the interest of popular sovereignty and more efficient government. The Jews overwhelmingly supported the House of Orange, if for no other reason than tradition, not to mention anti-Jewish sentiment among the Patriots. According to the chronicle of David Franco Mendes, the Jews not only supported the House of Orange but also showed no enthusiasm for French policy or the ideas of the Enlightenment, and were politically passive throughout the general political struggle.[8]

In 1795 the French invasion did indeed lead to the exile of the stadholder, the establishment of the Batavian Republic (on the French model), the separation of church and state, and the proclamation of the Rights of Man and the Citizen. Only at this juncture did a group of intellectuals, led by Moses Solomon Asser (1754–1825), influenced by the political ideals of the Haskalah, form a Patriotic club, Felix Libertate, which included a minority of Christians beside its Jewish majority. This club, as against the politics of the parnassim and office-holders in the communities, forced the issue of emancipation on to the national agenda, and the recognition of Jews as full Dutch citizens. Members of Felix Libertate, led by Asser, petitioned the newly elected National Assembly in March 1796 to grant to the Jews equality of rights with the country's other inhabitants. Asser himself received no more than 14 of the 30 Jewish votes in the Jewish quarter of Amsterdam, so enthusiasm for emancipation was limited. The Assembly, however, voted in favour of emancipation by a majority of 45 to 24 and this decree was accepted unanimously – supposedly through the influence of the French ambassador.[9] Henceforth

> No Jew shall be excluded from exercising any rights or advantages which are attached to Batavian citizen rights and which he might wish to enjoy, provided that he possesses the requirements and fulfils all conditions demanded by the general constitution from every active citizen of the Netherlands.

This was predicated, as in France, on the consideration that 'the right of voting and of citizenship belongs only to individuals and that it would be an absurdity to grant same to any collectively considered Association, since society is not a collection of *corpora* but of individual members'.[10]

This victory for Felix Libertate was only partial in so far as it removed none of the occupational barriers to the economic advancement of the poor; similarly, it left unaffected the authority of the parnassim and their power over the communal organizations. This was inherent in the very terms of the debate in the Batavian Republic in 1798. Here, as distinct from France, the Jews were largely considered as a religious minority, not as a distinct and separate nation, and their *kehillot* as a sort of church with which the state had no concern and which could therefore continue to exist undisturbed. This contradicted Asser's view that 'neither our customs and traditions nor our language and clothing should distinguish us from any of the non-Jewish citizens'.[11] In the end the members of Felix Libertate withdrew from the existing community and, in defiance of its regulations, established their own community, Adat Yeshurun, which acquired its own synagogue, cemetery, rabbi and ritual bath. Its conduct was irreproachably 'orthodox', but tension reached such a pitch that an armed body of the civic guard had to escort R. Isaac Abraham Graanboom to the first service of Adat Yeshurun in April 1797. By 1806 the new congregation had almost 600 members.

To the armies of the Revolution in the world of western Jewry the dominant reaction was caution and reserve. Albeit with certain notable exceptions (for example Venice and Rome) this was the case in Italy; in Holland all accounts emphasize the lack of enthusiasm for the Revolution, with the belated exception of the *maskilim*. In the Rhineland the fluctuating fortunes and policies of the French conquerors conduced to an opportunistic policy, alleviated by a growing Francophilia. Above all, in the major and old-established communities of Mainz, Speyer, Trier, Bonn and Worms awkward situations must be confronted and decisive encounters evaded. This applied even when the ghettos in Bonn (1797) and Mainz (1798) were ceremoniously removed, amidst the planting of liberty trees. Certain Jews, for example Abraham Levy of Mainz, hoped to find in the French their saviours from discriminatory taxation, especially the body tax on movement. Levy, in an open letter to the French general Custine in November 1792, hailed him as 'a great hero' and offered thanks to God for Custine's 'great victory'. To what extent other Jews shared in this identification with the French is quite uncertain. At a guess, not many. The city's Jacobin Club had *c*.500 members – one-twelfth of the adult male population – and only four Jews: Isaak Bär, Nathan Maas, Sussman and Seligman. The overwhelming majority of Mainz Jewry, *c*.150 families, held nervously aloof and imposed a *herem* on Maas for his Jacobin zeal. The following year those Jews who refused to take the civic oath were summarily expelled at the instigation of the French occupying forces and local revolutionaries.[12] In Worms considerable pressure was vainly applied to the community to coerce members into taking the oath.[13]

Only in *c*.1797–8 did Rhineland Jewry abandon its reserved, not to say negative, outlook *vis-à-vis* the French conquest. Perhaps, by now, the new regime had a more enduring air. In 1797 as part of the creation of the French-sponsored Cisrhenan Republic on the left bank of the Rhine, the authorities exempted the Jews from the Jewish poll tax. When the French discarded the idea of a satellite republic in favour of annexation, and arranged for the implementation of their new policy by a series of votes, the decision of the Jewish voters is unfortunately indeterminate since the number of Jewish household heads in the relevant *départements* is disputed: were there 4624 or an estimated 3000? The total who voted for union with France was an undisputed 1254, which represents either slightly less than one quarter of the former figure or *c*.42 per cent of the latter figure.[14] Even if the pro-French vote was indeed one-quarter, it will still in all probability have represented an accretion of Francophilia since 1792, say. This is certainly true of the urban areas, especially Mainz and Worms. The community in Krefeld remained loyal to the *ancien régime*, the return of which in 1793 R. Löb Carlburg greeted with a song of praise. The members held themselves aloof from French institutions while appreciating the benefits of the Revolution's Jewish policies.[15] The increased mobility that French rule and emancipation directly permitted made Joseph Isaac of Mülheim, a wealthy grain merchant, the first Jew to settle in Cologne since the expulsion of 1424. In obedience to Napoleonic legislation of 1806, Joseph Isaac became Joseph Stern. But it was as Joseph Isaac that on 26 Ventose Year VI/16 March 1798 he received the necessary permission to move. A month later on 17 April 1798 the family moved – 'on the second day of the new month of Iyyar 5558', according to Joseph Isaac's memoirs.[16] He was one of a number of wealthy Jews attracted by the superior economic opportunities that Cologne offered. Others included Salomon Oppenheim, a one-time court factor and future banker; Samuel Benjamin Cohen, a metal-dealer; and Heymann Cassel, a pawnbroker and cotton merchant.[17] This movement exemplifies the path taken by the wealthy to leave the congested Jewish quarters and withdraw their resources from the *kehillah*, diminishing its charitable potential.

In Prussia local conditions initially determined the state's Jewish policy, independently of events in France. Pressure for an extension of economic opportunities was unremitting. In 1787 Friedländer and his associates had taken advantage of the change of ruler to present the new king, Frederick William II (1786–97), with a memorandum calling for the amelioration of their status. This document, in emphasizing the material benefit that would accrue to the state through a more equitable treatment of the Jews, again took issue with the principle of their collective liability and argued forcefully for the removal of special taxes and of those restrictions that barred Jews from engaging in crafts or agriculture or purchasing landed property. This document also suggested that only those Jews whose industrial enterprises contributed to national prosperity and employment qualified for an extension of political and economic privileges. In their petition of 1793 submitted with the same aim by a group of 34 household heads from Königsberg the point was made that 'the wealthier, better and nobler' Jews would be the more tempted than 'the poorer and uncultured Jews' to undergo a spurious conversion (in order to be relieved of the burden borne by the Jews in general) and thus their tax yield would be lost to the state.[18] These appeals were premature. Military defeat in 1805 and the reorganization of the Prussian state were indispensable to any further degree of emancipation. In the meantime, in 1792, the grant of naturalization to the banker Daniel Itzig certainly signified an advance. That same year a number of leaders in Franconia (Wolf Neuburger, Isaak Marx and Jakob Haenle) joined with their Prussian confrères in calling for the removal of barriers to Jewish economic activities. Even with the support of Chancellor Hardenberg this could not overcome the opposition of King Frederick William: for such a reform to succeed 'quieter times' were needed, the king wrote.[19] But selected individuals could certainly achieve a degree of emancipation by way of government service, for example Itzig and Friedländer; the banker Lipmann Meyer Wulff was the lessee of the state lottery; Benjamin Veitel Ephraim, the son of Frederick the Great's collaborator, was sent on a diplomatic mission to Paris in 1791 to detach France from Austria and secure an alliance with Prussia. He campaigned against Marie Antoinette and was admitted to La Société des Amis de la Constitution. He was also apparently in touch with Frankists in Paris, before his expulsion.[20]

In the maskilic centres of Berlin, Königsberg and Breslau the Revolution was seen as part of an overall movement towards policies of rationalism and tolerance and Louis XVI as an enlightened monarch worthy to rank with Frederick II and Joseph II.[21] The maskilic periodical *Ha-Me'assef*, which was published only irregularly between 1784 and 1829, reported on events in France with a strong emphasis on developments favourable to French Jewry, especially where they could be associated with Louis XVI. The journal did not appear 1790–4; when it reappeared (1794–7) the sole mention of France is made in a reference to a patriotic prayer pronounced by Breslau Jewry for the victory of the Prussian king over the revolutionaries.[22]

17
Another Rabbi, Another Emperor: David Sinzheim and Napoleon

To Revolution, emancipation and war the *kehillot* of eastern France showed themselves resistant. Persisting antisemitism and the collective obligation to discharge communal debts contracted in pre-revolutionary days, and which, as distinct from those of other corporations, had not been nationalized were among the forces of cohesion. (In Strasbourg, Bischheim and Metz, Jews were hindered in taking the civic oath or in voting in local elections, and sometimes attacked by rioters.)

This was in any case a conservative area and attachment to the *kehillah* prevailed over disruption. This still left some room for a degree of movement and disengagement. Not only did small communities, hitherto subject to the authority of Metz or Nancy, assert an autonomy of their own; also, individuals increasingly detached themselves from their respective communities. In certain localities, in the interests of good order the prefects had to intervene. At Lixheim, near Sarreguemines, in 1802, a group of dissidents established their own synagogue, contrary to the wishes of fellow-Jews and the rabbi of Nancy. The consequent furore provoked the intervention of the prefect of Meurthe who kept Portalis, director of religions (*directeur des cultes*), informed of the affair. Such disputes did not cease, and over the next year or two communal leaders from Metz and other localities in the upper and lower Rhine and Lorraine complained to prefects and Portalis alike: 'Liberty of conscience has degenerated into licence. People think everything is permitted because there are no longer any leaders...' 'A false idea of the principle of liberty and equality led many people to suppose that they can act and behave as they please and that they were freed from paying communal dues...' In Metz young and old clashed over liability for the community's debts. Leaders pressured prefects and ministers for their support. The Metz leadership, in reply to a request from the local prefect, submitted a project of reorganization that would designate buildings for public worship, regulate the outgoings and income of the community, introduce a compulsory tax and authorize the 25 largest taxpayers to elect 5 administrators and the rabbi. This would amount to a re-establishment of the *Nation*. The charter granted to the Protestants in 1802 inspired Berr Isaac-Berr of Nancy to seek something similar for the Jews. Early in 1805, Jewish leaders in Paris, where also dissension and disorder prevailed, submitted to Portalis a plan for the reorganization of Jewish worship in France. This too gave supreme power, under the state, to the notables and presaged the future consistorial structure.[1]

At this precise juncture, in a not unrelated development, Napoleon came to reconsider projects for the reorganization of Jewish life. This notion had first emerged in the earliest years of the new century, at the time of a concordat with the Vatican and a reordering of the body of French Protestants. The case of the Jews was postponed on the grounds that, being less a religion than a people, further consideration was required. By 1805 Napoleon's earlier opportunism in religious matters had degenerated from a degree of pro-Jewish sympathy into distaste and even contempt. In 1797 he had personally intervened in favour of the emancipation of the Jews in the Papal territory of Ancona. But he now saw the Jews as 'caterpillars, locusts who are ravaging France'.[2] He came to advocate their ultimate disappearance through marriage with gentiles. At another time he encouraged the Ashkenazim not to disappear but to turn themselves into Sephardim – *'faites comme les Portugais, comme ceux de Bordeaux'*, he advised Jacob Lazard, the Paris jeweller.

This was not the mood in January 1806. When Napoleon passed through Strasbourg on his return from the battlefield of Austerlitz, the authorities seized the occasion to make the emperor familiar with the indebted peasants' grievances against their Jewish creditors. The economic and financial crisis of 1805 inflamed the tension, especially in upper Alsace, where the peasants had overextended themselves in the acquisition of land. It was in vain that ministerial reports themselves revealed a ubiquitous problem of rural credit, irrespective of Jewish involvement; in vain that the supposed Jewish control of nationalized property was shown to be unfounded; in vain that the Jewish economy by and large proved to be in no better shape than the peasant – in the summer and autumn of 1805 the peasant prejudices vented themselves in outbreaks of anti-Jewish violence.[3] On 8 February, 1806 the Catholic organ *Mercure de France* published an anti-Jewish tirade, the work of Vicomte de Bonald the publicist. He not only denounced the usurious Jews ('the high and mighty lords of Alsace') but also branded the Jews as incapable of citizenship under Christianity unless they became Christians. A divine curse weighed on them. At this time also the Parisian lawyer Louis Poujol argued that only the withdrawal of their citizenship and exceptional legal measures could cure the Jews of their usurious habits. In the Council of State this view found powerful advocates (as against those ministers who did reject discriminatory legislation).[4] Simon Mayer counterattacked de Bonald in terms of the integration that emancipation would bring.

Amidst these polemics, threats and violence, Napoleon resumed a policy of 'regeneration' that had been somewhat in abeyance since the early years of the Revolution. The French policy had much in common with that of Joseph II – in fact the French decree of 1808 requiring the Jews to take on fixed family names was modelled precisely on that of Joseph of 1787. The programme also included the use of military service as a means to integration, exposure to state education, encouragement to enter agriculture, and the inculcation of patriotism.

The Council of State took its first steps in May 1806 and imposed a moratorium of one year on the repayment of debts owed to Jews in eastern France, and summoned to Paris an Assembly of Notables. This would offer its advice whereby moneylenders could be directed into 'useful crafts and professions'. Napoleon conceived of this ad hoc body as 'the Estates General of the Jews'. The prefects were required to choose, 'among the rabbis, the landowners and other Jews, those most distinguished for their probity and their enlightenment [*lumières*]'. The two attributes belonged together because the Notables would be a vehicle to propagate that 'sense of civic morality' in which those Jews who engaged in moneylending were notoriously deficient.[5] The moratorium brought hardship to the peasants' creditors. The proposed Assembly of Notables created a concern of quite another kind. That they should be selected in proportion to the number of Jews in a given department was the intention, to be corrected however by a weighting that would favour the less numerous but supposedly more enlightened Sephardi Jews of the south-west. In actual fact the relatively small Italian Jewish population of *c.* 30 000 contributed about 25 per cent of the Notables and about 33 per cent of the rabbis in the subsequent Sanhedrin.[6] Very few of the prefects had time to make the necessary count. The weighting in favour of the Sephardim did not counterbalance the fears of those (for example David Gradis from Bordeaux) who feared the establishment of a framework going beyond the local, that is, that the Sephardim would be brought under the same rubric as the Ashkenazim.

In July 1806 when the Notables first met in Paris they numbered 111, including those delegates from Italy whose arrival was delayed. They were quite unrepresentative of the mass of peddlers, cattle-dealers and moneylenders. Most Notables were men of at least a modest substance – merchants, landholders, one or two manufacturers (for example Nathan Lippmann of Besançon, clock manufacturer; Berr Isaac-Berr, tobacco manufacturer, of Nancy), a shipowner (Furtado junior, of the lower Pyrenees), a banker or two (Rodrigues from Seine; Salomon Oppenheim from Roer). They also included physicians and horse-dealers and about 15 rabbis of whom some were among the most distinguished of the day: Sinzheim (Strasbourg), Deutz (Koblenz), Cologna (Mantua) and Cracovia (Venice). Sinzheim wrote dismissively of certain of his colleagues: the supposed rabbi of Bayonne was no more than a synagogue cantor who did not even know Hebrew; the so-called rabbi of Turin was a teacher in a small town near Turin.[7] Some Notables were not, without hardship, able to absent themselves from their affairs, and for some others the expenses of travel were a burden. Their local communities had to be prevailed upon to raise special support taxes. Even so, because the Notables were in session – not without interruption – from July 1806 to April 1807, some had to withdraw prematurely on grounds of financial hardship. A happy group of six deputies, sharing accommodation, was described by Abraham Furtado, one of their number, as 'bon vivans', enjoying visits to the countryside in the company of sundry *hommes de lettres*.[8] These were the *philosophes* and eighteenth-century deists among the Notables. All that they knew of the Bible came from Voltaire, it was popularly said. Abraham Furtado, who had been accused of treason for his Girondist affiliation, qualified his earlier enthusiasm for Rousseau and Voltaire with the more conservative thinking of Locke and Montesquieu.

The Notables constituted themselves as an organized body when they elected Furtado as their president by a majority of 62 votes to 32 for Berr Isaac-Berr. They also elected two secretaries, Isaac Samuel Avigdor (Nice) and Rodrigues the younger (Paris). Thus organized, the Notables faced a government intent on imposing on its Jewish subjects a clear commitment to their duties as citizens of the Napoleonic empire. In fact, no doubt unwittingly, Napoleon had orchestrated a confrontation that took on independent life and determined the guidelines of the Jewish relationship with the state for at least a century, not only in France but in western Europe generally. At the outset this was by no means apparent when there was little to suggest anything other than a convergence between the government's policy and that of many of the Notables. The government, however, perceived an obstacle to this commitment by virtue of the fact that 'religion … among the Jews includes everything which establishes and rules society. Therefore the Jews are a nation within a nation'.[9] This reproach has precedents of course and did not need to await the advent of the nation-state, for it flourished even under the *ancien régime* both in Prussia and in France. In the interval the reproach had lost none of its implication of conflicting loyalties and that is why Count Molé, one of Napoleon's commissioners to the Assembly, baldly told the Notables: 'The wish of His Majesty is that you should be Frenchmen … determined to conform in everything to the laws and to the morality which ought to regulate the conduct of all Frenchmen.' This wish found its epitome in Napoleon's project, outlined in a letter to Champagny that the Jews be made to 'find Jerusalem in France'.[10]

But this is not the whole truth. Disregarding for the moment differences inside the Council of State, the Napoleonic side had a more or less covert agenda, formulated by Champagny, minister of the interior. He did not reveal it in full lest, as he explained, it 'might frighten some rabbis who are too slavishly attached to their ancient practices'. In fact, Napoleon looked forward to a time when one-third of the marriages (performed under Jewish auspices) would be between Jew and Christian – then 'the Jews' blood will lose its particular character ... [and] when some of their youth are required to join the army they will stop having Jewish interests and sentiments; they will acquire French interests and sentiments'.[11] This recapitulated the position expounded in the first year of the Revolution (by Abbé Maury) that the Jew, *qua* Jew, could not become a Frenchman. It was not enough for Napoleon to introduce a division between the 'religious' and 'national' components of the Jew, for the simple reason that whichever component were removed the individual concerned would still survive as a Jew, albeit truncated. This was already a factor that must weaken the force of Mendelssohn's vision of the possibility of a 'religious' body shorn of its 'national' components. The removal, say, of the 'national' component, even in alliance with the rewriting of Jewish history, could by no means be equated with the separation of church and state (see above, p. 215). The same asymmetry must also weaken Furtado's argument, when he rhetorically asked:

> Is there no difference at all between a constituted political body and a people dispersed among all the peoples of the world? Between a national body which existed three thousand years ago and the descendants of that nation ... preserving of their former condition no more than the mode of adoring the Eternal?[12]

But the programme of regeneration was predicated precisely on the persistence of this distinction which it set out to remove. This was a problem for Napoleon, as it were.

The Notables, for their part, as a number of private letters to their constituents in Alsace and Italy make clear, were not insensitive to the need to find common ground with Napoleon and to the unspoken pressure exercised by the government.[13] At this early stage, the Notables had no reason to doubt the goodwill of Napoleon or to withhold their cooperation.

When Count Molé submitted to the Assembly the famous Twelve Questions, this cooperation was put to the test. The questions fell into four groups: the first group enquired into the compatibility of Jewish matrimonial law with that of the civil code; the second would clarify the relationship of Jews to their French homeland and the attitude prescribed by Jewish law towards those Frenchmen and 'fellow-citizens' who were not Jewish; third, how were rabbis nominated or appointed and how far did their jurisdiction extend? The final group of questions turned to matters of occupation, with special reference to usury and to its permissibility (or otherwise) in transactions with strangers, as compared with fellow-Jews.[14] The thrust of all the questions was directed at ascertaining to what extent, if at all, adherence to any tokens of Jewish 'separatism' compromised the eligibility of the Jews for French citizenship and this in turn was predicated on their capacity for an undivided national allegiance and for their regeneration where necessary to achieve this end.

The implication of defective or questionable patriotism aroused resentment among the Notables and the general tone of their response to the Twelve Questions rejected any such imputation. President Furtado deputed twelve of his colleagues to prepare answers to the questions. This group consisted of three rabbis and nine other Jews from France, Germany and Italy. This composition corresponded to the three languages of the Assembly and to the geographical origin of the Notables. It also points to the enhanced influence of the rabbinic party, especially to that of R. David Sinzheim from Strasbourg, as compared with the declining influence of the *philosophes*. From a letter dated 16 October 1806 sent by Sinzheim to a rabbinical colleague in Prague, Baruch (Benedict) Jeiteles (1762–1813), it appears that Sinzheim himself took charge of the drafting of the replies to the Twelve Questions. In so doing he made clear his resolve to counter unremittingly any attempt to undermine religious legislation; it was not, in any case, Sinzheim averred, part of Napoleon's thinking to affect Mosaic or Talmudic laws. As I hope to show, Sinzheim made the Assembly's response in the light of the traditional principle – 'the law of the land is the law'.[15]

Sinzheim's role in the ensuing debates can well be compared with that of Ezekiel Landau in Prague a generation earlier. Both rabbis confronted an assimilationist ruler, using change of name, military service, occupational restructuring and education as instruments of a policy of 'regeneration'. Whereas, however, Landau could respond to and even influence Habsburg policy, Sinzheim had no such possibility. Landau also had no Code Napoléon to contend with in his protest at the impact of Joseph's *Ehepatent* on Jewish marriage law. The emancipated rabbi had less freedom of action than the subject of an autocratic ruler, however enlightened. Also of course the need to reconcile Ashkenazim and Sephardim curtailed Sinzheim's freedom of action. But none of this removed his capacity to elaborate a *modus vivendi* with Napoleon which preserved a modicum of autonomy from the grasp of the new nation-state.

Polygamy and divorce were easily disposed of: in the case of the former the Assembly referred to the decree issued at Worms in the eleventh century by Rabbenu Gershom disallowing polygamy for a millennium in the Ashkenazi world; as for divorce, this was allowable, the Assembly decreed, but would not be valid in Jewish law 'if not previously pronounced by the French code'. They were able to assure the Commissioners that the Jews looked on non-Jewish Frenchmen as their brethren, and on France as their country which they were committed to defend; that rabbis now performed no other function than to preach, officiate at marriages and pronounce divorces (that is, that they had no political role to perform); that the laws did not prohibit the practice of any occupation; that a distinction must be made between loans to the poor where no interest was charged and loans for commercial purposes where interest might legitimately be charged.[16]

The debate on the third question – 'does the law require Jews to intermarry only among themselves?' – proved the most contentious. At one stage the tumult in the Assembly forced an adjournment. This matter was crucial to Jewish integrity and continuity, and if in Prague R. Ezekiel Landau had gone to the extreme in his opposition to Joseph II's marriage patent – in which the topic of marriage with gentiles took no part at all – how much more must the anxiety in Paris be justified in the Napoleonic context of assimilation. Mendelssohn had earlier gone so far as to declare that the gentile world, if 'civil union' were to be acceptable to the Jews, must accept the prohibition of intermarriage (see above, p. 216). In 1844, when the German reformers met in conference at Brunswick, only with a qualification that effectively rendered intermarriage impossible did they adopt a resolution that accepted their non-prohibition of intermarriage.[17]

In Paris one rabbi made an attempt to treat the question as one of theology so that it called for an exclusively rabbinic consideration. 'Is it not evident that if astronomical subjects were proposed you would consult only astronomers?', it was asked. Furtado refused to depart from the principle of majority voting, 'inherent to the nature of every deliberative assembly'. The law, it was ultimately agreed, 'does not...state that the Jews can only intermarry among themselves'. On the other hand, a mixed marriage was unacceptable to rabbinic opinion because, according to the Talmud, marriage required a religious blessing for a marriage to be religiously valid, and

> this could not be done towards persons who would not both of them consider their ceremonies as sacred; and in that case the married couple could separate without the *religious* divorce; they would then be considered as married *civilly* but not *religiously*.

The rabbis, this answer added, 'would be no more inclined to bless the union of a Jewess with a Christian, or of a Jew with a Christian woman, than Catholic priests themselves would be to sanction unions of this kind'. The Assembly also emphasized that a Jew who married a Christian woman did not on that account cease to be a Jew, any more than if he had married a Jewish woman under civil and not religious law.[18] This answer left in limbo the extent to which a civil marriage between a Jewish and a non-Jewish partner was a marriage at all; for example, while possible and permissible, by reason of the fact that it lacked all religious status, it left open the possibility that the Jewish partner in a civil marriage could at the same time enter into marriage with a Jewish partner. Besides, nothing at all was said of the religious status of children born to a couple united only by a civil marriage. An admirer of Sinzheim praised him for first 'revealing one handbreadth and then concealing two' (see below, p. 284). Perhaps this is an example.

These obscurities and uncertainties were necessary for Sinzheim and his colleagues to answer Napoleon with due regard for the principle that 'the law of the land is the law [*dina de malkhuta dina*]' – an indispensable accompaniment to exilic circumstances. 'In everything relating to civil or political interests', ran the Paris version, 'the law of the state is the supreme law'; and the Notables emphasized this with a reference to the oath of allegiance to the Republic they had taken in 1791 which committed them 'to acknowledge no other rules in all civil matters'.[19] Sinzheim and his colleagues evaluated the demands of the Napoleonic state from the standpoint of an inherited jurisprudence of equal standing and judged them to be acceptable. The Notables were certainly not unanimous. Marc Foy, for example, from the department of the Lower Pyrenees, objected and maintained that the answers (and Foy had in mind specifically the answers to questions 4–6 concerning attitudes to non-Jewish Frenchmen and the state) 'ought to be founded on the sentiments which animated the Israelite in common with all Frenchmen their brethren'. Since principles of religion were not involved, Foy continued, 'the Assembly ought to frame the answers rather as Frenchmen than as men of any particular religion'.[20] But this did not seriously hamper Sinzheim and his colleagues, as far as one can judge; at least, they had concerns other than the views of a dissident Jew.

Napoleon and the commissioners to the Assembly saw the answers as an apologia for French Jewry rather than as a sincere attempt scrupulously 'to expound the features [*points*] of their belief and the detail of their internal customs'.[21] Napoleon was however sufficiently satisfied with the answers to choose to convoke a Grand Sanhedrin, composed, like its ancient predecessor, of 70 members and a president, of whom two-thirds in this instance would be rabbis. This meant the addition of some 30 rabbis to the 15 already present among the Notables. It is not clear either why Napoleon resurrected a body that had not met for some seventeen centuries, or who first conceived the notion at all. There is a suggestion that the whole operation had foreign-political aims in that it would win to the French cause the mass of Jews living to the east – a not negligible consideration when war with Prussia and Austria might be thought imminent. Metternich, Austrian ambassador in Paris, certainly shared this view of Napoleon's intentions.[22] Napoleon planned to confer on the proceedings in general the greatest possible *éclat*. The members of the Sanhedrin had to dress completely in black, sport a black silk cloak and wear a three-cornered hat (*rabbat*). Their decisions 'would stand beside the Talmud to become articles of faith and principles of religious legislation'.

When the Notables discussed the invitation, it was to be sent 'to all the synagogues of France and Italy as well as to all the synagogues of the western world'. One member objected that 'it ought not to be sent into the countries now at war with France'. His colleagues overruled him on the ground that since the aim of the Sanhedrin was 'to attach more particularly the Israelites to the different countries they inhabit', and since it was in the interest of every government, whether hostile or friendly to France, to adopt the principles occupying the Assembly, the invitation should indeed be sent to all western synagogues. It was therefore translated into Hebrew and German.[23]

Foreign rabbis attended only from Frankfurt on Main and the Adat Yeshurun congregation of Amsterdam. In Austria, Baron Eskeles of Vienna received an invitation to take part in the Sanhedrin from his Parisian confrère, Rodrigues, secretary to the Assembly of Notables. This was not taken up. The Austrian government was at one with Metternich in viewing the proceedings in Paris with the gravest suspicion as a tool of French foreign policy. They therefore sought to counteract any influence it might have by supervising correspondence, bringing pressure to bear on the Viennese bankers Arnstein and Eskeles and using the services of the maskilic educator and government official Herz Homberg. The government's enquiries found that the overwhelming majority of the congregations in Vienna, Prague, Bohemia and Moravia regarded the Sanhedrin with either indifference or hostility. Only in Trieste did the community's Francophilia and proximity to Italy give cause for alarm.[24]

The Sanhedrin sat for no more than a month, precisely from 9 February to 9 March 1807, when Champagny put an end to its proceedings. The assembled rabbis had time enough to give their *hascamah* to the decisions of the Notables. These decisions have lately become controversial and partake of the debate on the Revolution in general and, in particular, of the alliance concluded between French nationalism and French Jewry. Echoes of the arguments raised by Spinoza and Mendelssohn are also audible. First, in its alleged subservience to Napoleon the Sanhedrin is said to have sacrificed Jewish law to the laws of the state; second, that both the Assembly of Notables and the Sanhedrin are said to have lacked, in the best of cases, any legitimate *locus standi*, simply because both included individuals quite unqualified to judge on legal issues – apart from which it was a gentile ruler who had summoned both bodies and determined their membership, procedure, agenda and timetable and even the dress of the rabbinical participants.[25]

At the time this debate would have been impolitic in the extreme. But it was certainly possible to have regrets and reservations, even on the part of those rabbis who gave the Twelve Answers their general approval. This was the position of R. Ishmael b. Abraham Ha-Cohen of Modena, one of the most renowned halachic authorities of the eighteenth century. R. Ishmael was 83 in 1806 and the infirmity of age made it impossible for him to join the deputies from Italy in Paris. But he followed events closely from home and, remote from local pressure, formulated his own answers to the Twelve Questions. These did not differ greatly from those prepared in Paris save for their greater emphasis on the loss of rabbinic autonomy. Even while admitting that rabbinical tribunals had always had to seek from gentile rulers charters that would allow rabbinic courts to impose punishments and fines, there was still, R. Ishmael of Modena maintained, a difference between 'former times' and now, 'when everyone does as he pleases and the rabbis lack all power to protest, they can do nothing but give appropriate answers to those who put to them questions of ritual. And to expound to the people matters of law and morality and the love of one's neighbour so that the people will hear and improve their ways'; R. Ishmael then referred to Exodus 18 ff. and Deuteronomy 16 ff., requiring the appointment of judges, a police force, and local leaders as institutions of government, 'but today we have no capacity to turn this potential into practice.'[26]

Other contemporaries viewed the work of the Assembly of Notables and the Sanhedrin as an exemplary formulation of the communal relationship to the state. This applied not only to Napoleon (on the whole) but also to sections of the Jewish world normally in bitter conflict with each other. This is because the Answers constitute a veritable *chef d'oeuvre* in their susceptibility to varying interpretations, which made them acceptable to the extremities of opinion. Sinzheim's work merited the unstinting praise of R. Moses Schreiber of Pressburg (the Hatam Sofer, 1787–1839), the stringent founder of modern orthodoxy and a rabbi with whom Sinzheim had been in correspondence: in a eulogy after Sinzheim's death in 1812, Schreiber spoke of the deceased's learning, his courage, and his qualities of leadership – 'he remained in authority through his valour, others did not dominate him and lead him astray, God forbid! After he had revealed one handbreadth, he concealed two handbreadths and his integrity stood firm'. But a leading reformer, Ludwig Philippson (1811–89), the very antithesis to Schreiber and bête noire of the orthodox, also endorsed Sinzheim's work and commended the Twelve Answers to the Brunswick rabbinical conference of 1844.[27] It was possible to emphasize either the upholding of tradition in the understanding of the relationship to the state – including, presumably, the relationship to the state's marriage law – which is what earned the praise of Schreiber, or, alternatively, to welcome Sinzheim's accommodation of that very tradition to the modern state – which is what appealed to Philippson.

This ambiguity was mirrored inside the Sanhedrin itself. Furtado read Jewish history in terms of a comprehensive religio-political legislation, transmitted by God through Moses, of which the second element had perforce lost its initial applicability following Israel's defeat, dispersion and submission to the laws of the nations where it dwelt. But this had freed Israel from the obligation 'to follow a civil code other than that of the nations which give us shelter'. This necessity was no evil, Furtado continued, and gave an opportunity to create 'a perfect conformity ... between the civil code and our religious usages'.[28] Sinzheim, on the other hand, looked on this necessity as indeed 'an evil'. In the understanding of his somewhat cryptic remarks extreme care is called for, because Sinzheim spoke in Hebrew whereas the official *procès-verbal* gives a French translation, now englished in part below.[29] It is still possible with due caution, I trust, to acknowledge not only that had Sinzheim defied the Napoleonic project of total assimilation, if at the price of certain sacrifices, but also that these could be 'contained', as it were, within a traditional structure and comprehended within the maxim 'the law of the land is the law.' The political laws remained in existence, though circumstances made it impossible to implement them. This is remote from Furtado's understanding of relief from those laws permitting of adoption of the civil code. In his closing presidential address to the assembled rabbis and laymen of the Sanhedrin, Sinzheim made much of the fact that its decisions had been arrived at in accordance with

> *les maximes de la loi* ... you have recognized religious and political dispositions; but you have declared that to go beyond the line of the former was nothing but confusion, sacrilege and profanation. You have acknowledged the validity of certain civil acts, but you have avowed their religious incoherence ... Conforming to the precepts of the God of Israel, who is a God of peace, you have permitted, in certain public acts, the civil sanction to precede the religious sanction in order to manifest your deference to the laws of the state. You have recognized that there are certain cases where dispensations from some points of the law became necessary: the protection of the sovereign and the safety of the state made it incumbent on you to grant them.[30]

By way of accompaniment to this process of accommodation to the demands of the state and as a means to give it legislative sanction and machinery Furtado and other Notables were engaged in negotiating with Napoleon's commissioners a consistorial system for the organization of Jewish worship in France and the Empire. This was a sequel to the abortive initiative of 1801/02 (see above, p. 276), but it took shape at a markedly less sympathetic period and the notion of regeneration came into conflict with that other notion of legal equality embodied in the Code Napoléon. In a published *mémoire* at the legislation under discussion in the Council of State Furtado argued forcefully that the state should support rabbis as it supported the dignitaries of other religions. Did the Jews not pay the same taxes as Christians? Were they not helping to support the bearers of other religions? Second, Furtado rejected the proposal that two-thirds of Jewish conscripts be required to serve in person or purchase only Jews as substitutes. Third, he took issue with the enforced delay in the repayment of debts due to Jewish creditors and with the restrictions to be imposed on entry into commerce. The first proposal was 'defective', the second 'useless', and the third 'dangerous', Furtado concluded.[31]

None of this activity had any success. In March 1808 Napoleon issued three decrees which seriously compromised the political and legal status of French Jewry. The first and second were comparatively innocuous in so far as they followed the *reglement* establishing the new communal structure worked out by the Notables in December 1806. This provided for the centralization of worship and its administration under a central consistory in Paris. This would supervise the activities of departmental consistories in every department with a minimum population of 2000 Jews. Each consistory comprised laymen and rabbis selected by the wealthy and with state approval. It functioned as a dedicated propagator of the teaching of the Sanhedrin of obedience to the laws of the empire and as watchdog over the conduct of consistory members. Despite the arguments of Furtado this decree refused all concession to the demand that the state make itself responsible for the financial upkeep of rabbis. The third decree soon became known as 'infamous' because of the restrictions it imposed on the economic role of the Jews, their residential rights and their liability to military service. The moratorium on the repayment of debts to Jews originally introduced in 1806 and renewed in 1807 was removed, but the decree replaced this measure by others which all but stifled credit operations by annulling certain categories of loans, requiring that the loan by a Jew to a gentile be taken up in full before repayment was sanctioned, reducing debts bearing interest above 5 per cent and empowering the courts to grant extensions of repayment dates. The decree further hampered commerce by demanding that a Jewish trader possess a licence to trade, which would be dependent on the recommendation of his local prefect and consistory. These licences had to be renewed annually and were revocable. As a means to control the Jewish population of Alsace no immigration into the departments of the upper and lower Rhine was permitted and no Jew who did not already live in the empire could settle inside Alsace unless he undertook to take up agriculture. The decree deprived French Jewry of a further facility by requiring each Jewish conscript to serve in person, without the freedom enjoyed by other Frenchmen of engaging a substitute to serve in their stead.

In July 1808 French Jewry suffered a further blow to its integrity when Napoleon took another leaf from the Habsburg book of Joseph II and, in the interests of assimilation, ordered the Jews to adopt within three months fixed forenames and family names, on pain of expulsion from the empire. This command was directed to those subjects of the empire 'who follow the Hebraic cult' and had no fixed family names or forenames. Apart from certain exceptions, every Jew in this position was now required, on pain of expulsion, to take on a fixed name, but not a name taken from the Old Testament or the name of any town. This meant that the names of the Jews would approximate to those of their Christian compatriots.

'The infamous decree' was limited in time and space: its validity was limited to ten years and it completely exempted the Portuguese Jews of Bordeaux and the south-west departments of the Gironde and the Landes. To a large extent, exemption or inclusion was a class matter. Those Jews on whom restrictions would be imposed, Champagny, the minister of the interior, reported to Napoleon during the drafting of the decree, would be 'all those who are not bankers, wholesalers, large-scale merchants, owners of property or factory directors', which left all the peddlers, hawkers, horse- and cattle-dealers and small-time moneylenders, concentrated in Alsace.[32]

Financial-economic status was not the only criterion for exemption. Their excellent army record, abstention from usury, no less than their economic prowess, won exemption for the Paris Jews of the department of the Seine. The Jews of the south-east, with the support of the local prefects, also agitated for exemption which, after about a year's delay, they did indeed obtain. In the end about 14000 Jews secured exemption.[33]

Primarily the Jews of Alsace had to bear the burden of 'regeneration' – in other words, endure the consequences of Napoleonic departure from equality before the law. The decade-long validity of the 'infamous decree' took it into the early years of the Restoration, when the new Bourbon regime allowed it to lapse, defying the explicit wish of Alsatian public opinion. With the increase in Jewish loans in the early 1820s this opposition persisted and at times turned to anti-Jewish violence. But the government of the Restoration held firm and refrained from any attempt to extend or renew the discriminatory legislation of 1808.[34]

The first rabbis of the central consistory in Paris were the chairman and vice-chairmen of the Sanhedrin – Sinzheim (Strasbourg), Salvator Segré (Vercelli) and Abraham Cologna (Mantua). Two Ashkenazim – Baruch Cerf Berr (son of *the* Cerf Berr) and the Paris jeweller Jacob Lazard – flanked and counterbalanced the rabbinical officers. No sooner had these dignitaries taken their oath of obedience and allegiance to the imperial constitution and to the emperor, and sworn to make known whatever 'might be contrary to the interests of the sovereign', than they set about organizing consistories in the various circumscriptions of the empire. Adherence was voluntary and could only apply to those Jews who, as the Notables put it, were 'attached to religious practices'.[35] The first consistorial synagogues were established in 1809 and their spread matched the extension of the empire and French rule. By 1812 they existed not only in the major French centres (Paris, Strasbourg, Metz, Nancy, Bordeaux and Marseilles) but also in Turin, Cassel, Livorno, Florence, Rome, Amsterdam, Bonn, Koblentz, Emden and Hamburg and Venice. The consistories had powers of taxation which provided the financial resources essential to the performance of their roles. To maintain the synagogues, schools, cemeteries and so on and their personnel in each circumscription was the chief task. They employed a *commissionaire surveillant* charged with reporting the existence of any unauthorized *minyan* and notifying the consistory of the personal details of the Jews of the circumscription (including their change of name) and especially of those liable to conscription. The responsibility of the *commissionaire* included the collection of the taxes due to the consistory. A casual and random dip into the records of the central consistory (referring to Italy) shows the enormously wide range of concerns: harbouring stolen property; rabbis' salaries; family names; mediating among the three congregations in Turin of Italian, German and Spanish Jews; electoral irregularities in Koblenz; establishing a consistory in Rome; limiting to a synagogue the locale of a religious marriage ceremony; keeping track of potential conscripts; urging vaccination against smallpox. Other sources show the consistory's concern for the state of the smaller Dutch synagogues, perhaps only a room; students' requests for exemption from conscription; notification of public prayers for the emperor, including a Hebrew canticle composed by Solomon Haym Crémieux of Aix in honour of Napoleon and Josephine. The central consistory in Paris gave the rabbinate a base from which to fight against discrimination.[36]

The central consistory in Paris crowned a hierarchy of lesser consistories throughout the empire but it was by no means omnipotent and had to contend with local and countervailing forces in virtually every part of the empire. Even in Paris there was dissension; for example the issue of limiting the marriage ceremony to the synagogue brought Sinzheim into conflict with his 'lay' fellow-officials.[37]

The consistorial system served as an instrument of French government policy, at home and throughout the empire. Its mission was to assimilate the Jews, in a Napoleonic spirit. But none of the consistories made it their *raison d'être* to take assimilation to the extremity sought by Napoleon, that is that it was the duty of each department where there was a consistory to ensure that of the marriages it authorized one-third must be between Jew and Christian. Not only in this negative sense but also positively in the range of activities undertaken by the consistories had a species of communal autonomy been recreated – not indeed to the extent of 'a nation within a nation', but recognizable in those terms. Had Spinoza and those other thinkers who had denied to Judaism a political dimension – Mendelssohn and Hourwitz – written in vain ? Was the 'sceptre of Judah' reborn on French soil? To some extent this was indeed the case. Moreover, Mendelssohn's demand that the state must accept the Jews' condition for acceptance in relation to the refusal to permit intermarriage was vindicated. His distinction between *Glaubensvereinigung* and *Civilvereinigung* is paralleled in the rejection by the consistorial rabbi R. Abraham Cologna that 'fusion … is only a matter of civil and political association which has nothing and can have nothing in common with belief in the messiah who has come or who is to come'.[38]

18
From Paris to Vienna

Was Napoleon's invasion of Russia in 1812 part of the wars of Gog and Magog heralding the messiah (Ezek. 28–29)? Or was the expectation premature and even impious? Should Jews pray for Napoleon's defeat and the victory of the Tsar, or vice versa? The Hassidic masters of Rymanov and Lublin in Poland took strongly conflicting views and directed their prayers accordingly.[1] In western and central Europe, communities and individuals had similar divergent views, though without the messianic enhancement. Amidst invasion and war one constant remained – poverty. There were certainly those (few) Jews who profited from war (bankers, financiers, military suppliers and outfitters), but for the overwhelming majority poverty and indigence remained the norm.[2] In certain areas (primarily urban) the progress of emancipation added to the incidence of poverty when greater freedom of movement enabled the wealthier families to leave their confined and insalubrious accommodation, thus depriving the *kehillah* of their resources and support. This happened early on in Carpentras and Avignon (see above, p. 268). Venice would suffer similarly; also Amsterdam, when the *kehillah* lost its authority over the kosher meat market and those annexed taxes, earmarked for charitable and welfare purposes.

The great change concerned the political context of poverty. In the years after 1805, say, and until the end of the empire the movement of frontiers and their political entities rewrote the Jewish map. Those Jews in the former Batavian Republic became subjects of Louis Napoleon, king of Holland; those in Baden, Bavaria and Württemberg found themselves adherents of the Confederation of the Rhine (Rheinbund); then there were the Jews in the kingdom of Westphalia formed of portions of Hanover, the former Rhineland territories of Prussia, Brunswick and Hesse-Cassel; the Jews of Italy formed part of the local Napoleonic kingdom; outside the French empire the defeat of Prussia at the battle of Jena (1806) created unprecedented opportunity for change; only a few years later the community in Hamburg found itself annexed to the empire at the same time as were the other Hanseatic ports of Lübeck and Bremen.[3]

Only in theory to these disparate entities did the Napoleonic exports of emancipation and the consistorial system bring a degree of unity. In the actual implementation of these ideals most important was the local context formed of its Jewish component as much as of its territorial component. No more consistent picture results. In most territories local and foreign factors interacted to create confusion and uncertainty. But it is probably true to say that on balance the French influence was welcome.

In 1805 almost 80 per cent of Amsterdam Jewry was dependent on poor relief and by 1810 there was no change for 14 300 of the *c.*22 000 Jews in Amsterdam.[4] The reasons for this poverty do not differ from those in the German states, that is exclusion from the guilds and the flow of immigrants from those states in an illusory search for a more secure existence. This influx would be all the stronger given the persuasive absence of restrictions on entry or residence, in contrast to the limitations enforced elsewhere. The emancipation of 1796 referred to no more than legal status, so that it had only limited influence, apart from which its provisions were disregarded. This formed the background to a petition that six communal leaders, led by those of the new Adat Yeshurun congregation, submitted to the Batavian Republic. This petition stigmatized four types of discrimination: in terms of taxation; the economy (emphasizing the inequity in barring Abraham Levi, a trained blacksmith, from membership of the appropriate guild); the exclusion of Jews from official positions; the refusal of integration by singling out the Jews as 'The Jewish Nation'.[5] On no score did the Amsterdam city council give the petitioners any satisfaction. Only in 1806, with the advent of the Kingdom of Holland under Louis Napoleon, did two of the petition's signatories – Carel Asser and Daniel Jonas Meyer – receive senior positions in the government. A Sephardi, Immanuel Capadoce, became the king's personal physician. The more benign turn of events showed itself in the exemption of Dutch Jewry from the provisions of the *décret infâme* and also allowed them to engage substitutes in case of conscription.[6] This legislation required not only the adoption of family names but also the renaming of the two communities. The Hoog-Duitsche (High German) Jews became Dutch Jews and the Portuguese Jews became Dutch Portuguese Jews. A campaign against the use of Yiddish and in favour of Dutch accompanied the patriotic inspiration. It went still further when the consistory ordered that even in synagogue ceremonies the new family name be used.[7]

In their efforts further to advance the cause of emancipation, Asser and Meyer procured the establishment of a Supreme Consistory for the Dutch High-German Jews. This deprived the erstwhile congregational leaders, the parnassim, of their autonomy and their related capacity to impose fines and, in particular, of their capacity to limit the purchase of meat to the communal meat market. This caused a decline in the revenue derived from the tax imposed on meat, which could now be supplied more cheaply by private butchers. This loss of revenue had the most catastrophic effect on the system that had hitherto provided some sort of relief for the indigent. This was the underside of emancipation. 'The bill for the emancipation and its reforms, for the separation of church and state was, consequently, paid by the paupers of Amsterdam.'[8] When the French left, in 1813–14, the centralized consistorial system accompanied their departure and ostensibly gave way to a more diffuse machinery of 12 synagogues (10 Ashkenazi, 2 Sephardi). In fact, however, through the Ministry for the Reformed and Other Religions, the government appointed members of the so-called General Committee for Israelite Affairs and it was this body which maintained liaison with the government in relation to the conduct of the congregations. The French influence showed itself also in the encouragement of Dutch as against the prevailing Yiddish vernacular.[9]

In the Italian states and communities the French influence had none of the quasi-uniform character evident in Holland. Some ten consistories were established of which the most important were in Rome, Florence and Venice, following the decree of March 1808. Perhaps the most fortunate community was that of the Duchy of Parma, where the Napoleonic legislation remained practically intact. Here Jews could enter the liberal professions and take up posts in the public services. Less happy was that of Mantua. It was recaptured by the French in 1801 and did not return to Austrian rule until 1814. This did lead to the loss of the right to occupy public office, but the Austrians made no attempt to restore the ghetto. At the other extreme stood Rome and the Papal States, where the ghetto was re-established with all the limitations this system imposed on the Jews' economic life. Venice, with a population of some 1600 Jews, took up an intermediate position. The provisional government had abolished the ghetto in 1791. The subsequent period of Austrian rule brought little benefit to the Jews until the establishment of the Kingdom of Italy in 1805 and the conquest of Venice in 1806 brought full emancipation to the Jews, who now enjoyed rights and obligations equal to those of the Christian population. This was reconcilable with a reality in which the living conditions of the ghetto deteriorated, in a process identical to that at work in Amsterdam and Carpentras when the wealthy withdrew their support and communal government disintegrated (see above, p. 290):

> With the ending of the Venetian Republic , the Jewish community had in fact stopped concerning itself with the ordinary maintenance of the houses, roads, bridges and canals that constituted the Ghetto. The municipal authorities had for a long time shown little interest, so that the quarter was deteriorating progressively into a state of general neglect. Many houses, particularly in the New Ghetto, had been abandoned by families who preferred healthier living conditions and who tended to move to the Cannareggio quarter to be nearer to the synagogue. Those families who continued to live in the Ghetto were either the poorest or … non-Venetians who had moved to the city in search of better economic opportunities.[10]

In Livorno the large community of *c.*4600 early secured exemption from the *décret infâme*, but this did not halt poverty and financial collapse in the Jewish economy any more than in the general, as a consequence of Napoleon's continental blockade. This was not his only unpopular measure; the marriage regulations as accepted by the Sanhedrin were another. In the Tuscan departments of the Napoleonic empire these came into effect on 1 May 1808. In order to circumvent the need for a civil ceremony, in addition to the Jewish, in April 1808 the unusually large number of 37 marriages was celebrated as against the average total of 6 to 7. In the period up to the collapse of the French regime in 1814, consistorial regulations were evaded and clandestine marriages took place in private and in the presence of witnesses alone. When the French left and Livornese Jewry lost their status as citizens they could still employ the argument from utility to discourage any reversion to the *ancien régime*.[11] The community also acted in concert with the local bishop to suppress the work of Aron Fernando. He was one of the Jewish revolutionaries whom the Austrians had exiled in 1799–1801. In 1810 Fernando published the first part of a work that called for the abolition of many of the commandments and *una completa reforma del culto* – which would have reduced Judaism to a deistic faith. It was this that brought about the suppression of the second part. In general, it seems that only through their participation in revolutionary movements for Italian unification (for example the Carbonari) could Jewish hopes for improved conditions be realized.[12]

To the north, in the German states, the same variety of circumstances existed, also the same urge for removal of those barriers that hindered entry to the body of citizens. In some states (for example Prussia) Jews could serve as municipal councillors; in others (the Duchy of Sachsen-Altenburg) they were totally excluded; in the Duchy of Anhalt-Cöthen they enjoyed the protection of the Code Napoléon; in Frankfurt the new Stättigkeit of 1808 issued by the prince-primate of the Rheinbund, Baron Dalberg, again required Jews to live inside the *Judengasse*, limited the number of families and marriages and reinstituted the poll tax.

In the German states, and including Austria, political activity was very much the preserve of the economic elite, even more so than in Italy, and it was their resources and connections which, on the classical model, appreciated that governmental discrimination was no more than a means to enrichment, and which, accordingly, made discrimination into a negotiable commodity that could be converted into hard cash. In the purchase by Cerf Berr from Strasbourg of the city's right to levy *péage corporel* there was a precedent: in 1811 Mayer Amschel Rothschild bought from Baron Dalberg the emancipation of the Jews in the newly formed Duchy of Frankfurt, at a cost of 440000 gulden (20 times the annual sum the Jews were charged for their 'protection'). Earlier, together with Wolf Breidenbach, the Hesse court factor, Rothschild had been active in securing the abolition of the body tax in Bavaria. This paralleled the success in Baden of Israel Jacobson, court factor in Brunswick.[13]

In the newly established kingdom of Westphalia ruled by Jerome, the youngest brother of Napoleon, the legal status of the Jews was at its most favourable. From 1808 the approximately 16000 Jews enjoyed complete emancipation. Under the dominating influence of Israel Jacobson, Westphalia with its capital at Cassel became the seat of the 'Royal Westphalian Consistory of the Mosaic Religion'. It enjoyed the favour of King Jerome, no doubt through his heavy indebtedness to Jacobson. The latter used this favourable position to promote the Jewish cause elsewhere and this included a notable (but unavailing) protest at the Frankfurt Stättigkeit of 1808. His consistory required rabbis to inculcate through their sermons obedience to their laws and appreciation for military service. Jewish scholars would train the children of the poor for agriculture and the army. The synagogue service was to be marked by decorum and praying in unison, with the 'call-up' to the Torah reading to be by family name and not by the father's name. In the interests of assimilation, Jerome's associate Israel Jacobssohn, following Napoleon's law of 1808, germanized his own name to Jacobson (i.e., he would no longer bear the Hebrew name 'Israel, son of Jacob').[14] Private services for prayer were forbidden. This reform programme had very little popular support – one estimate puts it at less than 5 per cent of the Jewish population. Local Jewish leaders complained to the king that the consistory was both costly and unnecessary and should be amalgamated with the Christian. The programme also of course caused outrage in Paris and illustrates some of the problems Sinzheim had to contend with. The central consistory had more than once to challenge the decrees issued by its nominally subordinate Westphalian consistory.[15] Tradition-minded rabbis shunned Westphalia. Thus R. Abraham Auerbach in Bonn, whom Jacobson invited to take the post of chief rabbi in Westphalia, refused on the grounds that his orthodoxy would be unfitted for Cassel. He was related by marriage to Sinzheim, was well connected in Paris and knew French and German.[16]

Emancipation came to the *c.*6000 Jews of Hamburg (*c.*6 per cent of the total population) when the city was incorporated into the French empire (December 1810). The inclusion of the *décret infâme* of 1808, with the other legislation affecting Jews, was successfully forestalled through a petition presented by Moses Isaac Hertz and Jacob Oppenheimer. The accession to equal citizenship brought with it liability to military service and to the financial demands made by the French authorities. When, in December 1813, the French demanded from the Jews a special contribution they forfeited much of their initial popularity – even though the demand was made in vain. In May 1814, when the French finally left, the rejoicing of the communal presidium was undisguised. The community also took the occasion of the French withdrawal to proclaim its 'devotion to the state in which we live, pure love of the fatherland', as a basis for the hope that a return to autonomy would not entail the loss of that equality granted by the French.[17]

In Berlin and Prussia the French influence was indirect and blended with an existing struggle for a greater degree of legal and economic freedom. To some extent the result followed from Jewish pressure, and to some extent from the efforts of the Prussian bureaucracy to remodel the Prussian state, by way of sequel and reaction to the defeat at Jena (1806). For their part the Jewish remodelling of Judaism, the defusing of the messianic idea, the unremitting assertion of identification with the state and the educational initiatives all failed to bring about even the prospect of any substantial political change until 1806. The state's continuing concern with the assimilation of the Jews and their supervision showed itself in 1792 and again in 1797 when reform proposals were made dependent on the assumption of a fixed family name together with the use of German and Roman characters in business and public documents.[18]

The Prussian reforms post-Jena took in the system of serfdom and municipal government. The latter had most to offer the Jewish towndwellers, at least those few who could claim citizen status (that is, Bürgerrecht) and satisfied the property qualifications. At the first elections in 1809 in Prussia, David Friedländer and the banker Solomon Veit were elected to the Berlin municipality, and a little later the baptized Baron Delmar. Also in Potsdam and Königsberg and in Beuthen and in Gross-Strelitz (Upper Silesia) and in Glogau (Lower Silesia), Jews were elected to municipal office.[19] Pressure on the government persisted, taking a variety of forms, all intended to demonstrate the capacity of the Jews to contribute equally with any other subject to the welfare of the state. In 1809 their membership of the Berlin civil guard comprised 84 Jewish privates (*Gardisten*), 2 corporals, 2 sergeants, 3 second-lieutenants and 1 first-lieutenant. Most of the volunteers were merchants, but they also included 6 bankers, 2 money-changers and 1 copper-engraver. This was a noteworthy demonstration, for the anticipation of Jewish recruits was one motive that impelled the government to consider at all any relaxation in the status of the Jews. The Königsberg banker Caspar wrote to Schrötter, the Prussian minister, extolling the Jews 'not only as soldiers but also as excellent soldiers' and referring to an article in the journal *Shulamith* detailing the exploits of the Polish Corps established by Berg under the command of Kosciuszko. Schrötter, in his report to the king, looked forward to conscripting the unlikely total of 50000 'Jewish souls'.[20]

The anticipation of Jewish recruits was congruent with the general observation that to remove the legislation that excluded the Jew from the general body of the population would in itself function as a sort of regeneration on the eighteenth-century model. Thus the 'Edict Concerning the Civil Condition of the Jews in the Prussian State' of March 1812 is couched in conditional terms in return for the fulfilment of which the Jews were recognized as 'inhabitants and Prussian citizens' subject to the same taxes, laws, and obligations as other citizens and enjoying the same rights to purchase landed property, settle in town and countryside and exercise all lawful crafts and trades. It withdrew any residual judicial power from the rabbis; required Jews to take on fixed family names and to use German 'or another living language' in their trading accounts and contracts; and although the Edict granted freedom of marriage it limited population increase by denying to a foreign Jew who married a Prussian Jewess the right to settle in Prussia. The Edict left open for future consideration what public appointments and state offices Jews might take up; they were admitted to academic, school and communal positions. This Edict, although addressed to individuals, did not remove the obligation to contribute to communal expenses and it also preserved the incapacity to secede from communal bodies.[21] The Edict applied to the Jews living in the four provinces of Brandenburg, Pomerania, Silesia and East Prussia as determined by the Treaty of Tilsit. There is no doubt of the enthusiasm it met with; and deservedly so, for with all its limitations in terms of geography it created a remarkable free legal framework for the Jews of the four provinces who fulfilled the statutory conditions of the Edict.

The enthusiasm showed itself at its most forthright in the participation of Jewish volunteers in the wars of liberation from Napoleonic rule, 1813–14. In the allied armies and hospitals 24 Jewish doctors are known to have served; in Prussia alone 10 Jews were decorated; Jewish women and girls were active in caring for the sick and wounded and for the widows and orphans of the fallen. The Berlin salonière Henriette Herz helped to collect cash, linen and bedding for a Berlin hospital. In 1813 in Prague Rahel Levin (another former salonière and Beethoven's *unsterbliche Geliebte*) cared for the wounded from the battle of Dresden. Rabbis and publicists became recruiting officers. In the Breslau synagogue the chief rabbi of Silesia, R. Aaron Karfunkel, blessed the Jewish volunteers and freed them from certain religious duties – 'God will accept as a prayer your service for the fatherland and restore you to your families garlanded with honour.' In Berlin the acting chief rabbi, R. Meyer Simeon Weyl, ordered daily prayers calling on God to protect the king, his counsellors, the army and all the inhabitants of Prussia. In Hamburg the ladies sewed flags and the young men served in the Hanseatic Legion. Central and southern German records tell of volunteers in Hesse, Hanau, Cassel and Bavaria. Patriotism in many cases took the form of donations in cash and military equipment; for example, Jacob Hirsch, the court factor in the Grand Duchy of Würzburg, fitted out 75 volunteers at his own expense. A rough calculation for Prussia gives a volunteer total of 2 per cent of the Jewish population as compared with 2.4 per cent in the population as a whole. 71 of the Jewish soldiers were awarded the Iron Cross for combatants. No less striking is the social status of the volunteers. 'The names of the sons of the most respected and wealthiest Jewish households are met with on the lists of all the volunteer battalions', wrote one Prussian official in May 1813. This was often remarked on.[22]

Amidst the confusion of the French withdrawal from the German states and the crumbling of the Napoleonic empire, patriotism went unrewarded.

In a broad sense, the general sympathy of the late eighteenth century for Jewish aims (with all its limitations), was in the process of yielding to a renewal of antisemitism. Even in Westphalia emancipation remained only a short episode, it is said.[23] In Prussia ministers were in general agreement that not even to Jewish volunteers who had been awarded the Iron Cross should positions in state service be opened up. The Napoleonic *décret infâme* of 1808 was extended indefinitely in the new Prussian territories in the Rhineland acquired after 1815. In fact the Prussian Edict of 1812 marked the climax, for the time being, of the extension of Jewish political rights. The Edict's provisions for the putative entry into state service on the part of Jewish aspirants to, say, an academic, administrative or military career were whittled down.[24] In 1813 in Mecklenburg-Schwerin an emancipation law on the Prussian model was swiftly rescinded. In Hamburg, even before the final collapse of the French empire, the Council proclaimed in July 1814 that 'the public cannot be attuned to the general acceptance [of the Jews] as equal to other citizens'. Certain forces in Hamburg favoured the notion of Jewish equality, but they lacked the power to overcome the opposition of craftsmen, the guilds and small shopkeepers. In Lübeck after the final withdrawal of the French in December 1813 the Senate removed all the legislation introduced by the French and restored the inequality as between Jew and Christian. In Bremen in July 1814 the Jews had to submit to the Senate a demand for civil rights in order to avert their expulsion – this secured a reprieve for six years.[25]

In the southern German states of Württemberg, Baden and Bavaria the general legislative trend was directed at limiting both the mobility of the Jewish population and also any increase. The Bavarian Edict of 1813, for example, contained provisions reminiscent of the pharaonic legislation of the eighteenth century. The emigration and settlement of foreign Jews was not only forbidden but the number of families in a particular location must not, as a general rule, be increased. Thus, to establish a family a 'matricular number' was needed as a condition of permission to marry. But as the total of matricular numbers in any one location was limited to the existing total, only one son could marry, and then he must await the death of his parents. Peddlers and petty traders and petty moneylenders required special permission to marry, even if they were in possession of a 'matricular number'. With all the repressiveness of this decree of 1813, in its defence it is still said that to the children of the lower classes it gave the chance of education in the state schools and to the few artisans (bakers, tailors) the chance to work for non-Jewish employers. All would much prefer to live in the age of emancipation and not of absolutism.[26]

Amidst this generally hostile atmosphere the Jewish economic elite in the German states and Austria set itself to prevent any further deterioration in the Jewish situation and even, if at all possible, to bring about the restoration of those rights secured during the Napoleonic regime and now in the process of being lost. It was very much an ad hoc affair and in no way a coordinated effort. The battleground was the Congress of Vienna (1814–15), called in order to settle the affairs of Europe after the Napoleonic upheavals and collapse. It stands out as the first great European conference in which Jews put on the agenda their liberties and status.

Caroline, the wife of Salomon, one of the five sons of Mayer Amschel Rothschild, founder of the banking house, was apparently among the first to appreciate the temper of the time and the opportunity it presented. 'It does not look rosy for us as regards our citizenship', she wrote to her husband (then in London) in July 1814:

> As far as I can see from a distance, we still have a long struggle before us ... Can't you, my dearest Salomon, contribute to this through your acquaintances over there? ... Perhaps a minister there would give you an introduction to Austria, Russia, or whomsoever has a say in this matter. You may ask, what has a woman to do with public affairs? Better she should write about soap and needles. However, I see what I am doing as necessary. Nobody is doing anything about this matter.[27]

Within a few months the Jewish presence at Vienna would be selective, formidable, and dominated by the financial elite. This included Simon Edler v. Lämel of Prague, and from Vienna Leopold Hertz, Arnstein, Eskeles, and Solomon Levy. From the banking revolution in Vienna, inflation and governmental bankruptcy (1811) the house of Arnstein and Eskeles emerged more powerful than ever.[28] The house of Rothschild took a special interest in the fate of Frankfurt am Main, its home town. The house, at the time of the congress, was in the process of developing a relationship with the Austrian chancellor, Metternich.[29] Wilhelm v. Humboldt, the Prussian liberal and educationalist, had already urged in 1809 that Jewish emancipation be the subject of 'a leap, a sudden declaration'. This would be just, politically expedient and consistent. Humboldt also looked forward to the effect of toleration in bringing about the disintegration of Judaism.[30] Much hope was centred on the Prussian chancellor v. Hardenberg, who had been instrumental in the passage of the Prussian Edict of 1812 and was not insensitive to the financial-diplomatic nexus. In a letter intended to persuade the Hamburg authorities to withdraw their anti-Jewish measures, Hardenberg made much of the

> influence which Jewish houses exert upon the system of credit and commerce of the various German states, which cannot escape the notice of the Congress. The commercial interest of the cities themselves suggests a milder treatment of their Jewish inhabitants ... continued persecution would merely incline [the Jewish houses] to remove with their capital, which is so valuable to the Hansa towns, to other cities, in which the

same rights as the Christian inhabitants enjoy would be accorded to them.[31]

At the personal level Friedrich Gentz, secretary to the Congress and confidant of Metternich, was the grateful recipient of *douceurs* from Lämel and perhaps also from Hertz. In April 1815 Lämel made him *'un beau présent pour le mémoire en faveur des Juifs'*; in June 1815, *'après beaucoup de négotiations Lämel se chargea du payement des autres 2000 ducats, que m'a valu l'affaire des Juifs'.*[32]

In Vienna, in April 1815, a group of wealthy bankers and financiers, native to the Habsburg empire, made a direct appeal to the emperor. Eskeles, Nathan v. Arnstein and Edler v. Herz for the Austrian Jews, Simon Ritter v. Lämel for the Bohemians and Lazar Auspitz for the Moravians stressed the Jews' economic contributions as industrialists and exporters and their combatant role, and appealed for equality with other subjects in relation to occupation, trade and the acquisition of property. The appeal made no mention of the pharaonic laws and the group has justifiably been dismissed as 'in reality an economic interest group'.[33] In any case, the fact that the Arnstein and Eskeles families left Vienna for their respective country estates in Baden and Hietzing only three days after the submission of the appeal, and removed themselves from the scene of action, suggests that their enthusiasm was limited. But the receptions, balls and concerts that Fanny v. Arnstein organized for the delegates were highly appreciated for their taste and lavishness.[34]

At the diplomatic level intervention bore most heavily on the situation in Frankfurt and the Hansa cities of Hamburg, Bremen and Lübeck. In the latter two the task was to avert the threatened expulsion of those Jews who had entered during the French period. In Hamburg it was necessary, against the opposition of artisans and shopkeepers, to avert a reversion to the pre-war limits on residence and occupation. In Frankfurt the task was to secure the unconditional maintenance in its whole scope of 'the solemn contract' concluded in 1811 between Frankfurt Jewry and the grand duke.[35] In general terms the spokesmen for the Jews strove to ensure that the confederal constitution of the proposed federation of German states included provision for the attainment of equality of rights and for the preservation of those rights already secured in the individual federated states.

An ad hoc representative council of seven members of the Hamburg community engaged a young Christian advocate, Dr Carl August Buchholz, to argue the case of Hanseatic Jewry. The Frankfurt community nominated two of its own members as spokesmen – J. J. Gumprecht and Jakob Baruch; the latter had earlier represented the community before the Reichstag in Regensburg and also at Vienna in a dispute concerning the rights of Jewish traders at the Frankfurt fair. They had to travel to Vienna in the guise of merchants.

Gumprecht, Baruch and Buchholz had the support of Metternich, v. Hardenberg and Wilhelm v. Humboldt, but they were unable to prevail against the campaign led by Senator Smidt of Bremen (1773–1857), an orthodox Lutheran, and Danz of Frankfurt. 'Metternich, Wessenberg, Hardenberg and I', Humboldt wrote to Caroline his wife, on 4 June 1815, 'maintained the cause as well as we could. Rechberg, Darmstadt, Saxony and the Hanseatic cities constituted the principal opposition.'[36] This had two sources: first, resistance to any measure that would infringe the sovereignty of the states and the free cities; second, an inveterate antisemitism. At one session, chaired by Metternich, when the 'Jewish' clause in the draft constitution was read out, 'Count Rechberg was the first to begin to laugh, and the laughter became infectious and went the rounds, except for a few.'[37] The Congress failed to bring about any alleviation in the situation of the Jews. The great-power intervention of Austria, Prussia, Great Britain and Russia was couched in only the vaguest of terms. In 1816 Castlereagh instructed the Earl of Clancarty, the British representative at Frankfurt, 'to encourage the general adoption of a liberal system of toleration with respect to the individuals of Jewish persuasion throughout Germany, in order that they may not be deprived of those indulgences they have lately enjoyed'. The next year the Prussian king instructed v. Hardenberg no longer to support the Jewish cause at the Federal Diet.[38] In Frankfurt, although the ghetto was not reinstituted, the eventual *Judengesetz* of 1824 to emerge from trilateral negotiations among the community, the Senate and a commission of the federal diet excluded the Jews from free citizens' rights, whilst recognising them as 'Israelite citizens' with the right to purchase property throughout the city; limited the number of permitted marriages for the 3300-strong community to 15 per annum; and restricted the activities of traders and artisans.[39]

19
Epilogue: 1819

This was the year when the recent past became the present; that is to say, when the process of change took on a certain static quality and what had been perhaps inchoate became structured and articulate. In 1819 in Hamburg a rabbinical symposium expounded certain teachings of a new form of Jewish theory and practice entitled *These are the Words of the Covenant [Eleh Divrei Ha-Brit]*. The same year the so-called 'Hep-Hep' riots brought fear and destruction to communities in Germany from Würzburg in the south to Hamburg in the north. To confront both phenomena was the task assumed by a 'Society for the Culture and Science of Judaism' (Verein für die Cultur und Wissenschaft des Judentums), constituted in Berlin in 1819. The seven young intellectuals and scholars who founded the society had an outlook that encompassed their twin enemies; on the one hand, the society's scholarly research would destroy precisely that 'rabbinism' to which the upholders of the Covenant had dedicated themselves. But scholarship had political ramifications also and in so far as it rescued Judaism from rabbinic hands would establish the intellectual acceptance of Judaism, destroy stereotypes and thus remove a barrier to the further extension of Jewish liberties, as against the antisemitism of the Hep-Hep rioters. The proclamation of orthodoxy, the foundation of the Verein and the outburst of mass antisemitism make 1819 a year *sui generis*. One era is closing and another unfolding.

In the Jewish context the term 'Orthodox' is clearly a misnomer since its meaning of 'right belief' hardly suits a context where belief is subordinate to practice and where, consequently, 'orthoprax' would be the more fitting term. In his inaugural address at the opening of the Orthodox rabbinical seminary in Berlin (1873), R. Esriel Hildesheimer emphasized that not in 'philosophical or theological theorems or dogmas' had the heart of Judaism been formulated. Rather, 'it seizes hold of the life of its adherents...This is our conception of Orthodoxy in Judaism...'[1] Nevertheless, the former usage is prevalent to the extent that it is inescapable.[2] As an analytical tool the term was first used, it seems, by Saul Ascher, the *maskil*, in his *Leviathan*

300

(1792) to place 'Orthodox' Judaism in opposition to 'Reform' Judaism, particularly in so far as the former's laws and commandments compromised the autonomy of the individual, according to Ascher's Kantian doctrine. A generation later this conflict of Orthodox vs. Reform was transcended by far in a local Hamburg dispute that rapidly and unexpectedly took on all the dimensions of an irreconcilable *Kulturkampf*. How and why did this come about – not only in Germany of course but, it is true to say, also throughout large parts of the West (with the singular exception of France)? One argument has it that 'Orthodoxy only emerged in response to Reform; it appeared at the time of the Hamburg Temple controversy (1818 and after), when its first programmatic statement proclaimed its existence.'[3]

To suggest, however, that Orthodoxy emerged fully formed from one particular controversy does not seem to me to do justice to the work of the past, still less account for the particular characteristics Orthodoxy displays. (For this reason any discussion of those characteristics is best postponed, pending a tentative elucidation of their past.)

Two motives were at work in the making of Orthodoxy, decades before the Hamburg Temple: first, in sociological terms, it would reverse the declining status of the rabbi and make him the embodiment and exponent of 'right belief'; second, it would repress the fear that intellectual developments in the gentile world had generated. In the particular context of time and place, certain themes are evoked to combat an unwelcome present, and in so doing a certain degree of coalescence takes place – in other words, an ideology is created. Ancient themes are reborn to take on a fresh meaning in a changed environment.

Not only had the traditional role of the rabbi been progressively diminished during the eighteenth century, but the institution itself had become a target for the anticlericalism of Friedländer and the Haskalah, which denigrated the rabbi as no more than 'a supervisor of kashrut'.[4] Nuances are obviously called for here, in view of the political responsibilities undertaken by R. Ezekiel Landau in Prague and R. David Sinzheim in Paris. Even so, the rabbinic loss of control over education in the new maskilic schools at Karlsruhe, Halberstadt, Seesen and elsewhere, the decline of the *kehillah* into a state-dominated organism, and the general transition from a text-centred community to a national community will necessarily devalue rabbinic expertise in Talmud and Codes.[5] As a consequence – to quote R. Ishmael Ha-Cohen of Modena – a rabbi now had not much more to do than 'expound to the people matters of law and morality and the love of one's neighbour so that the people will hear and improve their ways'. The decline in prestige is reflected in the relative unpopularity of rabbinical students as marriage partners; in 1812 in the whole of the French empire only three candidates presented themselves for the rabbinate: Isaac Bernays of Mainz, Lambert Lambert of Metz and Samuel Azaria of Livorno. This is all the more remarkable as such candidacy carried with it exemption from military service.[6]

As part of the governing body the rabbis could not but suffer, albeit indirectly, at the *kehillah's* loss of power, its growing subordination to the state, its internal disintegration through diminished resources. It is also obvious that the growing interest taken, from the early eighteenth century, in the governance of the *kehillah* by the state must *mutatis mutandis* diminish the power of the rabbi and reduce his authority to impose financial or social penalties (for example exclusion from the community). This is manifest above all in Prussia at least from the 1730s.[7] 'Thank God, rabbis have no power,' wrote David Friedländer in 1792.[8] Disregard for the rabbinic courts is epitomized in resort to the civil courts.

These varied developments in the framework of rabbinic 'politics' and communal role took place amidst an atmosphere increasingly inimical to 'rabbinism'. In Ascher's *Leviathan* and the works of his *maskilic* colleagues are refracted the biblical criticism of Spinoza, the Kantian critique of heteronomy and Voltairian deism. In more extreme terms stands the conversion movement among contemporary Prussian Jewry, especially among the 20 Berlin salonières of whom at least 17 converted and 10 married gentiles. Of the 3493 Jews resident in Berlin in 1812, it seems that 245 later converted, that is somewhere between 7 and 8 per cent.[9]

With the moderate Haskalah of Mendelssohn, say, it was certainly possible for traditionally minded scholars and rabbis to find common ground. There existed what has been called an 'uncertain demarcation' between rabbinic culture at its most open and the Haskalah. Pre-eminently did this apply in Bohemia, Moravia and Hungary. Yeshivot double as centres of Haskalah, rabbis instruct their pupils in the natural sciences and Mendelssohn's Biblical commentary is studied sympathetically.[10] More to the west, however, where the Enlightenment vastly sharpened the intellectual threat to Judaism and attracted many more Jews, this openness and even hospitality was experienced as a danger. Not everywhere of course: self-criticism marks Saul Berlin's justified rebuke to his rabbinical colleagues that in the last two centuries they had held themselves aloof from disciplines other than their own; in the curriculum of the Jewish school R. Asher Ginsburg of Wallerstein (Minsk, 1754; Karlsruhe, 1837), deplored the ignorance of Hebrew grammar and secular studies.[11] These two rabbis came from the heart of the rabbinic establishment: Berlin was the son of R. Hirsch Levin, chief rabbi of Berlin and younger brother to R. Solomon Hirschel, chief Ashkenazi rabbi in London; Asher Ginsburg was the son of the renowned Aryeh Leib Ginsburg of Metz. But their openness to 'Greek wisdom' could not endear them to their colleagues of Orthodox belief. Here, the notion of 'regenerating' the Jews, assimilating them to the gentile world, frenchifying them or, as the case may be, germanizing them, held unforeseeable dangers. Secular studies, for example foreign languages, might in themselves be not undesirable and even welcome in the interests of earning a livelihood but in the view of authorities such as R. Jonathan Eibeschütz of Metz, R. Ezekiel Landau of

Prague and R. Raphael Cohen of Hamburg they facilitated intercourse with the gentile world of the intellect and by taking time away from study of the Torah threatened Jewish survival and continuity.[12] Both in Trieste and Prague rabbis expressed their apprehension at the doubts that familiarity with literature in the vernacular might arouse in the minds of members.

The tense relationship inside the Napoleonic consistoire between Sinzheim in Paris and Jacobson in Westphalia foreshadowed the situation in Hamburg where the Westphalian model was paramount. In 1819 Hamburg had no chief rabbi; in his stead a court of three judges governed the community. This Bet Din viewed with alarm the foundation of a Reform temple and hoped to prevail on the Senate to procure its collapse. Their reasons were simple and obvious. The ritual and service of the temple introduced some worship as well as a sermon in German, redefined the divine relationship to Israel in favour of a universalist modification and introduced a choir and accompanying organ into the service.

In reaction, the views of leading contemporary rabbis were solicited as a source and instrument of pressure on the Senate. Not only did the 40 rabbis who responded reject unanimously all the temple's innovations in ritual and worship but, in so doing – in the prevailing ambience of diminished power and prestige, of internal Jewish indifference or hostility to an inherited tradition, of changing values and a threatening intellectual environment, mediated by a rapprochement with the gentile world – they also gave birth to Orthodoxy.

The rabbis saw themselves as guardians of an unchanged and unchangeable heritage. Three rabbis from Prague denounced the reformers for 'lacking faith and seeking only to make a name for themselves among the peoples'; they were accused of altering prayers 'formulated for us by the Men of the Great Assembly' (*c*.300 BCE); to R. Abraham Tiktin (Breslau) it was 'an absolute prohibition to change anything from the customs of our forefathers'; R. Abraham Eliezer Halevy (Trieste) said of the reformers that it was their sole aim 'to throw off the yoke of the Torah'; the rabbis from Padua declared it was 'not in their power to change what the Talmud had decreed even by a hair's breadth'. The consistory of Wintzenheim (Upper Alsace) asked, 'Whence came the authority to sing to the accompaniment of an organ, to desecrate the Sabbath ... if not only to imitate the peoples?'; to R. Samuel (Amsterdam and Amersfoort) 'the man who does not believe in the coming of the Messiah has no portion or inheritance among the children of Israel and by the name Israel he will no longer be called ... the House of Israel is obliged to believe in the thirteen principles of faith' ... 'every man and woman in Israel, old and young, is obliged to believe in everything that we have received from our fathers ... as transmitted to us, mouth to mouth, from Sinai.'[13] It was in the state's own interest not to permit divisions inside religious groups, maintained R. Jacob Lorbeerbaum (Lissa), in an evident appeal to the Hamburg Senate. He took a somewhat Erastian view of church–state relations and referred to Proverbs 24:21: 'Fear the Lord, my son, and the king and with dissidents do not mingle.' The Erastian link between the enforcement of unity and the state's interest is explained in terms of the consequences should 'sectarianism' be permitted. R. Lorbeerbaum wrote:

> We have seen that the kingdom and the authorities in each and every state take heed that everyone is bound into the faith of his own religion so that groups are not formed in which everyone does what his heart desires, for on this depends the existence of the state.[14]

Of all the respondents dominant was the charismatic figure of R. Moses Schreiber (the Hatam Sofer) of Frankfurt am Main and Pressburg. It seems that his influence turned a local dispute into one of general significance. The issue was no longer the form of worship in a particular Reform institution but the Jewish destiny as a whole.[15] Schreiber held to the traditional view that since the fall of the Temple the Jews were 'the prisoners of the nations' and that is why he inveighed against the reformers' refusal to pray not for redemption but 'for our peace among the nations'. They, the reformers, had indeed recalled the words of Jeremiah (29:7): 'Seek the welfare of the city to which I have exiled you and pray to the Lord on its behalf'; but, Schreiber continued, the reformers had dismissed Isaiah's call to the watchmen on the walls of Jerusalem, 'not to rest and give no rest to Him until He establish Jerusalem and make her renowned on earth' (62:6–7).[16] In fact, Schreiber's reasoning showed his awareness, not of a localized struggle, but of a struggle for the very future of Judaism. In this conviction of a critical junction, Orthodoxy, under Schreiber's guidance, espoused the idea of deliberate stringency as a means to subdue the threat of wholesale dissolution. In the same vein, in dismissing Reform Jewry as a source and symptom of dissolution, Schreiber hoped to have the power to forbid marriage between 'our' children and the children of the Reform Jews. 'Let their community be as that of the Sadducees and the Karaites. They should keep to themselves and we to ourselves.' His right not to confer rabbinic status on any of his students at the yeshivah in Pressburg until the student had found a community agreeing to accept him served the same separatist purpose, that is, Schreiber would not allow any of his students to take office in a Reform congregation.[17] In political terms Schreiber demanded absolute, utmost loyalty to the temporal ruler, whom he exalted to a status beyond criticism; 'for the king is the choice of the Lord and we are obliged to fear and to respect him because of awe and the honour due to Heaven'. The king below stands for the ruler above. Schreiber sought in return absolute toleration and certainly not emancipation, for this, as I earlier explained, allegedly entailed the danger of assimilation through contact with 'the peoples' and, moreover, this contact caused antisemitism.[18]

The type of Orthodoxy that R. Moses Schreiber and his followers proclaimed was soon joined by other versions, in which the fear of change and
intellectual challenge became transformed into an unremitting affirmation
of an unbroken continuity which linked, supposedly, the Men of the Great
Assembly (*c.*300 BCE) to contemporary Europe.

Orthodoxy was never uniform, homogeneous or monolithic. Nevertheless,
three basic features distinguish Orthodoxy from earlier modes of practice. First
a break from the traditional principle, or at least convention, that a *kehillah*
functions as a unity encompassing both the transgressors and the observant.
This all-embracing formation the Orthodox rejected in favour of a formation
limited to their own followers. Second, Orthodoxy is marked by its quasi-
absolute rejection of 'secular' studies and culture and their political manifestation in the form of emancipation. This complex of phenomena supposedly
entailed the danger of assimilation through contact with 'the peoples', and,
so some of the Orthodox maintained, this was precisely the process that had
occasioned the expulsion from Spain. Third, Orthodoxy insists on the most
stringent and punctilious performance of the commandments. Lastly, there
were circumstances when, rather than drawing on the sources of the law in
the Codes, commentaries and so on, Orthodoxy preferred to base itself on the
piety of the decisor (and thus go some way to restoring rabbinic authority).[19]

Precedents can be found for all these positions – for example, in the rejection of 'Greek wisdom', or in the concept of 'faith in the sages'. As for the
notion that a minority of members within a given community may separate
themselves from the majority on the grounds of that majority's lax and
intolerable conduct, this has a precedent in the Sephardi community in
Bevis Marks, London, in the early 1700s, when, in essence, a group of
disturbed members consulted Haham Zvi of Amsterdam. These people were
alarmed, to the extent of wishing to leave their congregation,

> when they saw that sons of our nation who perform acts that should not
> take place among the Israelites … attend prayer services there and go up
> to read from the Torah and [participate in] all the other rituals that are
> customary in the synagogue.

Were these members, alarmed in this way, authorized to leave their
community, despite the prohibition of so doing, and join the Ashkenazi
community in London? In his responsum Haham Zvi did in these circumstances sanction withdrawal, for 'any man whose heart has been touched by
God has the right to separate and leave that congregation and pray with a
quorum in whatever place that he chooses'.[20] There are parallels to this
situation in the seventeenth-century congregations of Amsterdam and
Livorno, for example uncircumcised Jews were prohibited from holding a
scroll of the Torah, or denied the right of burial in a Jewish cemetery or the
right to be included in communal prayers for the deceased.[21]

The parallel between these prohibitions and the ostracism which Orthodoxy exercised *vis-à-vis* Reform Jews, say, must not be exaggerated. Nineteenth-century port-Jews in Hamburg certainly stand out from seventeenth-century port-Jews in Livorno or Amsterdam. But the juxtaposition strikes me as fruitful – all the more so as the authorities in both situations had to contend with similar religio-philosophical challenges to tradition. Deistic thinking, for example, or naturalistic doctrines of religion, prevail throughout the whole period.

By the 1860s differences concerning the role of the rabbinic courts and the value of secular culture had already emerged among Orthodox circles in Germany.[22] But it was at the level of scholarship that Orthodoxy was most vulnerable, and not its variations. Hardly did '*These are the Words of the Covenant*' appear than it was subjected to vehement attack by the 25-year-old Leopold Zunz, an independent scholar (1794–1886). He had been a student at the newly founded University of Berlin and had attended courses given by August Boeckh and F. A. Wolf on Plato's Republic, ancient philosophy (which had a strong philological emphasis), Greek antiquities and literature. Zunz was introduced to Biblical criticism by August de Wette. He owed his early Jewish education to the *Freischule* and *Gymnasium* in Wolfenbüttel. He developed into one of the foremost Jewish scholars of the nineteenth century. In a Berlin journal in 1819 Zunz denounced *These are the Words of the Covenant* and its rabbinic authors as the epitome of 'ignorance, arrogance and fanaticism'. Not 'rabbinism' *per se* did Zunz assail but its contemporary exponents. 'They do not understand even their own Talmud.' They were no more than the decadent heirs to a tradition of learning that had ceased to flourish with the Reformation.[23]

At this point the scholarship and politics of 1819 became involved with each other. Zunz's scholarship and critique had a political dimension to which contemporary events in the form of antisemitism gave crucial impetus. Zunz was outraged not only by the alleged 'fanaticism and ignorance' of the rabbis but also by the antisemitic pamphlet published in 1815 by Rühs, a professor at Berlin in ancient history and one of Zunz's teachers. Rühs argued that Jewish arrogance, economic parasitism and intellectual backwardness unfitted the Jews to become German citizens. This was why only one of the antisemitic manifestations of an inchoate movement that had early shown itself in the treatment of Jewish emancipation at the Congress of Vienna and been expressed, both before and after the Congress, in publications and pamphlets by Fichte among others. This message was reinforced by the exclusion of Jewish students from the 'Christian-German' *Burschenschaften*; the outburst of 'Germanomania' (to quote the *maskil* Saul Ascher) at the Wartburg festival of 18 October 1817, commemorating the third centenary of Luther's protest and the French defeat at the battle of Leipzig. The books burned on that occasion typically included Ascher's *Die Germanomanie*, first published in 1815. Its message of rationalism and universalism as against the nationalist and romantic mysticism of the students could not but be provocative. Also during these years the limits to the Prussian emancipation edict of 1812 were clarified, especially in regard to the entry of Jews into public life, for example senior army ranks and academe. In the summer of 1819 the movement took a violent turn with an outburst of antisemitism that spread from south to north in Germany. The so-called Hep-Hep riots began in Würzburg in early August and in a spontaneous chain of discontent, violence and disorder spread to the Jewish quarters in Bamberg, Karlsruhe, Frankfurt, Heidelberg, Darmstadt, Mannheim and as far north as Hamburg and Danzig. Metternich, at the Carlsbad conference, arranged for federal troops to maintain order, should local authorities prove too weak.

In Würzburg (from which Jews had been excluded until 1803) gangs of rioters and looters, made up of pauperized and displaced handworkers and petty tradesmen, forced the 400 Jews of the city to flee for their lives and take refuge in the surrounding villages. Everywhere in the towns and cities mentioned Jews were molested, their windows broken, shop signs torn down, premises ransacked. Students often participated. The movement lasted till early October. Among the worst hit areas were Würzburg, Frankfurt am Main and Hamburg, which argues that the prospect or actuality of emancipation and the socio-political advancement of Jews was a principal operative factor. This was certainly the case in Frankfurt, where the mob smashed the windows of the Rothschild offices in the *Judengasse*, and Baron Amschel Rothschild (the recipient of death threats) contemplated quitting the city altogether.[24]

These events brought together Zunz and a group of half a dozen likeminded young intellectuals. They met in November 1819 in Berlin and 'constituted a society [*Verein*] for the improvement of the condition of the Jews in the German federation'. Eduard Gans, one of the seven, recalled the prevailing atmosphere:

> In many towns of the German fatherland those horrible scenes had taken place which made many envisage an unexpected return of the middle ages. We came together to help, where there was need, to discuss the means whereby best to help avert the deep-rooted danger.[25]

In 1821, about two years after the first meeting, this nucleus took a somewhat more formal shape in the Verein für Cultur und Wissenschaft der Juden (Society for the Culture and Science of the Jews). The term 'Science of Judaism' comprises the activity of treating Judaism and its culture with the methods of (historical) science. The seven founding members of the Verein had a background in middle-class German Jewry from which they were alienated. They were, with one exception, in their twenties and receptive to the intellectual ferment in early nineteenth-century Prussia generated by

Herder, Hegel, Schleiermacher, Savigny and the Romantic movement. They all looked forward to closer identification with German culture. Conversely, why should Christians not be active in Jewish research, it was asked? This was certainly Zunz's hope when he vainly tried to secure at the University of Berlin the establishment of a chair in Jewish history and literature. He found it deplorable that an exhibition of the printed book in Berlin in 1840 did not include a single work in Hebrew.

This was consonant with Zunz's political judgement which he carried into his scholarship. Under the rubric 'The Science of Judaism' his work transformed the nature of Jewish scholarship in the nineteenth century and immensely widened its scope to include the study of sermons, public discourse, poetry, ritual and historiography. In a certain sense the two endeavours were one in that the transformation of the negative Jewish image to be brought about by scholars would at the least conduce to an enhanced appreciation and understanding of Judaism in the gentile world and thus to its political acceptance, and diminish the possible recurrence of any Hep-Hep riots; a political upheaval (like that of 1848, which Zunz enthusiastically supported, Garibaldi being one of his heroes) might also reasonably be expected to remove the apparatus of Jewish suppression. In the introduction to his study of the Jewish sermon, preaching and public oratory, Zunz explicitly attributed the 'retarded civil state' of the Jews to the neglect of knowledge of the Jews – a neglect which left 'legislators and scholars' dependent on the authorities of the seventeenth century, such as the antisemite Eisenmenger.[26] After 1819 the science of Judaism moved away from the direct confrontation with Orthodoxy and towards an engagement with the Jewish past – primarily its literature – as a means to enlighten its gentile detractors. This was a continuing process of scholarship, likewise those other legacies of 1819, Orthodoxy and antisemitism.

Notes

Introduction

1. See A. Mittelman, *The Politics of Torah* (New York: SUNY, 1996), pp. 69 ff.; also the sixteenth-century legal code Shulhan Arukh, Hoshen Mishpat, Laws of Judges, 2:1.
2. See M. Elon, 'Le-Mehutan shel Takkanot Ha-Kahal Ba-Mishpat Ha-Ivri', in S. Tedeschi (ed.), *Mehkarei Mishpat le-Zekher A. Rosenthal* (Jerusalem: Magnes Press, 1964), pp. 1–54.
3. See B. J. Bamberger, 'Individual Rights and the Demands of the State: The position of Classical Judaism', *Central Conference of American Rabbis*, vol. 44 (1944), pp. 197–211.
4. L. Strauss, *What is Political Philosophy?* (Westport, 1973), p. 84.
5. See R. Judah Loewe b. Bezalel, *Netivot Olam* ii, repr. (London: Honig, 1961), pp. 38, 81; also the material quoted in B. L. Sherwin, *Mystical Theology and Social Dissent* (London: Associated University Presses, 1982), p. 165.
6. Joseph Dan, *Jewish Studies in a New Europe, Proceedings of the Fifth Congress of the European Association for Jewish Studies, Copenhagen* (1998), p. xxx; see also R. Loewe, *The Position of Women in Judaism* (London: SPCK, 1966), pp. 51–2; and Mittelman, *Politics of Torah*, pp. 76–7.
7. For sources of these and similar statements, see S. W. Baron, *A Social and Religious History of the Jews*, XII (New York: Columbia University Press, 1967), pp. 198–9; R. Israel Isserlein, *Trumat Ha-Deshen*, repr. (Bnei Brak, 5731 [1971]), No. 342.
8. R. Isaiah Horovitz, *Shnei Luhot Ha-Brit* (end commentary on pericope Va-Yishlach [Gen. 32:4–36:43]), repr. (Jerusalem, 1963), Bk II, Pt 3.
9. B. Ravid, *Economics and Toleration in 17th-Century Venice* (Jerusalem: American Academy for Jewish Research, 1978), p. 98.
10. D. Kaufmann, 'Rabbi Zevi Ashkenazi and his Family in London', *TJHSE*, III (1899) pp. 102–25, here pp. 102–3.
11. For the standard work on this subject see Samuel Shiloh, *Dina de-malkhuta Dina* (Jerusalem: Academic Press, 1974); see also N. Rakover, *Shilton Ha-Hok be-Yisrael* (Jerusalem: Sifriyat Ha-Mishpat Ha-Ivri, 1989), pp. 65ff.; and G. Blidstein, *A Note on the Function of the 'Law of the Kingdom Is Law'* (Jerusalem: Centre for Jewish Community Studies, n.d.).
12. D. Carpi (ed.), *Pinkas Va'ad Padua 1577–1603* (Jerusalem: Israel Academy of Sciences, 1973), No. 436; I. Halperin (ed.) and I. Bartal (rev.), *Pinkas Va'ad Arba Aratzot* (Jerusalem: Mossad Bialik, 1945); No. 297; Dov Avron (ed.), *Pinkas Ha-Ksherim shel Kehillat Pozna* (Jerusalem, 1961), pp. 132, 136; S. Schwarzfuchs (ed.), *Le Registre des Délibérations de la Nation Juive Portugaise de Bordeaux 1711–1787* (Paris: Fundacao Gulbenkian, 1981), No. 74, para. 2 (hereafter *Registre*, with the relevant document or page number); see also E. Carlebach, 'Attribution of Secrecy and Perceptions of Jewry', *JSS*, II (1996), pp. 115–136.
13. Quoted Sylvie-Anne Goldberg, 'Temporality as Paradox: The Jewish Time', *Proceedings of the Fifth Congress of the European Association of Jewish Studies*, pp. 284–92; see also R. Bonfil, *Jewish Life in Renaissance Italy* (Stanford: California University Press, 1994), p. 225.

14. D. Krochmalnik, 'Das Neue Weltbild in jüdischen Kontexten', in M. Graetz (ed.), *Schöpferische Momente des europäischen Judentums* (Heidelberg: Winter, 2000), pp. 249–70.
15. R. Moses di Trani, *She'elot u-Tshuvot* (Venice, 1629), No. 307.
16. R. Judah Loewe b. Bezalel, *Derekh Hayyim*, repr. (London: Honig, 1961), ch. 6, p. 305; see also Jacob Katz, 'Between 1096 and 1648–49', in S. Ettinger (ed.), *Sepher Yovel le-Yitzhak Baer* (Jerusalem: Israel Historical Society, 1960), pp. 318–37, esp. pp. 328–9.
17. Quoted E. Fram, *Ideals Face Reality* (Cincinnati, OH: Hebrew Union College Press, 1997), p. 32.
18. See B. Ravid, 'The First Charter of the Jewish Merchants of Venice, 1589', *AJS Review*, 1 (1976), pp. 187–222.
19. For an analysis of *La Livornina*, see Lionel Lévy, *La Nation Juive Portugaise* (Paris: L'Harmattan, 1999), pp. 25ff.; Deborah Hacohen, 'Ha-Kehillah be-Livorno u-Mosdotehah', in R. Bonfil (ed.), *In Memoria di Umberto Nahon* (Jerusalem: Fondazione Sally Meyer, 1978), pp. 107–27.
20. E. Mayer, *Die Frankfurter Juden* (Frankfurt am Main: Kramer Verlag, 1966), p. 19. For a similar demographic pattern but with different estimates, see M. Awerbuch, 'Alltagsleben in der Frankfurter Judengasse', in K. Grözinger (ed.), *Jüdische Kultur in Frankfurt am Main*, (Wiesbaden: Harrasowitz, 1997), pp. 1–24, esp. p. 2.

1 Central Europe in Peace and War, 1600–48

1. J. F. Battenberg, 'The Jewish Population in the Holy Roman Empire', WCJS, xi, Div. B, iii (Jerusalem, 1994), pp. 61–8.
2. Idem, 'Des Kaisers Kammerknechte', *HZ*, 245 (1987), pp. 545–9, esp. p. 584ff.
3. G. Veltri, 'Ohne Recht und Gerechtigkeit – Kaiser Rudolf II und sein Bankier Markus Meyzel', in G. Veltri and A. Winkelmann (eds), *An der Schwelle zur Moderne* (Leiden: Brill, 2003), pp. 233–55; see also Fugger Newsletter, 5 April 1601, in J. R. Marcus (ed.), *The Jew in the Medieval World, A Source Book* (New York: Harper & Row, 1965), nos. 325–6; G. Bondy and F. Dworsky (eds), *Zur Geschichte der Juden in Böhmen, Mähren and Schlesien von 906 bis 1620* (Prague, 1906), nos. 968, 971–3.
4. Daniel Cohen, 'Die Entwicklung der Landesrabbinate in den deutschen Territorien bis zur Emanzipation', in A. Haverkamp (ed.), *Zur Geschichte der Juden in Deutschland* (Stuttgart: Hiersemann, 1981), pp. 221–42, here pp. 235–6; see also R. Juspa Shamash, *Minhagim de-Warmeisa*, ed. Eric Zimmer, 2 vols, repr. (Jerusalem:Makhon Yerushalayim, 1992), no. 293.
5. Rabbi M. Horovitz, *Frankfurter Rabbinen* (with additions by R. Josef Unna), repr. (Jerusalem, 1969), pp. 40ff.; I. Kracauer, *Geschichte der Juden in Frankfurt am Main 1150–1824*, 2 vols (Frankfurt am Main: Kauffmann, 1925–27), I, pp. 337ff.
6. The issues are examined in V. Press, 'Kaiser Rudolf II und der Zusammenschluss der deutschen Judenheit', in Haverkamp (ed), *Geschichte der Juden*, pp. 243–93; and in A. Herzig, 'Die Jüdischheit teutscher Nation', *Aschkenas*, III (1994), pp. 127–32; see also Cohen, 'Die Entwicklung der Landesrabbinate', p. 224.
7. Joseph Hahn, *Yosef Ometz* (Frankfurt am Main, 1723), p. 170b.
8. I. Kracauer, *Die Geschichte der Judengasse in Frankfurt am Main* (Frankfurt am Main: Kauffmann, 1906), p. 320.
9. H. Turniansky, 'The Events in Frankfurt am Main (1612–1616) in Megillas Vints', in M. Graetz (ed.), *Schöpferische Momente des Europäischen Judentums* (Heidelberg: Winter, 2000), pp. 221–37); S. Eidelberg (ed.), *R. Juspa, Shammash of Warmaisa*

[Worms] (Jerusalem: Magnes Press, 1991), Engl. Sec., pp. 71–5 (Heb. Sec., pp. 71–4); G. Wolf, *Zur Geschichte der Juden in Worms* (Breslau: Schletterscher, 1862), pp. 16 ff.

10. Kracauer, *Geschichte der Juden in Frankfurt*, I, p. 397.
11. Press, 'Kaiser Rudolf', pp. 283 ff.; C. R. Friedrichs, 'Jews in Imperial Cities', in R. Po-Chia Hsia and H. Lehmann (eds), *In and Out of the Ghetto* (Cambridge University Press, 1995), pp. 275–88. Friedrichs also writes ('Anti-Jewish Policies in Early Modern Germany and the Uprising in Worms 1613–1617', *Central European History*, xxiii (1990), pp. 91–152): 'In the short term the Jews could never resist the acts of violence visited upon them in Worms and elsewhere. But they were just as capable as their Christian enemies of trying to use the institutions of the Holy Roman Empire to their advantage. Above all, they were able to secure the support of the Emperor himself with results that were eventually to their benefit.'
12. L. Rosenthal, *Zur Geschichte der Juden im Gebiet der ehemaligen Grafschaft Hanau* (Hanau: Hanauischer Geschichtsverein, 1963), pp. 50–2; G. Marwedel, *Die Privilegien der Juden in Altona* (Hamburg: Christians, 1976) pp. 119/120; G. Wolf, *Geschichte der Juden in Wien* (Vienna: Hölder, 1876) pp. 260–1; W. Laubenthal, *Die Synagogengemeinden des Kreises Merzig* (Saarbrücken: Saarbrücken Druckerei, 1984), pp. 27–9.
13. Battenberg, 'Jewish Population', p. 61.
14. R. Dunn, *The Age of Religious Wars, 1559–1689* (London: Weidenfeld, 1970), p. 111.
15. See H. Graetz, *Geschichte der Juden*, x (Leipzig: Leiner, 1868), ch. 2; J. Israel, 'Central European Jewry during the Thirty Years' War', *Central European History*, xvi (1983), pp. 3–30; W. McCagg, *A History of Habsburg Jews* (Bloomington: Indiana University Press, 1989), p. 15; Eidelberg, *R. Juspa*, Heb. Sec., pp. 91–2.
16. Kracauer, *Geschichte der Juden in Frankfurt*, II, p. 29; E. Zimmer (ed.), *Minhagim de K. K. Wermaisa*, 2 vols (Jerusalem: Makhon Jerusalem, 1992), II, nos. 264–5; R. Joel Sirkes, *Tshuvot Ha-Bakh Ha-Yeshanot* (Frankfurt am Main, 1697), No. 103.
17. R. Juspa Hahn, *Yosef Ometz*, p. 166b.
18. Kracauer, *Geschichte der Juden in Frankfurt*, II, pp. 32–5.
19. See his responsa, *Havot Ya'ir*, repr. (Jerusalem, 1987), no. 60.
20. A. Kober, 'Die deutschen Kaiser und die Wormser Juden', in Ernst Roth (ed.), *Die alte Synagoge zu Worms* (Frankfurt am Main: Ner Tamid, 1961), pp. 189 ff.; G. Wolf, *Geschichte der Juden in Worms*, Beilage XXV.
21. A. Landau and B. Wachstein (eds), *Jüdische Privatbriefe aus dem Jahre 1619* (Vienna: Braumüller, 1911). Some of the letters are available in an English translation in F. Kobler (ed.), *Letters of Jews through the Ages*, 2 vols (London: East and West Library, 1953), pp. 449–79.
22. See M. Popper, 'Les Juifs de Prague Pendant la Guerre de Trente Ans', *REJ*, nos. 29–30 (1894–5), pp. 127–41; G. Klemperer, 'The Rabbis of Prague', *HJ*, XII (1950), pp. 33–66, esp. p. 65.
23. K. Spiegel, 'Die Prager Juden zur Zeit des dreissigjährigen Krieges', in S. Steinherz (ed.), *Die Juden in Prag* (Prague: Bnai Brith, 1927), pp. 107–86, esp. pp. 138–43; H. Schnee, *Die Hoffinanz und der moderne Staat*, III (Berlin: Duncker & Humblot, 1955), pp. 235–7.
24. Spiegel, 'Die Prager Juden', p. 110.
25. Popper, 'Juifs de Prague', p. 135.
26. Spiegel, 'Die Prager Juden', pp. 168 ff.
27. Ibid., pp. 161–2.

312 *Notes*

28. Klemperer, 'Rabbis of Prague', p. 51; J. Davis, 'Ashkenazic Rationalism and Midrashic Natural History', *Science in Context*, x (1997), pp. 605–26.
29. J. Perles, 'Urkunden zur Geschichte der jüdischen Provinzialsynoden in Polen', *MGWJ*, 16 (1867), pp. 306–7.
30. Israel Halperin, 'Mahloket al Breirat Ha-Kahal be-Frankfurt', *Tsiyon*, XXI (1956), pp. 64–91.
31. Prague was notorious for its 'violence and disputes', according to the contemporary, R. Moses Isserles of Cracow. History has been no kinder. Heinrich Graetz, echoing Isserles, saw the *kehillah* of the seventeenth century as 'base, avaricious, without conscience, violent and quarrelsome'. 'Many members of the community did not shrink even from perjury. The elders and their relatives permitted themselves all manner of abuse and the oppressed received no justice.' (R. Moses Isserles, *She'elot u-Tshuvot*, ed. R. Asher Ziv, repr. (New York: Yeshivah University, 1972), No. 14; H. Graetz,*Geschichte der Juden*, IX (Leipzig: Oskar Leinen, 1866), p. 387.
32. The above is based on Heller's own account of his imprisonment, *Megilat Eivah* (Breslau, 1837); G. Klemperer, 'The Rabbis of Prague', *Historia Judaica*, XII (1950), pp. 33–66, 143–52; M. H. Friedländer, *Beiträge zur Geschichte der Juden Mähren* (Brünn, 1876), pp. 18 ff. G. Wolf, *Ferdinand II und die Juden* (Vienna, 1859), pp. 49–50.
33. R. J. W. Evans, *The Making of the Habsburg Monarchy, 1550–1700* (Oxford: Clarendon Press, 1979), p. 198.
34. See A. F. Pribram (ed.), *Urkunden und Akten zur Geschichte der Juden in Wien*, 2 vols (Vienna: Braumüller, 1918), I, no. 68 [hereafter referred to as Pribram, *Urkunden*]; J. Prokes und A. Blaschka, *Der Antisemitismus der Behörden*, *JGGJCR*, 1929, I, pp. 41–110, esp. pp. 59 ff. and fnn. 22–3, pp. 88–9.
35. Spiegel, 'Die Prager Juden', p. 161.
36. Judah Leib b. Joshua, *Sefer Milhama be-shalom* (Prague, 1650), p. 2b.
37. T. Haas, 'Statistische Betrachtungen über die jüdische Bevölkerung Mährens', in H. Gold (ed.), *Die Judengemeinden Mährens in Vergangenheit und Gegenwart* (Brünn: Jüdischer Buchverlag, 1929), p. 592.
38. M. Grünfeld, 'Äusserer Verlauf der Geschichte der Juden in Mähren', in Gold (ed.), *Judengemeinden*, pp. 12–13.
39. Haas, 'Statistische Betrachtungen', p. 592; see also A. Frankl-Grün, *Geschichte der Juden in Kremsier*, I (Breslau: Schlesische Buchdruckerei, 1896), pp. 96 ff.; and Friedländer, *Juden in Brünn*, pp. 19–20.
40. It is not unreasonable to suppose that, despite the censure of moralists and rabbis, dicing and mixed dancing accompanied these festivities (see Ruth Berger, 'Tanzt der Teufel mit?', *Kalonymos*, VI (2003), pp. 4–7).
41. See J. F. Battenberg, 'Schutz, Toleranz oder Vertreibung', in E. G. Franz (ed.), *Juden als Darmstädter Bürger* (Darmstadt: Roether Verlag, 1984), pp. 33–49, esp. pp. 39 ff.
42. See B. Altmann, 'The Autonomous Federation of Jewish Communities in Paderborn', *JSS*, III (1941), pp. 159–88, esp. pp. 161 ff.; also M. Evers, *Die Geschichte der Juden in der Stadt Warburg* (Warburg: Hermes, 1978), pp. 18–19; G. Marwedel, *Die Privilegien der Juden in Altona* (Hamburg, 1976), p. 50; Adolf Altmann, *Geschichte der Juden in Stadt und Land Salzburg* (Salzburg: Müller, 1990), pp. 223–4; N. Bamberger, *Geschichte der Juden von Kitzingen*, new imp. (Kitzingen: Högner, 1983), pp. 11–13; L. Rosenthal, *Juden in Hanau*, p. 50; H. Schmitt *et al.* (eds), *Juden in Karlsruhe* (Karlsruhe: Badenic Verlag, 1988), pp. 25–6; E. L. Ehrlich, 'Geschichte und Kultur der Juden in den rheinischen Territorialstaaten', in *Monumenta Judaica* (Cologne, 1963), p. 258.

43. *Pinkas Ha-Ksherim shel Kehillat Pozna, 1621–1835*, ed. D. Avron (Jerusalem, 1966), no. 190.
44. B. Brilling, *Geschichte der Juden in Breslau von 1454 bis 1702* (Stuttgart: Kohlhammer, 1960), pp. 15 ff., 69 ff.
45. P. Bloch, 'Ein vielbegehrter Rabbiner des Rheingaues, Juda Mehler Reutlingen', in *Martin Philippsohn Festschrift* (Leipzig: Fock, 1916), pp. 114–34.
46. G. Weill, 'L'Alsace', in B. Blumenkranz (ed.), *Histoire des Juifs en France* (Toulouse: Privat, 1972), pp. 144 ff.
47. G. Roos, *Relations entre le Gouvernement Royal et les Juifs du Nord-Est de la France au XVIIe Siècle* (Paris: Champion, 2000), pp. 101–2, 125, 127; see also G. Weill, 'Recherches sur la Démographie des Juifs d'Alsace du XVIe au XVIIIe siècle', *REJ*, nos. 129–30 (1970–1), pp. 53–4, 60–1.
48. See Graetz, *Geschichte der Juden*, x, p. 51; also F. Redlich, 'De Praedi Militari – Looting and Booty 1500–1815', in *VSW* (1956), Beiheft, no. 39, pp. 21, 55; for further references to the trade in the spoils of war, see B. Altmann, 'Jews and the Rise of Capitalism', *JSS*, v (1943), pp. 163–86, esp. fn. 29, p. 169.
49. For this I am deeply indebted to H. Turniansky (ed.), *Sefer Massah u-Merivah of Alexander b. Isaac Pappenhoffen* (Jerusalem: Magnes Press, 1985), esp. pp. 81, 117 ff.
50. Halperin, 'Mahloket', p. 111.
51. The above is based on G. Wolf, *Juden in Wien*, pp. 27 ff. and Beilage, xxviii; and M. Grunwald, *Vienna* (Philadelphia, PA: JPSA, 1936), pp. 80 ff.; see also the references cited in Pribram, *Urkunden*, i, p. xxviii; and what appears to be a fairly full list of loans up to 1670 in M. Grunwald, *Samuel Oppenheimer und sein Kreis* (Vienna: Braumüller, 1913), p. 20 ff.
52. Pribram, *Urkunden*, nos. 36, 37, 52.
53. Wolf, *Juden in Wien*, p. 43.
54. Wolf, *Ferdinand II*, p. 19.
55. Pribram, *Urkunden*, nos. 52, 54–7, 63.
56. Grunwald, *Jews in Vienna*, p. 89; Wolf, *Juden in Wien*, p. 46.
57. Ibid., Beilage, xxx.
58. Grunwald, *Jews in Vienna*, pp. 106–7.

2 'A Little Jerusalem' and 'A Great Jerusalem'

1. J. J. Schudt, *Jüdische Merckwürdigkeiten* (Frankfurt am Main, 1714), Bk iv, ch. xviii, p. 271.
2. H. P. Salomon, *Portrait of a New Christian, Ferrão Alvares Melo* (Paris: Fundacao Gulbenkian, 1982), p. 3.
3. S. Schwarzfuchs, *Les Juifs de France* (Paris: Albin Michel, 1975), p. 143; D. Sorkin, 'The port Jew: notes towards a social type', *JJS*, L (1999), pp. 87–97.
4. M. Studemund-Halévy, 'Sprachverhalten und Assimilation der portugiesischen Juden in Hamburg', in A. Herzig, ed., *Die Juden in Hamburg 1590–1990* (Hamburg: Dölling & Galiz Verlag, 1991), pp. 283–99, here p. 284.
5. Minna Rozen, 'La Vie Économique des Juifs du Bassin Méditerranéan', in S. Trigano (ed.), *La Société Juive à travers l'Histoire* (Paris: Fayard, 1992), pp. 296–352.
6. Jonathan Israel, 'The Sephardi contribution to economic life and colonisation in England and the New World (16th–18th centuries)', in Hayyim Beinart (ed.), *The Sephardi Legacy II* (Jerusalem: Magnes Press, 1992), pp. 365–98.

314   *Notes*

7. Lionel Lévy, *La Nation Juive Portugaise* (Paris: L'Harmattan, 1999), pp. 46 ff.
8. Flora Levi d'Ancona, 'The Sephardi Community of Leghorn', in R. Barnett and W. Schwab (eds), *The Sephardi Heritage II* (Grendon, Northants: Gibraltar Books, 1989), pp. 180–202.
9. The above is based on Sh. Toaff, 'Mahloket R. Jacob Sasportas u-Farnassei Livorno', *Sefunot*, ix (1965), pp. 169–91; for an English translation of some of the salient documents in this dispute, see M. Walzer *et al.* (eds), *The Jewish Political Tradition* (New Haven, CT: Yale University Press, 2000), i, pp. 424–9.
10. Generally, see Günter Böhm, 'Die Sephardim in Hamburg', in Herzig (ed.), *Die Juden in Hamburg*, pp. 21 ff; also H. Wallenborn, *Bekehrungseifer, Jüdische Angst und Handelsinteressen* (Hildesheim: Olms, 2003). p. 288.
11. It is certainly interesting to note that the first fictional Jewish shipowner had appeared a generation earlier, *c.*1592, in the figure of Barabbas, the villainous hero of Marlowe's *The Jew of Malta*: see B. Arbel, 'Shipping and Toleration', *Mediterranean Historical Review*, xv (2000), pp. 56–71.
12. Jonathan Israel, 'Duarte Nunes da Costa (Jacob Curiel) of Hamburg, Sephardi Nobleman and Communal Leader (1585–1664)', *SR*, xxi (1987), pp. 14–34, esp. p. 21; Arbel, 'Shipping and toleration', pp. 56–71, esp. pp. 63 ff.
13. Böhm, *Sephardim in Hamburg*, p. 23.
14. Israel, 'Duarte Nunes da Costa', pp. 14–34.
15. H. Kellenbenz, *Sephardim an der unteren Elbe* (Wiesbaden: Harrasowitz, 1958), pp. 257–8.
16. J. Cassuto (ed.), 'Aus dem ältesten Protokollbuch der Portugiesischen Jüdischen Gemeinde in Hamburg', *JJLG*, viii (1910–11), pp. 234–5 (Entry for 25 Nissan 5418 = 28 April 1658).
17. H. M. Graupe, *Die Statuten der drei Gemeinden, Altona, Hamburg und Wandsbek* (Hamburg: Christians Verlag, 1973), pp. 19 ff.
18. Kellenbenz, *Sephardim an der unteren Elbe*, pp. 53–4, 200; P. Kromminga, 'Duldung und Ausgrenzung. Schutzjuden und Betteljuden in Hamburg', in Herzig (ed.), *Juden in Hamburg*, pp. 187–93; J. Whaley, *Religious Toleration and Social Change in Hamburg 1529–1819* (Cambridge University Press, 1985), pp. 94–5.
19. O. Vlessing, 'The Portuguese Merchant Community in 17th Century Amsterdam', in C. Lesger and L. Noordgraf (eds), *Entrepreneurs in Early Modern Times* (The Hague: Stichting Hollandse Historische Reeks, 1995), pp. 223–43.
20. K. Sonnenberg-Stern, *Emancipation and Poverty* (Basingstoke: Macmillan, 2000), pp. 34–5; A. H. Huussen Jr, 'The legal position of Sephardi Jews in Holland, circa 1600', in *DJH*, iii (1993), pp. 19–41.
21. Quoted Miriam Bodian, 'Amsterdam, Venice and the Marrano diaspora', in J. Michman (ed.), *Dutch-Jewish History* (Jerusalem: Tel Aviv University, 1984), pp. 47–65, here p. 61.
22. H. Méchoulan, *Etre Juif à Amsterdam au temps de Spinoza* (Paris: Albin Michel, 1991), p. 28.
23. J. I. Israel, 'The Jews of Venice and their links with Holland and with Dutch Jewry (1600–1710)', in G. Cozzi (ed.), *Gli ebrei e Venezia* (Milan: Edizioni Comunita, 1987), pp. 95–111.
24. See also D. Swetchinski, *Reluctant Cosmopolitans* (London: Littman Library, 2000), pp. 357–67.
25. J. Michman, 'Historiography of the Jews in the Netherlands', in J. Michman (ed.), *Dutch-Jewish History* (Jerusalem: Institute for Research on Dutch Jewry, 1984), pp. 7–29, here p. 22.

26. R. Israel Shchepanski (ed.), *Ha-Takkanot be-Yisrael*, IV (Jerusalem: Mossad Ha-Rav Kuk, 1993), p. 317.
27. J. R. Marcus (ed.), *The Jew in the Medieval World: A Source Book 315–1791* (New York: Harper & Row, 1965), pp. 378–80. For a less sympathetic view of the Sephardi curriculum in the schools of Bordeaux, given the relative absence of a halakhic component, see above, p. 220.
28. For the organisation of this community see D. M. Sluys, 'Yehudei Ashkenaz be-Amsterdam mi-Shnat 1635 ad Shnat 1795', in J. Michman (ed.), *Mehkarim al Toldot Yahadut Holland* (Jerusalem: Magnes Press, 1975), pp. 69–121, esp. p. 81.
29. See the material quoted in G. M. Weiner, 'Sephardic Philo- and Anti-Semitism in the Early Modern Era', in R. H. Popkin and G. M. Weiner (eds), *Jewish Christians and Christian Jews* (Dordrecht: Kluwer, 1994), pp. 189–214.
30. R. H. Popkin, 'Rabbi Nathan Shapira's visit to Amsterdam in 1657', in Michman (ed.), *Dutch-Jewish History*, pp. 185–205.
31. J. Kaplan, 'Amsterdam and Ashkenazic migration in the seventeenth century', *SR*, XVII (1989), pp. 22–44.
32. Quoted H. Bloom, *The Economic Activities of the Jews of Amsterdam in the 17th and 18th Centuries*, repr. (NewYork: Kennikat, 1969), p. 203.
33. O. Vlessing, 'New Light on the Earliest History of the Amsterdam Portuguese Jews', in J. Michman (ed.), *Dutch-Jewish History*, IV (Jerusalem, 1993), pp. 43–75, esp. pp. 63–4.
34. See Israel, 'Duarte Nunes da Costa', pp. 14–34; idem., 'An Amsterdam Jewish Merchant of the Golden Age', *SR*, XVIII (1984), pp. 21–40.
35. J. Kaplan, 'Olamo ha-dati shel sokher benle'umi Yehudi bi-tekufat ha-merkantilizm', in M. Ben-Sasson (ed.), *Dat ve-khalkala* (Jerusalem: Zalman Shazar, 1995), pp. 233–51.
36. D. M. Swetchinski, 'The Portuguese Jews of 17th century Amsterdam: Cultural Continuity and Adaptation', in F. Malino and P. C. Albert (eds), *Essays in Modern Jewish History* (London: Associated University Presses, 1982), pp. 56–80.
37. Quoted in Moses Bensabat Amzalak, 'Joseph da Veiga and stock exchange operations in the seventeenth century', in I. Epstein *et al.* (eds), *Essays in Honour of the Very Rev. Dr J. H. Hertz, Chief Rabbi* (London: Edward Goldston, 1942), pp. 33–49; for other aspects of Pensa's work, see D. Penslar, *Shylock's Children* (California University Press, 2001), pp. 60 ff., and H. Kellenbenz (ed.), *Confusion de Confusiones* (Cambridge, MA: Harvard University Press, 1957).
38. Y. Kaplan, 'Die portugiesischen Juden und die Modernisierung', in A. Nechama *et al.* (eds), *Jüdische Lebenswelten* (Frankfurt am Main: Suhrkamp, 1992), pp. 303–17, esp. p. 310.
39. Mechoulan, *Etre Juif*, pp. 56–8.
40. This is an *avant-goût* of a future which will show the consequence if the synagogue is 'invested with the value of a substitute temple'. A place of transition becomes a place of permanence; in the age of emancipation, memory is modified – 'and it is with the force of logic that by dint of seeking to make itself out to be a sacred building the synagogue ends by aping the church' (Dominique Jarrassé, 'Les Mémoires du Temple', in E. Benbassa (ed.), *Transmission et Passages en Monde Juif* (Paris: Publisud, 1997), pp. 473–85, here p. 480.
41. Swetchinski, *Reluctant Cosmopolitans*, p. 179.
42. Quoted H. P. H. Nusteling, 'The Jews in the Republic of the United Provinces', in J. Israel and R. Salverda (eds), *Dutch Jewry* (Leiden: Brill, 2002), pp. 45–57, here p. 46.

43. See Y. Yerushalmi, *Anusim ha-hozrim la-yahadut ba-me'ah ha-17* (Jerusalem: PWCJS, 1972), II, pp. 201–9.
44. Talya Fishman (ed. and trans.), *Shaking the Pillars of Exile* (Stanford University Press, 1997), p. 91.
45. Ibid., pp. 140–1.
46. C. Gebhardt (ed.), *Die Schriften des Uriel da Costa* (Amsterdam: Curis Societatis Spinozanae, 1922), pp. 150 ff.
47. See Uriel da Costa's *Examination of Pharisaic Traditions*, ed. and trans. H. P. Salomon and I. S. D. Sassoon (Leiden: Brill, 1993), esp. ch. 1; there is a summary of da Costa's *Propostas* in J. J. Petuchowski, *The Theology of Haham David Nieto* (New York: Ktav, 1970), pp. 35 ff.
48. See da Costa's 'Exemplar humanae vitae' (1639), in Salomon and Sassoon, op. cit., appendix 3; also J. Kaplan, 'The intellectual ferment in the Spanish-Portuguese Community of 17th century Amsterdam', in H. Beinart (ed.), *The Sephardi Legacy*, II (Jerusalem: Magnes Press, 1992), pp. 288–314.

3 On French Soil

1. Jules Bauer, 'Un Commencement d'Insurrection au Quartier Juif d'Avignon au XVIIe Siècle', *REJ*, 38 (1899), pp. 123–36.
2. M. Calmann, *The Carrière of Carpentras* (Littman Library: Oxford University Press, 1984), p. 174.
3. Hugues Jean de Dianoux, 'Les Juifs d'Avignon et du Comtat Venaissin', in B. Blumenkranz (ed.), *Histoire des Juifs en France* (Toulouse: Privat, 1972), pp. 193–218; Armand Lunel, *Juifs du Languedoc, de la Provence* (Paris: Albin Michel, 1975), p. 127; Simone Mrejen-O'Hara, 'Pratiques Religieuses dans les "Quatre Saintes Communautés" d'Avignon et du Comtat Venaissin', *Archives Juives*, 28 (1995), pp. 12–13.
4. Calmann, *Carpentras*, pp. 62–3.
5. R. Anchel, *Les Juifs de France* (Paris: Janin, 1946), pp. 154–5 (Mémoire sur les Trois Evêchés, 1699–1700).
6. H. Graetz, 'Eine historische Notiz', *MGWJ*, XXI (1872), pp. 44–7; A. Hertzberg, *The French Enlightenment and the Jews* (Columbia University Press, 1968), p. 120.
7. Roos, *Relations*, pp. 175, 30–1.
8. B. Blumenkranz (ed.), *Documents Modernes sur les Juifs* (Toulouse: Privat, 1979), No. AN 0009 E 1995; hereafter referred to as Blumenkranz, *Documents*. For the total of 480, see also the letters edited by S. Kerner referred to in n. 27 below (pp. 244–8).
9. G. Weill, 'Recherches sur la démographie de juifs d'Alsace du XVI au XVIII Siècles', *REJ*, Nos. 129–30 (1970–1), pp. 51–67; see also F. Raphaël and R. Weyl (eds), *Juifs en Alsace* (Toulouse: Privat, 1977), p. 361.
10. Roos, *Relations*, p. 113.
11. Lemalet, 'Juifs et intendants au XVIIe Siècle', *XVIIe Siècle*, 46 (1994), p. 300; Roos, *Relations*, p. 115; see also Z. Szajkowski, *The Economic Status of the Jews in Alsace, Metz and Lorraine* (New York: Editions Historiques, 1954), p. 30.
12. Roos, *Relations*, pp. 148–9.
13. R. Néher-Bernheim (ed.), *Documents Inédits sur l'Entrée des Juifs dans la Société Française* (Diaspora Research Institute, Tel Aviv University, 1977), pp. 103 ff. (Hereafter referred to as Néher-Bernheim, *Documents*.)
14. J. R. Berkovitz, 'Patterns of rabbinic succession in modern France', *JH*, 13 (1999), pp. 59–82, esp. p. 74.

15. Szajkowski, *Economic Status of the Jews in Alsace*, p. 62; Raphaël and Weyl (eds), *Juifs en Alsace*, pp. 362, 372, 375; Archives Israélites, III, pp. 686–9; see also C. Hoffmann, *L'Alsace au dix-huitième siècle*, 4 vols. (Colmar: Huffel, 1906–7) IV, p. 370.
16. Szajkowski, *Economic Status of the Jews in Alsace*, pp. 52–3; for the text of the petition see ibid., pp. 146–9.
17. P. A. Meyer, *La Communauté Juive de Metz au XVIIIe Siècle* (Nancy: Serpenoise, 1993), p. 93.
18. Szajkowski, *Economic Status of the Jews in Alsace*, p.142; see also Blumenkranz, *Documents*, AN 0025 G7 380; AN 0040 G7 544.
19. Quoted Roos, *Relations*, p. 306.
20. Ibid., pp. 92ff; Lemalet, 'Juifs et intendants', pp. 287–302, esp. p. 296 ff; Szajkowski, *Economic Status of the Jews in Alsace*, p. 42, fn. 94; Blumenkranz, *Documents*, AN 0426 F12.
21. Quoted Lemalet, 'Juifs et intendants', p. 293.
22. For the origin of this term see Françoise Job, *Les Juifs de Lunéville aux XVIIIe et XIXe Siècles* (Presses Universitaires de Nancy, 1989), p. 19.
23. Blumenkranz, *Documents*, AN 0045 G7 1633; AN 0042 G7 1633; AN 0024 G7 378; Lemalet, 'Juifs et intendants', pp. 291ff.; see also Anchel, Juifs de France, p. 165.
24. Meyer, *Communauté Juive*, p. 95.
25. Ibid., p. 8; Lemalet, 'Juifs et intendants', pp. 290ff; Blumenkranz, *Documents*, AG 0034 AI 1583; AG 0056 AI 1754; AG 0064 AI 1851; Anchel, *Juifs de France*, pp. 178ff.
26. Blumenkranz, *Documents*, AN 0080 AI 1872; AG 0097 AI 1971; AG 0126 AI 2167; AG 0129 AI 2167; AG 0196 AI 2396.
27. S. Kerner, 'Les Démarches des Envoyés de la Communauté Juive de Metz à Paris et à Versailles Relative à la "Taxe Brancas"', *Annales de l'Est*, 26 (1974), pp. 217–64.
28. Blumenkranz, *Documents*, AG 0005 AI 1767; AG 0008 AI 1289; AG 0035 AI 1583; AG 0163 AI 2391; AG 0172 AI 2395; AG 0167 AI 2393; AG 0205 AI 2420; 'As for their enterprise in supplying the troops of the king', commented one report, otherwise unfavourable, on Alsatian Jewry, 'the frugality, industry and laborious activity of the Jews ... are an infinite and certain resource. It would be difficult for a French army to subsist without their help' (quoted Job, *Juifs de Lunéville*, p. 19).
29. Meyer, *Communauté Juive*, pp. 97–8.
30. Ibid., pp. 47 ff.
31. Blumenkranz, *Documents*, AG0216 AI 2679.
32. Meyer, *Communauté Juive*, p. 78.
33. Abraham Cahen, 'Le Rabbinat de Metz Pendant la Période Française (1567–1871)', *REJ*, VII-VIII (1883–4), pp. 111ff.
34. *The Life of Glückel of Hameln, 1646–1724, written by herself*, Eng. trans. (London: East and West Library, 1962), pp. 176–7; Cahen, 'Rabbinat de Metz', p. 219; Meyer, *Communauté Juive*, p. 67.
35. David Kaufmann, 'Extraits de l'Ancien Livre de la Communauté de Metz', *REJ*, XIX-XX (1889), pp. 115–30; N. Netter, 'Die Schuldennot der jüdischen Gemeinde Metz, 1791–1854', *MGWJ*, 57 (1913), pp. 593–619.
36. Abraham Cahen, 'Enseignement Obligatoire', *REJ*, I (1880), pp. 303–5.
37. Hertzberg, *French Enlightenment and the Jews*, pp. 168–9; S. Schwarzfuchs, 'The Metz Community in the 18th Century', manuscript lecture, pp. 5–6.
38. Quoted Meyer, *Communauté Juive*, p. 94.
39. Kaufmann, 'Extraits de l'Ancien Livré', p. 116.
40. Hertzberg, *French Enlightenment and the Jews*, p. 233; Simon Schwarzfuchs (ed.), 'Le Memorbuch de Metz', p. VIII (manuscript); Meyer, *Communauté Juive*, p. 70.

41. A. Cahen, *Règlements somptuaires de la Communauté Juive de Metz* (Versailles: Cerf et Fils, 1881); see also A. Rubens, *A History of Jewish Costume* (London: Vallentine Mitchell, 1967), pp. 196–200.
42. N. Netter, 'Die Schuldennot der Jüdischen Gemeinde Metz, 1791–1854', *MGWJ*, 57 (1913), *passim*; Szajkowski, *Economic Status of the Jews in Alsace*, p. 71.
43. Kerner, 'Les Démarches des Envoyés', *passim*.
44. Meyer, *Communauté Juive*, pp. 70–1.
45. Ibid., p. 104; Zosa Szajkowski, *Jews and the French Revolutions of 1789, 1830 and 1848* (New York: Ktav, 1970), pp. 757–8.
46. Hertzberg, *French Enlightenment and the Jews*, p. 128; Gilbert Cahen, 'La Région Lorraine', in Blumenkranz, *Juifs en France*, pp. 108 ff.
47. M. Lemalet, 'Vie et Mort de Marc Terquem, banquier Juif de Metz', *Archives Juives*, 29 (1996), pp. 36–47.
48. Hertzberg, *French Enlightenment and the Jews*, p. 127.
49. Blumenkranz, *Documents*, AG 0109 AI 2046; AG 0115 AI 2095; AG 0117 AI 2095 AG 0125 AI 2167; AN 0162; Roos, *Relations*, p. 298.
50. R. Jonathan Eibeschutz, *Ya'arot Dvash*, ed. R. Isaiah Pick, 2 vols, 2nd edn (Jerusalem: Machon Or Ha-Sefer, 1988), I, pp. 111, 289; II, p. 321; also M. Saperstein (ed. and trans.), *Jewish Preaching 1200–1800, An Anthology* (New Haven, CT: Yale University Press, 1989), pp. 329 ff.
51. F. Malino, 'Resistance and Rebellion in Eighteenth Century France', *TJHSE*, XXX (1987–8), pp. 55–70, here p. 67.
52. Cahen, 'Rabbinat de Metz,' p. 104.
53. Ibid., pp. 262–6; F. Malino, 'The Jews and the Parlement of Metz', in G. Dahan (ed.), *Les Juifs au Regard de l'Histoire* (Paris: Picard, 1985), pp. 327–41.
54. The headings of the 33 sections are listed in Blumenkranz, *Documents*, No. AN 0074 HI 1641.
55. For all the above see Cahen, 'Rabbinat de Metz'; and Malino, 'Resistance and Rebellion', *passim*.
56. See Françoise Hildesheimer, 'Une Créature de Richelieu: Alphonse Lopez, le "Seigneur Hebreo"', in Dahan, *Les Juifs au Regard de l'Histoire*, pp. 293–9; see also B. Bedos-Rezak, 'Tolérance et Raison d'État', in H. Méchoulan (ed.), *L'Etat Baroque* (Paris: Vrin, 1985), pp. 244–83; S. Simonsohn, 'Havat-Da'at Shel Ha-Sorbonne be-davar Yishuv Yishuv be-Tsarfat (1633)', *Tsiyon*, Nos. 23–4 (1958–9), pp. 98–101.
57. G. Nahon, 'Les Rapports des Communautés judéo-portugaises de France avec celles d'Amsterdam au XVIIe et au XVIIIe Siècles', *SR*, X (1976), pp. 37–78; Elie Szapiro, 'Le Sud-Ouest 1501–1789', in Blumenkranz, *Juifs en France*, pp. 221–61, esp. pp. 229 ff.
58. For some of the contrasting viewpoints, see the material cited in F. Malino, *The Sephardic Jews of Bordeaux* (Alabama: University of Alabama Press, 1978), p. 120, fn. 47; also Cecil Roth, 'Quatre Lettres d'Elie de Montalte', *REJ*, 87 (1929), pp. 137–65; idem, 'Aboab's Proselytisation of the Marranos', *JQR*, NS 23 (1932), pp. 121–62; S. Schwarzfuchs, *Les Juifs de France* (Paris: Albin Michel, 1975), p. 143.
59. H. Léon, *Histoire des Juifs de Bayonne* (Paris: Durlacher, 1893), p. 19; T. Malvezin, *Histoire des Juifs à Bordeaux* (Marseilles: Lafitte Reprint, 1976), pp. 113–14; Méchoulan, *Etat Baroque*, p. 250.
60. G. Nahon, 'The Sephardim of France', in R. Barnett and W. Schwab (eds), *The Sephardi Heritage*, II (Grendon, Northants: Gibraltar Books, 1989), pp. 46–74.
61. Mme. d'Aulnoy, 'Voyage d'Espagne', *Revue hispanique*, 67 (1926), pp. 140 ff.; Malvezin, *Les Juifs à Bordeaux*, pp. 124 ff.
62. Léon, *Juifs de Bayonne*, pp. 22–3; Hertzberg, *French Enlightenment and the Jews*, pp. 50–1.

63. One fortunate exception was the dancing master Quiros: the town-governor, Count de Gramont, gave him permission to have a room in town 'and to sleep there so that he might be on hand to give dancing lessons to his pupils, before and after supper, during winter' (Léon, *Juifs de Bayonne*, p. 67); generally, see Anne Zintz, 'Une niche juridique – l'installation des Juifs à Saint Esprit-lès-Bayonne au XVIIe siècle', *Annales*, 49 (1994), pp. 639–69.

64. Blumenkranz, *Documents*, AG0144, No. 241; AN0436F12; see also Léon, *Juifs de Bayonne*, pp. 36 ff., 63 ff.

65. J. Cavignac, 'A Bordeaux et Bayonne', in B. Blumenkranz (ed.), *Les Juifs en France au XVIIIe Siècle* (Paris: Commission française des Archives juives, 1994), pp. 53–72.

66. Lemalet, 'Juifs et *Intendants*', pp. 293 ff.

67. Malvezin, *Juifs à Bordeaux*, pp. 172 ff.

68. Ibid., p. 231.

69. Mlle, Giteau, 'Vie Économique et Classes Sociales dans le Monde Laïque', in R. Boutrouche (ed.), *Bordeaux de 1453 à 1715* (Bordeaux, 1966), pp. 455–506.

70. For the substance of this material I am indebted to Nahon, *Rapports*, and Evelyne Oliel-Grausz, 'La Circulation du Personel Rabbinque dans les Communautés de la Diaspora Sépharade au XVIIIe Siècle', in E. Benbassa (ed.), *Transmission et Passages en Monde Juif* (Paris: Publisud, 1997), pp. 313–34; see also the article by C. L. Wilke, 'Un Judaïsme Clandestin dans la France du XVIIe Siècle', ibid., pp. 281–311.

71. *Registre*, Nos. 9, 11.

72. Miriam Bodian, *Hebrews of the Portuguese Nation* (Bloomington: Indiana University Press, 1997), p. 140.

73. R. Menkis, 'Patriarchs and Patricians', in F. Malino and D. Sorkin (eds), *From East and West* (Oxford: Blackwell, 1990), pp. 11–45; G. Nahon, 'From New Christians to the Portuguese Jewish Nation in France', in Beinart, *Sephardi Legacy II*, p. 359.

74. See Bodian, *Hebrews of the Portuguese Nation*, p. 141; Nahon, *Rapports*, p. 61.

75. Malvezin, *Juifs à Bordeaux*, pp. 172–3, 200; *Registre*, No. 110.

76. Cavignac, 'A Bordeaux et Bayonne', pp. 53–72.

77. Blumenkranz, *Documents*, AN1496 Marine B7 204; Léon, *Juifs de Bayonne*, p. 140; Nahon, *Rapports*, pp. 158–9, fn. 301; Georges Cirot, *Les Juifs de Bordeaux* (Bordeaux: Feret, 1920), pp. 48–9.

78. *Registre*, App, II, pp. 599–605.

79. Malino, *Sephardic Jews of Bordeaux*, p. 6; Malvezin, *Juifs à Bordeaux*, pp. 172 ff., 183.

80. Blumenkranz, *Documents*, AN0427 F12; AN0004 E1839; AN0005 E1955.

81. Danièle and Carole Iancu, *Les Juifs du Midi* (Avignon: A. Barthélemy, 1995), pp. 160 ff.

82. Blumenkranz, *Documents*, AN0430 F12, AN0461–62 F12, AN0464–5 F12, AN0467 F12.

83. René Moulinas, 'Le Conseil du Roi et le Commerce des Juifs d'Avignon en France', *18e Siècle*, No.13 (1981), pp. 169–79.

84. Malvezin, *Juifs à Bordeaux*, pp. 174–5; *Registre*, No. 33.

85. Malvezin, *Juifs à Bordeaux*, p. 177; see also Moulinas, 'Conseil du Roi', p.171.

86. Hertzberg, *French Enlightenment and the Jews*, p. 95, fn. 47.

87. Malvezin, *Juifs à Bordeaux*, pp. 191 ff.

4 Resettlement in London

1. J. I. Israel, 'The Dutch Sephardic Colonization Movement', in Y. Kaplan *et al.* (eds), *Menasseh ben Israel and His World* (Leiden: Brill, 1989), pp. 139–63; L. Wolf, 'American Elements in the Re-Settlement', *TJHSE*, III (1899), pp. 76–93, esp. pp. 80 ff.

2. See G. Lloyd-Jones, *The Discovery of Hebrew in Tudor England* (Manchester University Press, 1983); W. Horbury, 'John Spencer (1630–93) and Hebrew study', *Corpus Christi College (Cambridge) Association Newsletter*, no. 78 (1999), pp. 12–23.
3. J. Gwyer, 'The case of Dr Lopez', *TJHSE*, XVI (1945–1951), pp. 163–84; Edgar Samuel, 'Dr Rodrigo Lopes' Last Speech from the Scaffold at Tyburn', ibid., XXX (1987–88), pp. 51–3; F. D. Zeman, 'The Amazing Career of Dr Rodrigo Lopez', *Bulletin of the History of Medicine*, 39 (1965), pp. 295–308; Charles Meyers, 'Debt in Elizabethan England: The Adventures of Dr Hector Nunez, Physician and Merchant', *TJHSE*, XXXIV (1997), pp. 125–40.
4. Christopher Marlowe, *The Jew of Malta*, I, 2; see also John Gross, *Shylock* (London: Chatto & Windus, 1992), *passim*.
5. Israel Abrahams, 'Joachim Gaunse', *TJHSE*, IV (1899–1901), pp. 83–101; Lewis Feuer, 'Francis Bacon and the Jews: who was the Jew in the New Atlantis?', *TJHSE*, XXIX (1982–6), pp. 1–25; R. Jan van Pelt, 'The Instauratio Magna and the Jews', in J. Michman and T. Levie (eds), *Dutch Jewish History* (Jerusalem, 1984), pp. 53–68; generally, see David Katz, *Philosemitism and the Readmission of the Jews to England 1603–1655* (Oxford: Clarendon Press, 1982).
6. Quoted Louis Hyman, 'The Jews of Ireland' (London: JHSE, 1972), p. 11; see also T. Rabb, 'The Stirrings of the 1590s and the Return of the Jews to England', *TJHSE*, XXVI (1979), pp. 26–33.
7. E. N. Adler, *About Hebrew Manuscripts* (Oxford University Press, 1905), pp. 67–77.
8. Rivka Schatz, 'Emdato shel Menasseh b. Israel klapei Ha-Meshihiyut', *Bar-Ilan Annual*, XXII–XXIII (1988), pp. 429–47.
9. L. Wolf, *Menasseh b. Israel's Mission to Oliver Cromwell* (London, 1901), pp. 73–103, esp. p. 100; see also Israel, 'Dutch Sephardic Colonization Movement', pp. 139–63.
10. Avrom Saltman, *The Jewish Question in 1655 – Studies in Prynne's Demurrer* (Ramat-Gan: Bar-Ilan University Press, 1995), pp. 116ff.; see also N. Osterman, 'The Controversy over the Proposed Re-admission of the Jews to England (1655)', *JSS*, III (1941), pp. 301–28.
11. Quoted David Katz, *The Jews in the History of England 1485–1850* (Oxford: Clarendon Press, 1994), p. 136; L. Wolf, 'The First English Jew', *TJHSE*, II (1894–5), pp. 14–48.
12. Menasseh b. Israel, 'Vindiciae Judaeorum', in Wolf, *Mission…*, pp. 144–5.
13. W. Bray (ed.), *The Diary of John Evelyn* (London: Warne, n.d.), p. 245.
14. For examples, see Lucien Wolf, 'Status of the Jews in England after the Re-settlement', *TJHSE*, IV (1903), pp. 177–93, esp. p. 184.
15. W. S. Samuel, 'The First London Synagogue of the Resettlement', *TJHSE*, X (1924), pp. 1–147, and appx. I, pp. 49ff.
16. L. D. Barnett (ed.), *El Libro de los Acuerdos* (Oxford University Press, 1931), p. 15.
17. R. C. Latham and W. Matthews (eds), *The Diary of Samuel Pepys* (London: HarperCollins, 1995), IV, p. 335 (entry for 14 October 1663).
18. H. S. Q. Henriques, 'Proposals for Special Taxation of the Jews after the Revolution', *TJHSE*, IX (1918–20), pp. 39–66, esp. p. 65; J. M. Ross, 'Naturalisation of the Jews in England', ibid., XXIV (1970–3), pp. 59–72; Norma Perry, 'Anglo-Jewry, the Law, Religious Conviction and Self Interest (1655–1753)', *Journal of European Studies*, XIV (1984), pp. 1–23.
19. H. S. Q. Henriques, *Jews and the English Law* (Oxford University Press, 1908), pp. 170–1; James Picciotto, *Sketches of Anglo-Jewish History*, ed. Israel Finestein (London: Soncino, 1956), p. 100.
20. See Katz, *Jews in the History of England*, p. 321.

21. C. Tucker, 'Jewish marriages and divorces in England until 1940', *Genealogists' Magazine*, 24, no. 3 (September 1992), pp. 87–93.
22. Picciotto, *Sketches*, pp. 87, 456; Henriques, *Jews and the English Law*, pp. 22–3.
23. Picciotto, *Sketches*, pp. 33–4.
24. R. D. Barnett, 'The Correspondence of the Mahamad', *TJHSE*, xx (1964), pp. 1–50, esp. pp. 2–3.
25. M. Bodian, 'Biblical Hebrews and the Rhetoric of Republicanism', *AJSR*, xxii (1997), pp. 199–221, esp. p. 207; L. Barnett, *El Libro*, p. 3.
26. See I. Epstein, 'Ascama I of the Spanish and Portuguese Jewish Congregation of London', in M. Ben-Horin (ed.), *Studies in Honour of Abraham A. Neuman* (Leiden: Brill, 1962), pp. 170–214, esp. p. 174.
27. See Barnett, *El Libro*, pp. 1–14.
28. Perry, 'Anglo-Jewry, the law, religious conviction', p. 5. Samuel Sasportas later had a chequered career as a broker on the Royal Exchange: *TJHSE, Miscellanies*, iii (1937), pp. 81–2.
29. Haham Dr Moses Gaster, *History of the Ancient Synagogue of the Spanish and Portuguese Jews* (London: published by author, 5661–1901), p. 88.
30. *The Economic Writings of Sir William Petty* (Cambridge University Press, 1899), p. 84.
31. Katz, *Jews in the History of England*, pp. 137 ff.; Barnett, *El Libro*, pp. 58–9; L.Wolf, 'The Jewry of the Restoration', *TJHSE*, v (1902–05), pp. 5–33; Edgar Samuel, 'Antonio Rodrigues Robles, *c*.1620–1688', *TJHSE*, xxxvii (2001), pp. 113–15.
32. I. Tishby (ed.), 'Yediot Hadashot al kehilat Ha-'anusim' be-London', in A. Mirsky *et al.* (eds), *Galut ahar Golah* (Jerusalem: Ben-Zvi Institute, 1988), pp.470–96, here p. 475. (This is a selection of Sasportas's letters from London, 1664–5.)
33. Wolf, 'Status of the Jews in England', pp. 177–93; R. D. Barnett, 'Mr Pepys' contacts with the Spanish and Portuguese Jews of London,, *TJHSE*, xxix (1988), pp. 27–33; L. D. Barnett (ed.), *Bevis Marks Records* (Oxford University Press, 1940), I, pp. 1–15.
34. Henriques, 'Proposals for Special Taxation', pp. 39–66; Oscar Rabinowicz, *Sir Solomon de Medina* (London: JHSE, 1974), ch. 6.
35. G. Yogev, *Diamonds and Coral – Anglo-Dutch Jews and 18th Century Trade* (Leicester University Press, 1978); Eli Faber; *Jews, Slaves and the Slave Trade* (New York University Press, 1998), pp. 22 ff.; M. Woolf, 'Foreign trade of London Jews in the 17th century', *TJHSE*, xxiv (1975), pp. 38–58; for the activities of an individual trader, see Edgar Samuel, 'Manuel Levy Duarte, 1631–1714, An Amsterdam merchant jeweller', *TJHSE*, xxvii (1982), pp. 11–31.
36. Sir Josiah Child, *A New Discourse of Trade* (London, 1693), ch. 7, pp. 1 ff.
37. G. Cantor, 'The Rise and Fall of Emanuel Mendes da Costa', *EHR* cxvi, no. 467 (2001), pp. 584–603, esp. p. 585.
38. Barnett, *El Libro*, pp. 28, 78–9.
39. A. S. Diamond, 'The Community of the Resettlement 1656–1684', *TJHSE*, xxiv (1975), pp. 134–50.
40. Tishby, 'Yediot Hadashot', pp. 476 ff.; A. S. Diamond, 'The Cemetery of the Resettlement', *TJHSE*, xix (1960), pp. 163–90, esp. p. 185.
41. Y. Kaplan, 'The Jewish Profile of the Spanish-Portuguese Community of London during the Seventeenth Century', *Judaism*, xli (1992), pp. 229–40; T. Endelman, 'Jewish Communal Structure in Britain from the Resettlement to the Present', in *Festschrift Julius Carlebach* (Heidelberg: Winter, 1992), pp. 1–16; Barnett, 'Mr Pepys' contacts', p. 30.
42. This letter is quoted at length in M. Goldish, 'Jews, Christians and Conversos', *JJS*, xlv (1994), pp. 227–57, here p. 238.

5 At Peace in the Post-War World

1. Joseph Ha-Cohen, *Divrei Ha-Yamim* (Amsterdam: Proops, n.d.), p. 48b; R. David Gans, *Tsemah David* (Frankfurt/Amsterdam, 5452 [1692]), pp. 69a–b.
2. See C. M. Clark, *The Politics of Conversion* (Oxford: Clarendon Press, 1995), *passim*.
3. J. R. Wolf, 'Zwischen Hof und Stadt', pp. 50–79; G. Wolf, *Zur Geschichte der Juden in Worms* (Breslau, 1862), p. 92; J. F. Battenberg, 'Zwischen Integration und Segregation', *Aschkenas*, VI (1996), pp. 421–54, esp. pp. 421 ff.; H. Franke, *Geschichte und Schicksal der Juden in Heilbronn*, Stadt Archiv, 1963, p. 49 ff.; Daniel Cohen, 'Die Landjudenschaften in Hessen-Darmstadt', in *Neunhundert Jahre Geschichte der Juden in Hessen* (Wiesbaden: Kommission für die Geschichte der Juden in Hessen, 1983), pp. 151–214.
4. Generally, see R. J. W. Evans, *The Making of the Habsburg Monarchy* (Oxford: Clarendon Press, 1979), ch. 4.
5. Ivo Cerman, 'Anti-Jewish Superstition and the Expulsion of the Jews from Vienna, 1670', *Judaica Bohemiae*, XXXVI (2001), pp. 5–30.
6. G. Wolf, *Geschichte der Juden in Wien* (Vienna: Holder, 1876), p. 49.
7. G. Scholem, *Sabbatai Sevi, The Mystical Messiah 1626–1676*, Engl. trans. (London: Routledge, 1973), pp. 559 ff.
8. Rabbi M. M. Krochmal, *Tsemah Tsedek*, repr. (Jerusalem, 1982), No. 106 (final paragraph).
9. D. Kaufmann, *Die Letzte Vertreibung der Juden aus Wien* (Vienna: Konegen, 1889), pp. 60 ff.; M. Grunwald, *Samuel Oppenheimer und sein Kreis* (Vienna: Braumüller, 1913), pp. 10 ff., 27; for living conditions in the ghetto, see M. Grunwald, *Vienna* (Philadelphia, PA: JPSA, 1936), pp. 107 ff.
10. Pribram, *Urkunden*, I, Nos. 108, 110; 115: 1–3; see also Grunwald, *Oppenheimer*, p. 270.
11. Grunwald, *Oppenheimer*, pp. 30 ff.; see also R. Gershom Ashkenazi, *Avodat Gershuni*, repr. (Jerusalem, 1982), No. 48.
12. J. Bérenger, 'Les Juifs et l'Antisémitisme dans l'Autriche du 17e Siècle', in *Etudes Européennes* (Paris: Publications de la Sorbonne, 1973), pp. 181–92.
13. Pribram, *Urkunden*, I, No. 115: 3.
14. Ibid., No. 155: 4, fn. 6.
15. See Kaufmann, *Letzte Vertreibung*, p. 113.
16. R. Jacob Sasportas, *Ohel Ya'akov*, Nos. 77–8; see also Kaufmann, *Letzte Vertreibung*, pp. 129–135.
17. See F. Kobler (ed.), *Juden und Judentum in deutschen Briefen* (Vienna: Saturn, 1935), pp. 37–8.
18. Pribram, *Urkunden*, I, No. 118; see also Wolf, *Juden in Wien*, pp. 52 ff.
19. Battenberg, *Des Kaisers Kammerknechte*, pp. 580–1; M. Breuer, *German-Jewish History in Modern Times*, I (New York: Columbia University Press, 1996), pp. 155 ff.; see also H.-J. Schoeps, *Barocke Juden, Christen, Judenchristen* (Berne: Francke, 1965).
20. *The Life of Glückel of Hameln Written by Herself*, Engl. trans. (London: East and West Library, 1962), pp. 77 ff.; R. Yair Hayyim Bachrach, *Havot Ya'ir*, repr. (Jerusalem, 1987), No. 136; see also E. Schohat, *Im Hilufei Tekufot* (Jerusalem: Mossad Bialik, 1960), ch. 3, *passim*.
21. See Nos. 5, 9, 11 in Juspa's *Ma'aseh Nissim*, in Eidelberg, *R. Juspa*.
22. See Jakob Horovitz, 'Aus der Oxforder Handschrift des Josif Omez', in *Festschrift Jakob Freimann* (Berlin, 1937), pp. 92–3.

23. Bachrach, *Havot Ya'ir*, No. 1, Hasaga 11–12, end; see also E. Schohat, 'Hitarut Shel Yehudei Germaniya ba-svivotam', *Tsiyon*, XXI (1956), pp. 207–35, esp. pp. 229 ff.
24. See N. Römer, *Tradition und Akkulturation* (Münster: Waxman, 1995), p. 21.
25. S. Volkov, *Die Juden in Deutschland 1780–1918* (Munich: Oldenburg, 1994), p. 4; M. Breuer, 'Jüdische Religion und Kultur in den ländlichen Gemeinden 1600–1800', in M. Richarz and R. Rürüp (ed.), *Jüdisches Leben auf dem Lande* (Tübingen: Mohr, 1997), pp. 69–78.
26. Priebatsch, 'Die Judenpolitik', pp. 564–651, esp. pp. 598–9.
27. F. Battenberg, 'Schutz, Toleranz oder Vertreibung', in E. G. Franz (ed.), *Juden als Darmstädter Bürger* (Darmstadt: Roether, 1984), pp. 33–49, here p. 47; J. R. Wolf, 'Zwischen Hof und Stadt', ibid., pp. 50–79, here p. 66; R. Kestenberg-Gladstein, 'Wirtschaftsgeschichte der böhmischen Landjuden', *Judaica Bohemiae*, III (1967), pp. 101–33, here p. 109.
28. R. Kiessling, 'Zwischen Vertreibung und Emanzipation', in R. Kiessling (ed.), *Judengereinden in Schwaben* (Berlin: Academie, 1995), pp. 154–80; F. Hundsnurscher und G. Taddey (eds), *Die Jüdischen Gemeinden in Baden* (Stuttgart: Kohlhammer Verlag, 1968), pp. 6, 56, 122, 172; Utz Jeggle, *Judendörfer in Württemberg* (Tübingen: Tübinger Verein für Volkskunde, 1999), pp. 12–3.
29. Kiessling, 'Zwischen Vertreibung', p. 157.
30. See the material cited in M. Hildesheimer, 'Yahadut Ashkenas ba-me'ah ha-17 al pi Ha-She'elot u-Tshuvot', MA Thesis, University of Bar-Ilan, Ramat-Gan, 1972, pp. 176 ff.
31. Quoted I. Zinberg, *A History of Jewish Literature*, Engl. trans. (New York: Ktav, 1975), VII, pp. 298–9; see also S. Rohrbacher, 'Stadt und Land', in Richarz and Rürüp (eds), *Jüdisches Leben auf dem Lande*, pp. 37–58, esp. p. 45 and the literature quoted there; R. Samuel Halevy, *Nahlat Shivah* (Fürth, 1692), No. 77.
32. A. Kober, 'Die deutschen Kaiser und die Wormser Juden', in Ernst Roth (ed.), *Die alte Synagoge zu Worms* (Frankfurt am Main: Ner Tamid, 1961), pp. 182–98.
33. M. Freudenthal, 'Die Verfassungsurkunde einer reichsritterlichen Judenschaft', *ZGJD*, I (1929), pp. 44–68, esp. p. 53.
34. H. J. Behr, 'Judenschaft, Landstände und Fürsten in den geistlichen Staaten Westfalens im 18. Jahrhundert', in P. Freimark (ed.), *Gedenkschrift für B. Brilling* (Hamburg: Christians, 1988), pp. 121–5; M. Evers, *Die Geschichte der Juden in der Stadt Warburg* (Warburg: Hermes, 1978), pp. 16 ff.
35. L. Trepp, *Die Oldenburger Judenschaft* (Oldenburg: Holzberg, 1973), pp. 23–4.
36. Breuer, *German-Jewish History in Modern Times*, p. 199.
37. Daniel Cohen (ed.), *Die Landjudenschaften in Deutschland als Organe jüdischer Selbstverwaltung* (Jerusalem: Israel Academy of Sciences, 1996), I, No. 7:2:10.
38. Ibid., No. 8: 21. In Bayreuth the marriage broker received 2 per cent of the first 100 units of the sum settled on the bride, then 1 per cent of the remainder (Cohen, *Landjudenschaften in Deutschland*, II, No. 22:3; see also L. Munk, 'Die Constitution der sämmtlichen hessischen Judenschaft 1690', in *Jubelschrift zum siebzigsten Geburtstag Dr. I. Hildesheimer* (Berlin: 1890), pp. 69–82.
39. B. Altmann, 'The autonomous federation of Jewish communities in Paderborn', *JSS* III (1941), pp. 159–88; D. Aschoff, 'Das Münsterländische Judentum', *Theokratia*, III (1973–75), pp. 125–84, Docs Nos. 10–11; Cohen, *Landjudenschaften in Deutschland*, I, No. 7:2:42.
40. Cohen, *Landjudenschaften in Deutschland*, I, No. 7:1:12–15.
41. Ibid., No. 8:43; J. R. Wolf, 'Zwischen Hof und Stadt', p. 54.
42. Altmann, 'The autonomous federation', pp. 159–88, esp. p. 167.

43. Cohen, *Landjudenschaften in Deutschland*, ι, 7:2:6; Idem, 'Ha-Va'ad Ha-Katan shel bnei Medinat Ansbach', in Sh. Ettinger *et al.* (eds), *Sefer Yovel le-Yitzhak Baer* (Jerusalem: Israel Academy of Sciences, 1986), pp. 351–75.
44. Cohen, 'Die Entwicklung der Landesrabbinate'.
45. Juspa, Minhagim, ιι, No. 293.
46. F. Battenberg, 'Schutz, Toleranz, oder Vertreibung', in E. G. Franz (ed.), *Juden als Darmstädter Bürger* (Darmstadt: Roether, 1984), pp. 33–49, esp. p. 48.
47. Cohen, 'Die Entwicklung der Landesrabbinate'.
48. G. Renda, 'Fürth, das "bayerische Jerusalem"', in M. Treml (ed.), *Geschichte und Kultur der Juden in Bayern* (Munich: Saur, 1988), pp. 225–44, esp. pp. 228–9.
49. N. Ferguson, *The Cash Nexus* (Harmondsworth: Penguin, 2001), pp. 29 ff., 43 ff.
50. Hundsnurscher und Taddey (eds), *Jüdische Gemeinden in Baden*, pp. 186 ff. It is worth pointing out that in 1691 the Mannheim authorities abolished the compulsory wearing by Jews of a yellow wheel (G. Kisch, 'The Yellow Badge in History', *HJ*, ιv (1942), pp. 95–144.
51. Schnee, *Hoffinanz*, ιιι, 19, 75–6; ι, 192.
52. F. Redlich, 'The German military enterpriser and his workforce', *Vierteljahrschrift für Sozial- und Wirtschaftgeschichte*, Beiheft 47 (1961), ι, p. 166.
53. Battenberg, 'Schutz, Toleranz, oder Vertreibung', in Franz (ed.), *Juden als Darmstädter Bürger*, p. 40.
54. Schnee, *Hoffinanz*, v, p. 25.
55. E. Herzfeld, 'Förderung gewerblicher Entwicklung durch Juden in Hinterpommern im 18. Jahrhundert', in M. Heitman and J. H. Schoeps (eds), *Geschichte und Kultur der Juden in Pommern* (Hildesheim: Olms, 1995), pp. 239–54; idem., *Jüdische Kaufleute in Hinterpommern*, pp. 265–77; S. Stern (ed.), *Der Preussische Staat und die Juden* (Tübingen: Mohr, 1962). ι, pt. 2, No. 442. (Hereafter Stern, Akten, followed by volume, part and document number, or page reference where appropriate.)
56. B. Schedlitz, *Leffmann Behrens* (Hildesheim: August Lax, 1984), p. 89; for Behrens's mediatory activities see M. Wiener, 'Der Hof und Kammeragent Leffmann Behrens', *Magazin für die Wissenschaft des Judentums*, 6 (1879), pp. 48–63.
57. Pribram, *Urkunden*, No. 159.
58. Grunwald, *Oppenheimer*, p. 99.
59. Ibid., pp. 133, 168–9; for additional material on the scope of Oppenheimer's activities, see J. Bérenger, *Finances et absolutisme autrichien* (Paris: Imprimerie Nationale Sorbonne, 1975), pp. 437–9.
60. *Life of Glückel*, pp. 146–7.
61. S. Berger (ed.), 'The Desire to Travel – A Note on Abraham Levy's Yiddish Itinerary, 1719–1723', *Aschkenas*, vι (1997), pp. 497–506.
62. Pribram, *Urkunden*, Nos. 132, 134, 135, 137.
63. Grunwald, *Oppenheimer*, p. 183.
64. See Schedlitz, *Leffmann Behrens*, pp. 137 ff.
65. Danby translates the relevant verse as follows: 'Be heedful of the ruling power for they bring no man nigh to them save for their own need: they seem to be friends such time as it is to their gain, but they stand not with a man in his time of stress': Herbert Danby (ed.and trans.), *The Mishnah* (Oxford University Press, 1933), p. 448. The reference to Stadthagen comes from his commentary on *Shulhan Arukh*, Yore Deah, Nos. 20–1.
66. J. Toury, 'Der Eintritt der Juden ins deutsche Bürgertum', in H. Liebeschütz und A. Paucker (eds), *Das Judentum in der deutschen Umwelt 1800–1850* (Tübingen: Mohr, 1977), pp. 139–242, here p. 152.

67. Bachrach, *Havot Yair*, No. 157.
68. Priebatsch, 'Judenpolitik des fürstlichen Absolutismus', 599–600; see also Kober, *Worms*, pp. 192–94; Schudt, *Merckwürdigkeiten*, Book VI, ch. 17, pp. 319–20; ch. 19, pp. 161–2.
69. F. Battenberg, 'Gesetzgebung und Judenemanzipation im Ancien Regime', *Zeitschrift für Historische Forschung*, 13 (1986), pp. 43–63; J. R. Wolf, 'Zwischen Hof und Stadt', in Franz (ed.), *Juden Darmstadt*, pp. 50–79; A. Eckstein, *Geschichte der Juden im Markgrafentum Bayreuth* (Bayreuth: Seligsberg, 1907), pp. 45 ff.; Guido Kisch, *Rechts- und Sozialgeschichte der Juden in Halle, 1686–1730* (Berlin: De Gruyter, 1970), No. 23, pp. 149–51.
70. *Shulhan Arukh*, Yore De'ah, Laws of Idolatry, No. 151, para. 6.
71. See Krochmal, *Tsemah Tsedek*, Nos. 10 and 15; also Halperin (ed.), *Takkanot Mähren*, Nos. 220 ff.; A. M. Fuss, 'The Eastern European Shetar Mamran re-examined', *Dinei Yisrael*, IV (1973), pp. li–lxvii.
72. Sh. Eidelberg (ed.), *Tshuvot Rabbenu Gershom Me'or Ha-Golah* (New York: Yeshivah University, 1955), No. 68.
73. Cohen, *Landjudenschaften in Deutschland*, I, Nos. 7:2:49; 8:21; idem., 'Landjudenschaften in Hessen-Darmstadt', pp. 190, 213 fn. 414.
74. Bachrach, *Havot Yair*, No. 163.
75. This fortunate bride was Rebecca, the only daughter of Liebmann Bär, president of the *kehillah* in Breslau. She married David Baruch, the court factor in Bayreuth in 1785. Her trousseau included a gold clock set with rubies, emeralds and sapphires; pearl necklaces; diamond rings; a porcelain egg set in gold; sundry items in silver and 1000 gold ducats. This good fortune did not survive Liebmann Bär's death in 1799 and the *kehillah* had to care for the daughter of the marriage (Eckstein, *Geschichte der Juden im Markgrafentum Bayreuth*, pp. 124 ff.).
76. Selma Stern, *Der Hofjude im Zeitalter des Merkantilismus* (Tübingen: Mohr, 2001), pp. 174–5. I have quoted the extract from the English version, *The Court Jew* (Philadelphia, PA: JPSA, 5710–1950), pp. 189–90.
77. W. Sombart, *Die Juden und das Wirtschaftsleben* (Munich: Duncker & Humblot, 1922 – first published 1911), p. 50; see also F. Raphael, *Judaisme et Capitalisme* (Paris: PUF, 1982), chs 2 and 3.

6 Prague and Bohemia: From Recovery to Reduction

1. Popper, 'Les Juifs de Prague', pp. 79–93; M. Grünfeld, 'Ausserer Verlauf der Geschichte der Juden in Mähren', in H. Gold (ed.), *Die Juden und Judengemeinden Mährens in Vergangenheit und Gegenwart* (Brünn: Jüdischer Buchverlag, 1929).
2. N. Brüll, *Zur Geschichte der Juden in Mähren, Jahrbuch für Israeliten*, 2nd Ser., vol. 3, pp. 181–220, esp. p. 195.
3. For all the above, see Krochmal, *Tsemah Tsedek*, Nos 42, 45, 70, 78, 38. (There is a ruling to the effect that a wife is entitled to sue for divorce if her husband plans a lengthy absence; see, for example, Maimonides, *Mishneh Torah*, *Hilkhot Ishiyut*, 14:2); for examples of the random murder, assault and robbery of Jews, see A. Putik, 'The Prague Jewish Community in the late 17th and early 18th centuries', *JB*, XXXV (1999), pp. 4–121, here pp. 21–26.
4. Friedländer, *Materialien* (Brünn, 1888), p. 4; T. Jakobowitz, 'Die jüdischen Zünfte in Prag', *JGGJCR*, VIII (1936), pp. 57–131.
5. But Prince Schwarzenberg reserved the right to admit Jews to his estates, despite the decree (see R. Kestenberg-Gladstein, 'Differences of estates within pre-emancipation Jewry', *JJS*, X (1954), pp. 156–66, esp. p. 164).

6. A. M. Drabek, Das Judentum der böhmischen Länder vor der Emanzipation'; *Judaica Austriaca*, x (1984), pp. 5–30, esp. pp. 14ff.; Prokes und Blaschka, 'Antisemitismus der Behörden', pp. 41–94, esp. pp. 71–2; Vladimir Lipscher, *Zwischen Kaiser Fiskus Adel Zünften* (Zurich, 1983), pp. 35ff.

7. M. Rachmuth, 'Zur Wirtschaftsgeschichte der Prager Juden', *JGGJCR*, v (1933), pp. 9–78. Between Count Franz Maximilian Czernin and the Jews on his estate in Schwihau a friendly rapport existed at the end of the seventeenth century and the beginning of the eighteenth century, according to Lipscher, *Zwischen Kaiser*, p. 80.

8. G. Wolf, 'Gemeindestreitigkeiten in Prag, 1567–1678', *ZGJD*, i (1887), pp. 309–20; T. Jakobovits, 'Die Erlebnisse des Oberrabbiners Simon Spira-Wedeles in Prag 1640–1679', *JGGJCR*, iv (1932), pp. 253–332.

9. S. H. Lieben, 'Oppenheimiana', *JGGJCR*, vii (1935), pp. 409–55.

10. For a French translation of the declaration, see Popper, 'Juifs de Prague pendant la Guerre de Trente Ans', pp. 92–3.

11. T. Jakobovits, 'Das Prager und Böhmischer Landesrabbinat', *JGGJCR*, v (1933), pp. 79–136. Conflict between major communities and their lesser subordinates was normal – for example the relationship between Berlin and the Prussian communities or between Nancy and Lunéville and Saarguemines.

12 B. Nosek, 'Soziale Differenzierungen und Streitigkeiten in jüdischen Kultusgemeinden im 17.Jahrhundert', *Judaica Bohemiae*, xii (1976), pp. 59–92; T. Jakobovits, 'Jüdisches Gemeindeleben in Kolin, 1763–1768', *JGGJCR*, i (1929), pp. 332–68.

13. See his *Haskamah* to Rabbi Abraham Broda, *Eshel Abraham* (Frankfurt am Main, 1747).

14. Jakobovits, 'Das Prager Landesrabbinat', pp. 83ff.; Putik, 'Prague Jewish Community', pp. 69ff., 93ff.; see also S. H. Lieben, *David Oppenheim* (Frankfurt am Main, n.d.).

15. R. J. W. Evans, *The Making of the Habsburg Monarchy, 1550–1700* (Oxford: Clarendon Press, 1979), p. 117.

16. Kisch, 'Zensur jüdischer Bücher', esp. pp. 462–4; Prokes, 'Antisemitismus der Behörden', pp. 80–1; R. Jacob Emden, *Megilat Sefer*, ed. Abraham Bick, repr. (Jerusalem: Moreshet, 1979), p. 108; Jacob Koppel Duschinsky, *R. David Oppenheimer* (Budapest, 1922), p. 3; for the odyssey of this library and its eventual move to Oxford, see Lieben, *David Oppenheim*, p. 29.

17. Putik, 'Prague Jewish Community', pp. 38ff.

18. See M. Komorowski, *Bio-Bibliographisches Verzeichnis Jüdischer Doktoren im 17. und 18.Jahrhundert* (Munich: Saur, 1991), pp. 7–8.

19. G. Kisch, *Die Prager Universität und die Juden 1348–1848* (Mährisch-Ostrau: Kittl, 1935), chs vii–viii; N. Brüll, 'Zur Geschichte der Juden in Mähren', from *Jahrbuch für Israeliten*, ser. 2, vol. iii, pp. 181–220, here pp. 204–5.

20. S. Adler, 'Das älteste Judicial-Protokoll des Jüdischen Gemeinde-Archivs in Prag (1682)', *JGGJCR*, iii (1931), pp. 217–56, nos. 69, 95, 104.

21. M. R. Rachmuth, 'Der Plan einer Verlegung des Prager Ghettos nach Lieben, 1680', *JGGJCR*, vi (1934), pp. 145–56; Prokes, 'Antisemitismus der Behörden', p. 102.

22. V. L. Tapié, 'The Habsburg Lands 1618–57', *New Cambridge Modern History IV* (Cambridge University Press, 1970), pp. 503–30; Lipscher, *Zwischen Kaiser*, p. 101.

23. Quoted R. Kestenberg-Gladstein, 'Differences of Estates within Pre-emancipation Jewry', *JSS*, vi (1955), pp. 35–49.

24. Quoted R. Kestenberg-Gladstein, 'Wirtschaftsgeschichte der böhmischen Landjuden des 18. Jahrhunderts', *Judaica Bohemiae*, iii (1967), pp. 105ff.; Lipscher, *Zwischen Kaiser*, pp. 76, 92ff.

25. Ibid., pp. 74 ff.; see also Kestenberg-Gladstein, 'Toldot Ha-Kalkalah shel Yehudei Boehm she-mi-hutz le-Prag ba-me'ot ha-17 ve-ha-18', *Tsiyon*, XII (1947), pp. 49–69, 160–89.
26. Kestenberg-Gladstein, 'Wirtschaftsgeschichte', pp. 116–17.
27. 'A Seventeenth-Century Autobiography', ed. and trans. A. Marx, *Studies in Jewish History and Booklore* (New York: Jewish Theological Seminary of America, 1944), pp. 178–97, here p. 184.
28. Kestenberg-Gladstein, 'Wirtschaftsgeschichte', p. 112.
29. Lipscher, *Zwischen Kaiser*, 94 ff.; B. Bretholz, 'Die Judenschaft einer mährischen Kleinstadt. Markt Pirnitz im 18. Jahrhundert', *JGGJCR*, II (1930), pp. 403–55.
30. Krochmal, *Tsemah Tsedek*, nos. 31, 35. There is another version of the latter responsum which identifies the carters employed as Moslems – see Halperin, *Takkanot Mähren*, p. 84, fn. 4. Despite Krochmal's ruling in this case it was possible to devise a procedure whereby a customs post or toll booth, where the lessee was Jewish, could still be operated on the Sabbath by a non-Jew (Ibid., no. 257).
31. Halperin, *Takkanot Mähren*, nos. 259, 485.
32. Ibid., nos. 254, 256.
33. See B. Nosek and V. Sadek, 'Sotsialniye Protivorechiya v yevreiskikh religioznikh obschchestvakh v Moravii i ikh otrazheniye v sochineniyakh M.M.Krochmala (okolo 1600–1661)', *Judaica Bohemiae* XIII (1977), pp. 59–73; and vol. III, ch. 2 of Rabbi Dr Adolf Frankl-Grün, *Geschichte der Juden in Kremsier 1322–1848*, vols. I–III (Breslau/Frankfurt am Main, 1896–1901). A rabbi and historian talks of London Jewry in the early eighteenth century in the same terms. See p. 5 in this volume.
34. Krochmal's social concerns are a main theme in Horodetzky's account of his activities as a respondent. Horodetzky also points out that Krochmal responded not only to local problems but also to those from abroad, for example Tiberias (no. 16): S. A. Horodetzky, *Lekorot Ha-Rabbanut* (Warsaw: Tushiya, 1911), pp. 201–6.
35. Krochmal, *Tsemah Tsedek*, Nos. 1, 2, 18, 34; see also Frankl-Grün, *Juden Kremsier*, pp. 89 ff.
36. Putik, 'Prague Jewish Community', p. 97; G. Wolf, 'Zur Geschichte des jüdischen Gemeindewesens in Prag', *AZJ*, 27 (1863), No. 17, pp. 255–7; Halperin, *Takkanot Mähren*, pp. 11–12.

7 Early Decades in Brandenburg-Prussia: The Last Resettlement

1. G. Kisch, *Die Prager Universität und die Juden*, repr. (Amsterdam: Grüner, 1969), p. 25.
2. Schnee, *Hoffinanz*, I, pp. 48ff; Moritz Stern, 'Die Niederlassung der Juden im Berlin in Jahre 1671', *ZGJD*, II (1930), pp. 131–49; O. Lassally, 'Israel Aaron, Hoffaktor des Grossen Kurfürsten', *MGWJ*, 79 (1935), pp. 20–31, esp. p.24.
3. Selma Stern (ed.), *Der Preussische Staat und die Juden*, 7 vols (Tübingen: Mohr, 1962–75), 1/2 Nos. 50–1. This work is referred to hereafter as Stern, *Akten*, followed by volume and document (or page) number.
4. Stern, *Court Jews*, p. 52; Stern, *Akten*, 1/1 p.150; see also D. Hertz, 'The Despised Queen of Berlin Jewry', in R. Cohen and V. Mann (eds), *From Court Jews to the Rothschilds* (New York: Jewish Museum, 1996), pp. 68–77. For the 'Jews' Commission', see this volume, p. 133.
5. Stern, *Akten*, 1/2 Nos. 363–4; 369–70; for Liebmann and Lehmann, see Schnee, *Hoffinanz*, I, pp. 64 ff.; II, pp. 86, 169–222.

6. G. Renda, 'Das bayerische Jerusalem', in M. Treml (ed.), *Geschichte und Kultur der Juden in Bayern* (Munich: Saur, 1988), pp. 225–36; Frankl-Grün, *Juden in Kremsier*, I, p. 108; III, pp. 3–4.

7. The above is based on Kaufmann, *Letzte Vertreibung*, pp. 206 ff.; and Stern, 'Niederlassung', pp. 131 ff.

8. Stern, *Akten*, 1/2, No. 12; for Halberstadt model, ibid., No. 104.

9. In general see S. Jersch-Wenzel, *Juden und Franzosen in der Wirtschaft des Raumes Berlin/Brandenburg zur Zeit des Merkantilismus* (Berlin: De Gruyter, 1978); P. Baumgart, 'Absoluter Staat und Judenemanzipation in Brandenburg-Preussen', *Jahrbuch für die Geschichte Mittel- und Ost Deutschlands*, 13–14 (1965), pp. 60–87.

10. Stern, *Akten*, 1/2, Nos. 24, 28, 121, 148.

11. Ibid., 2/2, Nos. 16, 18–21.

12. See A. A. Bruer, *Geschichte der Juden in Preussen (1750–1820)* (Frankfurt am Main: Campus Verlag, 1991), pp. 413–14, n. 31.

13. E. Landshut, *Toldot Anshei Shem u-Fe'ulatam be-Edat Berlin* (Berlin: Poppelauer, 1884), pp. 6–7; see also the report of the Jews' Commission, Stern, *Akten*, 2/2, No. 4.

14. Ibid., 1/2, No. 327.

15. For the text, see *Juden in Berlin 1671–1945 Ein Lesebuch* (Berlin: Nicolai, 1988), p. 23.

16. Landshut, *Toldot Anshei Shem*, p. 12; L. Geiger, *Geschichte der Juden in Berlin*, 2 vols (Berlin: Guttentag, 1871), I, pp. 20 ff.

17. Stern, *Akten*, 2/2, No. 448; see also Miriam Bodian, 'Ha-Yazmim Ha-Yehudim be-Berlin', *Tsiyon*, 49 (1984), pp. 159–84, esp. pp. 165 ff.

18. Stern, *Akten*, 1/2, Nos. 216, 218–19, 221, 266. See also ibid., No. 203.

19. Stern, *Akten*, 1/2, No. 293.

20. Ibid., 2/2, Nos. 193–5.

21. Stern, *Akten*, 2/2, No. 7.

22. Stefi Wenzel, *Jüdische Bürger und Kommunale Selbstverwaltung* (Berlin: De Gruyter, 1967), p. 20.

23. R. Kaelter, *Geschichte der Jüdischen Gemeinde zu Potsdam*, repr. (Berlin, 1993), pp. 12 ff.; Stern, *Akten*, 2/2 No. 263.

24. Ibid., 2/2, No. 273.

25. Stern, *Akten*, 1/2 No. 31; 2/2, No. 332.

26. Landshut, *Toldot Anshei Shem*, pp. 4–5.

27. Shiloh, *Dina de-Malkhuta Dina*, pp. 430–31.

28. Stern, *Akten*, 2/2, Nos. 10, 12.

29. Landshut, *Toldot Anshei Shem*, pp. 27–30, 35 ff.; this version of Falk's dismissal is accepted, it seems, by Marcus Horovitz, in his *Frankfurter Rabbiner* (Jerusalem, 1969), p. 127.

30. Stern, *Akten*, 2/2, Nos. 206, 217–27; J. Meisl (ed.), *Pinkas Kehillat Berlin, 1723–1854* (Jerusalem: Rubin Mass, 1962), No. 46; Geiger, *Geschichte der Juden in Berlin*, II, pp. 85 ff.

31. See e.g. M. R. Cohen, 'Leone da Modena's Riti'; *JSS*, 34 (1972), pp. 287–317, esp. p. 308 and fn. 117.

32. See also Stern, *Akten*, 1/2, No. 496, paras 43–44.

33. Stern, *Akten*, 2/1, p. 33; 2/2 Nos. 72, 74.

34. Stern, *Akten*, 1/2, No. 244; see also H. Seeliger, 'Origin and Growth of the Berlin Jewish Community', *LBYB*, III (1958), pp. 159–68. esp. pp. 160–1; I. Freund, *Die Emanzipation der Juden in Preussen*, 2 vols (Berlin: Poppelauer, 1912), I, p. 15.

35. Stern, *Akten*, 1/1, p. 141, 1/2, No. 435; G. Salinger, 'Jüdische Gemeinden in Hinterpommern', in M. Heitman *et al.* (eds.), *Geschichte der Juden in Pommern* (Hildesheim: Olms, 1995), p. 38; O. Lassally, 'Zur Geschichte der Juden in Landsberg an der Warthe', *MGWJ*, No. 80 (1936), pp. 403–5.
36. This did not in fact arrest the growth of the local Jewry which from 175 persons c.1700 advanced to 448 by 1752. (Erika Herzfeld, 'Aus der Geschichte der Hinterpommerscher Juden bis zum Ende des 18ten Jahrhunderts', in Heitman und Schoeps, *Juden in Pommern*, pp. 19–35; Stern, *Akten*, III/2, no. 766. For the general situation in the German states see A. Sinyelnikov, *Sotsialno-demografich-eskiye posledstviya ogranichenieya brakov mezhdu yevreyami v nemetskikh gosudarst-vakh v XVII–XIX vekov* (Moscow/Jerusalem: Vestnik yevreyskovo universiteta v Moskve No. 3, 1993), pp. 22–55.
37. Moritz Stern, 'Jugendunterricht in der Berliner Jüdischen Gemeinde während des 18ten Jahrhunderts', *JJLG*, 19(1928), pp. 39–68, esp. p. 40. The Privilege for Berlin Jewry of 1750 permitted 2 teachers for the girls' school, of whom both must be married.
38. Stern, Akten, 2/2, No. 173 and fn. 1.
39. Ibid., 2/2, No. 97; J. Meisl (ed.), *Pinkas (Protokollbuch) der jüdischen Gemeinde Berlin (1723–1854)* (Jerusalem: Rubin Mass, 1962), pp. 420–2.
40. Stern, *Akten*, 2/2, Nos. 190–1.
41. Freund, *Emanzipation der Juden*, II, Urkunder pp. 15–22.
42. Stern, *Akten*, 2/2, No. 191.
43. See S. M. Lowenstein, *The Berlin Jewish Community* (Oxford University Press, 1994), p. 13.
44. Stern, *Akten*, 2/2, Nos. 308, 316, 319; Seeliger, 'Origin and Growth', p.161.
45. Stern, *Akten*, 2/2, No. 676.

8 Amsterdam: From Turmoil to Decline

1. Jonathan Israel, 'The Sephardi Contribution to Economic Life in England and the New World (16th–18th centuries)', in H. Beinart (ed.), *The Sephardi Legacy II* (Jerusalem: Magnes Press, 1992), pp. 365–98, esp. pp. 391 ff.
2. See Dominique Jarrassé, 'Les Mémoires du Temple', in Benbassa, *Transmission*, pp. 473–97, here p. 474.
3. See N. Rosenbloom, 'Discreet theological polemics in Menasseh b. Israel's Conciliador', *PAAJR*, 58 (1992), pp. 143–91.
4. M. Awerbuch, 'Spinoza in seiner Zeit', in H. Delf *et al.* (eds), *Spinoza in der europäischen Geistesgeschichte* (Berlin: Hentrich, 1994), pp. 39–74, esp. pp. 47 ff.; see Fishman, *Shaking the Pillars*, ch. 3.
5. Swetchinski, *Reluctant Cosmopolitans*, pp. 225 ff.
6. P. Mendes-Flohr and J. Reinharz (eds), *The Jew in the Modern World. A Documentary History*, 2nd edn (Oxford University Press, 1995, 2:1); A. Kasher and S. Bidermann, 'Why Was Spinoza Excommunicated?', in D. S. Katz and I. Israel (eds), *Sceptics, Millenarians and Jews* (Leiden: Brill, 1990), pp. 98–144, here pp. 132 ff.
7. I. S. Revah (ed.), *Spinoza et le Dr. Juan de Prado* (Paris: Mouton, 1959), pp. 31–2.
8. D. S. Katz, 'The Marginalization of Early Modern Anglo-Jewish History', in T. Kushner (ed.), *The Jewish Heritage in British History* (London: Cass, 1992), pp. 60–77; Kasher and Bidermann, 'Why Was Spinoza Excommunicated?' pp. 132 ff.; see also Bodian, *Hebrews of the Portuguese Nation*, pp. 123 ff., 129 ff.; and Julian Weill, 'Spinoza et le Judaïsme', *REJ*, 49–50 (1904–5), pp. 161–180.

9. S. Nadler, *Spinoza's Heresy* (Oxford: Clarendon Press, 2001), *passim*.
10. See the material cited in B. Septimus, 'Ethical Religion and Political Rationality', in I. Twersky (ed.), *Jewish Thought in the 17th Century* (Cambridge, MA: Harvard University Press, 1987), pp. 399–433, esp. p. 429, fn. 130.
11. See A. Altmann, 'Eternality of Punishment: A Theological Controversy within the Amsterdam Rabbinate in the Thirties of the 17th century', *PAAJR*, XL (1972), pp. 1–88; also H. Méchoulan, 'La Mort comme Enjeu Théologique, Philosophique et Politique à Amsterdam au 17e siècle', *XVIIe Siècle*, 46 (1994), pp. 337–48.
12. B. Spinoza, *A Theologico-Political Treatise*, trans. R. H. M. Elwes (London: Bell, 1889), p. 8.
13. Ibid., end ch. III.
14. Gerson Cohen, 'Messianic Postures of Ashkenazim and Sephardim', *Leo Baeck Memorial Lecture*, 9 (1967), pp. 9 ff.; Lionel Kochan, *The Jew and His History* (London: Macmillan, 1977), pp. 32 ff.
15. See Moses Wall's English translation (1652) of *Spes Israelis/Esperança de Israel*, ed. H. Méchoulan and G. Nahon (Oxford: Littman Library/Oxford University Press, 1987), p. 102.
16. G. D. Hundert, 'Reflections on the Whig Interpretation of Jewish History', in H. Joseph *et al.* (eds), *Truth and Compassion* (Ontario: Wilfred Laurier University Press, 1983), pp. 115–16.
17. See for example, D. S. Katz, 'Henry Jessey and the Jews', in J. Kaplan *et al.* (eds), *Menasseh b. Israel and his World* (Leiden: Brill, 1989), pp. 117–38.
18. See J. Kaplan, 'The Portuguese Jews in Amsterdam: From Forced Conversion to a Return to Judaism', *SR*, XV (1981), pp. 37–51.
19. Ram Ben-Shalom, 'The Converso as Subversive', *JJS*, L (1999), pp. 259–83; J. Barnai, 'Christian Messianism and Portuguese Marranos', *JH*, VII (1993), pp. 119–126; see also idem, 'The Spread of the Sabbatean Movement in the 17th and 18th Centuries', in S. Menache (ed.), *Communication in the Jewish Diaspora*, pp. 313–37.
20. R. Jacob Sasportas, *Tzitzat Novel Zvi*, ed. I. Tishby (Jerusalem: Mossad Bialik, 1954), p. 17.
21. 'Aus dem ältesten Protokollbuch der Portugiesisch-Jüdischen Gemeinde in Hamburg', trans. J. Cassuto, *JJLG*, X (1913), pp. 292–3.
22. Sasportas, *Tzitzat Novel Zvi*, p. 75. For the Portuguese propensity to gamble see Swetchinski, *Reluctant Cosmopolitans*, p. 216.
23. *Diary of Samuel Pepys*, VII, p. 47 (entry for 19 February 1666).
24. Sasportas, *Tzitzat Novel Zvi*, pp. 18–19, 131, 142–3, 170, 320; for the reference to Maimonides, see his Mishneh Torah, Laws of Kings, XI: 4.
25. J. Kaplan, ' "Karaites" in early Eighteenth Century Amsterdam', in Katz and Israel (eds), *Sceptics*, pp. 196–236.
26. Evelyne Oliel-Grausz, 'La Circulation du Personnel Rabbinique', in Benbassa, *Transmission*, pp. 330–4, esp. pp. 330–1.
27. See J. Kaplan, *Onesh Ha-Herem ba-Kehillah ha-Sephardit be-Amsterdam ba-meah Ha-18*, Proceedings of the Tenth World Congress of Jewish Studies, Div. B, I (Jerusalem, 1990), pp. 1–7.
28. R. Moses Hagiz, *Sfat Emet*, repr. (Jerusalem: Sha'ar, 1987), pp. 17–18, 30, 33, 40, 76.
29. Jonathan Israel, 'The Changing Role of the Dutch Sephardim in International Trade, 1595–1715', in J. Michman and T. Levie (eds), *Dutch Jewish History* (Jerusalem: Tel-Aviv University, 1984), pp. 31–51; I. Schorsch, 'Portmanteau Jews', in D. Cesarani (ed.), *Port Jews* (London: Cass, 2002), pp. 59–74, here p. 59.

30. Robert Cohen, 'Passage to a New World: The Sephardi Poor of 18th Century Amsterdam', in Lea Dasberg and J. N. Cohen (eds), *Neveh Ya'akov* (Assen: Van Goreum, 1982), pp. 31–42; see also W. C. Pieterse, 'The Sephardi Jews of Amsterdam', in R. Barnett and W. Schwab (eds), *The Western Sephardim, II* (Grendon, Northants: Gibraltar Books, 1988), pp. 75–99.
31. Bloom, *Economic Activities*, p. 214.
32. Cohen, 'Passage to a New World', *passim*.
33. Quoted Bodian, *Hebrews of the Portuguese Nation*, p. 158.
34. Bloom, *Economic Activities*, pp. 70, 213–14; F. Egmond, 'Poor Ashkenazim in the Dutch Republic', in J. Michman (ed.), *Dutch-Jewish History* III (Jerusalem, 1993), pp. 205–25.
35. Sluys, *Yehudei Ashkenaz*, p. 91.

9 From London to the Provinces

1. This report is No. 18 in the *She'elot u-Tshuvot of Haham Zvi* (Amsterdam, 1712). There is a fairly full English translation by Leon Roth in *Chronicon Spinozanum*, I (The Hague, 1921), pp. 278–82, and a German translation in J. Winter and A. Wünsche (eds), *Geschichte der Rabbinischen Litteratur* (Berlin: Poppelauer, 1897), II, pp. 572–5; see also D. Ruderman, 'The Career and Writings of David Nieto', *PAAJR*, 58 (1992), pp. 193–219; and J. J. Petuchowski, *The Theology of Haham David Nieto* (New York: Ktav, 1970).
2. *Matteh Dan*, Warsaw, 5644 (1884), pp. 1–2. Rav and Shmuel are two of the great controversialists of the Talmud.
3. I have taken this part-translation of responsum No. 38 from A. S. Ferziger, 'Between Ashkenaz and Sefarad', *SR*, xxxv (2001), pp. 7–22, here p. 9; I. Epstein, 'Ascama 1 of the Spanish and Portuguese Jewish Congregation of London', in M. Ben-Horin *et al.* (eds) *Studies and Essays in Honor of A. A. Neumann* (Philadelphia PA: Dropsie College, 1962), pp. 170–214, esp. p. 181; see also pp. 305 ff. above.
4. T. Endelman, *Radical Assimilation in English Jewish History, 1656–1945* (Bloomington: Indiana University Press, 1990), *passim*; Comte de Mirabeau, *Sur Moses Mendelssohn, sur la Réforme Politique des Juifs* (London, 1787), p. 108.
5. E. R. Samuel, 'Dr Meyer Schomberg's Attack on the Jews of London', *TJHSE*, xx (1964), pp. 83–111, esp. pp. 102 ff.
6. See A. P. Arnold, 'Apprentices of Great Britain 1710–1773', with an Introduction by R. D. Barnett, *TJHSE*, xxii (1970), pp. 145–57.
7. R. D. Barnett, 'Dr Samuel Nunez Ribeiro and the Settlement of Georgia', in *Migration and Settlement* (London: JHSE, 1971), pp. 63–100; see also Y. Kaplan, 'Wayward New Christians and Stubborn New Jews', *JH*, viii (1994), pp. 27–41.
8. A. S. Diamond, 'Problems of the London Sephardi Community, 1720–1733', *TJHSE*, xxi (1968), pp. 39–63, esp. p. 61.
9. H. E. S. Fisher, 'Jews in England and the 18th Century English Economy', *TJHSE*, xxvii (1982), pp. 156–65. (This is a review of G. Yogev, *Diamonds and Coral – Anglo-Dutch Jews and 18th Century Trade* [Leicester University Press, 1978].)
10. Charles Wilson, *New Introduction to W. A. Cunningham, Alien Immigrants in England*, 2nd. edn (London: Cass, 1969), p. xvii.
11. Lucy Sutherland, 'Samson Gideon: Eighteenth Century Jewish Financier', *TJHES*, xvii (1953), pp. 79–90. Only that Balzac who wrote *La Messe de l'Athée* could do justice to Gideon's conjunction of allegiances.

12. See Perry, 'Anglo-Jewry, the Law, Religious Conviction', esp. pp. 13–14; for an account of these economic disabilities see also J. M. Ross, 'Naturalisation of Jews in England', *TJHSE*, xxiv (1975), pp. 59–72.
13. Quoted Faber, *Jews, Slaves*, pp. 277–8, fn. 3.
14. Henriques, *Jews and the English Law*, p. 241, fn. 2
15. A. M. Hyamson, *The Sephardim of England* (London: Methuen,1951), p. 125.
16. A. Gilam, *The Emancipation of the Jews in England, 1830–1860* (New York: Garland, 1982), pp. 10–11.
17. R. Liberles, 'The Jews and Their Bill', *JH*, ii (1987), pp. 29–36; see also Mirabeau, *Sur Moses Mendelssohn*, p. 101.
18. C. Roth (ed.), *Anglo-Jewish Letters* (London: Soncino, 1938), pp. 128–30; Liberles, 'Jews and Their Bill', p. 34.
19. Mirabeau, *Sur Moses Mendelssohn*, p. 107; the 'zealots' are not identified.
20. Hyamson, *Sephardim of England*, p. 128, fn. 1; Roy Wolper, 'Circumcision as Polemic in the Jew Bill of 1753', *Eighteenth Century Life*, vii (1982), pp. 28–36. It is also suggested that the anti-Jewish uproar was such that it led to the curbing and later revision of Handel's Israelite oratorios – see Ruth Smith, *Handel's Oratorios and Eighteenth Century Thought* (Cambridge University Press, 1995), chs. 8, 15. I owe this reference to the erudition of Dr Susan Wollenberg of Lady Margaret Hall, Oxford.
21. Board of Deputies Minute Book 2, March 1829–January 1838, pp. 8–9.
22. Roth, *Anglo-Jewish Letters*, p. 30.
23. For the experience of one particular family see N. Perry, 'La Chute d'une Famille Séfardie – Les Mendes da Costa de Londres', *18ème Siècle*, No. 13 (1985), pp. 11–25; Cantor, 'Emanuel Mendes da Costa', *English Historical Review*, cxvi, No. 467 (2001), pp. 584–603.
24. Endelman, *Jews of Georgian England*, p. 172; Diamond, 'Problems of the London Sephardi Community', pp. 39–63; Hyamson, *Sephardim of England*, pp. 71, 170, 190; Neville Laski, *The Laws and Charities of the Spanish and Portuguese Jews Congregation of London* (London: Cresset, 1952), pp. 33, 99, 113.
25. Picciotto, *Sketches*, pp. 162–3.
26. Hyamson, *Sephardim of England*, p. 224.
27. L. D. Barnett (ed.), *Bevis Marks Records*, I (Oxford University Press, 1940) pp. 30–33; C. Roth, *History of the Great Synagogue* (London: Edward Goldston, 1950), pp. 8 ff.
28. Katz, *Jews in the History of England*, p. 273.
29. V. D. Lipman, 'Sephardi and other Jewish Immigrants in England in the 18th century', in *Migration and Settlement* (London: JHSE, 1971), pp. 37–63.
30. R. D. Barnett, 'Anglo-Jewry in the Eighteenth Century', in V. D. Lipman (ed.), *Three Centuries of Anglo-Jewish History* (Cambridge: Heffer, 1961), pp. 45–68, esp. pp. 60 ff.; Endelman, *Jews of Georgian England*, p. 119.
31. Roth, *Great Synagogue*, pp. 17, 30; R. Johanan Holleschau, *Ma'aseh Rav* (Amsterdam, 1707), f. 16a; see also Lipman, 'Sephardi and Other Jewish Immigrants', pp. 38–9.
32. Holleschau, *Ma'aseh Rav*, f. 16a.
33. Kaufmann, 'Rabbi Zevi Ashkenazi', pp. 102–25.
34. Holleschau, *Ma'aseh Rav*, p. 1; G. W. Busse, 'The Herem of Rabenu Tam in Queen Anne's London', *TJHSE*, xxi (1968), pp. 138–47; Roth, *Great Synagogue*, ch. iv; R. J. D'Arcy Hart, 'The Family of Mordecai Hamburger and Their Association with Madras', *JHSE, Miscellanies*, iii (1937), pp. 57–75.

35. A. Barnett, *The Western Synagogue through Two Centuries (1761–1961)* (London: Vallentine Mitchell, 1961), pp. 41–42.
36. Levi Nathan, *A Short Account of the Life and Transactions of Levi Nathan* (London, 1776), p. 3. Nathan had been a pupil of R. Jonathan Eibeschütz in Hamburg and later became an itinerant preacher in Germany, Italy and France.
37. Quoted Rev. H. Mayerowitsch, 'The Chazanim of the Great Synagogue, London', *JHSE*, Miscellanies, IV (1942), p. 85.
38. For all the above see C. Duschinsky, *The Rabbinate of the Great Synagogue London, 1756–1842* (Oxford University Press, 1921), pp. 21 ff.; Letters 4–5, pp. 162–6 (see also p. 232); Holleschau, *Ma'aseh Rav*, f. 6d; R. David Tevele Schiff, *Lashon Zahav*, I (Offenbach, 1822), pp. 26a–27a; see also R. Markus Horovitz, *Frankfurter Rabbinen*, p. 199. ('The seven principles of the sons of Noah' traditionally comprise the prohibition of idolatry, blasphemy, bloodshed, sexual unchastity, theft, eating flesh from a living animal, and require the establishment of a legal system. These principles are incumbent on all mankind.)
39. Roth, *Great Synagogue*, pp. 68–70.
40. Siegfried Stein, 'Some Ashkenazi Charities in London at the End of the Eighteenth and Beginning of the Nineteenth Centuries', *TJHES*, XX (1964), pp. 63–81.
41. G. Godden, *Minton Pottery and Porcelain of the first period* (London: Jenkins, 1968), p. 82 and plate 128; Betty Naggar, 'Jewish Pedlars and Hawkers, 1740–1940', *Porphyrogenitus* (1992), p. 41; Lipman, 'Sephardi and other Jewish Immigrants', pp. 45–6.
42. Naggar, 'Jewish Pedlars', pp. 55 ff.
43. G. L. Green, *The Royal Navy and Anglo-Jewry, 1740–1820* (Ealing: Geoffrey Green, 1989), pp. 29, 110; Barnett, 'Anglo-Jewry in the Eighteenth Century', p. 62; C. Roth, 'The Portsmouth Community and its Historical Background', *TJHSE*, XIII (1936), pp. 157–87; A. Jacob, 'The Jews of Falmouth', *TJHSE*, XVII (1953), pp. 63–72.
44. Ibid.; see also C. Roth, 'The Chief Rabbinate of England', in I. Epstein *et al.* (eds), *Essays in Honour of the Very Rev. Dr J. H. Hertz* (London: Edward Goldston,1943), pp. 371–84.
45. Liberles, 'The Jews and Their Bill', p. 32.
46. For Hart Lyon's sermon, see M. Saperstein (ed.), *Jewish Preaching, 1200–1800 – An Anthology* (New Haven, CT: Yale University Press, 1989), pp. 350–8; for a mention of numerous other sermons on notable national occasions in peace and war, see Hyamson, *Sephardim of England*, pp. 135–6, fn. 1; Schiff, *Lashon Zahav*, II, p. 32a; Duschinsky, *Rabbinate of Great Synagogue*, p. 114; I. Abrahams, 'Hebrew Loyalty under the First Four Georges', *TJHSE*, IX (1922), pp. 103–30.

10 Expulsion from Prague (1745–8)

1. S. Schweinburg-Eibenschutz, 'Une confiscation de livres hébreux à Prague', *REJ*, 29 (1894), pp. 261–71; G. Kisch, 'Die Zensur jüdischer Bücher in Böhmen', *JGGJCR*, II (1930), pp. 456–90.
2. For all the above see Prokes, 'Antisemitismus der Behörden'; Anita Frankova, 'Erfassung der jüdischen Bevölkerung in Böhmen', *Judaica Bohemiae*, VI (1970), pp. 55–69.
3. See the material cited in Kestenberg-Gladstein, 'Differences of Estates', esp. pp. 164–5, fn. 5.

4. M. H. Friedländer, Beiträge zur Geschichte der Juden in Mähren (Brünn, 1876), p. 27; A. Frankl-Grün, 'Die Folgen des österreichischen Erbfolgekriegs für die Juden Kremsiers', MGWJ, 38 (1894), pp. 330–1.

5. Simonsohn, Jews in Duchy of Mantua, p. 147; J. R. Wolf, 'Zwischen Hof und Stadt', in Franz, Juden als Darmstädter Bürger, p. 68; for a broad outline of this theme, see Frankova, 'Erfassung der jüdischen Bevölkerung', passim; also R. Jacob Emden, She'ilot Yavetz (Altona, 1759) II, No. 15; H. Adelman, 'Servants and Sexuality', in T. M. Rudavsky (ed.), Gender and Judaism (New York University Press, 1995), pp. 91–7, esp. p. 94; E. Horowitz, 'The Worlds of Jewish Youth in Europe 1300–1800', in Giovanni Levi (ed.), A History of Young People in the West (Harvard University Press, 1977), ch. 4.

6. H. J. Kieval, Languages of Community (California University Press, 2000), pp. 21–2.

7. Frankl-Grün, 'Die Folgen des österreichischen Erbfolgekriegs', pp. 326, 330.

8. J. Bergl, 'Die Ausweisung der Juden aus Prag im Jahre 1744', in S. Steinherz (ed.), Die Juden in Prag (Prague: Bnei Brith, 1927), pp. 187–247, here p. 247, fn. 26; see also A. M. Drabek, 'Das Judentum der böhmischen Länder vor der Emanzipation', Judaica Austriaca, X (1984), pp. 3–30, esp. p. 24.

9. B. Mevorah, 'Die Interventionsbestrebungen in Europa zur Verhinderung der Vertreibung der Juden aus Böhmen und Mähren, 1744–45', Tel Aviver Jahrbuch für deutsche Geschichte, IX (1980), pp. 15–81, esp. pp. 31, 35, 73.

10. Robinson to Lord Harrington (Secretary of State) 27 March 1745 – Appendix to A. Newman, 'The Expulsion of the Jews from Prague in 1745 and British Foreign Policy', TJHSE, XXII (1970), pp. 30–41.

11. S. Vind, Rabbi Yehezke'el Landau (Jerusalem: Hotsa'at da'at Torah, 1961), p. 14; see also J. Bergl, 'Das Exil der Prager Judenschaft von 1745–1748', JGGJCR, I (1929), pp. 263–331; and the material cited in Drabek, 'Das Judentum der böhmischen Länder', p. 22, fn. 68.

12. G. Wolf, 'Die Vertreibung der Juden aus Böhmen im Jahre 1744', in Jahrbuch für die Geschichte der Juden und des Judentums (Leipzig, 1869), IV, pp. 159 ff.

13. Ibid., pp. 222 ff., p. 273; see also S. Plaggenborg, 'Maria Theresa und die böhmischen Juden', Bohemia, 39 (1998), pp. 1–16, passim.

14. Robinson, 'The Expulsion of the Jews from Prague', p. 38; Bergl, 'Ausweisung der Juden', p. 227.

15. F. Kobler (ed.), Letters of Jews through the ages, Engl. trans., 2 vols. (London: East and West Library, 1953), II, pp. 591–2. This is one of four surviving letters mostly written in Yiddish and apparently assembled by Wolf Wertheimer. They were originally discovered and edited by S. H. Lieben, and published in JGGJCR, IV (1932), pp. 353–479. The Kobler version has been used here with slight variations. Lieben also collected and edited 'Briefe von 1744–1748 über die Austreibung der Juden aus Prag', JGGJCR, IV (1932), pp. 353–479.

16. Kobler, Letters of Jews, pp. 592–3; see also A. Goldmann et al. (eds), 'Quellen und Forschungen zur Geschichte der Juden' in Deutsch-Österreich-Nachträge (Vienna: Selbstverlag der historischen Kommission, 1936), xi, p. 64.

17. Kobler, Juden und Judentum in deutschen Briefen, pp. 46–8.

18. This extract from the Pope's letter is taken from Samuel Wertheimer's report to his father, dated 27th Adar II (5)505 (= March 31, 1745), in Lieben, Briefe, no. 68, pp. 451–2.

19. Bergl, Exil, pp. 267 ff.

20. Mevorah, 'Die Interventionsbestrebungen', p. 30.

21. Kobler, Letters of Jews, pp. 607–8.

22. Bergl, *Exil*, p. 330, fn. 4.
23. This case is argued by Mevorah, 'Die Interventionsbestrebungen'; see also idem, 'The Imperial Court-Jew Wolf Wertheimer as diplomatic mediator', *Scripta Hierosolymitana*, XXII (1972), pp. 184–201.
24. Kobler, *Letters of Jews*, pp. 607–8; Bergl, *Exil*, p. 277.
25. Ibid., p. 291.
26. Wertheimer (in Regensburg) to Moses Hart (London), 8 December 1747, in Kobler, *Letters of Jews*, pp. 609–10.
27. Bergl, *Die Ausweisung*, pp. 312–13.
28. Bergl, *Exil*, p. 314; T. Jakobovits, 'Die Zünfte während der Austreibung der Juden aus Prag', *JGGJCR*, VIII (1936), pp. 111–18.
29. Kobler, *Letters of Jews*, pp. 609–10; Lieben, 'Briefe von 1744–1748', No. 79, dated Av [5]508 = July 1748.
30. Bergl, *Das Exil*, pp. 320–5.
31. See S. Krauss, *Joachim Edler v. Popper* (Vienna: Selbstverlag des Verfassers, 1926), pp. 78–9; and G. Wolf, 'Die Vertreibung', pp. 169, 223.
32. S. H. Lieben, 'Die von Maria Theresa projektierte Esrogim-Steuer', *MGWJ*, 53 (1909), pp. 720–2; Bergl, *Exil*, pp. 327–9.
33. See the material cited in J. Karniel, *Die Toleranzpolitik Kaisers Josephs II* (Gerlingen: Bleicher, 1985), p. 32; Gerson Wolf, *Aus der Zeit der Maria Theresa* (Vienna: Hölder, 1871), pp. 63, 71.
34. See M. Saperstein, 'War and Patriotism in Sermons to Central European Jews: 1756–1815', *LBYB*, XXXVIII (1993), pp. 3–14, esp. pp. 7 ff.; Vind, *Yehezke'el Landau*, pp. 16–17, 20; M. Popper, 'Die Juden in Prag und der Siebenjährige Krieg', *MGWJ*, 38 (1894), pp. 415–21.
35. Pribram, *Urkunden*, I, No. 199.
36. J. Karniel, 'Zur Auswirkung der Toleranzpatente', in P. Barton (ed.), *Im Zeichen der Toleranz* (Vienna: Institut für Protestantische Kirchengeschichte, 1981), pp. 204–20.
37. Schnee, *Hoffinanz*, III, p. 247; IV, pp. 316–17; Grunwald, *Oppenheimer*, pp. 282, 295 ff.; Wachstein, *Quellen*, II, pp. 312 ff.
38. Pribram, *Urkunden*, I, p. 391.
39. Rabbi Dr M. Papo, 'The Sephardi community of Vienna', in J. Fraenkel (ed.) *The Jews of Austria* (London: Vallentine Mitchell, 1967), pp. 327–46; N. M. Gelber, 'Al Reshita Shel Ha-Kehillah Ha-Sephardit be-Vienna', in *Sefer Ha-Zikaron le Bet Ha-Midrash la-rabbanut be-Vienna* (Jerusalem: Reuben Maas, 1946), pp. 105–11; Grunwald, *Vienna*, pp. 391–2; N. M. Gelber, 'The Sephardic community in Vienna', *JSS*, X (1948), pp. 359–96.
40. Pribram, *Urkunden*, I, Nos. 149, 150; Grunwald, *Vienna*, pp. 185–7; see also S. Mayer, *Die Wiener Juden 1700–1900* (Vienna: Löwit Verlag, 1917), p. 263.
41. Pribram, *Urkunden*, I, No. 174; Grunwald, *Vienna*, p. 139.
42. P. G. Dickson, *Finance and Government under Maria Theresa 1740–1780*, II (Oxford: Clarendon Press, 1987), pp. 304–5; perhaps Lazar Oesterreicher also belonged to this group. After the Seven Years' War he took on the task of army supply in Austria and Bohemia but his resources were unequal to the demands made on them; see C. Duffy, *The Army of Maria Theresa* (London: David & Charles, 1977), p. 127.
43. Pribram, *Urkunden*, I, No.161, III, para. 8; see also Krauss, *Popper*, p. 30.
44. W. O. McCagg, 'Jewish Wealth in Vienna 1670–1918', in M. Silber (ed.), *Jews in the Hungarian Economy* (Jerusalem: Magnes Press, 1992), pp. 53–91, here p. 57; Mayer, *Wiener Juden*, p. 99; Grunwald, *Vienna*, p. 143.

45. Karniel, *Toleranzpolitik*, pp. 247–8; for a list of members, see B. Wachstein, 'Die Gründung der Wiener Chevrah Kadishah', *Mitteilungen zur jüdischen Volkskunde*, XIII (1910), pp. 9–12.
46. For the significance of this phenomenon see p. 242 above.
47. Pribram, *Urkunden*, I, No. 202, v.
48. Ibid., Nos. 175, 179; McCagg, 'Jewish Wealth', p. 63; see also Wolf, *Juden in Wien*, p. 70.
49. Karniel, *Toleranzpolitik*, p. 116.
50. Pribram, *Urkunden*, I, No. 185.
51. Wetzlar, formerly one of 'Frederick the Great's Jews', made his fortune in the Seven Years' War and later moved to Vienna. He became a convert in 1777 and was raised to the nobility as Karl Abraham Wetzlar Freiherr von Plankenstern. In his mansion in 1783 Mozart first met his future librettist, Lorenzo da Ponte, né Emanuele Conegliano, in the ghetto of Ceneda (S. Hodges, *Lorenzo da Ponte* [London: Grafton, 1985], pp. 3 ff., 47).
52. Pribram, *Urkunden*, I, No.185, v, vi (esp. fn. 2) XVIII; Grunwald, *Vienna*, pp. 142, 191; Wolf, *Juden in Wien*, p. 72.
53. A. Tartakower, 'Jewish Migratory Movements', in Fraenkel, *Jews of Austria*, p. 286; McCagg, 'Jewish Wealth', p. 56.

11 The Old and the New *Kehillah*

1. In other words, the static and abstract sociological categories of 'traditional' and 'modern' society postulated by Jacob Katz (see his *Tradition and Crisis*, Engl. trans., Schocken Books, New York, 1993) fail to do justice to the evolutionary factor, especially where the impact of poverty as an agency of social change, which Katz largely ignores, is concerned. Poppel has described this work as 'schematic' and also pointed out that 'there is little social data on the great mass of Jews whose fate was at issue in the great struggle for emancipation, or on the limited elites who expounded the ideologies that Katz describes' (S. M. Poppel, 'New Views on Jewish Integration in Germany', *Central European History*, IX (1976), pp. 86–108).
2. M. Dienemann, 'Die Geschichte der Einzelgemeinde als Spiegel der Gesamtgeschichte', in E. Roth (ed.), *Die alte Synagoge zu Worms* (Frankfurt am Main: Ner Tamid Verlag, 1961), p. 171.
3. Néher-Bernheim, *Documents*, pp. 40 ff.; H. Monin, 'Les Juifs de Paris à la fin de l'Ancien Régime', *REJ*, xxiii (1891), pp. 85–98; cases from eastern France in Hertzberg, *French Enlightenment*, pp. 56 ff.; Iancu, *Juifs du Midi*, p. 219; C. Casper-Holtkotte, *Juden im Aufbruch* (Hanover: Hahnsche, 1996), pp. 181 ff.
4. M. Shulvass, *From East to West* (Detroit: Wayne State University Press, 1971), pp. 108 ff.
5. Sergio Della Pergola, 'An Overview of Demographic Trends', in J. Webber (ed.), *Jewish Identities in the New Europe* (London: Littman, 1994), pp. 57–73. See the data cited in A. Polonsky, *The Jews in Old Poland* (London: Tauris, 1993), p. 4; also R. Mahler, *Yidn in amolikn Polin im Likht fun Ziffern* (Warsaw, 1958), *passim*.
6. Breuer, *German-Jewish History*, p. 151; R. Liberles, 'Future Research', *LBYB*, XLV (2000), p. 212.
7. See the remarks by G. Otruba in F. Seibt (ed.) *Die Juden in den böhmischen Ländern* (Munich: Oldenbourg, 1983), p. 325.
8. R. Judah Hurwitz, *Amudei Beit Yehudah* (Amsterdam, 1766), p. 13b; see also B.-Z. Katz, *Rabbanut, Hassidut, Haskalah*, 2 vols (Tel-Aviv: Dvir, 1956), II, pp. 122–8.
9. Simonsohn, *Jews of Mantua*, 1977, p. 403.

10. Kracauer, *Frankfurter Juden*, II, p. 145; see also U. Kaufmann, 'Jüdische Handwerker', in K. Grözinger (ed.), *Jüdische Kultur in Frankfurt am Main* (Wiesbaden: Harassowitz, 1997), pp. 47–71, esp. pp. 57–8; P. Hildenfinger, *Documents sur les Juifs à Paris au XVIIIe Siècle* (Paris: Champion, 1913), pp. 26, 44.

11. J. Maitlis, 'London Yiddish Letters of the Early 18th Century', *JSS*, VI (1955), pp. 153–65; J. Michman, 'The Impact of German-Jewish, Modernization on Dutch Jews', in J. Katz (ed.), *Towards Modernity* (Oxford: Transaction, 1987), p. 175; D. Penslar, *Shylock's Children* (California University Press, 2001), pp. 35–6.

12. Naggar, *Jewish Pedlars*, passim; V. D. Lipman, 'Sephardi and Other Jewish Immigrants in England', in *Migration and Settlement* (London: JHSE, 1971), pp. 37–62; R. D. Barnett, 'Anglo-Jewry in the Eighteenth Century', in V. D. Lipman (ed.), *Three Centuries of Anglo-Jewish History* (London: JHSE, 1961), pp. 45–68; Endelman, *Jews of Georgian England*, pp. 231 ff.

13. Raphael and Weyl, *Juifs en Alsace*, p. 374.

14. *Life of Glückel*, pp. 43–4; H. Rachel, 'Die Juden im Berliner Wirtschaftsleben', *ZGJD*, 2 (1930), pp. 175–96, esp. p. 179; Grunwald, *Oppenheimer*, p. 35; Cohen, *Landjudenschaften*, I, p. 231; R. Ezekiel Landau, *Noda Biyehudah*, I, No. 34, p. 29; A. Frankl-Grün, 'Die Folgen des österreichischen Erbfolgekrieges für die Juden Kremsiers', *MGWJ*, 38 (1894), p. 275; M. Ginsburger, 'Strasbourg et les Juifs', *REJ*, 79 (1924), p. 173; Naggar, *Jewish Pedlars*, pp. 36 ff.

15. Blumenkranz, *Juifs en France*, p. 113; see also Meyer, *Communauté Juive*, p. 94; K. E. Demandt, *Bevölkerungs- und Sozialgeschichte der jüdischen Gemeinde Niedenstein 1653–1866* (Wiesbaden: Kommission für die Geschichte der Juden in Hessen, 1980), pp. 43–4.

16. M. Grunwald, *Hamburgs deutsche Juden* (Hamburg: Janssen, 1904), p. 4; B. Wachstein (ed.), *Urkunden und Akten zur Geschichte der Juden in Eisenstadt* (Vienna: Braumüller, 1926), No. 137, pp. 157–8.

17. *Registre*, No. 173.

18. S. M. Lowenstein, 'Two Silent Minorities, Orthodox Jews and Poor Jews in Berlin, 1770–1823', *LBYB*, XXXVI (1991), p. 23.

19. Meisl, *Pinkas*, No. 169; S. Maimon, *Geschichte des eigenen Lebens* (Berlin: Schocken, 1936), pp. 127 ff., 141 ff.; J. R. Marcus, *Communal Sick Care in the German Ghetto* (Cincinnati: Hebrew Union College Press, 1947), pp. 193–4.

20. I take these examples from S. W. Baron, *The Jewish Community*, 3 vols (Philadelphia, PA: JPSA, 5706-1945), II, pp. 332–3.

21. D. Kaufmann, 'Die Schuldennot der Gemeinde Posen', *MGWJ*, 39 (1895), pp. 38–46; D. McEwan, 'The Fischer Family Archives in London', *German History*, 5 (1987), pp. 74–81; Stern, *Akten*, I/2, No. 368; Grunwald, *Hamburgs deutsche Juden*, p. 125; J. Jacobson, *Jüdische Trauungen in Berlin 1759–1813* (Berlin: De Gruyter, 1968), pp. xxi ff.; S. M. Lowenstein, 'Ashkenazic Jewry and the European Marriage Pattern', *JH*, viii (1994), pp. 155–75, esp. p. 157; Elkan Henle, 'Über die Verbesserung des Judentums', *Shulamit*, 2 (1808), pp. 361–83, esp. pp. 374 ff.

22. G. D. Hundert, 'Shkiot Yirat Kavod be-kehillot beit Yisrael be-Lita', *Bar-Ilan Annual*, XXIV–XXV (1989), pp. 41–50.

23. Breuer, *German-Jewish History*, p. 247.

24. Shulvass, *From East to West*, p. 67; R. Glanz, *Geschichte des niederen Jüdischen Volkes in Deutschland* (New York: Leo Baeck-Yivo, 1968); Calmann, *Carpentras*, p. 99; Z. Szajkowski, *Poverty and Social Welfare among French Jews* (New York: Editions Historiques, 1954), p. 6.

25. Cohen, *Landjudenschaften in Deutschland*, I, No. 8:71; Meyer, *Communauté Juive*, p. 49.

26. S. Rohrbacher, 'Räuberbanden', in J. Bohnke-Kollwitz (ed.), *Köln und das rheinische Judentum* (Cologne: Bachem, 1984), pp. 117 ff.
27. See the description in Marcus, *Communal Sick Care*, p. 177.
28. See J. Toury, *Der Eintritt der Juden ins deutsche Bürgertum* (Tel Aviv: Diaspora Research Institute, 1972), p. 165; see Mendelssohn's comment in Part II of C. W. Dohm, *Uber die bürgerliche Verbesserung der Juden* (Berlin/Stettin, 1783), II, p. 72. ('Protection' [*Schutz*] is used here in the sense of membership of a community which has paid 'protection money' [*Schutzgeld*] for the right to live on certain conditions for a certain period in a certain locality.)
29. F. Egmond, 'Crime in Context: Jewish Involvement in Organised Crime in the Dutch Republic', *Jewish History*, IV (1998), pp. 75–100; Rohrbacher, *Räuberbanden, passim*; G. Friess, 'Zur Lebenswelt jüdischer Räuberbanden unter besonderer Berücksichtigung Pommerns', in M. Heitman and H. J. Schoeps (eds), *Geschichte der Juden in Pommern*, 1995, pp. 299 ff.; Endelman, *Jews of Georgian England*, p. 196.
30. Glanz, *Leben des niederen Jüdischen Volkes*, pp. 97, 303 fn.19, 168, 94, 101; Malino, 'Resistance and Rebellion', p. 65; see also C. Küther, *Räuber und Gauner in Deutschland* (Göttingen: Vandenhoeck & Ruprecht, 1987), p. 76.
31. Rabbi I. N. Mannheimer, *Gottesdienstliche Vorträge* (Vienna, 1835), p. 422. I owe this reference to the kindness of Professor D. Penslar.
32. M. Richarz (ed.), *Jewish Life in Germany*, Engl. (slightly modified) trans. (Bloomington: Indiana University Press, 1991), p. 3.
33. C. Clark, *The Politics of Conversion* (Oxford: Clarendon Press, 1995), pp. 59–60.
34. Quoted H. Pollack, *Jewish Folkways in Germanic Lands* (Cambridge, MA: MIT Press, 1971), p. 164.
35. A. Berliner, *Geschichte der Juden in Rom*, repr. (Hildesheim: Olms, 1987), II, p. 104.
36. Gaster, *History of the Ancient Synagogue*, p. 88; *Registre*, No. 13; Swetchinski, *Reluctant Cosmopolitans*, p. 193; Jonathan Israel, *Jews in Mercantilism*, p. 244; B.-Z. Ornan Pinkus, *Die Portugiesische Gemeinde in Hamburg*, in M. Studemund-Halevy (ed.), *Die Sephardim in Hamburg*, I (Hamburg: Buske, 1997), pp. 7–9; G. Marwedel (ed.), *Die Privilegien der Juden in Altona*, (Hamburg: Christians, 1976), No. 85; D. Cohen, *Landjudenschaften in Deutschland* I, Nos. 6:21–7.
37. S. Singer, 'Jews and Coronations', *TJHSE*, V (1902–05), pp. 79–114.
38. This is a quotation from a Harvard PhD thesis entitled 'Becoming French: Patriotic Liturgy and the Transformation of Jewish Identity in France, 1706–1815', submitted by R. B. Schechter, September 1993, pp. 11–12; see also A. Shohat, 'Hitarutam shel Yehudei Germaniya Ba-Svivotam', *Tsiyon*, 21 (1956), pp. 207–35, esp. p. 227.
39. Schechter, 'Becoming French', pp. 50 ff.
40. M. Saperstein, 'War and Patriotism in Sermons to Central European Jews, 1756–1815', *LBYB*, XXXVIII (1993), pp. 3–14.
41. For a convenient summary of Mendelssohn's views, see Michael Meyer, *The Origins of the Modern Jew* (Detroit: Wayne State University Press, 1967), pp. 24–5.
42. Hagiz, *Sfat Emet*, pp. 13, 18, 30, 33, 106.
43. R. Jacob Emden, *Siddur Amudei Shamayim* (Altona, 1735), I: 35a; see also J. J. Schacter, 'Echoes of the Spanish Expulsion in 18th Century Germany', *Judaism*, 41 (1992), pp. 180–9.
44. R. Jacob Emden, *Megilat Sefer*, repr. (Jerusalem: Jewish Classics, 1979), pp. 40, 62, 116–17, 147; see the material cited in A. Bik, *Rabbi Ya'akov Emden* (Jerusalem: Mossad Ha-Rav Kuk, 1974), p. 142, and in Shohat, *Im Hilufei Tekufot*, pp. 117–18; also A. Bik, 'Rabbi Ya'akov Emden u-Milhamato be-Shulhanei Altona,' *Tarbitz*, 42 (1973), pp. 461–8.

45. See the extracts quoted in B.-Z. Katz, *Rabbanut, Hassidut, Haskalah*, II, pp. 126–7.
46. M. Faierstein (ed. and trans.), *The Libes Briv of Isaac Wetzlar* (Brown University, 1996), *passim*; see also idem, 'The Liebes Brief – A Critique of Jewish Society in Germany (1749)', *LBYB*, XXVII (1982), pp. 219–41, here p. 227.
47. H. M. Graupe (ed.), *Takkanot Shlosh Kehillot* (Hamburg: Christians, 1973), II, No. 3, p. 188; R. Jonathan Eibeschütz, Urim Ve'Tummim, 26, quoted A. Schreiber, *Jewish Law and Decision-Making* (Philadelphia, PA: Temple University Press, 1979), pp. 336–7.
48. Stein, 'Some Ashkenazi Charities in London', p. 64.
49. C. Abramsky, 'The Crisis of Authority within European Jewry in the Eighteenth Century', in S. Stein and R. Loewe (eds), *Studies in Jewish Religious and Intellectual History* (Tuscaloosa: Alabama University Press, 1979), pp. 13–28.

12 'Jerusalem' in Berlin

1. I. M. Jost, *Geschichte des Judentums und seiner Sekten* (Leipzig: Dörfling, 1859), iii, pp. 285–92.
2. Meisl, *Pinkas*, Intro., ch. 2, pt. iii; and no. 312; Stern, *Akten*, III/2–1, nos. 96, 110.
3. See S. Jersch-Wenzel, *Juden und Franzosen in der Wirtschaft des Raumes Berlin/Brandenburg zur Zeit des Merkantilismus* (Berlin: De Gruyter, 1978), ch. 5.
4. Stern, *Akten*, III/2–1, nos. 99, 118.
5. Meisl, *Pinkas, passim*. For the loans raised by the community in 1761 see ibid., nos. 142–3.
6. Moritz Stern, 'Zur Geschichte der Fleischgebühren', *Soncino Blätter*, II (1927); S. Lowenstein, 'Two Silent Minorities', *LBYB*, XXXVI (1991), pp. 3–27, esp. p. 5; see also idem, *The Berlin Jewish Community* (Oxford University Press, 1994), pp. 15–16.
7. Dolf Michaelis, 'The Ephraim Family', *LBYB*, XXI (1976), pp. 201–28, esp. p. 215; Meisl, *Pinkas*, p. viii; M. Stern, 'Das Vereinsbuch des Berliner Beth Hamidrasch 1743–1783', *JJLG*, XXII (1931–2), pp. 401–20, pp. I–XVIII (Heb. section).
8. Meisl, *Pinkas*, pp. lxxii–lxxiii, fn. 152.
9. Schnee, *Hoffinanz*, I, p. 190; J. Jacobson, *Jüdische Trauungen in Berlin*, p. xix; H. Seeliger, 'Origin and Growth of the Berlin Jewish Community', *LBYB*, III (1958), pp. 161–2.
10. See table 3 in J. Toury, *Kavim le-heker knisat Ha-Yehudim la-Hayyim Ha-Ezrahiim be-Germaniya* (Tel Aviv: Ha-Makhon le-Heker Ha-Tfutsot, 1972), p. 19.
11. See Miriam Bodian, 'Mishpakhat Gomperts be-Germaniya ba-Me'ot 17–18', *Proceedings of the 10th World Congress of Jewish Studies*, Div. B, I (Jerusalem, 1990), pp. 177–82; idem, 'Ha-Yazmim ha-Yehudiim be-Berlin'; H. C. Johnson, *Frederick the Great and his Officials* (Newhaven, CT: Yale University Press, 1975), p. 92.
12. F. Oppeln-Bronikowski (ed. and trans.), *Friedrich der Grosse: Politische Testamente* (Munich: Treu, 1941), pp. 28, 35, 141.
13. Stern, *Akten*, III, 2–1, no. 64; see also Freund, *Emanzipation der Juden*, I, pp. 18–19, fn. 5.
14. Geiger, *Geschichte der Juden in Berlin*, p. 145.
15. The *reglement* is reproduced in full in Freund, *Emanzipation der Juden*, II, Urkunden pp. 22–5; see the remarks by S. Jersch-Wenzel, 'Die Herausbildung eines "Preussischen" Judentums 1671–1815', in P. Freimark (ed.), *Juden in Preussen – Juden in Hamburg* (Hamburg: Christians, 1983), pp. 11–31, esp. p. 17.
16. Stern, *Akten*, III/2–1, nos. 63, 68.

17. Ibid., III/2–1, nos. 65, 75, 78, 91; Marcus, *Jew in the Medieval World*, pp. 92–3.
18. Stern, *Akten*, III/1, p. 120; III/2–1, no. 97.
19. For the text of the *reglement* see Freund, *Emanzipation der Juden*, II, Urkunden pp. 22–60; there is a fairly free English translation in Mendes-Flohr and Reinharz, *Jew in the Modern World*, pp. 22–7; see also Stern, *Akten*, III/2–1, nos. 113, 450.
20. Stern, *Akten*, III/2–1, nos. 106–7; for a brief sketch of the extent to which the political views of Spinoza and Mendelssohn converge, see pp. 215 ff. above. In 1750 Cocceji attended a session of the rabbinic court in Cleves and to his dismay found it exceeding its powers (ibid., no. 98). As for the lacunae Cocceji supposedly perceived in the laws of the person whom he called the 'honourable Moses', he had evidently overlooked the conditions of inheritance in the situation raised by the daughters of Zelophehad (Num. 27:1–11).
21. Stern, *Akten*, III/2–1, no. 145.
22. The various interchanges are summarized in Stern, *Akten*, III/1, pp. 121–2; cf. also III/2–1, no. 454 and particularly no. 466; Geiger, *Geschichte der Juden*, II, p. 125; Landshut, *Toldot Anshei Shem*, p. 40.
23. Stern, *Akten*, II/2, no. 253; see also S. Stern, 'Die Juden in der Handelspolitik Wilhelm I von Preussen', *ZGJD*, V (1935), pp. 207–15.
24. See Michaelis, 'Ephraim Family', pp. 221–8; F. v. Schröter, *Das Preussische Münzwesen* (Berlin: Parey, 1908), II, pp. 208, 227, 251, 255; III, pp. 82, 85, 110; Johnson, *Frederick the Great*, pp. 183–4; see also P. Baumgart, 'Die Stellung der jüdischen Minorität im Staat des aufgeklärten Absolutismus', *Kairos*, XXII (1980), pp. 226–45, esp. p. 244.
25. See S. M. Lowenstein, 'Jewish Upper Crust and Berlin Jewish Enlightenment', in F. Malino and D. Sorkin (eds), *From East to West* (Oxford: Blackwell, 1990), pp. 182–201; idem, *Berlin Jewish Community*, p. 22.
26. This is based on M. Saperstein, *Your Voice like a Ram's Horn* (Cincinnati: Hebrew Union College Press, 1997), pp. 151–2.
27. Jersch-Wenzel, 'Herausbildung eines "preussischen" Judentums', pp. 12, 30–1. 'Fritzische Gesinnung' might very roughly be translated as a 'feeling' for Frederick combined with a nuance of sympathy.
28. For a short summary of the tax position, see H. Holeczek, 'Die Judenemanzipation in Preussen', in B. Martin and E. Schulin (eds), *Die Juden als Minderheit in der Geschichte* (Munich: DTV, 1981), pp. 136–7; also S. Jersch-Wenzel, *Juden und Franzosen*, p. 165; Stern, *Akten*, III/2–1, no. 279.
29. This erroneous view is put forward by Priebatsch, 'Judenpolitik des fürstlichen Absolutismus', p. 651; Selma Stern (Stern, *Akten*, II/1, pp. 20, 149); and Schnee (*Hoffinanz*, IV, p. 346). The same view also colours Baumgart, 'Absoluter Staat und Judenemanzipation'. For a balanced presentation of the argument, see J. Toury, 'Der Eintritt der Juden ins deutsche Bürgertum', in H. Liebeschutz and A. Paucker (eds), *Das Judentum in der deutschen Umwelt, 1800–1850* (Tübingen: Mohr, 1977), pp. 139–242, esp. pp. 153 ff.
30. Stern, *Akten*, III/2–1, nos. 515, 548, 548a; for a characterization of Marcus, see idem, *Akten*, III/1, p. 203.
31. Ibid., III/2–1, no. 124.
32. Schnee, *Hoffinanz*, V, pp. 36–7; I, pp. 186–7; Moritz Stern, 'Der Oberlandesälteste Jacob Moses', *Mitteilungen des Gesamtarchivs der deutschen Juden*, VI (1926), pp. 14–40.
33. See Stern, *Akten*, III/1, pp. 188–9 and III/2–1, nos. 374, 377, 380; also Bodian, *Ha-Yazmim Ha-Yehudiim*, p. 165.

34. Stern, *Akten*, III/2–2, nos. 1115, 1128; Stern, 'Jacob Moses', pp. 39–40; W. W. Hagen, *Germans, Poles and Jews* (Chicago University Press, 1980), p. 46.
35. See the material quoted in Shohat, *Im Hilufei Tkufot*, pp. 272–3.
36. S. M. Lowenstein, 'Two Silent Minorities', *LBYB*, XXXVI (1991), pp. 24–5.
37. W. I. Cohn, 'The Moses Isaac Family Trust', *LBYB*, XVIII (1973), pp. 267–80.
38. Meisl, *Pinkas*, no. 234; see also ibid., p. xlviii; Stern, *Akten*, III/2–1, no. 537.
39. For all above, see S. Rawidowicz (ed.), *Moses Mendelssohn Gesammelte Schriften*, (Berlin: Akademie, 1930) VII/I, *passim*; also M. Stern, 'Die Anfänge von Hirschel Löbels Berliner Rabbinat', *Jeschurun*, XVII (1930), pp. 364–5; and idem, 'Meyer Simon Weyl, der letzte Kurbrandenburgische Landrabbiner', *Jeschurun*, XIII (1926), pp. 290–1.
40. Stern, *Akten*, III/2–1, no. 491; ibid., III/1, pp. 288–9.
41. See Isaac Abraham Euchel's dedication to his translation of the liturgy, Königsberg, 1786, pp. 4a–b; W. Weinberg, 'Language Questions Relating to Moses Mendelssohn's Pentateuch Translation', *HUCA*, LV (1984), pp. 197–242. This article fully documents the alarming decline in knowledge of Hebrew; Landshut, *Toldot Anshei Shem*, p. 81.
42. L. Geiger, 'Ein Brief Moses Mendelssohns und sechs Briefe David Friedländers', *ZGJD*, I (1887), pp. 268, 271.
43. A. Gotzmann, 'The Dissociation of Religion and Law in Nineteenth Century German-Jewish education', *LBYB*, XLIII (1998), *passim*; see also J. Petuchowski, 'Manuals and Catechisms of the Jewish Religion in the Early Period of Emancipation', in A. Altmann (ed.), *Studies in Nineteenth Century Jewish Intellectual History* (Cambridge, MA: Harvard University Press, 1964), pp. 47–64.
44. F. Rosenzweig, *Vorspruch zu einer Mendelssohn-Feier, Kleinere Schriften* (Berlin: Schocken, 1937), p. 53.
45. See M. Mendelssohn, 'Einleitung zur Ubersetzung der Schrift des R. Menasse b. Israel – Rettung der Juden', in M. Brasch (ed.), *Moses Mendelssohns Schriften* (Leipzig: Voss, 1880), I, pp. 475–500.
46. M. Mendelssohn, *Jerusalem*, trans. A. Arkush (Brandeis University Press, 1983), p. 70.
47. For a sympathetic exposition of the relationship between Spinoza and Mendelssohn, see J. Guttmann, 'Mendelssohn's Jerusalem and Spinoza's Tractatus', in *Bericht der Hochschule für die Wissenschaft des Judentums*, no. 48 (Berlin, 1931), pp. 33–67.
48. Mendelssohn, *Jerusalem*, pp. 132, 130–1, 100–1, 134.
49. Ibid., p. 135.
50. Maimon, *Geschichte des eigenen Lebens*, p. 157.

13 On the Eve, in France

1. See R. Néher-Bernheim, 'Jacob Rodrigues Péreire', *REJ*, 142 (1983), pp. 373–449, here pp. 408–9.
2. *Registre*, p. 591.
3. Camille Bloch, 'Un Épisode de l'Histoire Commerciale des Juifs en Languedoc (1738)', *REJ*, XXIV (1892), pp. 272–80; Françoise Hildesheimer, 'La Présence Juive en Provence à la Fin de l'Ancien Régime', in Blumenkranz, *Les Juifs en France au XVIIIe Siècle*, pp. 111–23.
4. Ibid., pp. 162 ff.
5. Iancu, *Juifs du Midi*, p. 164.
6. For all these data see Cavignac, *A Bordeaux et Bayonne*, pp. 56 ff.

342 *Notes*

7. Elie Szapiro, 'Le Sud-Ouest', in Blumenkranz, *Juifs en France au xviiᵉ siècle*, pp. 221–61, here pp. 241 ff.
8. Cavignac, *A Bordeaux et Bayonne*, p. 68; *Registre*, pp. 588, 592, 593.
9. Léon, *Juifs de Bayonne*, p. 147; *Registre*, No. 85; Malino, *Sephardic Jews of Bordeaux*, p. 24; S. Schwarzfuchs, 'Notes sur les Juifs de Bayonne', *REJ*, Nos. 125–6 (1966–67), pp. 353–64.
10. R. Hayyim Joseph Azulai, *Sefer Ma'agal Tov*, (Jerusalem, 1934), p. 114.
11. *Registre*, Nos. 280, 422; Menkis, 'Patriarchs and Patricians', pp. 39–40.
12. Néher-Bernheim, *Documents*, p. 157.
13. R. B. Schechter, 'Becoming French: Patriotic Liturgy and the Transformation of Jewish Identity in France, 1706–1815', D.Phil. thesis, Harvard University, 1993, pp. 24 ff.; *Registre*, Nos. 504–5.
14. Zalkind Hourwitz, *Apologie des Juifs*, repr. (Paris: Editions d'Histoire Sociale, 1989), pp. 3, 34, 39, 61, 65; see also F. Malino, *A Jew in the French Revolution* (Oxford: Blackwell, 1996).
15. I take this description from R. Néher-Bernheim, 'Cerfberr de Medelsheim: Le Destin d'une Famille Durant la Révolution', *REJ*, 137 (1978), pp. 61–75.
16. J. Weil, 'Contribution à l'Histoire des Communautés Alsaciennes au 18e Siècle', *REJ*, 81 (1925), pp. 169–80; M. Ginsburger, 'Une Fondation de Cerf Berr', ibid., 74–7 (1922), pp. 47–57; Néher-Bernheim, *Documents*, pp. 175–9.
17. Néher-Bernheim, *Documents*, ii, p. 325; see also Blumenkranz, *Documents*, AN 0169 No. 139.
18. For the Protocols of the assembly of 1777, see *Blätter für jüdische Geschichte und Litteratur*, 2 (1901), pp. 18–22, 28–9, and, for a comprehensive study of the topic, J. Berkovitz, 'Social and Religious Controls in Pre-Revolutionary France', *JH*, xv, No. 1 (2000), pp. 1–40, esp. pp. 20 ff.; see also G. Weill, 'Rabbins et Parnassim dans l'Alsace du XVIIIe Siècle', in M. Yardeni (ed.), *Les Juifs dans l'Histoire de France* (Leiden: Brill, 1980), pp. 96–109; Néher-Bernheim, *Documents*, pp. 95 ff. M. Ginsburger, 'Un Emprunt de la Nation Juive d'Alsace', *REJ*, 81 (1925), pp. 83–6.
19. Néher-Bernheim, *Documents*, p. 97.
20. Meyer, *Communauté Juive*, pp. 98–9.
21. Ibid., pp. 103 ff.; Hertzberg, *French Enlightenment and the Jews*, pp. 128–30; Netter, 'Schuldennot Metz', passim.
22. Meyer, *Communauté Juive*, pp. 45–6, 70, 187 ff.
23. Blumenkranz, *Documents*, AE 0984, pp. 111–12.
24. See pp. 155–200 of the Berlin edition of 1781 of Dohm's work; also A. Altmann, *Moses Mendelssohn* (London: Routledge, 1973), pp. 449 ff.; R. Liberles, 'Dohm's Treatise on the Jews', *LBYB*, xxxiii (1988), pp. 29–42; S. Weill, 'Les Juifs d'Alsace à la Veille de l'Emancipation', *Les Nouveaux Cahiers*, No. 97 (1989), pp. 23–8.
25. D. Feuerwerker, *L'Emancipation des Juifs en France* (Paris: Albin Michel, 1976), pp. 30 ff.; Hertzberg, *French Enlightenment and the Jews*, pp. 318–19.
26. Weil, *Rabbins et Parnassim*, p. 106; idem, 'L'Intendant d'Alsace et la Centralisation de la Nation Juive', *Dix-Huitième Siècle* No. 13 (1981), pp. 181–205; Néher-Bernheim, *Documents*, pp. 97 ff.
27. Ibid., pp. 62, 77–8; P. E. Hyman, *The Emancipation of the Jews of Alsace* (New Haven, CT: Yale University Press, 1991), pp. 12, 30.
28. M. Liber, 'Les Juifs et la Convocation des Etats Généraux', *REJ*, 65 (1912), pp. 89–133, esp. pp. 111 ff.; G. Weill, 'Recherches sur la Démographie des Juifs d'Alsace du XVI au XVIII Siècle', *REJ*, 129–130 (1970–1), pp. 51–67. Certain localities (for example Haguenau-Wissembourg) proposed in their *cahiers de doléances*

to retain these marriage restrictions – see Z. Szajkowski, *Jews and the French Revolutions of 1789, 1830, 1848* (New York: Ktav, 1970), pp. 48 ff.

29. See M. Yardeni, 'Les Juifs dans la Polémique sur la Tolérance des Protestants en France à la Veille de la Révolution', *REJ*, 132 (1973), pp. 79–94.

30. Malesherbes, *Second Mémoire sur le Mariage des Protestants en 1786*, 2nd edn (London, 1787), p. 101; generally, see P. Grosclaude, *Malesherbes* (Paris: Fischbacher, 1961), pp. 631–49.

31. On the whole episode of the Malesherbes Commission see Schwarzfuchs, *Du Juif à l'Israélite*, ch. 4; and Z. Szajkowski, 'Mishlahotehem shel Yehudei Bordeaux el ve'idat Malesherbes (1788) ve-el Ha-Asefa Ha-Le'umit (1790)', *Tsiyon*, XVIII (1953), pp. 31–79.

14 The Rabbi and the Emperor: Ezekiel Landau and Joseph II

1. Feuerwerker, *Emancipation des Juifs*, pp. 15, 169.

2. See for example the extracts from the Nikolsburg chronicle of Abraham Trebitsch quoted in Kestenberg-Gladstein, *Juden in den böhmischen Ländern*, p. 94.

3. Pribram, *Urkunden*, I, no. 205; for substantial extracts from the Edict of Toleration of 1782 and that referring to Vienna, see Mendes-Flohr and Reinharz, *Jew in the Modern World*, I, No. 9.

4. Lois Dubin, *The Port Jews of Habsburg Trieste* (Stanford: California University Press, 1999), pp. 73 ff.

5. H. Gold, *Gedenkbuch der untergegangenen Judengemeinden Mährens* (Tel Aviv: Olamenu, 1974) p. 93; V. Sadek, 'La Chronique Hébraique de l'Histoire des Juifs pragois', *Judaica Bohemiae*, No. 1 (1965), pp. 59–68.

6. Pribram, *Urkunden*, I, No. 205.

7. V. Sadek and J. Sedinova, 'Peter Berr – Penseur Eclairé de la Vieille Ville Juive de Prague', *Judaica Bohemiae*, XIII (1977), pp. 7–28; K. Schubert, 'Der Einfluss des Josefinismus auf das Judentum in Osterreich', *Kairos*, XIV (1972), pp. 82–97. *Ha-Meassef* (*'The Gleaner'*), founded in 1783 in Königsberg, was the Hebrew-language journal of the early *Haskalah*.

8. Quoted M. Breuer, 'Emancipation and the Rabbis', *Niv Hamidrashiya*, 13–14 (5738/9–1978/9), p. 28.

9. See on this point K. Lohrmann, 'Die Entwicklung des Judenrechts in Osterreich', in K. Lohrmann *et al.* (eds), *1000 Jahre Osterreichisches Judentum* (Eisenstadt: Roetger, 1982), pp. 25–54, esp. pp. 45 ff.; regarding Moravia, Brüll points out 'that Joseph's legislation did little to alleviate the pressure on the Jews' (*Juden in Mähren*, pp. 206–7).

10. W. O. McCagg Jr, *A History of Habsburg Jews, 1670–1918* (Bloomington: Indiana University Press, 1989), pp. 49–50; idem, 'Jewish Wealth in Vienna, 1670–1918', in Silber, *Jews in the Hungarian Economy*, pp. 53–91.

11. See B. Heilig, 'Aufstieg und Verfall des Hauses Ehrenstamm', in *BLBI*, X (1960), pp. 101–22.

12. Subsequent decades strongly suggest that this was just as well, or that at least the 'productivization' of the Jewish masses by means of artisanry and agriculture would have been a retrograde pursuit, that the economic programme of the absolutist monarchs and the *maskilim* was ill-conceived. Under the *ancien régime* in Bohemia and Moravia, the Jewish social structure corresponded to that of 'a future

bourgeois-industrial urban middle-class', writes one economic historian. Between the late eighteenth century and 1910 the occupational distribution of the Jews in Bohemia and Moravia changed remarkably little. 50 per cent continued to be engaged in trade, finance and commerce; 20 per cent in industry and crafts; a significant increase in the numbers of free professionals and officials took the proportion from 14 per cent to 25 per cent; an equally significant decline took the proportion of tenant-farmers (*Pächter*) from 13 per cent to 3 per cent. These data and the comment are quoted by G. Otruba in his 'Der Anteil der Juden am Wirtschaftsleben der böhmischen Länder', in Seibt (ed.), *Juden in den böhmischen Ländern*, pp. 209–68, esp. p. 219. They come originally from an article by Jan Hermann, 'Evolution of the Jewish population in Bohemia and Moravia 1754–1953' (which I have not been able to consult).

13. Quoted Kestenberg-Gladstein, *Juden in den böhmischen Ländern*, p. 32.
14. Ibid., p. 350; L. Singer, 'Die Entstehung des Juden – Systemalpatentes von 1797', *JGGJCR*, VII (1935), pp. 191–263, esp. p. 221.
15. M. Mendelssohn, *Gesammelte Schriften*, 20.2 (Stuttgart: Frommann, 1994), Nos. 248, 254, 282.
16. For a general study, see A. Kober, 'Jewish Names in the Era of Enlightenment', *HJ*, V (1943), pp. 165–81.
17. Pribram, *Urkunden*, I, No. 245.
18. Meisl, *Pinkas*, no. 209; for the further transition to Mendelssohn-Bartholdy, note the letter of Abraham, the son of Moses Mendelssohn, to *his* son, the composer, Felix: 'My father's father was called Mendel Dessau. When his son, my father, began to make a name for himself and to tear his brethren out of the deep humiliation in which they had sunk, through the spreading of a higher culture, he felt that it would be too much of a burden for him, as Moses Mendel Dessau, to come closer to those at that time in possession of this higher culture: he called himself Mendelssohn. ... But in the same way as necessity had imposed itself on my father to modify his name in a sense appropriate to his position, so did it appear to me out of piety and considerations of prudence to act in the same way... You cannot and must not be called Felix Mendelssohn ... you must therefore call yourself Felix Bartholdy because the name is a garment and this must be in accord with the epoch, the need, the status if it is not to become a hindrance or laughable ... If you are called Mendelssohn then you are *eo ipso* a Jew and that does not help you at all, precisely because it is not true'. This letter was sent to the twenty-year-old Felix while he was on a concert tour in England, in explanation of Abraham's decision to become a convert to Christianity and to have his four children baptized; see the extract in P. Peterson, 'Juden im Musikleben Hamburgs,' in A. Herzig (ed.), *Die Juden in Hamburg 1590–1990* (Hamburg: Dölling und Galitz Verlag, 1991), p. 299; see also J. Jacobson, 'Von Mendelssohn zu Mendelssohn-Bartholdy', *LBYB*, V (1960), pp. 251–61.
19. W. Stern, 'Jewish Surnames'. *LBYB*, XXII (1977), pp. 221–36; M. Liber, 'Les Juifs et la Convocation des Etats Généraux', *REJ*, LXIV (1912), p. 270; Max Warschawski, 'Enigmes dans un Cimetière', *Archives Juives*, 24 (1988), pp. 59–81.
20. H. Pollack, *Jewish Folkways in Germanic Lands* (Cambridge MA: MIT Press, 1971), pp. 25–7.
21. W. Zacek, 'Eine Studie zur Entwicklung der jüdischen Personennamen in neuerer Zeit', *JGGJCR*, VIII (1936), pp. 309–97, here p. 312; for another example, see M. Rachmuth, 'Zur Wirtschaftsgeschichte der Prager Juden', *JGGJCR*, V (1933), pp. 9–78, here pp. 76–7, fn. 60.

22. See Y. Kaplan, From *Christianity to Judaism*, Engl. trans. (Oxford University Press for the Littman Library, 1989), p. v; and 'The "De Pinto" Manuscript: A 17th century Marrano Family History', *SR*, IX (1975–6), p. 39, fn. 120.
23. See A. Büchler, *The Political and the Social Leaders of the Jewish Community of Sepphoris in the Second and Third Centuries* (Oxford University Press, n.d.), p. 47; Amos Funkenstein, 'The Dialectics of assimilation', *JSS*, I, No. 2 (1995), pp. 1–14, here p. 4.
24. The three root letters *sh*, *l*, *m* stand respectively for *shem* – name; *lashon* – language; *malbush* – attire.
25. Zacek, 'Studie zur Entwicklung', pp. 318 ff.; D. McEwan, 'Jüdisches Leben im Mährischen Ghetto', *Mitteilungen des Instituts für österreichische Geschichtsforschung* (1991), pp. 83–145, here pp. 109 ff.
26. See J. V. H. Melton, *Absolutism and the Eighteenth Century: Origins of Compulsory Schooling in Prussia and Austria* (Cambridge University Press, 1988), introduction and *passim*.
27. C. Ozer, 'Jewish Education in Transition', *HJ*, 9 (1947), pp. 75–94, 137–58.
28. See Edward Breuer, 'Naphtali Herz Wessely and the Cultural Dislocations of an Eighteenth-Century Maskil', in D. Sorkin and S. Feiner (eds), *New Perspectives on the Haskalah* (London: Littman, 2001), pp. 27–47.
29. Landshut, *Toldot Anshei Shem*, pp. 82–3; see also this volume p. 165.
30. M. Saperstein (ed.), *Jewish Preaching 1200–1800 – An Anthology* (New Haven, CT: Yale University Press, 1989), pp. 359–73, esp. p. 365; see also M. Eliav, *Ha-Hinukh Ha-Yehudi Be-Germaniya* (Jerusalem: Jewish Agency, 1960), pp. 39–51; M. Samet, 'Mendelssohn, N. H. Weisel ve-rabbanei doram', in *Mehkarim be-toldot am Yisrael* (Haifa, 1970), pp. 223–57.
31. Duschinsky, *Rabbinate of the Great Synagogue*, pp. 249–50.
32. Pribram, *Urkunden*, II, p. 605.
33. M. Silber, 'The Historical Experience of German Jewry and its Impact on Haskalah and Reform in Hungary', in J. Katz (ed.), *Towards Modernity* (Oxford: Transaction, 1987), pp. 107–57, esp. p. 147, fn. 29.
34. Lois Dubin, 'Trieste and Berlin: The Italian Role in the Cultural Politics of the Haskalah', in Katz, *Towards Modernity*, pp. 189–224, here p. 197.
35. Quoted M. Saperstein, 'Chief Rabbi Ezekiel Landau', in S. Gilman and J. Zipis (eds), *Yale Companion to Jewish Writing* (New Haven, CT: Yale University Press, 1997), pp. 84–7, here p. 86.
36. H. Kieval, *The Making of Czech Jewry* (Oxford University Press, 1988), p. 5 ff.
37. Dohm, *Bürgerliche Verbesserung*, II, pp. 237 ff.; see also the chapter devoted to army service in Y.-Z. Kahana, *Mehkarim be-sifrut ha-tshuvot* (Jerusalem: Mossad Ha-Rav Kuk, 1973), pp. 163–94.
38. See the letter of the Triestine to the Polish rabbis in Dubin, *Port Jews of Trieste*, pp. 149–50, and the rabbinic declaration quoted in S. K. Padover, *The Revolutionary Emperor*, 2nd edn (London: Eyre & Spottiswoode, 1967), pp. 184–85; Simonsohn, *Jews in Mantua*, p. 75.
39. S. Dubnow, *Weltgeschichte des Jüdischen Volkes*, German trans. (Berlin: Jüdischer Verlag, 1929), IX, pp. 188 ff.; see also M. Stanislavsky, *Tsar Nicholas and the Jews* (Philadelphia: JPSA, 5743–1983), pp. 28 ff; and J. Katz, 'Towards a Biography of the Hatam Sofer,' in Malino and Sorkin, *From East and West*, pp. 223–66, here p. 238.
40. Richarz, *Jewish Life in Germany*, p. 57.
41. H. Teufel, 'Ein Schüler Mendelssohns – Herz Homberg', in G. Ammerer *et al.* (eds), *Ambivalenzen der Aufklärung* (Munich: Oldenburg, 1997), pp. 187–202; H. Homberg, *Bne-Zion* (Vienna, 1812), No. 397.

42. For the text and eye-witness account of Landau's address, see Kestenberg-Gladstein, *Juden in den böhmischen Ländern*, pp. 70–72; for his later views, ibid., pp. 339–40.

43. Dubin, *Port Jews of Habsburg Trieste*, p. 193.

44. Pribram, *Urkunden*, I, No. 231, iii; see also ibid., vi.

45. R. Shlomo Vind, *Ha-Rav Yehezke'el Landau* (Jerusalem: Hatzalat Da'at Ha-Torah, 1961), appx. II, pp. 95 ff.; see also the quoted extracts from the memoranda of rabbis from Bohemia and Galicia in Pribram, *Urkunden*, I, No. 231, iv; G. Graff, *Dina de'malkhuta Dina in Jewish Law, 1750–1848* (Alabama University Press, 1985), p. 47.

46. Pribram, *Urkunden*, I, No. 231, XII.

47. S. D. Munk, *Toldot Rabbenu Yehezke'el Landau* (Jerusalem, 1953), pp. 12, 14.

48. R. Ezekiel Landau, *Noda Bi'Yehudah: Even Ha-Ezer*, repr. (Jerusalem, 1969), no. 88; for an account of Landau's modus operandi, see A. L. Gilman, *Ha-Noda Bi'Yehudah U-Mishnato* (Jerusalem: Mossad Ha-Rav Kuk, 1960), ch. 2; and Y. Kamelhar, *Sefer Mofet Ha-Dor* (Piotrkow, 1934), p. 76.

49. *Noda Bi'Yehudah* ii: *Orekh Hayyim*, nos. 29, 38, 33.

50. Vind, *Ha-Rav Landau*, pp. 34–5. Eibeschütz had left Prague in 1743 under French protection, while the city was under siege from the French, to become chief rabbi in Metz. For this apparent act of disloyalty the Habsburgs had banned him from their territories. In 1760, aged *c.*70, through the good offices of the Danish ambassador, Eibeschütz hoped to secure the annulment of the banishment order and return to Prague in a private capacity.

51. Landau, *Noda Bi'Yehudah* I: *Yoreh Deah* No. 93; Kamelhar, *Mofet Ha-Dor*, pp. 60 ff. Landau's successor, R. Eleazar Fleckeles (1754–1826) had to contend with heretics, 'epicureans', 'calculators of the end', followers of the pseudo-messiah Sabbatai Zvi and those who denied creation and the reality of God (see E. Fleckeles, *Ahavat David*, Prague, 1800, Introduction and pp. 3a, 30a–b).

52. Saperstein, *Ram's Horn*, ch. x. For an English version of the responsum on hunting, see S. B. Freehof (ed.), *A Treasury of Responsa* (Philadelphia, PA: JPSA, 1963), pp. 216–19; for the original Hebrew, see Landau, *Noda Bi'Yehudah*, II: *Yoreh De'ah*, No. 10.

53. L. Singer, 'Zur Geschichte der Juden in Böhmen in den letzten Jahren Josefs II und unter Leopold II', *JGGJCR*, VI (1934), pp. 189–280, esp. pp. 233 ff.; Pribram, *Urkunden*, II, nos. 257, 261–iii, 297, 348.

54. Dubin, *Port Jews of Habsburg Trieste*, pp. 184, 194.

55. Gilman, *Ha-Noda Bi'Yehudah*, p. 95; in another sermon Landau reviled money-lenders who added interest to capital, charged extortionate rates of interest, 'as though there were no prohibition against usury in the Torah' (*Ahavat Tsiyon*, Prague, 1827, pp. 156 ff.).

56. For a succinct presentation of Homberg's views, see Teufel, 'Ein Schüler Mendelssohns', and L. Singer, 'Die Entstehung des Juden-Systemalpatents von 1797', in *JGGJCR*, VII (1935), pp. 199–263, esp. pp. 211–19.

15 Revolution and War, 1789–1805

1. See David Ruderman, 'Was there an English Parallel to the German Haskalah?' in M. Brenner and D. Rechter (eds), *Two Nations: British and German Jews in Comparative Perspective* (Tübingen: Mohr, 1999).

2. Board of Deputies Minute Book 2, March 1829–January 1838, pp. 8–9.

Notes 347

3. See the remarks by D. Bourel in his comment on 'Jewish Enlightenment in Berlin and Paris', in M. Brenner *et al.* (eds), *Jewish Emancipation Reconsidered* (Tübingen: Mohr, 2003), p. 37.
4. Mendes-Flohr and Reinharz, *Jew in the Modern World*, III, No. 1.
5. S. Schwarzfuchs (ed.), *Le Journal Révolutionnaire d'Abraham Spire* (Paris: Verdier, 1989), introduction.
6. The best guide to these *cahiers de doléance* still remains M. Liber, 'Les Juifs et la Convocation des Etats Généraux', *REJ*, Nos. LXIII–LXVI (1912–14); see also Hertzberg, *French Enlightenment and the Jews*, pp. 350 ff.; Meyer, *Communauté Juive*, p. 82.
7. Schwarzfuchs, *Le Journal Révolutionnaire*, pp. 90–91; Feuerwerker, *Emancipation des Juifs*, pp. 288 ff.
8. Malvezin, *Juifs à Bordeaux*, pp. 253–54; Liber, 'Les Juifs et la Convocation', *REJ*, LXIV (1912), pp. 255–61; Schwarzfuchs, *Du Juif*, pp. 123–4.
9. For a succinct presentation of Abbé Grégoire's views, see S. Trigano, 'The French Revolution and the Jews', *Modern Jewish Studies*, X (1990), pp. 171–90.
10. Olry Terquem, *Archives Israélites*, IV, (1843), pp. 725–6.
11. For all the above, see R. Weyl et J. Daltroff, 'Le Cahier de Doléance des Juifs d'Alsace', *Revue d'Alsace*, 109 (1983), pp. 65–80; R. Weyl, 'Un rabbin alsacien engagé', in M. Hadas-Lebel and E. Oliel-Grausz (eds), *Les Juifs et la Révolution française* (Louvain: Peeters, 1992), pp. 85–95; Schwarzfuchs, *Du Juif*, pp. 107–8; M. Lemalet, 'L'Emancipation des Juifs de Lorraine', in D. Tollet (ed.), *Politique et Religion dans le Judaisme moderne* (Paris: PUPS, 1987), pp. 63–83.
12. 'La Révolution Francaise et l'émancipation des Juifs' (Paris: EDHIS, 1968), V, No. 3.
13. Ibid., V, Nos. 3–4; Malino, *A Jew in the French Revolution*, p. 75.
14. This letter is reprinted in Szajkowski, 'Mishlahotehem', doc. 5.
15. Quoted Zosa Szajkowski, *Jews and the French Revolutions of 1789, 1830 and 1848* (New York: Ktav, 1970), p. 579.
16. R. Ayoun (ed.), *Les Juifs de France de L'Emancipation à l'integration; Documents, Bibliographie et Annotations* (Paris: L'Harmattan, 1997), pp. 66–71.
17. 'La Révolution Française et l'Emancipation des Juifs', *EDHIS*, V, No. 8.
18. Szajkowski, 'Mishlahotehem', pp. 66–7.
19. 'La Révolution Française et l'Emancipation des Juifs', *EDHIS*, V, No. 11 (esp. pp. 81, 95). This is the French version of the distinction that Mendelssohn had earlier made between *Civilvereinigung* and *Glaubensvereinigung*.
20. Blumenkranz et Soboul, *Juifs et la Révolution Française*, p. 214.
21. Issue for Pericope Jethro (Ex. 18:1–20:26), 31 January – 5 February 1790.
22. Lemalet, 'L'Emancipation des Juifs de Lorraine', pp. 72–74; *EDHIS*, VIII, pp. 18–19.
23. K. Stillschweig, 'Das Judentum im Lichte des französischen Nationsbegriffs', *MGWJ*, 81 (1937), pp. 457–8.
24. Mendes-Flohr and Reinharz, *Jew in the Modern World*, III, No. 5.
25. Ibid., III, No. 6.
26. For a succinct discussion of this issue, see Malino, *Sephardic Jews of Bordeaux*, pp. 61–2; also Szajkowski, *Jews and the French Revolutions*, pp. 586 ff.
27. Szajkowski, *Jews and the French Revolutions*, p. 639, fn. 106; Netter, 'Die Schuldennot der Jüdischen Gemeinde Metz.'
28. For the gist of the appeal see J. R. Berkovitz, 'The French Revolution and the Jews: Assessing the Cultural Impact', *AJSR* XX, No. 1 (1995), pp. 25–86, here p. 53.
29. R. Schechter, 'Translating the "Marseillaise"', *Past and Present*, Nos. 142–3 (1994), pp. 108–35.

30. R. Necheles, 'L'Emancipation des Juifs 1787–1795', in B. Blumenkranz et A. Soboul (eds), *Les Juifs et la Révolution Française* (Toulouse: Privat, 1976), pp. 71–86, esp. p. 83; Jacques Godechot, 'Les Juifs de Nancy de 1789–1795', *REJ*, 96 (1928), pp. 1–35, esp. p. 14.

31. See R. Marx, 'La Régénération économique des Juifs d'Alsace', in Blumenkranz et Soboul, *Juifs et la Révolution Française*, pp. 105–20, here p. 112. Schneider, an unfrocked German monk, was a member of the Jacobin Club in Strasbourg and publisher-editor of the journal *Argos*.

32. Max Polonovski, 'Un Aventurier Mythomane sous L'Empire – Samson Cerf Berr', *REJ*, 154 (1995), pp. 43–76; R. Néher-Bernheim, 'Cerf Berr de Medelsheim: Le Destin d'une Famille durant la Révolution', *REJ*, 137 (1978), pp. 61–75.

33. F. Barbier, 'Les Origines de la Maison Fould', *RH*, 281 (1989), pp. 159–92.

34. Hyman, *Emancipation of the Jews of Alsace*, p. 15.

35. For all the above, see Roland Marx, 'Régénération Economique', pp. 114 ff. Seligmann Alexandre is also described as a banker, with manufacturing interests in tobacco and textiles in Strasbourg and the upper Rhine. He was imprisoned from May–August 1794, during the Terror; See Néher-Bernheim, 'Cerf Berr de Medelsheim', pp. 69–70; also Jean Daltroff, 'Samuel Levy de Balbronn, Un riche prêteur d'argent Juif de Basse-Alsace', *REJ*, 148 (1989), pp. 53–68.

36. Marx, 'Régénération Economique', p. 117; Jean Daltroff, 'Les Ratisbonne', *REJ*, 159 (2000), pp. 461–77, here p. 466.

37. Lemalet, 'L'Emancipation des Juifs de Lorraine', p. 68. There is a slightly expanded version of this article in *Les Nouveaux Cahiers*, 97 (1989), pp. 29–35.

38. Néher-Bernheim, *Documents*, pp. 323, 330, 349; R. Reuss, 'Quelques Documents Nouveaux sur l'antisémitisme dans le Bas-Rhin, de 1794–9', *REJ*, 59 (1910), pp. 275–6.

39. See on this point Berkovitz, 'French Revolution and Jews'.

40. Introduction to *Yad David*, Offenbach, 1799, quoted S. Schwarzfuchs, *Napoleon, the Jews, and the Sanhedrin* (London: Routledge, 1979), p. 20; see also Robert Weyl, 'Le Grand Rabbin David Sinzheim', in Hadas-Lebel and Oliel-Grausz, *Révolution Française*, pp. 85–95.

41. S. Diezinger, 'Französische Emigranten und Flüchtlinge', in V. Rödel (ed.), *Die Französische Revolution und die Oberrheinlande* (Sigmaringen: Thorbecke, 1991), pp. 275–84.

16   Beyond the Rhine and Over the Alps

1. D. Bourel, 'Moses Mendelssohn, Markus Herz und die Akademie der Wissenschaften zu Berlin', *Mendelssohn Studien*, 4 (1979), pp. 223–34, here p. 234.

2. R. Moulinas, 'Les Juifs d'Avignon et du Comtat', in Blumenkranz and Soboul, *Juifs et la Révolution française*, pp. 143–82, esp. pp. 171 ff.; A. Lunel, *Les Juifs du Languedoc, de la Provence et des Etats Français du Pape* (Paris: Albin Michel, 1975), pp. 178 ff.; H. Chobaut, 'Les Juifs d'Avignon et du Comtat et la Révolution Française', *REJ*, 102 (1937), pp. 3–39; see also S. Posener, 'The Social Life of the Jewish Communities in France in the 18th century', *JSS*, 7 (1945), pp. 195–232, esp. p. 206.

3. Dubin, *Port Jews of Trieste*, p. 220; see also Dan Segre, 'The Emancipation of Jews in Italy', in P. Birnbaum and I. Katznelson (eds), *Paths to Emancipation* (Princeton University Press, 1995), pp. 206–37, esp. pp. 215 ff.

4. See Carlo Mangio, 'La Communauté Juive de Livourne face à la Revolution Française', in Blumenkranz et Soboul, *Juifs et La Révolution Française*,

pp. 191–209; Ulrich Wyrwa, *Juden in der Toskana und in Preussen im Vergleich* (Tübingen: Mohr, 2003), pp. 140 ff.

5. B. Mevorah (ed.), *Napoleon u-Tekufato* (Jerusalem: Mossad Bialik, 1968), pp. 36–7; Simonsohn, *Jews in Mantua*, pp. 95 ff.

6. This chronicle is reprinted in Mevorah, *Napoleon u-Tekufato*, pp. 17–36.

7. Berliner, *Juden in Rom*, II, pp. 138 ff.

8. See for example, L. and R. Fuks, 'Preface to David Franco Mendes, Memories', *SR*, IX (1975), p. x.

9. J. Michman, *Dutch Jewry during the Emancipation Period, 1787–1815* (Amsterdam University Press, 1995), p. 24.

10. R. Mahler (ed.), *Jewish Emancipation – A Selection of Documents* (New York: American Jewish Committee, 1944), No. 11.

11. Quoted Sonnenberg-Stern, *Emancipation and Poverty*, p. 52. See also A. Halff, 'Diyunei Ha-Asefah Ha-Le'umit shel Ha-Republika Ha-Batavit be-davar Ha-Emanzipatsiya ha-Yehudim 1796', in J. Michman (ed.), *Mehkarim al Toldot Yahadut Holland* (Jerusalem: Magnes Press, 1975), pp. 201–40.

12. W. Grab, 'Deutscher Jakobinismus und Jüdische Emanzipation', in W. Grab (ed.), *Der deutsche Weg der Judenemanzipation 1789–1938* (Munich: Piper, 1991), pp. 41–72; H. Molitor, 'Die Juden im französischen Rheinland', in J. Bohnke-Kollwitz *et al.* (eds), *Köln und das rheinische Judentum*, pp. 87–94.

13. J. Hansen (ed.), *Quellen zur Geschichte des Rheinlandes im Zeitalter der Französischen Revolution 1780–1801* (Bonn: Hanstein, 1933) II, 760, No. 345, fn. 3.

14. See A. Kober, 'The French Revolution and the Jews in Germany', *JSS*, 7 (1945), pp. 294–322, here p. 312, fn. 76; and Molitor, *Juden im Rheinland*, p. 93, fn. 46.

15. A. Zittartz, 'Die französische Herrschaft und die Juden in Krefeld (1794–1814)', *Aschkenas*, Jg. 6 (1996), pp. 87–116.

16. Quoted Shulamit Magnus, *Jewish Emancipation in a German City* (Stanford University Press, 1997), p. 26; see also E. Weyden, *Geschichte der Juden in Köln am Rhein*, repr. (Osnabrück: Kuballe, 1984), pp. 274–5.

17. Magnus, *Emancipation in a German City*, p. 31.

18. See Bodian, 'Ha-Yazmim Ha-Yehudiim be-Berlin'; Freund, *Emanzipation der Juden*, II, Urkunden, pp. 91–6.

19. See the correspondence in F. Morgenstern, 'Hardenberg and the emancipation of Franconian Jewry', *JSS*, XV (1952), pp. 253–74; generally on this period, R. Rürup, 'The Tortuous and Thorny Path to Legal Equality', *LBYB*, XXI (1986), pp. 3–33.

20. Néher-Bernheim, *Documents*, pp. 276–8.

21. This view is contested, but see the article by S. Feiner, 'Bein ha-Mapekha Ha-Tsarfatit le-ven Tmurot be-Haskalat Berlin', *Tsiyon*, LVII (1992), pp. 89–92.

22. The above is based on the work of Janine Strauss, in her 'Echos de la Révolution Française dans la Littérature de la Haskalah', *Archives Juives*, XXIV (1988), pp. 40 ff. According to A. Kober ('French Revolution and Jews in Germany', p. 298), *Ha-Me'assef* reported on events in France in such a way that it 'not only refrained from giving offence in Prussia but emphasised its loyalty towards king and country'.

17 Another Rabbi, Another Emperor

1. See R. Anchel, *Napoléon et les Juifs* (Paris, 1928), pp. 42 ff.; M. Graetz, *Les Juifs en France au XIXe Siècle* (Paris: Seuil, 1989), pp. 52–3; Szajkowski, *Jews in the French Revolutions*, pp. 682–3.

2. Baron Pelet de la Lozère, *Opinions de Napoléon* (Paris: Firmin Didot, 1833), pp. 215–17.

3. See Berkovitz, 'French Revolution and Jews', pp. 53 ff.
4. Graetz, *Juifs en France*, pp. 50–1.
5. See the preamble to the decree in R. Mahler, *A History of Modern Jewry*, Engl. trans. (London: Vallentine Mitchell, 1971), p. 61.
6. S. Simonsohn, *Tshuvot ahadot shel Yehudei Italiya al Ha-Emantzipatiyah Ha-Rishonah ve-al Ha-Haskalah, Italia Judaica* (Rome: University of Tel Aviv), 1989, pp. 47–68, here p. 60.
7. N. M. Gelber, 'La Police Autrichienne et le Sanhédrin de Napoléon', *REJ*, 83 (1927), pp. 1–21, 113–45. The proceedings of the grand Sanhedrin were edited by D. Tama under the title *Collection des Procès Verbaux et Decisions du Sanhédrin* (Paris, 1807). In the contemporary English translation, *Transactions of the Parisian Sanhedrim (sic)*, also edited by Tama (London, 1807), pp. 110–16, there is a comprehensive list of the participating Notables and their occupations.
8. Malino, *Sephardic Jews of Bordeaux*, p. 83.
9. See Schwarzfuchs, *Napoleon, Jews*, p. 55, where this report is quoted at length.
10. *Correspondance de Napoléon* (Paris: Imprimerie Impériale, 1863), xiii, pp. 122 ff.
11. Quoted Schwarzfuchs, *Napoleon, Jews*, pp. 78, 100–01; for part of the French text, see ibid., p. 207 fn. 31.
12. This is an extract from Furtado's speech to the Grand Sanhedrin that followed the first sessions of the Assembly of Notables; for Furtado's remarks, see Tama, *Transactions*, p. 106.
13. See the material quoted in Mevorah, *Napoleon u-Tekufato*, pp. 82–3.
14. Tama, *Transactions*, pp. 132–5.
15. Gelber, 'Police Autrichienne', pp. 119, 138–40.
16. For the text of the Answers, see Tama, *Transactions*, pp. 150–207, and the analyses and discussion in Schwarzfuchs, *Napoleon, Jews*, pp. 68 ff.
17. Michael A. Meyer, *Response to Modernity* (Oxford University Press, 1988), p. 135.
18. Tama, *Transactions*, pp. 155–6.
19. Ibid., pp. 152–3.
20. Ibid., pp. 207–11.
21. Quoted from the Commissioners' report in F. Delpech, 'Les Juifs en France et dans l'Empire', in B. Blumenkranz et A. Soboul (eds), *Le Grand Sanhédrin de Napoléon* (Toulouse: Privat, 1979), pp. 1–26, here p. 10.
22. Gelber, 'Police Autrichienne', pp. 113–45.
23. Tama, *Transactions*, pp. 263–5.
24. Gelber, 'Police Autrichienne', pp. 122 ff.
25. C. Touati, 'Le Grand Sanhédrin de 1807 et le droit rabbinique', in Blumenkranz et Soboul, *Grand Sanhédrin de Napoléon*, pp. 27–48; J. M. Chouraqui, 'La Loi du Royaume est la Loi; les Rabbins, la Politique et l'Etat en France (1807–1905)', *Pardès* 2 (1985); E. Smilevitch, 'Halakha et Code Civil. Questions sur le Grand Sanhédrin de Napoléon', ibid., 3 (1986). In 1974 Chief Rabbi Ernest Gugenheim agreed that the Sanhedrin's teachings were in conformity with Jewish law (see the remarks of G. Nahon in Blumenkranz et Soboul, *Grand Sanhédrin de Napoléon*, p. 215).
26. Mevorah, *Napoleon u-Tekufato*, p. 116. The Notables correctly related the loss of rabbinical power to citizenship: 'The Jews, raised to the rank of citizens, have conformed in everything to the laws of the state; and accordingly the functions of the rabbis, wherever they are established, are limited to preaching morality in the temples, blessing marriages and pronouncing divorces' (Tama, *Transactions*, p. 195).
27. R. Schreiber's memorial address is reprinted in R. Joseph David Sinzheim, *Minhat Ani*, repr. (Jerusalem: Makhon Yerushalayim, 1974), pp. 29–32; Meyer, *Response to Modernity*, pp. 134–5.

28. Tama, *Procès-verbaux*, pp. 41–3.
29. For an example of the divergence between the French and Hebrew versions, see G. Graff, *Separation of Church and State* (Alabama University Press, 1985), p. 182, fn. 74.
30. Tama, *Procès-verbaux* ... , pp. 124–6. Sinzheim was not of course isolated among his rabbinical colleagues. R. Aaron Worms (1754–1836) of Metz was evidently a supporter; see J. Berkovitz, 'Jewish Scholarship and Identity in 19th Century France', *Modern Judaism*, 18 (1998), pp. 1–33.
31. Malino, *Sephardic Jews of Bordeaux*, pp. 106 ff.; Schwarzfuchs, *Napoleon, Jews*, pp. 120 ff.
32. See Magnus, *Jewish Emancipation*, p. 44.
33. Anchel, *Napoléon et les Juifs*, pp. 352–411; Iancu, *Juifs du Midi*, pp. 234 ff.
34. Hyman, *Emancipation of the Jews of Alsace*, pp. 18–19; *L'Israélite Français*, I (1817), pp. 358–69.
35. Tama, *Transactions*, p. 154.
36. S. Schwarzfuchs, 'Les Communautés Italiennes et le Consistoire Central, 1808–1815', *Michael*, I (1972), nos. 10, 15, 59, 133, 160, 218, 243, 390, 540, 1032; Blumenkranz, *Documents Modernes*, AN 0540, 0543, 0548, 0618; U. R. Kaufmann, 'The Jewish Fight for Emancipation in France and Germany', in M. Brenner (ed.), *Jewish Emancipation Reconsidered* (Tübingen: Mohr, 2003), pp. 79–92.
37. Sinzheim, *Minhat Ani*, II, 71–3.
38. Berkovitz, 'French Revolution and Jews', p. 55, fn. 86.

18 From Paris to Vienna

1. Mendes-Flohr and Reinharz, *Jew in the Modern World*, I, No. 17.
2. See the material quoted in Toury, *Kavim le-heker knisat Ha-Yehudim la-Hayyim Ha-Ezrahiim*, ch. 1.
3. It may be that these changes in sovereignty encouraged a name change to suit any eventuality: in 1808 Salomon Abraham of Coblenz in the Rhine-Mosel department became the Franco-German Jacques Kauffmann. (See H. Mathy and E. Bucher (eds), 'Die Juden in der französischen Zeit von 1798/1801 bis 1814', in G. F. Böhm (ed.), *Zur rechtlichen Situation der Juden im 18ten Jahrhundert* – XII, pt. I (Koblenz, 1982), No. 57.
4. Sonnenberg-Stern, *Emancipation and Poverty*, pp. 220 ff.
5. Michman, *Dutch Jewry*, pp. 30 ff.
6. Ibid., p. 200, fn. 54.
7. Sonnenberg-Stern, *Emancipation and Poverty*, pp. 66 ff., 71; Michman, *Dutch Jewry*.
8. J. Michman, 'The Conflicts between Orthodox and Enlightened Jews', *SR*, XV (1981), pp. 20–36, here p. 23.
9. R. G. Fuks-Mansfeld, 'Arduous Adaptation', in J. C. H. Blom et al. (eds), *The History of the Jews in the Netherlands*, Engl. trans. (Oxford: Littman Library, 2002), pp. 196 ff. See also S.W. Baron, 'Moses Cohen Belinfante – A Leader of the Dutch-Jewish Enlightenment', *HJ*, V (1943), pp. 1–35.
10. Gadi Luzzatto Voghera, 'Italian Jews', in R. Liedtke and S. Wendehorst (eds), *The Emancipation of Catholics, Jews and Protestants* (Manchester University Press, 1999), pp. 169–87, here p. 175.
11. See G. Laras, 'Le Grand Sanhédrin de 1807 et ses Conséquences en Italie', in Blumenkranz et Soboul, *Juifs et la Révolution Française*, pp. 100–18, esp. pp. 109 ff.; P. Filippini, 'La Nation Juive de Livourne', in M. Hadas-Lebel et E. Oliel-Grausz, *Juifs et la Révolution française*, pp. 237–47.

12. Mario Rossi, 'Emancipation of the Jews of Italy', in A. Duker and M. Ben-Horin (eds), *Emancipation and Counter-Emancipation* (New York: Ktav, 1974), pp. 209–35.
13. Niall Ferguson, *The World's Banker* (London: Weidenfeld, 1998), pp. 80–1; B. Brilling, 'Mayer Amschel Rothschild und die Abschaffung des Leibzolls in Bayern', *BLBI*, VII, No. 26 (1964), pp. 165–71; Schnee, *Hoffinanz*, II, pp. 109 ff., III, pp. 127 ff.
14. G. Samuel, 'Die Namengebung der Westfälischen Judenschaft von 1808', *ZGJD*, VI (1935), pp. 47–51; Sulamith, *Jg*, II (1808), p. 170.
15. For a general picture of Jacobson's rule see A. Herzig, *Judentum und Emanzipation in Westphalen* (Münster: Aschendorff, 1973), pp. 12 ff.; see also J. R. Marcus, *Israel Jacobson* (Cincinnatti: Hebrew Union College Press, 1972); and Meyer, *Response to Modernity*, p. 37.
16. See Sinzheim, *Minhat Oni*, pp. 13–14, fn. 8.
17. M. Zimmermann, *Hamburgischer Patriotismus und deutscher Nationalismus* (Hamburg: Christian, 1979), pp. 22 ff.
18. D. Bering, *Der Name als Stigma* (Stuttgart: Klett-Cotta, 1987), pp. 45–6; W. Z. Tannenbaum, 'A Town on the Volkach', *LBYB*, XLV (2000), pp. 93–117.
19. J. Toury, 'Der Anteil der Juden an der Städtischen Verwaltung im vormärzlichen Deutschland', *BLBI*, No. 23 (1963), pp. 265–86.
20. L. Geiger, 'Berliner Bürgergarde 1809', *ZGJD* IV (1890), p. 372; I. Freund, *Emanzipation der Juden*, II, Urkunden, pp. 208–11.
21. Ibid., pp. 454–9; see also R. Liberles, 'Emancipation and the Structure of the Jewish Community in the Nineteenth Century', *LBYB*, XXXI (1986), pp. 51–67.
22. For the above I am greatly indebted to E. Lindner, *Patriotismus deutscher Juden* (Frankfurt am Main: Lang, 1997), esp. pp. 61, 62, 65, 67–8, 73, 77–9, 85–90, 99; H. G. Reissner, 'Henriette Mendelssohn', *LBYB*, XXI (1967), pp. 247–58; Rolf Vogel, *Ein Stück von uns*, (Mainz: Hase-Koehler, 1977), p. 30; Jersch-Wenzel, 'Die Herausbildung eines 'Preussichen' Judentums 1671–1815', in Freimark, *Juden in Preussen*, p. 31; M. Philippson, 'Der Anteil der jüdischen Freiwilligen an dem Befreiungskriege 1813 und 1814', *MGWJ*, No. 50 (1906), pp. 1–21.
23. Herzig, *Judentum und Emanzipation*, p. 15.
24. Freund, *Emanzipation der Juden*, II, Urkunden, pp. 465–7.
25. Zimmermann, *Hamburgischer Patriotismus*, p. 26; H. Krohn, Die Juden in *Hamburg 1800–1850* (Frankfurt am Main: 1967), p. 21.
26. C. Prestel, 'Jüdische Unterschicht im Zeitalter der Emanzipation', *Aschkenas*, I (1991), pp. 95–134.
27. Quoted Ferguson, *The World's Banker*, p. 184.
28. W. O. McCagg, 'Jewish Wealth in Vienna', in Silber, *Jews in the Hungarian Economy*, pp. 64–5.
29. N. Ferguson, 'Metternich and the Rothschilds', *LBYB*, XLVI (2001), pp. 19–54.
30. E. Timms, 'Metternich and Jewish emancipation', ibid., pp. 3–18, esp. p. 9; Freund, *Emanzipation der Juden*, II, Urkunden, pp. 275 ff.
31. Max Kohler, 'Jewish Rights at International Congresses', *AJYB*, XXVI (5678 = 1918), pp. 113–15).
32. F. Gentz, *Tagebücher* (Leipzig: Brockhaus, 1861), pp. 371, 386; see also pp. 285, 354, 370, 382.
33. Kestenberg-Gladstein, *Juden in den böhmischen Ländern*, p. 346.
34. S. W. Baron, *Die Judenfrage auf dem Wiener Kongress* (Vienna: Löwit, 1920), p. 145; Ludwig Bato, *Die Juden im alten Wien* (Vienna: Phaidon, 1928), pp. 166 ff.
35. S. Carlebach, *Geschichte der Juden in Lübeck und Moisling* (Lübeck, 1898), pp. 51, 61; Baron, *Judenfrage auf dem Wiener Kongress*, pp. 51 ff., 65, 110–11; Schnee, *Hoffinanz*, VI, p. 147.

36. Rechberg was a Bavarian representative and Wessenberg an Austrian.
37. Quoted Baron, *Judenfrage auf dem Wiener Kongress*, p. 156; for Rechberg's defence of Bavarian sovereignty, see his letter to the king (June 1815) and his pride in having saved *'les droits de souveraineté de Votre Majesté'* (I. Klemmer, *Aloys v. Rechberg (1766–1849)* (Munich: Stadtarchiv, 1975), p. 77.
38. Kohler, *Jewish Rights at International Congresses*, pp. 130–1.
39. P. Arnsberg, *Die Geschichte der Frankfurter Juden*, I (Darmstadt: Roether, 1983), pp. 376–79.

19 Epilogue: 1819

1. See M. Eliav (ed.), *Rabbiner Esriel Hildesheimer – Briefe* (Jerusalem: Maas, 1965), p. 213.
2. See J. Katz, *Orthodoxy in Historical Perspective, Studies in Contemporary Jewry* (Bloomington: Indiana University Press, 1986), II, pp. 3–17; also C. Schulte, 'Saul Ascher's Leviathan, or the Invention of Jewish Orthodoxy in 1792', *LBYB*, 45 (2000), pp. 25–34.
3. David Sorkin, 'Religious Reform and Secular Trends in German-Jewish Life', *LBYB*, 40 (1995), pp. 169–84, here p. 174; for the general background see also S. M. Poppel, 'The Politics of Religious Leadership, the Rabbinate in Nineteenth Century Hamburg', *LBYB*, 28 (1983), pp. 439–70.
4. See the material cited in Ismar Schorsch, 'The Emergence of the Modern Rabbinate', in W. E. Mosse *et al.* (eds), *Revolution and Evolution: 1848 in German-Jewish History* (Tübingen: Mohr, 1981), pp. 205–53, esp. pp. 228 ff.
5. See M. Halbertal, *People of the Book* (Cambridge, MA: Harvard University Press, 1997), *passim*.
6. S. Schwarzfuchs, 'Correspondance du Consistoire Central', *Michael* I (1972), pp. 109–62, here p. 147; see also Giuseppe Laras, 'Le Grand Sanhédrin de 1807 et ses conséquences sur Italie', in B. Blumenkranz et A. Soboul (eds), *Le Grand Sanhédrin de Napoléon* (Toulouse: Privat, 1979), pp. 101–18, here p. 109.
7. This is the theme of a remarkable article by A. Gotzmann, 'Strukturen jüdischer Gerichtsautonomie in den deutschen Staaten des 18. Jahrhunderts', *HZ*, no. 267 (1998), pp. 313–56; idem, *Eigenheit und Einheit* (Leiden: Brill, 2002), pp. 38 ff.
8. L. Geiger (ed.), 'Briefe David Friedländer 1789–1799', *ZGJD*, I (1887), pp. 268, 271.
9. D. Hertz, *Jewish High Society in Old Regime Berlin* (New Haven, CT: Yale University Press, 1988), p. 244.
10. M. Silber, 'The Historical Experience of German Jewry and its Impact on the Haskalah and Reform in Hungary', in J. Katz (ed.), *Towards Modernity* (Oxford: Transaction, 1987), pp. 107–57, esp. pp. 113 ff.
11. Ha-Me'asef, VI, 1790, p. 370; M. Pelli, 'Maskilim and the Talmud', *LBYB*, 27 (1982), p. 249, fn. 19; J. Helphand, 'The Aborted Candidacy of Rabbi Asher Ginsburg', *Jewish History*, XV (2001), pp. 44–57.
12. See H. Pollack, 'Précurseurs de l'Emancipation Juive en Europe Centrale', *XVIIIe Siècle*, XIII (1981), pp. 149–60. In a sermon in 1745 Eibeschütz warned against 'false prophets who arose and learned from the sages of the idolaters among them and mingled with the people and learned from their seductive words to go after vanity' (Ya'arot Dvash, I, p. 136, col. 2).
13. These quotations are from Letters no. 5, 8, 9, 14, 20 published in the symposium *Eleh Divrei Ha-Brit* (Hamburg: Bet Din, 1819).
14. Ibid., no. 19, p. 80.

15. S. P. Rabinowitz, *R. Yomtov Lippmann Zunz* (Warsaw, 1896), p. 42.
16. *Eleh Divrei Ha-Brit*, second letter, p. 42.
17. J. Katz, 'Towards a biography of the Hatam Sofer', in Malino and Sorkin, *From East and West*, pp. 223–66. This also applied to the graduates of the Orthodox Rabbinical Seminary in Berlin – see S. Schwarzfuchs, 'The Making of the Rabbi', in J.Carlebach (ed.), *Das Aschkenasische Rabbinat* (Berlin: Metropol, 1995), pp. 133–40.
18. *Eleh Divrei Ha-Brit*, p. 41; see also above p. 194 for the attitude of eighteenth-century French Jews to the Bourbon monarchs.
19. For all the above, I am deeply indebted to M. Samet, 'Ha-Ortodoxiya', *Kivunim*, XXVI (1987), pp. 99–114; idem, 'The Beginning of Orthodoxy', *Modern Judaism*, VIII (1988), pp. 249–69.
20. This responsum is no. 38 in Haham Zvi's collected responsa. I have used the translation and analysis in A. S. Ferziger, 'Between "Ashkenazi" and Sepharad', *SR*, XXXV (2001), pp. 7–22. London is not positively identified as the scene of this encounter but internal evidence makes it virtually certain.
21. Miriam Bodian, 'Men of the Nation', *Past and Present*, 143 (1994), pp. 48–76, esp. pp. 71–2.
22. D. Ellenson, *Rabbi Esriel Hildesheimer and the Creation of a Modern Jewish Orthodoxy* (Tuscaloosa: Alabama University Press, 1990), pp. 62ff.
23. Zunz's review ('Ankündigung eines Werkes: Geist der Rabbiner') appeared in *Berlinische Nachrichten der Haude und Spenerschen Zeitung*, no. 88 (1819). It was 'one of the most aggressive outbursts against orthodox rabbinism published in the nineteenth century', according to a student of Zunz: L. Wallach (ed.), *Liberty and Letters – The Thoughts of Leopold Zunz* (London: East and West Library, 1959), p. 31 fn. 63.
24. For a comprehensive study of the riots in their historical context, see J. Katz, 'Para'ot Hep-Hep shel shnat 1819 be-Germaniya al Reka'an Ha-Histori', *Tsiyon*, 38 (1973), pp. 62–115; see also Uriel Tal, 'Young German Intellectuals on Romanticism and Judaism', in S. Liebermann and A. Hyman (eds), *S. W. Baron Jubilee Volume* II (Jerusalem: American Academy for Jewish Research, 1974), pp. 919–38; Ferguson, *World's Banker*, pp. 150, 176, 188.
25. A. Strodtmann, *Heines Leben und Werke* (Berlin: Duncker, 1887), I, pp. 245, 381.
26. L. Zunz, *Die Gottesdienstlichen Vorträge der Juden* (Berlin: Asher, 1832), p. vii.

Bibliography

Rabbinic responsa, sermons, correspondence

Ashkenazi, R. Gershom, *Avodat Gershuni*, repr. (Jerusalem, 1982).

Ashkenazi, Haham Zvi, *She'elot u-Tshuvot* (Amsterdam, 1712).

Bachrach, R. Ya'ir Hayyim, *Havot Ya'ir*, repr. (Jerusalem, 1987).

Bezalel, R. Judah Loewe b., *Derekh Hayyim*, repr. (London: Honig, 1961.

——, *Netivot Olam*, repr. (London: Honig, 1961).

Carlebach, J., *Das Aschkenasische Rabbinat* (Berlin: Metropol, 1995).

Duschinsky, C. *The Rabbinate of the Great Synagogue London, 1756–1842* (repr. Farnborough: Gregg, 1971).

Eibeschütz, R. Jonathan, *Ya'arot Dvash*, ed. R. Isaiah Pick, 2 vols., 2nd edn (Jerusalem, 1988).

Eidelberg, S. (ed.), *Tshuvot Rabbenu Gershom Me'or Ha-Golah* (New York: Yeshivah University, 1955).

Eleh Divrei Ha-Brit (Hamburg: Bet Din, 1819).

Eliav, M. (ed.), *Rabbiner Esriel Hildesheimer – Briefe* (Jerusalem: Maas, 1965).

Emden, R. Jacob: *Siddur Amudei Shamayim* (Altona, 1735).

——, *She'ilot Yavetz* (Altona, 1759).

Ferziger, A.S., 'Between "Ashkenazi" and Sepharad', *SR*, xxxv (2001), pp. 7–22.

Freehof, S.B. (ed.), *A Treasury of Responsa* (Philadelphia: JPSA, 1963).

Gans, R. David, *Tsemah David* (Frankfurt/Amsterdam, 5452 [1692]).

Halevy, R. Samuel, *Nahlat Shivah* (Fürth, 1692).

Horovitz, R. Isaiah, *Shnei Luhot Ha-Brit*, repr. (Jerusalem, 1963).

Hurwitz, R. Judah, *Amudei Beit Yehudah* (Amsterdam, 1766).

Israel, R. Menasseh b., *Spes Israelis/Esperança de Israel*, ed. H. Méchoulan and G. Nahon (Oxford: Littman Library/Oxford University Press, 1987).

Isserlein, R. Israel, *Trumat Ha-Deshen*, repr. (Bnei Brak, 5731 [1971]).

Isserles, R. Moses, *She'elot u-Tshuvot*, ed. R. Asher Ziv, repr. (Jerusalem, 1970).

Kahana, Y.-Z., *Mehkarim be-sifrut ha-Tshuvot* (Jerusalem: Mossad Ha-Rav Kuk, 1973).

Krochmal, R. Menaham Mendel, *Tsemah Tsedek*, repr. (Jerusalem, 1982).

Landau, R. Ezekiel, *Noda Bi'Yehudah*, repr. (Jerusalem, 1969).

Modena, R. Judah, *Voice of a Fool – Shaking the Pillars of Exile*, ed. and trans. Talya Fishman (Stanford University Press, 1997).

Moses di Trani, R., *She'elot u-Tshuvot* (Venice, 1629).

Nosek B. and V. Sadek, 'Sotsialniye Protivorechiya v yevreiskikh religioznikh obschchestvakh v Moravii i ikh otrazheniye v sochineniyakh M.M. Krochmala (okolo 1600–1661)', *Judaica Bohemiae*, xiii (1977).

Petuchowski, J.J., *The Theology of Haham David Nieto* (New York: Ktav Publishers, 1970).

Saperstein, M. (ed. and trans.), *Jewish Preaching 1200–1800, An Anthology* (New Haven, CT: Yale University Press, 1989).

Sasportas, R. Jacob, *Tzitzat Novel Zvi*, ed. I. Tishby (Jerusalem: Mossad Bialik, 1954).

——, *Ohel Ya'akov*, ed. Samuel Halperin, 2nd edn (Bnei Brak, 1986).

Schorsch, Ismar, 'The Emergence of the Modern Rabbinate', in W.E. Mosse *et al.* (eds), *Revolution and Evolution: 1848 in German-Jewish History* (Tübingen: Mohr, 1981), pp. 205–53.

Shiloh, Samuel, *Dina de-Malkhuta Dina* (Jerusalem: Academic Press, 1975).
Sinzheim, R. Joseph David, *Minhat Oni*, repr. (Jerusalem, 1974).
Sirkes, R. Joel, *Tshuvot Ha-Bakh Ha-Yeshanot* (Frankfurt am Main, 1697).
Zunz, L., *Die gottesdienstlichen Vorträge der Juden* (Berlin: Asher, 1832).

Documentary collections

Ayoun, R. (ed.), *Les Juifs de France de l'Emancipation à l'Integration* (Paris: L'Harmattan, 1997).
Blumenkranz, B., *Documents Modernes sur les Juifs* (Toulouse: Privat, 1979).
Bondy, G. and F. Dworsky (eds), *Zur Geschichte der Juden in Böhmen, Mähren and Schlesien von 906 bis 1620* (Prague: Bondy, 1906).
Cassuto, J. (ed.), 'Aus dem ältesten Protokollbuch der Portugiesischen Gemeinde in Hamburg', *JJLG*, viii (1910–11).
Freund, I., *Die Emanzipation der Juden in Preussen*, ii, Urkunden (Berlin, 1912).
Hildenfinger, P., *Documents sur les Juifs à Paris au xviiie siècle* (Paris: Champion, 1913).
Kaufmann, David, 'Extraits de l'ancien livre de la Communauté de Metz', *REJ*, 19–20 (1889), pp. 115–30.
Komorowski, M., *Bio-Bibliographisches Verzeichnis Jüdischer Doktoren im 17. und 18. Jahrhundert* (Munich: Saur, 1991).
Mahler, R. (ed.), *Jewish Emancipation – A Selection of Documents* (New York: American Jewish Committee, 1944).
Marcus, J.R. (ed.), *The Jew in the Medieval World: A Source Book 315–1791* (New York: Harper & Row, 1965).
Mendes-Flohr, P. and J. Reinharz (eds), *The Jew in the Modern World. A Documentary History*, 2nd edn (Oxford: Oxford University Press, 1995).
Mevorah, B. (ed.), *Napoleon u- Tekufato* (Jerusalem: Mossad Bialik, 1968).
Néher-Bernheim, R. (ed.), *Documents inédits sur l'Entrée des Juifs dans la Société Française* (Diaspora Research Institute, Tel Aviv University, 1977).
Pribram, A.F. (ed.), *Urkunden and Akten zur Geschichte der Juden in Wien*, 2 vols (Vienna: Braumüller, 1918).
Schwarzfuchs, S. (ed.), *Le Registre des délibérations de la Nation Juive Portugaise de Bordeaux 1711–1787* (Paris: Fundacao Gulbenkian, 1981).
Shamash, R. Juspa, *Minhagim de-Warmeisa*, ed. Eric Zimmer, 2 vols, repr. (Jerusalem, 1992).
Stern, Selma (ed.), *Der Preussische Staat und die Juden*, 7 vols (Tübingen: Mohr, 1962–1975).
Tama, D. (ed.), *Transactions of the Parisian Sanhedrin*, Engl. trans. (London, 1807).
Wachstein, B. (ed.), *Urkunden und Akten zur Geschichte der Juden in Eisenstadt* (Vienna: Braumüller, 1926).
Walzer, M. *et al.* (eds), *The Jewish Political Tradition* (New Haven, CT: Yale University Press, 2000).

Memoirs, biography, autobiography, letters

Altmann, A., *Moses Mendelssohn* (London: Routledge, 1973).
d'Aulnoy, Mme, 'Voyage d'Espagne', *Revue Hispanique*, 67 (1926).
Azulay, R. Hayyim Joseph, *Sefer Ma'agal Tov* (Jerusalem, 1934).
Barnai, J. 'Christian Messianism and Portuguese Marranos, *JH*, vii (1993), pp. 119–26.
——, 'The Spread of the Sabbatean Movement in the 17th and 18th Centuries', in S. Menache (ed.), *Communication in the Jewish Diaspora* (Leiden: Brill, 1996), pp. 313–37.

Ben-Shalom, Ram, 'The Converso as Subversive', *JJS*, L (1999), pp. 259–83.

Bik, A., *Rabbi Ya'akov Emden* (Jerusalem: Mossad Ha-Rav Kuk, 1974).

——, *Rabbi Ya'akov Emden u-Milhamato be-Shulhanei Altona* (Tarbitz, 42, 1973), pp. 461–68.

—— (ed.), *Rabbi Ya'akov Emden, Megilat Sefer* (Jerusalem: Jewish Classics, 1979).

Bourel, D. 'Moses Mendelssohn, Markus Herz und die Akademie der Wissenschaften zu Berlin', *Mendelssohn Studien*, 4 (1979), pp. 223–34.

Breuer, Edward, 'Naphtali Herz Wessely and the Cultural Dislocations of an Eighteenth-Century Maskil', in D. Sorkin and S. Feiner (eds), *New Perspectives on the Haskalah* (London: Littman Library, 2001), pp. 27–47.

Brilling, B. 'Mayer Amschel Rothschild und die Abschaffung des Leibzolls in Bayern', *BLBI*, VII (1964), pp. 165–71.

Cantor, G. 'The Rise and Fall of Emanuel Mendes da Costa', *English Historical Review*, CXVI, no. 467 (2001), pp. 584–603.

Cohen, Mark (ed. and trans.), *Leon Modena's Life of Judah* (Princeton University Press, 1988).

Duschinsky, Jacob Koppel, *R. David Oppenheimer* (Budapest, 1922).

Ellenson, D., *Rabbi Esriel Hildesheimer and the Creation of a Modern Jewish Orthodoxy* (Alabama University Press, 1990).

Faierstein, M. (ed. and trans.), *The Libes Briv of Isaac Wetzlar* (Brown University, 1996).

——, 'The Liebes Brief – A Critique of Jewish Society in Germany (1749)', *LBYB*, XXVII (1982).

Geiger, L. (ed.), 'Briefe David Friedländer 1789–1799', *ZGJD*, I (1887), pp. 256–73.

Gentz, F., *Tagebücher* (Leipzig: Brockhaus, 1861).

Gilman, A.L. *Ha-Noda Bi'Yehudah U-Mishnato* (Jerusalem: Mossad Ha-Rav Kuk, 1960).

The Life of Glückel of Hameln, 1646–1724, written by herself, Eng. trans. (London: East and West Library, 1962).

Grosclaude, P., *Malesherbes* (Paris: Fischbacher, 1961).

Hagiz, R. Moses, *Sfat Emet*, repr. (Jerusalem, 1987).

Hart, R.J. D'Arcy, 'The Family of Mordecai Hamburger and their Association with Madras', *JHSE*, Misc. III, 1937.

Heller, Rabbi Yomtov Lipmann, *Megilat Eiva* (Breslau, 1837).

Helphand, J. 'The Aborted Candidacy of Rabbi Asher Ginsburg', *Jewish History*, XV (2001), pp. 44–57.

Hodges, S., *Lorenzo da Ponte* (London: Grafton Books, 1985).

Holleschau, R. Johanan, *Ma'aseh Rav* (Amsterdam, 1707).

Horodetzky, S.A., *Lekorot Ha-Rabbanut* (Warsaw, 1911).

Horovitz, R.M. *Frankfurter Rabbinen (with additions by R. Josef Unna)*, repr. (Jerusalem, 1969).

Jakobovits, T., 'Die Erlebnisse des Oberrabbiners Simon Spira-Wedeles in Prag 1640–1679', *JGGJCR*, IV (1932), pp. 253–332.

Kasher, A. and S. Bidermann, 'Why was Spinoza Excommunicated?', in D.S. Katz and I. Israel (eds), *Sceptics, Millenarians and Jews* (Leiden: Brill, 1990), pp. 98–144.

Kauffmann, David, 'Rabbi Zevi Ashkenazi and his Family in London', *TJHSE*, III (1899) pp. 102–25.

Klemperer, G., 'The Rabbis of Prague', *HJ*, XII (1950), pp. 33–66.

Kobler, F. (ed.), *Juden und Judentum in deutschen Briefen aus drei Jahrhunderten* (Vienna: Saturn Verlag, 1935), pp. 46–8.

——, *Letters of Jews through the Ages*, 2 vols (London: East and West Library, 1953).

Landau, A. and B. Wachstein (eds), *Jüdische Privatbriefe aus dem Jahre 1619* (Vienna: Braumüller, 1911).

Landshut, E., *Toldot Anshei Shem u-Fe'ulatam be-Edat Berlin* (Berlin: Poppelauer, 1884).
Latham, R. and W. Matthews (eds), *The Diary of Samuel Pepys*, VII (London: Harper Collins, 1995).
Leib, R. Judah b. Joshua, *Sefer Milhama be-Shalom* (Prague, 1650).
Lieben, S.H., *David Oppenheim* (Frankfurt am Main, n.d.).
——, 'Oppenheimiana', *JGGJCR*, VII (1935), pp. 409–55.
McEwan, D., 'The Fischer Family Archives in London', *German History*, 5 (1987), pp. 74–81.
Maimon, S., *Geschichte des eigenen Lebens* (Berlin; Schocken Verlag, 1936).
Malino, F., *A Jew in the French Revolution* (Oxford: Blackwell, 1996).
Marcus, J.R., *Israel Jacobson* (Cincinnati: Hebrew Union College Press, 1972).
Marx, A. (ed. and trans.), 'A Seventeenth-century Autobiography', *Studies in Jewish History and Booklore* (New York: Jewish Theological Seminary of America, 5704–1944), pp. 178–97.
Mevorah, B. 'The Imperial Court-Jew Wolf Wertheimer as Diplomatic Mediator', *Scripta Hierosolymitana*, XXII (1972), pp. 184–201.
Munk, S.D., *Toldot Rabbenu Yehezk'el Landau* (Jerusalem, 1953).
Nadler, S., *Spinoza's Heresy* (Oxford: Clarendon Press, 2001).
Néher-Bernheim, R., 'Cerfberr de Medelsheim: Le Destin d'une famille durant la Révolution', *REJ*, 137 (1978), pp. 61–75.
——, 'Jacob Rodrigues Péreire', *REJ*, 142 (1983), pp. 373–451.
Perry, N., 'La Chute d'une famille Séfardie – Les Mendes da Costa de Londres', 18ème siècle, 13 (1985), pp. 11–25.
Petty, Sir William, *Economic Writings* (Cambridge University Press, 1899).
Rabinowitz, S.P., *R. Yomtov Lippmann Zunz* (Warsaw, 1896).
Revah, I.S. (ed.), *Spinoza et le Dr. Juan de Prado* (Paris: Mouton, 1959).
Ruderman, D., 'The Career and Writings of David Nieto', *PAAJR*, 58 (1992), pp. 193–219.
Samet, M. 'Mendelssohn, N.H. Weisel ve-rabbanei doram', in *Mehkarim be-toldot am Yisrael* (Haifa, 1970).
Saperstein, M., 'Chief Rabbi Ezekiel Landau', in S. Gilman and J. Zipis (eds), *Yale Companion to Jewish Writing* (New Haven, CT: Yale University Press, 1997), pp. 84–7.
Schedlitz, B., *Leffmann Behrens* (Hildesheim: August Lax, 1984).
Schiff, Rabbi David Tevele, *Lashon Zahav* (Offenbach, 1822).
Schoeps, H. -J., *Barocke Juden, Christen, Judenchristen* (Berne: Francke Verlag, 1965).
Scholem, G., *Sabbatai Sevi, The Mystical Messiah 1626–1676*, Engl. trans. (London: Routledge, 1973).
Schudt, J.J. *Jüdische Merckwürdigkeiten* (Frankfurt am Main, 1714).
Sherwin, B.L., *Mystical Theology and Social Dissent* (London, Toronto: Associated University Presses, 1982).
Stern, M., *Meyer Simon Weyl, der letzte Kurbrandenburgische Landrabbiner'*, *Jeschurun*, XIII (1926), pp. 290–1.
——, 'Die Anfänge von Hirschel Löbels Berliner Rabbinat', *Jeschurun*, XVII (1930), pp. 364–5.
Strodtmann, A., *Heines Leben und Werke* (Berlin: Duncker, 1887).
Teufel, H., 'Ein Schüler Mendelssohns – Herz Homberg', in G. Ammerer *et al.* (eds), *Ambivalenzen der Aufklärung* (Munich: Oldenburg, 1997), pp. 187–202.
Vind, R. Shlomo, *Ha-Rav Yehezke'el Landau* (Jerusalem: Hotsa'at Da'at Ha-Torah, 1961).
Wallach, L. (ed.), *Liberty and Letters – The Thoughts of Leopold Zunz* (London, 1959).
Warschawski, Max, 'Enigmes dans un cimetière', *Archives Juives*, 24 (1988), pp. 59–81.

Zeman, F.D., 'The Amazing Career of Dr Rodrigo Lopez', *Bulletin of the History of Medicine*, 39 (1965), pp. 295–308.

Historical

England

Abraham, Israel, 'Joachim Gaunse', *TJHSE*, IV (1899–1901), pp. 83–101.
——, 'Hebrew Loyalty under the First Four Georges', *TJHSE*, IX (1922), pp. 103–30.
Arnold, A.P., 'Apprentices of Great Britain 1710–1773', with an introduction by R.D. Barnett, *TJHSE*, XXII (1970), pp. 145–57.
Barnett, A., *The Western Synagogue through Two Centuries* (1761–1961) (London: Vallentine Mitchell, 1961).
Barnett, R.D., 'Anglo-Jewry in the Eighteenth Century', in V.D. Lipman (ed.), *Three Centuries of Anglo-Jewish History* (Cambridge: Heffer, 1961), pp. 45–68.
——, 'Dr Samuel Nunez Ribeiro and the Settlement of Georgia', in *Migration and Settlement* (London: JHSE, 1971), pp. 63–100.
Busse, G.W., 'The Herem of Rabbenu Tam in Queen Anne's London', *TJHSE*, XXI (1968), pp. 138–47.
Child, Sir Josiah, *A New Discourse of Trade* (London, 1693).
Diamond, A.S., 'Problems of the London Sephardi Community, 1720–1733', *TJHSE*, XXI (1968), pp. 39–63.
Duschinsky, C., *The Rabbinate of the Great Synagogue London, 1756–1842* (Oxford University Press, 1921).
Endelman, Todd, *The Jews of Georgian England* (Philadelphia: JPSA, 5739/1979).
——, *Radical Assimilation in English Jewish History, 1656–1945* (Bloomington: Indiana University Press, 1990).
——, 'Jewish Communal Structure in Britain from the Resettlement to the Present', in *Festschrift Julius Carlebach* (Heidelberg: Carl Winter, 1992), pp. 1–16.
Epstein, I., 'Ascama 1 of the Spanish and Portuguese Jewish Congregation of London', in *Studies and Essays in Honor of A. A. Neumann*, ed. M. Ben-Horin *et al.* (Philadelphia: Dropsie College, 1962), pp. 170–214.
Feuer, Lewis, 'Francis Bacon and the Jews: Who was the Jew in the New Atlantis?', *TJHSE*, XXIX (1982–6), pp. 1–25.
Fisher, H.E.S., 'Jews in England and the 18th Century English Economy', *TJHSE*, XXVII (1982), pp. 156–65.
Gaster, Dr Moses, *History of the Ancient Synagogue of the Spanish and Portuguese Jews* (London, 5661 = 1901).
Gilam, A., *The Emancipation of the Jews in England, 1830–1860* (New York/London: Garland Publishing, 1982).
Green, G.L., *The Royal Navy and Anglo-Jewry, 1740–1820* (Ealing, 1989).
Gwyer, J., 'The Case of Dr. Lopez', *TJHSE*, XVI (1945–51), pp. 163–84.
Henriques, H.S.Q., *Jews and the English Law* (Oxford: Oxford University Press, 1908).
——, 'Proposals for Special Taxation of the Jews after the Revolution', *TJHSE*, IX (1918–20), pp. 39–66.
Horbury, W., 'John Spencer (1630–1693) and Hebrew Study', *Corpus Christi College, Cambridge, Association Newsletter*, no. 78 (1999), pp. 12–23.
Hyman, Louis, 'The Jews of Ireland' (London: JHSE, 1972).
Jacob, A., 'The Jews of Falmouth', *TJHSE*, XVII (1953), pp. 63.

Kaplan, Y., 'Wayward New Christians and Stubborn New Jews', *JH*, VIII (1994), pp. 27–41.

Katz, David, *Philosemitism and the Readmission of the Jews to England 1603–1655* (Oxford: Clarendon Press, 1982).

——, 'Henry Jessey and the Jews', in J. Kaplan *et al.* (eds), *Menasseh b. Israel and His World* (Leiden: Brill, 1989), pp. 117–38.

——, 'The Marginalization of Early Modern Anglo-Jewish History', in T. Kushner (ed.), *The Jewish Heritage in British History* (London: Cass, 1992), pp. 60–77.

——, *The Jews in the History of England 1485–1850* (Oxford: Clarendon Press, 1994).

Laski, Neville, *The Laws and Charities of the Spanish and Portuguese Jews Congregation of London* (London: Cresset Press, 1952).

Liberles, R., 'The Jews and Their Bill', *JH*, II (1987), pp. 29–39.

Lipman, V.D., 'Sephardi and Other Jewish Immigrants in England in the 18th Century', in *Migration and Settlement* (London: JHSE, 1971), pp. 37–63.

Lloyd-Jones, G., *The Discovery of Hebrew in Tudor England* (Manchester University Press, 1983).

Mayerowitsch, Rev. H., 'The Chazanim of the Great Synagogue, London', Miscellanies, *JHSE*, IV (1942).

Meyers, Charles, 'Debt in Elizabethan England: The Adventures of Dr. Hector Nunez, Physician and Merchant', *TJHSE*, XXXIV (1997), pp. 125–40.

Mirabeau, Comte de, *Sur Moses Mendelssohn, sur la Réforme Politique des Juifs* (London, 1787).

Naggar, Betty, 'Jewish Pedlars and Hawkers, 1740–1940', *Porphyrogenitus* (1992).

Osterman, N, 'The Controversy over the Proposed Re-admission of the Jews to England', *JSS*, III (1941), pp. 301–28.

Perry, Norma, 'Anglo-Jewry, the Law, Religious Conviction and Self Interest (1655–1753)', *Journal of European Studies*, XIV (1984), pp. 1–23.

Petty, Sir William, *Economic Writings* (Cambridge University Press, 1899).

Picciotto, James, *Sketches of Anglo-Jewish History*, ed. Israel Finestein (London: Soncino Press, 1956).

Rabb, T., 'The Stirrings of the 1590s and the Return of the Jews to England, *TJHSE*, XXVI (1979), pp. 26–33.

Rabinowicz, Oscar, 'Sir Solomon de Medina' (London: JHSE, 1974).

Ross, J. M. 'Naturalisation of the Jews in England', *TJHSE*, XXIV (1970–3), pp. 59–72.

Roth, Cecil, 'The Portsmouth Community and its Historical Background,' *TJHSE*, XIII (1936), pp. 157–87.

——, 'The Lesser London Synagogues of the 18th Century', *Miscellanies*, III (London: JHSE, 1937).

——(ed.), *Anglo-Jewish Letters* (London: Soncino Press, 1938).

——, 'The Chief Rabbinate of England', in I. Epstein *et al.* (eds), *Essays in Honour of the Very Rev. Dr J. H. Hertz* (London: Edward Goldston, 1943), pp. 371–84.

——, *History of the Great Synagogue* (London: Edward Goldston, 1950).

Ruderman, David, 'Was there an English Parallel to the German Haskalah?', in M. Brenner and D. Rechter (eds), *Two Nations: British and German Jews in comparative perspective* (Tübingen: Mohr, 1999).

Saltman, Avrom, *The Jewish Question in 1655 – Studies in Prynne's Demurrer* (Ramat-Gan: Bar-Ilan University Press, 1995).

Samuel, E.R., 'Dr. Meyer Schomberg's Attack on the Jews of London', *TJHSE*, XX (1964), pp. 83–111.

Samuel, W.S. 'The First London Synagogue of the Resettlement', *TJHSE*, x (1924), pp. 1–147.

Singer, S., 'Jews and Coronations', *TJHSE*, v, (1902–05), pp. 79–114.

Smith, Ruth, *Handel's Oratorios and Eighteenth-Century Thought* (Cambridge University Press, 1995).

Stein, Siegfried, 'Some Ashkenazi Charities in London at the End of the Eighteenth and Beginning of the Nineteenth Centuries', *TJHSE*, xx (1964), pp. 63–81.

Sutherland, Lucy, 'Samson Gideon: Eighteenth Century Jewish Financier', *THJSE*, xvii (1953), pp. 79–90.

Tishby, I. (ed.), 'Yediot Hadashot al Kehilat Ha-Anusim be-London', in A. Mirsky *et al.* (eds), *Galut ahar Golah* (Jerusalem: Ben Zvi Institute, 1988), pp. 470–96.

Tucker, C., 'Jewish Marriages and Divorces in England until 1940', *Genealogists' Magazine*, September 1992, pp. 87–93.

Wolf, Lucien, 'The First English Jew', *TJHSE*, ii (1894–5), pp. 14–48.

——, 'American Elements in the Re-Settlement', *TJHSE*, iii (1899), pp. 76–93.

——, *Menasseh b. Israel's Mission to Oliver Cromwell* (London, 1901).

——, 'The Jewry of the Restoration', *TJHSE*, v (1902–05), pp. 5–33.

——, 'Status of the Jews in England after the Re-Settlement', *TJHSE*, iv (1903), pp. 177–93.

Wolper, Roy, 'Circumcision as Polemic in the Jew Bill of 1753', *Eighteenth Century Life*, vii (1982), pp. 28–36.

Woolf, M., 'Foreign Trade of London Jews in the 17th century', *TJHSE*, xxiv (1975), pp. 38–58.

Yogev, G., *Diamonds and Coral–Anglo-Dutch Jews and 18th Century Trade* (Leicester: Leicester University Press, 1978).

France

Anchel, R., *Napoléon et les Juifs* (Paris, 1928).

——, *Les Juifs de France* (Paris: Janin, 1946).

Bauer, Jules, 'Un commencement d'Insurrection au quartier juif d'Avignon au xviie siècle', *REJ*, 38 (1899), pp. 123–36.

Berkovitz, J.R., 'The French Revolution and the Jews', *AJSR*, xx (1995), pp. 25–8.

——, 'Jewish Scholarship and Identity in 19th Century France', *Modern Judaism*, 18 (1998), pp. 1–33.

——, 'Patterns of Rabbinic Succession in Modern France', *JH*, 13 (1999), pp. 59–82.

——, 'Social and Religious Controls in Pre-revolutionary France', *JH*, xv (2000), pp. 1–40.

Bloch, Camille, 'Un épisode de l'histoire commerciale des Juifs en Languedoc (1738)' *REJ*, xxiv (1892), pp. 272–80.

Blumenkranz, B. (ed.), *Histoire des Juifs en France* (Toulouse: Privat, 1972).

Cahen, Abraham, 'Enseignement Obligatoire', *REJ*, i (1880), pp. 303–5.

——, *Règlements somptuaires de la Communauté Juive de Metz* (Versailles: Cerf et fils, 1881).

——, 'Le Rabbinat de Metz pendant la période francaise (1567–1871)', *REJ*, vii–viii (1883–1884), pp. 111 ff.

Cahen, Gillbert, 'La Région Lorraine', in Blumenkranz (ed.), *Histoire des Juifs en France* (Toulouse: Privat, 1979), pp. 1–26.

Calmann, Marianne: *The Carrière of Carpentras* (Littman Library-OUP, 1984).

Chobaut, H. 'Les Juifs d'Avignon et du Comtat et la Révolution Française', *REJ*, 102 (1937), pp. 3–39.

Chouraqui, J.M. 'La Loi du Royaume est la loi; les rabbins, la politique et l'Etat en France (1807–1905)', *Pardès*, 2 (1985).

Daltroff, Jean, 'Samuel Levy de Balbronn, Un riche prêteur d'argent Juif de Basse-Alsace', *REJ*, 148 (1989), pp. 53–68.

de Dianoux, Hugues Jean, 'Les Juifs d'Avignon et du Comtat Venaissin', in Blumenkranz (ed.), *Histoire des Juifs en France* (Toulouse: Privat, 1979), pp. 193–218.

Feuerwerker, D., *L'Emancipation des Juifs en France* (Paris: Albin Michel, 1976).

Gelber, N.M., 'La Police Autrichienne et le Sanhédrin de Napoléon', *REJ*, 83 (1927), pp. 1–21, 113–45.

Ginsburger, M., 'Une Fondation de Cerf Berr', *REJ*, 74–7 (1922), pp. 47–57.

——, 'Un Emprunt de la Nation Juive d'Alsace', *REJ*, 81 (1925), pp. 83–6.

Godechot, Jacques, 'Les Juifs de Nancy de 1789–1795', *REJ*, 96 (1928), pp. 1–35.

Graetz, M., *Les Juifs en France au xixe siècle* (Paris: Seuil, 1989).

Hertzberg, A., *The French Enlightenment and the Jews* (New York/London: Columbia University Press, 1968).

Hildesheimer, Françoise; 'La Présence Juive en Provence à la fin de l'Ancien Régime', in B. Blumenkranz (ed.), *Les Juifs en France au xviiie siècle* (Paris, 1994), pp. 111–23.

Hyman, Paula, E., *The Emancipation of the Jews of Alsace* (New Haven, CT: Yale University Press, 1991).

Iancu, Danièle et Carole, *Les Jifs du Midi* (Avignon: A Barthélemy, 1995).

Job, Françoise, *Les Juifs de Lunéville aux xviiie et xixe siècles* (Nancy: Presses Universitaires de Nancy, 1989).

Kaufmann, U.R., 'The Jewish Fight for Emancipation in France and Germany', in M. Brenner (ed.), *Jewish Emancipation Reconsidered* (Tübingen: Mohr, 2003), pp. 79–92.

Kerner, S., 'Les démarches des envoyés de la communauté juive de Metz à Paris at à Versailles relative à la "taxe Brancas"', *Annales de l'Est*, 26 (1974), pp. 217–64.

Lemalet, M., 'L'Emancipation des Juifs de Lorraine', in D. Tollet (ed.), *Politique et Religion dans le Judaisme moderne* (Paris: PUPS, 1987), pp. 63–83.

——, 'Juifs et Intendants au XVIIe siècle', *xviie siècle*, 46 (1994), pp. 287–302.

——, 'Vie et Mort de Marc Terquem, banquier Juif de Metz', *Archives Juives*, 29 (1996), pp. 36–47.

Léon, M., *Histoire des Juifs de Bayonne* (Paris: Durlacher, 1893).

Liber, M., 'Les Juifs et la Convocation des Etats Généraux', *REJ*, nos. LXIII–LXVI (1912–1914).

Lunel, Armand, *Les Juifs du Languedoc, de la Provence et des Etats français du Pape* (Paris: Albin Michel, 1975).

Malesherbes, *Second Mémoire sur le Mariage des Protestants en 1786*, 2nd edn (London 1787).

Malino, F., The Jews and the Parlement of Metz', in G. Dahan (ed.), *Le Juifs au Régard de i'histoire* (Paris: Picard, 1985), pp. 327–41.

——, '*The Sephardic Jews of Bordeaux* (Tuscaloosa: Alabama University Press, 1987).

——, 'Resistance and Rebellion in Eighteenth Century France', *TJHSE*, xxx (1987–8), pp. 55–70.

Malvezin, T., *Histoire des Juifs à Bordeaux*, repr. (Marseilles: Lafitte, 1976).

Marx, R., 'La Régénération économique des Juifs d'Alsace', in B. Blumenkranz et A. Soboul (eds), *Les Juifs et la Révolution française* (Toulouse: Privat, 1976), pp. 105–20.

Méchoulan, H. (ed.), *L'Etat Baroque* (Paris: Vrin, 1985).

Meyer, P.A., *La Communauté Juive de Metze au xviiie siècle* (Nancy: Serpenoise, 1993).

Moulinas, René, 'Les Juifs d'Avignon et du Comtat', in B. Blumenkranz et A. Soboul (eds), *Les Juifs et la Révolution française* (Toulouse: Privat, 1976), pp. 143–82.

——, 'Le conseil du roi et le Commerce des Juifs d'Avignon en France', *18e Siècle*, 13 (1981), pp. 169–79.

Mrejen-O'Hara, Simone, 'Pratiques Religieuses dans les "quatre saintes communautés" d'Avignon et du Comtat Venaissin', *Archives Juives*, 28 (1995), pp. 12–13.

Necheles, R., 'L'Emancipation des Juifs 1787–1795', in B. Blumenkranz and A. Soboul (eds), *Les Juifs et la Révolution française* (Toulouse: Privat, 1976), pp. 71–86.

Néher-Bernheim, R., 'Cerf Berr de Medelsheim: Le Destin d'une famille durant la Révolution', *REJ*, 137 (1978), pp. 61–75.

Netter, N., 'Die Schuldennot der jüdischen Gemeinde Metz, 1791–1854', *MGWJ*, 57 (1913), pp. 593–619.

Polonovski, Max, 'Un Aventurier Mythomane sous L'Empire – Samon Cerf Berr', *REJ*, 154 (1995), pp. 43–76.

Posener, S., 'The Social Life of the Jewish Communities in France in the 18th Century', *JSS*, 7 (1945), pp. 195–232.

Raphael, F. and R. Weyl, *Juifs en Alsace* (Toulouse: Privat, 1977).

Roos, G., *Relations entre le gouvernement royal et les Juifs du nord-est de la France au XVIIe siècle* (Paris: Champion, 2000).

Schechter, R.B., 'Becoming French: Patriotic Liturgy and the Transformation of Jewish Identity in France, 1706–1815', D.Phil. thesis, Harvard, Mass. (1993).

——, 'Translating the 'Marseillaise', *Past and Present*, 142–3 (1994), pp. 108–35.

Schwarzfuchs, S., 'Notes sur les Juifs de Bayonne', *REJ*, 125–6 (1966–7), pp. 353–64.

——, *Les Juifs de France* (Paris: Albin Michel, 1975).

——, (ed.), *Le registre des délibérations de la Nation Juive Portugaise de Bordeaux (1711–1787)* (Paris: Centro Cultural Portuguêse, 1981).

——, (ed.), *Le Journal révolutionnaire d'Abraham Spire* (Paris: Verdier, 1989).

——, (ed.), 'Le Memorbuch de Metz' (manuscript).

——, 'The Metz Community in the 18th Century', Manuscript lecture.

Stillschweig, K., 'Das Judentum im Lichte des französischen Nationsbegriffs', *MGWJ*, 81 (1937), pp. 457–8.

Strauss, Janine, 'Echos de la Révolution Francaise dans la littérature de la Haskalah', *Archives Juives*, XXIV (1988), pp. 40 ff.

Szajkowski, Zosa, 'Mishlahotehem shel Yehudei Bordeaux el ve'idat Malesherbes (1788) ve-el Ha-Asefa Ha-le'umit (1790)', *Tsiyon*, XVIII (1953), pp. 31–79.

——, *The Economic Status of the Jews in Alsace, Metz and Lorraine* (New York: Editions Historiques, 1954).

——, *Poverty and Social Welfare among French Jews* (New York: Editions Historiques, 1954).

——, *Jews and the French Revolutions of 1789, 1830 and 1848* (New York: Ktav, 1970).

Szapiro, Elie, 'Le Sud-Ouest', in B. Blumenkranz (ed.), *Historie des Juifs en France* (Toulouse: Privat, 1972), pp. 221–61.

Tollet, D. (ed.), *Politique et Religion dans le Judaisme Moderne* (Paris: PPPS, 1987).

Trigano, S., 'The French Revolution and the Jew' *Modern Jewish Studies*, X (1990), pp. 171–90.

Weil, J., 'Contribution à l'histoire des communautés alsaciennes au 18e siècle', *REJ*, 81 (1925), pp. 169–80.

Weill, G., 'Recherches sur la Démographie des Juifs d'Alsace du XVII au XVIII siècles', *REJ*, 129–30 (1970–1), pp. 51–67.

——, 'L'Alsace', in B. Blumenkranz (ed.), *Histoire des Juifs en France* (Toulouse: Privat, 1972).

——, 'Rabbins et Parnassim dans l'Alsace du XVIIIe Siècle', in M. Yardeni (ed.), *Les Juifs dans l'histoire de France* (Leiden: Brill, 1980), pp. 96–109.

Weill, G., 'L'intendant d'Alsace et la centralisation de la Nation Juive', *Dix-Huitième, Siècle*, 13 (1981), pp. 181–205.

Weill, S., 'Les Juifs d'Alsace à la Veille de l'Emancipation', *Les Nouveaux Cahiers*, 97 (1989), pp. 23–28.

Weyl, R., 'Un rabbin alsacien engagé', in M. Hadas-Lebel and E. Oliel-Grausz (eds), *Les Juifs et la Révolution française* (Louvain/Paris: Peeters, 1992), pp. 85–95.

—— et J. Daltroff, 'Le Cahier de Doléance des Juifs d'Alsace', *Revue d'Alsace*, 109 (1983), pp. 65–80.

Yardeni, M., 'Les Juifs dans la polémique sur la tolérance des Protestants en France à la veille de la Révolution', *REJ*, 132 (1973), pp. 79–94.

In the German states

Altmann, B., 'The Autonomous Federation of Jewish Communities in Paderborn', *JSS*, III (1941), pp. 159–88.

Aschoff, D., 'Das Münsterländische Judentum', *Theokratia*, III (1973–5), pp. 125–84.

Awerbuch, M., 'Alltagsleben in der Frankfurter Judengasse', in K. Grözinger (ed.), *Jüdische Kultur in Frankfurt am Main* (Wiesbaden: Harrasowitz Verlag, 1997), pp. 1–24.

Bamberger, N., *Geschichte der Juden von Kitzingen*, new imp. (Kitzingen: Verlag Högner, 1983).

Battenberg, J.F., 'Gesetzgebung und Judenemanzipation im Ancien Régime', *Zeitschrift für Historische Forschung*, 13 (1986), pp. 43–63.

——, Des Kaisers Kammerknechte, *HZ*, 245 (1987), pp. 545–99.

Baumgart, P., 'Absoluter Staat und Judenemanzipation in Brandenburg-Preussen', *Jahrbuch für die Geschichte Mittel und Ost-Deutschlands*, 13/14 (1965), pp. 60–87.

Behr, H.J. 'Judenschaft, Landstände und Fürsten in den geistlichen Staaten Westfalens im 18. Jahrhunder', in P. Freimark (ed.), *Gedenkschrift für B. Brilling* (Hamburg: Christians Verlag, 1988), pp. 121–35.

Berger, Ruth, 'Tanzt der Teufel mit?', *Kalonymos*, VI, 2003, pp. 4–7.

Bloch, P., 'Ein vielbegehrter Rabbiner des Rheingaues, Juda Mehler Reutlingen', in *Martin Philippsohn Festschrift* (Leipzig: Fock, 1916).

Bodian, Miriam, 'Ha-Yazmim Ha-Yehudiim be-Berlin', *Tsiyon*, 49 (1984), pp. 159–84.

Breuer, M., 'Jüdische Religion and Kultur in den ländlichen Gemeinden 1600–1800', in M. Richarz and R. Rürüp (eds), *Jüdisches Leben auf dem Lande* (Tübingen: Mohr, 1997).

——, German–Jewish History in Modern Times, I (New York: Columbia University Press, 1996).

Brilling, B., *Geschichte der Juden in Breslau von 1454 bis 1702* (Stuttgart: Kohlhammer Verlag, 1960).

Carlebach, S., *Geschichte der Juden in Lübeck und Moisling* (Lübeck, 1898).

Casper-Holtkotte, C., *Juden im Aufbruch* (Hanover: Hahnsche Verlag, 1996).

Cohen, Daniel, 'Die Entwicklung der Landesrabbinate in den deutschen Territorien bis zur Emanzipation', in A. Haverkamp (ed.), *Zur Geschichte der Juden in Deutschland* (Stuttgart: Hiersemann, 1981), pp. 221–42.

Cohn, W.I., 'The Moses Isaac Family Trust', *LBYB*, XVIII (1973), pp. 267–80.

Demandt, K.E., *Bevölkerungs- und Sozialgeschichte der jüdischen Gemeinde Niedenstein 1653–1866* (Wiesbaden: Kommission für die Geschichte der Juden in Hessen, 1980).

Dienemann, M., 'Die Geschichte der Einzelgemeinde als Spiegel der Gesamtgeschichte', in E. Roth (ed.), *Die alte Synagoge zu Worms* (Frankfurt am Main: Ner Tamid Verlag, 1961), pp. 167–72.

Eckstein, A., *Geschichte der Juden in Markgrafentum Bayreuth* (Bayreuth: Seligsberg, 1907).

Ehrlich, E.L., 'Geschichte und Kultur der Juden in den rheinischen Territorialstaaten', in *Monumenta Judaica* (Cologne, 1963), pp. 242–81.

Eidelberg, S. (ed.), R. *Juspa, Shammash of Warmaisa* [Worms] (Jerusalem: Magnes Press, 1991).

Eliav, M., *Ha-Hinukh Ha-Yehudi Be-Germaniya* (Jerusalem: Jewish Agency, 1960).

Evers, M., *Die Geschichte der Juden in der Stadt Warburg* (Warburg: Hermes Verlag, 1978).

Feiner, S., 'Bein ha-Mapekha Ha-Tsarfatit le-ven Tmurot be-Haskalat Berlin', *Tsiyon*, LVII (1992), pp. 89–92.

Franke, H., 'Geschichte und Schicksal der Juden in Heilbronn' (Stadt Archiv, 1963).

Franz, E.G. (ed.), *Juden als Darmstädter Bürger* (Darmstadt: Roether, 1984).

Freudenthal, M., 'Die Verfassungsurkunde einer reichsritterlichen Judenschaft', *ZGJD*, I (1929), pp. 44–68.

Freund, I., *Die Emanzipation der Juden in Berlin*, 2 vols (Berlin: Poppelauer, 1912).

Friedländer, M.H., *Beiträge zur Geschichte der Juden Mähren* (Brünn, 1876).

Friedrichs, C.R., 'Anti-Jewish Policies in Early Modern Germany and the Uprising in Worms, 1613–1617', *Central European History*, XXIII (1990), pp. 91–152.

——, 'Jews in Imperial Cities', in R. Po-Chia Hsia and H. Lehmann (eds), *In and Out of the Ghetto* (Cambridge University Press, 1995).

Friess, G., 'Zur Lebenswelt jüdischer Räuberbanden unter besonderer Berücksichtigung Pommerns', in M. Heitman and H.J. Schoeps (eds), *Geschichte und Kultur der Juden in Pommern* (Hildesheim: Olms, 1995), pp. 297–314.

Glanz, R., *Geschichte des niederen Jüdischen Volkes in Deutschland* (New York, 1968).

Gotzmann, A., 'Strukturen jüdischer Gerichtsautonomie in den deutschen Staaten des 18. Jahrhunderts', *HZ*, 267 (1998), pp. 313–56.

Grab, W., 'Deutscher Jakobinismus und Jüdische Emanzipation', in W. Grab (ed.), *Der deutsche Weg der Judenemanzipation 1789–1938* (Munich: Piper, 1991), pp. 41–72.

Hahn, Joseph, *Yosef Ometz* (Frankfurt am Main, 1723).

Halperin, Israel, 'Mahloket al Breirat Ha-Kahal be-Frankfurt', *Tsiyon*, XXI (1956), pp. 64–91.

Hertz, D., *Jewish High Society in Old Regime Berlin* (New Haven, CT: Yale University Press, 1988).

Herzfeld, E., 'Förderung gewerblicher Entwicklung durch Juden in Hinterpommern im 18. Jahrhundert', in M. Heitman and H.J. Schoeps (eds), *Geschichte und Kultur der Juden in Pommern* (Hildesheim: Olms, 1995), pp. 239–54.

Herzig, A., *Judentum und Emanzipation in Westphalen* (Münster, 1973).

——, (ed.), *Die Juden in Hamburg* (Hamburg: Dölling und Galiz, 1991).

——, 'Die Jüdischheit teutscher Nation', *Aschkenas*, III (1994), pp. 127–32.

Hildesheimer, M., 'Yahadut Ashkenas ba-me'ah ha-17 al pi Ha-She'elot u-Tshuvot', unpublished MA Thesis, University of Bar-Ilan, Ramat-Gan, (1972).

Holeczek, H., 'Die Judenemanzipation in Preussen', in B. Martin and E. Schulin (eds), *Die Juden als Minderheit in der Geschichte* (Munich: DTV, 1981), pp. 136–7.

Horovitz, Jakob, 'Aus der Oxforder Handschrift des Josif Omez', in *Festschrift Jakob Freimann* (Berlin, 1937).

Hundsnurscher, F. and G. Taddey (eds), *Die Jüdischen Gemeinden in Baden* (Stuttgart: Kohlhammer Verlag, 1968).

Jacobson, J., *Jüdische Trauungen in Berlin 1759–1813* (Berlin: De Gruyter, 1968).

Jeggle, Utz, *Judendörfer in Württemberg* (Tübingen: Tübinger Verein für Volkskunde, 1999).

Jersch-Wenzel, S., *Juden und Franzosen in der Wirtschaft des Raumes Berlin/Brandenburg zur Zeit des Merkantilismus* (Berlin: De Gruyter, 1978).

——, 'Die Herausbildung eines "Preussischen" Judentums 1671–1815', in P. Freimark (ed.), *Juden in Preussen – Juden in Hamburg* (Hamburg: Hans Christians Verlag, 1983).

Johnson, H.C., *Frederick the Great and His Officials* (New Haven, CT: Yale University Press, 1975).

Katz, Jacob, 'Between 1096 and 1648–49', in S. Ettinger (ed.), *Sepher Yovel le-Yitzhak Baer* (Jerusalem: Israel Historical Society, 1960).

——, 'Paraot Hep-Hep shel shnat 1819 be-Germaniya al Reka'an Ha-Histori', *Tsiyon*, 38 (1973), pp. 62–115.

Kaufmann, D., 'Die Schuldennot der Gemeinde Posen', *MGWJ*, 39 (1895), pp. 38–46.

Kaufmann, U., 'Jüdische Handwerker' in K. Grözinger (ed.), *Jüdische Kultur in Frankfurt am Main* (Wiesbaden, 1997), pp. 47–71.

Kisch, Guido, *Rechts- und Sozialgeschichte der Juden in Halle, 1686–1730* (Berlin: De Gruyter, 1970).

Klemmer, I., *Aloys v. Rechberg (1766–1849)* (Munich: Stadtarchiv, 1975).

Kober, A., 'The French Revolution and the Jews in Germany', *JSS*, 7 (1945), pp. 294–322.

——, 'Die deutschen Kaiser und die Wormser Juden', in Ernst Roth (ed.), *Die alte Synagoge zu Worms* (Frankfurt am Main: Ner Tamid Verlag, 1961).

Kracauer, I., *Die Geschichte der Judengasse in Frankfurt am Main* (Frankfurt am Main: J. Kauffmann Verlag, 1906).

——, Geschichte der Juden in Frankfurt am Main 1150–1824, 2 vols (Frankfurt am Main: J. Kauffmann Verlag, 1925–1927).

Kromminga, P., 'Duldung und Ausgrenzung. Schutzjuden und Betteljuden in Hamburg', in A. Herzig (ed.), *Juden in Hamburg* (Hamburg: Dölling und Galiz, 1991), pp. 187–93.

Küther, C., *Räuber und Gauner in Deutschland* (Göttingen: Vandenhoeck und Ruprecht, 1987).

Laubenthal, W., *Die Synagogengemeinden des Kreises Merzig* (Saarbrücken: Saarbrücken Druckerei, 1984).

Lowenstein, S.M., 'Jewish Upper Crust and Berlin Jewish Enlightenment', in F. Malino and D. Sorkin (eds), *From East to West* (Oxford: Blackwell, 1990), pp. 182–201.

——, 'Two Silent Minorities, Orthodox Jews and Poor Jews in Berlin, 1770–1823', *LBYB*, XXXVI (1991).

——, 'Ashkenazic Jewry and the European Marriage Pattern', *JH*, VIII (1994), pp. 155–75.

——, *The Berlin Jewish Community* (Oxford University Press, 1994).

Magnus, Shulamit, *Jewish Emancipation in a German City* (Stanford University Press, 1997).

Marcus, J.R., *Communal Sick Care in the German Ghetto* (Cincinnati: Hebrew Union College Press, 1947).

Mayer, E., *Die Frankfurter Juden* (Frankfurt am Main: Kramer Verlag, 1966).

Melton, J.V.H., *Absolutism and the Eighteenth Century: Origins of Compulsory Schooling in Prussia and Austria* (Cambridge University Press, 1988).

Meyer, Michael, *The Origins of the Modern Jew* (Detroit: Wayne State University Press, 1967).

Michaelis, Dolf, 'The Ephraim Family', *LBYB*, XXI (1976), pp. 201–28.

Molitor, H., 'Die Juden im französischen Rheinland', in J. Bohnke-Kollwitz *et al.* (eds), *Köln und das rheinische Judentum* (Cologne: Bachem, 1984), pp. 82–94.

Morgenstern, F., 'Hardenberg and the Emancipation of Franconian Jewry', *JSS*, XV (1952), pp. 253–74.

Philippson, M., 'Der Anteil der jüdischen Freiwilligen an dem Befreiungskriege 1813 und 1814', *MGWJ*, 50 (1906), pp. 1–21.

Pollack, H., *Jewish Folkways in Germanic Lands* (Massachusetts: MIT Press, 1971).

Poppel, S.M., 'New Views on Jewish Integration in Germany', *Central European History*, IX (1976), pp. 86–108.

Press, V., 'Kaiser Rudolf II und der Zusammenschluss der deutschen Judenheit', in A. Haverkamp (ed.), *Geschichte der Juden* (Stuttgart: Hiersemann, 1981), pp. 243–93.

Priebatsch, F., 'Die Judenpolitik des fürstlichen Absolutismus im 17. und 18. Jahrhunderten', in *Festschrift für D. Schäfer* (Jena: Fischer, 1915), pp. 564–651.

Rachel, H., 'Die Juden im Berliner Wirtschaftsleben', *ZGJD*, 2 (1930), pp. 175–96.

Renda, G., 'Fürth, das "bayerische Jerusalem"', in M. Treml (ed.), *Geschichte und Kultur der Juden in Bayern* (Munich: Saur, 1988), pp. 225–44.

Rohrbacher, S., 'Stadt und Land', in M. Richarz und R. Rürüp (eds), *Jüdisches Leben auf dem Lande*, pp. 37–58.

——, 'Räuberbanden', in J. Bohnke-Kollwitz (ed.), *Köln und das rheinische Judentum*, (Cologne: Bachem, 1984), pp. 117–24.

Römer, N., *Tradition und Akkulturation* (Münster: Waxman Verlag, 1995).

Rosenthal, L., *Zur Geschichte der Juden im Gebiet der ehemaligen Grafschaft Hanau* (Hanau: Hanauischer Geschichtsverein, 1963).

Roth, E. (ed.), *Die alte Synagoge zu Worms* (Frankfurt am Main: Ner Tamid, 1961).

Rürüp, R., 'The Tortuous and Thorny Path to Legal Equality', *LBYB*, XXI (1986), pp. 3–33.

Samuel, G., 'Die Namengebung der Westfälischen Judenschaft von 1808', *ZGJD*, VI (1935), pp. 47–51.

Schacter, J.J., 'Echoes of the Spanish Expulsion in 18th Century Germany', *Judaism*, 41 (1992), pp. 180–9.

Schmitt, H. *et al.* (eds), Juden in Karlsruhe (Karlsruhe: Badenic Verlag, 1988).

Schnee, H., *Die Hoffinanz und der moderne Staat* (Berlin: Duncker und Humblot, vols 1–6, 1953–67).

Schohat, E., 'Hitarut Shel Yehudei Germaniya ba-svivotam', *Tsiyon*, XXI (1956), pp. 207–35.

——, *Im Hilufei Tekufot* (Jerusalem: Mossad Bialik, 1960).

Schudt, J.J., *Jüdische Merckwürdigkeiten* (Frankfurt am Main, 1714).

Seeliger, H., 'Origin and Growth of the Berlin Jewish Community', *LBYB*, III (1958), pp. 161–2.

Shulvass, M., *From East to West* (Detroit: Wayne State University Press, 1971).

Silber, M., 'The Historical Experience of German Jewry and its Impact on the Haskalah and Reform in Hungary', in J. Katz (ed.), *Towards Modernity* (Oxford: Blackwell, 1987), pp. 107–57.

Sorkin, David, 'Religious Reform and Secular Trends in German-Jewish Life', *LBYB*, 40 (1995), pp. 169–84.

Stern, Moritz, 'Der Oberlandesälteste Jacob Moses', *Mitteilungen des Gesamtarchivs der deutschen Juden*, VI (1926).

——, 'Zur Geschichte der Fleischgebühren', *Soncino Blätter*, II (1927).

Stern, Selma, 'Die Juden in der Handelspolitik Wilhelm I von Preussen', *ZGJD*, V (1935), pp. 207–15.

——, *The Court Jew* (Philadelphia: JPSA, 5710–1950).

——, *Der Hofjude im Zeitalter des Merkantilismus* (Tübingen: Mohr, 2001).

Tal, Uriel, 'Young German Intellectuals on Romanticism and Judaism', in *S.W. Baron Jubilee Volume*, II (Columbia University Press, 1974), pp. 919–38.

Tannenbaum, W.Z., 'A Town on the Volkach', *LBYB*, XLV (2000), pp. 93–117.

Toury, J., 'Der Eintritt der Juden ins deutsche Bürgertum', in H. Liebeschütz und A. Paucker (eds), *Das Judentum in der deutschen Umwelt 1800–1850* (Tübingen: Mohr, 1977).

——, 'Der Anteil der Juden an der Städtischen Verwaltung im vormärzlichen Deutschland', *BLBI*, 23 (1963), pp. 265–86.

Trepp, L., *Die Oldenburger Judenschaft* (Oldenburg: Holzberg Verlag, 1973).

Turniansky, H., 'The Events in Frankfurt am Main (1612–1616) in Megillas Vints', in M. Graetz (ed.), *Schöpferische Momente des Europäischen Judentums* (Heidelberg: Winter, 2000).

Vogel, Rolf, *Ein Stück von uns* (Mainz: Hase-Koehler, 1977).
Volkov, S., *Die Juden in Deutschland 1780–1918* (Munich: Oldenburg, 1994).
Weyden, E., *Geschichte der Juden in Köln am Rhein*, repr. (Osnabrück: Kuballe, 1984).
Whaley, J., *Religious Toleration and Social Change in Hamburg 1529–1819* (Cambridge University Press, 1985).
Wolf, G., *Zur Geschichte der Juden in Worms* (Breslau: Schletterscher Verlag, 1862).
Wolf, J.R., 'Zwischen Hof und Stadt', in E.G. Franz (ed.), *Juden als Darmstädter Bürger* (Darmstadt: Roether Verlag, 1984).
Wyrwa, Ulrich, *Juden in der Toskana und in Preussen im Vergleich* (Tübingen: Mohr, 2003).
Zittartz, A., 'Die französische Herrschaft und die Juden in Krefeld (1794–1814)', *Aschkenas*, VI, (1996), pp. 87–116.

Habsburg empire

Adler, S., 'Das älteste Judicial-Protokoll des Jüdischen Gemeinde-Archivs in Prag (1682)', *JGGJCR*, III (1931), pp. 217–56.
Altmann, Adolf, *Geschichte der Juden in Stadt und Land Salzburg* (Salzburg: Müller Verlag, 1990).
Barson, S.W., *Die Judenfrage auf dem Wiener Kongress* (Vienna: Löwit, 1920).
Bato, Ludwig, *Die Juden im alten Wien* (Vienna: Phaidon Verlag, 1928).
Battenberg, J.F., 'The Jewish Population in the Holy Roman Empire', WCJS XI Div. B, iii (Jerusalem, 1994), pp. 61–8.
——, 'Zwischen Integration und Segregation', *Aschkenas*, VI (1996), pp. 421–54.
Bérenger, J., 'Les Juifs et l'antisémitisme dans l'Autriche du 17e siécle', in *Etudes Européennes* (Publications de la Sorbonne, Paris, 1973), pp. 181–92.
——, *Finances et absolutisme autrichien* (Paris: Imprimerie Nationale Sorbonne, 1975).
Berger, S. (ed.), 'The Desire to Travel – A Note on Abraham Levy's Yiddish Itinerary, 1719–1723', *Aschkenas*, VI (1996), pp. 497–506.
Bergl, J., 'Die Ausweisung der Juden aus Prag im Jahre 1744', in S. Steinherz (ed.), *Die Juden in Prag* (Prague: Bnei Brith, 1927), pp. 187–247.
——, 'Das Exil der Prager Judenschaft von 1745–1748', *JGGJCR*, I (1929), pp. 263–331.
Bretholz, B., 'Die Judenschaft einer mährischen Kleinstadt: Mark Pirnitz im 18. Jahrhundert', *JGGJCR*, II (1930), pp. 403–55.
Breuer, M., 'Emancipation and the Rabbis', *Niv Hamidrashiya*, vols 13–14 (5738/9–1978/9), pp. 26–51.
Brüll, N., *Zur Geschichte der Juden in Mähren*, *Jahrbuch für Israeliten*, 2te Folge, 3, pp. 181–220.
Cerman, Ivo, 'Anti-Jewish Superstition and the Expulsion of the Jews from Vienna, 1670', *Judaica Bohemiae*, XXXVI (2001), pp. 5–30.
Davis, J., 'Ashkenazic Rationalism and Midrashic Natural History', *Science in Context*, X (1997), pp. 605–26.
Dickson, P.G., *Finance and Government under Maria Theresa 1740–1780*, II (Oxford: Clarendon Press, 1987).
Drabek, A.M., 'Das Judentum der böhmischen Länder vor der Emanzipation', *Judaica Austriaca*, X (1984), pp. 5–30.
Duffy, C., *The Army of Maria Theresa* (London: David & Charles, 1977).
Evans, R.J.W., *The Making of the Habsburg Monarchy, 1550–1700* (Oxford: Clarendon Press, 1979).
Ferguson, N., 'Metternich and the Rothschilds', *LBYB*, XLVI (2001), pp. 19–54.

Frankl-Grün, Rabbi Dr. Adolf, 'Die Folgen des österreichischen Erbfolgekriegs für die Juden Kremsiers', *MGWJ*, 38 (1894).

——, *Geschichte der Juden in Kremsier 1322–1848*, vols I–III (Breslau/Frankfurt am Main, 1896–1901).

Frankova, Anita, 'Erfassung der jüdischen Bevölkerung in Böhmen', *Judaica Bohemiae*, VI (1970), pp. 55–69.

Gelber, N.M., 'La Police Autrichienne et le Sanhédrin de Napoléon', *REJ*, 83 (1927), pp. 1–21, 113–45.

Gold, H., *Gedenkbuch der untergegangenen Judengemeinden Mährens* (Tel Aviv: Olamenu, 1974).

Grünfeld, M., 'Ausserer Verlauf der Geschichte der Juden in Mähren', in H. Gold (ed.), *Judengemeinden Mährens in Vergangenheit und Gegenwart* (Brünn: Jüdischer Buchverlag, 1929).

Grunwald, M., *Samuel Oppenheimer und sein Kreis* (Vienna/Leipzig: Braumüller, 1913).

——, *Vienna* (Philadelphia: JPSA, 1936).

Hass, T., 'Statistische Betrachtungen über die jüdische Bevölkerung Mährens', in H. Gold (ed.), *Die Judengemeinden Mährens in Vergangenheit und Gegenwart* (Brünn: Jüdischer Buchverlag, 1929).

Heilig, B., 'Aufstieg und Verfall des Hauses Ehrenstamm', *BLBI*, X (1960), pp. 101–22.

Homberg, Herz, *Bne-Tsiyon* (Vienna, 1812).

Israel, J., 'Central European Jewry during the Thirty Years' War', *Central European History*, XVI (1983), pp. 3–30.

Jakobovits, T., 'Jüdisches Gemeindeleben in Kolin, 1763–1768', *JGGJCR*, I (1929), pp. 332–68.

——, 'Das Prager und Böhmischer Landesrabbinat', *JGGJCR*, V (1933), pp. 79–136.

——, 'Die Zünfte während der Austreibung der Juden aus Prag', *JGGJCR*, VIII (1936) pp. 111–18.

Karniel, J., 'Zur Auswirkung der Toleranzpatente', in P. Barton (ed.), *im Zeichen der Toleranz* (Vienna, 1981).

——, *Die Toleranzpolitik Kaisers Josephs II* (Gerlingen: Bleicher Verlag, 1985).

Kaufmann, D., *Die Letzte Vertreibung der Juden aus Wien* (Vienna: Carl Konegen, 1889).

Kestenberg-Gladstein, R., 'Toldot Ha-Kalkalah shel Yehudei Boehm she-mi-hutz le-Prag ba-me'ot ha-17 ve-ha-18', *Tsiyon*, XII (1947), pp. 49–69, 160–89.

——, 'Differences of Estates within Pre-emancipation Jewry', *JJS*, X (1954), pp. 156–66.

——, 'Wirtschaftsgeschichte der böhmischen Landjuden', *Judaica Bohemiae*, III (1967), pp. 101–33.

Kieval, H.J., *The Making of Czech Jewry* (Oxford University Press, 1988).

——, *Languages of Community* (California University Press, 2000).

Kisch, G., 'Die Zensur jüdischer Bücher in Böhmen', *JGGJCR*, II (1930), pp. 452–90.

——, *Die Prager Universität und die Juden*, repr. (Amsterdam: Grüner, 1969).

Klemperer, G., 'The Rabbis of Prague', *HJ*, XII (1950), pp. 33–66.

Kohler, Max, 'Jewish Rights at International Congresses', *AJYB*, XXVI (5678 = 1918), pp. 113–15.

Krochmalnik, D., 'Das Neue Weltbild in jüdischen Kontexten', in M. Graetz (ed.), *Schöpferische Momente des europäischen Judentums* (Heidelberg: C. Winter, 2000), pp. 249–70.

Lieben, S.H. (ed.), 'Die von Maria Theresa projektierte Esrogim-Steuer', *MGWJ*, 53 (1909), pp. 720–2.

——, 'Briefe von 1744–1748 über die Austreibung der Juden aus Prag', *JGGJCR*, IV (1932), pp. 353–479.

370   Bibliography

Lipscher, Vladimir, *Zwischen Kaiser Fiskus Adel Zünften* (Zurich, 1983).

Lohrmann, K., 'Die Entwicklung des Judenrechts in Osterreich', in K. Lohrmann *et al.*, (eds), *1000 Jahre Osterreichisches Judentum* (Eisenstadt: Edition Roetger, 1982).

McCagg, W.O., *A History of Habsburg Jews* (Bloomington: Indiana University Press, 1989).

——, 'Jewish Wealth in Vienna 1670–1918', in M. Silber (ed.), *Jews in the Hungarian Economy* (Jerusalem 1992), pp. 53–91.

McEwan, D., 'Judisches Leben im Mährischen Ghetto', *Mitteilungen des Instituts für österreichische Geschichtsforschung* (1991), pp. 83–145.

Mayer, S., *Die Wiener Juden 1700–1900* (Vienna: Löwit Verlag, 1917).

Mevorah, B., 'Die Interventionsbestrebungen in Europa zur Verhinderung der Vertreibung der Juden aus Böhmen und Mähren, 1744–45', *Tel Aviver Jahrbuch für deutsche Geschichte*, ix (1980), pp. 15–81.

Nosek, B., 'Soziale Differenzierungen und Streitigkeiten in jüdischen Kultusgemeinden im 17. Jahrhundert', *Judaica Bohemiae*, xii (1976), pp. 59–92.

Ozer, C., 'Jewish Education in Transition', *HJ*, 9 (1947), pp. 75–94, 137–158.

Padover, S.K., *The Revolutionary Emperor* (London: Eyre & Spottiswoode, 2nd edn, 1967).

Pollack, H., 'Précurseurs de l'Emancipation Juive en Europe Centrale', *XVIIIe siècle*, xiii (1981).

Popper, M., 'Les Juifs de Prague pendant la guerre de Trente Ans', *REJ*, 29–30 (1894–5), pp. 127–41.

Prokes, J. and A. Blaschka, 'Der Antisemitismus der Behörden', *JGGJCR*, i (1929), pp. 41–110.

Putik, A., 'The Prague Jewish Community in the late 17th and early 18th centuries', *JB*, xxxv (1999), pp. 4–121.

Rachmuth, M.R., 'Zur Wirtschaftsgeschichte der Prager Juden', *JGGJCR*, v (1933), pp. 9–78.

Sadek, V., 'La Chronique Hébraique de l'histoire des Juifs pragois', *Judaica Bohemiae*, i (1965), pp. 59–68.

Sadek, V. and J. Sedinova, 'Peter Beer – Penseur Eclairé de la vieille ville Juive de Prague', *Judaica Bohemiae*, xiii (1977), pp. 7–28.

Schubert, K., 'Der Einfluss des Josefinismus auf das Judentum in Österreich', *Kairos*, xiv (1972), pp. 82–97.

Singer, L., 'Die Entstehung des Juden – Systemalpatenten von 1797', *JGGJCR*, vii (1935), pp. 191–263.

Spiegel, K., 'Die Prager Juden zur Zeit des dreissigjährigen Krieges', in S. Steinherz (ed.), *Die Juden in Prag* (Prague: Bnai Brith, 1927).

Stern, W., 'Jewish Surnames', *LBYB*, xxii (1977), pp. 221–36.

Veltri, G., 'Ohne Recht und Gerechtigkeit – Kaiser Rudolf II und sein Bankier Markus Meyzel', in G. Veltri and A. Winkelmann (eds), *An der Schwelle zur Moderne* (Leiden: Brill, 2003), pp. 233–55.

Wachstein, B., 'Die Gründung der Wiener Chevrah Kadishah', *Mitteilungen zur jüdischen Volkskunde*, xiii (1910), pp. 9–12.

Wolf, G., *Ferdinand II und die Juden* (Vienna, 1859).

——, 'Zur Geschichte des jüdischen Gemeindewesens in Prag', *AZJ*, 27 (1863).

——, 'Die Vertreibung der Juden aus Böhmen im Jahre 1744', in *Jahrbuch für die Geschichte der Juden und des Judentums* (Leipzig, 1869).

——, *Aus der Zeit der Maria Theresa* (Vienna, 1871).

——, *Geschichte der Juden in Wien* (Vienna: Hölder Verlag, 1876).

——, 'Gemeindestreitigkeiten in Prag, 1567–1678', *ZGJD*, i (1887).

Holland

Blom, J.C.H. *et al.* (eds), *The History of the Jews in the Netherlands*, Engl. trans. (Oxford: Littman Library, 2002).

Bloom, H., *The Economic Activities of the Jews of Amsterdam in the 17th and 18th centuries*, repr. (London: Kennikat Press, 1969).

Bodian, Miriam, 'Men of the Nation', *Past and Present*, 143 (1994), pp. 48–76.

Cohen, Robert, 'Passage to a New World: The Sephardi Poor of 18th Century Amsterdam', in Lea Dasberg and J.N. Cohen (eds), *Neveh Ya'akov* (Assen: Van Gorcum, 1982), pp. 31–42.

Egmond, F., 'Poor Ashkenazim in the Dutch Republic', in J. Michman (ed.), *Dutch-Jewish History III* (Jerusalem, 1993), pp. 205–25.

——, 'Crime in Context: Jewish Involvement in Organised Crime in the Dutch Republic', *Jewish History*, IV (1998), pp. 75–100.

Halff, A., 'Diyunei Ha-Asefah Ha-Le'umit shel Ha-Republika Ha-Batavit be-davar Ha-Emanzipatsiya ha-Yehudim 1796', in J. Michman (ed.), *Mehkarim al Toldot Yahadut Holland* (Jerusalem: Magnes Press, 1975).

Kaplan, J., 'Amsterdam and Ashkenazic Migration in the Seventeenth Century', *SR*, XVII (1989).

——, 'Die Portugesieschen Juden und die Modernisierung', in A. Nechama *et al.* (eds), *Jüdische Lebenswelten* (Frankfurt am Main: Suhrkamp, 1992), pp. 303–17.

Méchoulan, H., *Etre Juif à Amsterdam au temps de Spinoza* (Paris: Albin Michel, 1991).

Michman, J. (ed.), *Mehkarim al Toldot Yahadut Holland* (Jerusalem: Magnes Press, 1975).

——, 'The Conflicts between Orthodox and Enlightened Jews', *SR*, XV (1981), pp. 20–36.

——, 'The Impact of German-Jewish Modernization on Dutch Jews', in J. Katz (ed.), *Towards Modernity* (New Brunswick: Transaction Books, 1987), pp. 171–87.

——, *Dutch Jewry during the emancipation period, 1787–1815* (Amsterdam University Press, 1995).

Nusteling, H.P.H., 'The Jews in the Republic of the United Provinces', in J. Israel and R. Salverda (eds), *Dutch Jewry* (Leiden: Brill, 2002), pp. 45–57.

Popkin, R.H., 'Rabbi Nathan Shapira's visit to Amsterdam in 1657', in J. Michman (ed.), *Dutch-Jewish History* (Jerusalem: Institute for Research in Dutch Jewry, 1984), pp. 185–205.

——, and G.M. Weiner (eds), *Jewish Christians and Christian Jews* (Dordrecht: Kluwer, 1994).

Sluys, D.M., 'Yehudei Ashkenaz be-Amsterdam mi-Shnat 1635 ad Shnat 1795', in J. Michman (ed.), *Mehkarim al Toldot Yahadut Holland* (Jerusalem: Magnes Press, 1975).

Sonnenberg-Stern, K., *Emancipation and Poverty* (Basingstoke: Macmillan, 2000).

The Sephardi world

Adler, E.N., *About Hebrew Manuscripts* (Oxford University Press, 1905).

Altmann, A., 'Eternality of Punishment', *PAAJR*, XL (1972), pp. 1–88.

Amzalak, Moses Bensabat, 'Joseph da Veiga and Stock Exchange Operations in the Seventeenth Century', in I. Epstein *et al.* (eds), *Essays in Honour of the Very Rev. Dr J. H. Hertz, Chief Rabbi* (London: Edward Goldston, 1942).

Arbel, B., 'Shipping and Toleration', *Mediterranean Historical Review*, XV (2000), pp. 56–71.

Barnett, R.D., 'The Correspondence of the Mahamad', *TJHSE*, XX (1964), pp. 1–50.

——, 'Mr Pepys' contacts with the Spanish and Portuguese Jews of London', *TJHSE*, XXIX (1988), pp. 27–33.

Barnett, R.D. and W. Schwab (eds), *The Sephardi Heritage*, i–ii (Grendon: Gibraltar Books, 1989).

Beinart, H. (ed.), *The Sephardi Legacy*, i–ii (Jerusalem: Magnes Press, 1992).

Bodian, Miriam, 'Amsterdam, Venice and the Marrano Diaspora', in J. Michman (ed.), *Dutch-Jewish History*, (Jerusalem: Tel Aviv University, 1984), pp. 47–65.

——, *Hebrews of the Portuguese Nation* (Bloomington: Indiana University Press, 1997).

——, 'Biblical Hebrews and the Rhetoric of Republicanism', *AJSR*, xxii (1997), pp. 199–221.

Cantor, G., 'The Rise and Fall of Emanuel Mendes da Costa', *EHR*, cxvi, 467 (2001), pp. 584–603.

Cesarani, D. (ed.), *Port Jews* (London: Frank Cass, 2002).

Cirot, Georges, *Les Juifs de Bordeaux* (Bordeaux: Feret et fils, 1920).

Da Costa, Uriel, *Examination of Pharisaic Traditions*, ed. and trans, H.P. Salomon and I.S.D. Sassoon (Leiden: Brill, 1993).

Diamond, A.S., 'The Cemetery of the Resettlement', *TJHSE*, xix (1960), pp. 163–90.

——, 'The Community of the Resettlement 1656–1684', *TJHSE*, xxiv (1975), pp. 134–50.

Gebhardt, C. (ed.), *Die Schriften des Uriel da Costa* (Amsterdam, 1922).

Gelber, N.M., 'Al Reshita Shel Ha-Kehillah Ha-Sephardit be-Vienna', in *Sefer Ha-Zikaron le Bet Ha-Midrash la-rabbanut be-Vienna* (Jerusalem: Reuben Maas, 1946).

Giteau, Mlle, 'Vie économique et classes sociales dans le monde laïque', in R. Boutrouche (ed.), *Bordeaux de 1453 à 1715*, (Bordeaux: Fédération Historique du Sud-Ouest, 1966), pp. 455–506.

Goldish, M., 'Jews, Christians and Conversos', *JJS*, 45 (1994), pp. 227–57.

Hildesheimer, Françoise, 'Une Créature de Richelieu: Alphonse Lopez, le "Seigneur Hebreo"', in G. Dahan (ed.), *Les Juifs au Regard de l'Histoire* (Paris: Picard, 1985), pp. 293–99.

Israel, J., 'An Amsterdam Jewish Merchant of the Golden Age', *SR*, xviii (1984), pp. 21–40.

——, 'The Changing Role of the Dutch Sephardim in International Trade, 1595–1715', in J. Michman and T. Levie (eds), *Dutch Jewish History* (Jerusalem: Tel-Aviv University, 1984), pp. 31–51.

——, 'Duarte Nunes da Costa (Jacob Curiel) of Hamburg, Sephardi Nobleman and Communal Leader (1585–1664)', *SR*, xxi (1987), pp. 14–34.

——, 'The Jews of Venice and their Links with Holland and with Dutch Jewry (1600–1710)', in G. Cozzi (ed.), *Gli ebrei e Venezia* (Milan: Edizioni Comunita, 1987), pp. 95–111.

——, 'The Dutch Sephardic Colonisation Movement', in J. Kaplan *et al.* (eds), *Menasseh ben Israel and His World* (Leiden: Brill, 1989), pp. 139–63.

——, 'The Sephardi Contribution to Economic Life and Colonisation in England and the New World (16th–18th centuries)', in H. Beinart (ed.), *The Sephardi Legacy II* (Jerusalem: Magnes Press, 1992), pp. 365–98.

Kaplan, J., *From Christianity to Judaism*, Engl. trans. (Oxford University Press – Littman Library, 1989).

——, *Onesh Ha-Herem ba-Kehillah ha-Sephardit be-Amsterdam ba-meah Ha-18*, Proceedings of the Tenth World Congress of Jewish Studies, Div. B, i (Jerusalem, 1990), pp. 1–7.

——, ' "Karaites" in Early Eighteenth Century Amsterdam', in D. Katz and J. Israel (eds), *Sceptics, Millenarians and Jews* (Leiden: Brill, 1990), pp. 196–236.

——, 'The Intellectual Ferment in the Spanish-Portuguese Community of 17th Century Amsterdam', in H. Beinart (ed.), *The Sephardi Legacy*, ii (Jerusalem: Magnes Press, 1992), pp. 288–314.

——, 'The Jewish Profile of the Spanish-Portuguese Community of London during the Seventeenth Century', *Judaism*, XLI (1992), pp. 229–40.

——, 'Die portugiesischen Juden und die Modernisierung', in A. Nechama *et al.* (eds), *Jüdische Lebenswelten* (Frankfurt am Main: Suhrkamp, 1992).

——, 'Olamo ha-dati shel sokher benle'umi Yehudi bi-tekufat ha-merkantilizm', in M. Ben-Sasson (ed.), *Dat ve-khalkala* (Jerusalem: Zalman Shazar, 1995), pp. 233-51.

Kellenbenz, H. (ed.), *Confusion de Confusiones* (Harvard University Press, 1957).

——, *Sephardim an der unteren Elbe* (Wiesbaden, 1958).

Léon, H., *Histoire des Juifs de Bayonne* (Paris: Durlacher, 1893).

Lévy, L., *La Nation Juive Portugaise* (Paris: L'Harmattan, 1999).

Malino, F., *The Sephardic Jews of Bordeaux* (University of Alabama Press, 1978).

Malvezin, T., *Histoire des Juifs à Bordeaux*, repr. (Marseilles: Lafitte, 1976).

Méchoulan, H., 'La Mort comme enjeu théologique, philosophique et politique à Amsterdam au 17e siècle', *XVIIe Siècle*, 46 (1994), pp. 337–48.

Menkis, R., 'Patriarchs and Patricians', in F. Malino and D. Sorkin (eds), *From East and West* (Oxford: Blackwell, 1990), pp. 11–45.

Nadler, S., *Spinoza's Heresy* (Oxford: Clarendon Press, 2001).

Nahon, G., 'Les Rapports des communautés Judéo-Portugaises de France avec celles d'Amsterdam au XVIIe et au XVIIIe Siècles', *SR*, X (1976), pp. 37–78.

——, 'From New Christians to the Portuguese Jewish Nation in France', in H. Beinart (ed.), *Sephardi Legacy II* (Jerusalem: Magnes Press, 1992).

Oliel-Grausz, Evelyne, 'La Circulation du personnel rabbinique dans les communautés de la diaspora sépharade au XVIIe siècle', in E. Benbassa (ed.), *Transmission et Passages en monde juif* (Paris: Publisud, 1997), pp. 313–34.

Papo, Rabbi Dr M., 'The Sephardi Community of Vienna', in J. Fraenkel (ed.), *The Jews of Austria* (London: Vallentine Mitchell, 1967), pp. 327–46.

Pieterse, W.C., 'The Sephardi Jews of Amsterdam', in R. Barnett and W. Schwab (eds), *The Western Sephardim II* (Grendon: Gibraltar Books, 1988), pp. 75–99.

Roth, Cecil, 'Quatre Lettres d'Elie de Montalte', *REJ*, 87(1929), pp. 137–65.

Rozen, Minna, 'La vie économique des Juifs du bassin méditerranéan', in S. Trigano (ed.), *La Société Juive à travers l'Histoire* (Paris: Fayard, 1992), III, pp. 296–352.

Salomon, H.P., *Portrait of a New Christian Ferrão Alvares Melo* (Paris: Fundacao Gulbenkian, 1982).

Samuel, Edgar, 'Manuel Levy Duarte, 1631–1714, An Amsterdam Merchant Jeweller', *TJHSE*, XXVII (1982), pp. 11–31.

——, 'Dr. Rodrigo Lopes' Last Speech from the Scaffold at Tyburn', *TJHSE*, XXX (1987–1988), pp. 51–3.

——, 'Antonio Rodrigues Robles, c.1620–1688', *TJHSE*, XXXVII (2001), pp. 113–15.

Schatz, Rivka, 'Emdato shel Menasseh b. Israel klapei Ha-Meshihiyut', *Bar-Ilan Annual*, XXII–XXIII (1988), pp. 429–47.

Sorkin, David, 'Port Jew: Notes towards a Social Type', *JJS*, L (1999), pp. 87–97.

Studemund-Halévy, M., 'Sprachverhalten und Assimilation der portugiesischen Juden in Hamburg', in A. Herzig, ed., *Die Juden in Hamburg 1590–1990* (Hamburg: Dölling und Galiz Verlag, 1991), pp. 283–99.

Swetchinski, D.M., 'The Portuguese Jews of 17th century Amsterdam: Cultural Continuity and Adaptation', in F. Malino and P.C. Albert (eds), *Essays in Modern Jewish History* (London/Toronto: Associated University Presses, 1982), pp. 56–80.

——, *Reluctant Cosmopolitans* (London: Littman Library, 2000).

Vlessing, O., 'New Light on the Earliest History of the Amsterdam Portuguese Jews', in J. Michman (ed.), *Dutch-Jewish History*, IV (Jerusalem, 1993), pp. 43–75.

374   Bibliography

Vlessing, O., 'The Portuguese Merchant Community in 17th Century Amsterdam', in C. Lesger and L. Noordgraf (eds), *Entrepreneurs in Early Modern Times* (The Hague: Stichting Hollandse Historische Reeks, 1995), pp. 223–43.

Weiner, G.M., 'Sephardic Philo- and Anti-Semitism in the early modern era', in R.H. Popkin and G.M. Weiner (eds), *Jewish Christians and Christian Jews* (Dordrecht/London: Kluwer, 1994).

Wilke, C.L., 'Un judaïsme clandestin dans la France du XVIIe siècle', in E. Benbassa (ed.), *Transmission et Passages en monde juif* (Paris: Publisud, 1997), pp. 281–311.

Italy

Berliner, A., *Geschichte der Juden in Rom*, repr. (Hildesheim: Olms, 1987).

Bonfil, R., *Jewish Life in Renaissance Italy* (California University Press, 1994).

—— (ed.), *In Memoria di Umberto Nahon* (Jerusalem: Fondazione Sally Mayer, 1978).

Cozzi, G. (ed.), *Gli Ebrei e Venezia* (Milan: Edizioni Comunita, 1987).

Dubin, Lois, *The Port Jews of Habsburg Trieste* (Stanford: California University Press, 1999).

Fishman, Talya (ed. and trans), *Shaking the Pillars of Exile* (Stanford University Press, 1997).

Hacohen, Deborah, 'Ha-Kehillah be-Livorna u-Mosdotehah', in R. Bonfil (ed.), *In Memoria di Umberto Nahon* (Jerusalem: Fondazione Sally Meyer, 1978), pp. 107–27.

Laras, G., 'Le Grand Sanhédrin de 1807 at ses conséquences en Italie', in B. Blumenkranz et A. Soboul (eds), *Les Juifs et la Révolution française* (Toulouse: Privat, 1976), pp. 100–18.

Levi d'Ancona, Flora, 'The Sephardi Community of Leghorn', in R. Barnett (ed.), *The Sephardi Heritage II* (Northants: Gibraltar Books, 1989).

Lévy, Lionel, *La Nation Juive Portugaise* (Paris-Montreal: L'Harmattan, 1999).

Mangio, Carlo, 'La Communauté Juive de Livourne face à la Révolution Française', in B. Blumenkranz et A. Soboul (eds), *Les Juifs et La Révolution Française* (Toulouse: Privat, 1976), pp. 191–209.

Ravid, B., 'The First Charter of the Jewish Merchants of Venice, 1589', *AJS Review*, 1 (1976), pp. 187–222.

——, *Economics and Toleration in 17th century Venice* (Jerusalem: American Academy for Jewish Research, 1978).

Rossi, Mario, 'Emancipation of the Jews of Italy', in A. Duker and M. Ben Horin (eds), *Emancipation and Counter-Emancipation* (New York: Ktav, 1974), pp. 209–35.

Schwarzfuchs, S., 'Les Communautés Italiennes et le Consistoire Central, 1808–1815', *Michael*, I (1972).

Segre, Dan, 'The Emancipation of Jews in Italy', in P. Birnbaum and I. Katznelson (eds), *Paths to Emancipation* (Princeton University Press, 1995), pp. 206–37.

Simonsohn, S., *Tshuvot ahadot shel Yehudei Italiya al Ha-emantzipatiyah Ha-rishonah ve-al Ha-Haskalah* (Rome: Italia Judaica, University of Tel Aviv, 1989).

Toaff, Sh., 'Mahloket R. Jacob Sasportas u-Farnassei Livorno', *Sefunot*, IX (1965), pp. 169–91.

Voghera, Gadi Luzzatto, 'Italian Jews', in R. Liedtke and S. Wendehorst (eds), *The Emancipation of Catholics, Jews and Protestants* (Manchester University Press, 1999).

Communal Records and Ordinances

Avron, D. (ed.), *Pinkas Ha-Ksherim shel Kehilat Pozna, 1621–1865* (Jerusalem, 1966).

Barnett, L.D., *El Libro de los Acuerdos* (Oxford University Press, 1931).

——,(ed.), *Bevis Marks Records* (Oxford University Press, 1940).

Board of Deputies Minute Book, London, March 1829–January 1838.

Carpi, D. (ed.), *Pinkas Va'ad Padua 1577–1603* (Jerusalem: Israel Academy of Sciences, 1973).

Cohen, Daniel (ed.), *Die Landjudenschaften in Deutschland als Organe jüdischer Selbstverwaltung* (Jerusalem: Israel Academy of Sciences, 1996).

——, 'Die Landjudenschaften in Hessen-Darmstadt bis zur Emanzipation', in *900 Jahre Geschichte der Juden in Hessen* (Wiesbaden: Kommission für die Geschichte der Juden in Hessen, 1983).

——, 'Ha Va'ad Ha-Katan shel Bnei Medinat Ansbach', in Sh. Ettinger (ed.), *Sefer Yovel le- Yitzhak Baer* (Jerusalem: Israel Academy of Sciences, 1986), pp. 351–75.

Elon, M., 'Le-Mehutan shel Takkanot Ha-Kahal Ba-Mishpat Ha-Ivri', in S. Tedeschi (ed.), *Mehkarei Mishpat le-Zekher A. Rosenthal* (Jerusalem: Magnes Press, 1964), pp. 1–54.

Graupe, H.M., *Die Statuten der drei Gemeinden, Altona, Hamburg und Wandsbek* (Hamburg: Hans Christians Verlag, 1973).

——, (ed.), *Takkanot Shlosh Kehillot* (Hamburg: Hans Christians Verlag, 1973).

Halperin, I., *Takkanot Medinat Maehren* (Jerusalem: Mekitsei Nirdarmim, 1962).

——, (ed.) and I. Bartal (rev.), *Pinkas Va'ad Arba Aratzot* (Jerusalem: Mossad Bialik, 1945).

Jacobson, J., *Jüdische Trauungen in Berlin* (Berlin: De Gruyter, 1968).

Marwedel, G., *Die Privilegien der Juden in Altona* (Hamburg: Hans Christians Verlag, 1976).

Meisl, J. (ed.), *Pinkas Kehillat Berlin, 1723–1854* (Jerusalem: Mass, 1962).

Perles, J., 'Urkunden zur Geschichte der Jüdischen Provinzialsynoden in Polen', *MGWJ*, 16 (1867).

Schwarzfuchs, S. (ed.), *Le Registre des Deliberations de la Nation Juive Portugaise de Bordeaux, 1711–1787* (Paris: Centre Cultural Portuguèse, 1981).

Shchepanski, R. Israel (ed.), *Ha-Takkanot be-Yisrael*, IV (Jerusalem: Mossad Ha-Rav Kuk, 1993).

Stern, M., 'Das Vereinsbuch des Berliner Beth Hamidrasch 1743–1783', *JJLG*, XXII (1931–2), pp. 401–20.

Miscellaneous

Abramsky, C., 'The Crisis of Authority within European Jewry in the Eighteenth Century', in S. Stein and R. Loewe (eds), *Studies in Jewish Religious and Intellectual History* (Alabama University Press, 1978), pp. 13–28.

Awerbuch, M., 'Spinoza in seiner Zeit', in H. Delf *et al.* (eds), *Spinoza in der europäischen Geistesgeschichte* (Berlin: Hentrich, 1994), pp. 39–74.

Bamberger, B.J., 'Individual Rights and the Demands of the State: The Position of Classical Judaism', *Central Conference of American Rabbis*, LIV (1944), pp. 197–211.

Baron, S.W., *A Social and Religious History of the Jews*, XII (Columbia University Press, 1967).

——, *The Jewish Community*, 3 vols (Philadelphia: JPSA, 5706 - 1945).

Baumgart, P., 'Die Stellung der jüdischen Minorität im Staat des aufgeklärten Absolutismus', *Kairos*, XXII (1980), pp. 226–45.

Bering, D., *Der Name als Stigma* (Stuttgart: Klett-Cotta, 1987).

Birnbaum, P. and I. Katznelson (eds), *Paths to Emancipation* (Princeton University Press, 1995).

Blidstein, G., *A note on the function of the 'law of the kingdom is law'* (Jerusalem: Centre for Jewish community studies, n.d.).

Büchler, Adolph, *The Political and the Social Leaders of the Jewish community of Sepphoris in the second and third centuries* (Oxford University Press, n.d.).

Carlebach, E., 'Attribution of Secrecy and Perceptions of Jewry', *JSS*, II (1996), pp. 115–36.

Clark, C.M., *The Politics of Conversion* (Oxford: Clarendon Press, 1995).

Cohen, Gerson, 'Messianic Postures of Ashkenazim and Sephardim', *Leo Baeck Memorial Lecture*, 9 (1967).

Dahan, G. (ed.), *Les Juifs au Regard de l'Histoire* (Paris: Picard, 1985).

Dan, Joseph, 'Jewish Studies in a New Europe', *Proceedings of the 5th Congress of the European Association for Jewish Studies* (Copenhagen, 1998).

Diezinger, S., 'Französische Emigranten und Flüchtlinge', in V. Rödel (ed.), *Die Französische Revolution und die Oberrheinlande* (Sigmaringen: Thorbecke Verlag, 1991), pp. 275–84.

Dunn, R., *The Age of Religious Wars, 1559–1689* (London: Weidenfeld, 1970).

Faber, Eli, *Jews, Slaves and the Slave Trade* (New York University Press, 1998).

Ferguson, Niall, *The World's Banker* (London; Weidenfeld, 1998).

——, *The Cash Nexus* (Harmondsworth: Penguin Books, 2001).

Fram, E., *Ideals Face Reality* (Cincinnati: HUC Press, 1997).

Funkenstein, Amos, 'The dialectics of assimilation', *JSS*, I, 2 (1995).

Fuss, A.M., 'The Eastern European Shetar Mamran Re-examined', *Dinei Yisrael*, IV (1973), pp. li–lxvii.

Goldberg, Sylvie-Anne, 'Temporality as Paradox: The Jewish Time', *Proceedings of the 5th Congress of the European Association of Jewish Studies*, pp. 284–92.

Goldish, M., 'Jews, Christians and Conversos', *JJS*, XLV (1994).

Gotzman, A., 'The Dissociation of Religion and Law in nineteenth century German-Jewish education', *LBYB*, XLIII (1998).

——, *Eigenheit und Einheit* (Leiden: Brill, 2002).

Graff, G., *Dina de-Malkhuta Dina in Jewish Law, 1750–1848* (Alabama University Press, 1985).

Gross, John, *Shylock* (London: Chatto & Windus, 1992).

Guttmann, J., 'Mendelssohn's Jerusalem und Spinoza's Tractatus', *Jahresbericht der Hochschule für die Wissenschaft des Judentums*, Berlin, 28 (1931), pp. 33–67.

Hagen, W.W., *Germans, Poles and Jews* (Chicago University Press, 1980).

Halbertal, M., *People of the Book* (Harvard University Press, 1977).

Horowitz, E., 'The Worlds of Jewish Youth in Europe, 1300–1800', in Giovanni Levi (ed.), *A History of Young People in the West* (Harvard University Press, 1977).

Hundert, G.D., 'Reflections on the Whig Interpretation of Jewish history', in H. Joseph *et al.* (eds), *Truth and Compassion* (Ontario: Wilfred Laurier University Press, 1983), pp. 115–16.

——, 'Shkiot Yirat Kavod be'kehillot beit Yisrael be-Lita', *Bar-Ilan Annual*, XXIV–XXV (1989), pp. 41–50.

Jacobson, J., 'Von Mendelssohn zu Mendelssohn-Bartholdy', *LBYB*, 5 (1960), pp. 251–61.

Jarrassé, Dominique, 'Les Mémoires du Temple', in Esther Benbassa (ed.), *Transmission et Passages en monde juif* (Paris: Publisud, 1997), pp. 473–97.

Katz, B.-Z., *Rabbanut, Hassidut, Haskalah*, 2 vols (Tel-Aviv: Dvir, 1956).

Katz, J., *Orthodoxy in Historical Perspective, Studies in Contemporary Jewry*, II (Indiana University Press, 1986), pp. 3–17.

Kisch, G., 'The Yellow Badge in History', *HJ*, IV (1942), pp. 95–144.

Kober, A., 'Jewish Names in the Era of Enlightenment', *HJ*, V (1943), pp. 165–81.

Kochan, Lionel, *The Jew and his History* (London: Macmillan, 1977).

Liberles, R., 'Emancipation and the structure of the Jewish Community in the nineteenth century', *LBYB*, XXXI (1986), pp. 51–67.

——, 'Dohm's Treatise on the Jews', *LBYB*, XXXIII (1988), pp. 29–42.

Loewe, R., *The Position of Women in Judaism* (London: SPCK, 1966).

Mahler, R., *Yidn in amolikn Polin im Likht fun Ziffern* (Warsaw, 1958).

Mendelssohn, M., 'Einleitung zur Ubersetzung der Schrift des R. Menasse b. Israel – Rettung der Juden', in M. Brasch (ed.), *Moses Mendelssohns Schriften* I (Leipzig: Voss, 1880), pp. 475–500.

——, *Jerusalem*, trans. A. Arkush (Brandeis University Press, 1983).

——, *Gesammelte Schriften*, 20.2 (Stuttgart: Frommann Verlag, 1994).

Meyer, Michael, A., *Response to Modernity* (Oxford University Press, 1988).

Mittelman, A., *The Politics of Torah* (New York: SUNY Press, 1996).

Oppeln-Bronikowski, F. (ed. and trans.), *Friedrich der Grosse: Politische Testamente* (Munich: Treu Verlag, 1941).

Pelli, M., 'Maskilim and the Talmud', *LBYB*, 27 (1982), pp. 243–60.

Penslar, D., *Shylock's Children* (California University Press, 2001).

Pergola, Sergio Della, 'An Overview of Demographic Trends', in J. Webber (ed.), *Jewish Identities in the New Europe* (London/Washington: Littman Library, 1994).

Petuchowski, J., 'Manuals and Catechisms of the Jewish Religion in the Early Period of Emancipation', in A. Altmann (ed.), *Studies in Nineteenth century Jewish Intellectual History* (Harvard University Press, 1964).

Polonsky, A., *et al.* (eds), *The Jews in Old Poland* (London, New York: Tauris, 1993).

Prestel, C., 'Jüdische Unterschicht im Zeitalter der Emanzipation', *Aschkenas*, I (1991), pp. 95–134.

Rakover, N., *Shilton Ha-Hok be- Yisrael* (Jerusalem: Sifriyat Ha-Mishpat Ha-Ivri, 1989).

Raphael, F., *Judaisme et Capitalisme* (Paris: PUF, 1982).

Rosenbloom, N., 'Discreet Theological Polemics in Menasseh b. Israel's Conciliador', *PAAJR*, 58 (1992), pp. 143–91.

Rosenzweig, F., *Vorspruch zu einer Mendelssohn-Feier, Kleinere Schriften* (Berlin: Schocken, 1937).

Rubens, A., *A History of Jewish Costume* (London: Vallentine Mitchell, 1967).

Rudavsky, T.M., (ed.), *Gender and Judaism* (New York University Press, 1995).

Samet, M., 'Ha-Ortodoxiya', *Kivunim*, XXVI (1987), pp. 99–114.

——, 'The Beginning of Orthodoxy', *Modern Judaism*, VIII (1988), pp. 249–69.

Saperstein, M., 'War and Patriotism in Sermons to Central European Jews: 1756–1815', *LBYB*, XXXVIII (1993), pp. 3–14.

Schreiber, A., *Jewish Law and Decision-Making* (Philadelphia: Temple University Press, 1979).

Schröter, F.V., *Das Preussische Münzwesen* (Berlin: Paul Parey, 1908).

Schulte, C., 'Saul Ascher's Leviathan, or The Invention of Jewish Orthodoxy in 1792', *LBYB*, 45 (2000), pp. 25–34.

Schwarzfuchs, S., 'The Making of the Rabbi', in J. Carlebach (ed.), *Das aschkenasische Rabbinat* (Berlin: Metropol Verlag, 1995), pp. 133–40.

Septimus, B., 'Ethical Religion and Political Rationality', in I. Twersky (ed.), *Jewish Thought in the 17th Century* (Harvard University Press, 1987), pp. 399–433.

Sombart, Werner, *Die Juden und das Wirtschaftsleben* (Munich: Duncker und Humblot, 1922 – first published 1911).

Spinoza, B., *A Theologico-Political Treatise*, trans. R.H.M. Elwes (London: Bell & Sons, 1889).

Stanislavsky, M., *Tsar Nicholas and the Jews* (Philadelphia: JPSA, 5743–1983).

Strauss, L., *What is Political Philosophy?* (Westport, 1973).

Tartakower, A., 'Jewish Migratory Movements', in J. Fraenkel (ed.), *Jews of Austria* (London: Vallentine Mitchell, 1967).

Zacek, W., 'Eine Studie zur Entwicklung der jüdischen Personennamen in neuerer Zeit', *JGGJCR*, VIII (1936), pp. 309–97.

Zalkind Hourwitz, *Apologie des Juifs* (Paris: Editions d'Histoire Sociale, repr. 1989).

Zimmermann, M., *Hamburgischer Patriotismus und deutscher Nationalismus* (Hamburg: Hans Christian Verlag, 1979).

Zunz, L., 'Ankündigung eines Werkes: Geist der Rabbiner', *Berlinische Nachrichten der Haude und Spenerschen Zeitung*, 88 (1819).

——, *Die Gottesdienstlichen Vorträge der Juden* (Berlin: Asher, 1832).

Index